The Dispossessed Majority

The Dispossessed Majority

Wilmot Robertson

HOWARD ALLEN   CAPE CANAVERAL

To my co-author. No other title adequately describes your inestimable assistance.

Fourth Paperback Printing
International Standard Book Number: 0–914576–04–6
Library of Congress Catalog Card Number: 71–167649
Second Revised Edition

In order to possess what you do not possess
You must go by the way of dispossession.

—T. S. ELIOT, *Four Quartets*

Contents

Contents

PART X

Prospects and Perspectives

Foreword

THE MOST TRULY disadvantaged are those who are hated for their virtues, not their vices, who insist on playing the game of life with opponents who have long ago abandoned the rules, who stubbornly go on believing that a set of highly sophisticated institutions developed by and for a particular people at a particular point in time and space is operational for all peoples under all circumstances.

The intent of this book is to supply members of this discomfited and threatened group—here provisionally defined as the American Majority—with a systematic diagnosis of the diseases and debilities which have laid them low and a probative regimen for their recovery.

So many liberals having become minority racists and so many conservatives having become rootless cranks, so much religion having become social science and so much social science having become intellectual sleight-of-hand, the thoughtful Majority member has had nowhere to turn but to himself. This, however, may be his salvation. In isolation the critical faculty cuts deeper. Only now is it possible to understand the tragic and humiliating fate of the American Majority because only now are a few Majority minds, deepened by decades of solitary contemplation and sharpened by the grim chronicle of events, finally tuning to the emergency wavelength of collective survival.

On the surface America appears lost. But the animalization of the body and the brutalization of the spirit, the desecration of the environment, the venality of politics, the drug plague, the ghetto savagery, the apostasy of the professors and journalists, the mindlessness of the students, the phobic materialism and Babbittry of their parents—all these, perhaps, are not the irreversible regressions they seem. They may be merely short-term roadblocks or detours on the Great Trek to a higher and more luminous life form. In the sequence of organic rebirth, what is to be done must first be undone. Unthinking must precede rethinking. According to the sine curve of human activity, degeneration alternates with regeneration. Quite possibly, the present phase is one of _reculer pour mieux sauter._

On the hopeful side, the chromosomal material, the first and fundamental requirement for an American resurgence, is still in abundant supply. Life scientists and those few social scientists worthy of the name are seething with insights and breakthroughs that cannot help but unbait some of the dogmatic traps lately cretinizing the more active Majority intellects. From the raked-over ashes of burnt-out historicism flashes a spark or two of authentic history. There is even the glimmer of a new religion (or the rejuvenation of the old) in the Promethean utterances and riddles of the new ontology.

At all events, the Majority will soon be out of limbo. There is nowhere for it to go but up—or all the way down. It is really a matter of timing, a race between the encroaching jungle and the ripening harvest. The moon walk may turn out to be the last mile, or the crossing of the Rubicon.

PART I

Racial Dynamics

Chapter 1

The Concept of Race

NOTHING HAS RAISED man to higher peaks of creativity or lowered him to greater depths of destructiveness than the dual notion of human similarity and dissimilarity.

Every man is like every other man in that he belongs to the same species, *Homo sapiens*. The seven-foot Watusi and the four-foot Pygmy, the milk-white Swede, the coffee-colored Latin American mestizo and the almond-eyed and almond-tinted Oriental are all capable of interbreeding. The idea of human likeness consequently has biological origins. But so does the idea of human unlikeness. Every man differs physically and mentally from every other man, which accounts both for human individuality and group differences.[1] As Shakespeare wrote:

> "Strange is it that our bloods,
> Of colour, weight, and heat, pour'd all together,
> Would quite confound distinction, yet stand off
> In differences so mighty." [2]

The average person probably starts life as a similarist and ends as a dissimilarist. The child grows older and wanders

---

1. Even identical, one-egg twins differ slightly in height, weight, head length and head width. L. C. Dunn and Th. Dobzhansky, *Heredity, Race and Society*, New American Library, New York, 1960, p. 27. "Deux jumeaux identiques, provenant du même oeuf, possédant la même constitution génétique, manifestent chacun une personnalité différente." Alexis Carrel, *L'homme, cet inconnu*, Librarie Plon, Paris, 1935, p. 336.
2. *All's Well that Ends Well*, Act II, Scene 3.

from the family hearth, only to find that all fathers do not look like his father, all mothers are not like his mother, all children are not like his brothers and sisters. As he strays farther afield, he discovers noticeable physical and cultural differences among the populations of big cities and foreign countries.[3] Inevitably he recognizes that some human beings have a set of physical and cultural characteristics similar to his own while others do not. With or without the help of father, mother, teacher, book or television, he has separated one group of people from another. Whether he likes it or not, whether he knows it or not, he has subscribed to the concept of race.

The belief that every man belongs to a distinct human breed is a persistent one—and the despair of physical anthropologists. For a hundred years they have been trying to eradicate such "loose thinking" by developing more rigorous definitions of race. So far their efforts have been concentrated on the accumulation and classification of biometrical data, and have produced as much controversy as agreement. Even if they eventually succeed in establishing the physiological component of race on firm scientific ground, they will still be faced with the mysteries and complexities of the psychological component. Race, as every American politician is well aware, goes far beyond the realm of the physical.

Unfortunately for those anthropologists who work with tape measures and computers, the concept of race leans as heavily on the *awareness* of blood relationship as it does on the *fact* of blood relationship. The physical anthropologist will only permit genetic factors to enter into the determination of race. The statesman, poet and prophet take a less scientific approach. They know the immense power that feelings of kinship exert in human affairs, and the vast political and social transformations which take place when these feelings are kindled or rekindled in large numbers of human hearts. When men cannot appeal to anthropology to

3. One social scientist, George Murdock, has found 73 elements common to all cultures, among them: courtship, dancing, division of labor, education, family, folklore, games, hair styles, hospitality, law, magic. *The Science of Man in the World Crisis,* edited by Ralph Linton, Columbia University Press, New York, 1945, p. 124.

justify the existence of a race, they will often appeal to history. "The device of myths to establish a common ancestry for an ethnic group," sociologist E. K. Francis noted, "is a very ancient one." [4]

Ethnic group is the favorite term of those anthropologists and biologists who wish to drain race of its emotional content and subjectivity. Even more anemic is *cline,* a graded series of characteristics of a species. But changing man's vocabulary does not necessarily change his thinking. *Ethnic group, population group, cline,* and the like, are handy labels for classifying certain segments of mankind with minimal friction, but they by no means tell the whole story.

There are other, less watered-down synonyms for race, of which the most common are *stock, breed* and *nationality.* They still hit rather wide of the mark. More descriptive, though awkward, are such sociological neologisms as *we-feeling* and *we-group.* William Graham Sumner, a pillar of the almost extinct conservative school of sociology, had a particular fondness for *ethos,* the Greek word for the collection of ideas, standards and habits which differentiated one human group from another.[5] *Ethos,* however, leaves much to be desired because of the small emphasis it places on the physical stratum.

Perhaps the word which most closely approximates race is *people,* either modified by a possessive (my, your) or as Oswald Spengler defined it when he wrote, "The Roman name in Hannibal's day meant a people, in Trajan's time nothing more than a population." [6] More highly charged expressions for race are the crude but communicative *blood brother* and *soul brother,* which Negro store owners paint on their windows during ghetto riots to escape the wrath of arsonists and looters.

So meaningful and at the same time so meaningless, the concept of race encompasses so many facts and fancies, so much love and hate, so much reason and unreason that it is

4. E. K. Francis, "The Nature of the Ethnic Group," *American Journal of Sociology,* March, 1947, p. 396.
5. William Graham Sumner, *Folkways,* Ginn & Co., Boston, 1906, p. 12.
6. *The Decline of the West,* trans. C. F. Atkinson, Knopf, New York, 1957, Vol. II, p. 165.

more easily sensed than understood. In some respects, race is similar to certain other four-letter words in English. It throws a hard emotional punch and its use is studiously avoided in polite and academic circles. For all its semantic sloppiness, however, race exerts a profound influence over men's minds. As Edgar T. Thompson stated, "The absence among the people of a clearly formulated definition of race, far from weakening it, actually adds to the potency of the race idea." [7]

Man is the amalgam of his physiological inheritance and his sociological acquisitions. He can shed the latter, but not the former. He can give up his religion, his country and his culture. He cannot give up his race. Or, more precisely, he cannot give up the physical side of his race, which, apart from superficial alterations by plastic surgeons or beauticians, is inexorably determined by the laws of genetics. [8]

7. "Race in the Modern World," *Journal of Negro Education,* Summer, 1944, p. 272.

8. Even the rare phenomenon of *passing* is primarily involved with non-physical aspects of race. Essentially the man who passes is trading the cultural trappings of one community for those of another. Biologically speaking, the alleged Negro who "looks" so white that he is accepted as a white by the white world could hardly be described as a Negro in the first place.

Chapter 2

Racism

As the idea is to ideology,[1] so the concept of race is to racism. This leads to the definition of racism as a belief in the race idea. But belief implies some measure of assent, some inward or outward activation of the belief. Racism, accordingly, can be described as the overt or covert expression of the concept of race at one or more levels of human activity—in politics, art and religion, in business, in community life, in the privacy of the home.

Racism, which presupposes a common ancestry, is not identical with nationalism, which presupposes a common citizenship. It is usually, but not invariably, associated with such an exalted form of nationalism as patriotism, such extreme forms as chauvinism and jingoism, such localized forms as sectionalism, regionalism and provincialism. Racism is present both in the foundation and in the dissolution of empires. It may reenforce nationalism in homogeneous societies and oppose it in multiracial states. In proletarian

---

1. "An ideology is a complex of ideas or notions which represents itself to the thinker as an absolute truth for the interpretation of the world and his situation within it; it leads the thinker to accomplish an act of self-deception for the purpose of justification, obfuscation, evasion, in some sense or other to his advantage." Karl Jaspers, *The Origin and Goal of History*, trans. Michael Bullock, Yale University Press, New Haven, 1968, p 132. "Roughly defined, an ideologist is a thinker convinced he has discovered clear solutions to certain human problems or predicaments—solutions capable of expression in general theoretical terms." *Times Literary Supplement* (London), Jan. 29, 1970, p. 1

revolutions and fascist counterrevolutions, it may play a far more important role than class.[2]

When races are geographically separated or isolated, racism is likely to be directed externally, across and beyond the boundaries of one province, region or state to another province, region or state. Where races live side by side, in the same neighborhood or in the same school district, racism is apt to be directed internally, to the city block and the classroom. Racism of both types is present in most large nations. But while Russia, for example, with its autonomous and somewhat homogeneous republics has more of the externalized variety, racism in the United States with its numerous and widely dispersed racial elements is more implosive than explosive.

As far as can be ascertained, practically every society, people or nation has passed through one or more racist cycles. In spite of their endless internecine wars and political and economic rivalry, the ancient Greeks, according to H. A. L. Fisher, "believed themselves to be one in race, language and institutions," designating all foreigners as barbarians and generally treating them as such.[3] The mass of Romans considered the Greeks corrupt weaklings. Many Jews have clung to the idea of the Chosen People even to this day. Prototypal racist attitudes were exhibited by the Spanish conqueror and the American settler toward the Indians and the Negroes. The traditionally hostile sentiments of the Chinese toward the non-Chinese need no elaboration, nor does the white supremacy once practiced by the French and British toward the native populations of their all but defunct empires.[4]

Like national defense or the balance of payments, racism is frequently regulated by outside events and influences. A homogeneous or even a heterogeneous society may display few signs of racism in peacetime. But once a neighboring state becomes aggressive, once a few thousand fellow na-

---

2. See Chapter 25.

3. As quoted by T. J. Haarhoff, *The Stranger at the Gate*, Longmans Green, London, 1938, p. viii.

4. For a more detailed summary of racist manifestations among the peoples of the world, see Sumner, *Folkways*, p. 29.

tionals or racial cousins abroad become the victims of oppression, the dormant racism of the society or of one or more
population groups within the society may be quickly aroused
and assume a dynamic instead of a static character.

Racism, it should also be mentioned, operates in different
orbits in different locations. Consider two American soldiers,
one of Scandinavian, the other of South Italian origin, guarding a lonely outpost facing the North Koreans or North Vietnamese. At home the first might have called the second a
Latin or an Italian when he was trying to be polite, a Wop
or a Greaser when he wasn't. Now he feels himself in the
presence of a fellow white.

Perhaps the first law of racism is that racism begets
racism. Paradoxically, so does anti-racism, which focuses so
much attention on racial news and implants it so deeply in
the public consciousness that the net amount of racism is
greatly increased. Anti-racism, moreover, permits many people to practice racism vicariously by adopting the cause of
every race but their own.

In one respect, racism is a form of group morale. It provides a protective psychic shell for the most defenseless and
defensive peoples. It is also largely responsible for the high
aggression quotient of dynamic peoples. Promoting tribalism
both in the most retarded and most advanced nations, racism
makes the modern tribal state with its sophisticated technology a fearsome opponent. Everything else being equal—
manpower, industrial plant, scientific proficiency and natural
resources—a racist state can muster a deadlier military
machine than a non-racist state.[5] In the matter of fighting
spirit, the tribe or race may be regarded as the extension of
the family, and death comes easier to those who believe
they are dying for their people as well as for their country.
The lonely, hermetic soldier with only a modicum of race
consciousness has more difficulty being brave. Conscientious
objectors, pacifists and draft evaders are in short supply in
racially oriented societies.

So much of racism remains below the surface in any given
historical setting that the student of the past seldom gives it

5. See Chapter 33.

proper emphasis. Quite possibly it is the most compelling force in the record of human achievement—and human failure. Who can prove the contrary? Who can prove that racism is not a better clue to the rise and fall of civilizations than economics, religion, organic growth and decay, weather, great men or even fate? [6]

Take the United States with the unusually homogeneous genetic substrate of the Founding Fathers, the racial struggle with the Indians, the racial overtones of the Civil War, the racial differences of the Old and New Immigration, the racial mechanics of big-city and Southern politics, the mounting tempo of minority demands and agitation. Take the United Nations, now coalescing into a conglomeration of racial blocs. Take the twentieth-century revolt of the colored peoples of Asia and Africa against white colonialism. Weigh all this evidence, and then wonder at the liberal and conservative historians who grind out their thickly annotated histories which either avoid racism altogether or treat it as a disease rather than as a basic element of human nature.

At present, worldwide movements are afoot to abolish racism. But as indicated by events in the United States and abroad, far from being abolished anywhere, it is becoming intensified everywhere. All that is happening is that one form of racism is being replaced by another or by several others.

Instead of attempting to destroy the indestructible, it might be wiser to learn more about man's racial reflexes. A greater knowledge of the sources of racism might produce effective ways of civilizing and controlling it and directing it into more creative and constructive channels. Such knowledge might also aid in distinguishing between the racial behavior that helps to build nations and the racial behavior that tears them down.

----

6. "The application of this principle [racism] has governed the evolution of all advancing societies since soon after the beginning of agriculture." C. D. Darlington, *The Evolution of Man and Society*, Allen and Unwin, London, 1969, p. 607.

Chapter 3

Racial Metaphysics

THE CONCEPT OF RACE and the racial ideologies which flow from it permeated the great civilizations of antiquity. The Bible divided the races of mankind into the sons of Shem (Semites), Ham (non-Semitic Mediterraneans) [1] and Japheth (northern peoples). Among the sons of Shem were the Jews, who were warned by Jehovah to preserve their racial identity, as they were "a special people unto himself, above all the people that are upon the face of the earth." [2]

The Aryans who invaded India were so concerned with race that they set up a complex caste system by means of which the priestly Brahmans succeeded in preserving their original physical type over a period of 2500 years, although their once fair complexions, through mutations and some miscegenation, are now better adapted to the blasting Indian sun.[3] The wall paintings of the Egyptians depicted a simpler and less sophisticated form of racism. The gods and pharaohs were always larger than life while Negroes and other outlanders were posed in cringing obeisance.[4]

---

1. Christian theologians later gratuitously added Negroes to this category.
2. In some respects the Book of Deuteronomy is a racial tract. The above quotation is from 7:6. Strictures against intermarriage and dealing with foreigners are found in 7:3, 15:3, and 23:3–6, 20.
3. "The first caste division . . . was not by status but by color; it divided long noses from broad noses, Aryans from Nagas and Dravidians . . . The caste system had the eugenic value of keeping the presumably finer strains from dilution. . . ." Will Durant, *Our Oriental Heritage*, Simon and Schuster, New York, 1954, pp. 398, 487.
4. References to Negroes in the English captions of these wall paintings on view at the British Museum in 1968 had been partially erased. Ap-

As might be expected, the Greeks were the first to look for natural causes of racial differences and to philosophize about racial matters. Hippocrates' essay, *Airs, Waters, Places,* gave climate and geography as possible reasons for variations in human physiology and temperament.[5] Plato thought it would be good to inculcate ideas of racial purity in the youth destined for the future leadership of the commonwealth. Such ideas (he described them as "noble lies") would develop a greater measure of pride and responsibility in the young elite—qualities which presumably made for better statesmanship.[6] Aristotle helped institutionalize slavery with his hypothesis of the "natural-born" slave.[7]

But full-blown, "scientific" racial theories did not take form for another two thousand years. It was not until the late eighteenth and the first half of the nineteenth century that enough data had been collected to permit a few intrepid anthropologists and systematizers to categorize all mankind according to race. Along with the classifications came the value judgments. Since whites had now conquered or settled much of the earth and were remaking it in their image, an innately superior bloodline was proposed for the conquerors, who, after the decline of Spain and Portugal, were variously described as Anglo-Saxons, Nordics, or Teutons and who came from Britain, Germany, Scandinavia and neighboring areas in Europe.

The theory of Northern European racial supremacy was assisted and expanded by the discovery of a surprising linguistic relationship between the Aryans, Persians, Hittites, Kassites, Greeks and Romans of the ancient world, and the French, English, Germans, Slavs and other peoples of modern Europe. Although a common language does not necessarily presuppose a common race, the Indo-European languages,[8] as they came to be called, and the Indo-European

parently some modern descendants of the victims of ancient Egyptian racism had not wanted to be reminded of past indignities.

5. *Hippocrates,* William Heinemann, London, 1923, Vol. I, pp. 71 ff.

6. *The Republic of Plato,* trans. Francis MacDonald Cornford, Oxford University Press, New York, 1945, pp. 106–7.

7. Ernest Barker, *The Politics of Aristotle,* Clarendon Press, Oxford, 1950, pp. 13–14.

8. One Indo-European root word: name (English), *nama* (Old Persian), *nama* (Sanskrit), *onoma* (Greek), *nomen* (Latin), *nome* (Italian), *nombre* (Spanish), *nom* (French), *Name* (German), *eemya* (Russian).

speakers gave birth to a racial hypothesis in which a blond, light-complexioned people with rare creative gifts continuously refertilizes dying and decadent civilizations.[9]

Among the chief advocates of this hypothesis, often designated as the Aryan theory, were Arthur de Gobineau (1816–1882), a French count and Germanophile who wrote the first coherent, though highly fanciful, racial interpretation of history;[10] Houston Stewart Chamberlain (1855–1927), an Englishman who became a naturalized German and whose grandiose *Weltanschauung* detected Teutonic genes in almost all the great men of the past, including Jesus Christ; Madison Grant (1865–1937), American lawyer and naturalist who expounded a Spenglerian pessimism of world history by alleging the decline of the great culture-bearing, culture-creating Nordic peoples and whose arguments were helpful in securing the passage of restrictive United States immigration laws in the early 1920's; and Lothrop Stoddard (1883–1950), American political philosopher, also active in the immigration issue, who warned that whites would soon be overwhelmed by the fecundity of the colored races.[11]

Although his Spanish ancestry and his Puritan associations in New England precluded any special affection for the Teuton, the philosopher Santayana was one of the most vigorous subscribers to the idea of racial hierarchies. "Some races," he stated, "are obviously superior to others. A more thorough adjustment to the conditions of existence has given them spirit, vitality, scope and a relative stability. . . . It is therefore of the greatest importance not to obscure this superiority by intermarriage with inferior stock, and thus nullify the progress made by a painful evolution and a prolonged sifting of souls. Reason protests as much as instinct against any fusion, for instance, of white and black peoples.

---

9. Some examples of such refertilization: Aryan invasion of India; Dorian invasion of Greece; Italic invasion of Italy; Germanic overrunning of the Western Roman Empire; Norman conquest of Normandy and Sicily. For more on the Indo-European peoples, see Chapter 9.

10. "Là où l'élément germanique n'a jamais pénétré," de Gobineau declared, "il n'y a pas de civilization à notre manière." *Essai sur l'inégalité des races humaines*, Librarie de Firmin-Didot, Paris, 1884, Vol. I, p. 93.

11. Chamberlain's principal work was *Die Grundlagen des neunzehnten Jahrhunderts;* Grant's, *The Passing of the Great Race;* Stoddard's *The Rising Tide of Color.*

. . . The Jews, the Greeks, the Romans, the English were never so great as when they confronted other nations . . . but this greatness falls whenever contact leads to amalgamation." [12]

In the 1930's for the first time in history, theories of race superiority became state doctrine when the National Socialist German Workers Party took command in Germany.[13] But after the inventory of Hitler's racial excesses was published at the close of World War II, all arguments for racial supremacy were placed beyond the pale of permissible thought by the Western intellectual community.

Race being so deeply personal a subject, it comes as no surprise that advocates of racial superiority usually belong to, or think they belong to, the race they consider superior. It is equally no surprise that in America the opposition to theories of Nordic or Northern European superiority was led by anthropologists, scientists and social scientists who were in most cases members of minority groups. Perhaps in the belief that one good myth deserves another, Franz Boas (1858–1942), a scholar of German-Jewish origin and late professor of anthropology at Columbia University, put forward the first comprehensively developed theory of racial equality. In the same vein as nineteenth-century British historian Henry Buckle, who singled out environment as the determining factor of history, Boas hypothesized that nurture, not nature, was the chief determinant of important racial differences. He went so far as to assert that even such a persistent genetic trait as head shape (cephalic index)[14] could be altered by an environmental change in one or two genera-

12. *The Life of Reason,* Scribner's, New York, 1922, Vol. II, pp. 166–7.

13. Or was it the second time? Alexander Stephens, Vice-President of the Confederacy, once declaimed: "This our new government is the first in the history of the World based upon this great physical, philosophical, and moral truth . . . that the Negro is not equal to the white man, that slavery —subordination to the superior race—is his natural and normal condition." Charles and Mary Beard, *The Rise of American Civilization,* Macmillan, New York, 1930, Vol. 2, p. 68.

14. Cephalic index is head breadth divided by head length times 100. The lower the index, the longer the head. Like physical scientists, anthropologists have a fondness for using complicated Greek derivatives for simple and precise English expressions. Dolichocephalic is long-headed and brachycephalic is round-headed.

tions.[15] Ashley Montagu, a physical anthropologist of Anglo-Jewish origin, became the great popularizer of racial equalitarianism with a seemingly endless series of best-selling books, television appearances and speeches before learned and unlearned societies.[16] Other leading members of the equalitarian school were Otto Klineberg, Melville Herskovits, Alexander Goldenweiser, Isador Chein, Theodosius Dobzhansky, Gene Weltfish and Negro psychologist Kenneth Clark.[17]

The theory of racial equality received the official sanction of the United Nations with the publication of the 1950 and 1962 UNESCO statements on race. Sounding more like a declaration of faith than a reasoned scientific document, the UNESCO papers produced the following axioms: "The scientific evidence indicates that the range of mental capabilities in all ethnic groups is much the same. . . . As for personality and character, these may be considered raceless . . . given similar degrees of cultural opportunity to realize their potentialities, the average achievement of the members of each ethnic group is about the same."

Although really intending to describe the credo of the behaviorist school of psychology, which worked hand in glove with the equalitarian anthropologists by stressing human malleability, sociologist Horace Kallen aptly summed up the UNESCO statements in words which deserve to be carved on Boas' and Montagu's tombstones: *At birth human infants, regardless of their heredity, are as equal as Fords.*[18]

---

15. Franz Boas, "Changes in Bodily Form of Descendants of Immigrants." *American Anthropologist,* New Series, 14:530–562. A refutation of Boas' position can be found in Henry Pratt Fairchild's *Race and Nationality,* Ronald Press, New York, 1947, p. 105.

16. As one of the sponsors, together with the late Bishop James Pike and British-born Zen Buddhist Alan Watts, of a computer dating service, Montagu has been able to encourage the application of his theories. *San Francisco Sunday Examiner & Chronicle, Date Book,* Jan. 19, 1969, p. 24.

17. The school also included a few vociferous Anglo-Saxon females, Ruth Benedict and Margaret Mead. In his scholarly monographs, Dobzhansky, a White Russian, tactfully admitted there were some differences in racial capabilities, but practically denied them in his writings for public consumption. Leslie White's evolutionist school of anthropology and W. H. Sheldon's attempts to equate temperament and body form have received scant recognition because of their anti-Boas stance.

18. See Kallen's article, "Behaviorism," *Encyclopedia of Social Sciences,* Macmillan, New York, 1963, Vols. 1–2, p. 498. J. B. Watson, the founder of behaviorism, wrote, "There is no such thing as an inheritance of capacity, talent, temperament, mental constitution and characteristics." *Behaviorism,* W. W. Norton, N.Y., 1930, p. 94.

By the early 1960's, the idea of innate racial equality had become so firmly established in modern education and in the communications media that no one could question it and still maintain his academic or professional respectability. Nevertheless, a small but persistent reaction set in, stimulated by school desegregation and the violence which accompanied Negro demands for a place in the American sun.

Carleton Putnam, American air transport pioneer and historian, declared that the Boas school of anthropology based its conclusions concerning racial equality on a misconceived self-interest. He advocated a realistic acceptance of the differential in Negro thought patterns and learning capacity, arguing that Negro integration on all but the economic level leads to a steady, relentless deterioration of American education, social life and national power, as well as to the deterioration of the Negro himself.[19]

Henry E. Garrett, former professor of psychology at Columbia University, went further than Putnam by calling the equalitarian dogma "the scientific hoax of the century." Garrett accused social scientists of relying on moral denunciation when their real evidence regarding Negro mental abilities became feeble. He also blamed church leaders for falsifying science to bolster their ethical arguments for racial equality.[20]

William Shockley, who won the Nobel prize in physics for co-inventing the transistor, joined the controversy when he suggested that all contemporary programs for Negro betterment were based on false premises. "The major deficit in

---

19. See Putnam's *Race and Reason* (1961) and *Race and Reality* (1967), both published by Public Affairs Press, Washington, D.C. The most destructive aspect of equalitarianism, Putnam maintained, lies "in teaching that the greater part of the differences in status of individuals and groups among us is due to social injustice, whereas the scientific fact remains that, frequent as injustice is, these differences are primarily attributable to innate differences in capacity. Nowhere has the damage been more serious than in the incitement of the Negro to insurrection against the white man's law and culture."

20. See Garrett's article, "The Equalitarian Dogma" in *Perspectives in Biology and Medicine*, Summer, 1961, and his article on "Differential Psychology," *Ency. Brit.* (1963), Vol. 7, p. 368. For reasons of its own, the *Encyclopaedia Britannica* concealed for years all references to its 14th edition or date of publication. The copyright date, 1963, is the only way to identify those volumes cited extensively in this study. In 1974, however, with great fanfare Editor Mortimer Adler announced the publication of a 15th edition.

Negro intellectual performance," Shockley asserted, "must be primarily of hereditary origin and thus irremediable by practical improvements in environment." [21] Other supporters of the theory of Negro intellectual differences included Wesley C. George, R. Ruggles Gates, Audrey Shuey and Arthur Jensen. With scant regard for consistency, Julian Huxley, the noted British biologist who helped prepare the UNESCO statements on race, went on record as stating that it was probably "true Negroes have a slightly lower average intelligence than the whites or the yellows." [22]

A few leading twentieth-century anthropologists and sociologists attempted to stand above or straddle the question of racial differences.[23] Some of this reticence was doubtless due to fear, some to the natural reluctance of bona fide scientists to generalize on what they considered to be insufficient data. One of the greatest modern anthropologists, Carleton Coon, wrote, "The subject of racial intelligence . . . has not progressed far enough to merit inclusion in a general work of racial history." [24]

Nevertheless, Coon provided powerful ammunition for the anti-equalitarian school with a startling and illuminating theory on the origin of races. Since Darwin, and even before Darwin, it had been taken for granted that the races of man had descended or branched out from a single species, *Homo sapiens*. In direct and iconoclastic contradiction to this traditional doctrine, Coon stated that the five living races of mankind, which he named Caucasoid, Mongoloid, Australoid, Capoid and Congoid, had evolved separately into *Homo sapiens* following different timetables. If Coon was

21. Speech before National Academy of Sciences, April 24, 1968.
22. By the early 1970's Robert Ardrey, Richard Herrnstein and Raymond Cattell in America, H. J. Eysenck in England and Konrad Lorenz in Germany were propounding the biological aspects of behavior or intelligence so convincingly that the equalitarians were considering more effective means of refutation than libel.
23. Principally A. L. Kroeber, Aleš Hrdlička and Pitrim Sorokin. Hrdlička warned of the danger of a mass inflow of Negro genes into the Amercian population, but refused to say why it was a danger. *Proceedings of the Third Race Betterment Conference*, Jan., 1928, pp. 84–5. Sorokin admitted the evidence of mental differences among races, but would not ascribe the cause to heredity. *Contemporary Sociological Theories*, Harper & Bros., New York, 1929, pp. 291–3.
24. *The Races of Europe*, Macmillan, New York, 1954, p. vii.

right about the parallel genesis of races, there now existed an evolutionary basis for racial differences, and the case against the equalitarians was strengthened. Even more damaging to the equalitarian viewpoint was Coon's assertion that the Negro race, which he assigned to the Congoid group, was the last of the world's races to evolve. The blacks, according to Coon, had been in a *sapiens* state for a shorter time (he estimated some 210,000 years) than races nearer the center of evolutionary activity.[25] This led inexorably to the conclusion that Negroes were the least developed and least articulated of mankind's principal racial divisions.

The violent and vituperative reaction which greeted Coon's theories vividly demonstrated the metaphysical nature of the race question. Ashley Montagu, who previous to the publication of Coon's work had said that the multiracial origin of man was "inadmissible," declared that Coon's facts were fraudulent and compared the former president of the American Association of Physical Anthropologists to "the racial anthropologists [of] a hundred years ago."[26] Marvin K. Opler, another anthropologist of the Boas persuasion, was equally vehement, stating, "it is easy to see why Coon's theory should make him the darling of segregationist committees and racists everywhere . . . he cannot convincingly write human history, even racial history. He will have to acquire more knowledge, more compassion and more humility for that."[27]

Instead of invective, which is often self-defeating because it publicizes the target, the silent treatment was given to another great modern anthropologist, Sir Arthur Keith (1866–1955). It was Keith's view that the greatest outburst of man's biological progress occurs in the hunting band, when a combination of geographical isolation and group cohesion produces the balanced gene pool necessary for the efficient functioning of the evolutionary process. Keith was afraid

25. Coon, *The Origin of Races*, Knopf, New York, 1962, pp. 3, 4, 85, 655–59 and *The Story of Man*, Knopf, New York, 1962, 2nd Edition, pp. 35–38.
26. *Man in Process*, New American Library, New York, 1961, p. 103 and *Man's Most Dangerous Myth*, World, Cleveland, 1964, p. 86.
27. *New York Herald-Tribune, Book Section*, Dec. 9, 1962, p. 7.

that the total racial integration demanded by the more dedicated equalitarians might have a dysgenic effect on man by swamping beneficial mutations before they have a chance to take hold. The British anthropologist also pointed out that prejudice, discrimination, xenophobia and certain other human characteristics now considered sinful may actually serve an important evolutionary purpose. They may be nature's chief tools for race-building and for creating favorable growth conditions for the variegated cultures and peoples which have made the mosaic of man so rich and colorful.[28]

If professional anthropologists can descend to the lowest levels of polemics, vindictiveness and thought control, how, it may be asked, can the layman have enlightened ideas about race? The answer is that at least a ray of enlightenment is provided by the historical evidence, which points inescapably to the fact that certain races or peoples have accomplished far more than others in the fields of technology, material comfort and popular government. If these accomplishments are due to genetic causes, the low-achieving races in Western-dominated cultures will always be saddled, as they have been in the past, with the stigma of underperformance, even though they may be perfectly capable of overperformance in their ancestral societies, many of which are still extant.

Much of the bitterness of the present-day racial debate stems from some races being forced to compete, or choosing to compete, in a world they never made. The all-important question of whether heredity or environment has the upper hand in the shaping of human destiny hardly enters into the argument, which has degenerated into a quasi-theological dispute involving such crucial psychological ingredients as pride and face-saving. One side appeals to heredity to explain past successes and the other to environment and "historical accidents" to excuse past failures.

If heredity were proved beyond a shadow of a doubt to be the central factor in human achievement, the proof would

---

28. See Keith's *A New Theory of Human Evolution,* Watts, London, 1950; *Essays on Human Evolution,* Watts, 1948; various essays included in Watts' *Form Series 5, 8, 18, 20;* the essay, *Ethnos or the Problem of Race,* in *Today and Tomorrow Series,* Kegan Paul, London, 1931. A reprint of *A New Theory of Human Evolution* can be obtained from Howard Allen Enterprises, Cape Canaveral, Florida.

nonetheless be rejected in the present climate of modern thought. Environmentalists have too much at stake, both physically and spiritually, to abandon their cause for any reason, least of all a negative scientific verdict on the validity of their ideas and programs. They are only too well aware that the acceptance or acknowledgment of important genetic diversities in man would seriously undermine the entire foundation of prevailing political and social dogma, the fountainhead of the miraculous changes which have been wrought in the status of privileged and underprivileged minorities.

Nonetheless, time seems to be working unflaggingly in the service of the hereditarian party. Investigations into racial intelligence are still largely taboo,[29] but research teams keep approaching the subject tangentially with significant new discoveries relating to racial divergence in brain structure, resistance to disease, blood group distribution, glandular function, hormone activity and gene composition.[30]

Also, as environment becomes increasingly man-made, its effect in creating and perpetuating racial differences, either in the long-term Darwinian sense or in the short-term, discredited Lamarckian sense, is bound to shrink. Human surroundings are growing increasingly similar, particularly in highly civilized areas where a common technology, a common educational system, a common communications network and common occupations are prescribing a common way of life. According to equalitarian theory, the performance and achievement levels of different races will converge as their environments converge. Consequently, the supreme

29. Nobel laureate William Shockley has had many of his college addresses disrupted or cancelled by the violence of black and white radicals. H. J. Eysenck was physically assaulted during a lecture in London. Richard Herrnstein, who never mentioned race, has been continuously harassed because he discussed the meritocracy that might derive from high I.Q. matings. The trials and tribulations of Arthur Jensen, who published a paper indicating that Negroes are less fitted for the contemporary educational process than whites, will be recorded in Chapter 20. The only allegations of racial differences which do not provoke a bitter reaction from the intellectual establishment, conservative and liberal, are those proposing the superiority of Jews. Since such statements are better described as racial propaganda than rational argument, they will be dealt with in Chapter 15.

30. See p. 216.

test of environmentalism may come in the not too distant future.

Meanwhile, the issues raised by the hereditarians are given more relevance with each day's events. It is hard to believe that the scientific curiosity of the world's most scientifically-curious society can be prevented much longer from cracking one of the last and most exciting frontiers of knowledge. But the metaphysics of racial equality, although so far having failed to provide any workable solutions for modern man's most insoluble problem, still fires the hearts of tens of millions—tens of millions who can be forgiven for refusing to accept the harsh possibility that nature practices a form of racial Calvinism.

Because the faithful are certain not to let go of their cherished equalitarian dream without a fight, there is likely to be a Galileo of genetics before there is a Newton.[31]

31. The counterattack against equalitarian anthropology moved out of first gear in 1974 with the publication of *Race* by Dr. John R. Baker, an internationally renowned Oxford biologist and a Fellow of the Royal Society, which to a British scientist is the next best thing to a Nobel prize. Dr. Baker minced no words and ducked no issues in what the respected journal *Social Biology* asserted was "perhaps the best-documented book on human races ever published." In contrast to the Boasites, Baker found significant mental as well as physical differences among the races, which he classified, analyzed and evaluated with such professional skill that hardly anyone rose to challenge him. In the United States the book was deliberately ignored by the mass media except for the *Washington Post,* which ran a splenetic review by a sociologist and former Israeli commando named Amitai Etzioni.

Chapter 4

The Physiological Stratum of Race

IT HAS BEEN REMARKED that race begins with the physical. To provide a clearer picture of the physiology of race, a few of the better-known systems of racial classification will be briefly summarized in the first part of this chapter. The second part will be concerned with the race-sorting methods of the man in the street, whose amateurish yet appraising eye is sometimes more perspicacious in such matters than the cold professional scrutiny of the physical anthropologist.

According to zoologists, there are some 1,116,300 living species of animals. Man, as *Homo sapiens,* is one of them. The derivation is as follows: [1] Animal Kingdom; Phylum Chordata; Subphylum Vertebrata; Class Mammalia; Order Primates; Family Hominidae; Genus *Homo;* Species *sapiens.* Here zoology stops and anthropology takes over. After the species comes the race.

Serious attempts at racial classification began almost two centuries ago. Most have been based on skin color with primary emphasis on the three most common and most noticeable shades of pigmentation: White (Caucasoid), Yellow (Mongoloid), Black (Negroid). J. F. Blumenbach, the father of physical anthropology, decided that the Brown (Malayan) and Red (Amerindian) races should be included in the color spectrum.[2] Using such criteria as nose form,

---

1. R. W. Hegner and K. A. Stiles, *College Zoology,* Macmillan, New York, 1959, pp. 2, 8.
2. J. F. Blumenbach, *The Anthropological Treatises,* trans. Thomas Bendyshe, Longmans, London, 1865.

stature and head shape as well as skin color, J. Deniker devised a sophisticated catalog of eighteen races.[3] A. L. Kroeber, late professor of anthropology at the University of California, added four races to the basic three: Australoid, Veddoid, Polynesian, Ainu.[4] Carleton Coon's classification has already been given. One or two anthropologists have classified races according to hair form: straight, wooly and curly.[5] By means of the latest techniques of blood type analysis, W. C. Boyd divided man into thirteen races.[6]

In regard to a racial classification of whites, the most popular, if not the most accurate, is that of William Z. Ripley, an influential American anthropologist whose three categories deserve some attention because of their effect on racial theories in the early part of the century. Ripley's white races, together with their "racial markers" and Old World homelands are listed below: [7]

Nordic.[8] Physical characteristics: long head, narrow or elliptic face, fair complexion, light-brown or blond hair, light-colored eyes, narrow nose, regular features, tall and slender physique. Old World habitat: Scandinavia, Northern Germany, Netherlands, Scotland, England. There are also scattered Nordic populations in Ireland, Belgium, Northern France, Central and Southern Germany, Switzerland, Austria, Northwest Russia (including the Baltic states) and Poland.

Alpine. Physical characteristics: round head, broad face, brown hair and eyes, ruddy complexion, stocky, average height. Old World habitat: Ireland, Belgium, France, Ger-

---

3. Coon, *The Races of Europe,* pp. 281–2.
4. A. L. Kroeber, *Anthropology,* Harcourt Brace, New York, 1948, p. 132.
5. *Ency. Brit.,* Vol. 18, pp. 864 ff.
6. Coon, *The Living Races of Man,* pp. 18–9.
7. W. Z. Ripley, *The Races of Europe,* Appleton, New York, 1910, Chapter 6.
8. Most contemporary anthropologists are quite leery of racial designations. When speaking of races they always deal in frequencies and averages, mindful of the intensive racial overlapping that makes classification of the white races so difficult and so frustrating. A Nordic in anthropological language merely means an individual who possesses more Nordic traits than Alpine or Mediterranean. After millennia of racial mixing, pure races are hard to come by, although there are still many individuals who closely approximate idealized racial models.

many, Switzerland, Northern Italy, Central Europe and the Slavic-speaking countries.

Mediterranean. Physical characteristics: long head, thin face, dark brown hair and eyes, olive complexion, regular features, small to medium height. Old World habitat: Spain, Southern France, Southern Italy, Greece, the Middle East, North Africa and the Mediterranean islands.

Many anthropologists, both before and after Ripley, developed more complicated, more subtle and often contradictory classifications for the white portion of mankind. Carleton Coon, who added seven more white races to Ripley's original three, made a special point about the Alpines, stressing not only their physical dissimilarities, but their different origin in time and place. According to Coon and a school of European anthropologists, Alpines are descended from Upper Paleolithic races which retreated to the remote areas and mountain fastnesses of Europe upon the arrival of Neolithic (Nordic and Mediterranean) invaders. In Coon's view, the Alpine represents the reemergence of the ancient European, a racial reincarnation increasing in intensity and seemingly favored by urbanization.[9]

Of special interest to Americans is the ethnological research of E. A. Hooton, who proposed nine separate racial divisions for the white population of the United States. In the list below only the races, their physical traits and their European points of origin are given.[10] Their quantitative distribution will be found in Chapter 8.

Nordic-Mediterranean. Long-headed with light eyes, dark hair, or dark eyes, fair hair. Old World habitat: British Isles.

Nordic-Alpine. Round-headed with high concentration of blondism or Nordic features and physical build. Old World habitat: Slavic lands, Germany, France.

Predominantly Nordic. Not quite the pure Nordic. Old World habitat: Britain, Scandinavia.

9. Coon, *The Races of Europe,* pp. 220, 289–93, 510, 560.
10. E. A. Hooton, *Twilight of Man,* G. P. Putnam, New York, 1939, pp. 203–10. The above classification was based on the physical studies of some 29,000 adult American males by the Harvard Anthropological Museum.

Dinaric. Round-headed, narrow nose, with great range of pigmentation. Old World habitat: Poland, France, Germany, Scotland, Near East.

Keltic.[11] Long-headed, red or reddish hair with blue eyes, or dark hair with blue eyes. Old World habitat: Southern Ireland.

Pure Mediterranean. Long-headed, dark eyes, dark hair. Old World habitat: Portugal, Spain, Italy.

East Baltic. Pure blond round heads with short, broad noses. Old World habitat: Germany, Russia, Poland.

Pure Alpine.[12] Dark-haired, dark-eyed round heads with broad noses. Old World habitat: France, Spain, Portugal, Poland, Balkans, Near East.

Pure Nordic. Long heads, ash blond or golden hair, pure blue or pure grey eyes. Old World habitat: Britain, Scandinavia.

The formal terminology of Hooton's racial table has by no means penetrated the popular idiom. While the average layman may agree in principle with some of the broad racial categories of the professional anthropologist, he uses a shorter and more pungent nomenclature. To the ordinary American, Mediterranean is the name of a sea between Europe and Africa and has no racial significance. The popular synonym for Mediterranean, in its anthropological sense, is "Latin." "Foreign-looking," even more vague and ambivalent, also describes the American who has darker than average skin, hair and eye coloration. But not too dark a coloration! The American Negro, for instance, is never "foreign-looking."

Popular anthropology is not afraid to subdivide its "Latin race." When someone is called "Italian-looking" or "Spanish-looking" or "Greek-looking," it means that persons of Italian, Spanish or Greek descent can presumably be recognized on sight. Other popular attempts at identifying Mediterraneans, by nationality group as well as by race, are represented

---

11. Some anthropologists prefer the term *Atlantic* for this category.

12. Hooton, unlike many of his colleagues, does not subdivide his Alpine category to include *Armenoid,* the dark, round-headed Alpine-Mediterranean hybrid of East-Southeast Europe and the Middle East.

by such slur words as "Wop" (Italian), "Dago" (Spaniard or Italian), and "Spic" or "Greaser" (applied to all Latins and to the even darker-hued, part-Mediterranean, Mexican-American mestizo). Occasionally, even American Indians are categorized as Latins by urbanites who have never been near a reservation.

Alpine is another racial term never used by the general public. The stocky, round-headed assembly line worker from Central and Eastern Europe, the barrel-necked bartender from Ireland [13] and the mill hand from French Canada are too blurred a racial type to have earned separate racial status from the people at large. They may still bear the peasant look of their Old World ancestors, but they no longer have a peasant's occupation. In general, the popular classification of Alpines in the United States has been limited to localized slang expressions (Bohunks, Canucks, etc.) based largely on national and geographic origins.

Nordic is the only white racial designation of the professional anthropologists to have found a place in the vernacular of popular anthropology. Although the term is most frequently applied to Scandinavians, many Americans, particularly the more willowy and blonder film stars, are described as "Nordic-looking." But because of its association with old theories of racial supremacy and Hitler's master race, Nordic is used rather sparingly and is being replaced by the acronym WASP (White Anglo-Saxon Protestant). Unflattering and imprecise, WASP is now a common tag for Americans with at least some Northern European physical traits, although millions of fair-complexioned Americans are not Protestants and additional millions not Anglo-Saxons. Since there is no such thing as a nonwhite Anglo-Saxon, a less redundant and equally stinging acronym would be ASP.

Majority is another term of increasing importance in the American racial dictionary. Completely ignored by professional anthropologists, the American Majority comprises the Nordic, Alpine, Nordic-Alpine and Nordic-Mediterranean elements of the population, as distinguished from the darker Mediterranean and colored elements. It is far from

---

13. An Alpine racial specimen. The red-headed, freckled-face Irish American and the blue-eyed colleen are Keltic in origin.

being a race, but it does contain demonstrable traces of an "American" physical norm. When traveling abroad, Majority members will "look like Americans" to the local populace, to whom U.S. citizens of Mediterranean, Oriental or Negro extraction will not look "American." Even on the home front—among the towheaded school children of the Midwest farm belt, among air force officers, airline pilots and astronauts, among the membership of ski clubs—there are those who appear more "American" than others, meaning that the former are within the racial parameters of the Majority physical model. If there is an American racial type in the making, it will almost certainly emerge from the Majority gene pool.[14]

Professional anthropology is as reluctant to extend racial recognition to the American Majority as it is to bestow racial status on American Jewry. Not one physical anthropologist in a hundred will admit that there is a Jewish race, although Carleton Coon has found some uniformity of cephalic index, facial structure and coloration among Russian and Polish Jews, who account for 80 percent of the American Jewish population.[15] Some ethnologists have detected a certain "nostrility" in Jews, but deny there is a unique set of Jewish facial expressions and gestures.[16] "Although Jews in Europe," writes C. D. Darlington, "always have different frequencies of blood groups from the Christian populations around them, they depart from the average Jewish frequencies in the direction of these populations."[17]

Historically, Jews were Semites and belonged to the Near Eastern branch of the Mediterranean race. Many Sephardic Jews still retain Near Eastern physical traits, often characterized as Jewish in the United States because there are so few Arabs. Many Northern and Central European Jews, including some Sephardim who went to Holland after their expulsion from Spain in 1492, possess a few Nordic traits and a measure of blondism. Eastern European Jews, who

14. For Wyndham Lewis' discovery of a "Super-European" American physical type, see p. 116.
15. *The Races of Europe*, pp. 643–4.
16. George Eaton Simpson and J. Milton Yinger, *Racial and Cultural Minorities*, Harper, New York, Revised Edition, 1958, pp. 57–9.
17. Darlington, *The Evolution of Man and Society*, footnote 3, pp. 467–8.

also exhibit occasional signs of light coloration, are racially distant from the olive-skinned, long-headed Sephardim of the Mediterranean area. Their round-headedness is probably due to their descent from the Armenoid Khazars, who converted to Judaism in the first millennium, A.D., or to intermarriage with other Armenoids and Alpine Slavs.

In spite of the findings of physical anthropologists, a sizable part of the American public, as well as many Jews themselves, continue to think of Jews as a separate and distinct race. All they have to go on are Biblical references to a common Jewish historical origin and various sets of physical traits which have a higher incidence among Jews than among members of any other American population group. The concentration of Jews in the more visible occupations and their irrepressible group solidarity nourish the popular idea of Jewish racehood.

In classifying the Mongoloid population groups in the United States, amateur and professional anthropology again part company. The general public considers American Indians a race apart, in line with traditional white attitudes toward the "Red Man," but physical anthropologists put them in the broader Mongoloid racial category.[18] To the man in the street, the Mongoloid race is the yellow race and is composed entirely of Orientals—Chinese, Japanese and other Eastern Asiatics—who "all look alike," presumably because popular techniques of identifying Mongoloids do not proceed much beyond the slanted eye (epicanthic fold).[19] Professional anthropologists also place Eskimos, Mexicans and Polynesians generally in the Mongoloid racial niche, recognizing the Mediterranean factor in the Mexican population and the Australoid presence in the Polynesian racial background.[20]

---

18. In the frontier days, because of their war paint and the sun's reflection on their highly-toned skin, Indians were called Red Men. From this came the concept of a Red race, an ethnological oversimplification that was later abandoned. Actually, Indian skin color varies from light yellow to mahogany. Coon, *The Living Races of Man,* p. 153.

19. Americans who have had firsthand experience in the Far East or Hawaii or who have lived in San Francisco have learned to detect certain racial differences among Mongoloids, particularly the darker coloration of the Southeastern Asiatics as compared to that of Chinese, Japanese and Koreans.

20. Coon, *op. cit.,* pp. 138, 184, 294.

Nonprofessionals consider Eskimos, Hawaiians and Mexicans as comprising separate races.

In the darkest area of the racial palette, professional and popular anthropologists are in some agreement. When they talk about the Negro race, they both mean approximately the same thing. Many professionals, however, believe that American Negroes as a whole are 20 percent to 30 percent white [21] and talk of coffee-tinted Mulatto strains and diverse tribal origins. The public has adopted a less subtle approach. It simply designates as a Negro anyone with enough telltale traces of Negro features, hair form and pigmentation. Except in a few urban areas where they have been given a distinct racial status of their own, Puerto Ricans are generally labeled Negroes, even though they may often have a much greater proportion of Mediterranean than Negro genes. In general, sensitivity to Negro coloration is so great that many Americans would call a high-caste Hindu with narrow face, long nose and other aristocratic features a Negro because of his dark skin.

The main variances in the popular and professional racial classification of the U.S. population are summed up in the following Pigmentation Spectrum, designed and constructed to reemphasize the overriding importance both anthropologists and laymen attach to skin color.

PIGMENTATION SPECTRUM

SKIN COLOR	Light White	White	Dark White	Yellow to Mahogany	Light Tan to Black
PHYSICAL ANTHRO- POLOGY	Nordic Nordic-Alpine Keltic Nordic-Medi- terranean	Alpine East Baltic Dinaric	Mediterra- nean Armenoid	Mongoloid	Negro Mulatto
POPULAR ANTHRO- POLOGY	Wasp		Latin	Mexican Oriental Indian	Colored Negro Black

21. Geneticist C. Stern estimates 20 percent. B. Glass and C. C. Li on the basis of blood group and other tests estimate 30 percent. Coon, *op. cit.,* p. 305.

Broadly approximate and far from rigorous in its presentation of the American racial amalgam, the Pigmentation Spectrum, in addition to illustrating the spectroscopic method of racial identification, does serve to clarify in graphic fashion the four cardinal rules of American race relations and racial etiquette:

a) The farther apart races are in the Spectrum, the more race-conscious will be the behavior of their members toward each other, and the more they will treat each other as stereotypes rather than as individuals.

b) The closer together races are in the White area of the Spectrum, the more easily their members may submerge or ignore their racial differences, even to the point of claiming the same racial affiliation.

c) The farther a race is to the right of the Spectrum the more it will vary from the American physical norm as defined by Majority racial parameters. In this respect, the Spectrum serves as an "assimilation meter." With one important exception,[22] the more races differ from the Majority in skin color, the less chance their members will have of assimilation.

d) The farther apart races are in the Spectrum the more the members of one race will accentuate the color differences of the other. Whites will find Latins darker, Orientals yellower, and Negroes blacker than they really are. Conversely, members of colored races will think whites much paler than their pigmentation merits.

Rule (a) above refers to the extensive use which the ordinary citizen makes of stereotypes in racial classification. The bane of professional anthropology, stereotypes often come in pairs: the idealized version of one's own race and the caricature of the other man's. The degree of caricature may depend on the degree of tension between any two races at any particular moment.

In the Philadelphia suburbs, for example, the Main Line family of old American lineage may identify with the Nordic stereotype of the tall, handsome blond with regular features, light eyes, high brow and long head. In Philadelphia proper, Negroes may have a different image of their Main Line

22. See Chapters 8, 15.

neighbors. The neck is thicker, the head rounder, the build shorter and stockier. Cruel lips, cold eyes and a frigid expression add up to an almost brutish appearance. The blond beast instead of Prince Charming.

Alpine stereotypes, many imported from the Old World, range (depending on who is doing the stereotyping) from the bloated Milwaukee burgher to Santa Claus, from the thick-jointed, flat-faced trucker to the nutbrown maid. Latin stereotypes are divided between grimacing gangsters and soulful Valentinos, Carmens and Carmelites. To many non-Jews, the Jew is often a squat, plutocratic vulgarian or a bespectacled, hothouse egghead. The Jew himself clings to the stereotype of an aristocratic, white-maned Moses or a swashbuckling Israeli sabra. Negroes like to identify with towering black athletes, charismatic preachers, Emperor Jones and rifle-toting Black Panthers. Many whites, on the other hand, cannot dissociate the Negro image from Uncle Tom, Aunt Jemima, Stepin Fetchit, urban muggers or head-hunting cannibal chiefs with bones through their noses.

The physiological stratum of race also includes character [23] and intelligence,[24] insofar as such traits have a genetic origin. No matter how controversial and unpleasant, racial stereotypes which go beyond surface physical characteristics cannot be ignored if they provide meaningful clues to popular

---

23. Is there a direct relationship between physical appearance and character? Plato equated the beautiful with the good. Lysis, 216 d, trans. J. Wright, *The Collected Dialogues,* Bollingen Series LXXI, Princeton University Press, Princeton, N.J., 1969. Hippocrates found that people with fair complexions had stubborn and independent attitudes. *Airs, Waters, Places,* p. 135. Hansen's famous study of the temperamental and character differences of the fair and dark populations of Norway was cited by Havelock Ellis in his comparison of skin color with performance. *A Study of British Genius,* Houghton Mifflin, Boston, 1926, pp. 306–7.

24. The low forehead and the pointed head have long been accepted as signs of stupidity or imbecility. In Elizabethan England there was a proverb, "Very round head, forgetful and stupid. Long head, clever and attentive." Thomas Hill, *Pleasant History,* London, 1613. In Shakespeare's *Anthony and Cleopatra,* his heroine asks, "Bears't thou her face in mind? Is it long or round?" The messenger: "Round even to faultiness." Cleopatra: "For the most part, too, they are foolish that are so." The Englishman's poor opinion of brachycephalism may be explained by the fact that the English have a lower incidence of round-headedness than any other Northern European population. Coon, *The Living Races of Man,* p. 399. Cromwell's Roundheads were so called because of their bowl-shaped haircuts, which contrasted sharply with the long flowing hair of the Cavaliers.

conceptions of racial differences. A case in point is the average white American of Northern European extraction who indulges in character and intelligence stereotypes by considering himself and "his kind" to be wise, hard-working, brave, dedicated, honest and God-fearing—on the whole a slightly deflated combination of Puritan divine, Virginia planter and Western pioneer. On the intelligence scale he rates the Orientals and Jews rather high, but finds more craftiness than wisdom. He views Latins as frivolous, sexually volatile, superficial and prone to organized crime and treachery. He considers Indians, Mexicans and Negroes as stupid, shiftless, unclean and overfond of alcohol or narcotics.[25]

In return, the more sophisticated Latins and Jews classify the average Majority member as a plodding, credulous, loutish Philistine, while viewing themselves as the inheritors of a superior religion and culture. To the non-Jew, Jews are often as avaricious as Shylock. Jews, as might be surmised, consider themselves extremely charitable. Both Indians and Negroes are likely to typecast whites as unbridled horse traders, paragons of insensitivity, specialists in genocide and sexually repressed Horatio Algers and Simon Legrees.

Many such stereotypes dissolve and many new ones emerge as the political, economic and social status of Americans alters. Status changes, however, usually occur long before stereotype changes, and it may take some time for the public stereotype to catch up with the publicized stereotype. In less than a century, the Jewish pawnbroker has yielded to the affectionate Jewish supermother; the shuffling and obsequious Negro to the champion prizefighter; the drunken Irish brawler to the kindly priest; the opium-smoking, pig-tailed coolie to Charlie Chan. In many a television and stage drama the blond hero has become the blond villain. The repulsive traits, both physical and psychological, now heaped upon Germans, Russians and Arabs were once reserved for the "unspeakable" Turks.

---

25. Medill McCormick's statement that Theodore Roosevelt understood the "psychology of the mutt" reveals another common attitude of oldline Americans toward all other Americans, white or colored. Richard Hofstadter, *The American Political Tradition*, Knopf, New York, 1949, p. 230.

In recent times, racial stereotypes have come under as sharp an attack as racism itself. But those most opposed to stereotypes usually have their own, and in the end all that is accomplished is the substitution of one set of stereotypes for another. Rather than concentrate on the abolition of stereotypes—as impossible a task as abolishing the human tendency to generalize—social scientists might welcome them as instructive signposts to the study of intergroup behavior. They have an impressive pedigree, deriving not only from gossip, hearsay and the lower depths of human depravity, but from folklore, myth, religion, literature, art and music. Some of the most sublime expressions of human creativity have made liberal use of racial stereotypes.

Carleton Coon is one of the very few modern anthropologists who is not too disturbed about stereotypes: "Popular, subjective labels in the designation of races, used among persons ignorant of the existence of physical anthropology, are often truer than the hesitant results of erudite wanderings in the labyrinth of numbers." [26]

But it is now time to enter "the labyrinth of numbers." To arrive at a broader understanding of American racial dynamics, the emphasis now shifts from the qualitative to the quantitative aspects of race.

---

26. *The Races of Europe,* p. 335.

PART II

Racial Composition of the United States

Chapter 5

White Immigration

IT IS TRUE that all Americans—Indians included—are either immigrants or the descendants of immigrants. It is equally true that radically different kinds of immigrants came to America for radically different reasons. One thinks of the Indian inching his way over the Aleutian land bridge in search of food . . . the Pilgrim building his city of God in the New England wilderness . . . the Negro chained to the hold of a slave ship.

From the earliest colonial times to almost the middle of the nineteenth century, white immigrants were motivated by love of fame and adventure, by land hunger, by fortune hunting, by the hope of retaining and expanding their religious identity,[1] by misgivings about the governments of their homelands and their governments' misgivings about them, by a concern for liberty,[2] and by the nagging and endemic

---

1. The religious motivation must not be overrated. Only 5 percent of white Americans at the time of the War of Independence were church members. Franklin Littell, *From State Church to Pluralism*, Anchor Books, Garden City, N.Y., 1962, p. 32. One reason for the Pilgrims' transatlantic passage was the fear that their sons and daughters would "wed out in the world" if they extended their period of refuge in the "swinging" Netherlands. *Ibid.*, p. 5.

2. D. H. Lawrence asserts the Puritans were running away from liberty, that they simply could not stand the ever-increasing personal freedom and humanity of post-Renaissance England, that there was far more religious freedom in the England they left than in the New England they founded. *Studies in Classical American Literature*, Viking Press, New York, 1964, pp. 3, 5.

Northern European wanderlust. The immigration was made up of farmers, artisans, tradesmen and soldiers of fortune, with a light froth of dissident aristocrats and a thin sediment of jailbirds. Though it is often forgotten, many of the early white immigrants had already enjoyed a fair measure of prosperity in their native lands.[3] Where it existed the economic drive was important, but it was directed more toward economic gain than economic security.

Natural selection was extremely hard on the pioneering vanguard. More than half the Mayflower's passengers died either on the sea voyage or during their first year in Massachusetts.[4] In Jamestown, the first permanent English colony in America, there were more than five hundred colonists in 1609. No more than sixty were alive a year later.[5] On the morning of March 22, 1622, an Indian war party fell upon colonial settlements in the upper reaches of Virginia's James River. In a few hours, 347 whites were killed without respect to age or sex.[6] Elsewhere, famine, disease, Indian raids and the rigors of the frontier carried on a relentless winnowing, culling and sifting of a people whose principal elements, from the outset, had never been a cross section of the English or of any other Old World population.[7]

In 1689, the number of whites in the thirteen colonies was approximately 200,000. By 1754, it had grown to a million—300,000 in New England, 300,000 in the Middle Colonies, 400,000 in the South. In 1790, the year of the first Federal Census, the national origins of American whites and their percentage of the total white population were estimated as follows: British (77), German (7.4), Irish (4.4), Nether-

3. Alexis de Tocqueville, *De la démocratie en Amérique*, Gallimard, Paris, 1961, Tome 1, p. 31.

4. Ellsworth Huntington, *The Character of Races*, Scribner's, New York, 1925, p. 304.

5. William Sweet, *Story of Religion in America*, Harper, New York, 1939, pp. 42, 51.

6. *Ibid.*, p. 34.

7. The Puritans came largely from East Anglia, one of the blondest regions of England. Ellis, *A Study of British Genius*, footnote, p. 39. Selective processes were apparently going on during all phases of immigration. Polish immigrants, for example, were taller and thinner than the Poles who remained at home. Coon, *The Races of Europe*, p. 565.

lands (3.3), French (1.9), Canadian (1.6), Belgian (1.5), Swiss (0.9), Scandinavian (0.9), other (1.1).[8]

The profoundly Protestant character of white immigration persisted until the 1840's, when the Irish, driven out by a potato blight, began crossing the Atlantic by the hundreds of thousands, together with large contingents of Central Europeans, including political refugees from the abortive 1848 revolutions.[9] Although its religious balance may have shifted a little over the next three or four decades—three million Irish arrived, plus millions of continental Catholics—the United States still remained overwhelmingly Northern European in racial background. The Alpine, Keltic and Dinaric genes which had been injected into the American bloodstream were of the light-complexioned variety, and the few Irish and Central European racial traits that were at odds with Northern European physical norms did not clash in the critical area of skin color. Even so, the *old* Old Immigrants mounted a large-scale, crypto-racial attack against the *new* Old Immigrants, chiefly the Irish, who in a revival of classic Reformation polemics were charged with "Popery." [10]

Long before the Old Immigration came to an end, descendants of the original settlers began a new mass migration which took them to Western New York and the Midwest—eventually to Texas and the Far West—and denuded New England of half its Anglo-Saxon population. It was this migration, as historically important as the one from England to New England, which fixed the present racial character of much of the trans-Appalachian United States.[11]

---

8. See Appendix.

9. The Catholic Irish are to be distinguished from the Protestant Scotch-Irish, most of whom originated in the lowlands of Scotland and later moved to Northern Ireland. 200,000 Scotch-Irish arrived in the fifty years preceding American independence. Maurice Davie, *World Immigration,* Macmillan, New York, 1949, pp. 21–24.

10. The American party, whose members were called Know Nothings by the political opposition, claimed 43 representatives, 5 senators and 7 state governors shortly before the outbreak of the Civil War. The increasing urgency of the slavery issue, however, played havoc with a political party which, in addition to its Protestant bias, was drawing subtle racial distinctions among whites. Davie, *op. cit.,* p. 88.

11. Stewart Holbrook, *The Yankee Exodus,* Macmillan, N.Y., 1950, p. 4.

The 1880's marked the start of the New Immigration, which brought millions of Jews, Slavs, Italians and other Eastern and Southern Europeans to the United States. This time the character of white immigration, which had been changing very slowly for almost half a century, underwent a rapid and deep transformation. Most New Immigrants were brunet, olive-hued Mediterraneans or belonged to the darker-complexioned divisions of the Alpine race. They came to escape starvation, not to risk it—to crowd the cities, not to clear the land. Old Immigrants had been more than willing to trade security for insecurity. The new arrivals had reverse priorities. Both groups were overloaded with dreams, but those of the New Immigrants were more mundane. Whether the fault of genetics or environment or both, the mental traits of the Old and New Immigrant types were often in sharper contrast than their physical characteristics.

The last, organized, nationwide manifestation of what might be called Old Immigrant solidarity was an attempt to dam the flood of the New Immigration, and culminated in the 1924 Immigration Act. Total immigration from Europe was limited to approximately 150,000 annually, as compared to the all-time high of 1,285,000 in 1907.[12] Furthermore, the legislation was racially selective in that European countries were given quotas according to their relative contribution to the American population as of 1920.[13] As Congress planned it, whatever small amount of immigration still trickled in was to be weighted in favor of the Northern European racial matrix.

But events took a different course. Many Northern European countries left their quotas partly unfilled or filled them with persons in transit from other parts of Europe. Congressional and presidential dispensations were given to anti-Nazi[14] and anti-Communist refugees, World War II displaced persons, and 120,432 "war brides," many of whom were

12. Total immigration from Southern and Eastern Europe for the period 1820–1930 was 13,944,454.
13. Davie, *op. cit.*, p. 377.
14. 140,000 German and Austrian Jews came to the U.S. between 1933 and 1940. 150,000 more European Jews, most of them survivors of concentration camps, arrived in the postwar period (1945–54). James Yaffe, *The American Jews,* Random House, New York, 1968, p. 8.

Asiatics.[15] There were no quota restrictions on the hundreds of thousands of Cubans who fled Castro, on Puerto Ricans (American citizens), on Mexicans or on other inhabitants of the Western Hemisphere.[16]

As of 1965, approximately ten million legal immigrants had arrived in the United States under the quota system.[17] If the number of illegal immigrants is added (estimated at almost 175,000 annually in the 1920's),[18] the sum is not inconsiderable. The problem is compounded by the presence of aliens, of whom 3,669,000 registered with the Immigration Service in 1967 and 2,000,000 did not.

Both in regard to type and number, the immigrants who came to the United States under the quota system violated the letter and the intent of the Immigration Acts of 1921 and 1924 and the McCarran Act of 1952. The primary aim of all this legislation had been to preserve the racial profile of the United States as it had been defined and defended by the Founding Fathers [19] and had become "fixed" in the late

---

15. *Ency. Brit.*, Vol. 15, pp. 467–8.

16. Puerto Rican and Mexican immigrants more properly belong to the nonwhite immigration, the subject of the following chapter. Cuban refugees were largely upper and middle class and therefore came from the whiter elements of the Cuban population, whose lower class has a strong Negro strain. For an estimate of the present size of these minorities, see Chapter 14 and Table V, p. 60.

17. *Statistical Abstract of the U.S.*, 1969, p. 91.

18. Davie, *op. cit.*, p. 400. Besides demonstrating the difficult task of immigration enforcement, the 500,000 individuals apprehended by U.S. government agencies for illegally crossing the Mexican border in the single year of 1950 dramatize the wide gap between immigration statistics and immigration facts. *One America,* edited by Francis J. Brown and Joseph S. Roncek, Prentice-Hall, Englewood Cliffs, N.J., 1962, p. 387.

19. Washington was opposed to unrestricted immigration because he wanted to protect the "American character." Jefferson feared that, since the bulk of European immigration would eventually have to come from Central, Southern and Eastern Europe, the newcomers would import with them the ideas and principles of absolute government under which they and their ancestors had lived for so many centuries. Charles Beard, *The Republic*, Viking Press, New York, 1962, pp. 10–11. Another argument against immigration was that it limited the natural increase of the native population. According to "Walker's Law," which assumes that the fecundity of indigenous groups is cut down by immigrant competition, the 3,500,000 American whites of 1790 would have increased to a number equivalent to the present-day population if the Constitution had forbidden all immigration. Madison Grant, *The Conquest of a Continent*, Scribner's, New York, 1933, p. 276.

nineteenth century. It was much too late for laws that would permit a privileged caste of fair-haired Nordics to lord it over a bottom layer of black slaves and white serfs. But it was not too late for Congress to prevent the Northern European racial nucleus from being physically and culturally submerged by continuing mass migrations of Southern and Eastern Europeans.

Quotas both succeeded and failed in the accomplishment of the grand Congressional design. The Northern European preponderance was safeguarded in the quantitative sense. But immigration continued at more than a trickle, and most of it was composed of the very racial elements which Congress had sought to bar. Concurrently, the political, economic and social impact of the Southern and Eastern European immigrants was greatly magnified.

It goes without saying that the quota system had always been an open sore to liberal and minority organizations. It was an outrage to those who sincerely believed in racial equality, and a stumbling block to those who were beginning to promote other than Northern European brands of racism. In 1965, bowing to an unprecedented lobbying effort that had been gathering momentum for more than half a century, President Johnson signed a new immigration act which kept the quota system, but radically changed the quotas. The national origins provisions, so hateful to the liberal-minority forces, were abolished and immigration limited to: relatives of American citizens and permanent residents (74 percent); members of professions and others of "exceptional ability" (10 percent); skilled and unskilled workers certified by the Secretary of Labor (10 percent); refugees from political persecution or national calamities (6 percent). The first category, which crowded out all others, was immediately dominated by the spouses and unmarried children of first-generation citizens from Greece, Italy and the Philippines.[20] With respect to numbers, an annual ceiling of 170,000 and 120,000 was placed on immigrants from the Eastern and Western Hemispheres, re-

---

20. *New York Times,* Aug. 31, 1970, pp. 1, 37.

spectively, thereby imposing a quota for the first time on Canadians and Latin Americans.[21]

When the Johnson immigration bill came before the Senate, only eighteen votes were cast against it, all from Southern Senators whose constituencies contained the nation's largest concentrations of old-fashioned white supremacists.[22] The great immigration debate, which had become the great racial debate, was over. At the urging of a British-descended, Southern-minded, Texas-born President, Congress had decided that the British or Northern European preponderance, which had both created and given unity and direction to American civilization, no longer deserved legislative sanction.

21. *Britannica Book of the Year,* 1966, p. 368.
22. *Time,* Oct. 1, 1965, p. 27.

Chapter 6

Nonwhite Immigration

IF THE ENGLISH began the Old Immigration, the Indians, who arrived some twenty thousand years earlier, initiated what could be described as the Prehistoric Immigration. In the year 1500, there were supposedly 850,000 Indians within the geographic limits of the present-day continental United States and Canada.[1] By 1770, the Indian inhabitants of the areas occupied by the thirteen colonies had been for the most part exterminated or evicted. During and after the Winning of the West, Indians were placed on reservations and at one time their total number was reduced to less than 250,000.[2]

The Mongoloid migration to North America—American Indians are classified as Mongoloids—was revived after more than a score of centuries with the arrival of the Chinese coolie in California. The Chinese, who first worked in the gold mines and then helped build the Western end of the transcontinental railroads, provoked a hostile reaction from whites. From time to time, Western state legislatures and Congress passed acts of exclusion against the Chinese, whose number reached 107,000 in 1890.

The Japanese immigration did not begin until after the Civil War and never quite reached the proportions of the

---

1. *Our American Indians at a Glance,* Pacific Coast Publishers, Menlo Park, Calif., 1961, p. 6.
2. In recent times the Indian population group has made a substantial recovery. See *American Indian* section, Chapter 16.

Chinese. In 1907 it was brought to a halt by the "Gentleman's Agreement" worked out with Japan by President Theodore Roosevelt. After World War I, Asiatic immigration was such a rarity that the annual quota of one hundred set for China and Japan by the 1924 Immigration Act actually resulted in an increase in the number of legal immigrants from these two countries.[3]

Not aliens in the terminology of the 1924 Immigration Act, Filipinos were later so designated by Congress. By 1930 some 45,000 had come to the United States. When the Philippine Islands were granted independence in 1934, Filipinos were put in the same category as other Orientals and their annual immigration quota fixed at fifty.[4] A large and unexpected Asiatic migration occurred in 1975, when 150,000 Vietnamese refugees arrived in the United States.

The nonwhite immigration which has had the most lasting effect on the nation's racial composition has of course been that of the Negroes. Blacks from Africa were never categorized as Old Immigrants because of their different skin color and because of the different set of circumstances which brought them to America. Negroes could not be considered New Immigrants, because most stopped coming long before the New Immigration started. In point of fact, some Negroes arrived in the colonies almost as soon as the first whites. Like many whites, they came as indentured servants. But while the whites were able to work off their servitude (the average term in the Southern colonies was four years), the Negroes' status hardened into one of permanent and perpetual indenture, otherwise known as slavery. By far the greater number of blacks, however, were slaves upon arrival.

In 1790, according to the first Federal Census, there were 697,623 Negro slaves and 59,538 free Negroes in the United States. Few African Negroes came after 1820, when the British outlawed the slave trade. But in 1860 there were supposedly 3,953,760 Negro slaves and 488,070 free Ne-

---

3. The immigration picture outside the continental U.S.—i.e., the Hawaiian Islands—is a very different one and will be briefly examined in Chapter 16.
4. Davie, *op. cit.,* pp. 342–7.

groes. If true, this means that the Negro population increased almost six-fold during the slavery period.[5] In the next hundred years it more than quadrupled.

The largest influx of immigration since World War I has originated not in the Old World, but below the Rio Grande and in the West Indies. Although they cannot be classified as 100 percent nonwhite, the millions of Mexican-Americans who live in California and the Southwest—most of them having moved there since 1924—are certainly more Indian than Caucasian. Also largely in the nonwhite category are the vast numbers of part-Negro, part-Mediterranean Puerto Ricans who migrated to the United States, principally to New York City, after 1945.[6]

The 1965 Johnson Act, which purportedly ended racial quotas, had the effect of favoring nonwhite over white immigration. Now that the colored peoples of Europe and Asia are no longer excluded from America by the device of national origins, it is certain that Europeans will comprise a smaller proportion of future immigrants. Although the Western Hemisphere quota should theoretically reduce the genetic flow from Mexico and the Caribbean, Mexicans and colored West Indians have never paid much attention to immigration controls in the past and are not likely to change in the near future. Of the four to twelve million illegal immigrants or aliens estimated to be in the U.S. in 1975, probably eighty percent were Mexicans. As citizens, Puerto Ricans continue to have free entry.

The Eastern Hemisphere quota, as well as the priorities given to relations of American citizens and to professional and skilled workers, has resulted in an increase of Asiatics, but not Negroes. African blacks are not noted for their occupational skills and have been separated far too long from American Negroes to have maintained any family ties.[7]

How the Johnson Act, which did not take full effect until 1968, is changing the pattern of American immigration, is

5. Mooney, *Smithsonian Miscellaneous Collection*, XXX, 1928.
6. Simpson and Yinger, *Racial and Cultural Minorities*, p. 136.
7. On the other hand the number of legal and illegal Negro immigrants from the Caribbean area has risen sharply.

best shown by listing the number of immigrants in fiscal years 1965 and 1970 from the ten principal immigration sources.[8]

IMMIGRANTS AND COUNTRY OF ORIGIN

1965		*1970*	
Canada	40,013	Mexico	43,034
Mexico	37,432	Philippines	25,425
Britain & No. Ireland	29,747	Italy	24,481
Germany	26,357	Cuba	16,684
Cuba	20,086	Greece	16,542
Dominican Republic	10,851	China	16,297
Italy	10,344	Jamaica	15,309
Colombia	9,790	Britain & No. Ireland	13,925
Poland	7,458	Portugal	13,297
Argentina	5,629	Canada	12,263

It is noteworthy that only two of the countries in the 1970 column, the United Kingdom and Canada, have populations of Northern European racial origin, and both are well down the list. The two leading countries, Mexico and the Philippines, have mestizo and Mongoloid populations, and the next three, Italy, Cuba and Greece, specialize in Mediterranean immigrants.

Since the new quota system only adds up to 270,000 annually, this by itself does not indicate an immediate shift in the racial makeup of the American population as a whole. But there are other factors to be considered.[9] Thousands of Mediterraneans and nonwhite immigrants come to the United States each year outside the Johnson quotas as a result of various Congressional "deals." [10] Countless numbers of illegal immigrants—almost all of them nonwhite—also continue to

---

8. *New York Times,* Aug. 31, 1970, p. 37.

9. According to George H. Brown, Director of the Census Bureau, immigration is expected to remain at 400,000 per year for the foreseeable future —270,000 Johnson Act immigrants and the remainder refugees and other special cases. By 1985, some 6,000,000 persons will probably have entered the country after 1970 and will have had some 1,500,000 children. *Washington Post,* Dec. 29, 1970. The Census Bureau reported at the end of 1970 that nonwhite immigration had jumped from 4.4 percent in 1950–60 to 13.6 percent in 1960–70. *Washington Post,* Dec. 31, 1970.

10. In one such deal a Congressman introducing a special law to permit the entry of 5,000 Sicilians obtained the support of another Congressman by promising to vote for the latter's bill to let in 3,000 Iraqi Jews. *Time,* Nov. 21, 1969, p. 86.

arrive. Admittedly, the present rate and type of immigration is not leaving as deep an imprint on the American racial mold as the soaring birthrates of dark-white and nonwhite native Americans. But times change—and time changes—and over a period of decades even small genetic infusions from abroad add up. Perceptibly or imperceptibly, the national complexion is darkening.

Chapter 7

The Fusion and Mosaic Fallacies

THE GREAT AMERICAN DREAM has been a collection of dreams, one of the wilder variety being that of the Melting Pot. The Melting Pot visionary prophesied that any immigrant, no matter what his race, nationality or social background, once immersed in the giddy liquefaction of American life would be transformed into a uniquely American solute with all the Old World heritage of caste and cultural disparity dissolved away.[1]

That dream, long dying, is now dead. The Melting Pot, which worked to some extent in the time of the Old Immigration when the ingredients were more racially and culturally harmonious, refused to function when the New Immigration was added to the solution. Melting Pot advocates seemed to forget that different races thrown together in the same environment instead of dissolving or fusing tend to stratify or

---

1. Israel Zangwill wrote a book entitled *The Melting Pot* (Macmillan, New York, 1909) in which he defined America "as a crucible in which divers races and nationalities are being fused into a new and greater race with a superior culture." If Zangwill was the high priest of the Melting Pot, Emma Lazarus was the high priestess. Never much of a poet, Miss Lazarus was even less of a prophet. She may have invited the "teeming refuse" of Europe to American shores, but when they arrived they did not perform as she had predicted. In later life, she turned out to be something of a racist, with her uncharitable remarks about Russians and ancient Greeks and her glowing Semitism. See *The Poems of Emma Lazarus*, Houghton Mifflin, Boston, particularly "The Crowing of the Red Cock," "The Banner of the Jew" and "Gifts." Also see her ethnocentric communication to Rabbi Gottheil in H. E. Jacob's *The World of Emma Lazarus*, Schocken Books, New York, 1949, p. 78.

separate.[2] "The more two different peoples grow alike in externals," Santayana wrote, "the more conscious and jealous they become of diversity in their souls . . ."[3]

What population mixing there has been in the United States has largely taken place among nationality, not racial groups. As one sociologist, R. J. R. Kennedy, put it, ". . . Irish, Italians and Poles intermarry mostly among themselves and British-Americans, Germans and Scandinavians do likewise, while Jews seldom marry Gentiles."[4] Some integrationists expected an upswing in the intermarriage rate after the 1967 Supreme Court decision overturning a miscegenation law in Virginia.[5] But only a small increase has been noted.

This is not to say that racial crossing in the United States has stopped. It began with Pocahontas and it did not end with the marriage of former Secretary of State Dean Rusk's daughter to a Negro. It has either been highly publicized, as with the interracial marriages of screen stars and celebrities, or clandestine, as with white liaisons with Indian maids on the frontier, slave girls on the plantation or fancy Mulatto mistresses in Charleston and New Orleans. It is a sign of the times, and of the lengthening shadow of the minority presence, that the male role in racial crossing is now being monopolized by minority members, except in the case of American G.I.'s stationed abroad.

But sexual role-changes in interracial socializing do not necessarily mean more mixed offspring. Negro-white dating, now a commonplace in a few prestigious and avant-garde colleges, has not been accompanied by an equivalent rise in Negro-white mating. Modern education is apodictically color-

---

2. In 1930, 51 percent of all Detroit Negroes lived in predominantly white areas. In 1960, only 15 percent lived in white areas. *Time,* Nov. 9, 1962, p. 62.

3. *The Life of Reason,* Vol. II, p. 166.

4. Simpson and Yinger, *Racial and Cultural Minorities,* pp. 546–7. The last statement in the quotation needs some clarification. Jews *are* marrying Gentiles in the upper reaches of "society," in the professional and entertainment world, and in the middle-sized cities, where marital opportunities within the Jewish community are limited. Some statistics show that 25% of Jewish marriages now involve a non-Jewish spouse.

5. There are still miscegenation statutes in a score of states, but none has been enforced since the Supreme Court ruling. In 1960–70 there were 67,000 marriages between Negroes and whites.

blind, yet classroom violence works for the separation rather than the integration of races. Rock concerts, the rallying points of the nation's supposedly unbigoted youth, are often as segregated as Metropolitan Opera performances.

In direct contradiction to Melting Pot theory, the children of interracial couples do not become any generalized American type or the progenitors of a new race. They remain Negroes or Indians or Orientals. Only in marriages between Americans of Northern European descent and "Latins" is it possible for the offspring to lose their minority status.

In the slavery era, when tremendous social and psychological barriers separated whites from Negroes, a wave of interracial breeding in the South introduced white genes into a large segment of the Negro population.[6] Today, when many of these barriers have been lowered, there is much less Negro-white mixing. Today, in spite of the hold that race leveling has on education and the news media, the races of America instead of disappearing in some theoretical solvent are actually precipitating out.

With the passing of the Melting Pot fantasy has come the anti-fantasy—the American Mosaic. The intellectual *mise-en-scène* has suddenly been rearranged to accommodate a new sociological fad, the *pluralistic society,* in which all races and nationality groups live harmoniously side by side, all maintaining and strengthening their racial and cultural identity, each making its own contribution in its own way to the total picture of American life.

Like the promoters of the Melting Pot, the salesmen of pluralism have misread history, which teaches that pluralistic societies are static and caste-ridden and a standing invitation to disorder and disaster. Historically disoriented, the voices of pluralism are also dramatically contradictory. They are opposed to racism in theory, but support minority racism in practice. They uphold group identity, but demand integration. They approve of racial quotas, but are against racial discrimination. The Negro leadership is split down the middle concerning these issues. One group advocates an increasing

------

6. See footnote 21, p. 29.

participation in white society, while the other demands withdrawal and apartheid.

Meanwhile, the American social order totters along in the grip of rising racial tension, which is both a cause and effect of pluralism. The Mosaic has turned out to be as great a failure, as great a misfiring of the imagination, as the Melting Pot. Mosaics are bits and pieces of inorganic matter which once put in place stay in place. Races are pulsating, organic continuities altering in size and status, now dynamic, now static, as the age dictates and as they dictate to the age. The Darkening Immigrant is not evidence that America is entering an age of pluralism. He is a harbinger of changing racial hierarchies.

Chapter 8

A Racial Census of the United States

A RACIAL CENSUS of the United States must begin with whatever applicable statistics are available from the Census Bureau. In this regard, the following figures were contained in the 1970 Federal Census:

TABLE I

White.	177,748,975
Negro.	22,580,289
Indian.	792,730
Japanese.	591,290
Chinese.	435,062
Filipino.	343,060
All Other *.	720,520
Total	203,211,926

* The category, "All Other," includes Polynesians, Koreans, Malayans, Hawaiians, Aleuts, Eskimos, Thais, etc.

A quick reading of Table I might indicate that most of the work of a racial census has already been done. The American population has been divided into one white and several nonwhite categories. A second look, however, discloses that only two of the main categories, White and Negro, would be considered acceptable racial designations by professional anthropologists, while amateur anthropologists would prefer that Japanese, Chinese, Filipinos and most "All Others" be grouped under an Oriental heading. Amateur anthropologists, with the backing of some professionals, would also insist on a breakdown of the White classification. They would insist in vain. Only when it is realized that the Census Bureau does not publish statistics on the various white races in the United States will the difficulty of compiling an accurate racial census be understood.

There are, nevertheless, some non-racial population studies that can be used for determining the ethnic composition of American whites. The Census Bureau does collect demographic data on some nationality groups and on the foreign born. Many minority organizations keep a running census of their own minorities. Experts on minority affairs are also deeply interested in the accumulation of minority statistics. All such figures, if handled with discretion, can be of help in taking up the Census Bureau's unfinished business.

But no meaningful white statistics can be obtained without first making two adjustments in Table I. The Federal Census counts most Mexicans and Puerto Ricans as whites. The American public and most anthropologists emphatically do not. Consequently, Mexicans and Puerto Ricans should be subtracted from the white total.

An estimate of the Mediterranean element in the American population can be obtained by the national origins method. The membership of population groups from preponderantly Mediterranean countries (Portugal, Spain, Greece, etc.) can be added up and the total assigned to a Mediterranean entry. The same process can be applied to population groups from preponderantly Alpine countries (the Slavic lands, Baltic states and Hungary). The estimated size of all these population groups is listed in *One America,* generally conceded to be the best source book on American minorities and nationality groups.[1] In cases where the European mother country has more than one significant racial component, Alpine allocations can usually be made according to the racial composition of the homeland, as estimated in Carleton Coon's *The Races of Europe* or in Carl Brigham's *A Study of American Intelligence* (see Appendix).

---

1. *One America,* edited by Francis J. Brown and Joseph S. Roncek, Prentice-Hall, Englewood Cliffs, N.J., 1962.

The number and racial affiliation of the rest of the white
population can be obtained by subtracting the Mediterranean
and Alpine totals from the White entry in Table I. This remainder represents a broadly approximate count of the largest
segment of Americans of Northern European descent—the
very few pure and very many impure Nordics from preponderantly Nordic Britain and Scandinavia, partially Nordic Ireland, Germany, Switzerland, Holland and Belgium, and frac-
tionally Nordic France and Austria. The indirect approach
to the enumeration of the Nordic category is necessitated by
the absence of reliable estimates in *One America* or elsewhere
for these population groups.[2] Those who wish to see a calcu-
lation of the Northern European element by the national
origins method may consult the Appendix, which also contains a statistical interpretation of America's white racial history and tabulated racial allocations of all nationality groups.

In line with the procedures, changes and corrections proposed so far, the short-form Federal Census (Table I) has
now been "reconstituted" into Table II.

TABLE II

Race	Number	% of White Population	% of Total Population
White			
Nordic	112,775,000	65.86	55.50
Alpine	46,290,000	27.04	22.78
Mediterranean	12,157,000	7.10	5.98
Sub-total	171,222,000	100.00	84.26
Nonwhite			
Mexican	5,073,000		2.49
Oriental	2,090,000		1.03
Indian	793,000		.39
Puerto Rican	1,454,000		.72
Negro	22,580,000		11.11
Sub-total	31,990,000		15.74
Total	203,212,000	100.00	100.00

2. The nationality groups which comprise the Northern European racial
amalgam have generally lost their separate identities and in a minority-
conscious era no longer draw the attention of privately-financed census
takers. A recent Census Bureau study, however, finally did get around
to some of these neglected groups, but the results were very misleading.
See p. 546.

In Table II percentages have been introduced; Mexican and Puerto Rican entries added; Asiatics and "All Others" collected under a single "Oriental" heading. The White category has been removed and apportioned among Ripley's white racial divisions.[3] Minority statistics and racial allocations to substantiate the apportionment will be found in the appropriate sections of Part IV and in the Appendix.

There is no point in denying that, mathematically speaking, Table II leaves much to be desired. Unofficial minority statistics, some up to date, some perhaps twenty years old, have sometimes been substituted for official Census Bureau figures.[4] White racial allocations have been arrived at by a combination of educated guesswork, arbitrary anthropological definitions and wide-ranging projections. Whole population groups have been assigned to a Nordic, Alpine or Mediterranean category on the basis of their national origin, although no European country contains such an unadulterated population. Also, in compiling the white racial estimates, no account has been taken of the varying birthrates of different population groups or selective immigration from the motherland.

But even if it should contain errors as great as 10–20 percent, Table II serves a purpose. It quantifies the Pigmentation Spectrum in Chapter 4 by attaching numbers to population groups of differing skin coloration, the chief criterion of popular racial classification. Table II also demonstrates, in a rough way, how many people are black, brown, red, yellow and white; how many whites (Nordics and Alpines) are white enough to be considered white; and how many whites (Mediterraneans) are not.

As a partial confirmation of the white allocations in Table II, reference is again made to E. A. Hooton's racial classification of the white population of the United States.[5] Hooton's racial divisions, it will be recalled, were not based on national origins data or population group statistics, but on a Harvard-sponsored anthropological study of 29,000

3. See pp. 23–4.
4. See pp. 40, 62.
5. See pp. 24–5.

A Racial Census of the United States 57

adult American males. In addition to dividing whites into nine separate races, Hooton estimated the proportion of each race to the total white population. These percentages, previously omitted, are now given in Table III below. In columns 3, 4 and 5, they are distributed among the racial categories of the Pigmentation Spectrum and the results compared with Table II percentages.

TABLE III

E. A. HOOTON'S RACIAL DIVISIONS	HOOTON'S % OF TOTAL U.S. WHITE POPULATION	PIGMENTATION SPECTRUM CATEGORIES		
		LIGHT WHITE *Nordic* Nordic-Alp. Nordic-Med. Keltic	WHITE *Alpine* Dinaric E. Baltic	DARK WHITE *Medit.* Armenoid
(1)	(2)	(3)	(4)	(5)
Nordic-Mediterranean	25	25		
Nordic-Alpine	23	12	11	
Predominantly Nordic	17	17		
Dinaric	13.3		13.3	
Keltic	8.48	8.48		
Pure Mediterranean	4.38			4.38
East Baltic	3		3	
Pure Alpine	2.68		2.68	
Pure Nordic	2.44	2.44		
Percentage Total		64.92	29.98	4.38
Table II Percentages		65.86	27.04	7.10

The close correlation of the percentages of Tables II and III can hardly be described as a coincidence. But as always in the case of racial allocations, accuracy has been sacrificed on the altar of generalization. Hooton's East Baltics, in spite of their Alpine physique and circular crania, are probably blonder and fairer than many Nordic-Mediterraneans, who were assigned to the Light White column principally because they represent a common British racial type.[6]

Given greater authority and credibility by the Hooton estimates, Table III will now undergo one further revision to bring it in closer agreement with the American racial picture as seen by the roving anthropological eye of the man in the street. Since the public does not distinguish, or does not care to distinguish, between Nordics and Alpines and the various Nordic-Alpine shadings, these two white categories have been combined and designated "White" in Table IV below. Also, in keeping with the dictates of popular anthropology that Mediterraneans are only dubiously white, the Dark White entry has been changed to Latin.

TABLE IV

Race	Number	% White Population	% Total Population
"White"	159,065,000	92.90	78.28
Latin	12,157,000	7.10	5.98
Mexican	5,073,000		2.49
Oriental	2,090,000		1.03
Indian	793,000		.39
Puerto Rican	1,454,000		.72
Negro	22,580,000		11.11
Total	203,212,000	100.00	100.00

However offensive it may be to the political sensibilities of the Census Bureau and to the professional sensibilities of physical anthropologists, Table IV presents a more instructive and realistic statistical summary of the American population than the Federal Census (Table I). It portrays the United States as a moderately heterogeneous nation, with about 15.7 percent of its population nonwhite and about 7.1 percent of its whites on the racial borderline. Looking at Table IV, an atomic physicist might compare the country's racial com-

---

6. See Hooton's description of the Nordic-Mediterranean on p. 24.

position to a white nucleus with six electrons whose orbital radius increases linearly with skin color.

But Table IV, unfortunately, is still not the end of the racial numbers game. As stated earlier in this study, race has its cultural and psychological side. In the words of one controversial American ethnologist, there is a "blood-race" and a "thought-race" [7]—which is to say that population groups who act as a race must be defined and treated as such even if they do not qualify as a race in the accepted anthropological, biological and zoological meaning of the word. Just as dark coloration excluded some whites from the "White" racial category in Table IV, certain cultural "colorations" would exclude others.

Consequently, one more table is necessary—one which takes into account the non-physiological stratum of race. To satisfy this requirement, Table V is offered as a "culturally corrected" version of Table IV. The physical basis of race has been retained by using, where possible, the various categories and numerical totals of the previous Tables. The cultural basis has been introduced by classifying population groups according to their degree of assimilation. The several Latin and nonwhite groups have become Unassimilable Minorities. Central and Eastern Europeans and French-Canadians, as well as a considerable number of Irish-Americans, have been designated Assimilable Minorities. Jews, most of whom qualify physically for Assimilable status, have been classified as an Unassimilable Minority because of their long history of non-assimilation everywhere.[8]

---

7. Lothrop Stoddard, *The New World of Islam*, Scribner's, New York, 1921, p. 160. It is the "thought-race" which made it possible for Congressman Adam Clayton Powell, who genetically could hardly be distinguished from a Mediterranean, to call himself a Negro. It is the same "thought-race" which permits Israeli premier and former chief of staff Major General Itzhak Rabin, with his fair complexion, light eyes and many other Northern European characteristics, to designate himself a Jew. When Stoddard wrote, "For his blood-race he will not stir; for his thought-race he will die," he apparently believed that in a test of strength between the physical and the psychological sides of race, the latter would often be the winner.

8. Only China ever succeeded in assimilating its Jewish population. Nathaniel Peffer, *The Far East*, University of Michigan Press, Ann Arbor, 1958, p. 43.

TABLE V

RACIAL COMPOSITION OF THE UNITED STATES (1970)

Designation	Assimilation Status	Number	% Total Population	Source
Majority	Assimilated	128,273,000	63.12	White entry, Table IV, less Assimilable White Minorities and Jews.
White Minorities	Assimilable			
Irish	"	13,000,000	6.39	Irish-American section, Chap. 13.
Polish	"	3,000,000	1.48	Polish section, Chap. 13.
French-Canadian	"	3,000,000	1.48	French-Canadian section, Chap. 13.
Other	"	6,722,000	3.31	Baltic, Slavic and Hungarian sections, Chap. 13.
Sub-total		25,722,000	12.66	
Jewish	Unassimilable	5,869,000	2.89	Chap. 15.
Southern Italian	"	7,011,000	3.45	Southern Italian section, Chap. 14.
Other Medit.	"	4,347,000	2.14	Portuguese, Spanish, Greek, Lebanese, Armenian, Cuban sections, Chap. 14.
Sub-total	"	17,227,000	8.48	
Nonwhite Minorities	Unassimilable			
Mexican	"	5,073,000	2.49	Mexican section, Chap. 16.
Oriental	"	2,090,000	1.03	Chinese, Japanese, Filipino sections, Chap. 16.
Indian	"	793,000	.39	Indian section, Chap. 16.
Puerto Rican	"	1,454,000	.72	Puerto Rican section, Chap. 16.
Negro	"	22,580,000	11.11	Chap. 17.
Sub-total		31,990,000	15.74	
RECAPITULATION	Assimilated	128,273,000	63.12	
	Assimilable	25,722,000	12.66	
	Unassimilable	49,217,000	24.22	
TOTAL		203,212,000		

The thinking that went into the construction of Table V will be explained more fully in Parts III and IV. Here it might be pointed out that assimilation, although the dictionary defines it as the merging of cultural rather than biological traits, has physical as well as psychological overtones and is a decisive factor in American race relations.

Finally, within the somewhat arbitrary confines of Table V, the demography of the United States is presented in a form which both identifies and numbers the principal participants in the present-day racial confrontation. The American Majority, briefly mentioned in Chapter 4, now takes its place as the protagonist of this study and of the American racial drama. A huge, unwieldy, ungainly population mass, six times larger than the largest minority and comprising 63.1 percent of all Americans, the Majority is physically defined by its Nordic and Alpine racial affiliations, the former strain being predominant. Whatever Mediterranean ancestry is present must be well diluted.

Psychologically defined, the Majority is the only fully assimilated population group. Until recently every minority, willy-nilly, has gravitated toward it and around it. The cultural definition of the Majority is given by its central position in American society, by its dominant role in the shaping of the American state and by its historic task as the New World propagator of the at first Anglo-Saxon, then Northern European,[9] now Americanized version of Western civilization.

But Table V, it should be noted, carries a 1970 dateline. The question may be reasonably asked if the Majority and minority proportion of the total population will not be substantially altered by 1990, when there may be 256,000,000 Americans, or by 2020, when there may be 298,000,000.[10] The answer is that if Puerto Ricans, Mexicans and Negroes maintain their present high birthrates America's racial mix

---

9. Northern European, although a geographical term, is perhaps the best racial description for the American Majority. It is broad enough to include the various Nordic and Alpine crosses, yet narrow enough to exclude the darker Southern Europeans and the nonwhite population groups.

10. Census Bureau projections from *U.S. Book of Facts, Statistics & Information* (*1969*), p. 7, and *Miami Herald*, Dec. 18, 1972, p. 34-A.

will slowly be transformed. A 1971 Census Bureau report indicated that Mexican-American females between 35 and 44 had an average of 4.4 children each and Negro females in the same age group averaged 3.6 children each, as compared to the national average of 2.9 children.[11] In another report the Census Bureau estimated there may be as many as 35,000,000 nonwhites in 1990, an almost twofold increase in three decades.[12] Even so, according to one population expert, it will not be until 2050 that nonwhites will regain the proportion (19 percent) of the total population that Negroes held in 1790.[13] But since most Mexicans and Puerto Ricans are defined as members of the white race in these projections, they are woefully conservative.

In contrast to the Unassimilable Minorities, whose growth is now due in large part to natural processes and only in small part to immigration, the American Majority, although its share of the total population will probably remain the same, continues to grow by a process of accretion. Half of all Assimilable Minority members will probably be absorbed into the Majority in one or two generations. Barring nuclear war, revolution, famine, genocide and nationwide epidemics, the racial composition of the United States at the start of the twenty-first century may be estimated as follows: Majority (62 to 64 percent); a reduced Assimilable Minority (5 to 7 percent): a bigger ratio of Unassimilable whites (9 to 11 percent) with a greater concentration of Mediterraneans; a much larger proportion of nonwhites (20 to 22 percent).[14]

But the power and durability of a race do not depend on numbers. A healthy morale, a healthy biology and a consciousness of kind are much more important factors. Its large size, at least for the time being, is one of the Majority's great

---

11. Associated Press, Nov. 28, 1971.

12. *Statistical Abstract of the U.S.* (1969), p. 7.

13. Daniel J. Bogue, *The Population of the United States,* The Free Press of Glencoe, Ill., 1959, p. 767. In the next twenty years, Negroes, now an urban as well as a rural population group, are likely to outnumber whites in Detroit, Cleveland, Baltimore, Chicago, St. Louis and Philadelphia. They already compose almost 75 percent of the population of the nation's capital. Theodore White, "Racial Collision in the Big Cities," *Life,* Nov. 22, 1962, p. 106 and *Time,* Nov. 23, 1970, p. 14.

14. The possibility of a significant increase in the nonwhite population by hybridization has already been discounted. See pp. 50–1.

handicaps. The multitude of its members, aggravated by their wide dispersal and the steady addition of only partly related genetic elements, make the Majority extremely susceptible to various forms of deracination.[15]

American racial dynamics have now entered a phase where most of the spirit, most of the drive, most of the competitiveness and most of the will to power are on the side of the smaller battalions, the dynamic minority battalions that have seized the racial initiative.

---

15. Particularly to that form of deracination known as proletarianization. See Chapter 25.

PART III

The Majority at Bay

Chapter 9

Majority Origins

AN UNMISTAKABLE SIGN of racelessness, a synonym for powerlessness in a multiracial state, is a general apathy toward the subject of racial origins. As Macaulay put it, "A people which takes no pride in the noble achievements of remote ancestors will never achieve anything worthy to be remembered by noble descendants."[1] At present, the American Majority is little inclined to examine its racial history or prehistory. It is even less inclined to compose, embroider and propagate the myths which are the taproots and symbols of race consciousness.

In general, Majority members have satisfied their search for ethnic identity by tracing their ancestry to a European mother country. It was this emphasis on national origins which led to the assumption that the United States was an Anglo-Saxon nation, a term still used by many foreign and a few American journalists and historians when they refer, anachronistically, to America as an "Anglo-Saxon power." In the first century of American independence, the Anglo-Saxon component[2] of the population was numerically predominant, so the assumption was well founded. It was supported by a strong cultural link, as well as by the English origin of most of the citizenry. But today, although the

---

1. Macaulay, *History of England from the Accession of James II*, Macmillan, London, 1914, Vol. 3, p. 1526.
2. Included in this component were many Americans of Welsh, Scotch, and Scotch-Irish descent who had the right to object to an Anglo-Saxon pedigree.

language has come through without overmuch damage and although other cultural vestiges are still recognizable, the British-American plurality, the root of the Anglo-Saxon connection, no longer exists.

The Anglo-Saxon element of the American white population (77 percent in 1790) is today less than 41.4 percent.[3] It may still comprise a majority of the Majority (55 percent), but otherwise it has become a minority (only 35 percent of the entire population).[4] It has also become racially unidentifiable. Other population groups of Northern European origin are now so undifferentiated, so thoroughly a part of the Majority racial colloid, that Americans of Scandinavian, German, Belgian and Dutch descent, as well as the assimilated segments of the Irish, French, Italian, Central European and Slavic immigration, can scarcely be distinguished from WASPs. Even the American aristocracy is by no means an Anglo-Saxon monopoly. Any American *Almanach de Gotha* or *Debrett's* would have to include Du Ponts, Vanderbilts, Astors, Rockefellers and Roosevelts, as the *Social Register* currently does. The founders of these enterprising families were anything but Anglo-Saxons.[5]

To find more solid ancestral moorings, the Majority, including the English-descended portion of it, will have to delve much deeper in time and space. The dwarfed perspectives of British and other Northern European "national histories" will have to be considerably broadened and lengthened. The genetic and cultural contribution of England to American civilization was undeniably much more important than that of any other single nation or group of nations. Nevertheless, the English are only one offshoot of a great ethnic division to which other Majority members can claim equal kinship. Since Majority unity can never rest on national origins, which are inherently divisive, it might be well for Majority historians to stop treating the Majority past as a

3. See United Kingdom entry in Appendix table.
4. Obtained by applying United Kingdom percentage in Appendix table to the appropriate population totals on p. 60.
5. Rudyard Kipling once heard Theodore Roosevelt, who would have been a Prince if there had been an American nobility, "thank God in a loud voice that he had not one drop of British blood in him." Kipling, *Something of Myself*, Doubleday, Garden City, N.Y., 1937, p. 131.

chronological patchwork of petty Old World rivalries, inter-larded with tendentious sociological dogma, and start treat-ing it as a discrete genetic and cultural continuum.

One of the great difficulties of this approach is not the unearthing of the anthropological evidence. Enough of it is already at hand. The principal deterrent is the formidable opposition of the intellectuals who dictate the shape and con-tent of contemporary historical interpretation. A single step in the direction of establishing common Majority racial roots would be, in their eyes, a direct challenge to one or more of the currently accepted fashions in historicism—the materi-alistic fixations of Marx, the religious ecstasies of Toynbee, the morphological prophecies of Spengler, the liberal plati-tudinizing of the Schlesinger school and the anti-history of Popper.

The curious and opportunistic double standards of the intellectual community actually encourage a certain amount of *minority* dabbling in racial history. There is no outcry when American Jews, bypassing the European countries from which they came, claim descent from a Semitic race of Hebrews in ancient Palestine.[6] This is a large concession con-sidering that contemporary social science is dead set against the derivation of bloodlines from cultural and religious simi-larities. Nor are there loud objections from academicians when blacks write volumes about the ethnic ties of American Negroes, not to the West African tribes from which they sprang, but to *négritude* and to the "African soul." The same historical license is freely granted to romantic Irish and Welsh Americans who dream of the departed glories of the Kelts (despite glaring evidence of their Nordicism),[7] and to American Indians and Mexican-Americans who speculate about noble forebears in a pre-Columbian golden age.

But all such flights of racial fancy, all such imaginative attempts to establish racial identity, are forbidden to the Ma-jority. From a minority standpoint this taboo is quite under-standable. The farther back Majority racial history is pur-

6. Ludwig Lewisohn's *This People* (Harper, New York, 1933) is perhaps the classic example of modern Jewish racial mysticism.
7. Coon, *The Races of Europe*, pp. 378, 397.

sued, the more inevitable is its collision with the Aryan theory.[8]

Assuming for the sake of argument that the Aryan theory deserves some credibility, it then follows that an Indo-European or Nordic proto-race was the primary source of many of the world's principal civilizations—Aryan (India), Kassite, Hittite, Persian, Mycenaean, Greek, Roman, Keltic, Teutonic, Slavic and the latter-day Western European. Moreover, if a racial as well as a linguistic connection is admitted between the ancient Indo-European peoples [9] and present-day Northern Europeans and their racial cousins overseas, then Majority members can claim as their ancestors the authors of the *Vedas,* Homer, Darius, Plato and Caesar, as well as many of the greatest figures in medieval and modern history. They can also claim an art almost as old as the Egyptian and Sumerian and a literature that antedates that of the Hebrews by more than a millennium.[10]

Although it is not generally known, several top-rated historians and scholars have lent their support to the Aryan theory. V. Gordon Childe, described by the *Encyclopaedia Britannica* as "easily the greatest prehistorian in Britain of his generation, and probably in the world," [11] wrote that Aryans "appear everywhere as promoters of true progress and in Europe their expansion marked the moment when the prehistory of our continent begins to diverge from that of Africa or the Pacific." [12] Another British academician not only agreed that the various Indo-European peoples possessed a related language but also discovered traces of a

8. Some of the more vigorous advocates of the Aryan theory have already been mentioned in Chapter 3, as well as the surprising similarity of certain Indo-European root words. Hitler's espousal of the Aryan theory, it is unnecessary to add, did nothing to improve its already low standing in the eyes of the Western intellectual community.

9. A recent intriguing effort at historical synthesis identifies the island of Helgoland in the North Sea as Atlantis and its inhabitants as sea-roving Northmen, who took part in history's first documented naval battle—an attack on the fleet of Ramses III off the mouth of the Nile in the thirteenth or twelfth century B.C. Jürgen Spanuth, *Atlantis,* Grabert-Verlag, Tübingen, 1965.

10. The Vedic hymns go back to 2,000 B.C. The oldest parts of the Bible to 850 B.C. See footnote 9, p. 152.

11. *Ency. Brit.,* Vol. 5, p. 502.

12. As quoted by Darlington, *The Evolution of Man and Society,* p. 146.

common mythology.[13] Toynbee did the Aryan cause no harm with some flattering remarks about the historical acumen of the Aryanist, de Gobineau.[14]

More recently, Oxford Professor C. D. Darlington stated of the Aryans: "Although they are stretched across two continents we attribute to them a common ancestry and a common origin, somewhere between the Danube and the Don and at some time before the end of the third millennium, B.C." [15]

Firmer evidence in support of the Aryan theory includes the genetic imprint of properly dated skulls with the proper cephalic index in areas where Indo-European languages were spoken, and a wealth of literary and artistic allusions attributing fair coloration and blondness to the gods and heroes of the early Indo-European cultures.[16] The sensitivity of the Aryan invaders of India to skin color—the basis of their caste system—might have been a genetic rather than an acquired trait since it is still prevalent among Northern Europeans and Majority Americans.

Finally, to the dismay and extreme discomfort of orthodox racial equalitarians, anthropologist Carleton Coon reawakened and gave new life to the Indo-European speech-race correlation by stating the "Indo-European languages were, at one time, associated with a single, if composite, racial type, and that . . . racial type was an ancestral Nordic." [17] Coon went on to say that the patricians of the Roman Republic were mostly Nordic in race,[18] and brought the genetic connection up to date by describing North America as the world's "greatest Nordic reservoir." [19]

From any scholarly standpoint the Aryan theory is an oversimplification. A few oblong skulls, a few Nordic pro-

13. Rev. Sir George Cox, *Mythology of the Aryan Nations*, Kegan Paul, London, 1903.
14. *A Study of History*, Vol. VI, pp. 216–17.
15. Darlington, *op. cit.*, p. 140.
16. Coon, *The Races of Europe*, Chapters V and VI. Also see Chapter 12 of this study.
17. Coon. *op. cit.*, p. 221.
18. *Ibid.*, p. 554. So, perhaps, were some of the early emperors. Suetonius speaks of Augustus' hair as "inclining to golden," of Nero's "light blond hair" and Galba's "blue eyes." *De Vita Caesarum*, 2, 79.
19. Coon, *op. cit.*, p. 651.

files on crumbling statuary, a few literary references to blondism do not prove the existence of a great culture-bearing Indo-European race. But neither do they disprove it. At all events, if the Majority intelligentsia is too cautious or too intimidated to subscribe to a remote Indo-European lineage, it can hardly ignore the Majority's more readily traceable descent from the Indo-European-speaking Germanic peoples, who began to play a commanding role in world history during and after the fall of the Western Roman Empire.

In the 4th, 5th and 6th centuries, A.D., *Völkerwanderungen* from the German forests released a torrent of Northern European genes over much of the continent, some even spilling over to Africa. For Majority members of English descent in particular and for American history in general, the most eventful part of this migration was the Germanizing or "Nordification" of England by the Teutonic Angles and Saxons. Similar genetic influences were introduced into the British Isles over the next four or five centuries by the incursions of Danes and other Northmen.

Even as the wave of Germanic expansion was contracting and the Ostrogoths, Visigoths and Vandals [20] were losing their kingdoms in Italy, Spain and North Africa, a new Northern European migration was in the making. In the next six hundred years the Scandinavian Vikings and Normans conquered Normandy, Sicily, Southern Italy, England and parts of Ireland, and settled Iceland, the coast of Greenland and, briefly, Newfoundland. [21] In the east, in about the same time sequence, bands of roving Swedish warriors and merchants known as Rus and Varangians became lords of the Russian riverways. Apart from giving the country their name,

---

20. Eighty thousand Vandals, according to the count of their king, Genseric, disappeared after three generations, presumably by indiscriminate mating. Darlington, *op. cit.*, p. 317.

21. The Northmen almost, but not quite, captured London (895), Paris (885–886) and Constantinople (860). In *A Study of History,* Toynbee has inserted an entrancing piece of historical speculation in which he envisions what might have happened if the pagan Scandinavians had captured these European capitals, gone on from Iceland to permanently settle America and, instead of being converted to Christianity, had outlawed it. Vol. II, pp. 438–43.

they set up one of their own leaders, Rurik, as the first Russian Czar. In 1042, Varangians sailing west through the Aegean and Normans sailing east from Sicily marked the Scandinavian encirclement of Europe by engaging each other in a Mediterranean sea battle.[22]

The racial drive of the Northmen, before it was enervated in *douce France* and in warmer, lemon-scented lands farther south, catalyzed the Crusades, an ill-fated but Herculean effort to found a vast Teutonic fief in the Near East. The ostensible purpose of the Crusaders, under such Norman leaders as Tancred, Bohemund and Richard I of England, was to make the Holy Land safe for Christianity.

In other crusading movements taking place in Europe in these times, the motives were more specifically racial. In the east and northeast, the Teutonic Knights were pushing back the Balts and Slavs. In Spain, the Visigothic aristocracy had reemerged after centuries of hiding in the mountain fastnesses of Galicia and Asturias and was mounting a counterattack to drive the Arabs from the Iberian peninsula —a military operation which culminated in the founding of the Spanish Empire and the discovery of the New World.[23] Needless to say, none of these Crusades was conducted according to the teachings of the New Testament. Whatever moral restraints and humane acts were exhibited could as well be ascribed to chivalry as to Christianity.[24]

---

22. For centuries the Varangians formed the personal bodyguard of the Byzantine emperors. After the battle of Hastings, they were replaced by Englishmen fleeing the Norman conquest of Britain. Eric Oxenstierna, *The Norsemen*, trans. Catherine Hutter, New York Graphic Society Publishers, Greenwich, Conn., 1965, p. 279.

23. The Visigoths and their identifiable progeny are all but gone from the racial map of Spain. But if they have vanished into Spain's overwhelmingly Mediterranean ethnic solvent, some racial memories still stirred in one of the finest minds of modern Spain. Ortega y Gasset in his *Meditación Preliminar* has written (p. 121): "¿Quién ha puesto en mi pecho estas reminiscencias sonoras, donde—como en un caracol—perviven las voces íntimas que da el viento en los senos de las selvas germánicas?"

24. Chivalry is a refined mixture of stylized military courtesy, honor and courtly love which is still faintly recognizable in the unwritten rules of what in England and America is known as fair play. Tacitus detected one chivalric rite in pagan German society. "Tum in ipso concilio vel principum aliquis vel pater vel propinquus scuto frameaque iuvenem ornant." *De Germania*, 13, 5–6. For a fairly comprehensive modern survey of chivalry, see F. W. Cornish, *Chivalry*, Swan Sonnenschein, London, 1901. For a

Before the Middle Ages ended,[25] the Holy Land was lost.
The Turks began their march to Constantinople, Budapest
and the outskirts of Vienna. The Popes, who were largely of
Lombard (Germanic) origin,[26] placed themselves at the head
of the populations of Southern Europe and humiliated the
German emperors. Meanwhile, the Teutonic and Norman aristocracy, having developed national loyalties, began to marry
into rich mercantile families. And in the east, the Nordic
Slavs were being "Alpinized" as they mixed with neighboring peoples and underwent other undetermined genetic and
adaptive processes.[27]

The large-scale colonial undertakings of Spain and Portugal, beginning in the fifteenth century, could hardly be
called manifestations of Northern European racial energy,
although more than a few *conquistadores* displayed an unusual disproportion of non-Mediterranean traits.[28] The racial

less reverent and somewhat hilarious view of the same subject, see Robert
Briffault, *The Mothers,* Macmillan, New York, 1927, Vol. 3, pp. 382–423,
or later one-volume edition of same title.

25. Will Durant has some pertinent remarks about the racial composition
of Europe at the height of the Middle Ages. "The Germans, by a millennium
of migrations and conquests, had made their type prevail in the upper classes
of all Western Europe except central and southern Italy, and Spain. The
blond type was so definitely admired in hair and eyes that St. Bernard
struggled through an entire sermon to reconcile with this preference the 'I
am black but beautiful' of the Song of Songs. The ideal knight was to be
tall and blond and bearded; the ideal woman in epic and romance was
slender and graceful, with blue eyes and long blond or golden hair." *The
Age of Faith,* Simon and Schuster, New York, 1950, p. 832.

26. Hildebrand, who as Gregory VII was the most temporal of all Popes,
was a Lombard from Tuscany. Before Germans in the Papal office put their
religious preferences above their racial ties, their pro-Teutonic sentiments
often approached those of Hitler. See particularly Bishop Liutprand's tenth-
century polemic on the "baseness and cowardice and avarice and effeminacy
and mendacity" of the Romans in Toynbee's *A Study of History,* Vol. IV,
pp. 522–23.

27. "The Slavs, like all the other Indo-European-speaking peoples whom
we have been able to trace, were originally Nordic, and there is no suggestion in their early remains, in the regions studied, of the numerically predominant brachycephalic racial increments which today are considered
typically Slavic." Coon, *The Races of Europe,* p. 220.

28. Vasco da Gama's great grandmother was a Hereford, a member of
the highest echelon of English nobility. Henry Hart, *Sea Road to the Indies,*
Macmillan, New York, 1950, p. 97. Columbus, a North Italian, was tall
with long head, blue eyes and red hair. Samuel Morison, *Admiral of the
Ocean Sea,* Little, Brown, Boston, 1942, p. 47. Cortés traced his lineage
back to the Lombard kings of Italy and Pedro de Alvarado, his bravest

lineaments of the Reformation, however, were unmistakable. In the words of Macaulay: "The Reformation had been a national as well as a moral revolt. It had been, not only an insurrection of the laity against the clergy, but also an insurrection of all the branches of the great German race against an alien domination." [29] Macaulay might better have said Northern European instead of German, because after the Reformation Southern and Austrian Germans remained solidly Catholic.

Protestantism, the religious emancipation of the North, helped inspire and accelerate the most massive Northern European expansion of all time. In a succession of great, seafaring "Folkwanderings," which lasted from the seventeenth to the end of the nineteenth century, British, Germans, Scandinavians and Irish shipped out by the millions to North America, South Africa, Australia and New Zealand, and by the tens of thousands to the outposts of empire in Black Africa, South America, Asia and the Pacific Islands.

At the start of the twentieth century, despite the French Revolution which had all but demolished the old Teutonic ruling class in most of Latin Europe, Northern European power and influence were never greater. The British and German Empires with their invincible land and sea forces, their near monopoly of world commerce, their technical efficiency and the boundless energy of their industrious citizenry constituted a concentration of military and economic strength that no other nation or group of nations could match.

This immense power, it might be noted, rested on more than guns and butter. It was the end product of a set of unique institutions, among which was representative government, whose origins Montesquieu had detected in the behavior and practices of ancient German tribal assemblies.[30]

---

lieutenant, was so blond that the Aztecs called him *Tonatiuh,* the Sun. Prescott, *Conquest of Mexico,* Modern Library, New York, pp. 128, 258. Balboa, the discoverer of the Pacific, was fair with reddish-golden hair and beard. Kathleen Romoli, *Balboa of Darien,* Doubleday, Garden City, N. Y., 1953, p. 31.

29. *The History of England from the Accession of James II,* Vol. 1, p. 58.
30. *De l'esprit des lois,* 11, 6–8. Iceland had a parliament, the Althing, as early as the tenth century.

A fondness for personal freedom, an independence of spirit, the unusually high status accorded women and a deep affection for the land were considered typical characteristics of Teutonic-speaking peoples by Tacitus in his essay, *De Germania*. Such attitudes and habits were probably the seeds of the Magna Carta and of the subsequent British emphasis on individual rights and liberties. Perhaps the greatest institutional achievement of all was the legal system—including that Scandinavian or Teutonic invention known as trial by a jury of one's peers, a rudimentary form of which was carried to England by the Normans.[31]

All these milestones of social evolution seemed to have sprung from an almost instinctive recognition that "the basis of . . . society was the free man."[32] The highest refinement and expression of this political reflex was embodied in the activity and legislation of the British Parliament, making for a climate of political and economic stability unparalleled in history. It was the comparatively stable social environment produced by these institutions which was the basic precondition for Northern European leadership in government, art, science, industry, agriculture and almost every other sector of human endeavor.

It was only natural that these institutions were carried across the Atlantic and further refined and developed by the English and other Northern Europeans who settled in North America. If a special biological inheritance had accounted for the progress and prosperity of the Northern European states in the Old World, it would have been reasonable to expect that a New World country with an overabundance of the same genetic resources would become an even greater nation—perhaps the greatest nation of all.

It took less than two centuries of national independence and two World Wars for this prophecy to come true. The irony was that by the time the United States had become the dominant force in world affairs, the American Majority, the principal agent of American greatness, was no longer the dominant force in America.

---

31. See p. 378.
32. J. R. Green, *A Short History of the English People,* Harper, New York, 1892, Vol. 1, p. 2.

Chapter 10

The Decline of the Majority

THE DECLINE OF the Majority began with the political and military struggle between the North and South.

In addition to nationalistic and cultural differences, Northern Europeans in Europe were divided by geography, principally the Baltic and North Seas and the English Channel. In the United States, the great divider was weather. The mean July temperatures of Massachusetts and Pennsylvania are 73.5°F and 75.5°F, respectively. The mean July temperatures of Virginia and Mississippi, 79°F and 80°F. These few extra degrees of summer heat made it impossible for Southern plantation owners to recruit a labor force within their own ranks. In a hot climate the Northern European is worthless as a field hand. The South would never have obtained anything like its flourishing antebellum prosperity without a large supply of Negroes.

To meet the demands of their environment, Southerners created their own unique *modus vivendi*—a highly romanticized and heavily scented version of which still haunts American history. Northerners, prompted in part by what has been described as the Anglo-Saxon's "sentimental flaw" [1] and in part by extending the concern for their own individual rights to others, first tried to alleviate slavery, then to end it. Southerners reacted to Northern meddling much as both they and the Northern colonists had reacted to King George's meddling a century earlier. They seceded.

1. Madison Grant, *The Passing of the Great Race*, Scribner's, New York, 1916, pp. 14, 77.

If the North had been more patient and had been willing to "wait out" slavery a little longer—it was already doomed by the mechanization of cotton growing, overplanting and other causes—there might never have been a Civil War. In that event, the American Majority today would be substantially more numerous. The death toll in the war was 610,000 —compared to 4,435 in the War of Independence—and almost all the dead were of Northern European descent. In spite of the greater number of Northern casualties,[2] the war's dysgenic effects fell much more heavily on the South. The North had a population of 22,000,000, nearly all white, as against 12,000,000 in the South, one-third of whom were slaves.[3] The Southern officer class, in its reckless chivalry, was decimated, while in the North the purchase of substitutes was a thriving business. Seventeen percent of the Confederate generals were killed, compared to 2.5 percent of the Union generals.[4]

After the carnage ended, the Southern branch of the Majority became for all intents and purposes an oppressed minority. Northern carpetbaggers and Southern scalawags, using unknowing Negroes as tools, made a successful, though short-lived, bid for political and economic control—historians called it Reconstruction—which exasperated more Southern feelings than the war itself. The passage of time and surges of national unity during World Wars I and II served to cool Southern resentment, until it was rekindled in the 1950's by the North's reopening of the Negro question. The use of Army paratroopers and Federal marshals to enforce Supreme Court rulings was hardly calculated to let sleeping animosities lie.

Second only to the tragic polarization of North and South

2. There were 360,000 deaths on the Northern side; 250,000 on the Southern. The war costs amounted to about $5 billion, with an additional $3 billion outlay for postwar rehabilitation. Beard, *The Rise of American Civilization*, Vol. 2, pp. 98–9.

3. John Hope Franklin, *From Slavery to Freedom*, Knopf, New York, p. 386.

4. Nathaniel Weyl, *The Creative Elite in America*, Public Affairs Press, Washington, D.C., 1966, p. 57. "The cost in blood to the Union," Weyl added, "was paid chiefly by the poorer classes and by those without much education and influence. The Confederacy, by contrast, enacted draft laws which bore on rich and poor equally. . . ."

as a cause of Majority decline was the tremendous development of the national economy. If too much money is the seedbed of corruption, it is also the hotbed of racial amnesia. The great wealth generated before the Civil War by Majority plantation owners and shipping tycoons, and after the war by industrial and financial magnates, tended to concentrate their minds and energies on such mundane matters as money-making, profit-taking and business organization. Majority plutocrats gave little thought to the effect their demands for an ever larger labor force would have on the American racial makeup.

"As the Nordic planter of the South," Charles Beard explained, "in his passionate quest for wealth, was willing to sabotage his own kind in a flood of Negroes from the wilds of Africa, so the Nordic mill owner of New England, with his mind on dividends, took little thought about the nationality or color of those who stood patiently at his spindles and looms or huddled into the tenements of his cities." [5]

The political consequences of this indiscriminate call for manpower were not long in coming. Even before the Civil War, the Irish presence began to make itself felt in a few of the biggest cities, where the Majority first tasted defeat at the polls. The defeat became national many decades later when the white minorities in the North combined with still embittered Southerners to win presidential elections.

It was the Majority's obsessive materialism, its habit of putting the tangibles before the intangibles of civilization, which made possible and perhaps made certain the Great Depression. Rugged individualism, laissez-faire, the separation of powers and many, many other cherished possessions in the Majority hope chest went up in the smoke of emergency legislation to save the national economy. The New Deal, the first administration to inject sizable amounts of non-Majority personnel and non-Majority ideology into the federal government, marked the coming of age of the liberal-minority coalition.

Minority participation in politics and in every other sector of American life has now increased to where it can be said

---

5. Beard, *op. cit.*, Vol. 1, p. 640.

that the Majority is no longer the racial Establishment of the United States.[6] The Majority image—that of Western man as derived from Northern European (principally Anglo-Saxon) antecedents and as modified by the frontier and other peculiarly American environmental conditions—is being effaced by other racial and cultural imprints. And as Majority power and influence continue to decline, American civilization, as is daily becoming more apparent, is losing much of its cultural glue. The old forms remain, but the content is either going or gone.

Because the forms remain, the American Majority is but vaguely aware of its dispossession. It still votes, but no longer chooses. It is still free to speak, but not to speak freely. It still patronizes the arts, but the arts have become a minority wasteland. It still has economic strength, but it no longer directs the economy. It is still a major influence in determining local policy, but only a minor influence in determining vital areas of national and foreign policy. Most Majority members still lead private lives that are the envy of the world. In public, however, they are circumspect to the point of pusillanimity.

Those inclined to deny the Majority's dispossession may well adopt the following line of questioning. How, they may ask, can the Majority be dispossessed when there are so many rich Americans of impeccable Majority lineage . . . when there are so many Majority politicians, writers, artists, lawyers, doctors, scientists and FBI agents . . . when the president, most congressmen and most of the governors still belong to the Majority . . . when the armed forces are still in Majority hands . . . when the Majority, still the largest population group, can easily swing the vote?

The answers to these and similar questions will constitute much of the remaining subject matter of this book. Here they will merely be summarized.

---

6. This decline has been misinterpreted by liberal sociologists as an exclusively WASP phenomenon. "[There] is a White Anglo-Saxon Protestant establishment which . . . has been gradually losing its power and authority in the course of the twentieth century." E. Digby Baltzell, *The Protestant Establishment*, Random House, New York, 1964, p. ix. Some minority writers have not only described but exulted over the Majority's fall from power. See Peter Schrag, *The Decline of the Wasp*, New York, 1972.

One of the principal proofs of the Majority's dispossession is that there is no Majority political party as such. For most of the twentieth century the dynamic force in American politics has been the Democratic party, largely financed by minorities,[7] the party of Franklin D. Roosevelt, who "headed a government of minorities."[8] Unreconstructed Southern Majority members still support the Democratic party, though in ever diminishing numbers, while continuing to subscribe to a white supremacy that by definition includes the minority whites, mostly in the North, who represent all that is most hateful to Southern prejudices.

Northern Majority members are mostly Republican, but millions still vote the Democratic ticket, and Eastern Majority liberals are often in closer intellectual agreement with minority liberals than Majority conservatives. The latter scatter their political effectiveness by belonging to the Democratic, Republican and Wallace parties in the South and the anti-liberal wing of the Republican party in the North. As for President Nixon's "Silent Majority," it is built on politics and decibels, not race. White or colored, Majority member or minority member, Christian or Jew, anyone who keeps his voice down and votes Republican automatically qualifies for membership. There are, however, some genuine racial connotations in the Republican "Southern strategy"—a move to gather Majority members in the South into the Republican fold. But the Southern strategy stands little chance of enduring success as long as minority members occupy high places in Republican party councils and anti-Southern Republican liberals try to out-liberal and out-minority the Democratic party leadership.

Even that inner sanctum of Majority privilege, the presidency, has come under successful attack. Al Smith lost the 1928 presidential race, but another Irish Catholic,[9] John F. Kennedy, won the 1960 election. Barry Goldwater, one-

---

7. See Chapter 15.

8. "Archbishop Spellman" by Robert I. Gannon, *Look,* Aug. 1962, p. 103.

9. Smith worked his way up the political ladder as a pure, unadulterated Irish Catholic, although his paternal grandfather was almost certainly an Italian and his paternal grandmother quite possibly a German. Matthew and Hannah Josephson, *Al Smith,* Houghton Mifflin, Boston, 1969, pp. 13–15.

quarter Jewish, was the Republican standard bearer in the 1964 presidential contest.[10] Lyndon Johnson, the winner, was an authentic Majority member and as Senator from Texas fought hard against civil rights legislation.[11] But when President, he completely reversed himself, once solemnly intoning the minority rallying cry, "We shall overcome," on a national television broadcast.[12] It is also significant that in 1976 the leading contenders for the Democratic presidential nomination were, except for Wallace, as concerned about minority interests as they were about the national interest.[13]

When a man like Lyndon Johnson, with all the power of the presidency behind him, feels compelled to change his beliefs so radically and to proclaim his minority sympathies so publicly and shrilly, the lower-level Majority politician, in sharp contrast to the priorities of most minority politicians, can hardly be blamed for placing party above race. Obviously, if he represents an overwhelmingly Majority district, the Majority congressman will support the aims and aspirations of those who voted for him in regard to local and some of the less controversial national issues. But the moment he is forced to take a stand on the wider questions that may crucially affect the nation as a whole, he usually bends and sways to the will and whim of lavishly-financed, minority-oriented organizations and lobbies which seem dedicated to every interest but those of his constituents.

Turning to the field of foreign affairs, the emotional ties of some minorities to their old and new homelands overseas— kept on the warming oven by the mechanics of racism— have produced a totally disproportionate minority influence. The recent history of American foreign policy reveals example after example of diplomatic, economic and military commitments which were the direct outcome of official sensitivity to minority pressure.

---

10. See footnote 40, p. 161.
11. In 1948, Senator Johnson said: "The civil rights program is a farce and a sham—an effort to set up a police state in the guise of liberty." Clarke Newton, *LBJ, The Man from Johnson City,* Dodd, Mead, New York, 1964, p. 112.
12. March 15, 1965.
13. President Nixon's remote Irish ancestry and Vice-President Agnew's Greek father will be mentioned later in a more appropriate context.

The unconditional surrender of Germany, which handed Eastern Europe over to Russia at the end of World War II and may have caused a million unnecessary casualties, is one such example.[14] American support of Israel, which cost the United States the friendship and goodwill of over a hundred million Arabs and smoothed the way for Russia's entrance into the Middle East, is another.[15] Still another is America's massive military and financial assistance to the emerging African nations, while leading newspapers and periodicals continue their harassment of white-controlled South Africa, the only stable political entity on the continent. Concurrently, America joins the United Nations in sanctions against the beleaguered whites of Rhodesia.[16]

Whether minority interests coincided with Majority and national interests in these major foreign policy decisions is a matter for debate. What is not debatable are the racial motivations inherent in such decisions. The Majority, having no longer any motherland but the United States, tends to view foreign affairs from a purely national perspective. Certain minorities, on the other hand, advocate a foreign policy based almost entirely on their emotional attachments to Old World homelands.

It is partly, if not wholly, for this reason that America is now disengaging from its anti-communist defensive war in Southeast Asia, where minority interests are inconsequential, while emphasizing and reemphasizing its commitments in the Middle East, where minority interests are paramount. In Cuba, for which the more influential minorities have little concern but where the threat to America's defenses is real, the continuing presence of Russian armed forces is all but ignored.

The two principal achievements of Majority foreign policy—the Monroe Doctrine and non-entanglement in Old World power politics—have now been scrapped, and it is doubtful if their scrapping has made America or the world a better place in which to live. They have been replaced by a foreign policy without a center of gravity, a jumble of diplomatic *non sequiturs* which flies off on one tangent to satisfy

14. See p. 449.
15. See pp. 481–8.
16. See p. 497.

minority emotionalism, on another to placate the liberal's impassioned anti-fascism, on another to soothe the conservative phobia of communism.

For better or worse, Majority control of foreign affairs was the only means of obtaining a coherent foreign policy. Once American diplomacy became pluralistic, the succession of disasters which has taken place in the last sixty years was inevitable. Until the reign of Henry Kissinger there was no branch of government where the Majority had a greater per capita representation than in the State Department. Yet it was precisely in the area of foreign policy that the Majority interest was and is most studiously ignored.

The greatest objection to the thesis of the Majority's dispossession is bound to arise from the undeniable fact that many of the nation's largest fortunes and many of the leading corporations are still in Majority hands. Here it is sufficient to say, along with Harvard economist John K. Galbraith, that wealth is no longer equivalent to power,[17] and that the average Majority member is considerably less opulent than the average member of a few minorities, particularly the Jews, who have now begun to challenge the Majority's hold on the big corporations.[18] That these same corporations, the principal sources of Majority wealth, are forbidden by law to contribute money to political parties, while labor unions, many under direct minority control, can contribute millions of tax-exempt dollars through their political action com-

---

17. Professor Galbraith, one of the nation's leading liberals, exposed himself to a charge of caste disloyalty when he attempted to bury the old chestnut of a conspirational Majority plutocracy tying up American politics and the American economy in its purse strings. As proof of his thesis that the power of private wealth has greatly declined, Galbraith cites the tremendous growth of the Federal government, the rise of the trade unions, the drying up of the servant class, which robs the rich of their prerogatives, and the ever increasing multitude of new rich, who, by spreading wealth around more evenly have greatly diminished the exclusive hunting grounds of the ultra-rich. John Galbraith, *The Affluent Society,* Houghton Mifflin, Boston, 1958, pp. 88–90.

18. Jewish wealth, a survey of which will be found in Chapter 15, is an exception to Galbraith's rule (see footnote 78, page 171). Figures on the economic status of the Armenian, Chinese and Japanese minorities are not readily available, but the indications are that, on the average, members of these minorities have a greater net worth than Majority members. The incalculable wealth of the Mafia probably raises the per capita income of the Southern Italian minority above the national mean.

mittees, is merely one more indication of the downward curve of Majority influence.

Ironically, many of the largest Majority fortunes have now passed into the possession of vast trusts and foundations, which frequently spend much of their income and capital on minority causes.[19] Also, some of the richest Majority members, instead of using their wealth for the benefit of the Majority, seemed to make a fetish of non-involvement and invisibility. Of the two authentic Majority billionaires, one, J. Paul Getty, who occasionally wrote economic homilies for a sex magazine, died in splendid isolation in a baronial English mansion and had not been in the U.S. for decades. The other, Howard Hughes, led a secretive, cloistered life in foreign hotels after erecting the world's largest gambling empire in Las Vegas.[20] The minority super-rich, it goes without saying, are far less inclined to dissociate themselves from what they consider to be their ethnic obligations.

Not surprisingly, the dispossession of the Majority becomes most apparent in the field of public opinion. If Ortega y Gasset is right in saying, "Never has anyone ruled on this earth by basing his rule essentially on any other thing than public opinion," [21] then minority domination of the present-day United States is incontestable. Minority members now own, control or operate the three major television and radio networks, almost every large motion picture company, the nation's three most influential newspapers, the largest newspaper chain, at least half of the important publishing houses and many, if not most, opinion-making periodicals.[22]

But this remarkable concentration of power does not stop here. There are several aggressively censorious minority organizations which scan radio and TV broadcasts, newspapers, magazines and books for even the most subtle anti-minority allusions.[23] Should any be found, the owner or

---

19. See p. 367.
20. See *Fortune,* May 1968, for a recent box score of American billionaires and centimillionaires. That many opulent Majority members contribute to conservative causes does not mean they are supporting the Majority. See Chapter 24.
21. *La rebelión de las masas,* Espasa-Calpe, Madrid, 1966, p. 116.
22. Specifics on pp. 164–9.
23. Among them the Catholic-controlled Legion of Decency, and the B'nai B'rith's Anti-Defamation League. For more on the latter organization, see pp. 189–90.

editor of the offending media and, if necessary, the writer, advertisers and stockholders are so advised and admonished.[24] All such literary bowdlerizing means the playing down, omission or twisting of news vital to the public interest. Not only is the news itself distorted, but also its presentation and interpretation.[25] The Majority, to its great loss, has no similar watchdog organizations.

Being a compound of what people read, see, feel and think, public opinion is only partly the creation of the minority-dominated channels of information. No reporter, commentator, author, philosopher or prophet can make a normally intelligent adult accept as true what he knows to be false. But as public opinion moves from local to national issues, it becomes less informed. A fool knows more at home than a wise man at his neighbor's, runs the Spanish proverb. Firsthand knowledge is supplanted by secondhand information and even thirdhand gossip. Finally, in the realm of foreign affairs, public opinion rests largely on "organized" opinion, the opinion of those who have a direct or indirect interest in conditioning public attitudes toward the events being reported and the policies under discussion.

---

24. Some less prestigious minority organizations even censor the classics. See pp. 236–8.

25. A *New York Times* reporter has written, "The media manufactured dramatic events and colossal characters out of many small incidents and minor men." Gay Talese, *The Kingdom and the Power,* World, New York, 1969, p. 194. Glaring examples of media distortion in recent decades were: the diabolization of Senator Joseph McCarthy; the apotheosis of the assassinated Kennedy brothers and Martin Luther King; the sniggering affection for the posturing white and black Neanderthals of the New Left and the more monstrous hippies; the whitewash of Chappaquiddick. "Has one ever heard a balanced discussion of the situation in South Africa? Or a reasonable presentation of the 'hawk' view on Vietnam? Or of the actions of a police force confronted with unruly crowds?" asks Ernest van den Haag in *The Jewish Mystique,* Stein and Day, New York, 1969, p. 142. The tendentiousness of the media is most obvious in the technique of editorializing by headline. "Let me control the headlines and I shall not care who controls the editorials," said Frederick Birchall, a one-time *New York Times* managing editor. Talese, *op. cit.,* p. 168. In the 1950's, when the slightest mention of communist or communism brought forth the Pavlovian response of "McCarthyism," President Truman accused presidential candidate Eisenhower of "being willing to accept the principles that identify the so-called master race." *New York Times,* Oct. 18, 1952, p. 1. Reporters and columnists were unanimously mute at this muffled charge of Nazism. In the 1972 presidential race George McGovern, who promised to adhere to the issues, twice associated President Nixon with Hitler in public speeches.

As for public opinion polls, they are often more effective in influencing public opinion than measuring it, more revealing of the pollsters' state of mind than the public's. The newspapers who subscribe to the polls have an important influence on what kinds of questions are asked and the size and composition of the sample. On the occasion of national and state elections, the press has developed the habit of using polls for bandwagon electioneering, in which statistics favorable to the preferred candidate are played up, while unfavorable statistics are played down or buried.[26]

In the event the control of the news media is regained by the Majority, public opinion will not undergo any overnight transformation. News treatment shapes people's minds, but the dogma and dogmatic boundaries that define and circumscribe news treatment flow from the domain of culture, of which public opinion is often but a servile adjunct. At the lower echelons of American culture—the Broadway stage, Hollywood films and television shows—minority dominance is scarcely challenged. At the higher reaches—poetry, serious novels, literary criticism, off-Broadway theater, modern music, painting and sculpture—the minorities have also assumed a commanding position.[27]

It has often been remarked, maliciously rather than accurately, that America's only original contribution to art was a minority contribution—Negro jazz. Now it is said that the minorities have taken over all American culture, and books are being written to document this theme. According to essayist Leslie Fiedler, the basic tone of the creative intellectual life of the United States has become Jewish.[28] Nathaniel Weyl not only proclaims the supremacy of Jews in modern American culture, but gives biological reasons for this supremacy.[29] Expanding on Weyl's genetic approach, Ernest van den Haag, Professor of Social Philosophy at New York University, asserts that "American sensibility itself has be-

---

26. The Louis Harris Poll predicted Hubert Humphrey would win the 1968 presidential election. Without a single exception, every major American newspaper and periodical predicted a sweeping Labour victory in the 1970 British general election.

27. See pp. 238–42.

28. *Time*, Aug. 19, 1966, p. 80.

29. *The Creative Elite in America*, Chapter XVIII.

come in part Jewish." [30] Van den Haag admits the domination of the news media by "Jewish liberals," the cultural
domination exercised by the "Jewish cultural establishment"
and, in a paroxysm of ethnic flattery which conveniently by-
passes the Greeks, the Renaissance and the masterworks of
Western art and science, declares that Jews "have given the
essential meaning to the last two thousand years of Western
history." [31]

As if blinded by their concentration on one cultural
phenomenon, the learned Semitists mentioned above seem to
have downgraded the significance of artistic stirrings from
another minority quarter. Jews may have Majority culture on
the run, but Negroes have it cornered. The recent surge of
Negro drama and semi-biographical racist tracts is not merely
remolding and redirecting Majority culture, but is attempting
to wound it mortally. The new Negro literary celebrities have
one-track minds and simple, recurring themes: [32] white women
are fair game for rape; white males have serious sexual de-
ficiencies; [33] looting, arson, mayhem, murder, insurrection and
even massacre are often worthy and understandable goals.
The language employed relies heavily on racial slurs and
repetitive incantations of profanity.

In spite of such artistic limitations, the Negro literary
and dramatic naissance is actively promoted by leading publishers and producers and often seen on educational television. [34] Majority writers, of course, cannot reply in kind

30. *The Jewish Mystique,* p. 98.
31. *Ibid.,* pp. 14, 41, 129–33.
32. For a list of some of these works and their authors see Chapter 18.
33. This assertion seems especially inappropriate considering that the physiological state known as "feminization" is far more prevalent among
Negroes than whites. Atrophy of the testicles and gynaecomastia (enlarge-
ment of the male breasts) are a fairly common Negro affliction. J. C.
Carothers, *The African Mind in Health and Disease,* World Health Organization, Geneva, 1953, p. 64. The myth of white unmanliness is now being
picked up and circulated by a few white publications. The following was
printed in *Playboy,* October, 1967 (p. 25): "Question—What do you call
it when a prostitute services a white client? Answer—The Naked and the
Dead."
34. Perhaps the most violently racist drama ever to reach any stage was
Slave Ship, presented in Brooklyn in the fall of 1969. Its author was LeRoi
Jones, a Negro who married a white. Anti-white libels and "literary" appeals
to racial violence are a frequent theme of black television talk shows.

since any public exhibition of Majority racism, cultural or otherwise, falls under an automatic and all-pervasive ban.[35] As might be expected, since there is no counterattack or rebuttal, the Negro cultural *putsch* is moving relentlessly toward establishing the thesis that whites are a race "accursed" and "the cancer of history." [36]

With respect to religion, the highest manifestation of culture, it is not so much that the Majority has lost its church as that the church, a few fundamentalist sects excepted, has lost the Majority. Majority Protestants cannot feel too enthusiastic at the spectacle of their ministers' devoting much of their time and their congregations' money to minority causes, including the sheltering and feeding of revolutionary street gangs.[37] Majority Catholics have had the same experience, and in addition must face the problem that the American branch of their church has traditionally been a pillar of minority support.

Predictably, the Catholic and Negro Protestant clergy has provided many of the more charismatic minority leaders— Father Groppi, the Berrigan brothers, Adam Clayton Powell, Martin Luther King—all of whom learned to feed their followers a heady mixture of social Christianity and minority racism. In contrast, no great defender of the Majority has arisen from any religious body, or is likely to as long as the Reverend William S. Coffin, who preached civil disobedience at home and disengagement in the Far East, while keeping silent about the Mideast, holds an Episcopalian sinecure, and Billy Graham and other evangelists bemuse their audiences with their own special brands of religious fossilism.

An assault on a people's culture necessarily includes an assault on a people's history, history being both the store-

---

35. The selective ban on the use of racial expletives is not limited to literary endeavors and what appears in the communications media. In Washington, where most of the population makes liberal use of "pig," "honky," "beast," etc. when addressing whites, the police have received formal orders to avoid the following expressions: boy, wop, kike, chink, dago, polack, bohunk, limey, frog, kraut, nigger, burrhead and spic. *San Francisco Sunday Chronicle and Examiner, This World,* May 5, 1968, p. 12.

36. The latter phrase is the creation of the white minority social critic, Susan Sontag, and is quoted by Benjamin DeMott in *Supergrow,* E. P. Dutton, New York, 1969, p. 74.

37. See p. 253.

house and arsenal of culture. Minority muckrakers [38] began rewriting the Majority past many years ago, but only recently have school texts, ably assisted by television "Westerns" and documentaries, made it a point to deliberately discredit the Majority's starring role in American history. Majority children are still permitted to learn that their ancestors (always with the help of minority groups) opened up the wilderness, but they are no longer permitted to forget that these same ancestors burned witches and committed atrocities against defenseless Indians. It is still admitted, somewhat grudgingly, that Majority industrial giants built the railroads and steel mills and developed the oilfields,[39] but they have long been characterized as lawless moneygrubbers and brutal exploiters of labor. The South, it is taught, produced most of the world's cotton and a gracious civilization, but at the price of mass lynching bees, night riders, slave gangs and genocide in the hot sun. Little, it turns out, that the Majority did was right, and even less was decent.

---

38. One of the foremost was Gustavus Myers, who went to great lengths in his celebrated study, *The History of the Great American Fortunes,* to detail the fabulous wealth of the richest Majority families, while practically ignoring minority millionaires like August Belmont, who as the American representative of the Rothschilds probably had more hard money at his disposal than any of his native-born competitors. Nor did Myers balance his roster of Majority financial coups by calling attention to Jesse Seligman, who helped persuade Americans and others to put $400,000,000 into an abortive French venture to build a canal across Panama. No one got a cent back, but Seligman kept his $300,000 advance and the additional huge profits he made as an underwriter. Stephen Birmingham, *Our Crowd,* Dell, New York, 1967, pp. 273–5. Also, Myers failed to mention the possible minority ancestry of his principal villain, Jay Gould, who was descended from Nathan Gold of Fairfax, Connecticut, the "u" being added in 1806. Birmingham, *op. cit.,* p. 132. Matthew Josephson presents the same dreary catalog of grand-scale Majority peculations in his book, *The Robber Barons,* and almost totally omits the financial juggling of the minority tycoons. The latest work of this genre is Ferdinand Lundberg's *The Rich and the Super-Rich.* Pages, sometimes even chapters, are devoted to Rockefellers, Mellons, Fords, Du Ponts, Hunts and Vanderbilts, but only a few words are given the Rosenwalds, Blausteins, Zellerbachs, Loebs, Seligmans and Warburgs and the index does not even mention the Guggenheims, Zemurrays, Baruchs, Schiffs, Sarnoffs, Annenbergs, Sulzbergers and Hirshhorns.

39. Dr. Lucy Rockefeller Hamlin, daughter of Laurance Rockefeller, said: "I never studied American history because I didn't want to sit in a class and risk hearing my great-grandfather described as a robber baron." *San Francisco Examiner and Chronicle,* March 2, 1969, Section A, p. 21.

Conceding that the Majority has no effective political representation, that its part in the making of domestic and foreign policy is less than decisive, that its economic influence is in eclipse, that its religious leaders have turned against it, that its culture has been shredded and its history demeaned—conceding all this, it may nevertheless be argued that the Majority cannot really be dispossessed until it loses command of the ultimate source of power, the Armed Forces. But the United States is not nineteenth-century Prussia. It has no military tradition which permits its officer corps to exercise an irresistible influence in politics. Due largely to the endurance of Majority institutions, the American military is still firmly under the civilian thumb.

If there are doubts about this, the verbal lashing accorded the military by the news media in the last several decades should dispel them. President Truman's curt dismissal of General MacArthur, General LeMay's "bad press" in the 1968 presidential contest, the ups and downs of Major General Edwin Walker [40] and the uproar over General George Brown's attack on the Israel lobby are proof that, as always in America, the pen is mightier and sharper than the sword.

The Armed Forces, moreover, are not as Majority-ridden as they appear. There are Jewish admirals in the Navy, Negro generals in the Air Force and a growing number of Negro revolutionary cadres in the Army. [41] The liberal-minority coalition, not the Pentagon, presided over the Korean stalemate. Majority, not minority, soldiers did most of the dying in Vietnam, where an installment-plan defeat had already been

---

40. Walker was a popular figure, at least in the North, when he commanded the troops which enforced the desegregation of Little Rock high schools in 1957. Later when he resigned from the Army and began to criticize the laws he had previously been called upon to execute, he was temporarily committed to an insane asylum, shot at by Lee Harvey Oswald and effortlessly transformed into a crackpot by the opinion makers.

41. "But now there is another war being fought in Vietnam—between black and white Americans . . . 'Ju Ju' and 'Mau Mau' groups have been organized . . . tanks fly black flags . . . elaborate training in guerrilla warfare has not been lost upon them, and many officers, black and white, believe that Vietnam may prove a training ground for the black urban commando of the future." *Time*, Sept. 19, 1969, p. 22. Young radicals and old-school Marxists look upon this army within the army as the vanguard of revolution.

set in motion, and victory, thanks to the television coverage, had been ruled out in advance.

At home, as violence and crime reach levels beyond the control of the police and National Guard, the Armed Forces may eventually be reduced to the status of a massive law enforcement agency, something like the Federal Bureau of Investigation, another organization with the hopeless mission of trying to force a diseased society to function as an orderly society. Rather than serving as an instrument to restore the Majority to greatness, the military, as meek, permissive and acquiescent as any other branch of government, is busily engaged in carrying out the commands of its enemies.[42]

But of all the proofs of Majority decline, none was more conclusive than the anthology of liberal-minority post mortems on the moon landing. Here was the great Majority enterprise of the century, perhaps the most memorable moment of mankind, yet after it was over, after the television coverage had ended, it was generally treated with veiled hostility and even described as a deliberate trick to divert attention from the plight and needs of the minority poor.

The definitive intellectual and academic line on the Apollo 11 mission was laid down in a rambling, three-part dissertation in a mass-circulation magazine by the Jewish novelist, Norman Mailer.[43] The author's theme was that Neil Armstrong's epic flight was a sort of wacky, unjustifiable, wasteful, semi-Nazi adventure insulting to the aspirations of Negroes. The Nazi taint, presumably, was due to the participation of German-born scientists in the space program. The whole affair, according to Mailer, was a lugubrious foretaste of the cold, computerized age to come, an age whose only salvation would be the drugs, drums and dharma of a

---

42. The My Lai massacre trial, initiated by the lurid reporting of minority correspondent Seymour Hirsch, was staged in such a way as to allow the military to preside over its own hara-kiri. When minority military planner Daniel Ellsberg stole the top-secret "Pentagon Papers," he was treated more like a hero than a criminal. Later all charges against him were dropped and he was practically canonized by the media, after it was learned that White House investigators had broken into his psychiatrist's office in search of damaging information. The spy went free. The counterspies were indicted. Ellsberg was last heard of as a member of a defense committee for Abbie Hoffman, arrested in 1973 for trying to sell $500,000 worth of cocaine. *Miami Herald*, Aug. 30, 1973, p. 16A.

43. *Life*, Aug. 29, 1969, Nov. 14, 1969 and Jan. 9, 1970.

different and better breed of men than the astronauts. The choice of Mailer, whose clownish forays into politics had earned him bigger headlines than his literary affectations, to appraise an almost unappraisable Majority exploit was in itself a sign of the Majority's disestablishment.[44]

So now with the downgrading of the astronauts and the upgrading of repentant rapists like Eldridge Cleaver, inspired militants like Huey Newton and stone-age throwbacks like Abbie Hoffman and Jerry Rubin, the wheel of Majority history has turned full circle. The Northern European element of the American population, dominant from earliest colonial times until after the turn of the century, has now been demoted to a secondary place in the American scheme of things. The Majority's institutions and its loyalties to these institutions, its work habits and its physical presence still keep the country together, but with less success each year.

The overall process of the Majority's dispossession is not too difficult to summarize. America's dominant population group, fragmented by the Civil War, then softened into a humanitarian mood by an era of peace and plenty and driven by an overpowering desire for cheap labor, decided to share the benefits of its laboriously developed political institutions with newcomers of different races and cultures. Since these new Americans were almost totally unpracticed and unskilled in the mechanics of self-government and in their own historical experience were quite unfamiliar with such ideas as equality and individual rights, they were all the more eager to gorge themselves on this rich libertarian feast, although more for their own private and collective appetites than for the public good.

Full social equality, however, was held back by residual feelings of Majority racial superiority. To help overcome this final impediment, minority anthropologists introduced and publicized "scientific evidence" to the effect that all races were inherently equal. The theories developed from such evidence (or preceding it) were promoted relentlessly

---

44. Mailer called WASPs "the most Faustian, barbaric, draconian, progress-oriented and root-destroying people on earth"—a racial slur that earned him high marks with the intelligentsia. He said WASP "nihilism found its perfect expression in the odyssey to the moon . . ." *Time*, Feb. 8, 1971.

by an alliance of liberal and minority intellectuals and public opinion merchants. It was not long before racial equalitarianism became established dogma and was taken up with a vengeance by nonwhites, whose historical experience was even more alien to Majority social organization than that of New Immigration whites.

In its zeal for racial leveling, the equalitarian school lost sight of the fact that the very dynamism which spurs a race to obtain equality forces it to go beyond equality. After decades of struggle, the vested interests in racial climbing become too great to be shut off arbitrarily by resolutions of the American Civil Liberties Union or the Americans for Democratic Action. Inevitably, equality edges toward superequality and superequality laps over into superiority.

Theories proposing the racial superiority of certain minorities are now being published by leading book firms, featured in the news media and discussed seriously in the highest circles of the liberal-minority intelligentsia.[45] It should come as no surprise to those who understand the real motivations of the racial levelers that the very same anthropologists who have been preaching equalitarianism most vigorously seem the least disturbed by this new trend. In fact, minority member Ashley Montagu, for many years the leading advocate of the equalitarian school of anthropology, has actually recommended a recent literary *tour de force* that describes Jews as a master race innately equipped with an intellectual apparatus that makes them superior to all other races and peoples everywhere.[46]

And so it has transpired that the once dominant Majority has been given the status—and stigma—of inferiority, not only by the facts of American life and the racial dynamism of minorities, but by the *ex cathedra* pronouncements of influential social scientists. There is hardly a greater form of dispossession than becoming a servant in one's own house.

---

45. Three cases for Jewish racial superiority, as well as one for Jewish inferiority, will be examined on pp. 182–6. Marshall McLuhan's allegations of Negro racial superiority will be briefly discussed on p. 219.

46. See full page advertisement for Ernest van den Haag's *The Jewish Mystique* in *New York Times*, Jan. 5, 1970.

Chapter 11

The Split in the Ranks

Is IT NOT INCREDIBLE that the largest American population group, the group with the deepest roots, the most orderly and the most technically proficient group, the *nuclear* population group of American culture and of the American gene pool, should have lost its preeminence to weaker, less established, less numerous, culturally heterogeneous and often mutually hostile minorities?

With all due allowance for minority dynamism and for the other external or historical causes given in earlier chapters, this miraculous shift of power could never have taken place without a Majority "split in the ranks"—without the active assistance and participation of Majority members themselves.

It has already been pointed out that race consciousness is one of the great social binding forces, from which it follows that when the racial gravitational pull slackens people tend to spin off from the group nucleus. Some drift aimlessly through life as human isolates. Others look for a substitute nucleus in an intensified religious and political life or an expanded class consciousness. Still others, out of idealism, romanticism, inertia or perversity, attach themselves to another race in an attempt to find the solidarity they missed in their own.

Strictly speaking, as has also been suggested previously, no one can change or trade his race. This is precluded by the physical stratum of race. But one can lose or give up his race-mindedness, his racial pride, his racism. One can acquire the cultural trappings, the language and the religion of another race. One can marry a person of a different race and have hybrid children. By taking one or more of these steps, the Majority member withdraws for all practical purposes from his own group and becomes, if not a bona fide, at least an *ad hoc* member of a minority.

Majority members split their ranks for a multitude of reasons, the chief one probably being ignorance—ignorance of the modern world about them and the ancient world behind them, ignorance derived from an unwillingness or inability to recognize the osmotic influence of race on matters that touch their day-to-day existence. Paradoxically, this ignorance is greater among the higher levels of Majority intelligence, for the literate man who reads nothing but nonsense is more ignorant than the illiterate who reads nothing. Prosperity, which increases social mobility while diluting race consciousness, is also an important factor in dividing the Majority from within. Overconcern for the material comforts and conveniences provided by modern technology serves to dull both the reason and the instincts. But no matter what the circumstances, those who leave the racial fold weaken the racial fold. It is not so much that there is strength in numbers. There is weakness in defection.

Who exactly are the Majority Splitters of the Ranks? Generally speaking, they can be broken down into five categories.

1. *The Gracchites.* The name is derived from the Gracchi, two brothers who, although belonging to one of the great patrician families of Rome, could not feed their ambition sufficiently within the orbit of their own aristocratic caste. Tiberius and Gaius Gracchus found that in times of stress in a relatively tolerant republic a descent of one or two steps in the social ladder is equivalent to an ascent of several steps in the political ladder. Accordingly, they became the standard bearers of revolution and agrarian revolt and were adulated by the plebeians. The Gracchi's political *modus operandi*, it might be added, was by no means limited to stirring up class against class, peasant against landlord,[1] exploited against

---

1. There were traces of populism in the Gracchi's revolutionary program. But the racial dynamics of populism are unifying rather than divisive. It is

exploiters. The patricians, the descendants of the Italic invaders, differed racially from the plebs, the offspring of earlier and later immigrations.[2] The Gracchi's appeal, consequently, was directed to oppressed races as well as to oppressed classes.

In a multiracial state, the well-born, ambitious member of a dominant race is constantly tempted to take the Gracchite route to power. It is harder for the patrician to win the respect of the patrician than to win the respect of the plebeian. It is also much easier to give money away than to earn it; to relax discipline than to enforce it; to be a hero to one's valet than to one's mirror.

History is full of Gracchites and the list includes famous popes, monarchs and princes. Philippe d'Orléans, who voted for the death of Louis XVI, his own cousin, to curry favor with the revolutionary mob, is perhaps the most notorious case. Teutonic aristocrats like Leo IX, who as Pope stirred up the Italian masses against the Holy Roman Emperor, certainly fit the description. So do those kings and reigning dukes who in late feudal times established absolute rule by crushing their fellow noblemen with the help of the bourgeoisie and the urban rabble. A noted twentieth-century Gracchite was Prince Valerian Obolensky, who switched allegiance from the Czar to the Bolsheviks and served as a high Soviet official until he was purged by Stalin.[3]

Gracchites have been particularly numerous in the United States since the 1930's. Franklin D. Roosevelt, Averell Harriman and Adlai Stevenson are three who come immediately to mind. All were born millionaires and the scions of good Majority families. None was particularly successful in any realm of private endeavor.[4] In their public careers all specialized in catering to minorities and all surrounded themselves

---

the reformer appealing to the farmers and yeomanry of his own race rather than the political extremist whose own proposals for land reform are only one item in a large package of revolutionary change and racial and class agitation.

2. See footnote 18, Chapter 9.

3. *Ency. of Russia and the Soviet Union*, p. 403.

4. The long, ludicrous string of FDR's financial speculations in the early 1920's in New York included a $26,000 loss with Louis Howe in a scheme to fatten lobsters! Alfred B. Rollins, Jr., *Roosevelt and Howe*, Knopf, New York, 1962, pp. 196–7.

with minority advisers, assistants and ghost-writers.[5] Their natural stamping ground was and is the Democratic party, previously described as the party of the minorities.

But there are also Republicans who come very close to being Gracchites. Nelson Rockefeller can match his Democratic counterparts in birth, wealth and all the other accouterments of what passes in America for aristocracy, having based his career on a reputation for liberalism, tolerance, friendship for labor and a highly publicized concern for the downtrodden. But since the voter base of the Republican party consists of Majority rather than minority members, the comparison with Democratic Gracchites is only valid when restricted to the Republican Gracchites' state or city fiefs. In New York, for example, Governor Rockefeller operated almost exactly as President Roosevelt operated on the national level—that is, he was dutifully responsive to the will of the liberal-minority coalition.[6] In the field of foreign relations, however, Republican Gracchites are more likely to uphold Majority interests.

The Gracchite makes considerable use of the family fortune to attack or undermine the system in which his family prospered. He capitalizes on his aristocratic mien, cultivated voice and fine manners to charm and win over the proletariat, much as the polished English actor, who was just another actor in London, "lays them out in the aisles" in the Iowa hustings. Cringing adulation from the lower depths is heady wine to the upper level Gracchite.

---

5. Gracchites to watch are Adlai Stevenson III, elected Senator from Illinois in 1970, and John D. Rockefeller IV, a rising power in West Virginia Democratic politics. A Gracchite whose star is presently setting is John Lindsay, a crypto New Leftist who ran under the Republican banner until repudiated by his party in the 1969 New York City mayoralty race, which he won as an independent. In 1970, Lindsay told a gathering of University of Pennsylvania students, "The ones I have unending admiration for are the guys who say, 'I simply will not serve in the Army of the U.S. in Vietnam and I am willing to take the consequences for it.' These are the guys who are heroes." *Human Events*, May 16, 1970, p. 374. His father a British-born banker, his mother a member of one of the nation's oldest families, Lindsay gave his daughter in marriage to a Jewish graduate student. *New York Times*, June 7, 1970, p. 80. In spite of an expensive television campaign advertising his Nordic physical traits, Lindsay finished out of the running in the 1972 contest for the Democratic presidential nomination.

6. Nelson Rockefeller became a middle-of-the-road mainstreamer in the 1970 New York gubernatorial contest in order to capitalize on a conservative groundswell in the ranks of the Irish and Italians.

All this is not to say that Gracchite politics is necessarily or always bad. There may come a time in the life span of every nation when certain issues become so critical they must be resolved even at the risk of revolution or racial conflagration. If no genuine leader can be found in a moment of crisis, as is often the case in a demoralized society, the Gracchite is sometimes a happier solution than the psychotic nihilist or head-rolling revolutionary. There usually remains at least a spark of feeling in the Gracchite heart for the people on whom he has turned his back.

It goes without saying that Gracchites are to be found in fields other than politics. Marshall Field III, the grandson of the Chicago merchant prince and subsidizer of the defunct minority racist New York daily newspaper, *PM,* was a dyed-in-the-wool Gracchite. So is Michael Straight, son of a Morgan partner and one-time editor-publisher of the *New Republic.* So is the son of another Morgan partner, Corliss Lamont, the well-known apologist and philosopher of Marxism. There are Gracchite lawyers, doctors and philanthropists. There are stage and screen Gracchites. There is a surprisingly large number of Gracchite diplomats. There are numerous female Gracchites, the most notable being the late Eleanor Roosevelt. There are also matrimonial Gracchites— men and women of established Majority families who marry minority members for money, for a racial lark or for the flattery and attention that social climbers extend to those with taller family trees.

The Gracchite usually pays a high price for his measure of glory. The adoration and fawning of the mob never quite compensate for the implacable hatred every group reserves for the defector.[7] In war the desertion of a general causes a much greater stir than the desertion of a private. In times of racial troubles, the desertion of an aristocrat, the guardian of the race, raises emotions to a much higher pitch than the

---

7. It was exactly this brand of hatred which prevented Nelson Rockefeller, potentially the strongest candidate, from securing the Republican nomination in 1964. It also gave rise to the stentorian booing of Rockefeller at the Republican convention in San Francisco by conservative activists, who for years had felt outraged by his Eastern habit of working harder for minority than for Majority votes. The memory of these boos probably induced Rockefeller to present a somewhat "deliberalized" image to the American people in 1974, when he was appointed vice-president of the United States.

desertion of a commoner. Not only were both Tiberius and Gaius Gracchus assassinated, so were two later Roman aristocrats of the Gracchite stamp, Catiline and Clodius.[8]

The Gracchite, even more than most liberals, has the peculiar habit of fomenting wars, but seldom fighting in them.[9] He loudly denounces the wealth of others, but keeps his own. He sneers at the upper classes, but still identifies with them. In the United States he is publicly in favor of integrated schools, but sends his own children to segregated schools. It is probably asking too much of any man, particularly a Gracchite, to practice what he preaches. Giovanni di Bernadone, who became St. Francis after a brief fling as the richest young man in Assisi, and Gautama Siddhartha, who evolved from princeling into Buddha, were the rarest of mortals, and certainly no Gracchites. They were humanitarians in the fullest and best sense of the word. The Gracchite's humanitarianism, however, always seems to be accompanied by an accumulation of power and by a torrential outpouring of

---

8. It is not quite accurate to call Clodius and Catiline Gracchites since they were both cut down in the middle of their conspiracies and rebellions, and historians never had a chance to plumb their real intentions. They might have been imitating Caesar, who practiced a far more sophisticated form of politics. Caesarism is the use of the mob to obtain the power to destroy the mob.

9. In World War I, Franklin Roosevelt, then in good health and of military age, was Assistant Secretary of the Navy. Harriman and Stevenson sat out World War II as Washington bureaucrats, though both were extremely active interventionists. Thomas Jefferson, who lived at a time when being a Gracchite was almost unthinkable, nevertheless had some noticeable Gracchite tendencies. His father was a self-made man of uncertain lineage, but his mother was a Randolph. No one was more responsible for the War of Independence than Jefferson, yet he never once heard a gun go off in anger. His single military exploit was an ignoble and hasty retreat into the Virginia mountains when the British made a sudden descent on Monticello. "Where is Jefferson?" wrote Washington bitterly while at Valley Forge. It was this same Jefferson, so heedful of his own life, who was inspired by Shay's Rebellion to write: "God forbid! we should ever be 20 years without such a rebellion. . . . What country can preserve its liberties if their rulers are not warned from time to time that their people preserve the spirit of resistance? Let them take arms! . . . What signify a few lives lost in a century or two? The tree of liberty must be refreshed from time to time with the blood of patriots and tyrants. It is its natural manure. . . ." See Jefferson's letter to Smith, Nov. 13, 1787. Also see Nathan Schachner, *Thomas Jefferson*, Thomas Yoseloff, New York, 1957, p. 216 and Albert Beveridge, *The Life of John Marshall*, Houghton Mifflin, Boston, 1916, Vol. 1, pp. 126, 303.

hatred upon all and sundry who dare to challenge this power.

What precisely are the Gracchite's true motives? Is he merely a man whose ambition outweighs his character— a man who, in spite of the immense advantages of his birthright, fails to make the first team, and consequently decides to abandon his teammates, go over to the opposing side, change the rules of the game and try to win anyway? Could it be that fear of competition with his peers is always his greatest concern? Is he not, in the long run, taking out his own failings on his own kind?

2. *The Trucklers*. These are the Majority members who are not born rich like the Gracchites and do not exude any of the aristocratic aroma that delights the olfactory organs of the *hoi polloi*. They come from the middle and lower layers of the Majority. If they are men of wealth—and many are— they made their money themselves, either in business, the professions or, in the not unusual case of Lyndon Johnson, in politics.

Trucklers play an active role in public life and in the formation of public opinion, while at the same time almost formally abjuring their own racial niche in society. The only racism they will abide is minority racism, which they do much to foster by their zealous interest and meddling in minority matters. But their reasons for playing the minority game are more opportunistic than idealistic. They know from long experience it will gain them prestige and respectability, give them a favorable image in the press and, if they are politicians, bring them more financial backing and more votes. They are also well aware of what would happen if they ever associated themselves in the slightest way with Majority racism.

A typical Truckler is the young, naive Majority journalist who, after writing his first important newspaper or magazine story about some international or domestic event from a purely Majority viewpoint, is suddenly called into the front office and handed a sheaf of indignant and even threatening letters from minority organizations with fancy letterheads and illustrious signatures. At that moment he can: (1) re-

fuse to be pressured and be discharged on the spot, (2) resign before he is discharged, (3) promise to be more
"objective" in the future and keep his position. Having
spent a great deal of time and money on becoming a journalist and not wanting to abandon his career at the outset,
he chooses course (3). He acquires more "objectivity" by
tailoring his reporting in such a way as to eliminate further
letters. Another Truckler is born.[10]

A second type of Truckler is the young Majority politician
or bureaucrat who, during his first stay in Washington or in
a state capital, inadvertently makes an off-the-cuff remark
critical of some outlandish exhibition of minority racism.
Immediately he finds himself pilloried and in danger of
becoming a social outcast. He apologizes and never makes
the same mistake again. Now he understands the score. Now
he may engage the services of a minority adviser to keep
him on his toes on minority issues and a minority ghost-
writer to prepare his speeches. He will thereby avoid the
possibility of any further embarrassing remarks, while at the
same time improving his oratory. The dynamic language of
minority racism shows up very well in audience reaction, in
contrast to the listless, canned phrases of Majority speech
writers.[11]

One of the most curious aspects of Truckling is its dependence on geography. Harry Truman, a chipper haberdasher
who fell on hard times and flirted with the Ku Klux Klan,
made his debut in politics as a member of the corrupt

10. The *ne plus ultra* Truckler in the newspaper field is Turner Catledge,
a native Mississippian and long-time Managing Editor of the *New York
Times.* As another Timesman wrote, Catledge's "home state had been
denigrated regularly in the press for a decade . . ." Talese, *The Kingdom
and the Power*, p. 143. The *Times,* of course, had been the principal deni-
grator.
11. Judge Sam Rosenman, later Chairman of the Board of Twentieth
Century-Fox, wrote many of the Roosevelt and Truman speeches. Many
famous Kennedy and Johnson addresses were ghosted by minority writers,
Theodore Chaikin Sorensen and Richard Goodwin. The dull and turgid
Eisenhower speeches were generally written by Majority professorial types.
As for phrase-making, FDR's "Happy Warrior" epithet for Al Smith was
dreamed up by Justice Joseph Proskauer and Kennedy's "New Frontier"
was the simultaneous brainchild of Walt Rostow and Max Freedman. Ernest
K. Lindley, *Franklin D. Roosevelt*, Bobbs-Merrill, New York, 1931, p. 223
and *San Francisco Chronicle, This World,* Aug. 17, 1965.

Pendergast political machine.[12] By the time he had moved into the White House he was a champion of civil rights. Finally, having retired from Washington and safely back in the Majority-dominated Kansas City suburbs, he heaped vitriolic remarks on the civil rights movement and its leader, Martin Luther King.[13] In California, as State District Attorney, Earl Warren urged and supported the 1942 roundup and transportation to California concentration camps of 75,000 American citizens of Japanese descent—the greatest mass violation of the Bill of Rights in American history.[14] In Washington, however, Chief Justice Warren became the revered protector of the Bill of Rights.

Trucklers are not only found in the executive, judiciary and legislative branches of the government. They abound in every bright and dark corner of American life. There is the novelist who is careful to make his minority characters "inoffensive". . . the playwright or scenarist who methodically gives the villain a Majority pedigree and Majority physical traits . . . the businessman who lends his company's name to any number of minority lobbies . . . the clergyman who preaches the righteousness of minority causes and is not averse to making his point by leading street demonstrations and sit-ins.

Aware of the immense rewards passed out to the faithful, many Trucklers become full-time minority enthusiasts, for which they not only receive numerous academic kudos and a prefabricated market for their books and articles, but also ready cash. Minority fund-raising events pay up to $1,000 a night for prominent Majority speakers. The late Vice-President Alben Barkley, Eleanor Roosevelt and her son, Elliott, and a host of lesser Majority notables made small

---

12. Truman paid $10 for his initiation fee into the Missouri Ku Klux Klan in 1922. He got his $10 back when he opposed the Klan's anti-Catholic policies—certainly the decent and loyal thing to do in view of Boss Pendergast's religion. Alfred Steinberg, *The Man from Missouri*, Putnam, New York, 1962, p. 64.

13. President Johnson's chameleon attitude toward civil rights has been mentioned in a previous chapter. For an example of Truman's post-presidential attacks on civil rights, see *New York Times*, April 13, 1965, p. 24.

14. *Washington Post*, Oct. 5, 1965, p. 1.

fortunes or sizable grubstakes as the star attractions of
Bonds for Israel dinners.[15]

Trucklers frequently render greater service to minority
projects than minority leaders themselves. Many legislative
Trucklers have been so well trained in racial matters they are
often more sensitive to minority interests than to those of
their own constituents. In regard to voter appeal, a handsome, imposing Majority member is sometimes more of a
political and social asset to minorities, providing he is properly "minority-broken," than a minority candidate. The
latter may lack the clean-cut appearance so handy in attract-
ing widespread support for minority-slanted legislation.

No Majority member is born a Truckler. Truckling is the
result of an educational process—sometimes years in the
making, sometimes an overnight conversion—in which the
young Majority member has drilled into him the modern
catechism of success. He learns he must be tactful rather
than truthful, may question the non-controversial but not the
controversial, must sail before the winds of "public opinion"
but not head into them. He is taught to fear the taboos of
present-day American society as thoroughly as primeval man
was taught to fear the taboos of his day. He is instructed to
explain his Truckling on moral and humanitarian grounds,
although it has never been known to retard the advancement
of his career.

One can admire a person who by changing his ideas and
principles risks death, disgrace or severe financial loss. One
reserves the right to adopt a certain skepticism toward those
whose ideological skin-shedding, often conveniently and
beautifully timed, makes them rich, powerful and celebrated.
Perhaps Truckler is too strong a word for those political
and moral trimmers who, at least superficially, are perform-
ing the age-old trick of sacrificing integrity to ambition.
But the Truckler, as here defined, oversteps this common
vice. He goes further than making a fetish of self-interest. He

---

15. As a Gracchite, Mrs. Roosevelt did not need the money, but Elliott,
one of the five offspring and often in financial straits, did. Patricia Roosevelt,
I Love a Roosevelt, Doubleday, New York, 1967, pp. 250–51. Also see
Time, Nov. 19, 1956, p. 27.

puts the interests of other peoples above the interests of his own.

3. *The Pussyfooters.* These are the Majority members who take no positive action against their own group but who seldom, if ever, defend it. They comprise the second and third echelons of Majority leadership—lawyers, doctors, scientists, small-time newspaper editors, professors, teachers, preachers, big and small businessmen, local, state and federal officials.

In contrast to Gracchites and Trucklers, who betray and violate Majority interests, Pussyfooters soft-pedal and subordinate them. Immersed in their own day-to-day problems, obsessed with the material aspects of existence, often isolated in areas where the Majority is overwhelmingly predominant, Pussyfooters have less direct contact with the minority challenge and consequently are less concerned about it. When and where they come face to face with minority dynamism, in social gatherings or in community affairs, instead of standing up for the Majority viewpoint, they simply keep quiet.

Pussyfooters know that something is wrong, but they don't know what, and they do not have the time, the inclination, the courage or the intellectual initiative to find out. Some Pussyfooters tread softly because they dislike argument, while others are fearful of their livelihood. Some are just temperamentally unsuited for the verbal screaming matches and hysterical logic-chopping in which their liberal and minority neighbors like to engage them.

So long as things go relatively well for them economically, so long as their stomachs are full, Pussyfooters may be expected to go on pussyfooting. Only a solar plexus variety of racism is ever likely to rouse them from their racelessness.

But every day there are countless little economic and social clashes, countless little unattractive slices of American life that eat away at Pussyfooter noninvolvement. Every day the Majority assistant manager at the expensive resort hotel welcomes a greater and greater influx of minority millionaires. Every day the Majority artist, poet, playwright or novelist must cope with an even tighter minority monopoly of art, literature and drama. Every day a larger and larger share of federal and local taxes is allocated to minority welfare projects. With its sit-ins, lie-ins, lootings and muggings at home and its military crusade in the Middle East, minority racism is becoming so shrill even the deaf are beginning to hear.

But hearing is a long way from understanding. Unlike members of the dynamic minorities who seethe and quiver as a single organism at the slightest crack in the social order, Pussyfooters continue to drift supinely on the edge of the great social vortex, whirling clockwise or counterclockwise as public opinion dictates.

4. *The Old Believers.* The American political tradition is a rare and delicate blend of English Whiggery, French egalitarianism, classic Stoicism and social Christianity. This complex doctrinal amalgam was once the exclusive ideology of the American Majority. Today, considerably altered in substance and given the name of liberalism, it has been eagerly adopted, if not taken over, by the minorities.[16] Nevertheless, a great many Majority members still call themselves liberals. Those who honestly subscribe to liberalism, not in its perverted modern form, but in its original Lockean, Jeffersonian and Lincolnian version, are here designated as Old Believers. Gracchites and Trucklers are pseudo, hypocritical, opportunistic or fearful liberals. Pussyfooters are reluctant or fitful liberals. Old Believers belong to the disappearing breed of honest liberals.

Old Believers seldom become particularly prominent or successful in present-day America. On the rare occasions they do, it is not for long. The plain truth is that the liberal establishment cannot stand liberalism in its pure, undiluted form. Old Believers, for example, not only pretend to believe in but *do* believe in the freedom of the printed and spoken word, an intolerable superstition to minority organizations who have drawn up certain critical boundaries for American thought, and equally intolerable to the politicians and opinion molders whose careers are built on a one-dimensional, one-sided, simplistic view of modern society.

Increasingly out of fashion, Old Believers are now mostly

16. The metamorphosis of liberalism is both the title and the subject of Chapter 23.

found in small universities or among the non-fundamentalist, non-violent, non-permissive clergy. The most vocal are often the descendants of families with roots in the New England town meeting or Populist tradition. In general, they are trying to transplant a faded, withered liberalism which functioned adequately under a special set of historical and genetic conditions to a different age and an often hostile and alien environment—a transplant that is being continuously rejected by the American body politic. All their hopes and convictions to the contrary, liberalism is not independent of time and race.

Two of the most prominent Old Believers in recent times were Dorothy Thompson, the columnist, and Charles Beard, the historian. Dorothy Thompson won nationwide acclaim when she was condemning Nazi persecution of the Jews with Old Testament vehemence. But when, after World War II, she used the same principles and arguments to denounce Jewish dispossession of the Palestinian Arabs, she lost her most important newspaper outlets and died in Portugal in relative obscurity. Charles Beard, in early New Deal days considered America's greatest living historian and an exemplar of liberalism, was cast out of the American intellectual community after he had accused President Roosevelt of unconstitutional acts in the handling of American diplomacy and foreign policy prior to Pearl Harbor.[17]

Old Believers also come in groups, the most influential being the Society of Friends or Quakers. Practicing almost total religious, political and social tolerance and driven by a compulsion for "good works," the Quakers pour their efforts and money (of which they have considerable) into projects which actively promote minority racism, although Quaker doctrine bristles at the very concept of race. The Quakers' uncritical acceptance of oldtime, Anglo-Saxon liberalism as applicable to a modern, racially heterogeneous society has given birth to some strange ideological hybrids within the Quaker community. Drew Pearson, the most vituperative of columnists, Alger Hiss, the most subtle of communist conspirators, Klaus Fuchs, the most dedicated of atomic spies,

17. Charles Beard, *President Roosevelt and the Coming of the War, 1941*, Yale University Press, New Haven, Conn., 1948, pp. 580 ff.

as well as a few of the more notorious, non-minority members of revolutionary bomb, kidnap and murder squads, had Quaker backgrounds.[18]

Quakers and other Old Believers are to be commended for their unshakable faith in human nature. But they must be sharply criticized for their meddlesome, misdirected charity and the warped compassion which have earned them the name of Bleeding Hearts. In some respects, the Old Believer may be compared to the captain of a ship in distress. In another century and with another crew his stubborn courage might have piloted his vessel safely into port. But now, the prisoner of his own outdated seamanship, he steers blindly from reef to reef.

5. *The Proditors.*[19] The fifth and final category of those who have brought about the split in the Majority ranks is unique in that its members are tainted with outright disloyalty—not only to the Majority, their population group, but to the United States, their nation. The Gracchite or Truckler, while often going against the best interests of the American people, will not knowingly stray beyond the frontiers of high treason. Franklin D. Roosevelt would compromise with Communists, promote them to high office, give them far more than he received at the conference tables of Teheran and Yalta, but would never join them. Lesser politicos and public figures pampered them for years, but finally denounced them. The Proditor, on the other hand, seems to take a savage delight in severing all his previous ties, deliberately seeking out his country's enemies, foreign and domestic, and joining enthusiastically in the upending and destruction of everyone and everything once closest to his heart and mind.

The Proditor, in short, takes up permanent residence in

---

18. Perhaps there should be a special category for the Majority college students, many of them coeds, who surrender their minds to the schizoid Svengalis of the social science faculties. Worse than the ordinary Truckler because they are willing to shoot as well as to write and orate, most eventually return to the Majority fold once they discover their minority cohorts are not radicals at all, but anti-Majority racists.

19. The word, which means a particularly nasty form of traitor, is used here in the Shakespearean sense: "Thou most usurping proditor and not protector of the king."

that far country where the Gracchite and Truckler dare not penetrate. Though he may fancy himself a Robin Hood, though he may manufacture the most plausible and idealistic excuses for his great and small treacheries, the Proditor—there is no point in being euphemistic—is a common or, better, an uncommon criminal.

The circumstances which produce the Proditor do not defy analysis. As with the Gracchite, there is often the preliminary personal failure. The accompanying drift into exotic political philosophies is more of an indicator than a cause of the treason to come.

Thomas Paine deserted his wife and then filed for bankruptcy. Next he deserted his country, England, went to America, then returned to Europe, where he helped stir up the revolutionary terror in France. In 1796 Paine accused Washington of treachery,[20] a libel which in no way has shaken Paine from his lofty pedestal in the modern liberal pantheon, though recent charges of treason against high officials by non-liberals have not been received so warmly.[21]

John Brown also went through bankruptcy before he found his true vocation: helping to foment the Civil War. He first tasted blood during the Kansas land settlement disputes, when he and his four sons attacked five sleeping men and hacked them to death with sabers.[22] At Harper's Ferry, he seemed as eager to incite the slaves to revolution as he was to free them.

It is inherent in the renegade profession that betrayal is easier the second time around. With scarcely a qualm the defector becomes the redefector and the agent the double agent. Almost ritualistically, the Proditor makes a new career out of confessing his previous sins and informing against his previous co-workers and accomplices.

Whittaker Chambers was perhaps the prime example of

20. Perhaps in retaliation, Theodore Roosevelt called Paine "a dirty little atheist." Alfred Aldridge, *Man of Reason, The Life of Thomas Paine,* Lippincott, Philadelphia, 1959, pp. 244–5, and Beard, *The Rise of American Civilization,* Vol. 1, p. 270.

21. Namely, Senator Joseph McCarthy's charges against General Marshall and Robert Welch's against Eisenhower.

22. *Dictionary of American Biography,* Scribner's, New York, 1929, Vol. III, p. 132. In all there were eight members of Brown's homicide team, one of them, Theodore Weiner, an Austrian Jew.

the redefector. A sad piece of flotsam as a young man, yet gifted with a certain tasteless intellectuality, he became in succession: drifter, Marxist, Communist courier, high-paid news magazine editor, star witness against Alger Hiss and, in the autumn of his years, author of an agonizing, best-selling confessional. If the theme of *Witness* had not been so banal, Chambers, a late-blooming Quaker, might have reached the autobiographical heights of St. Augustine and Rousseau. With tortured introspection and in soap opera detail, he recounted how he first betrayed himself, then his people, then his country, then his adopted country (Russia), and finally his friends.

Oregon-born John Reed, another noteworthy Proditor, actually became a member of the Communist Party Executive Committee in Moscow. He died, aged thirty-three, at the peak of the Bolshevik ferment and lies in a grave by the Kremlin wall [23]—eight thousand miles from home, but only a stone's throw from the bones of Stalin.

Alger Hiss, who almost deserves a special category of his own, dwarfs all other American traitors, past and present, both in the essence and extent of his treason. Benedict Arnold, whose forebears were English, who married a Loyalist and who betrayed a country that was only a few years old, could not be accused of the higher treason of betraying his racial and cultural antecedents. Aaron Burr's treason was not total, since it might possibly have resulted in the establishment of an American empire in Mexico.

Alger Hiss, on the other hand, directly served a revolutionary totalitarian power whose political, social and economic philosophy and strategy, at least at the time, were unalterably anti-American. Although he moved in the highest circles and had received many of the rewards and honors his country was able to bestow, he put his wide-ranging talents and valuable connections at the disposal of an international complot, whose aim was the destruction or mutation of everything that had made his own success possible. Hiss is the supreme case of the brilliant mind, cut loose from all racial moorings, turning against itself. In his *Divine Comedy*,

23. Granville Hicks, *John Reed*, Macmillan, New York, 1936, pp. 4, 8, 394, 400.

Dante reserved the greatest torments for Judas, Cassius and Brutus, the betrayers of their benefactors. He might have been hard put to conceive of a circle of hell adequate for the likes of Alger Hiss.[24]

All Splitters of the Ranks—Gracchites, Trucklers, Pussyfooters, Old Believers and Proditors—damage the Majority not so much by their activity or passivity, their secret complicity or open collaboration with the opposition, as they do by the confusion with which they surround the Majority-minority confrontation. The mere presence of a Majority member in minority gatherings or street demonstrations, the mere appearance of a Majority name on the executive roster of minority lobbies or fund-raising organizations, helps disguise their essentially racial character. Also, by appealing to carefully selected principles of liberalism and conservatism and carefully chosen tenets of religion and ethics, Majority Splitters of the Ranks pose as the only legitimate heirs of a great Western humanitarian tradition. In this guise, they can more easily lend the gloss of moral respectability and a sense of Christian urgency to minority *Realpolitik*.

The number and influence of Splitters of the Ranks will not substantially decrease until the Majority member who encourages, defends or excuses minority-oriented liberalism and minority racism can no longer make a successful career out of depreciating the Majority stake in American civilization. Until such time, the lower ranks of the Majority will have to carry the main burden of the Majority defense, relying chiefly on their instincts, their unbrainwashed common sense, their inexpungible consciousness of kind—in other words, on their genetic resources.

24. The treason of atomic spies Julius and Ethel Rosenberg, Harry Gold, Morton Sobell and David Greenglass, even though it may have had a deadlier impact on the American future (see Chapter 38), lacked the racial and cultural depravity and the self-abasement of the Majority traitors. The Rosenbergs *et al.* were members of an Unassimilable Minority. Since they started out with fewer real and sentimental attachments to their country of residence, the Gordian knot they had to cut was tied more loosely and made of weaker rope.

Chapter 12

The Esthetic Prop

O NE SUCH GENETIC resource is what might be designated as the Esthetic Prop.

Even the most committed racial equalitarian can hardly deny that the physical traits of the idealized Nordic stereotype[1] are considered desirable by most whites and many nonwhites. The current sociological line, partly derived from Marxism, is that these traits are not favored because of any inborn or universal esthetic preference, but because they are typical of the dominant group and *ipso facto* bestow higher social status upon their possessors.

It is not difficult to disprove this materialistic conception of esthetics. The first documented evidence of blondism is an Egyptian wall painting of a daughter of Cheops, Queen Hetep-Heres II.[2] If one of the earliest and greatest Egyptian Pharaohs had a blond daughter, both he and his wife must have had some blond genes.[3] Blondness, conse-

---

1. See p. 23.
2. Hetep-Heres II may have derived her golden locks from Libyan ancestors, for there were Libyans in the Delta even in prehistoric times. These Libyans were ultimately descended from early European invaders of North Africa. There are still blond Berbers in Morocco, Algeria and in present-day Libya. Coon describes them as Nordics. *The Races of Europe*, p. 98.
3. Blondism is due to a recessive trait which must be present in both parents or in their family trees. It may be indicated by light brown hair or light eyes, as well as by blond hair, which even in the purest Nordic is likely to turn brown with advancing age.

quently, must have been attractive or prestigious as far back as 3075 B.C. in a highly civilized land populated almost entirely by brunet Mediterraneans.

In classical times there were constant references to the blondism of Greek and Roman gods and demigods.[4] The conventions of the Greek theater called for a black-wigged and black-haired tyrant, red hair for the dishonest slave, and fair curls for the youthful hero.[5] Ovid and Martial declared that light hair was preferred by Roman matrons for wigs, a preference which spread to America nineteen hundred years later.[6] Pope Gregory the Great called Anglo-Saxon captives he happened to see in Rome not Angles but "angels" because they were "bright-beautied" and of "gracious outward sheen."[7]

The *Rigsthula,* a cultural poem of the Vikings, describes early Scandinavian society as consisting of a black-haired, wrinkled-skinned lower class, a yeoman class with sturdy bodies and ruddy faces and a nobility with blond hair and skin whiter than the driven snow.[8] Of the medieval Caliphate of Cordova, it has been written, "Most of the Caliphs were fair or ginger-haired with blue eyes. . . ."[9] Perhaps this light coloration was due to intermarriage with the earlier Visigothic nobility. The most noble families in Christian Spain, who claimed direct descent from the Visigoths, had skin so white that the blue network of their veins was highly visible. For this reason, *sangre azul* (blue blood) became a synonym for aristocrat. The veins of more plebeian

4. The Latin word *flavens,* meaning yellow, golden or auburn, was "the color universally ascribed to the hair of heroic persons by the ancients." J. B. Greenough, *Virgil and the Other Latin Poets,* Ginn & Co., Boston, 1930, note 590, p. 133.

5. A. E. Haigh, *Attic Theater,* Clarendon Press, Oxford, 1907, pp. 221, 239.

6. "We're paying $10 a pound for Oriental hair and as much as $350 a pound for the best blond European hair," said Adolph Jacoby, an officer in a New York wig firm. *Wall Street Journal,* Oct. 17, 1962, p. 1.

7. Will Durant, *The Age of Faith,* p. 522.

8. Coon, *The Races of Europe,* p. 321.

9. Enrique Sordo, *Moorish Spain,* Crown, New York, 1962, p. 24. Although it is not generally known, Arabs have always drawn a very distinct color line. In present-day Iraq a citizen can obtain a legal judgment against a person falsely accusing him of Negro ancestry. Coon, *Caravan,* Henry Holt, New York, 1951, p. 161.

Spaniards were obscured by their darker Mediterranean skin.[10]

More tenuous evidence of the esthetic appeal of light coloration is offered by the legend of Quetzalcoatl, the Aztec god of the air, who allegedly instructed the copper-skinned Mexicans in the use of metals and in the arts of government. He was said to have a white skin and a beard, the latter being practically unknown to the almost beardless natives. When he had incurred the wrath of another divinity he left Mexico and sailed east across the Great Ocean, saying he would return. In Peru, a somewhat similar myth has white, bearded men conquering the pre-Incan inhabitants and imparting to them the blessings of civilization.[11]

Today, the Esthetic Prop still persists in Latin America, including those areas where Negroes and Indians predominate. As remote a town as Ita on the upper Amazon has a simple rule of thumb for status: the lighter the skin, the higher the class, and a light complexion is acknowledged as the hallmark of beauty.[12] Even in Japan, pale complexions are favored. The Japanese expression for well-born is "deep window," which refers to the lighter pigmentation of people shielded from the sun by thick-walled houses.[13]

The purely esthetic attractiveness of Nordicism is glaringly evident throughout the contemporary United States. Light-haired, long-headed, narrow-faced males still appear in most men's fashion ads, while in the so-called Hippie subculture, supposedly a complete rejection of present-day tastes, the girl with the long, straight, blond hair is the symbol of femi-

---

10. Don Quixote says of the fictitious, not the real, Dulcinea, "Cabellos son oro . . . su blancura nieve." Cervantes, *Don Quijote*, E. Castilla, Madrid, 1966, p. 98.

11. William H. Prescott, *The History of the Conquest of Mexico and the History of the Conquest of Peru*, Modern Library, New York, pp. 39, 736. Other investigators of Mexico's prehistory deny that Quetzalcoatl had white physical traits. Cesar A. Saenz, *Quetzalcoatl*, Instituto Nacional de Anthropologia é Historia, Mexico, 1962. For a series of lively asides on the Mexican god, see D. H. Lawrence, *The Plumed Serpent*. Those inclined to wring history from myth can hardly escape feeling that Quetzalcoatl was a shipwrecked, homesick Viking.

12. Charles Wagley, *Amazon Town*, Macmillan, New York, 1953, pp. 128–40.

13. *Life*, Sept. 5, 1969, p. 42.

ninity. Each year millions of American women spend tens of millions of dollars on hair bleaches and hair straighteners. Everywhere it is proclaimed that "blondes have more fun," and the phrase "gentlemen prefer blondes" has become a twentieth-century proverb.[14]

The avalanche of artificial blondes set loose by such publicity, and the incongruous and often ugly contrast of platinum hair with dark eyes and eyebrows and olive skin, should have been enough to destroy the blond ideal forever. That it did not verified an enduring, deeply ingrained esthetic preference on the part of most Americans.[15] Many other ways of tampering with nature—nose straightening and nose bobbing, electrolysis to raise the hair line and heighten the brow and forehead, elevator shoes to increase body height—have been adopted or tried by minority members striving to give themselves a "Majority look." [16]

The power of the Esthetic Prop is also apparent in present-day American mating and dating habits. Although the Majority is in the descendant, the most dynamic and successful minority males often marry or at least seek out the company of Majority females. For proof one has only to look at the couples who throng the most expensive nightclubs and restaurants. Moreover, the Nordic physical ideal has not only been the marriage ideal of the minority "New Rich" in

---

14. *Gentlemen Prefer Blondes* was the title of a novel by brunette Hollywood film writer, Anita Loos, whose father was of French descent. Miss Loos later explained why she had written the book: "The satisfaction of getting even with Mae Davis for seducing the man I loved [H. L. Mencken] more than paid for the pains [of writing it]." She continued her vendetta against blondes in another novel, *But Gentlemen Marry Brunettes*. In spite of the author's best intentions, however, the "dumb" gold-digging Lorelei has entered American folklore as the knowing young blonde who usually gets her way. Anita Loos, *A Girl Like I,* Viking Press, New York, 1966, p. 274.

15. Blondism is most appealing when accompanied by other Nordic physical characteristics. If it were not for the color sensitivity of most Americans, Nordic pigmentation and skin shade might be less important than other Nordic traits as criteria of male handsomeness and female beauty. Certainly "tall, dark and handsome" Nordic-Mediterraneans are more attractive physical specimens than shorter, squatter, though blonder, types.

16. Suntan mania does not contradict the logic of the Esthetic Prop. The ultraviolet rays of the sun may darken the skin, but they also lighten the hair and provide a pleasing contrast to light eyes and other manifestations of light coloration. Basically, a suntan is a sign of health and wealth—a temporary camouflage and an exotic masquerade.

America, but of European social climbers for at least a thousand years.

The relatively small number of Nordics in the world has doubtlessly enhanced their esthetic appeal. Rarity per se exercises a special attraction, and what is beautiful generally contains an element of the uncommon and esoteric. Just as the pure Nordic is a rarity among the part-Nordics who make up most of the American Majority, so the American Majority represents a rare racial type to the world's population as a whole. To whites and nonwhites alike, Nordics are the personification of the white race because they are the "whitest" whites.

Perhaps the best description of the physical attractiveness of the Majority has been given by Wyndham Lewis. "It is a common experience in talking to Americans to hear some magnificent human specimen (who is obviously the issue of say a first-class Swede and a magnificent Swissess, with a little Irish and a touch of Basque) refer to himself as a 'mongrel.' It is inconceivable yet indeed that is how a 'mixed' product is apt to look upon this superb marriage of Scandinavian, Goth and Celt—all stocks as closely related in blood . . . as the Brahmanic caste in India. . . . All you have to do is to look at this sterling type of 'mixed' American to admire the purity of line and fine adjustment achieved by the conjunction of these sister stocks. Far from being a 'mongrel,' of course, he is a sort of super-European; the best of several closely allied stocks have met in him, in exactly the same way as was constantly happening in the noble European families—where the issue of marriage between nobles, whether from England and Italy or Spain and Russia, did not constitute a 'half-breed,' but rather a more exalted feudal product. . . ." [17]

The possibility that the Esthetic Prop goes beneath the skin, that there is a relationship between what Herbert Spencer called "beauty of character and beauty of aspect," raises problems which are beyond the scope of this study. [18]

---

17. Wyndham Lewis, *Pale Face,* Chatto and Windus, London, 1929, p. 278.
18. Herbert Spencer, *Essays,* Appleton, New York, 1910, Vol. II, p. 387. Schopenhauer was another philosopher who believed in a connection be-

However, without becoming too entangled in psycho-biological complexities, one must agree with Spencer's suggestion that beauty is "idealization away from the ape." Three principal sources of ugliness, according to Spencer, are recession of the forehead, jaw protuberances and large cheekbones. Ergo, only those human beings are handsome whose jaws and cheekbones have been pulled back and nasal depressions filled in. Other qualifications are the absence of any forward opening of the nostrils and a small mouth.[19] Since the idealized Nordic meets these requirements more closely than other racial stereotypes, it follows that Nordics are the least "apelike" and so the most deserving of first prize in the ethnic beauty contest.[20]

The Esthetic Prop, moreover, has often been carried over into the realm of ethics and even politics. Plato was neither the first nor the last to equate beauty with the good. All else being equal, the handsome (i.e., Nordic-looking) politician or statesman has usually been able to evoke more deference and dedication than his less handsome (i.e., less Nordic-looking) rival, whose unprepossessing appearance may be a severe handicap in winning and keeping a following. Realizing the force these esthetic standards still exert in Western society, a perceptive intellectual like Marxist philosopher George Lukács, who stands well outside the Northern European genetic and cultural locus, has reacted by having a

tween outward appearance and inner being. The mouth, he said, expresses the thought of man, while the face expresses the thought of nature and the thought of the species. "Vielmehr ist jedes Menschengesicht eine Hieroglyphe," is how Schopenhauer summed up his opinion of the matter. *Parerga und Paralipomena,* F. A. Brockhaus, Leipzig, 1877, pp. 670–1.

19. Spencer, *op. cit.,* pp. 390–2.

20. In a work that falls distressingly short of *Moby Dick* and *Billy Budd,* Melville carried this physical argument into the spiritual plane when he attempted to equate blondism with goodness. In *Pierre,* Melville has Isabel complain: "Oh, God! that I had been born with blue eyes, and fair hair! These make the livery of heaven! Heard ye ever yet of a good angel with dark eyes, Pierre?—no, no, no—all blue, blue, blue—heaven's own blue . . ." *Pierre,* Hendricks House, New York, 1957, p. 370. In contrast, Melville's novella, *Benito Cereno,* which has only been equalled by Joseph Conrad's *Heart of Darkness* in plumbing the dark side of Negro mentality, seemed to propose a correlation between blackness and evil. Montesquieu and Mozart were also charter members of the "Black is not Beautiful" school. In the latter's opera, *Die Zauberflöte,* his black villian, Monostatos, sings, "Weiss ist schön, weil ein Schwarzer hässlich ist."

"liberal fear of beauty, with [an] obsessive suspicion that beauty and, by inference, a good deal of art is a mask preventing a clear view of human evil and suffering." [21]

It was the Esthetic Prop which prolonged the survival of the decadent Teutonic aristocracy in Central and Southern Europe centuries after it had been stripped of its preeminence. It is the same Esthetic Prop which helps the American Majority to hold on to the trappings, but not the substance, of its former power.[22] Only in the sector of esthetics, through the pervasiveness of the idealized Nordic biological type and its continued acceptance as the national template of physical charm and attractiveness, has the Majority been able to mount a small but successful holding action in the present racial melee.

21. *Times Literary Supplement,* June 18, 1970, p. 660.

22. After trying to persuade Negro girls to go back to natural, woolly hairdos and give up bleaching creams and Western dress styles, Negro militants themselves still search out white girls, preferring, when they have enough money for vacations abroad, Scandinavia to Africa. Fletcher Knebel, "The Black Woman's Burden," *Look,* Sept. 23, 1969, pp. 77–9.

PART IV

The Minority Challenge

Chapter 13

Assimilable White Minorities

Iᴛ ʜᴀs ʙᴇᴇɴ sʜᴏᴡɴ that 25,722,000 Americans—12.6 percent of the population—belong to what have been described as Assimilable White Minorities.[1] In the terminology of physical anthropology, these minorities are predominantly Alpine, a designation which in this study also encompasses the Dinaric and East Baltic races. Geographically speaking, their countries of origin have been Ireland, France (in the case of the French-Canadians and the Louisiana French), Russia and the Slavic lands, and various Central European and Balkan states. Mostly descended from those who arrived in the New Immigration, Assimilable Minority members, due to their not too remote racial and cultural affinity to the Majority, have the possibility—and usually the certainty—of being absorbed into the Majority population matrix. Since hundreds of thousands are doing so each year, they might be more properly defined as assimilating rather than assimilable.

In the following sections which list and briefly examine the Assimilable Minorities, no Northern European population group, except the Irish and the Finns, will be found. This may seem strange, since many of the Germans, Dutch, Belgians and more than a few of the Scandinavians and British who came to America were Alpines and part of the New Immigration. But Alpinism by itself is no serious impediment to the assimilation process. Neither is late arrival. What

---

1. Table V, p. 60.

does retard or hinder the assimilation of Assimilable Minorities is a combination or, more precisely, a manifold of Alpinism, late arrival, religious and linguistic differences, a tradition of political absolutism and peonage and, in the case of the Slavic groups, an Eastern European rather than a Western cultural heritage.

Because Alpines of Northern European descent have not had this multiplicity of obstacles blocking their assimilation, most have been given Majority status and considered assimilated. The same dispensation has been extended to Alpines of Swiss, Austrian and Northern Italian origin.[2] But this is not to say that *all* Americans of Northern European descent, Nordic or Alpine, are Majority members in good standing. A substantial quota of Irish-Americans have so far successfully resisted full assimilation. Other Americans of equally authentic Northern European lineage and with family trees going back to the Old Immigration still retain such minority habits as clannishness and bloc-voting [3] and cling to the customs and speech of their Old World points of origin. A rapidly diminishing number of Pennsylvania Dutch and German Catholics in the Ohio Valley are two examples. Some Welsh and Scots, minorities in their own homelands, brought along a persistent minority consciousness that has only been partly eradicated. Certain religious sects teach their members the necessity of moral or physical secession from society at large. All these groups, except the Irish, are small in number, isolated geographically and exercise very little influence on the national or even on the regional scene. Their separateness more accurately classifies them as clans or cults than as bona fide minorities.

Another type of Northern European who cannot be described as fully assimilated is the first-generation and, oc-

2. Some French belong to this category, but most do not, as will be shown in the *French Section* in this chapter.

3. A nationwide but indecisive German vote was noted as late as World War II, when some German-Americans turned against President Roosevelt in protest against his interventionist policies. Both German Protestants, and German Catholics voted in large numbers for Eisenhower, but many of the latter switched back to the Democratic party when Catholic John Kennedy ran for the presidency. Kevin Phillips, *The Emerging Republican Majority*, Arlington House, New Rochelle, N.Y., pp. 296, 314, 339.

casionally, the second-generation American from Britain, Germany, Holland, Scandinavia or Canada. No matter how closely he approximates the Majority racial and cultural norm, the newcomer, as opposed to the latecomer, almost always retains some traces of minority consciousness—a consciousness which he often manages to pass on to his children and sometimes, depending on its intensity, to his grandchildren. The foreign birth of such contemporary left-leaning public figures as Cyrus Eaton, John Galbraith and James Reston has probably had more influence than they would admit on their political and social attitudes.[4] If Earl Warren's father had been born in America instead of Norway and if he had not been such an intransigent socialist, it is possible that his son, when Chief Justice of the Supreme Court, would have been more concerned with Majority than minority interests.

Since it is only a question of time until the progeny of most Northern European holdouts will be part and parcel of the Majority, attention will now be focused on the Assimilable Minorities proper. These are the population groups who pride themselves on their differences and are reticent about assimilation—a process they still regard as a cultural leap into the unknown and a form of ethnic surrender. It is exactly these differences, both real and imagined, which encourage their physical and occupational segregation, which in turn reinforces their separateness. As they pass in review, the diversity of these minorities will become obvious. So will their on-again, off-again participation in the war being waged against the Majority. Although Unassimilable Minorities have taken the lead in this conflict, the Assimilable Minorities, as if unaware they are being phased out by their accelerating rate of assimilation, still lend considerable conscious or unconscious support to the minority cause.

The Irish:[5] One of the major ironies of American history is that the minority which has wielded the most political power in the United States in the first half of the twentieth-

---

4. Reston was born in Scotland. Eaton and Galbraith in Canada. Like Warren, Senator Henry Jackson also had a Norwegian immigrant father.
5. For the distinction between the Catholic Irish and the Protestant Scotch-Irish from Ulster, see footnote 9, p. 39.

century had until its arrival in the New World a very limited experience with the democratic process.[6] Although it was not necessarily a personal failing or an innate antipathy to democracy—their British masters handed out freedom sparingly—the Irish were never able to establish a permanent representative government in Ireland until comparatively recently. Only in 1948, when the great Irish overseas migrations to America had long since ended, did Ireland after a few decades of commonwealth status achieve complete independence. Ireland or Eire may be a republic now, but the ancestors of present-day Irish-Americans had for the most part never passed through the long, exasperating, but richly instructive cycle of political apprenticeship which led from feudal aristocracy to absolute monarchy to representative democracy.

In the detailed racial study of ten thousand Irish males in Ireland by E. A. Hooton, 28.9 percent were classified as Nordic-Mediterranean, 25.3 percent as Keltic, 18.6 percent Dinaric, 18.4 percent Nordic-Alpine, 6.8 percent predominantly Nordic, 1.1 percent East Baltic, 0.6 percent Pure Nordic, 0.3 percent Pure Mediterranean.[7] Carleton Coon, whose racial terminology often differs from Dr. Hooton's, speaks of a relatively large Upper Paleolithic streak in the Irish racial makeup.[8] Irish physical types consequently range from a Nordic-flavored racial mix, scarcely distinguishable from most other Northern Europeans,[9] to the heavy-boned, heavy-set, broad-faced, large-framed Upper Paleolithic, supposedly the genetic remains of an older European race which fled to the outermost regions of Western Europe to escape the Kelts and other invaders. One distinctive breed is the "Black Irish," the inhabitants of the Emerald Isle with the

6. "The importance of immigrant groups in the history of American politics can hardly be overestimated and in this history the Irish have played the principal role." *One America*, p. 61.

7. E. A. Hooton and C. W. Dupertuis, *The Physical Anthropology of Ireland*, Papers of the Peabody Museum of Archaeology and Ethnology, Harvard University, Vol. XXX, Nos. 1–2, p. 143.

8. Coon, *The Races of Europe*, pp. 376–84.

9. Wyndham Lewis, describing a mixed Anglo-Irish demonstration in London, wrote, "I was never able to discover which were Irish and which were English . . . they looked to me exactly the same." *Pale Face*, pp. 284–5

most pronounced Mediterranean cast, the reputed descendants of prehistoric "Atlantic-Mediterraneans" who cruised up the Atlantic coast from Gibraltar and Portugal. Some Black Irish may be the distant offspring of sailors from the wrecked Spanish Armada.[10]

The racial balance of Ireland has been reproduced fairly closely by the rank and file of Irish-Americans, though possibly with less accent on the Nordic element. The Irish exodus was composed chiefly of the poorer segments of the population—the tenant farmers and the bog-dwelling Western Irish, who were most removed in time and place from the more Nordic Irish in the east, where Vikings, Normans and English had been settled for centuries. One set of physical traits—pug nose, freckles, red hair and the "world's bluest eyes"—although not exclusively Irish, has come to be accepted, at least in America, as the basic ingredients of a common Irish stereotype.[11]

The racial composition of the Irish in Ireland provides a clue to one of the greatest difficulties in the compilation of an accurate census of American minorities, the difficulty of determining how many of the sixteen million Irish-American Catholics [12] belong to the Assimilable category, and how many are already assimilated and are full-fledged members of the Majority.

One way of attacking the problem is to take the blonder elements among Catholics of Irish descent, the elements which more closely approximate the median Northern Euro-

10. President Nixon probably belongs to the Black Irish category. The Nixons came from County Cork; the Milhous family from County Kildare. Phillips, *op. cit.*, pp. 174–5.

11. Coon, *op. cit.*, pp. 371, 381, 383. Bushy eyebrows, large heads, prominent chins, long and convex upper lips and great malar breadth are other fairly common Irish traits.

12. According to *Life* (March 17, 1961, p. 114), 29,000,000 living Americans claim some Irish descent. The subject here, however, is not those Americans who have one or two remote Irish ancestors. It is those Irish-Americans who still remain firm Catholics, are usually Irish on both sides and are quite aware of their origins. These are the Irish-Americans Andrew Rolle and Paul Blanshard probably had in mind when they estimated their number at 15 million and 15–16 million, respectively. Rolle, *The Immigrants Upraised*, University of Oklahoma Press, 1968, p. 304 and Blanshard, *American Freedom and Catholic Power*, p. 263. Blanshard's higher figure has been taken to compensate for the healthy birthrate of a population group whose Church still forbids contraception.

pean physical type, and to consider them assimilated rather than assimilable. E. A. Hooton's racial studies of Ireland can be used as a guide. According to Hooton, the Nordic Alpines, the Predominantly Nordics and the Pure Nordics account for 25.8 percent of the Irish in Ireland. This might be reduced to 20 percent for the Irish immigration to allow for the allegedly smaller proportion of Nordic elements. If these horseback estimates are not unacceptable, then 3,200,000 Irish-Americans (20 percent of 16,000,000) are assimilated and 12,800,000 (80 percent) can be classified as assimilable.

The Irish voting record can also be of assistance in discovering the proportion of assimilated and assimilable Irish. In the 1952 presidential race, it was estimated that 38 percent of the Catholic vote went to Eisenhower, and that an even higher ratio of Catholics voted Republican in the 1956 election.[13] In 1960, however, a Gallup Poll stated that three out of five Catholics who voted for Eisenhower switched to Kennedy.[14] Applying these percentages to the Irish segment of the Catholic population and to the Irish-American population as a whole, as well as to Irish voters, this means that 6,080,000 Irish (38 percent) were in the Republican ranks in 1952 and perhaps as many as seven million in 1956. Then in 1960, 60 percent of these temporary Republicans and their families returned to the Democratic fold to support Kennedy. This left 2,800,000 Irish Republicans for Nixon, the non-Catholic loser—certainly an acid test of assimilation for Irish-Americans.[15] Subtracting 2,800,000 from the total number of Catholics of Irish descent leaves 13,200,000 who can be counted as assimilable.

The 13,200,000 figure obtained by the Irish vote analysis

13. William Shannon, *The American Irish,* Macmillan, New York, 1963, pp. 410–11.

14. *Ibid.*

15. During the 1960 election Nixon, playing for the Majority vote, never talked about his Irish ancestry, while Kennedy with his unmistakable Keltic looks played his racial and religious background to the hilt in Northern urban areas and even mentioned it elsewhere. In the 1970 Congressional election campaign, however, Nixon took a trip to Ireland where much was made of his Irish forebears. As part of their "blue collar" and "law and order" strategy, the Republicans had decided to make an open bid for the Irish vote.

is very close to the 12,800,000 obtained by racial estimates and projections. Averaging the two yields 13,000,000 as a fair estimate of the size of the Irish-American Assimilable Minority. In general, these are the Irish-Americans who still congregate in the big cities, who faithfully back Irish-American political machines, who vote for Senator Kennedy despite Chappaquiddick, though in fewer numbers after South Boston, and who put their minority sentiments above their political judgment. These are the Irish-Americans whom Carl Wittke had in mind when he described their character as a "mixture of flaming ego, hot temper, stubbornness, great personal charm and warmth and a wit that shines through adversity. An irrepressible buoyancy, a vivacious spirit, a kindliness and tolerance of the common frailties of men . . . quick to anger and quick to forgive, frequently duped . . . generous, hospitable and loyal." Wittke also asserted that the Irish, although demonstrating a talent for art and literature, have never been particularly outstanding in the fields of science and invention.[16]

It was the great potato famine of the 1840's that first brought the Irish to the United States in large numbers. They carried with them bitter memories of starvation and centuries of humiliation and suppression under the heel of the English. Once they had finished their pick and shovel apprenticeship on the Erie Canal and on the railroads, they gathered together in large cities and often renewed their feuds with the British Empire by extending it to Americans of English extraction.

As Irish-Americans began to control the big city political machines and with them the Northern wing of the Democratic party, they often used it as a weapon of defense and revenge against the Republican party, which in many Irish-American eyes represented the interests of the English-descended establishment. Chicago Mayor "Big Bill" Thompson's well-publicized promise in 1927 to "make the King of England keep his snoot out of America" was a typical manifestation of Gaelic Anglophobia.[17] The most

16. *The Irish in America*, Louisiana State University Press, Baton Rouge, 1956, p. 233.
17. *Literary Digest*, Nov. 5, 1927, p. 5.

recent flare-up of this century-old hostility took place in the 1966 New York City subway strike when Michael Quill, head of the Transport Workers Union and a former member of the Irish Republican Army, attempted to turn the walkout into a personal vendetta against Mayor John Lindsay, who in spite of his Gracchite habits was deemed to be, if not as bad as an Orangeman, at least as bad as a WASP.[18]

It is almost impossible to write about the Irish in the United States without discussing the Roman Catholic Church. Irish Catholicism, in which both men and women participate, is vastly different from Catholicism in Spain, France and Italy, where the congregations consist almost entirely of women and where anticlericalism is a traditional male prerogative. The cherished place in their hearts that Irishmen everywhere reserve for the Catholic Church is due in great part to its loyal, unwavering support during the millennium-long struggle for Irish independence. Irish priests often had as high a price put on their heads as lay patriots and the Church used all its resources to keep Irish morale from sagging in the darkest hours of the Protestant occupation. Consequently, there is a secular as well as a religious link between the Catholic Church and most Irish-Americans, a stronger link than that between the Church and the common citizenry in Latin countries, where during much of medieval and modern history Catholic prelates allied themselves with aristocrats, monarchs and plutocrats.

Having helped keep Ireland alive for so many centuries, the Catholic Church has fought a dogged, rearguard action to insulate its Irish-American flock against the allurements and pressures of assimilation. The Church has always feared that joining the predominantly non-Irish, non-Catholic Majority may be the first step in abandoning the faith, or at least the kind of faith that fills pews and collection boxes to overflowing. Although the Irish account for less than half of all American Catholics, they remain the dominant Catholic congregation and furnish most of the money and most of the

---

18. *New York Times,* Jan. 2, 1966, p. 1 and Jan. 4, 1966, pp. 14, 17. The whole atmosphere surrounding the strike talks, according to one *Times* reporter was, "Down the English Protestant! Up the Irish!"

hierarchy.[19] Apart from the financial implications, a decline in Irish ethnocentrism and an accompanying decline in Irish religious fervor might expose the Church to a takeover by Poles, Italians or even Mexicans.

To preclude such a development, the Church has endeavored to keep the fires of Irish racism burning by a network of parochial schools, opposition to birth control, restrictions against marrying non-Catholics, and the subsidizing and promotion of a multitude of Irish political and social activities. Unquestionably, Catholicism must bear a great deal of the responsibility for the lingering, hyphenated status of many fifth- and sixth-generation Irish-Americans. But despite priestly qualms, most of the Irish who attached themselves to the Majority managed to take their religion along with them.

For obvious reasons, the Catholic Church is opposed to Marxism and communism, particularly their atheistic facets. But it does not follow that all Irish-Americans are. Inspired as much as by timeworn national and racial antipathies as by class antagonisms, Irish leaders have been in and out of the American Socialist and Communist movements since their beginnings. William Z. Foster, whose father was an "English-hating Irish immigrant," was the Grand Old Man of American Communism and Elizabeth Gurley Flynn was the Grand Old Lady.[20] Jim Larkin was a prominent Communist rabble-rouser in the 1920's and served a term in Sing Sing before being pardoned by Al Smith, one-time New York Governor and the first Catholic to run for president.[21] Vincent Sheean, who later became a devotee of Mahatma Gandhi, wrote a book, *Personal History,* which probably attracted more Americans to the Communist cause than anything written by Engels, Marx or Lenin.

---

19. In 1961, all but four of the fourteen American Cardinals were Irish-Americans. *Life,* May 17, 1961, p. 132.

20. Flynn once wrote, "The awareness of being Irish came to us as small children, through plaintive song and heroic story . . . we drew in a burning hatred of British rule with our mother's milk." Shannon, *The American Irish,* pp. 166–7. A more modern Irish-American lady radical is Kate Millett, married to a Japanese and the "philosopher" of the Women's Liberation Movement. *New York Times,* Aug. 27, 1970, p. 30.

21. See footnote 9, p. 81.

As might be expected of an extremely verbal, hard-fisted, hard-working immigrant group, the Irish have been deeply involved in American unionism, ranging from the most radical labor organizations [22] to the most conservative. John Mitchell was a founder of the United Mine Workers and P. J. McGuire one of the organizers of the American Federation of Labor. Other noted Irish-American labor leaders were P. H. Morrissey of the Brotherhood of Railway Firemen, Teddy Gleason of the International Longshoremen's Association, James O'Connell of the International Association of Machinists, Michael Quill of the Transport Workers Union and, neither last nor least, George Meany, present head of the AFL-CIO.

Irish brawn helped build industrial America and Irish blood helped defend it. There have been great Americans of Irish descent in every era of America history and every sector of American activity. The size of the Irish contribution is impossible to determine. Historian Samuel Eliot Morison says that it has been less than the German.[23] In any case it has been considerable, and America would not be the same without it.

While Irish-American political passions have been high, Irish political standards have frequently been low. The scandals of such mayors as Jimmy Walker and William O'Dwyer of New York, James Curley of Boston and John Houlihan of Oakland, California, attest to the success of the Irish in securing public office and their failure to dignify it.[24] For many years Boston, New York, Chicago, San Francisco and several other large American cities were little more than Irish political fiefs, where the party bosses turned out huge pluralities for the candidates of their choice regardless of the issues. Recently, however, the Irish have been forced to share their urban bailiwicks with other minorities, and in some cities their once undisputed political control seems to be ending.

Generally voting the straight Democratic ticket *en bloc*, Irish Catholics, as previously noted, left their party in large

---

22. For the most radical of all, the Molly Maguires, see footnote, p. 355.
23. *The Oxford History of the American People*, pp. 480–1.
24. See Chapter 30.

numbers in 1952, when they helped swing the election to Dwight Eisenhower. The Democratic allegiance of the party bosses remained unshaken, but the ivory-towered liberalism of presidential candidate Adlai Stevenson, veering more and more toward appeasement of the Soviet Union, was too much for many of the faithful, who for the first time had achieved a certain middle-class respectability and affluence in the postwar economic boom. It is this same respectability and affluence, when spread among other Assimilable Minorities, which so often gives birth to Republican voting habits.

But most of the Irish closed ranks again in the 1960 presidential election, when they had a chance to vote for one of their own, and a war hero at that. John F. Kennedy, with the aid of his father's great wealth and his proliferating relations, gave new life to Irish-American politics. The emergence of the Kennedy dynasty, despite the assassination of its two leading members within a six-year period, will probably provide a rallying point for old-fashioned Irish bossism for many years to come. The nomination of George McGovern as the 1972 Democratic standard bearer, however, provoked another mass defection to the Republican ticket.

More pragmatic than ideological, the typical Irish machine politician wants the people's votes, not the people's minds. Although liberalism is the official theology of the Democratic party, Irish bosses treat it largely as a vote-getting device and in the privacy of their homes their own political beliefs are likely to have a markedly anti-liberal tone. When foreign policy is involved, these beliefs are often brought into the open. Consequently, the Irish have exercised a steadying and conservative influence over American international relations in recent decades, first by helping to preserve American neutrality during the Spanish Civil War,[25] second by supporting Catholic anti-communist parties in Western Europe after World War II. Without this support a much larger portion of Europe might now be Sovietized.

At home, fear and hatred of communism inspired some

_____

25. Joseph Kennedy, while Ambassador to England, took the lead in defending the Embargo Act, which forbade the shipment of war materials to both the Franco and Republican forces, at a time most American officials were ready to lift it. Hugh Thomas, *The Spanish Civil War*, Harper & Row, New York, 1961, pp. 536, 614.

132   *The Minority Challenge*

Irish-American mavericks to cross party lines and attack Marxism and Marxist apologists with the demagogic innuendo that had hitherto been the monopoly of communists and ultra-liberals. Two such individuals were Father Coughlin, the radio priest of the New Deal era, and Senator Joseph McCarthy, not to be confused with Eugene McCarthy, the eccentric Irish-Scandinavian Senator from Minnesota. A loftier intellectual tone was provided by William Buckley—like President Kennedy the son of an Irish multimillionaire—whose acerbic wit and recondite posing recalled such European conservatives as Léon Daudet and Charles Maurras of the *Action Française* clique.[26] True to the equalitarian philosophy of their Church, many of the leading Irish-American conservatives have staunchly supported racial integration. In speaking of the Irish component of conservatism, it must not be forgotten that President Nixon "was elected to the presidency in a campaign substantially planned by New York Irish conservatives." [27]

Because of their Northern European racial and cultural affinities, because they have become in so many ways so typically and so generically American, it is difficult to claim Irish-Americans still belong to a minority, even an assimilable one. On the surface, the American of Irish descent is a made-to-order Majority prototype. He is patriotic. He is willing to live and let live. He is not as obtrusive, acquisitive or aggressive as members of some other minorities. He does not crowd the professions. His economic worth is not above average. It is only when matters of faith, pride, machine politics and Ireland come into play—matters about which they are still supremely sensitive—that many Irish-Americans defiantly display their minority colors. And when they do, when they continue to play minority politics, when they are willing to join their own worst enemies against the Majority, then this

26. With James Buckley, William's brother, a Senator from New York, there are the makings of a conservative Irish political dynasty, but this time composed of Irish Majority members, not professional Irishmen.

27. Phillips, *op. cit.*, pp. 174–5. Nixon's campaign manager in 1968 was John N. Mitchell, later Attorney General, later a chief villain of Watergate. Mitchell is a Presbyterian with an Irish mother. Mitchell's deputy was banker Peter Marcus Flanigan. Many Nixon idea men, notably Patrick Buchanan, were also of Irish descent.

Irish hardcore of thirteen million must be classified as assimilable rather than assimilated.

But there is not much doubt that this number will continue to diminish. Many of the once-compelling reasons for Irish-American separateness have now evaporated. Time, distance and the decline and fall of the British Empire have mellowed the ancient grudge against England.[28] The American Majority, in which the Irish used to find so many distasteful English characteristics and customs, is no longer uniquely Anglo-Saxon and has acquired a more evenly distributed Northern European (including Irish) population base. As for religious differences, the hard-line Protestantism of the frontier, resonant with the anti-Catholic and anti-Papal overtones of the Reformation, has dissolved into a sweetness-and-light deism whose main concerns are tolerance and social justice. Liberalizing directives from Rome, questions about Papal infallibility, demands for an end to priestly celibacy, all part of the ecumenical movement, are undermining the age-old monolithic structure of Catholicism [29]—and in the process lowering the Church's prestige in the eyes and ears of those who prefer to take their religion with a large seasoning of dogma, dramaturgy and ritual.

Before the Romans came to the British Isles, the Kelts (early Nordics) of Ireland and Britain were similar in culture, civilization and race. After the departure of the Romans and the arrival of the Christian missionaries, Ireland and England shared the same religion for more than a thousand years, although for half of this period Irish Catholicism was more Keltic than Roman. If the two peoples cannot capitalize on their similarities in order to smooth over

28. Only Ulster remains a running sore and a daily reminder of the 900-year-old feud. So far, however, the Irish Republican Army has confined its fury and its bombs to the Old World.

29. The link between the Irish and Roman Catholicism is not congenital or unbreakable. Many of the greatest Irishmen, perhaps the very greatest, were Protestants or non-believers. The list includes Parnell, the dedicated nineteenth-century Irish freedom fighter, Douglas Hyde, Ireland's first president, Swift, Goldsmith, Sheridan, Wilde, Shaw, Yeats, Joyce, Synge and O'Casey. Paul Carroll, the modern Irish playwright, echoes in his *White Steed* the feelings of many of his countrymen when his heroine inveighs against the priests and the "little men" for depriving Irishmen of their primeval pride and virility.

their differences in the Old World, perhaps their descendants will in the New, as so many already have. At all events, it would not seem logical for *any* Irish-Americans to tie their future to the coattails of irresponsible ethnic dynasts, whose principal function is to serve as political stalking-horses for liberals and Unassimilable Minorities. But taking a perverse pleasure in doing the illogical is something for which the Irish have long been famous.

Assimilable Irish-Americans compose the largest white minority and the second largest of all minorities. When and how they choose sides in the growing racial confrontation will have a crucial effect on the final pattern of American society. It goes without saying that it is in their deepest interests to see that the Majority restores the traditional American racial and cultural mold. If the mold is permanently broken, the Assimilable Irish-American stands to lose as much as his already assimilated brother, and every other American of Northern Europe descent.

The Finnish and Baltic Minorities: Some Finns were associated with the original Swedish immigration which took place when Americans were still British colonials. But appreciable numbers did not arrive in the United States until 1864. Many went to Michigan to become miners and others started farms in Minnesota. Russian political repression in the late nineteenth century drove more Finns to America. According to one authoritative estimate, there are now 400,-000 Americans of Finnish descent.[30]

In spite of their difficult, agglutinative language and their supposed Eurasian origin, most Finnish-Americans are hardly to be distinguished from their Old World neighbors, the Swedes. They are nearly as Nordic and equally as Protestant. Only their late arrival in the United States and the nationalistic feelings still engendered by Russian bullying and aggression have delayed their complete assimilation. After World War I, Finnish-Americans were accorded a sort of honorary membership in the Majority when Finland became the only European nation to pay its war debt in full. The Puritan Ethic may have died in Boston, but it lived on in Helsinki.

Like the Finns, members of the Estonian, Latvian and Lithuanian minorities—numbering 60,000, 50,000 and 272,000, respectively[31]—came from countries situated on the shores of the Baltic. Unlike Finland, these countries no longer exist and Soviet imperialism and land hunger have kindled irredentist feelings in the Baltic minorities which tend to accent group solidarity and decelerate assimilation. From the racial standpoint, Estonians, Latvians and Letts (Lithuanians) have sufficiently light coloration for membership in the Majority. But as Eastern Europeans and as members of the New Immigration, most of them still remain in the Assimilable category. Of the three Baltic minorities, the Lithuanian-Americans, who are darker than the Latvians and Estonians, and are Catholic instead of Protestant, will probably be the last to be assimilated.

The Slavic Minorities: The Russians[32] were the only whites to migrate to America by an eastward route, arriving first in Alaska and then proceeding down the Washington, Oregon and California coast. By the time of Seward's Folly in 1867, however, the Czarist-sponsored expansion into North America had lost almost all its momentum and was recoiling to Siberia. Large-scale Russian migration, this time by the conventional westward passage, did not begin until the high-water mark of the New Immigration. After World Wars I and II, tens of thousands of Russian anti-Communists sought entry into the United States, most of them unsuccessfully.

Because millions of non-Slavic immigrants listed Russia as their homeland, it is extremely difficult to arrive at an accurate figure for Americans of bona fide Russian descent. One fairly reliable estimate puts the number at 350,000.[33] Most Russian-Americans are farmers and industrial workers,

---

31. *Ibid.*, pp. 186, 192, 196. There is also a high estimate of 455,000 for the Lithuanian minority. But the lower estimate has been taken on the grounds that the 455,000 figure includes many Lithuanian Jews.

32. By Russian is meant Great Russian, as opposed to Ukrainians, Byelo-Russians, etc. See pp. 451–2.

33. *One America*, p. 130.

though there were a few highly proficient artists and scientists among the escapees of the 1917 revolution.

Ukrainian sectional feelings, intensified by a thousand years of Russian domination or attempts at domination, are often as ardent in America as they are—or were—in the Soviet Union. Even so, what has been said about the Russian minority in America applies generally to the Ukrainian, except that the latter with some 600,000 members is much more numerous.[34] With a strong national tradition, reinforced by centuries of minority status in the Old World, Ukrainian-Americans comprise a more tightly knit population group than Russian-Americans and are accordingly less assimilated.

The Poles came earlier and took a more active part in American history than other Slavic minorities. Some ten thousand Polish political dissenters arrived in the United States from colonial times up to the Civil War. Two Polish officers, Kosciuszko and Pulaski, fought bravely under Washington. But the mass Polish migration occurred in the first thirteen years of this century, during which time 1,500,000 Poles passed through Ellis Island. Today there are approximately three million Americans of Polish descent,[35] a figure which does not include Polish Jews. This makes the Polish minority the largest and most powerful Slavic minority in the United States.

Like Ukrainians, Poles are anti-Russian by habit and instinct. Unlike Ukrainians and Russians, they are Catholics.[36] About 10 percent are farmers. The rest reside in large cities and are spread rather evenly through industry, commerce and the professions. Fifty years ago, the Polish minority voted the straight Democratic ticket. But recently many Poles, some influenced by America's soft Russian policy, others by Negro rioting, have turned Republican.

Some Czechs, notably members of the Moravian Brotherhood, landed in America in colonial days. But the great rush

---

34. *Ibid.*, p. 136.

35. *Ibid.*, p. 147.

36. As it does with the Irish, the Church helps keep alive Polish ethnic feelings and officially encourages the preservation of the Polish language, the "tongue of the soul," among its Polish-American communicants. Davie, *World Immigration*, p. 262.

of Czech and Slovak immigration did not get under way until the early 1900s, when nationalist ferment in the Austro-Hungarian Empire was at its strongest. Now numbering about 1,750,000,[37] the Czech and Slovak minorities, who mix as little in the New World as they did in Czechoslovakia, are heavily concentrated in the big cities of the Midwest. On the average, Czechs and Slovaks have a darker coloration than Poles and Russians. About half the Czech-Americans and Slovak-Americans are Roman Catholics.

The Southern Slavs consist chiefly of Serbs, Croats and Slovenes, collectively known as Yugoslavs. At present there are some 1,000,000 in the United States—400,000 Croats, 400,000 Slovenes and 200,000 Serbs.[38] The Croats and Slovenes are Catholics. The Serbs are Eastern Orthodox. Almost all Yugoslav-Americans are descendants of New Immigrants. Most of the breadwinners work in heavy industry, mines and quarries. It is usually the Balkan element in the Yugoslav population which accounts for evidences of Mediterranean coloration.

Many Slavs (Slav is not a racial but a linguistic designation) exhibit Northern European physical traits, particularly those with ancestral origins in Northwest Russia and Northern Poland. Some Russian-Americans have the blue eyes, blond hair and long heads of the Swedish Varangians who founded Russia ten centuries ago. But in general, Slavic faces tend to be broad, cheekbones high, heads round and noses snub. Though there are occasionally a few Mongolian traces, physical and mental, the Slavic minorities have found no insurmountable racial or cultural obstacles in the path of their assimilation. Even the Polish-Americans, who a decade ago had ten thousand literary, dramatic, singing, social, religious and athletic societies in the United States, are becoming slowly but thoroughly Americanized.

The Hungarian Minority: Americans of Hungarian origin cover a wide racial spectrum. Originating long ago in the Asiatic steppes, the proto-Hungarians are now thought to have been members of the white rather than the yel-

37. *One America,* p. 162.
38. *Ibid.,* pp. 171–2.

low race. Today there is no question about their whiteness and they are designated Alpines. As to the number of Hungarian-Americans, the racial potpourri of the old Austro-Hungarian Empire has again made worthwhile immigration statistics hard to come by. One source indicates that more than half of the 1,600,000 immigrants from Hungary were Jewish.[39] If the non-Jewish proportion is taken as 40 percent, then there are 640,000 non-Jewish Americans of Hungarian descent. This figure does not include some 35,000 who fled across the Atlantic after Hungary's abortive 1956 uprising against the Soviet occupation forces.

The French-Canadians and the Louisiana French: The French are the most difficult of all American minorities to categorize. On the Majority side of the ledger are the Huguenots, Protestants of Calvinist persuasion who began their migration to the United States when Louis XIV revoked the Edict of Nantes in 1685.[40] Although they composed a mere 0.5 percent of the original white colonial stock,[41] there are now perhaps as many as two million Americans of Huguenot descent. Another million descendants of Old and New Immigration Frenchmen,[42] mostly from North and Northwest France, may be assigned to the assimilated category.

This is not the case with the French-Canadian minority. About three million French-Canadians are now in the United States,[43] most of them concentrated in a belt stretching from Michigan to Maine. The greatest concentration is in the rural and industrial areas of New England. Not an economically aggressive people and not noted for attempting to dominate the thoughts or politics of others, French-Canadians cling tenaciously to their Catholic religion, and somewhat less tenaciously to their French-Canadian cultural heritage and

39. *Ibid.*, p. 234.
40. Davie, *World Immigration,* pp. 19–20, 40. Paul Revere and John Jay were the two most celebrated Huguenots of Revolutionary times.
41. *Ibid.*, p. 41.
42. The most notable of these was Pierre Samuel Du Pont de Nemours, the founder of the Du Pont company.
43. *One America,* p. 341. A lower estimate of 2,500,000 is also given, but the higher has been accepted in view of the French-Canadian predilection for large families.

the French language. Their proximity to their long-established homeland in French Canada acts as a brake on the assimilatory process. Like the Mexican-Americans, they present the United States with a minority problem on the European model—i.e., a frontier population group with closer emotional and historical links to the far side than to the near side of the national border.

In 1886 in Rutland, Vermont, delegates attempted to organize a French-Canadian "nationality" with its own flag and national anthem, which was to serve as a protection for all French-speaking people, both in Canada and the United States.[44] The project never worked out, but it is symptomatic of why an American diplomat was quoted as saying that French-Canadians are the "most difficult of all immigrant races to assimilate." [45] Although perhaps a shade or two darker than the American population norm, all but a die-hard handful of French-Canadians will probably be assimilated in the long run—despite their traditional separatist attitudes.

Of the 600,000 Louisianians of French descent, some 300,000 still speak a French patois inherited from the early settlers of the Mississippi delta, among them the Acadian exiles from Nova Scotia memorialized by Longfellow.[46] Some of these "Cajuns" have countenances which exhibit a dark Mediterranean cast,[47] and they lead an isolated, specialized life in the bayous which in the past has dimmed the hope and possibility of assimilation. As clannish as the French-Canadians, they seem to range from the Assimilable to the Unassimilable categories. But the rapid economic changes now taking place in Louisiana are prying them out of their solitude and severely modifying their endogamic marriage habits, provincial customs and geographical sectionalism.

---

44. Wilfred Bovey, *Canadien*, J. M. Dent, Toronto, 1934, p. 100.
45. *Ibid.*, p. 187.
46. *One America*, p. 103.
47. Alexis Carrel, the late French biologist and Nobel laureate, has stated that the Mediterranean elements of the French population are inferior to the Northern elements. He ascribes this to the fact that the acclimatization of white men to heat is accomplished at the expense of the development of the nervous system and the intellect. *L'homme, cet inconnu*, p. 300.

It is not proper to end a discussion of the Assimilable Minorities without saying that in many ways they are more definitely and dynamically American than the Majority. Most Assimilable Minority members, for instance, still *believe* in America—believe with a nineteenth-century intensity that has all but faded in the hearts of many with deeper roots in the American past. Numerous Assimilable Minority members, moreover, manage to hold on to this belief, even though as blue-collar workers and as the largest component of metropolitan police forces, they live and work in the ferment of the big cities, where they have learned much faster than other Americans what is happening to their country.

Because the Assimilable Minorities have suffered much more than the Majority from school desegregation, the rise in crime and the deterioration of white urban neighborhoods, it is quite possible that the leadership of a Majority resurgence will come from Assimilable Minority ranks, from the ranks of men and women whose lives and livelihoods have been more openly threatened than those of suburban and rural Americans. Face-to-face experience with problems often creates a greater interest in solutions.

But it is also possible, if the present torpidity of the Majority continues and the Assimilable Minorities are abandoned and left to their own devices, that in order to survive in the megalopolitan jungle they may revive rather than give up their old ethnic loyalties, thereby delaying or perhaps postponing indefinitely their progress toward full assimilation.[48] In such an event, the Majority would lose an ally that could easily tip the scales either way in determining the irreversibility of the Majority's dispossession.

48. In the spring of 1972, Michael Novak in *The Rise of the Unmeltable Ethnics* urged a political alliance of blacks and Assimilable Minorities. He said (p. 20) the latter group comprised 70,000,000 Americans of Irish, Italian, Slavic, Spanish, Greek and Armenian descent. Jerome Rosow, a former Ass't. Secretary of Labor, was quoted as the source for this figure. Rosow, however, had merely said that 70,000,000 Americans were members of "lower middle income" families. Later, perhaps as a reward for the scholarly feat of changing an income group into an agglomerate of ethnic groups, Professor Novak surfaced as a speechwriter for Sargent Shriver in the 1972 presidential campaign. Actually, there are at least 2,000,000 Negroes in the "lower middle income" bracket as well as tens of millions of Majority members. See Jerome Rosow, *Overcoming Middle Class Rage*, Westminster Press, Phila., 1971, p. 87.

Chapter 14

Unassimilable White Minorities

IN CONTRAST TO the Assimilable Minorities, whose assimilation is only delayed, the Unassimilable Minorities are permanently barred from Majority status. The color bar, in the case of nonwhites, is in itself an insurmountable obstacle. With respect to the Unassimilable White Minorities, the causes that prevent assimilation may be cultural or biological or both.

This does not imply that the Unassimilable Minorities are bound together by similar racial or cultural backgrounds or common economic or social status. On the contrary, Unassimilable Minorities, white and nonwhite, are likely to differ more from each other than from some Assimilable Minorities or even the Majority. Among the Unassimilable Minorities are found the most affluent and the most impoverished American population groups, the most verbal and the most taciturn, the most *physical* and the least *physical,* the most religious and the most irreligious. In fact, the divisions that bedevil the Unassimilable Minorities are so extreme they sometimes give rise to massive confrontations and violence.[1]

But in spite of all their divergences, Unassimilable Minorities have joined in an alliance which, with the assistance of Majority Splitters of the Ranks, has steered the march of American events for the greater part of the century. In addi-

---

1. The Negro-Jewish brawling during the 1968 teachers' strike in New York City was one such case.

tion to combining their votes for carefully selected political candidates, the more dynamic of these minorities have overcome their polar differences to forge the solid ideological front which is destroying the most sacrosanct American institutions.

What then is the unifying force strong enough to prevail against all this diversity, the centripetal force mighty enough to turn off the racial centrifuge in which these minorities should logically be imprisoned? To paraphrase Nietzsche, it probably has to do with the will to power and the will to powerlessness—the desire for power by those Unassimilable Minorities who have little, the desire for more power by those who have much, and the desire to give away power by deracinated Majority members. Feeding these desires are such old psychological imponderables and intangibles as envy, insecurity, fear, hate and even, perhaps, self-hate. These desires have also received some economic nourishment, but not as much as might be supposed. In recent years, in the ghettos of the big cities, one minority has been looting, robbing and burning the assets of another, yet the latter continues to put a significant amount of its brainpower and money at the disposal of the former.

The only safe assumption to make about the force that unifies and galvanizes the Unassimilable Minorities is that it is most apparent and most forceful when directed against the Majority. Accordingly, it may be said that the chief source of minority unity and coordination is that great, sick, floundering, demographic whale, which can be attacked, slashed, bitten and nipped at with impunity. Above all else, it is opposition to the Majority which has built the effective but uneasy alliance between the Unassimilable Minorities and Majority Gracchites, Trucklers, Pussyfooters, Old Believers and Proditors—an alliance that still enjoys the partial and often less than enthusiastic support of Assimilable Minorities.[2]

Before presenting the Unassimilable Minority order of

---

2. This alliance, in its purely minority aspects, has been described by a prominent political analyst as consisting of "large, cohesive ethnic communities still half-rooted in Cork, Calabria and Cracow." Phillips, *op. cit.*, p. 438.

battle, it might be wise to caution that there are always countless exceptions to all generalizations about masses of anything, particularly masses of human beings. Obviously, there are unassimilable members of every Assimilable Minority and assimilable members of every Unassimilable Minority. But in what follows the emphasis is on frequencies not individuals, on statistical averages not one-point curves.

The Southern Italians: By and large, Italy is a biracial nation. Alpines predominate in the north and center, while Mediterraneans are concentrated in the lower boot—Campania, Calabria and Sicily—from which came 80 percent of the Italian immigration.[3] There being an estimated 8,764,-000 Italian-Americans, simple mathematics and the rules of American racial classification would agree that 7,011,200 are unassimilable.[4]

Of all the New Immigrants, Italians were the most numerous. Although they were peasants in the Old Country, when they arrived in America they clustered in urban "Little Italies," where Italian speech, Italian cooking, Italian song, Italian custom and Italian exuberance still project an Italian flavor strongly resistant to assimilation. The Catholic Church does its part in preserving this flavor, but Southern Italians are not Catholic in the Irish-American or French-Canadian way. One author explains, "Perhaps the average Italian [has been] too close to Rome . . . to be awed by it."[5] Many Italian-Americans look askance at the Church because of its long association with Italy's landed interests.

New York City has 1,300,000 Italian-Americans,[6] many of them in the needle trades. It is the third largest Italian city in the world, surpassed only by Rome and Milan. Unlike Southern Italians, who remained in the urban east, the more adventurous Northern and Central Italians went west, quite a few to California, where they became farmers and wine growers and where one of them, A. P. Giannini of Genoese descent, founded the world's largest and, as recent

---

3. L. F. Pisani, *The Italian in America,* Exposition Press, New York, 1957, p. 143.

4. Bureau of the Census report, 1973. See p. 546. Some wild, politically inspired estimates go as high as 21,000,000.

5. Pisani, *op. cit.,* p. 54.

6. *New York Times Magazine,* Aug. 10, 1969, p. 56.

events have proved, the world's most dynamited bank.[7] Their dispersal, their gregariousness and an Alpine instead of a Mediterranean complexion have made most Northern and Central Italians easy candidates for assimilation.

The Italian minority contains within its ranks a criminal organization, in which race is the prime requirement for membership.[8] The ordinary Italian-American, however, has no connection with the 5,000 Southern Italians, mostly Sicilians, who dominate organized crime. To get this message across to the public, Italian pressure groups have succeeded in persuading television and film producers to "lighten up" their gangster characters and give them non-Italian, preferably Majority, names.[9]

Historically, Italian-Americans have voted the straight Democratic ticket,[10] although when a crypto-Communist like Vito Marcantonio or a crypto-Republican like Fiorello La Guardia, appeared on the ballot, racial loyalties took precedence over politics.[11] Lately, reacting to the radicali-

----

7. Other rich Italian-Americans, mostly of the assimilated or assimilable variety, are: The DiGiorgio family (the California fruit dynasty), Angelo Petri (wine), John Cuneo (one of the United States' largest printing establishments), Pio Crespi (Texas cotton king), Antonio Giaccione (paper), Ross Siracusa (television), Louis Pagnotti (coal), Joseph Martino (lead), Salvatore Giordano (air conditioning), Vincent Riggio (former president of the American Tobacco Co.), Lee Iacocca (Ford Motor Co.), the Pope family (newspapers), Bernard Castro (furniture). Michael Musmanno, *The Story of the Italians in America,* Doubleday, New York, 1965, pp. 247–9. A latecomer is Jeno Paulucci, food processor.

8. The record of the Mafia or Cosa Nostra will be reviewed in Chapter 30.

9. Italian ethnic sensitivities have also been aroused by the discovery of a "Viking" map which defined once-mythical Vinland as a part of North America. Professional Italian-Americans described the map as a fraud and a slur on the good name of Columbus. *Ency. Brit. Book of the Year,* 1967, p. 102. The map may be bogus, but not the Viking voyages to the New World.

10. Notable Italian-American politicians, in or out of office, include former governors Michael DiSalle of Ohio and Albert Rossellini of Washington, John Volpe, former Secretary of Transportation, Senator John Pastore of Rhode Island and former Senator Peter Dominick of Colorado, Anthony Celebrezze, ex-Secretary of HEW, Jack Valenti, President, Motion Picture Association of America, Congressman George Miller of California, ex-Mayor Hugh Addonizio of Newark and Mayor Joseph Alioto of San Francisco. Of the above, only Volpe and Dominick are Republicans.

11. Vito Marcantonio was sent to Congress by the American Labor party and his voting record revealed the often close alliance between Communism and the racial antipathies of Unassimilable Minorities. He provided the sole opposition when the House of Representatives voted 350 to 1 for the 1941

zation of other, more dynamic Unassimilable Minorities, particularly in New York City, Italian-Americans have been crossing party lines in ever greater numbers. The conservative Republican, John Marchi, won his party's nomination in the 1969 New York City mayoralty primary, thanks to a large-scale Italian defection from Democratic ranks. A *New York Times Magazine* article attributed the shift in part to the fear of Italian-Americans that Negroes were "after their women." [12] In 1970, the Italian votes usually earmarked for Democratic candidates helped bring about the surprising upset that made James Buckley, the Conservative party's nominee, Senator from New York.

In general, the Italian-American exerts relatively little political and social influence, except in areas where the Mafia is concentrated. He is content to live in a kind of self-imposed ethnic quarantine and has little desire to impose his way of life, his prejudices and his attitudes on others. He has more children than members of most other white minorities, less wealth and, like all Southern Europeans, displays a warm, emotional attachment to his country of origin.

Carleton Coon has found two readily identifiable subraces among Southern Italians in the United States. He calls one "coarse" Mediterranean, the other Armenoid.[13] The average Majority member is not aware of these racial subtleties. He only knows that Southern Italian pigmentation is darker than his own, that most Italian-Americans are "foreign-looking," that they are therefore predestined to the racial and cultural apartness reserved for all minorities of Mediterranean provenance.[14]

War Department Appropriations Act to build up American defenses in a world engaged in total war. La Guardia was the half-Italian, half-Jewish, three-term Republican Mayor of New York City (1934–1945).

12. Aug. 10, 1969, p. 62.

13. Coon, *The Races of Europe*, p. 558.

14. Judge Michael Musmanno writes touchingly—and accurately—of the predicament faced by almost all Southern Italians in regard to assimilation. As a boy, Musmanno proposed marriage to a young girl recently arrived from England. He was only twelve at the time, but she did not turn him down on account of his age. She said she could never marry a "foreigner." Musmanno had been born in America. The English girl had only been in the U.S. seven months. Musmanno, *op. cit.*, p. 7.

146   *The Minority Challenge*

The White Spanish-speaking Minorities: The Spanish arrived in Florida, Louisiana, the Southwest and California a century or so before the Pilgrims landed in Massachusetts. But Spanish colonization was so thin that not more than a hundred thousand Old World Spaniards or Mexicans of pure Spanish origin ever settled permanently within the limits of the present-day United States. Time and interbreeding have assimilated their descendants except for those who, like the Hispanos of New Mexico, married local Indians. Needless to say, the Spaniards who came over in the New Immigration have remained largely unassimilated. There are perhaps 125,000 members in this latter category.[15]

The small Cuban minority in the United States has been multiplied exponentially since 1959 by the arrival in Florida of hundreds of thousands fleeing the regime of Castro. There are now some 565,000 Cubans living in this country.[16] Although Cuba has a sizable Negro population, the anti-Communist Cuban refugees, who belonged to the more affluent segments of the population,[17] are largely Mediterranean.

One other minority that originated in Spain, but speaks a more ancient language than Spanish, is composed of ten thousand Basques. Most Basques live in Nevada, where they have become the American sheepherding caste. In 1966, they helped elect a fellow Basque, Paul Laxalt, as Governor. From the standpoint of pigmentation, Basques are on the borderline between Dark White and White. They have been designated unassimilable because they were never assimilated by the Spanish. It is doubtful if Americans will have better luck.

Census studies have revealed that there are 2,138,000 Americans of Central, South American or "other Spanish-American" origin. There is no way of knowing how many of these are Mediterranean in race, though all have been designated as such in this study in order to compensate for the classification of all

15. Census Bureau figures from *U.S. Book of Facts, Statistics and Information,* p. 92.
16. *Persons of Spanish Origin in the U.S.,* Bureau of the Census, Washington, D.C., Nov. 1969, p. 4.
17. An earlier Cuban arrival was Charles B. (Bebe) Rebozo, President Nixon's closest friend.

Americans of Mexican and Puerto Rican origin as nonwhites. These latter two population groups will be discussed in Chapter 16. The 2,138,000 figure, however, does include the New Immigration Spaniards and Basques, but not the Cuban minority, which the Census Bureau considers a separate entity.

Miscellaneous Mediterranean and Balkan Minorities: [18] The 176,000 Americans of Portuguese origin—mostly fishermen, farmers, cattle ranchers and textile workers—are typically Mediterranean in appearance and consequently too far on the brunet side of the Pigmentation Spectrum for assimilation.[19] Mediterranean racial influence, or at least dark coloration, is also quite evident among the 60,000 Albanians,[20] 65,000 Rumanians, 35,000 Bulgars, 5,000 Turks and 600,000 Greeks [21] in the United States, the last-named being particularly active in the tobacco, candy, sponge and shipping industries. Olive skin, black hair and dark brown eyes offer 151,000 Americans of Syrian descent (including Lebanese and Palestinians) small hope of assimilation.[22] The 150,000 Armenian-Americans, who have their own Armenian National Church, derive from one of the world's oldest peoples and their history of persecution often parallels that of the Jews,[23] as does their financial acumen. Their chance of assimilation is also relatively low.

18. Population figures in this section from *One America*.

19. The blond or red-haired Azoreans of Gloucester, Mass., are an exception to this rule. They are descended from Flemish colonists who settled in the Portuguese-owned Azores many centuries ago.

20. There were once 100,000 Albanians in the U.S., but many of them returned home.

21. Spiro Agnew is half Greek, his mother having been a Virginian. Had he been a dark, small Mediterranean like Aristotle Onassis he might have wed Jacqueline Kennedy, but he never would have been the 39th Vice-President. Agnew's minority side came out in his warm friendship with Frank Sinatra and with the minority bribers who destroyed him politically. Peter Peterson, former Secretary of Commerce, is also a Greek-American, as is Michael G. Thevis, the pornography magnate, who lives on a $1,200,-000 estate in Atlanta (*Reader's Digest,* Nov. 1975, pp. 105–9).

22. Danny Thomas, the television showman, Ralph Nader, the gadfly of the large corporations, and Judge Robert Merhige, who issued the order integrating the black schools of Richmond, Va., with suburban white schools, are among the more prominent Lebanese-Americans.

23. Charles Gary, the Armenian-descended lawyer of the Black Panthers, said he never forgot he was called a "goddamned Armenian" in school. *Time,* Jan. 12, 1970, p. 30. Richest Armenian-American is probably Kirk Kerkorian, an airline magnate and Las Vegas hotel owner, who admitted paying $21,300 to the Cosa Nostra. *New York Times,* Jan. 17, 1970, p. 1.

While Assimilable Minorities generally have culture working against them but race working for them in the assimilation process, the Mediterranean minorities have culture *and* race working against them. In Europe, Latin populations usually solved their differences with their Northern conquerors by intermarriage, by swallowing them up genetically. In the United States, where Northern Europeans greatly outnumber Mediterraneans, this system won't work. Neither will its opposite—the swallowing up of Mediterraneans by Northern Europeans. The color sensitivity of the latter, sharpened by the presence of Negroes, Indians, Mexicans and other nonwhites, is much greater than that of Northern Europeans in Europe and more like that of Northern Europeans in South Africa.

It would take only one or two generations of intermarriage with Majority members for most Mediterraneans to obtain the proper physical credentials for assimilation. But Southern Italians, Spaniards, Portuguese, Greeks, etc., are shut off from the American genetic drift by their own choosing as well as by Majority taboos. Under such conditions, it will be quite some time before any appreciable number of Majority members— the Nordics among them are 'bleached-out" Mediterraneans according to certain anthropologists [24]—recombine with the smaller, darker, but otherwise somewhat similar race from which their ancestors supposedly split off a hundred centuries ago.

24. Coon says, "The Nordic race in the strict sense is merely a pigment phase of the Mediterranean." *Races of Europe,* p. 83.

Chapter 15

The Jews

B Y RIGHTS THE Jewish minority should have been included in the previous chapter. It is white and unassimilable. But it is also the most influential, most organized and most dynamic minority. As such, it deserves a chapter of its own.

Everywhere in the public eye, solidly ensconced in the apex of the American pyramid, Jews represent an astonishingly minute 2.89 percent of the total population— 5,869,000 out of 203,211,926.[1] These statistics point up a rather extraordinary disproportion between the size of American Jewry and its influence—a disparity not new to history, not restricted to the United States and not well understood by non-Jews. Indeed, many Americans, awed by the ubiquity of the Jewish presence, are convinced that Jews are considerably more numerous than they really are. A B'nai B'rith survey of two thousand high school students in twenty-one cities, excluding New York, revealed that 82 percent overestimated the Jewish population—some students by as much as seventy million![2] To account for this widespread popular delusion and for many other strange sociological phenomena associated with Jews, it is both helpful and necessary to make a brief excursion into Jewish history.

The Jews were a tribe of Semitic shepherds who coalesced

---

1. U.S. population from 1970 Census. Jewish population from 1969 *American Jewish Yearbook*. Like all statistics compiled by private organizations, these numbers must be accepted with some reservations.
2. *New York Post*, March 20, 1962, p. 12.

into a nation in the second millennium, B.C. At one time—presumably after, not before, they had settled in Canaan—many went as desert raiders, settlers, captives or refugees to Egypt. There, as written in Exodus (1:7), "The children of Israel were fruitful, and increased abundantly, and multiplied, and waxed exceeding mighty; and the land was filled with them." It was in Egypt that the Jews acquired Moses, who gave them their law and instructed them in monotheism. By no means a Jewish or a Mosaic invention, the belief in one god had been forced on Egypt as early as the fourteenth century, B.C., by the Pharaoh Iknaton.

It is barely possible that Moses (an Egyptian name) was one of Iknaton's high priests and a member of the royal family; that after the Pharaoh's death and the reestablishment of polytheism Moses may have become a prophet without honor among his own countrymen. In the search for a new following, he may have preached Iknaton's "lost cause" to the Jews, whose status as bond servants could have made them quite susceptible to a new and revolutionary form of spiritual solace. This theory, proposed by one of the most celebrated of modern Jews, Sigmund Freud, is supported by Moses' mysterious birth, his royal upbringing and his use of Aaron as an interpreter.[3]

It was during their Egyptian sojourn that Jews experienced and survived the first of their countless persecutions, not fleeing Egypt until Jehovah had destroyed the firstborn of every Egyptian family. Today, three thousand years after the first Passover,[4] Jews in their reincarnation as Israelis are again chastising the Egyptians, but this time with American-built Phantom Jets instead of with lice, boils, swarms of locusts and other assorted plagues and afflictions.

---

3. *Moses and Monotheism*, trans. Katherine Jones, Hogarth Press, London, 1951. Concerning his Egyptification of Moses, Freud wrote, "To deny a people the man whom it praises as the greatest of its sons is not a deed to be undertaken light-heartedly—especially by one belonging to that people." *Ibid.*, p. 11.

4. Jehovah spared the Jews by "passing over" their houses, which they had marked with lamb's blood. As for the Egyptians, "there was not a house where there was not one dead." Passover is celebrated each year as a high Jewish holy day though it is difficult to find much religious content in an act of mass filicide. Exodus (12:35) also tells how the Jews before leaving, "borrowed of the Egyptians jewels of silver, and jewels of gold, and raiment."

Some centuries after they had reached and organized the Promised Land, Jews decided they were the Chosen People and history's most enduring ethnocentrism was in full flower. Although the Bible is filled with stirring battles, priestly fortitude, Solomonic glory and Assyrian and Babylonian captivities, the Jewish imprint on the world's conscience and consciousness did not develop overnight. Herodotus, the Greek historian, who made an extended tour of the Middle East in the fifth century, B.C., described in detail almost all the nations and peoples in the area. He made no mention, however, of the Jews, whom he either could not locate or thought too insignificant to bother with.

The Jewish state was overrun by the Persians under Cyrus in the sixth century, B.C., and by Greeks and Macedonians under Alexander two centuries later. Alexander's successor generals and their dynastic heirs maintained their occupation of Jewish territory, in spite of sporadic Jewish revolts, until the Romans arrived under Pompey. Fierce rebellions against Roman rule flared up from time to time, culminating in the conquest of Jerusalem by Titus in A.D. 70 and the dispersal and expulsion of those Jews who remained by Hadrian sixty-five years later.[5]

By the first century, B.C., Jews had given up Hebrew and were speaking Aramaic, the language of Jesus. The earliest extant version of the Old Testament, the Septuagint, is not in Hebrew, Aramaic or any Semitic tongue, but in Greek. Its translation was accomplished in Alexandria during the rule of the Ptolemies, traditionally by seventy Rabbis, who were isolated in separate huts, but nonetheless came up with seventy identical versions, exactly alike even in punctuation. The religious writings of the Jews were their only lasting contribution to ancient civilization, unless one insists on adding the chauvinistic philosophy of Philo and the allegorical histories of Josephus.[6] No Jewish painting or sculpture—

5. It was the Jews' intransigence toward Rome, the ancient world's most successful attempt at federation, and the Jews' rejection of the Pax Romana that caused Gibbon to blame them for "their irreconcilable hatred of mankind" and to call them a "race of fanatics." *Decline and Fall of the Roman Empire*, Lippincott, Philadelphia, 1878, Vol. 2, p. 4.
6. Philo tried unsuccessfully to prove that Greek philosophers had plagiarized Jewish prophets. After the destruction of the Temple, Josephus

against which there were Biblical injunctions—and only the
barest traces of Jewish music, architecture or science have
survived from classical times.[7]

In the matter of the Old Testament, the first five books,
the Pentateuch, are a collection of stories and legends,
many of them long established in Middle Eastern folklore.
The Mosaic Law, the flood, the woman-from-the-rib, the
Garden of Eden, the story of David, all derive from specifically non-Jewish sources.[8] The remaining thirty-four books
consist of genealogies and laws, racial history, the fulmina-
tions and transcendental wisdom of the prophets, miraculous
occurrences, gross libels and soulful poetry. When its leading character, Jehovah, is putting all his enemies to the
sword, the Old Testament is literature and religion at their
crudest. At other times, notably in Isaiah, Ecclesiastes, Job
and the Psalms, it resonates with the highest expressions of
human genius. The Old Testament has a special appeal to
the English-speaking world due to the resplendent and
evocative language of the King James version.

The oldest books of the Old Testament go back no further
than the ninth century, B.C., and some were written less
than two hundred years before the birth of Christ—well after
Greek literary influence had become predominant in the
Eastern Mediterranean.[9] Ecclesiastes and the Psalms, the
former the object of much rabbinical animosity because of

---

sided with Titus against his compatriots, yet later turned out a philo-Semitic
Jewish history.

7. In the *Ency. Brit.* there are separate articles on Greek Architecture,
Art, Literature and Music. There are also separate articles on Roman
Architecture, Roman Art and Latin Literature. The artistic activities of the
Jews have been limited to one article, Hebrew Literature.

8. P. E. Cleator, *Lost Languages*, Mentor Books, New York, 1962,
pp.109–12.

9. ". . . little in the Old Testament is more than a century or two earlier
than the Homeric poems . . . Herodotus was contemporary with Malachi
and Obadiah . . . Theocritus was singing in Sicily while the Song of Songs
was being compiled in Palestine." T. Eric Peet, *A Comparative Study of the
Literature of Egypt, Palestine and Mesopotamia*, Humphrey Milford, Oxford University Press, 1931, pp. 1–2. Peet states that when the first frag-
ments of the Old Testament took their present form about 850 B.C.,
". . . the literatures of Egypt and Babylonia were . . . already hundreds,
one might almost say thousands, of years old."

its Greek style and thought, were so late they were not even included in the Septuagint.

In classical times, as today, anti-Semitism stalked Semitism relentlessly. Long before the beginning of their official diaspora, the Jews had migrated throughout the Mediterranean and the Near East, and wherever they went, as the Book of Esther makes clear, the anti-Semite was soon a familiar figure. The first historically documented pogroms and anti-Jewish *bagarres* took place in Alexandria, the capital of Ptolemaic Egypt, where there were many more Jews than in Jerusalem.[10] In A.D. 19, perhaps because of their abiding unfriendliness toward all things Roman, Emperor Tiberius expelled them from the capital city.[11] But the ban was only temporary. Less than a century later, the Emperor Trajan was accused of being surrounded by "unholy Jews."[12] In the second century A.D., Jews carried their traditional anti-Hellenism to the point of genocide. "In Cyrene," wrote Gibbon, "they massacred 220,000 Greeks; in Cyprus 240,000; in Egypt a very great multitude."[13]

A chief source of anti-Semitism in the classical world was the high degree of Jewish participation in the field of banking and money lending. In Egypt, in the words of E. M. Forster, "They speculated in theology and grain. . . ."[14] Describing the economic conditions of Italy in the time of Julius Caesar, Theodor Mommsen wrote: "Alongside the estate husbandry unnaturally prospering over the ruin of the small farmers, private banking also assumed enormous proportions as the Italian merchants vying with the Jews spread over all the provinces and protectorates of the empire."[15]

---

10. Anti-Semitic tracts abounded in Greek and Roman times and one work (no longer extant) by the Greek, Apion, was so well-known and influential that Josephus devoted a whole book to its rebuttal.

11. ". . . they alone of all nations avoided dealings with any other people and looked upon all men as their enemies." Diodorus Siculus, trans. F. R. Walton, Harvard University Press, Cambridge, Mass., 1967, Vol. XI, p. 53.

12. *Oxyrhynchus Papyri X,* 1242, 1.42.

13. Gibbon, *op. cit.,* Vol. 2, p. 4, including footnotes.

14. E. M. Forster, *Pharos and Pharillon,* Knopf, New York, 1961, p. 17.

15. Theodor Mommsen, *The History of Rome,* edited by Saunders and Collins, Meridian, New York, 1961, p. 539.

But it was the Jews' religious practices and clannishness, rather than their financial acumen, which brought forth harsh comments from such "Old Romans" as Cicero, Seneca,[16] Juvenal and Tacitus. The same criticism was leveled against Jews much later in the nascent Arabic civilization, where Mohammed borrowed so much from their religion, but harried them so mercilessly. In the larger *suqs* and trading centers of Arabia, however, where "Jews controlled many of the local banks,"[17] the financial grounds for anti-Semitism probably outweighed all others.

The advent of Christianity was a mixed blessing for the Jews. It gave them a special importance as the "People of the Book"—the physical and spiritual forefathers of Jesus. But it also made them accessories to the crucifixion. It was Caiaphas, the high priests and the elders who stirred up the multitude to press for Christ's death and the release of Barabbas. Today, Jewish participation in the execution of Jesus is being de-emphasized and a Papal encyclical has absolved the Jews from deicide. But the Pope's absolutions are not likely to have much effect as long as Matthew (27:24–25) quotes Pilate as declaring, "I am innocent of the blood of this just person . . ." and Jews replying, ". . . his blood be on us, and on our children."

There was a possibility at the very beginning that Christianity and Judaism might merge, but the moment Gentiles were admitted to Christian services Jewish ethnocentrism forced a permanent cleavage between the two religions. At the time of Christ, Jews were longing for a Messiah to punish their enemies, not for a tolerant Son of Man who forgave everyone and welcomed everyone, Jew and non-Jew, into the brotherhood of God. Within a century, the gulf between the two faiths was so wide that a few anti-Semitic allusions were incorporated into the Gospels. Even Jesus himself is made to say of Nathanael (John 1:47), "Behold an Israelite indeed, in whom is no guile!"

All in all, Christianity provided non-Jews with new rea-

---

16. Seneca's feelings about the great influence of Judaism on his fellow Romans were vented in his epigram, *Victi victoribus leges dederunt*. Seneca, *Opera*, Teubner, Leipzig, 1878, Vol. III, p. 427.

17. R.V.C. Bodley, *The Messenger*, Doubleday, New York, 1946, p. 166.

sons for respecting Jews and new reasons for persecuting them. Perhaps in the final balance, Jews gained more than they lost. Christianity was their passport to Western civilization, in which they periodically sank to the depths of degradation and rose to the heights of preeminence. Moreover, it was by appealing to the social and moral teachings of Jesus, principally to the democratic and liberal offshoots of the shattering message in the Sermon on the Mount, that Jews managed to break out of their European ghettos in the late eighteenth and nineteenth centuries.

Jews survived the fall of Rome as adeptly as the fall of Jerusalem. In the Dark Ages they were alternately tolerated and persecuted by the invading Teutons. In Spain they obtained the highest public offices in the Moorish kingdom of Grenada in the eleventh century, and dominated commerce and owned one-third of the real estate in Christian Barcelona in the twelfth century.[18] In England, Aaron of Lincoln, a medieval precursor of the Rothschilds, amassed enough wealth to finance the construction of nine Cistercian monasteries and the Abbey of St. Albans.[19] But Jewish fortunes declined when Europe was seized by the fervor— often more Gothic than Christian—which built the great cathedrals and triggered the Crusades. From the German Rhineland, where overzealous Crusaders organized a series of pogroms, a violent anti-Jewish reaction spread irresistibly over medieval and renaissance Europe.[20] England expelled its Jews in 1290, France in 1306, Austria in 1420, Spain in 1492, Florence in 1495, Portugal in 1496–7, Naples in 1541 and Milan in 1597.[21]

Taking with them a rudimentary Teutonic dialect which

18. Will Durant, *The Age of Faith,* pp. 371–3.
19. *Ibid.,* pp. 377–8.
20. Generally in the Middle Ages, Jews supported monarchies because it was easier to deal with one king than scores of nobles. They were also partial to the Papacy, which alternately protected and humiliated them. In 1215, Innocent III ordered all Jews, men and women, to wear a yellow badge. Darlington, *op. cit.,* p. 459. The tension between Jews and the English aristocracy was revealed by the Magna Carta, which contained specific restrictions concerning the payment of debts and interest to Jews.
21. Dates of expulsion are taken from articles on the applicable countries and cities in the *Jewish Encyclopedia,* Ktav Publishing, New York, 1904.

later evolved into Yiddish, most German and Central European Jews moved east to Poland, the great medieval haven of Jewry. Those pushing farther east met and mixed with Jewish contingents who for centuries had been working their way north from the Caucasus, on the way converting the Khazars, an Armenoid people whose genes are still evident in many Russian and East European Jews.

The Jews in Slavic lands, the Ashkenazim, are to be distinguished from the Sephardim, the purer-blooded Mediterranean Jews expelled from Spain by Ferdinand and Isabella in the same year Columbus discovered America. The Sephardim found sanctuary in Holland, Leghorn and Turkey, a few even getting as far as Brazil, from which they were later deported by the Portuguese. Twenty-four of these deportees, captured by the French on their way back to Holland, were deposited in Nieuw Amsterdam in 1654.[22]

The widely variegated racial composition of the Ashkenazim and Sephardim has already been discussed, as have the important genetic changes wrought by twenty-five hundred years of intermittent miscegenation with non-Jewish peoples.[23] Nevertheless, modern Jews of Sephardic or Ashkenazic origin, indeed Jews of French, American, Yemenite or any other nationality, like to think they are all directly descended from the ancient Hebrews of Palestine. It is worth repeating that this belief in a common ancestry, reinforced by religious traditions handed down for thirty centuries, can overcome all sorts of inherited biological differences in cementing a strong race consciousness.

In the late Middle Ages, most European Jews lived completely apart in walled ghettos, and intercourse with non-Jews was limited mainly to economic matters. In many European countries and free cities there was a total ban against Jews for centuries. As a result, hardly an identifiable or professing Jew was to be found in Chaucer's or Shakespeare's England, Michelangelo's Florence or Cervantes's and Velásquez's Spain.

22. Peter Stuyvesant, the governor, did not want to let them remain, but Jewish directors of the Dutch West India Company caused him to change his mind. Sachar, *The Course of Modern Jewish History*, p. 161. Also see Stephen Birmingham, *The Grandees*, Harper & Row, N.Y., 1971, Chap. 4.
23. See pp. 27–8.

Jews were not permitted to return to England until Cromwell's time, and it was not until 1791 that the French Assembly granted French Jews full citizenship. From then on, Jewish destiny brightened. Beginning with the Napoleonic wars, Joseph Wechsberg writes, "The supremacy of the Rothschilds in international finance lasted one hundred years." [24] In 1858, Lionel Rothschild was the first British Jew to be elected to Parliament and in 1868 Disraeli became Britain's Prime Minister. As the liberalization and commercialization of the West continued through the latter part of the nineteenth century and into the twentieth, Jewish emancipation kept pace.

By the 1920's, it could be fairly said that Jews were setting the tone for much of Western culture. For proof one has only to mention Marx, Freud, Einstein, the philosophers Bergson and Wittgenstein, and the anthropologist Boas. After five hundred years of eclipse and a resurgence that required little more than a century, Jews had achieved more power and influence than ever before in their history.

Then came Hitler. Although World War II was another desperate attempt by Germany to set up a continental empire in Europe, it was also a racial war between Germans and Jews. The number of European Jews actually killed by the Germans and their allies has never been correctly established. The accepted and widely quoted figure of 6,000,000 is apparently based on hearsay evidence by an SS officer, Wilhelm Hoettl, who declared Adolf Eichmann had informed him 4,000,000 Jews had died in extermination camps and 2,000,000 elsewhere.[25] The *Encyclopaedia Britannica* (1963)

---

24. *The Merchant Bankers,* Little, Brown, Boston, 1966, p. 343. One aspect of Rothschild power was amply demonstrated during Wellington's campaign against the French in Spain. The British general was badly in need of gold, which the British Rothschilds had difficulty in transmitting because of the French land and sea blockade. The French Rothschilds solved the problem for their British relations by arranging for the transshipment of Wellington's gold through France. A few pages after relating this anecdote, Wechsberg praises the Rothschilds for their loyalty to the rulers of the countries in which they happened to reside. *Ibid.,* pp. 338, 342.

25. *Trial of the Major War Criminals before the International Military Tribunal,* Nuremberg, Germany, Vol. XXI, Doc. 2738-PS, p. 85. Another SS officer, Dieter von Wisliceny, said Eichmann told him that 4,000,000 Jews had been killed. At other times, according to Wisliceny, Eichmann increased the total to 5,000,000.

is more conservative and uses the phrase "more than 5,000,-000." [26] One Jewish historian has placed the figure between 4,200,000 and 4,600,000, one-third of whom died of disease and hunger. [27] On the other hand, Paul Rassinier, a French socialist and onetime inmate of Buchenwald, has written a series of books to the effect that there were only 1,000,000 to 1,600,000 Jewish victims of Nazism. [28] He specifically denies the existence of gas chambers and charges that the death camp story was deliberately and grossly exaggerated by Jews to secure reparations from Germany and obtain moral and military support for Israel.

World War II was disastrous for Jews in Germany and in most of Europe. But by strengthening Jewish unity outside the area of Axis supremacy, Nazi anti-Semitism helped to seal Germany's defeat. The massive and wholehearted support of world Jewry and particularly of American Jewry in the war against Hitler was an important factor in the ultimate Allied victory. [29]

In the postwar period, Jews reached new levels of prosperity in the non-Communist world. In Spain, for the first time since 1492, Jews were permitted to open a synagogue. Even in Germany, where 30,000 survived Hitler, Jewish communities were reconstructed in many of the largest cities. The greatest triumph of modern Jewry, however, was the establishment of Israel, which provided Jews with a psychological lift they had not had since the days of Judah Maccabee and Bar Cocheba. [30] To the amazement of non-Jews and Jews alike, the historic Jewish stereotype shifted almost overnight from the cringing, sly money changer to the fearless desert fighter. [31] But the settlement and conquest of Pal-

26. Vol. 13, p. 64.

27. Sachar, *The Course of Modern Jewish History*, p. 457.

28. See principally *Le drame des juifs européens,* Les Sept Couleurs, Paris, 1964.

29. The prominent role played by American Jews in the development of the atom bomb, the call for Germany's unconditional surrender in World War II, and the staging of the Nuremberg trials will be treated later.

30. The effect of Israel on American foreign policy will be covered in Chapter 35. Judah Maccabee and Bar Cocheba were Jewish heroes who led armed rebellions against the Greek and Roman occupying forces.

31. The Zionist pioneers of Palestine were mostly Ashkenazim. They were a select group, as pioneers generally are, which helped account for their

estine brought with it a new rash of anti-Semitism in an area which had been relatively free of it for ages.

Although Israel may be the spiritual home of Jewry, the United States remains the Jewish center of gravity. Just as no one can fully understand present-day world affairs without taking Jews into account, so no member of the American Majority can even begin to comprehend the pattern of current American events without a rudimentary knowledge of the aims, the habits and the political, economic and social status of American Jews. In many respects, the goals and attitudes of American Jewry are major clues to recent American history.

It was during the Civil War that Jews first came to the attention of the American public at large. The first Jew to hold an important government post was Judah Benjamin, the Confederate Secretary of State, who fled to England after Appomattox.[32] On the Northern side, while the Lincoln administration was leaning heavily on the Rothschilds for financial support,[33] General Grant created the first anti-Semitic furor by ordering his subordinate commanders to expel Jewish peddlers and commission merchants from behind the Union lines.[34] Yet it was Grant who as President

surprising display of martial valor. The "un-Jewish" temperament and character of these Zionists were accented by their "un-Jewish" appearance.

32. Benjamin sent a Catholic priest to Europe to spread tales about Yankee "atrocities." Much ado was made about a raid on Richmond, in which the city was burnt down, the women debauched, the entire Confederate government assassinated and all the churches destroyed. Beard, *Rise of American Civilization*, Vol. 2, pp. 86–7.

33. Through August Belmont, the Rothschilds' American agent, who "was able, thanks to the hugeness of the Rothschild reservoir of capital, to start out in America operating his own Federal Reserve System." Belmont was one of the first Jews to crack the inner sanctum of American high society when he married the daughter of naval hero Commodore Perry. Birmingham, *Our Crowd*, pp. 27, 79–80, 101.

34. *Ibid.*, p. 98. Up to the present, the story of American anti-Semitism has been unimportant, unimpressive and inflated. There have been a few notorious social incidents, such as the refusal of the Grand Union Hotel in Saratoga to take in Joseph Seligman (1877) . . . a few Dreyfus-accented trials in which American courts have been accused of wrongly convicting Jews, such as the Leo Frank rape case in Atlanta (1913–1915) and the Rosenberg atom spy case after World War II . . . a few anti-Jewish flare-ups, such as the resurrected Ku Klux Klan and Henry Ford's *Dearborn Independent* in the 1920's and Father Coughlin's radio oratory and *Social Justice* magazine in the late 1930's . . . a few anti-war movements, such

seriously considered appointing his close friend, Joseph Seligman, Secretary of the Treasury. When President Garfield was shot in 1881, he was taken to Elberon, N.J., where Jesse Seligman, Joseph's brother, opened his house to the dying man's family. At a Seligman Saturday get-together in Elberon, "it was never a surprise to find a former U.S. President, a Supreme Court Justice, several Senators and a Congressman or two." [35]

The relatively few Sephardic Jews and the larger number of German Jews viewed with mixed feelings the mass influx of Jews which began in the 1890's and which derived in most part from the extensive realm of the anti-Semitic Russian Czars—from Poland, Lithuania and Russia proper. But though they did not open their hearts to the newcomers or accept them socially, Jewish Old Immigrants did open their purses. This starting money, swiftly compounded by the New Immigrants' financial flair, allowed most of them to escape their Lower East Side tenements within a generation. Today, while Jews of Western and Central European descent still retain a great deal of their wealth, the Eastern European Jews, in addition to being affluent in their own right, have assumed the leadership not only of American Jewry, but of world Jewry as well.

The administration of Franklin Roosevelt was the first to introduce scores of Jews into the decision-making echelons of government.[36] It is true that Theodore Roosevelt had

---

as the German-American Bund, the Christian Front and the Christian Mobilizers. Huey Long was the only American political leader of sufficient shrewdness to have carried anti-Semitism effectively into politics, but he was assassinated by a doctor in 1935. The late Gerald L. K. Smith, one of Long's principal aides, published a wide range of anti-Semitic literature. Charles Lindbergh accused the Jews of warmongering in a nationwide radio address in 1941 and repeated the charge in his war memoirs published 29 years later (see footnote 14, p. 438 of this study). A few scattered organizations preached anti-Semitism in the post-World War II period. Of these the Georgia-based National States Rights party seems to show the most vitality. Its head is J. B. Stoner who gained national publicity in 1972 when minority organizations tried to censor his paid political announcements on television.

35. *Ibid.*, pp. 126, 308–9.

36. Jews were especially conspicuous in the Securities and Exchange Commission, National Labor Relations Board, Social Security Board and the Departments of Labor and Justice. *Reader's Digest*, Sept., 1946, pp. 2–3. Two Jewish governors during the Roosevelt era were Henry Horner of

made Oscar Straus Secretary of Commerce and Labor, just as
it is true that there had been scattered appointments of Jews
in the Wilson and Hoover eras, including such notable figures as Paul Warburg, Louis Brandeis, Benjamin Cardozo
and Felix Frankfurter.[37] But the roster of New Dealers contained many more, if less distinguished, Jewish names:
Henry Morgenthau, Jr., Benjamin Cohen, Sol Bloom, Emanuel Celler, Herbert Lehman, David Niles, Samuel Rosenman,
Isador Lubin, Mordecai Ezekiel, Anna Rosenberg, Morris
Ernst, Nathan Straus, Donald Richberg, Lawrence Stein-
hardt and Robert Nathan. Bernard Baruch, in whose New
York apartment Winston Churchill had been an overnight
guest when making state visits to America in World War II,
seemed to overlap all administrations, having been an adviser to five American presidents.[38] Like Baruch, bankers
Alexander Sachs and Sidney Weinberg attended important
policy sessions of both Republican and Democratic administrations.

After World War II, David Lilienthal and Lewis Strauss
served as Chairmen of the Atomic Energy Commission and
helped guide the United States into the nuclear age. In the
1950's, Senator Joseph McCarthy brought the public spot-
light to bear on his two young Jewish assistants, David
Schine and Roy Cohn.[39]

President Truman kept many of Roosevelt's Jewish ap-
pointees on the federal payroll. But President Eisenhower,
who only obtained a small fraction of the Jewish vote, let
most of them go. Eisenhower, however, did appoint Douglas
Dillon to a high State Department post. Although it was not
according to White House plan, the Eisenhower administration watched Republican Senators Barry Goldwater and
Jacob Javits expand into national political fixtures.[40]

Illinois and Julius Meier of Oregon. When Roosevelt died, one rabbi compared him to Moses. Barnet Litvinoff, *A Peculiar People,* Weybright and
Talley, New York, 1969, p. 41.

37. Warburg was largely responsible for devising the Federal Reserve
System and was made the Federal Reserve Board's first Vice-Chairman.

38. Baruch made most of his millions speculating in copper stocks. When
America entered World War I, Wilson named him head of the War Industries Board.

39. Cohn later became a notorious Wall Street operator. See pp. 420-1.

40. Is it really accurate to say that men like Dillon and Goldwater are

Jews returned to Washington in force when John F. Kennedy assumed the presidency in 1961. Arthur Goldberg was appointed Secretary of Labor and Senator Abraham Ribicoff, Secretary of Health, Education and Welfare. When Goldberg moved up to the Supreme Court, Willard Wirtz succeeded him. Other Kennedy appointments included Newton Minow, head of the Federal Communications Commission; Mortimer Caplin, chief of the Internal Revenue Service; and Pierre Salinger, presidential press secretary. Dillon stayed on as Kennedy's Secretary of the Treasury. Three of Kennedy's principal aides and mentors were Arthur Schlesinger, Jr., Theodore Chaikin Sorensen and Richard Goodwin.[41]

When Lyndon Johnson became President upon Kennedy's assassination, he shifted Goldberg from the Supreme Court to the United Nations. Other Johnson appointments were Walt Rostow, chief presidential foreign adviser; Wilbur Cohen, Secretary of Health, Education and Welfare; and Abe Fortas, Associate Justice of the Supreme Court.[42] Edwin

---

Jews? Both had Polish Jews as paternal grandfathers—Samuel Lapowski (Dillon's) came to Texas as a clothier and Michael Goldwasser (Goldwater's) arrived in the Southwest as a peddler. Both Dillon and Goldwater, as their fathers before them, married non-Jews. Ostensibly, both lead the life of well-to-do members of the Majority—Dillon, the banker, being much more well-to-do than Goldwater. But the residue of Jewish race consciousness runs deep. It is extremely difficult in a milieu of intense racial divisions, as in present-day America, to determine exactly when a Jew ceases to be a Jew. Even if an individual no longer wishes to consider himself a Jew, the world may force him to be one. Goldwater's racial background, for instance, might help account for his mystifying friendships with Jewish gangsters. For Dillon's and Goldwater's antecedents, see *Time,* Aug. 18, 1961, p. 13 and July 24, 1964, p. 22. For Goldwater's gangster friends, see p. 406 of this study.

41. Goodwin, who in his capacity as Kennedy's adviser on Caribbean affairs had much to do with the Bay of Pigs fiasco, was torn between Eugene McCarthy and Robert Kennedy in the 1968 primary race for the Democratic presidential nomination. "The trouble is, baby," he explained, "I don't know which one of them to make president." He told Seymour Hirsch, McCarthy's press secretary, "Just you and me and two typewriters, Sy, and we'll bring down the government." *San Francisco Sunday Examiner & Chronicle, Sunday Punch,* July 14, 1968, p. 2.

42. Both before and after Johnson took office, Abe Fortas was "on the telephone [with Johnson] at least once a day and often as many as three or four times." *Esquire,* June, 1965, p. 86. The phone continued ringing after Fortas joined the Supreme Court. This close, somewhat unconstitutional relationship between the executive and the judiciary was one of the main

Weisl, Chairman of the Executive Committee of Paramount Pictures, served as Johnson's personal financial consultant.[43]

After Watergate and the beginning of his second term, Richard Nixon was surrounded by more Jewish cabinet members and high-level advisers than any other American president. Henry Kissinger was Secretary of State; Caspar Weinberger, Secretary of Health, Education and Welfare; James Schlesinger, a Lutheran with Jewish family ties, Secretary of Defense; Arthur F. Burns, Chairman of the Federal Reserve Board;[44] Herbert Stein, chief economic adviser; Laurence Silberman, Deputy Attorney General; Leonard Garment, legal counsel and head of the White House Civil Rights Dep't.[45]

As the first appointed president, Gerald Ford fired Schlesinger, but added Edward Levi, an old fellow traveler, as Attorney-General, and replaced Stein with Alan Greenspan.[46]

In his 1968 campaign, Hubert Humphrey had as his closest adviser, E. F. Berman.[47] Eight of Humphrey's eleven largest financial contributors were Jews.[48] George McGovern's 1972 presidential try was heavily financed by Jews and his chief aide was Frank Mankiewicz.[49]

Considering that Jews are less than three percent of the American population, the number of Jews in the inner circles of government is clearly out of proportion.[50] But where Jewish overrepresentation is overwhelming is in the opinion-

---

reasons the Senate refused to confirm Johnson's nomination of Fortas as Chief Justice. Whether Johnson was privy to Fortas' monetary dealings with the convicted stock embezzler, Louis Wolfson, which later led to Fortas' resignation, is not known. See p. 418.

43. G. William Domhoff, *Who Rules America?* Prentice-Hall, Englewood Cliffs, N.J., 1967, p. 104.

44. "The Chairman of the Federal Reserve Board has greater influence over the daily lives of all U.S. citizens than almost anyone except the President . . ." *Time*, Oct. 24, 1969, p. 89.

45. *Newsweek*, Nov. 18, 1968, p. 44. Consequently, all communications about minority problems had to clear through Mr. Garment's office.

46. Meanwhile, a Jewish forebear was discovered in the family tree of Treasury Secretary William Simon, who is a Catholic.

47. *Time*, Sept. 27, 1968, p. 17.

48. *San Francisco Chronicle*, Nov. 23, 1968, p. 9.

49. *Time*, May 8, 1972, pp. 16–21.

50. The number of Jews elected to office, while increasing steadily, is not overly large for the reasons given on p. 104. Currently there were 22 Jews in the House of Representatives.

forming sanctuaries of American society. Theoretically, the politician and the bureaucrat are the servants of the public, when they are not the servants of the political boss. In practice, however, the politician, bureaucrat, political boss *and* the public are frequently the servants of the news media.

In the newspaper field, the large newspaper chains and mass circulation tabloids bear much of the responsibility for shaping the public mind. But only a very few select newspapers shape the minds of those who govern the public. By far the most important are the *New York Times* and the *Washington Post*. These are the two newspapers which are read and taken to heart by the powers that be. The news they carry and how they treat such news determine to a large extent what the leadership of America says, thinks and does.[51]

The controlling interest in both of these two publications is held by Jews. The *New York Times,* the national newspaper of record, has been in the hands of the Ochses and the Sulzbergers for several generations, as has the *Chattanooga Times.*[52] A member of this dynasty, Mrs. Arthur Hays Sulzberger, who controls two-thirds of the *Times'* voting stock, is one of America's centimillionaires.[53] Most of the voting stock of the *Washington Post* is owned by Katharine Graham, the daughter of Eugene Meyer, the late banker. Mrs. Graham, described as very much "the boss lady" of her publishing empire, also directs *Newsweek,* the second largest weekly news magazine, and a strategically situated Washington, D.C., television station.[54]

---

51. Fifty copies of the *Times* go to the White House each day. It is distributed in 11,464 American cities. Talese, *The Kingdom and the Power,* pp. 72, 346.

52. In 1970 the *Chattanooga Times* was the defendant in an antitrust suit for "unlawful attempts" to monopolize the newspaper business in Chattanooga. *New York Times,* May 8, 1970, p. 9.

53. *Fortune,* May, 1966, and Talese, *op. cit.,* p. 318. Mrs. Sulzberger is the daughter of Adolph Ochs, the founder of the dynasty. Adolph's brother, George, partly anglicized his name to Ochs-Oakes and John Oakes, his son, presently directs the *Times* editorial page. When other editorial writers have "views [which] conflict with his, they are not published." Talese, *op. cit.,* pp. 72, 79, 81.

54. The information concerning Mrs. Graham, like much other data on the news and communications media in these pages, was taken from the article, "America's Media Baronies," in *Atlantic,* July, 1969.

Another important newspaper, the *St. Louis Post-Dispatch* is controlled by a grandson of Joseph Pulitzer, the Hungarian-Jewish publisher who invented yellow journalism.[55]

Less influential, but still important because it is one of the three remaining New York City metropolitan news-papers, is the *New York Post,* whose principal owner is Dorothy Schiff, the granddaughter of banker Jacob Schiff. The *Philadelphia Inquirer,* one of the two important Phila-delphia dailies, was owned until recently by Walter Annen-berg, U.S. Ambassador to the United Kingdom, who still retains several TV stations, as well as the *Morning Tele-graph, Seventeen* and *TV Guide.* The *New York Times* has called *TV Guide* "the giant among weeklies with a circula-tion of 14 million and estimated advertising revenues of $55 million." [56] Present publisher of the *San Francisco Chronicle,* one of the most widely read newspapers in the Far West, is Charles de Young Thieriot, a descendant of Meichel de Jung (later de Young), the paper's founder.[57] The twenty-two daily newspapers of Samuel Newhouse represent America's third largest journalistic empire, following close behind the Chicago Tribune—N.Y. Daily News and Knight-Ridder newspaper chains.[58] Newhouse also runs six TV stations, as well as a stable of magazines which include *Vogue, Glamour, Made-moiselle* and *House and Garden.* Many small American cities have newspapers controlled or operated by Jews, and two of them, the *Las Vegas Sun* and the *Carolina Israelite,* exercise more than local influence. Even the Times-Mirror Co., which publishes the massive *Los Angeles Times,* has a Jewish direc-tor, Simon Ramo. The *International Herald-Tribune,* published in Paris and read daily by top-level officials of European governments, has as its editor, Murray Weiss.

The list of magazines controlled by Jews is voluminous and includes *American Home, Commentary, Esquire, La-dies Home Journal, McCall's, Nation, New York Review of*

55. Beard, *op. cit.,* Vol. 2, p. 461.
56. *New York Times,* Oct. 29, 1969, p. 26. The Annenberg family's evasion of income taxes will be covered in Chapter 30.
57. Stephen Birmingham, *The Right People,* Little, Brown, Boston, 1968, p. 24.
58. Size is based on circulation, not number of newspapers. The New-house chain, incidentally, is by far the most profitable. *Business Week,* Jan. 26, 1976, pp. 55–62.

Books, New Yorker and *U.S. News and World Report.* Even when magazines are not owned or operated by Jews, they often have Jewish editors, or their publishers have close corporate or even marital connections with Jews. The Chairman of the Board of Time, Inc. (*Time, Fortune, Sports Illustrated, Money,* thirteen TV stations, the publishing house of Little, Brown and large holdings in Metro-Goldwyn-Mayer) is Andrew Heiskel, married to a Sulzberger. Henry Grunwald, of Austrian-Jewish extraction, is Managing Editor of *Time.* In charge of 105 correspondents, 90 editors, writers and reporters and a large staff of researchers, he "may be the single most influential linear journalist in the world." [59] Another widely circulated magazine with a Jewish Managing Editor, Martin Goldman, was *Look,* which expired in 1971.[60] At last report *Saturday Review, New Republic* and *American Heritage* had Jewish editors or publishers.

But whatever the measure of Jewish control or non-control, practically all important American publications vie with each other in procuring the services of Jewish reporters, pundits and assorted interpreters of past, current and future events. Examples at the literate or semi-literate level have included Walter Lippman, David Lawrence, Max Lerner, Arthur Krock and Art Buchwald; at the peephole level, Walter Winchell, Leonard Lyons, Irv Kupcinet and Herb Caen;[61] at the lonely hearts level, Ann Landers and "Dear Abby." [62] The nation's most influential—and savage—newspaper cartoonist is Herblock (Herbert Block) of *The Washington Post.* One of the most popular comic strips is Al Capp's *L'il Abner.*[63]

---

59. *Atlantic,* July, 1969, p. 43.

60. In 1970, Cowles Communications, which published *Look,* twenty-nine trade journals and magazines, three newspapers, and owned three radio stations and three television stations, was in such sorry financial straits it had to sell many of its most profitable enterprises to the New York Times Co. Among them were *Family Circle,* third largest U.S. women's magazine, a Memphis television station, three daily newspapers in Florida and a textbook firm. *Time,* Nov. 9, 1970, p. 41.

61. When a West Coast newspaper carried the headline, "Killer Hurricane Nearing Texas," Caen set the all-time low for his profession by commenting, "Promises, promises." *San Francisco Chronicle,* Sept. 20, 1967, p. 25.

62. See Chapter 20.

63. By far the most amusing comic strip, *L'il Abner* is nevertheless a

In book publishing, Knopf and Random House (owned by RCA), Holt, Rinehart and Winston (owned by CBS), Liveright, Lyle Stuart, Viking Press and Simon and Schuster are the principal Jewish firms, though nearly all leading publishers promote works of Jewish authors and employ Jews in executive and editorial positions—i.e., Jeremiah Kaplan, current president of Macmillan, and Robert Markle, editor-in-chief of Grosset and Dunlap.

Meanwhile, it may be noted that the leading distributor of paperbacks, magazines and newspapers to newsstands and to drug stores is Henry Garfinkle's Ancorp National Services, Inc., which owns Union News. Garfinkle has a near monopoly on the news distribution field in New York and he receives what the *Wall Street Journal* has described as bribes of $30,000 and $26,000 a year from *The New York Times* and *Daily News,* respectively. A close associate of Mafia figures and a good friend of press lord Samuel Newhouse, Garfinkle has been known to boast about having "publishers in my hip pocket." [65] Another powerful force in the book distribution field is the Book-of-the-Month Club—close to 250 million books mailed out in forty years—which was founded by the late Harry Scherman, born in Montreal of Anglo-Welsh-Jewish parentage. Still another are the wholesale book firms, many of which are Jewish-controlled.[66]

Perhaps the most convincing evidence of the Jewish hold over the popular mind is furnished by the commanding positions of Jews in the television, radio and motion picture industries. William Paley, the son of a Philadelphia cigar maker, is the controlling voice and board chairman of the

grinding, serialized attack on Majority folkways—an upside-down version of Aesop in which the city mouse triumphs over his country cousin. In the character of Daisy Mae, however, Capp is careful to render due obeisance to the Esthetic Prop. In 1972 Capp entered a plea of guilty to a charge of attempted rape and was fined $500 by a Wisconsin judge. *Facts on File,* 1972, p. 335.

64. The incredible disproportion of Jewish writers in contemporary American literature, literary criticism and nonfiction will be taken up in Chapter 18, as will the role of one or two key Jewish-owned publications in determining a book's success or failure.

65. *Wall Street Journal,* July 3, 1969, pp. 1, 17.

66. To simplify their accounting procedures, many of the biggest bookstores will only order from book wholesalers.

Columbia Broadcasting System. For many, many years RCA, the parent company of NBC, was headed by David Sarnoff and his son, Robert, who finally quit as chairman in 1975. Martin Seretean and Herbert Schlosser, however, remained as RCA's largest stockholder (1.5 million shares) and head of NBC-TV, respectively. The present board chairman of ABC, which operates the nation's third largest television network, is Leonard Goldenson.[67]

As for TV programming, Jews write almost all the "specials" and documentaries, as well as the "ethnic" comedies which depict minority members sympathetically and Majority members as cloying liberals or rightwing morons. How effective these nightly sermons have been in squelching the Majority's *élan vital* is unknown. For those who think the minority sensitivities of board chairmen do not filter down to the news program level, it should be pointed out they do not need to. The heads of the three TV news departments are Jews: Richard Wald (NBC), Richard Salant (CBS), Avram Westin (ABC). The leading TV news commentators are mostly non-Jewish liberals, but many reporters are Jewish: Mike Wallace, Edwin Newman, Eli Abel, Irving R. Levine, Daniel Schorr, Marvin Kalb, Martin Agronsky, Herbert Kaplow, Morley Safer and Carl Stern to name a few.[68]

The close link between television and the motion picture industry does not diminish Jewish influence in the latter. Hollywood from its inception has been overwhelmingly Jewish. One has only to mention such companies as Metro-Goldwyn-Mayer, 20th Century-Fox, Paramount Pictures, Warner Brothers, Universal, Columbia Pictures, United Artists, and such mythic personalities as Samuel Goldwyn, William Fox, Carl Laemmle, Joe Schenck, Jesse Lasky, Adolph Zukor, Irving Thalberg, Harry Cohn, Louis Mayer, David Selznick and Harry and Jack Warner.[69] The above-named, of course, belong to an older Hollywood generation. But the new breed is also largely Jewish. According to *Time*,

---

67. Of the $2,275,000,000 in television revenues in 1967, 53 percent went to the "big three." *Atlantic,* July 1, 1969, p. 88.

68. Wallace and Safer now have their own weekly program.

69. The few important non-Jewish decision makers of Hollywood also had minority backgrounds, i.e., Darryl Zanuck, of Hungarian descent, and Spyros Skouras, of Greek origin. However, the greatest Hollywood director,

Arthur Penn, Stanley Kubrick and Mike Nichols were the
nation's three leading film makers in 1969.[70]

Hollywood's link to Broadway has always been close and
here again there has been an almost fantastic overrepresentation of Jews. A brief idea of the Jewish domination of the
American theater, past and present, is furnished by the
roster (in rough chronological order) of such entertainment
"giants" as producers David Belasco, Daniel Frohman,
Florence Ziegfeld, the Shuberts, Jed Harris, Billy Rose,
Mike Todd, Hal Prince and David Merrick . . . such
directors and comedy writers[71] as George Kaufmann, Moss
Hart, Elia Kazan, Garson Kanin and Neil Simon[72] . . .
such songsmiths as Irving Berlin, Richard Rodgers and Lorenz
Hart, Oscar Hammerstein II, and Lerner and Loewe . . .
such rasping show business personalities as Al Jolson, Fanny
Brice, Eddie Cantor, Sophie Tucker, George Jessel, Bert Lahr,
Ethel Merman, Eddie Fisher and Barbra Streisand . . . and
such celebrated "standup" Jewish comedians as Jack Benny,
Mort Sahl, Alan King and Don Rickles, who have made Jewish
jokes the touchstones of contemporary American humor.[73]

The publishing and entertainment industries feed on ideas
as well as events, and in the realm of ideas American Jews

D. W. Griffith, was not Jewish. Nor were the two other great figures to
emerge from Hollywood—Greta Garbo and Charlie Chaplin. The claim
that Chaplin is part-Jewish is a freewheeling fiction of the wildest pro- and
anti-Semites. His mother was three-quarters Irish and one-quarter Gypsy.
His father was a descendant of French Huguenots who had been in England
for centuries. Charles Chaplin, *My Autobiography,* Simon and Schuster,
New York, 1964, pp. 18–9, 37, 45, 109.

70. *Time,* July 4, 1969, pp. 46, 51.

71. Serious playwrights, Jewish and otherwise, will be discussed in Chapter 18. Writers of message plays and dramatized political and sociological
tracts are not listed at all, but a quick reference to newspaper files will show
that their producers and authors are almost all minority members, chiefly
Jewish and Negro. As for pornographic drama, it is sufficient to say that
the dirtiest plays of the 1969–1970 Broadway and off Broadway season—
Ché, Geese and *Oh, Calcutta!*—were all written, directed or produced by
Jews, as were most of the pornographic motion pictures.

72. Simon's 1970 income was estimated at $2,300,000. *Time,* Jan. 12,
1970, p. 65.

73. "American show business . . . owes most of its wit, animation and
emotional frankness to the ebullience of Jewish talent," wrote Kenneth
Tynan, Britain's highest paid dramatic critic and himself part-Jewish. Mr.
Tynan was the producer of *Oh, Calcutta!* The quotation is taken from the
June, 1961, issue of *Holiday* magazine.

are just as firmly embedded as elsewhere. Any representative list of leading mid-century economists would have to
include Paul Samuelson and Milton Friedman; of leading
historians and political scientists, Arthur Schlesinger, Sr. and
Jr., Richard Hofstadter, Hans Morgenstern and J. P. Warburg; of leading sociologists, David Riesman, Arnold Rose,
Nathan Glazer, Seymour Lipset and Oscar Handlin; of
leading jurists, Felix Frankfurter; of leading anthropologists,
Otto Klineberg, Ashley Montagu and Melville Herskovits; of
leading psychiatrists, Erich Fromm and Karen Horney; of
leading philosophers, Morris Cohen, Irwin Edman, Mortimer
Adler, Paul Weiss and Herbert Marcuse. Jews are also prominent in the physical sciences, as their long string of Nobel
prizes attests.[74]

Before probing other areas of Jewish influence and power,
it might be well to mention one of the many side effects of
the Jewish ascendancy in the mass media. This is the favorable tide of publicity which overflows on Jews, partly because of their strategic position in the selection and distribution of news, partly because unfavorable publicity is
often interpreted as anti-Semitism. The inevitable result of
such image-polishing is that when a Jew and a non-Jew have
established a record of similar accomplishments in a similar
line of work, the former is likely to receive more attention
and recognition than the latter.

A case in point is Max Planck and Albert Einstein, the
two men who gave modern physics its two seminal hypotheses, the Quantum theory and Relativity. Planck, a non-Jew,
was scarcely known in America except in scientific circles,
while Einstein, even when an uncritical supporter of Joseph
Stalin after World War II, was the object of the American public's warmest esteem.[75] Another case is Sigmund
Freud, still considered a semi-charlatan in many parts of
Europe, but written up in the United States to the point
where the popular mind thinks him a universal genius. On

---

74. In the period 1901–62, 16 percent of the 225 scientists who won
Nobel prizes were Jews. Weyl and Possony, *Geography of Intellect*, p. 143.

75. For Einstein's part in the promotion and construction of the first
atom bomb, see pp. 520–1. For some unsung criticism of Einsteinian
physics, see footnote 6, p. 296.

the other hand, C. G. Jung, the most eminent non-Jewish psychiatrist, has received only a fraction of Freud's publicity, some of it extremely hostile.[76] The wide acclaim given a Jewish anthropologist like Ashley Montagu and the narrow recognition granted a much greater non-Jewish anthropologist like Carleton Coon is another example of the Semitic bias[77] of public information channels. This same bias is carried over into the field of international relations—most noticeably in the "good press" accorded Israel.

Jewish ownership of the wellsprings and pipelines of modern thought has perhaps superseded Judaism itself as the most important *secondary* cause of Jewish endurance, unity and power. The *primary* cause remains, as always, Jewish wealth. Ever since the diaspora and even before, the Jewish financier, money-maker and moneylender have been identified by non-Jews as quasi-biological types. For almost two thousand years of Jewish history, survival of the fittest has meant survival of the richest.[78]

Jewish wealth is an extremely touchy issue. Not since *Fortune* somewhat half-heartedly examined the problem in February, 1936, has there been a full-scale study of the

---

76. See footnote 58, p. 268.

77. The Semitic "tilt" of present-day public relations is further illustrated by the outpouring of magazine articles and books stressing the Jewish enrichment of American culture but omitting such names as Arnold Rothstein, the Minsky brothers, Mickey Cohen, Serge Rubinstein, Julius and Ethel Rosenberg, Bugsy Siegel, Bernard Goldfine and Jack Ruby. Sometimes this one-sided approach dissolves into pure literary sycophancy, as in the case of a "biography" of Albert Lasker. One of the first advertising moguls, and certainly the richest, Lasker was the hero of a book-length encomium by an internationally known reporter, although the high points of Lasker's career were organizing the first soap operas and introducing millions of women to the smoking habit ("Reach for a Lucky instead of a sweet"). John Gunther, *Taken at the Flood, The Story of Albert D. Lasker,* Harper, New York, 1960, pp. 4–5.

78. In Chapter 10, J. K. Galbraith was quoted as saying wealth was no longer equivalent to power in the U.S. Insofar as he was referring to Majority wealth, he was correct. As stated previously, most of the great Majority fortunes have been scattered, wasted or given to foundations which support projects that often work against Majority interests. Most Jewish wealth, on the other hand, is pooled and concentrated on specific, ethnic goals—Israel, anti-anti-Semitism, minority causes and political, economic and social campaigns to remove the last vestiges of Majority privilege. Professor Galbraith to the contrary, great wealth directed toward *group advantage* is not only equivalent to power, but to great power.

subject in the United States. Even in 1936, *Fortune* found American Jews firmly established in certain economic areas. Now more than three decades later, it is time to take another look.

Some idea of present-day Jewish wealth is furnished by a national poll which attempted to correlate income with religious denomination. It found that 18.9 percent of all Americans enjoying an annual income over $10,000 were Jews. Episcopalians accounted for 14.1 percent, individuals with no religious affiliation 11.6 percent, Presbyterians 8.7 percent, Catholics 4.6 percent and Baptists 2.1 percent.[79] Translated into racial terms, the poll indicated that Jews were the most affluent Americans, Majority members next, Assimilable and Unassimilable White Minority members next, and Negroes, traditionally Baptists, the poorest.

Similar findings were obtained by a special 1950 Federal Census report which revealed that of thirty-nine different U.S. population groups "foreign-born Russians" had the highest median income. The median income of Americans of native white parentage was 40 percent less. The Census report explained the economic success of the foreign-born Russians by saying, "the Russian group contains large refugee and Jewish components." [80]

Since Jews are 2.9 percent of the American population, an unwary statistician might be foolish enough to predict that 2.9 percent of American millionaires would be Jewish and that Jews would own 2.9 percent of the country's wealth. In 1955, however, more than 20 percent of all American millionaires were Jewish and Jews accounted for 10 percent of the personal income of all Americans.[81]

Perhaps the best proof of the constant expansion of Jewish financial power in the United States is furnished by the activities of the great Jewish banking houses and investment

79. D. J. Bogue, *The Population of the U.S.*, The Free Press of Glencoe, Illinois, 1959, p. 706.

80. *Ibid.*, pp. 367–9, 371.

81. *Look*, Nov. 29, 1955, pp. 27–35. Also see Sachar, *op. cit.*, p. 346. A Detroit study showed Jewish median income to be $6,000 compared to $4,800 for Protestants, $4,650 for Catholics, $3,500 for Negroes. James Yaffe, *The American Jews*, Random House, New York, 1969, p. 229.

companies. Year by year, Goldman, Sachs and Co.,[82] Kuhn,
Loeb & Co., Lazard Frères, Lehman Brothers, Lehman
Corporation and others are pushing their financial control
deeper and deeper into the nation's economy. No one, of
course, can determine the extent of this control, but some
indication can be obtained by examining the roster of directors of America's leading corporations. Wherever and
whenever a partner or officer of these banking houses or
their associated investment companies appears as a director
of a large corporation, it usually means that he represents
a significant, though not necessarily controlling, financial interest. It might be added that although these private Jewish
banking houses may have non-Jewish partners, they nonetheless remain firmly in Jewish hands.[83]

82. Henry Ford, a hardshell Protestant, was averse to Wall Street,
liberals, foreigners, Jews and non-Protestants in general. One could well
imagine his reaction if he returned to earth and found: (1) Sidney Weinberg of Goldman, Sachs on the Board of Directors of Ford Motor Co., (2)
the Ford Foundation, the world's richest sponsor of liberal causes, (3) his
grandson, Henry Ford, II, a Catholic convert, now married for the second
time to an Italian divorcee, (4) his two great-granddaughters, Anne and
Charlotte, wed to foreigners, the former temporarily to a Greek shipping
magnate and the latter to a Florentine Jew, now a Wall Street stockbroker.
In regard to Goldman, Sachs, it might be mentioned that as late as 1969 the
financial house was named by the Securities and Exchange Commission for
violating security laws by illegally pushing up the price of the shares of
Roosevelt Raceway, Inc. *New York Times,* Oct. 7, 1969, p. 61.

83. *Poor's Register of Corporations, Directors and Executives* (1964 and
1968) lists Goldman, Sachs partners as directors of the following corpo-
rations: Ford, Continental Can, General Cigar, McKesson & Robbins,
Champion Papers, Cudahy Packing, Lehn & Fink, United Biscuit, Jewel Tea,
Van Raalte, Cluett Peabody, Bulova Watch, Cowles Communications, B. F.
Goodrich, National Dairy Products, Condé Nast Publications, Manhattan
Shirt, Brown Shoe, Pillsbury, Endicott Johnson, Braniff Airways, Diebold,
May Department Stores, New York Telephone, Great American, Eagle-
Picher, Kelsey-Hayes, Data Control Systems, Sperry-Hutchinson.

Kuhn, Loeb partners are directors of: Westinghouse Electric, Sears In-
dustries, U.S. Rubber, Anglo-Israel Bank, Revlon, Benrus Watch, Tish-
man Realty, International Telephone and Telegraph, Todd-AO, American
Export Lines, Polaroid, C.I.T. Financial, Brush-Beryllium, Getty Oil, Great
Atlantic and Pacific Tea, Kennicott Copper, Atlas, Marine Midland Trust,
Metromedia, Buckeye Pipe, General American Transportation.

Lehman Brothers partners or Lehman Corporation directors are directors
of: Pan American Airways, Goebel Brothers, 20th Century-Fox, United
Fruit, Commercial Solvents, Chesebrough-Pond's, Paramount Pictures,
Beckman Instruments, Singer Sewing Machine, Bristol-Meyers, General

Footnote 83 makes it evident that Jews now have more than a foothold in automobiles, steel, public utilities, railroads, airlines, insurance, oil and chemicals—the same blue chip corporations which supposedly have been most successful in resisting Jewish infiltration. In many other business fields the Jewish foothold has become a monopoly. The two largest distillers, Seagram's (Samuel Bronfman) and Schenley's (Lewis S. Rosenstiel) are Jewish-controlled as are many of the largest textile companies, shoe firms and two leading tobacco companies.[84] The clothing industry at the manufacturing, wholesale and retail level is predominantly Jewish. So are most of the nation's department and furniture stores and cosmetic firms. Jewelry and precious stones are practically a Jewish monopoly.[85]

The anonymity which surrounds the operations of the private banking companies is occasionally broken by effusive references to the wealth of their principal partners. Robert Lehman of Lehman Brothers, it was revealed before his death, had an art collection worth more than $150,000,-000.[86] Gustave Levy, a Goldman, Sachs partner, has been described as the "biggest money man on Wall Street." [87] André Meyer of Lazard Frères, founded more than one hundred years ago by a French-Jewish gold trader from New Orleans, did not even take up residence in the United

---

Cable, RCA, Federated Department Stores, Bulova Watch, Western Union, Shell Oil, General Analine and Film, Standard Oil of California, Greyhound, FMC, Jones & Laughlin Steel, Anchor-Hocking, Times-Mirror, United California Bank, Union Oil, Wells Fargo Bank, Hertz, Litton Industries, General Motors, Allied Chemical, Continental Can, United States Lines, Caterpillar Tractor, IBM, Southern Pacific, Chase Manhattan Bank, Pacific Gas and Electric, Air Reduction, Northern Pacific, Bendix, Studebaker-Packard, Smith-Corona-Marchant, Flintkote, Sperry-Rand, Allied Stores.

Lazard Frères partners are directors of: Jones & Laughlin, National Fire Insurance, Olivetti-Underwood, Owens-Illinois, Manufacturers Life Insurance, Chemical Bank-New York Trust, Harcourt Brace, Harper and Row, Libby-Owens-Ford Glass, Warner Lambert Pharmaceutical, Sun Insurance, RCA, Engelhard Industries.

84. One, Philip Morris, has taken over Miller Brewing, American Safety Razor and Clark Chewing Gum. The other, P. Lorillard, has been taken over by Loew's Theatres.

85. See footnote 15, p. 498.

86. Joseph Wechsberg, *The Merchant Bankers,* p. 333.

87. Martin Mayer, *Wall Street,* Harper, New York, p. 193.

States until 1940, yet is now "the most important investment banker in the world." [88]

Meyer is a director of RCA and Allied Chemical in the United States as well as Fiat and Montecatini Edison in Italy. Presidents Kennedy and Johnson appointed him to important government posts and his close friends include Robert McNamara, Henry Fowler, Johnson's Secretary of the Treasury, Eugene Black, former head of the World Bank, and Jacqueline Kennedy. Lyndon Johnson consulted him regularly and David Rockefeller joined him in several real estate ventures. Lazard's New York branch has participated in vast financial transactions involving American Metal Climax, Minnesota Mining and Lockheed Aircraft. In 1966, it arranged for the MacDonald-Douglas merger for a fee of $1,000,000. Lazard has a $40,000,000 interest in International Telephone and Telegraph, one of the nation's largest conglomerates, and its New York, London and Paris branches manage or advise investments totaling $3,000,000,000. [89]

In 1970, three of the richest American Jews were Leon Hess (chemicals), Jacob Blaustein (oil) and Mrs. Arthur Hays Sulzberger (*New York Times*), each of whom had a fortune in excess of $150,000,000. [90] Presumably as rich were the Shubert brothers who owned a $400,000,000 theater empire. [91] Other opulent Jews include Joseph Hirshhorn, who made over $100,000,000 in uranium; [92] Billy Rose, the late showman, who (as of May, 1963) was the largest single shareholder of American Telephone and Telegraph; [93] Henry

---

88. *Fortune*, Aug. 1968, pp. 101 ff.

89. *Ibid*. In the same article *Fortune* stated, "The hard financial core of capitalism in the free world is composed of not more than 60 firms, partnerships and corporations owned or controlled by some 1,000 men."

90. *Fortune*, May 1968. In 1948, when President Truman was wondering whether or not to seek a second term, he called in six people to advise him. Blaustein, who died in 1970, was one of them. *New York Times*, Nov. 17, 1970, p. 44.

91. *San Francisco Sunday Examiner, Date Book*, Dec. 15, 1968, p. 2, as quoted from *The Brothers Shubert* by Jerry Stagg. Jake and Lee Shubert, according to the author, controlled 75 percent of all American theaters.

92. *Current Biography*, 1966, pp. 177–8.

93. *Newsweek*, May 27, 1963, p. 80 and *New York Times*, Feb. 11, 1966, p. 1.

Crown, onetime owner of the Empire State Building and holder of an estimated 18 percent of the stock in General Dynamics, the company which has often managed to procure the biggest slice of national defense contracts; [94] the late Louis Mayer, for years the highest salaried American; [95] Jack Dreyfus, Jr. and Howard Stein of the $1.8 billion Dreyfus Fund; [96] John Loeb of Carl Loeb, Rhoades & Co., whose partners are directors of sixty American corporations and who is the husband of a Lehman and the father-in-law of Edgar Bronfman; [97] the Zellerbachs of the Crown-Zellerbach Corp.; Paul Block, who controls Inland Steel; Bernard Cornfeld, with a 15 percent holding in Investors Overseas Service, worth $140 million until the company half collapsed in 1970 taking with it a sizable portion of the savings of tens of thousands of Europeans; [98] the late Lester Avnet of Avnet Electronics ($252 million annual sales); [99] Alfred Roberts, President of Lydia O'Leary, married to Eleanor Block of Block Drug (Polident); [100] Saul P. Steinberg of Leasco (assets of $400 million); [101] Rudolf Sonneborn of Witco Chemical; and Harry Winston, the jewelry magnate.

Always to be found in the topmost echelons of American affluence are such old established families (some members of which have become Christians) as the Seligmans, Warburgs, Kahns and Guggenheims, and the not-so-well established Strauses, Gimbels, Kaufmanns and Magnins. The elite Jewish families of San Francisco—Hellmans (Wells Fargo Bank), Fleishhackers (Anglo-California Bank), Haases (Levi Strauss), Sutros (stockbrokers), Schwabachers (Bank of America and Pacific Telephone and

94. $2,239,000,000 for the fiscal year ending June 30, 1968. *U.S. News & World Report,* April 21, 1969, p. 63, and *New York Times,* May 28, 1970.
95. $949,765 in 1941. *Current Biography,* 1943, p. 521.
96. *Moody's Banks & Finances,* Aug. 14, 1970, p. 1565.
97. Birmingham, *Our Crowd,* p. 443–5. Liquor baron Samuel Bronfman, Edgar's father, is considered to be the richest man in Canada. *Ibid.,* p. 445.
98. *Time,* Oct. 3, 1969, p. 95.
99. *New York Times,* Jan. 4, 1970, p. 77.
100. *New York Times Magazine,* Sept. 7, 1969, p. 122. His son was one of the promoters of the Woodstock Festival. See footnote 60, p. 245.
101. *Time,* Oct. 24, 1969, p. 94.

Telegraph directorships)—also deserve mention in any census of inherited wealth.

As the giant industrial concerns grow unwieldy and operating costs go out of sight, as accounting, financing and labor relations take precedence over invention, production and quality control, Jews have thronged to the lucrative pastures of land speculation, housing, the new technology and the building of conglomerates. Among such are Milton Shapp, currently Governor of Pennsylvania, Albert List, Louis Wolfson,[102] Roy Chalk, Norman Tishman, Charles Bluhdorn, Mark Taper, Lou Chesler,[103] A. M. Sonnabend, Lester Selig, the Levitts, the Bakalars, and Alfred Strelsin.[104] The most meteoric of all these wheeler-dealers is Meshulam Ricklis, born in Istanbul, raised in Israel, naturalized an American, who in one week made $2 million in the stock market.[105] Richest member of the club is probably Norton Simon.[106] Not to be excluded are Max Palevsky, the computer king, Lew Wasserman of MCA, Lawrence Harvey, the aluminum magnate, and Michel Fribourg, owner of Continental Grain ($2.5 billion annual sales), one of America's two largest privately held companies and probably the biggest profiteer in the recent American-Russian grain deals.

Another important source of Jewish wealth is the seemingly congenital preference of Jews for the most highly paid occupations. For example, 35 to 40 percent of working Jewish adults are in commerce, as against 13.8 percent of non-Jews; 10 to 12 percent in the professions as against 6.8 percent of non-Jews; [107] 73 percent in "white collar"

---

102. See Chapter 30.

103. Chesler made $70,000,000 in two stock operations on the American Stock Exchange. Leslie Gould, *The Manipulators*, 1966, p. 123.

104. Late additions to this roster: Eli Black of United Brands and United Fruit, Leonard Stern of Hartz Mountain, Martin Seretean, owner of 1,500,000 shares of RCA.

105. *San Francisco Sunday Examiner*, March 12, 1968, p. 1.

106. At a 1968 London auction Simon, who once controlled Hunt Foods, Canada Dry, Talent Associates, Ohio Match and Glass Container, paid $1,555,000 for a Renoir. *New York Times*, Oct. 10, 1968, p. 1.

107. Nathan Ruck, *Economic Trends in the American Jew*, Oscar Janovsky (ed.), Harper, New York, 1942, pp. 162, 165. The occupational specialties of Jews do not include coal mining, ditchdigging and domestic

jobs compared to 43 percent of Protestants and 33 percent of Catholics;[108] 48 percent are self-employed as against 19 percent of Protestants and 10 percent of Catholics.[109]

Foreseeing a Jewish stranglehold on the professions, many American medical and law schools established a quota system at the turn of the century. Under the battering of liberal and minority pressure, quotas have now been largely abandoned,[110] with the result that the proportion of Jews in the professions is going up rapidly. At present, medical colleges receive about 14,000 entry applications a year, 5,000 to 7,000 from Jews,[111] and in New York City already half of the 15,000 doctors are Jewish. The spiraling tuitions of the medical and legal schools have given Jews an additional advantage in the race for professional degrees. Belonging to the most affluent American population group, Jews can absorb the costs of postgraduate education better than non-Jews.

To sum up the phenomenon of Jewish affluence, what is happening in the United States today is what has been happening throughout much of Western history. The Jews, finding themselves unrestricted and uncurbed in a land rich in resources and labor, are rapidly monopolizing its wealth. It is almost certainly the same historic process that took place in Visigothic, Arabic and Catholic Spain, in medieval England, France and Germany—and most recently in twentieth-century Germany. Yet no one cares—or dares —to notice it. Those who are so concerned about labor monopolies or business cartels, about the influence of the Roman Catholic Church or the military-industrial complex, about the WASP domination of the big corporations or the international Communist conspiracy, seem strangely silent and utterly unconcerned about the activities of an ever more

---

service, although in New York City American Jews still drive taxis, wait on tables, serve in the police force, have blue collar jobs and work with their hands in the garment district.

108. *Ibid.* Negroes were not included in these percentages.

109. *Ibid.*

110. Jews are ambivalent about quotas which raise the participation of nonwhites in industry, education and politics. First they supported the idea, then some of them began to have their doubts, as they considered what might happen if quotas were imposed in merchant banking, the garment trade and the communications media.

111. Simpson and Yinger, *op. cit.*, pp. 677–9.

powerful, ever more dominant, supranational ethnocentrism with almost unlimited financial resources at its command.

But the silence is not so strange when one reflects on what British political analyst R. H. S. Crossman has described as "the anti-anti-Semitic veto which has successfully suppressed any candid and effective writing about the Jewish problem. . . ." [112] Any critical discussion of Jewish wealth— or for that matter any critical discussion of any aspect of Jewish power—immediately exposes the author or speaker to charges of anti-Semitism.[113] Since anti-Semitism is the great heresy of modern times, a person so accused is immediately subjected to such doses of social ostracism and economic attrition that any normal private life or successful public career will be permanently closed to him. It is consequently small wonder that the entire Western intellectual establishment has shied away from such a thankless and unprofitable task. At present, one can only be objective about Jews when one is a Jew. A very few anti-Zionist Jews, who believe Zionism harms Jewry by exposing ambivalent Jewish loyalties, declaim against Israel. A very few Jewish thinkers and scientists, and a very few Jewish novelists who let their characters run away from them, occasionally show symptoms of the ancient Jewish neurosis of *selbsthass* (self-hatred) and vent their feelings in a manner inconsistent with the all-out Jewish effort to keep anti-Semitism under impenetrable wraps.[114]

The removal of all things Jewish from the arena of rational discussion automatically relegates unfriendly opinions

---

112. R. H. S. Crossman, *Partisan Review,* Fall, 1964, p. 565.
113. ". . . among all other ethnic groups, his [the Jew's] expressed thinking, his expressed concerns, are the most subjective. And the Jew is usually hypersensitive . . . you can't even say 'Jew' without him accusing you of anti-Semitism. I don't care what a Jew is professionally, doctor, merchant, housewife, student, or whatever—first he, or she, thinks Jew." *Autobiography of Malcolm X,* Grove Press, New York, 1966, p. 283.
114. One such thinker was Simone Weil, the French-Jewish poetess-philosopher who equated the spirit of Judaism with the spirit of Nazism and who complained that the worship of the "earthy, cruel and exclusive Jehovah had turned Jews into a nation of fugitive slaves." One such scientist was Dr. Karl Landsteiner, Nobel laureate, who unsuccessfully sought an injunction against *Who's Who in American Jewry* for calling him a Jew. Sachar, *op. cit.,* p. 404. One such novelist is Philip Roth, author of *Portnoy's Complaint.*

of Jews to the hushed whispers of office, living room and country club, to underground "hate sheets" and to the verbal musings of crackpots haunted by visions of bearded elders plotting world conquest. All this lends an aura of mysticism and romantic obscurantism to anti-Semitism, which it does not deserve and which endows it with a kind of kinetic and subterranean diabolism. The day anti-Semitism breaks out into the light again—as suppressed ideologies have the habit of doing—it cannot avoid becoming the stock-in-trade of the apocalyptic avenger who knows that emotion and dogma move more mountains than reason. The sudden release of tensions and hatreds pent up during decades of censorship and indoctrination will probably obviate any less explosive outcome.

Instead of submitting anti-Semitism to the free play of ideas, instead of making it a topic for debate in which all can join, Jews and their liberal supporters have managed to organize an inquisition in which all acts, writings and even thoughts critical of Jewry are treated as a threat to the moral order of mankind. The pro-Semite has consequently made himself a mirror image of the anti-Semite. The Tartuffe of the contemporary era turns out to be the Jewish intellectual who believes passionately in the rights of free speech and peaceful assembly for all, but rejoices when permits are refused for anti-Semitic meetings and rocks crack against the skulls of anti-Semitic speakers.

Admitting the almost incredible disparity between Jewish numbers and Jewish influence in the United States—and it is growing more difficult for anyone not to admit it—how does modern scholarship explain it? The answer is that most modern scholars do not try to explain it at all, or if they do, simply deny that there is anything more to the Jewish problem than environmental coincidence. Those with a more inquisitive mind or with a special ax to grind have a few interesting theories on the subject—theories, however, which are basically apologies since they are circumscribed by the present-day caveat that any discussion of Jews must never put them in an unfavorable light.

One well-circulated theory, advanced by Jewish scholar Ludwig Lewisohn, is that Jews were primarily an agricultural people who were driven into banking and commerce by papal edicts forbidding Christians to engage in usury.[115] The implication is that Jews, against their national inclinations, were forced to become rich by being compelled to set up an hereditary plutocratic caste. This proposition, however, is untenable for the obvious reason that Jews were very active in moneylending long before Christianity—not to mention the Papacy—had entered the arena of history.

The late A. L. Kroeber, eminent head of the University of California's Anthropology Department, took an unruffled approach to the Jewish question. Pointing to the "exceedingly spotty Jewish participation in the great civilizations," Kroeber defined the present Jewish ascendancy as a "transitional phenomenon." It was, he said, the "released mobility" of the Jews which had the effect of propelling them forward "more quickly than Gentiles in fields which they enter newly, and temporarily with brilliant success." [116] As the years go by, however, and the Jews' upward curve shows no signs of leveling off, Kroeber's thesis is losing much of its cogency.

A more plausible thesis has a Darwinian base. It was the richest Jew who had the best chance of surviving the pogroms and lesser persecutions which have dogged Jewish footsteps over the centuries. In most cases he could buy his way out. But the richest Jew was generally the most adroit Jew, the one best suited and best adapted to the peculiar conditions and requirements of urban and ghetto life. Consequently, the affluent citified Jew of today is the end product of two thousand years of a special form of natural selection, the fortunate possessor of an inbred cosmopolitanism which is a great competitive advantage in decadent, heterogeneous, urbanized societies incapable of guarding their citizens against the racial dynamism of newcomers.

---

115. Sachar, *op. cit.,* p. 533. Lewisohn, who taught at several American universities before becoming Professor of Comparative Literature at Brandeis, was a Jewish supremacist who inveighed against Germans, Slavs, Negroes, and Anglo-Saxon "barbarism." One might speculate on what would happen to a Majority professor who inveighed against Jewish "barbarism."

116. *Configurations of Cultural Growth,* University of California, Berkeley, 1944, pp. 737 ff.

It is only a short step from acknowledging that peoples or races have special gifts to the development of all-inclusive theories of racial inferiority or superiority. The most ardent contemporary advocate of Jewish supremacy is Nathaniel Weyl, who alleges that Jews are inherently more intelligent than other peoples because they have been breeding for intelligence since the diaspora. Gentile churchmen, the cream of the non-Jewish medieval intelligentsia according to Weyl, were usually celibate and died without issue, while the more sexually unrepressed rabbis and Talmudic scholars were eagerly sought after by the daughters of prominent Jewish merchants.[117] Weyl's point concerning the energetic combination and recombination rather than the ascetic stulitification of clever Jewish genes would have more validity if he did not confuse intelligence with verbalism and intellectual sheen.[118] Or if he did not forget that most of the kings, artists, writers, architects and warriors of the Middle Ages, as well as more than a few Popes, were as lusty and prolific as his rabbis and ghetto tycoons.

In *The Geography of Intellect,* which he wrote with Stefan T. Possony, Weyl supported his claims for Jewish intelligence by referring to seventeen studies, of which, the authors said, "Eleven found the Jews superior in mental test scores, four found them equal and two found them inferior. Of the third category, Brigham's study was based on a fatal methodological error." The authors only gave details on one study, a series of tests covering almost two

---

117. *The Creative Elite in America,* Chap. XVIII. Boccaccio and Rabelais would have smiled at Weyl's assertions regarding the celibacy and intelligence of the clergy. Part of Weyl's theme, incidentally, was taken from Sir Francis Galton, who was equally bitter about the dysgenics of religious bachelorhood. But in his own intelligence ratings Galton excluded Jews and gave first place to the Athenians, whom he placed two grades above the nineteenth-century British and four grades above African Negroes. Sir Francis Galton, *Hereditary Genius,* Macmillan, London, 1869, pp. 42, 257 ff, 342, 357 ff.

118. "All intellectuality is in the long run shallowness; never does it allow of probing to the very roots of a matter, never of reaching down to the depths of the soul, or of the universe. Hence intellectuality makes it easy to go from one extreme to the other. That is why you find among Jews fanatical orthodoxy and unenlightened doubt side by side; they both spring from one source." Werner Sombart, *The Jews and Modern Capitalism,* trans. M. Epstein, Dutton, New York, 1914, p. 269.

thousand Jewish and non-Jewish children in three London schools, one upper class, one poor and the third very poor. The Jewish scores were significantly higher.[119] Weyl and Possony moreover, did not elaborate on the "fatal error" ascribed to Brigham, a Princeton psychology professor, whose analysis of Army World War I intelligence tests showed that Americans of Northern European descent made better scores than Jews, who in turn did better than Americans of Southern European descent.[120]

Weyl failed to mention it, but he must be aware that tests seeking to compare Jewish intelligence with the intelligence of such broad-spectrum groups as whites, Gentiles or Christians are necessarily loaded in favor of Jews. Since the Jewish population is concentrated almost entirely in or around the largest cities, tests involving sizable numbers of Jews have to be conducted in areas where the white population is extremely heterogeneous, with a heavy emphasis on groups of other than Northern European origin. Many of these "whites" may in fact be nonwhites because the Census Bureau defines most Puerto Ricans and Mexicans as whites.

To obtain an accurate measurement of Jewish intelligence, it would seem reasonable to compare Jews, a select group within the white population, with other select white population groups rather than with the white population as a whole. An intelligence test restricted to Jews and Majority members might produce entirely different results than the tests cited by Weyl. Also, since many intelligence tests reveal more information about verbal agility, quick recall and educational levels than about intelligence itself, it might be wise to take into consideration the fact that Jews, being the wealthiest and most cosmopolitan population group, have readier access to education than other Americans and to such educational byproducts as memory training and vocabulary building. But a college degree, a subscription to *The New York Times* and a fondness for forensics are no

---

119. *The Geography of Intellect*, pp. 162–3.
120. Carl Brigham, *A Study of American Intelligence*, pp. 160–90. For Brigham's racial allocations of the American population, see Appendix.

proof of higher intelligence. It was educated city Jews, not hillbillies, who furnished most of the support for Henry Wallace's Progressive party in the 1948 presidential election [121] —the party that stood for the almost total appeasement of the Soviet Union.[122]

In spite of these objections, the case for Jewish intellectual superiority continues to gather momentum. Ernest van den Haag devoted the opening chapter of his best-seller, *The Jewish Mystique,* to wide-ranging generalizations about the finer-tuned cerebral apparatus of Jews.[123] Although in only one instance did he supply any documentation for his allegations [124] and although he never once referred to Weyl by name, Professor van den Haag was obviously expanding on Weyl's "breeding for intelligence" hypothesis and his writing breathed the spirit of the latter's arguments.

But the case for the genetically based superiority of Jewish brains did not receive national prominence until a 1969 press interview with the British scientist-turned-novelist C. P. Snow. Quoting from a speech he was preparing to deliver to the Hebrew Union College, Snow, whose novels have been called "stupendously bad" by the *London Spectator,*[125] stated that Jews were definitely superior to all

121. Phillips, *op. cit.,* footnote p. 65.

122. A 1947 Gallup Poll showed that blue-collar workers were far more suspicious and aware of Russian expansionism than college graduates, who were still clinging to the outworn notion that Russia would join the Western democracies in the establishment of One World. *New York Times,* March 23, 1947, IV, p. 6. It might also be noted that the educated classes could not conceive of the 1939 Russo-German Nonaggression Pact until it was signed.

123. Van den Haag's remarks about Jewish cultural domination have been quoted on pp. 87–8.

124. *The Jewish Mystique,* p. 24. The author relied on an old study by Lewis Terman, who in tests of California school children found there were twice as many gifted Jewish students as their proportion of the population warranted. Here again, the tests were conducted in the largest cities—San Francisco, Oakland and Los Angeles—where California Jews were concentrated and where the Majority was underrepresented both in quantity and quality. Other population groups produced extremely high scores, but van den Haag did not mention them. The Scots did even better than the Jews on a percentage basis. The most important lesson of the Terman study was the woefully poor performance of Negro, Mexican and Latin children. Lewis Terman, *Genetic Studies of Genius,* Stanford University Press, 1925, Vol. 1, pp. 55–6.

125. June 16, 1969, p. 705.

other living peoples and attributed the cause to inbreeding.[126]

Ironically, theories of Aryan, Nordic or Teutonic racial supremacy, which assigned Jews to the lowest rung of the white racial ladder, have now been completely reversed. Within twenty-five years of Adolf Hitler's death and following the imprisonment or ostracism of all Northern European racial supremacists, in and out of Germany, an internationally known writer like C. P. Snow, was given a handsome stipend and treated most generously by the American press after publicly proclaiming a theory of racial superiority. But all things considered, Snow's, van den Haag's and Weyl's line of reasoning does not prove Jewish intellectual superiority as much as it proves the reshuffling of America's racial power structure.

When it is a matter of appraising racial intelligence, the historical record, the accumulated evidence of the entire human experience, would seem to be more reliable than a few scattered, often self-serving academic *obiter dicta* and IQ tests. If Jews are truly superior to the rest of mankind, it might be asked why, with one exception, the greatest cultural achievements of civilization took place in exactly those areas where Jews were unknown, banned, segregated or actively persecuted.[127] If superiority is to be measured in political and economic rather than cultural terms, how is it that the greatest and most enduring empires, republics and city states of Western civilization were founded without

126. *Pittsburgh Post Gazette*, April 1, 1969, p. 26. In the same interview Snow refused to be drawn into a discussion of Negro intelligence. By sidestepping the Negro issue, Snow proved himself less courageous than Weyl, who after giving up communism wrote extensively on the subject of Negro intellectual inferiority. Professor van den Haag, who also has definite ideas about black capabilities, testified for Southern white children in legal proceedings instituted in 1963 to overturn (unsuccessfully) the Supreme Court's 1954 school desegregation ruling. Putnam, *Race and Reality*, pp. 87–8.

127. The list of countries and cities forbidden to Jews in different eras was given earlier in this chapter. Here the list may be lengthened by adding that there were no Jews in Pericles' Athens and very minor Jewish participation in the cultural life of the Roman Republic and Empire (in their great days), or in Goethe's Germany and Dostoyevsky's Russia. The single example of a great and uniquely Hebrew culture, though somewhat restricted in that Judaism specifically forbade painting and sculpture, evolved in ancient Palestine, where Hebrews were a majority in their own land.

Jewish assistance and reached their zenith before the appearance of influential Jewish establishments within their borders.[128] No Jews signed the Magna Carta or the Declaration of Independence, and no Jews were active in the Long Parliament, the Constitutional Convention in Philadelphia or in any other of the great deliberations which gave form and substance to man's most successful experiments with representative government.

The few historic instances, or at least all the relatively recent ones, where bodies of Jews have assumed outright political control—the Kurt Eisner regime in Bavaria (November 1918—February 1919), the short-lived Spartacus uprising in Berlin (December 1918—January 1919) and Bela Kun's sadistic orgy in Budapest (March–August 1919)—could hardly be classified as golden ages of statesmanship. Neither could the Russian Revolution, in which Jews took a commanding role until the Stalin purges. The Jewish autonomous region of Birobidzhan fizzled out almost before it started.[129] As for Israel, it has been at war since its foundation.

As for the economic advantages Jews are supposed to confer upon their host countries, there is no question that they bring with them a great deal of money and financial expertise. But an increasing flow of money is often accompanied by inflation and a flood of speculation. If Jews are as intrinsic to the good economic life as some economists claim, it seems odd that the Weimar Republic with its plethora of Jewish financiers was an economic miasma, while the economic miracle of West Germany took place in the one large Western nation almost free of Jewish financial domination and at the very time (1952–1962) it was

---

128. Zenith is not meant to signify the era of greatest territorial expansion, but the moment of the cresting of national morale, purpose and unity. In this sense the greatest days of England occurred in the sixteenth rather than the nineteenth century. America is either well past its zenith or a long way from it. Greatness is more likely to occur at the zenith of great art, not great politics. Gigantic military forces and accumulations of wealth are usually weather vanes of approaching national disintegration, not signs of national health.

129. For the Birobidzhan debacle, see *Encyclopedia of Russia and the Soviet Union,* McGraw-Hill, New York, 1961, p. 258.

paying Israel $900 million in reparations and billions to individual Jews throughout the world. A country with an equally dynamic economy in the post-World War II era is Japan, which has no Jews at all.

Another way of measuring the Jewish contribution to society is to examine the political, economic and social conditions of those areas where Jews presently exercise the greatest control. The two main centers of Jewish power and population in the modern world are New York City and Israel. The former can only be described as the greatest municipal catastrophe of the day—a scabrous pile of ugliness, tastelessness and lawlessness—certainly not the brilliant world capital one would expect from a people with superior civilizing gifts. Although they have failed to make New York bloom, Jews have nevertheless accomplished wonders in the Palestinian wilderness. But the true measure of a people's genius is not determined by its ability to cultivate the land and to wage war, however essential these factors may be. Its ultimate place in history is determined by its statecraft, that is, by the creation of a special, fertilizing environment in which its art and institutions can be developed to their highest pitch.

Modern Jews may be gifted above all other peoples. Or they may be, as Toynbee states, the remnants of a fossil civilization.[130] Or they may even be, as anti-Semites claim, a parasitic social organism that survives by feeding off other social organisms. Which of these descriptions is most realistic it is too early to tell. Modern Jewry has been emancipated for less than two centuries and not enough data have been collected. But if it should turn out that Jews are superior beings, as many of them feel and as their more enthusiastic scholars and well-wishers are attempting to prove, it is time for a more conclusive demonstration of their capabilities.

It is one thing to reshape and reorder the thinking habits and living patterns of a decadent United States. It

---

130. For saying this, Toynbee was accused by Jewish historian Maurice Samuel of perpetuating "demonological anti-Semitism." Toynbee, *A Study of History*, Vol. V, p. 76 and Samuel, *The Professor and the Fossil*, Knopf, New York, 1956, p. 194.

is another to give the world a greater writer than Shakespeare, a greater composer than Mozart, a greater artist than Michelangelo. It is not an easy task for Israel to exist as a minuscule military and cultural oasis in the midst of a hostile desert wilderness. But it is a much more difficult task to undertake a civilizing mission in the Middle East comparable to Spain's in Latin America, Britain's in North America and France's in North Africa. As final proof of Jewish superiority, Einstein's theories must become Einstein's laws, and the net effect on the evolutionary process of Marx, Freud and other modern Jewish prophets must be positive not negative, constructive not destructive.

Until all the evidence is in, the Jewish hegemony in the United States can be more convincingly explained by the tensions of race relations than by other less controversial causes. The truth seems to be that any organized minority with a given amount of intelligence can obtain supremacy over a disorganized majority of equal intelligence. A race-conscious population group is far more effective and successful in most forms of endeavor than a race-unconscious population group. Racial spirit, like team spirit, stimulates victory in all types of competition, athletic or political, intellectual or social. If the Majority were as race-conscious as the Jewish minority and had half as many organizations working for it, Jewish predominance in America would disappear overnight.

Where Jews diverge most sharply from the Majority, aside from important personality differences,[131] is in having a higher degree of ethnocentrism, not a higher degree of

---

131. According to James Yaffe, Jews have more interest in sex than non-Jews, less interest in athletics, less faith in an afterlife, a lower birthrate, take many more expensive vacations, live longer, spend more time in psychoanalysis and are much more likely to be hippies. In Hollywood, Jews get more divorces, commit more adultery and drink less than their non-Jewish neighbors. Jews use Jewish doctors 95 percent of the time; Jewish lawyers 87 percent of the time. Although they sometimes try to force themselves into non-Jewish country clubs, they are very exclusive about their own. One of them, the Hillcrest in Southern California, has the highest initiation fee ($22,000) of any golf club in the U.S. and bans non-Jews except for a few show business figures who are admitted as "honorary Jews." Jews, continues Yaffe, are noted for their "fear, obsequiousness, isolationism and belligerence"—a psychological chasm between Jew and non-Jew that may

intelligence. To put it in a different perspective, Jewish power may derive as much or more from Majority weakness and disorganization as from Jewish strength.

Since the anti-Semitic taboo has made it impossible to submit the Jewish question to free discussion and open inquiry,[132] Jews have only themselves to thank for having set themselves above and outside the rules of conventional democratic conduct. Considering their history and their memories, it is only human for Jews to have done so. But it is also only human on the part of Majority members to oppose the kind of organized group behavior for which their institutions were never designed. When the occasion arises, Jews may appeal to fair play and tolerance for themselves, but they seldom extend these traditional democratic prerogatives to others. Let Majority members who think differently take even the first faltering step toward a racial protective organization such as the B'nai B'rith Anti-Defamation League [133] and they

---

never be bridged. Traditionally dogmatic themselves, they demand rationalism in others. For the Jew "the intellect can't be just a tool . . . it has to be a weapon too. He doesn't use it simply to discover what the world is like or to create something beautiful, or to communicate his ideas. He must use it to beat down his competitors, to prove his superiority. For him controversy is inseparable from intellectual activity. Watch him at a party; note the vicious delight with which he backs lesser intellects into a corner. He's implacable; neither social decorum nor human compassion can soften his attack. If you want to observe this trait at a safer distance, read what he writes to the letters-to-the-editor pages. In all Jewish publications, from *Commentary* down to the most obscure Yiddish weekly, these pages bathe the reader in vitriol. Like his father, the garment manufacturer, the Jewish intellectual doesn't trade easy." *The American Jews*, pp. 38, 65, 68, 234–5, 268–9, 292–3.

132. These conspiracies of silence also extend to schools of thought and avenues of research which might strengthen Majority unity and thereby ultimately work to the Jews' disadvantage—i.e., racial interpretation of American history, genetic arguments for segregated education, statistical studies of minority crime, and so on.

133. On its 50th anniversary the Anti-Defamation League could point with pride to a New York headquarters, regional offices in thirty cities, a staff of 150 full-time lawyers, social scientists, educators and public relations specialists. Its budget for 1960 was $3,940,000. Thomas B. Morgan, "The Fight Against Prejudice," *Look*, June 4, 1963, pp. 66 ff. Although tax exempt, the ADL plays a highly political role and occasionally even usurps the power of the police. The New Orleans regional director of the ADL put up most of the money for the informers which the FBI used to entrap an alleged bomber of synagogues in Mississippi. A young female school teacher

will be hounded out of public life almost overnight by the news media, "private" investigators, law enforcement agencies and, if need be, Congressional committees—all prodded into action by a nationwide avalanche of Jewish protest.

In the long run, the Jewish place in American life cannot rest on the sanctity of institutions, dated dogmas, *argumenta ad misericordiam* or the divine right of minorities. It must rest on the cause-and-effect relationship between the rise of the Jewish establishment and the Majority's disestablishment. If Jews are chiefly responsible for the present grinding assault on the nation's racial backbone, then the Jewish minority must come under public scrutiny. America could survive forever without Jews. It could not last a day without the Majority.

Meanwhile, the cyclic reckoning which has marked the rhythm of Jewish survival in the past closes in on American Jewry. Although the accumulation and preservation of Jewish wealth are only feasible in an orderly society where private property is a right, not a crime, Jews seem bent on destroying the very political, economic and social climate that has made their success possible.[134] As if in the grip of a lemming-like frenzy, they have been in the forefront of every divisive force of the modern era, from class agitation to minority racism, from the worst capitalistic exploitation to

---

was shot to death during the arrest, but the ADL escaped the usual investigation given any individual or group involved in homicide. *Los Angeles Times,* Feb. 13, 1970. As for the B'nai B'rith itself, which was founded in 1843 and headed by a Grand Saar, it has 205,000 male members in 1350 lodges in forty-three countries and 130,000 female members in 600 chapters. Edward Grusd, *B'nai B'rith,* Appleton-Century, New York, 1966, pp. 283, 286. The B'nai B'rith is the only private agency to have been given official "consultation status" by the United Nations, where it acts as a strong lobby for Israel and other Jewish interests. *New York Times,* May 28, 1970, p. 21.

134. The final effect of collectivist or welfare-state economics on Jewry has been completely misunderstood not only by most Jews but by most anti-Semites. After the Communist regime in Russia had confiscated Jewish fortunes and outlawed finance capitalism, Russian Jews had none of the usual Jewish defenses to fall back on when Stalin decided to turn against them—no Jewish-owned press, no Jewish-oriented public opinion, no lavishly financed network of Jewish societies. Today in the Soviet Union, a country largely created by Jewish thought and Jewish revolutionary activity, Zionism is a crime and Jews have practically disappeared from high public office. See Chapter 25.

the most brutal collectivism, from blind religious orthodoxy to atheism and psychoanalysis, from total dogmatism to total permissiveness.

Moreover, as Jewish domination has become more pronounced, so has Jewish separateness—a dangerous trend for a minority which prospers best by concealing its differences. Such recent historical stimuli as Nazi anti-Semitism, the Israeli experience and the stepped-up tempo of social disintegration have filled the Jewish stockpile of race consciousness to overflowing. The appearance of ever more Jews in the top strata of public life inevitably produces a greater amount of Jewish self-identification, as well as a far greater awareness of Jews on the part of non-Jews. Intensified publicity, while revealing the extreme cultivation of a few Jews, also calls more attention to such unattractive Jewish traits as intrusiveness, disputatiousness and haggling, and to the incredible garishness which permeates the Catskills, Miami Beach, Las Vegas and other centers of Jewish resort life.

The same racial dynamics which have sporadically propelled Jews to the top of the social heap have also cast them down into the abyss. The penduluming, rags-to-riches swing of Jewish history may lead to the fairyland castles of the Rothschilds, but it also may lead to the barbed wire of Auschwitz. When viewed objectively, the story of Jewish wanderings through time is both fascinating and repulsive, ennobling and degrading—in part comic, in great part tragic.

The only last word that can be said about Jews is that there is no last word. Jews are such a mass of contradictions and encompass such extremes of human behavior that they are simply beyond the reach of pat formulas, casual generalizations or prophetic clichés. They are both the "People of the Book" and the inventors of the strip tease.[135] They were pioneers of plutocracy *and* communism. They originated and lived by the concept of the "Chosen People," yet are presently the most vociferous of anti-racists. They are the most God-fearing and God-hating, the most straitlaced and the most permissive, the most cosmopolitan and most narrow-minded, the most cultivated and the most vulgar of peoples.

---

135. *New York Times,* Feb. 25, 1937, p. 10.

Jewish sabras in Israel fight like ten thousand Lawrences of Arabia, but in Germany their brethren went like lambs to the slaughter.[136] Ironically, many of the greatest Jews, perhaps the very greatest, have been Jewish renegades or pseudo-Jews.[137]

Through all this mountain of inconsistency there glimmers but one thin, barely visible vein of logic. The Jewish nervous system bears the load of many passions, but always noticeable are traces of an implacable hostility to the peoples who at different times have sheltered and persecuted them, enriched and impoverished them, deified and satanized them. The Jewish fascination for political, economic and social experiments may not be, as often supposed, proof of a noble, unselfish desire to radically improve or save mankind by a race of professional Messiahs, but of a firmly-rooted, semiconscious, semi-coordinated vendetta—Bacon called it a "secret inbred rancour" [138]—against all things non-Jewish and, in the final countdown, possibly all things Jewish as well.

If the past is an indication, if what Acton said about individuals is applicable to groups, a sharp reduction of the Jewish racial vector is in the offing. This could be achieved most easily and most painlessly by assimilation. But there are few, if any, signs of this on the horizon. The three thousand-year record of Jewish non-assimilation has only

136. Jewish docility in Hitler's concentration camps has aroused the ire of militant Jews, particularly Israelis. "But why," asks an article in a prominant Jewish magazine, "was there no resistance? . . . At Auschwitz the ratio of prisoners to guards varied from 20 to 1 to 35 to 1. [Yet] the Jews meekly accepted every successive order which rendered them impotent, they queued up for the deportation trains. . . ." *Commentary*, April, 1962, p. 354.

137. Renegades in that they embraced Christianity (Berenson, Disraeli, Heine, Husserl, Mahler, Mendelssohn, St. Peter and St. Paul) or turned openly atheist (Marx, Trotsky and other leading dialectical materialists). The possibility that Moses was an Egyptian and the fact that Josephus was a turncoat have been previously mentioned. Spinoza, the greatest Jewish philosopher, was expelled from the Jewish community in Amsterdam in 1656 by Rabbinical order. Many Orthodox Jews and anti-Semites agree—or hope—that Jesus was not Jewish because he came from "Galilee of the Gentiles." A prevailing Talmudic tradition has it that Jesus was the adulterous offspring of Joseph Panthera, a Roman Centurion, and Miriam, the wife of a carpenter. *Jüdische Enzyklopädie*, Jüdischer Verlag, Berlin, 1930, Band IV/1, pp. 772–3.

138. *New Atlantis*, Great Books, Chicago, 1952, Vol. 30, p. 209.

been broken once.[139] One alternative to assimilation is repression, of which history provides many forms—Egyptian bondage, Assyrian and Babylonian captivities, mass deportations, forced baptism, ghetto quarantine, Russian pogroms and German concentration camps.

When and if a resuscitated American Majority has the strength and the will to put a stop to the Jewish envelopment of America, history should not be repeated. The operation ought to be accomplished with a finesse that is a credit to both parties. The guiding purpose should be moral as well as cultural and political—to transcend, for the first time, the ancient racial infighting by facing the issue with the head and the heart, not the club.

Solutions to massive problems require every drop of reason and imagination that exists in the overflowing well of the human spirit. Separation is obviously part of the solution. But how can this most delicate of all social operations be performed successfully? How can it be brought off without unbearable dislocations in the lands of exodus and intolerable sacrifices in the lands of the ingathering?

Theoretically, the answer is Israel. But Israel is the sputtering fuse of World War III.

---

139. See footnote 8, p. 59.

Chapter 16

Nonwhite Minorities

THE MEXICANS: The typical Mexican is neither Spanish nor Asian, white nor yellow.[1] Although Spanish-speaking and the heir of a laminate of Spanish culture, he does not dream of Spain and the glories of the Spanish past. He is conscious of no ties to Eastern Asia, the home of his Indian ancestors. Primarily a mestizo, a Spanish–Indian hybrid, the Mexican considers himself a unique racial specimen.

Aside from the genetic distinction, where Mexicans differ most from their northern neighbors is in the art of living. With its fiestas and flowers, its ancient and modern art forms, its rich and varied resources, its rugged *mesetas* and *barrancas* and its exuberant tropic beaches, Mexico adds grace and beauty to an increasingly drab world. After the revolutions and counterrevolutions of the early twentieth century, an intense wave of nativism swept over the country, bringing with it such cultural splendors as the mural painting of Orozco, certainly the most magnificent and the most dazzling pictorial art to come out of the New World. The sworn enemy of this art is the Madison Avenue and Hollywood *kitsch* exported to Mexico from the United States, a spurious culture which vulgarizes and degrades exporters and importers alike.

---

1. *Focus,* a publication of the National Geographic Society, states the population of Mexico is 55 percent mestizo, 29 percent Indian, 15 percent European and under 1 percent Negro and Mulatto. To the casual visitor the European estimate appears high. Certainly the mestizo element accounts for the overwhelming proportion of Mexican-Americans.

As of 1969, there were said to be 5,073,000 Mexican-Americans in the United States—almost all in California, Texas, Colorado and the Southwest.² Eighty-five percent are *pochos* or native-born citizens, as distinguished from *cholos* or newcomers. Although 600,000 are concentrated in East Los Angeles and 350,000 in San Antonio, most Mexican–Americans are still agriculturally minded and furnish a badly needed source of "stoop" labor in the Imperial and San Joaquin valleys of California, now the nation's richest farming areas. Members of the second largest nonwhite minority, Mexican-Americans are often less educated and poorer than Negroes. Their school drop-out rate is 34 percent in grades 7 to 12 in Texas. Their per capita income is $1,380 in the Los Angeles area, compared to $1,437 for other nonwhites.³ Even so, the educational and economic status of Mexican-Americans is far superior to that of Mexicans in Mexico.

Forever unassimilable because of their pigmentation, Mexican-Americans accentuate their minority status by holding fast to their language (vast stretches of the American Southwest are now Spanish-speaking), by bloc voting (90 percent Democratic) ⁴ and by their political agitation and unioneering. Emulating Negroes, Mexican-Americans had their first "Brown Power" conference in Sacramento, California, in 1967.⁵ In the California valleys and in Los Angeles

2. *Persons of Spanish Origin,* Census Bureau, pp. 4–5. This estimate excludes 250,000 Hispanos in New Mexico who have developed and are perpetuating a Spanish-speaking subculture as assimilation proof as that of Mexican-Americans, from whom they differ little racially. A self-appointed leader, Reies Tijerina, tried to capitalize on Hispano minority feelings when he led an armed raid on a New Mexico courthouse and kidnapped several state employees. Tijerina, a Mexican-American born in El Paso, was dramatizing Hispano claims for lands allegedly stolen by the United States. A combination of Don Quixote and Rap Brown, Tijerina was quickly arrested; but he was acquitted in 1968 by a local jury. He was later sent to jail for assaulting two forest rangers. *San Francisco Sunday Examiner, This World,* Dec. 22, 1968, p. 24 and *New York Times,* Aug. 30, 1970.

3. *New York Times,* April 20, 1969, p. 54.

4. A solid bloc of Mexican-American votes, some from voters long dead, won Lyndon Johnson the hotly disputed 1948 senatorial primary in Texas at a crucial moment in his political career. See p. 415.

5. *San Francisco Sunday Examiner & Chronicle,* March 19, 1967, p. 6. The Ford Foundation supports two Mexican-American racial protective organizations—the Mexican-American Legal Defense and Educational Fund and the Southwest Conference of La Raza.

and Denver *barrios*[6] there have already been a few serious confrontations with Anglos, but according to one view, "The *Chicano* (Mexican-American) revolt against the Anglo establishment is still in the planning stage." [7] Mexican-American ethnocentrism is otherwise nourished by constant reminders of American aggression against Mexico and by a demagoguery which holds that Mexican-Americans are now second-class citizens in a part of North America that once belonged to their forefathers.

There is a distinct possibility, if the legal and illegal seepage of Mexican genes across the Rio Grande and the high Mexican-American birthrate continue at present levels, that Mexican-Americans will regain their lost territories of Alta California and Texas—already being called the Serape Belt—not by violence or minority politics but simply by exercising squatters' rights.

The Chinese: The first large contingent of Chinese immigrants (13,100) arrived in California in 1854.[8] Of an utterly alien civilization and totally unfamiliar with the American environment, the Chinese started out under the most severe cultural and economic handicaps. They built railroad beds throughout the West, painstakingly worked placer mines and provided much of the household help. The pigtailed Chinaman in the backroom was an institution that endured in San Francisco for more than half a century.

Once the gold boom had subsided and the railroads were running, Congress responded to pressure from Westerners fearful of the competition of coolie labor and of the rising tide of color (123,201 Chinese arrived in California in the 1870's) by passing the Exclusion Act of 1882. It was Congress' first try at immigration legislation and preceded the establishment of white quotas by almost forty years.[9]

The 1970 Federal Census listed 435,062 Americans of Chinese extraction, of whom 52,039 resided in the Hawaiian

---

6. Denver is the headquarters of a Mexican-American movement whose symbol is a three-dimensional head representing Spanish father, Indian mother and mestizo offspring.

7. *New York Times,* April 20, 1969, p. 1.

8. Davie, *World Immigration,* p. 308.

9. *Ibid.,* p. 313.

Islands. The Chinese almost doubled in size between 1960 and 1970, partly due to the Johnson Immigration Act, which released the Chinese, as it did all Asians, from racial and national, though not geographical, quotas. In spite of the new flow of Chinese immigration, the present ratio of the Chinese minorities to the rest of the population (0.21 percent) is not likely to register any significant jump. If relations with mainland China continue to stabilize, Chinese-Americans may once again begin their vintage-year, homebound voyages across the Pacific, a *westward* migration which until recently managed to keep their rate of growth below that of most other minorities.

Chinese-Americans are the prime example of the self-sufficient, static minority. Although once the victims of almost intolerable persecution and discrimination,[10] they have now buried their old resentments instead of taking them out in racial agitation and minority lobbying.[11] Rather proud of their hyphenated status, they keep their family names, they keep many of their Far Eastern ways, and they keep to themselves. Their lives are characterized by a subdued, middle-class morality and respectability. When most other nonwhite minorities move into an urban area, it usually deteriorates into a slum. Chinese enclaves, on the other hand, become centers of attraction. San Francisco's Chinatown, the largest concentration of Chinese in the New World, is one of the cleanest and best-maintained sections of the city. Once the battleground of rival tongs it now boasts a relatively low incidence of crime and juvenile delinquency, though there was one gang slaying in 1977.

The Chinese minority, at least in the continental United States, is by any standard of race relations the ideal minority. It gives more than it takes. It preserves and develops its own

10. The entire Chinese population of 1,000 was ruthlessly driven out of Truckee, California, in 1878. The previous year in San Francisco there was almost open warfare between the Irish and the Chinese. Davie, *op. cit.*, pp. 311–2.

11. In Hawaii, where nonwhites are in the majority, the Chinese are more politically active, as demonstrated by the presence in the U.S. Senate of liberal Republican, Hiram Fong. In the continental U.S., the Chinese minority, like the Japanese minority, stands apart from the liberal-minority coalition by often voting for conservative candidates and taking an aggressive stand against the busing of school children.

culture without seeking to impose it on others. Above all, it does not ask for special treatment. In fact, in all the bright serenity of the Chinese-American future there is only one small note of gloom. If revolutionary or racial fervor should induce China to launch a military attack against the United States, the position of the Chinese minority might become as tenuous as that of the Japanese in World War II.

The Japanese: Much of what has been written about Chinese-Americans applies to Japanese-Americans, or at least to those Japanese-Americans in the continental United States. The Japanese came to America later than the Chinese, but they encountered the same hostility. Although Japan itself had banned all foreigners for two hundred and thirty years (1638–1868), except for a few Dutch, and had forbidden its citizens to go abroad on pain of death, the Japanese government objected strongly to Congressional plans to include Japanese in the ban against Chinese immigration.[12] To soothe Japanese pride, President Theodore Roosevelt negotiated a "Gentleman's Agreement" in 1907, by which Japan agreed to halt the Japanese exodus, provided Congress passed no restrictive immigration legislation that mentioned the Japanese by name.[13] By 1940 there were some 140,000 Japanese in the continental United States, 86 percent of them in the Far West, where many had become prosperous truck farmers.[14] In 1970, counting those in Hawaii, there were 591,290 Japanese-Americans.

Shortly after Pearl Harbor, which displayed the dangers of Japanese military bravado, 110,000 West Coast Japanese (70,000 of them U.S. citizens) were removed from their homes, farms and businesses and transported to Colorado "relocation camps," at an average loss of $10,000 per family.[15] The Japanese in Hawaii, where their proportion to the population was much larger and their potential threat to national security much greater, were left in comparative peace. In 1944 the 442nd Regimental Combat Team, composed largely

---

12. Davie, *op. cit.,* pp. 318–21.   13. *Ibid.,* p. 321.   14. *Ibid.,* p. 324.
15 Simpson and Yinger, *op. cit.,* pp. 132–3. After the war, claims were settled at an average rate of 10 cents on the dollar. *Washington Post,* Oct. 5, 1965, p. 1.

of Nisei, second-generation Japanese-Americans from Oahu, was sent to fight crack German troops in the Italian campaign and proceeded to rack up one of the finest records in American military annals.

Quiet and unobtrusive on the mainland, where many vote Republican, Japanese play racial politics with a vengeance in the Hawaiian Islands where, as the largest population group, they vote Democratic.[16] Hawaii's two Representatives in Congress are Japanese, as are Senator Daniel Inouye and Governor George Ariyoshi. Such bloc voting belies the claim there are no racial tensions in Hawaii. The fact is that until recently the 50th state was a territory and was ruled with a strong hand by the dominant white traders and planters and the United States Armed Forces.[17] Since the more vociferous American minorities are not found in large numbers in Hawaii, the headline-making variety of minority agitation was and is largely absent. But it does not follow that racism is non-existent or that in the future there will not be a bitter power struggle among the various population groups. Island paradises are no exception to the laws of racial dynamics.

Other Pacific Ocean and Asian Minorities: The population statistics in footnote 16 demonstrate the unfolding of a racial tragedy in Hawaii. One of America's most colorful and romantic minorities, the Polynesian, is rapidly becoming extinct. Perhaps only 12,000 pure Hawaiians remain. At present a concerted effort is being made to save them by maintaining a subsidized refuge on the island of Niihau, where they live in voluntary quarantine from whites and Asians, still speak the old Hawaiian tongue and are without benefit of telephones, television, motion pictures, automobiles or liquor stores.

Another nonwhite minority largely concentrated in Hawaii is the Filipino. Of the 205,073 Filipino-Americans only

16. The 1970 Federal Census showed 768,561 people in Hawaii, divided as follows: White, 298,160; Japanese, 217,307; Hawaiian and part-Hawaiian, 98,441; Filipino, 93,915; Chinese, 52,039; Negroes, 7,573; Other, 1,126. Many of the whites belong to transient military families.

17. National defense is Hawaii's largest industry. Tourism is second, sugar third, pineapples fourth.

111,000 reside in the continental United States. Filipinos once had easy entry to America when the Philippine Islands were an American possession, but they came under quota restrictions after they were given independence in 1946.[18] Other Mongoloid or semi-Mongoloid minorities, so small in number and so lacking in influence as to be practically invisible, are the Koreans and Indonesians (recent Asian immigrants) and the Eskimos and Aleuts (ancient Asian immigrants).[19] Questions concerning the assimilation probability of all these groups are best answered by Kipling's celebrated poetic dictum.

The American Indians: There are several theories concerning the racial origin of the American Indians, the most common being that they are descendants of fur-wearing, spear-carrying, mammoth-eating Mongolian tribesmen who island-hopped or perhaps walked across the Bering Sea some twenty thousand years ago, when part of it was a grassy plain. A few dissident anthropologists point to the possibility of a partial descent from Polynesians and Melanesians who may have reached the New World from Easter Island. There are also legends of refugees from Atlantis and the lost continent of Mu, and of shipwrecked sailors from Chinese junks washing ashore in Central and South America.[20] The pockets of puzzling A_1 blood group may be accounted for by Australoid elements, and there is even the possibility of far-off kinship with the segregated Ainus of Japan.

In the year 1500, North America (above the Rio Grande) contained an estimated 850,000 Indians.[21] By 1860, the Indian population of the United States had decreased to

---

18. Filipino immigration has recently picked up again in consequence of the preferred status the Johnson Act gives to citizens' wives and relations. See p. 47.

19. The Aleuts were members of the early migration from Siberia, but they never went further than the Aleutian Islands. There, 150 years ago, Russian fur traders found 25,000 of their descendants. When the Russians departed, there were only 2,950 Aleuts left. *Ency. Brit.,* Vol. 1, p. 565.

20. *The American Heritage Book of Indians,* 1961, pp. 9, 25.

21. *Our American Indians at a Glance,* Pacific Coast Publications, Menlo Park, California, 1961, p. 6.

44,000,[22] a decline which seemed to bear out the theory of the Vanishing American and historian Arnold Toynbee's half truth that the English-speaking peoples colonized by dispossession and genocide.[23] But today, according to the 1970 Federal Census, the United States has almost 800,000 Indians and the number is increasing each year. Of these, 70 percent live in 399 government reservations.[24]

The Indians of North America never formed the basis of a mestizo population as did the Indians of Latin America. The English settler, who often brought his family with him, was not as prone to miscegenation as the lonely Spanish soldier. Moreover, North American Indians were hunters, nomads and isolated farmer and fisher folk—less adept at the art of socializing than the more urban agglomerates of the Aztec and Incan empires. This is not to suggest, however, that there was no interbreeding of Indians with trappers, traders and other white "squaw men" in the West and with Negro runaways in Southern states.[25] One way of explaining what happened is to say that Southern European miscegenation in Latin America diluted the white stock, whereas Northern European miscegenation in North America diluted the Indian stock.

Indian history furnishes an excellent confirmation of the axiom that racial tension diminishes as the physical distance between races lengthens. In frontier days, despite Rousseau's well-publicized notion of the "noble savage" and Cooper's Plutarchian Mohicans, Indians were regarded as the lowest

---

22. Coon, *The Living Races of Man*, p. 307. Today the most numerous Indian tribe is the Navajo, with a population of 80,000. In 1860, the number of Navajos was 12,000.

23. *A Study of History*, Vol. V, p. 46. In the same exaggerated vein, Toynbee could have described the eternal warfare between many nomadic Indian tribes as equally genocidal.

24. *Time*, Sept. 3, 1965, p. 72. An Indian author, Vine Deloria, Jr., estimates there are 1,000,000 Indians in the U.S.—400,000 on reservations, 500,000 living in Eastern cities and 100,000 scattered throughout Eastern rural areas. *New York Times Magazine*, Dec. 7, 1969.

25. At least two hundred communities in the Eastern U.S. consist largely of triracial hybrids of mixed Indian, Negro and white ancestry. Coon, *op. cit.*, p. 307. Madison Grant estimated that half the American Indian population has some white blood.

and most debased of humanoids.[26] Now that there is little or no contact with them, they are flattered and cozened by new friends, the today generation of eleemosynary ideologues, and forgotten by erstwhile foes. Indeed, it has become a commonplace—and a measure of his depreciating race consciousness—for a white Westerner to boast of his "Indian blood." Not too much, of course, but enough to conjure up visions of wide open spaces and Remington scouts. *Halfbreed*, at one time the most contemptuous expression in the language, has been thinned down to so anemic a pejorative that it hardly raises a glint in the eye.

If present minority vociferousness were proportionate to past suffering, Indians would be quite justified in being the most clamorous of all American population groups. Once the sole and undisputed ruler of all he surveyed, the Indian has both fallen and been lowered to the bottom of the American social scale, where he still remains. He was herded onto reservations, dosed with alcohol, decimated by smallpox and only given full citizenship rights in 1924—rights which he still has trouble exercising. In 1966, the average Indian had the lowest income of any American, an unemployment rate of nearly 40 percent, housing 90 percent below accepted standards and a life expectancy twenty-one years less than that of the general population.[27] Reservation Indians are still the wards of the Bureau of Indian Affairs, an organization of 16,000 government functionaries distinguished by a long record of administrative ineptitude.[28]

Taking their cue from the more dynamic minorities, Indians have recently made some efforts to close ranks. But they still speak more than a hundred different languages and belong to more than 250 tribes.[29] As they were seldom able

---

26. In 1866, three years after Lincoln had freed the slaves, an Arizona county was still offering $250 for an Apache scalp. *American Heritage Book of Indians*, p. 384. Francis Parkman's detailed description of Indian cannibalism and Indian habits of torturing white prisoners of both sexes makes the reactions of white settlers to their Red neighbors more understandable. *The Works of Francis Parkman*, Little, Brown, Boston, 1892, Vol. III, especially Chapter XVIII.

27. *Time*, March 15, 1968, p. 20.

28. *San Francisco Examiner, This World*, April 14, 1968, p. 19.

29. The sacking of the Indian Bureau offices in Washington and the 1973 "uprising" at Wounded Knee, while proving Indian racism was on the uptake, were conclusive proof of White House pusillanimity.

to unite when the white man was evicting them from their fields and hunting grounds, their endemic tribalism will surely continue to hamper the organization of any effective national lobby. The last major attempt at an Indian revival was the Ghost Dance religion (1889–90), when Wovoka, a Paiute medicine man, promised the return of the Golden Age. Million-footed herds of bison would repopulate the prairies. The dead chiefs and braves would rise up and go on one final war path. The paleface would be rooted out of the land. The movement was easily put down by the Seventh Cavalry.[30]

Noblesse oblige demands that respect be accorded the oldest Americans, the majority that has become a minority, the sole American population group with a non-derivative culture. The Indian, although he has not always measured up to his role, is the tragic hero of the American epic. He was the enemy for more than 250 years.[31] It is only fitting that the honors of defeat should provide both for his physical survival and his spiritual continuity.

The Puerto Ricans: The original Puerto Ricans were 20,000 to 50,000 Arawak Indians who died off in the sixteenth century after a few unsuccessful revolts against the Spaniards who had been overworking them in the gold mines. The void in the labor supply was filled by Negro slaves from Africa. In consequence, many Puerto Ricans have Negro branches in their family trees, and since those who have migrated to the United States derive largely from the poorer elements of the population—in direct contrast to the recent Cuban immigration—their dark coloration and frequency of Negroid traits not only render them unassimilable, but make it difficult not to confuse them with blacks.[32]

---

30. *Ibid.*, p. 371.

31. The Indian wars came to an end in 1891 with the final pacification of the Sioux. *Ibid.*, p. 400. Compared to the struggle with the Indians, American wars against France and Britain in the colonial period and against Britain, Mexico, Spain, Germany, Japan, North Korea and North Vietnam in the nineteenth and twentieth centuries were relatively brief.

32. The 1950 Federal Census found 1,762,411 whites and 446,948 Negroes in Puerto Rico. The 1960 Census, which omitted a racial breakdown

As American citizens, Puerto Ricans come under no immigration quota. With few legal complications impeding their entry and with an extremely high birthrate, Americans of Puerto Rican descent now total 1,454,000, many of whom live in New York's Spanish Harlem.[33] Like the Mexicans, Puerto Ricans have brought with them a skin-deep Spanish culture which has little in common with the original except the language. Also like the Mexicans, Puerto Ricans generally vote *en bloc* for Democratic political candidates. To lose no time in garnering these votes, politicians have changed the literacy test for voters by permitting it to be taken in Spanish. As a result, Puerto Ricans can now arrive in New York City without speaking or reading a word of English, go on relief and with minimum delay cast their ballots in local and national elections.

Coming from one of the world's most beautiful islands and friendliest climates, Puerto Ricans somehow manage to adapt to one of the world's ugliest slum areas and cruelest weather zones. Their economic status approaches that of the Negro, whom they look down upon in spite of their own part-African ancestry. Those who break the language barrier, however, soon surpass blacks in most levels of achievement.

Puerto Ricans in Puerto Rico, now a Commonwealth of the United States, are too proud for statehood, but not proud enough for independence. A streak of fervent nationalism which runs through some segments of the population motivated one band of Puerto Rican "patriots" to attempt to assassinate President Truman in 1950 and another to shoot five Congressmen in 1954. Whether the separatist feelings of second- and third-generation Puerto Ricans in New York City will subside or whether their political alliance with non-Spanish-speaking blacks will develop into a racial and cultural merger cannot be forecast at this time. What can be predicted is that they stand no more chance of being assimilated than their Harlem neighbors.

of the population in Puerto Rico, counted most Puerto Ricans in the U.S. as whites.

33. *Persons of Spanish Origin*, Census Bureau, 1969, pp. 3–4.

Chapter 17

The Negroes

THE NEGRO MINORITY, the largest and most violent
minority, merits a special chapter because it confronts the
United States with a problem which seems beyond solution.
Fanned and overheated by both black and white agitators
for often different ideological purposes, Negro racism has
now reached the point where it has literally grounded the
once soaring American *Zeitgeist* and is threatening to muti-
late it beyond recognition. For the first time since the pacification of the Indians, who themselves are resorting to localized
violence, some self-anointed leaders of a minority are seriously talking about taking up arms against the authority of
the state. Simultaneously, there is multiplying within the
Negro community a large criminal caste and an even larger
caste of welfare recipients and dehumanized drug addicts.

The first Negroes to arrive in the British possessions in
North America were twenty indentured servants who disem-
barked from a Dutch ship in Jamestown, Virginia, in 1619.[1]
Blacks, it is evident, have been in America as long as the
Majority and longer than all other minorities except the
Indian. Overwhelmed by the white culture, Negroes quickly
traded their tribal dialects for English, their tribal gods for
Christianity and their tribal names for those of their white
masters. But they could not trade their skin.

---

1. Brewton Berry, *Race and Ethnic Relations,* Houghton Mifflin, Boston,
1958, p. 104.

Negro slavery, one of the oldest and most enduring of human institutions, was introduced into the New World at the behest of the pious Christian bishop, Bartolomé de las Casas, who urged that only Negroes could survive the yoke of peonage the Spaniards and Portuguese had fastened on the Indians.[2] Slavery did not become big business in the United States until the stirrings of the Industrial Revolution. When cotton became king and Blake's "dark Satanic mills" began to scar the landscapes of New and Old England, only Negroes were willing, able or available to endure the rigors of field work on Southern plantations.

Contrary to conspiratorial theories of Negro history, which blame black misfortunes entirely on whites, African tribal chiefs played a key role in the slave trade. They were the procurement agents who rounded up neighboring tribesmen, as well as many of their own subjects, and marched them off to white-owned slave ships.[3] Rum was the staple article of this dubious commerce and passed for currency on the African West Coast. There, according to Charles Beard, "to slake their fierce appetite, [Negroes] would sell their enemies, their friends, their mothers, fathers, wives, daughters, and sons for New England's scalding potion."[4]

Slavery was the inhumanity of the white man to the black man. But it was also the inhumanity of the black man to his own kind. For many Negroes transportation to America was simply giving up one form of servitude for another. Often it was a fortuitous escape from starvation, disease, human sacrifice and cannibalism. Whites who feel most guilt-ridden about slavery should also take into account that, although it has been proscribed for more than a century in the United States, it is still prevalent in Africa. In the 1960's,

---

2. Davie, *op. cit.*, p. 587. De las Casas' proposal was adopted too late. Almost all the natives of the large West Indian Islands were wiped out before the arrival of their replacements.

3. Negro historian John Hope Franklin points out, "Slavery was an important function of African social and economic life." *From Slavery to Freedom*, Knopf, New York, 1967, p. 31. One of the favorite roundup methods was to set fire to a village by night and capture the fleeing inhabitants. *Ency. Brit.*, Vol. 20, p. 780.

4. *Rise of American Civilization*, Vol. 1, pp. 93–4. The slaves were transported in ships from which the hogsheads had been temporarily removed.

$5.60 would buy a healthy, half-caste baby in Somaliland and $2,200 an attractive young girl in the Sudan.[5]

The slavery question began to divide Americans from the very moment of their independence. The best minds of the day—Franklin, Patrick Henry, Washington, Hamilton, Jefferson, Madison—were opposed to slavery but unwilling to come to grips with it because of the greater urgency of unifying the young republic. Opposition to slavery, it should be realized, did not necessarily signify a belief in the equality preached so eloquently in the Declaration of Independence. Thomas Jefferson, the author of most of that document, suggested that "blacks, whether originally a distinct race, or made distinct by time and circumstances, are inferior to the whites in the endowments both of body and mind."

Jefferson was particularly pessimistic about Negro intellectual proficiency. "Comparing them by their faculties of memory, reason, and imagination, it appears to me that in memory they are equal to the whites; in reason much inferior, as I think one could scarcely be found capable of tracing and comprehending the investigations of Euclid; and that in imagination they are dull, tasteless, and anomalous. . . . They astonish you with strokes of the most sublime oratory. . . . But never yet could I find that a black had uttered a thought above the level of plain narration. . . ."[6]

After the slavery issue had reached the inflammatory stage, Maryland-born Chief Justice Roger B. Taney, writing the majority opinion in the Dred Scott decision (1857),

---

5. Sean O'Callaghan, *The Slave Trade Today,* as reviewed in *San Francisco Chronicle, This World,* May 27, 1962.

6. *The Life and Selected Writings of Thomas Jefferson,* Modern Library, New York, pp. 257–8, 262. Jefferson was all for Negro emancipation, but warned that the black "when freed . . . is to be removed beyond the reach of mixture." *Ibid.,* p. 262. How Jefferson's ideas were edited to fit modern liberal notions of equalitarianism is shown by the inscription on the Jefferson Memorial in Washington, which reads, "Nothing is more certainly written in the book of fate than that these people are to be free." The stone mason put a period in place of the original semicolon. Jefferson's sentence continued, "nor is it less certain that the two races, equally free, cannot live under the same government." Putnam, *Race and Reason,* p. 62. Washington, whose concern for Negroes was not as verbal as Jefferson's, but perhaps more generous, arranged for his slaves to be freed at his death. Jefferson, who at one time had as many as 212, did not.

took judicial notice that Negroes were "beings of an inferior order." [7] Abraham Lincoln was another non-believer in the genetic equality of Negroes. In fact, he was firmly committed to the separation of the two races and a strong supporter of the Illinois law which made marriage between whites and Negroes a crime.[8]

In 1790, there were 697,624 Negro slaves and 59,557 free Negroes in the United States; in 1860, on the eve of the Civil War, 3,953,760 Negro slaves and 488,000 free Negroes.[9] Slavery was abominable to the body and spirit, but as the more than five-fold increase in the slave population in seventy years demonstrated, it was hardly genocide. Since Congress had outlawed the slave trade in 1808, most of the increase could only be accounted for by Negro fecundity.

The enormous casualties of the Civil War are proof that the curse of slavery descended on whites as well as blacks. After the war had ended and slavery was abolished by the 13th Amendment, twenty Negro representatives and two Negro senators were sent to Congress and Southern state capitals were filled with Negro officeholders and office seekers. For a time there was a distinct possibility that Northern military power and vindictiveness plus Negro numbers and Southern demoralization might change the color of Southern civilization. But Southern whites went underground and formed the Ku Klux Klan, whose night-riding troops taught

---

7. See p. 388.
8. Benjamin Quarles, *Lincoln and the Negro*, Oxford University Press, New York, 1962, pp. 36-7. In one of the 1858 Lincoln-Douglas debates Lincoln was quoted as saying: "What I would most desire would be the separation of the white and black races." In 1862 Lincoln called a group of free Negroes to the White House to explain the reasons behind one of his pet projects, the colonizing of people of African descent. "We have between us a broader difference than exists between almost any other two races . . . this physical difference is a great disadvantage to us both. . . . Your race suffers very greatly, many of them, by living among us, while ours suffers from your presence. . . . If this is to be admitted, it affords a reason, at least, why we should be separated." Carl Sandburg, *Abraham Lincoln, The War Years*, Harcourt Brace, New York, 1939, Vol. 1, p. 574. For a summary of Lincoln's attitudes toward Negroes, see the statement of Ludwell H. Johnson, Associate Professor of History at William and Mary College, in Putnam, *Race and Reality*, pp. 134-7.
9. Franklin, *op. cit.*, pp. 186, 217.

the occupational forces and their white and black collaborators a few things about terror tactics and guerrilla warfare.

The North, ever more immersed in financial speculation and industrial expansion, finally grew weary of trying to enforce equality where none existed. President Rutherford B. Hayes, a moderate Republican, withdrew the last Federal troops in 1877 and the South was returned to the Southerners. The Negro sank back into serfdom and sharecropping, and the Supreme Court acknowledged the constitutionality of postbellum segregation in the "separate but equal" doctrine of *Plessy vs. Ferguson* (1896).

A casual visitor to Mississippi or Alabama at the end of the century might have been forgiven for thinking that except for a few legal formalities slavery had been reinstituted. But the Industrial Revolution, now in its middle stages, was preparing to wrench Negro destiny in a new direction. America's entry into World War I was accompanied by a great shortage of industrial manpower. Tens of thousands of Negro tenant farmers and hired hands heard the call and began a mass migration to Northern cities which is still continuing, though at a slower clip. In 1900, ninety percent of the Negro population lived below the Mason-Dixon line. In 1970, almost half of America's 22,580,000 Negroes lived outside the South.[10]

The transformation of a considerable segment of the Negro minority into an urban population ended the blacks' political isolation and brought them for the first time within reach of the liberal-minority coalition which has dominated American politics for most of this century. In the North, and only much later in the South, Negroes were taught the secret of bloc voting.[11] As political careers became more dependent on these votes, citadel after citadel of white resistance began to crumble. Equally effective in the success of the civil rights

---

10. The current migration rate is 100,000 a year. As late as 1950, according to the Census Bureau, seven out of ten American Negroes lived in the South. In spite of the Negro exodus, however, the South's population is still 19 percent black, as against 11 percent for the U.S. population as a whole.

11. In the 1964 presidential election, Negroes voted 95 percent for Lyndon Johnson. *Time*, Nov. 4, 1964, p. 4. The vote is almost unanimous for Negro candidates in local, state and Congressional elections where opposing candidates are white.

or Black Power movement were the huge financial contributions of the foundations, churches and affluent white minority
organizations, as well as the legal maneuvering and lobbying
of Negro organizations financed and in large part directed
by white liberals and Jews.[12] The Supreme Court lent a helping
hand by striking down the poll tax and literacy tests, two
political safeguards which the South had erected against any
recurrence of the Black Power of Reconstruction days.

By the late 1950's, it appeared the Civil War was going
to be fought over again in miniature. Freedom marchers,
federal marshals, Department of Justice attorneys, preachers, teachers, leftists, ultra-liberals—in short a whole new
generation of carpetbaggers—converged on the South both
to contain and spread the violence which greeted the Supreme Court's school desegregation decision (1954). But
times—and geopolitics—had changed. The squalid desolation of the Northern ghettos was a daily reminder that the

---

12. Julius Rosenwald of Sears, Roebuck was for years the biggest financial contributor to the Negro cause. The first president of the Urban League,
the second largest Negro organization, was banker Edwin Seligman. For the
past twenty-five years, the president of the National Association for the Advancement of Colored People (450,673 dues-paying members and $3,300,-
000 annual income, as of 1969) has been Jewish. Current president is
Kivie Kaplan, 58 members of whose family hold $500 life memberships.
Present head of the NAACP legal defense fund is Jack Greenberg. Yaffe,
op. cit., p. 257, and Arnold Rose, *The Negro in America*, Beacon, Boston,
1961, p. 267. Before he was assassinated by black separatists, Negro activist
Malcolm X wrote, "I gave the Jew credit for being among all other whites
the most active, and the most vocal, financier, 'leader' and 'liberal' in the
Negro civil rights movement." *Autobiography of Malcolm X*, p. 372. Jewish
intellectual and financial support was just as generous to radical Negro
organizations as it had been to the Urban League and the NAACP. Such
groups as CORE and SNCC practically lived off Jewish contributions. In
January, 1970, Leonard Bernstein held a party in his Park Avenue apartment and raised $3,000, to which he added the fee from his next concert,
for twenty-one Black Panthers arrested for plotting to kill policemen and
dynamite a police station, department stores, and a railroad right-of-way.
Time, Jan. 26, 1970, p. 14. A week later former Supreme Court Justice
Goldberg helped form a special commission to investigate whether Chicago
police had violated the rights of Black Panthers. Previous to this time, the
press reported that Panthers had killed five policemen and wounded forty-
two more in "shoot-outs" in twenty states. *Human Events*, Feb. 7, 1970, p.
10. Jewish money was all-important in the election campaigns of Negro
Mayors Carl Stokes of Cleveland and Richard Hatcher of Gary, Indiana.
Phillips, *op. cit.*, p. 350.

Negro problem could no longer be relegated to the far side of a neat geographical bisection.

The white liberals and minority members who, in the tradition of nineteenth-century abolitionists, had enthusiastically used Negro deprivation as a political and economic club with which to beat the hated South, the last stronghold of Majority racism, were not half so enthusiastic when the same problem surfaced with even greater intensity in their own Northern cities. It is more comforting to tell others how to remedy their errors than to do something about one's own. Part of the liberal-minority solution for the Negroes' predicament was to inculcate them with a hatred of Southern whites. But to the Northern Negro all whites looked the same. Ironically, the scapegoat makers were becoming the scapegoats.

The wind had been sown and the whirlwind was reaped when Negroes finally sensed the hypocrisy and cowardice of their white allies. From 1964 to the first six months of 1968, Negro race riots,[13] most of them in large Northern cities, accounted for 215 deaths, 8,950 injured and $285,000,000 in claims to insurance companies.[14] Although they were not so reported in the news media, the insurrections were not always mad, irrational acts of self-immolation, but could also be regarded as a well-conceived strategy of burning out the white merchants, mostly Jewish, who in the view of ghetto residents had been gouging and overcharging them.[15] Also

13. Swedish sociologist Gunnar Myrdal, whose two-volume integrationist tract, *An American Dilemma,* ignited the intellectual fuse of Black Power, predicted (in 1944) there would be no "further riots of any significant degree of violence in the North." His co-author, Arnold Rose, said (in 1962) all formal segregation and discrimination would end in one decade and informal segregation would "decline to a shadow" in two. *New York Times Magazine,* Dec. 7, 1969, p. 152.

14. *U.S. News & World Report,* July 15, 1968, p. 31.

15. At the end of 1968, after several years of exposure to arson and looting, 39 percent of the stores in the fifteen largest ghettos were still Jewish-owned. *Wall Street Journal,* Dec. 31, 1968, pp. 1, 12. Black militants accompanied their attacks on Jewish business with occasional flare-ups of anti-Semitic propaganda. Will Maslow, Executive Director of the American Jewish Congress, resigned from CORE's Executive Committee after attending a school meeting in Mt. Vernon, N.Y., in the course of which a Negro educator stated that Hitler had not killed enough Jews. But most Jews were far too committed to the Negro movement to imitate or even approve Maslow's act. Yaffe, *op. cit.,* p. 261.

not generally known was the fact that the riots were not led by the poor or disadvantaged, but by the better-paid, better-educated Negroes.[16]

In 1969, the riots slackened off as white businesses in the ghettos no longer offered such tempting targets. At the direction of paramilitary cadres endeavoring to establish themselves as the elite guard of an improbable racial revolution, the attack was turned against the police, who were ambushed in ghetto streets or gunned down at point blank range when they stopped black militants for traffic violations. Armed Negro bands occupied the buildings or classrooms of several colleges, held administrative officials and professors as hostages and were later amnestied after forcing tremulous presidents, deans and faculties to bow to their demands. Other Negro groups levied tribute on churches as reparations for mistreatment in the slavery era. The sins of the fathers were being visited upon the children well beyond the third and fourth generations. The same Majority liberals and minority racists who could not abide Hitler's Nuremberg laws were being asked to agree—and many did agree—to a moral law holding races accountable for acts committed by individuals long since dead.

When not attributed to the purposeful malevolence of "white racism" in general,[17] black militancy is often explained as the expected and excusable outgrowth of the Negro's low economic state. Reference is made to government statistics

16. Suspects in the police lineup following the 1968 Washington riots were found to be "amazingly respectable." Most of them had never been in trouble with the law, had decent jobs and had more schooling than the average Negro. More than half were family men. *U.S. News & World Report,* April 22, 1968, p. 29.

17. White racism was specifically named as the chief villain in the plight of the American Negro by the government-sponsored *Kerner Report* (1967), compiled by Federal Judge Otto Kerner who, with his former associate, Theodore Isaacs, was later found guilty of bribery, fraud and extortion. *Time,* Dec. 13, 1971, p. 15. Such official denouncements inevitably intensify hatred of whites as a group, which rebounds by hardening white feelings toward Negroes. Malcolm X exemplified the end point of aroused racial hostility when he said of the plane crash which killed some thirty white Americans, mostly from Atlanta, "I've just heard some good news!" *Autobiography of Malcolm X,* p. 394. Such racial vehemence, of course, is not the sole property of Negroes. A similar strain was noticeable in the late Ben Hecht who wrote he had a "holiday in his heart" every time a Zionist killed a British soldier. *New York Times,* May 20, 1947, p. 1.

which show that (in 1967) the median Negro family income was $4,939 compared to $8,318 for whites;[18] that Negro unemployment was 6.7 percent compared to 3.6 percent for whites; that 58 percent of all Negroes, as against 75 percent of all whites, finished high school.[19] What these statistics do not show is that Negroes are advancing at a rate that would have been unthinkable a few decades ago. By 1968, young Negro working couples were earning 99 percent of the income of young white working couples. In the same year, 32 percent of all Negro families were earning $8,000 or more, as compared to 15 percent in 1960.[20] Negro militancy, it turns out, is as much a function of Negro progress as of Negro deprivation.

There is also an historical proof of the absence of any strong connective link between Negro violence and Negro poverty. No one can deny that the economic status of blacks was much worse in the slavery and sharecropping eras than today. Yet in all that time only three Negro revolts were known to have taken place, and even these were of little consequence. The biggest was led by Nat Turner in Southhampton County, Virginia, in 1831. If this rather ignoble event—the white death total was ten men, fourteen women and thirty-one children—was the greatest explosion of Negro fury in three centuries, it could be concluded that Negroes are either by nature nonviolent or were content with their lowly lot.[21] But elsewhere the Negro record is at variance with these assumptions. The French experience in Haiti, where the massacre of the white population was total, and the recent war between Nigeria and Biafra, in which a million people died, hardly indicate a Negro aversion to violence.

It is apparent that blacks become more militant when they

---

18. Nevertheless, the income of the average Negro family in the U.S. exceeded the income of the average British family. *Economist,* London, May 10, 1969, p. 19.

19. *San Francisco Sunday Examiner & Chronicle, This World,* Jan. 19, 1969, p. 10.

20. *New York Times,* March 1, 1970, p. 69. Also see footnote 36, p. 352, of this study.

21. Two of the three rebellions were betrayed by Negro household slaves and each was inspired by the French Revolution or by appropriate passages from the Old and New Testaments. Franklin Frazier, *The Negro in the U.S.,* Macmillan, New York, 1957, pp. 87–91.

are better off, not when they are badly off. But this is simply a secondary effect of the primary cause of the rise of black violence—weakening white resistance. Throughout American history white supremacy has been a basic premise of the country's social relationships. Even the most fiery abolitionists exuded the air of the Great White Father. In fact, white supremacy had such overwhelming acceptance, was so firmly entrenched and so thoroughly institutionalized that Negroes would scarcely dare to criticize it, let alone take more forceful measures. Today, however, white supremacy or, to give it its modern name, Majority racism is so debilitated that Negro militancy, especially in the North, is not only possible but profitable. That it would come to a halt once Negroes achieved equality is the purest form of wishful thinking. Who would determine the cut-off date? The black militants? And how is equality to be measured?

If Majority members would only comprehend that the whole point, the whole drive, the very essense of minority racism is not to obtain equality but superiority, most of the misunder-standings and misinterpretations of contemporary Negro behavior would be avoided. Racism simply cannot be bought off. In its dynamic stages, it can only be controlled or suppressed by superior force, a force most effectively provided by an opposing or countervailing racism. What is indisputable is that the one way not to stop Negro militancy is to reward it.

There is no better indication of the decline of the American Majority than the recent and continuing successes of the Black Power movement. Negroes belong to the most backward of the world's major races and to the most backward of America's large population groups. Nevertheless, in the past several years they have managed to erect a kind of state within a state and in so doing have removed themselves well outside the range of the democratic process. In the name of equality they have achieved a kind of superequality which has led to the establishment of a double standard—one for themselves, one for whites—in the judicial, educational and welfare sectors of American society. That all this has been accomplished so quickly is vivid confirmation of the power of racism. Negroes, as a few of their own leaders will admit in private, have little else working for them.

Several theories have been advanced to account for Negro backwardness. One of the most publicized was put forward by Arnold Toynbee, whose monumental *Study of History* logs twenty-one civilizations, most of them created by white men, some by yellow men, none by black men.[22] Toynbee explained the Negro's civilizing deficiency by the theory of challenge and response. Surrounded by nature's bounty in the lush African tropics, the Negro, Toynbee postulated, only had to lift his hand to gather in his subsistence. With a minimum of challenge, there was a minimum of response. Being, so to speak, spoon-fed, the Negro was not sufficiently stimulated to develop his mental apparatus to its full potential.[23]

Another hypothesis, based on what the late A. L. Kroeber called cultural diffusion, asserted that the Negro, having been shunted off the main track of social progress by geography, suffered from lack of contact with other civilizations and consequently was programmed for barbarism. A neater theory, so neat that it is practically unanswerable, states that the Negro's predicament is simply due to bad luck, that the fate of all races is the result of nothing more than blind chance and historical accident, that if fortune had not been so kind to whites, they would still be living in caves. Still another viewpoint, more rationalizing than rational, alleges that the present condition of Negroes is due to a cleverly rigged white plot. White slave traders are blamed for deliberately wiping out thriving Negro civilizations in Africa, and the white empire builders who followed them are accused of transforming the surviving tribal states into sordid financial enclaves and boss-ridden plantations.

Needless to say, some or all of these theories have found favor with the environmentalist schools of social science— not withstanding that most of them are loaded with *non sequiturs,* guesswork and racial ax-grinding. Toynbee's challenge and response hypothesis loses much of its credibility when it is recalled that many geographical zones occupied by African Negroes—such as the East African highlands—are quite untropical and similar in climate, flora and fauna to areas which produced some of Toynbee's

22. Vol. 1, p. 232.
23. Vol. 2, pp. 26–9.

twenty-one civilizations.[24] With respect to the cultural diffusion theory, a great number of Negroes were situated on the southern border of ancient Egypt. They were consequently the most proximate of all peoples—just a short sail down the Nile—to one of the world's earliest and greatest civilizations. Given this headstart, Negroes should be far ahead of other races in cultural attainments. As for the historical accident theory, there is little to say except that one might suppose that in six thousand years Negro luck would have changed at least once.

Those who find genetic grounds for Negro backwardness seem to have a much stronger case than the behaviorists and equalitarians. They point to Carleton Coon's thesis that the Negro race is younger in an evolutionary sense than other races.[25] They produce medical research to demonstrate that Negroes have a faster kinesthetic maturation rate than whites, just as animals have a faster kinesthetic maturation rate than human beings, and that, in regard to fissuration, supragranular layer thickness and number of pyramidal neurons, the frontal lobes and cortex of the brain are less developed in Negroes than in whites, an index of younger evolutionary grade.[26]

They submit a mass of documentation derived from decades of intelligence testing to show that the I.Q. of the average Negro is from 15 to 20 points below that of the average white.[27] They refer to studies attributing consistent

24. It may have been disease, not insufficient challenge, that has made the Negro so lethargic. Half of all African blacks suffer from sickle cell anemia, an endemic malady that helps immunize them against malaria, but slows down bodily and mental functions. Sickle cell anemia also afflicts 10 percent of all American Negroes. Many white doctors are now working on the problem and there is reason to believe that they will soon produce a cure, as they have for many other diseases that have afflicted Africans over the centuries.

25. See p. 18.

26. For maturation rates, see Marcelle Geber, *The Lancet*, June 15, 1957, Vol. 272, No. 6981, pp. 1216–19. For frontal lobe and cortex studies, see C. J. Connolly, *External Morphology of the Primate Brain*, 1950, Springfield, Ill. pp. 146, 203–4; C. W. M. Pynter and J. J. Keegan, "A Study of the American Negro Brain," 1915, *Journal of Comparative Neurology*, Vol. 25, pp. 183–212; Ward C. Halstead, *Brains and Intelligence*, 1947, Chicago, p. 149; F. W. Vint, "The Brain of the Kenya Native," 1934, *Journal of Anatomy*, Vol. 68, pp. 216–23.

27. Audrey M. Shuey, *The Testing of Negro Intelligence*, Social Science Press, New York, 1966. The book analyzes 240 such tests accumulated over a forty-year period.

Negro underachievement in education to inherent learning
disabilities.[28]

They compare the emancipation of Negroes in the United
States with the approximately simultaneous emancipation of
the Russian serfs, contrasting the social mobility of the
latters' descendants to the prolonged post-slavery sluggish-
ness of American Negroes.[29] They measure the performance
of Chinese coolies, who on their arrival in the United States
were as illiterate and penniless as postbellum Negroes and
far less familiar with American ways, yet who needed less
than a century to reach the median income level. They quote
Hegel, Conrad, Schweitzer and Faulkner to suggest that
Negro differences are due to nature not nurture.[30]

The upholders of heredity further substantiate their case
by referring to the Negro's political and cultural record. They
point out that neither in the Old World nor the New has the
Negro ever produced a system of government that went one
step beyond the most elementary form of absolutism; that
indigenous Negro societies have left behind no literature, no
inscriptions or documents, no body of law, no philosophy,
no science—in short, no history. Even in those fields of art
where Negroes have displayed some creativity and originality
the ultimate effect, at least on the West, has been anti-
cultural—the contorted ugliness of modern painting and
sculpture, the jungle screeching of jazz and rock music, the
grotesque shuffling and weaving of the latest dance crazes.

28. The most notable of these studies is that of Dr. Arthur R. Jensen,
who found that white students had a "significantly greater ability to grasp
abstract concepts." See p. 281.

29. Discussing the posterity of Russian serfs, Pitirim Sorokin wrote, they
"yielded a considerable number of geniuses of the first degree, not to mention the eminent people of a smaller calibre . . . the American Negroes
have not up to this time produced a single genius of great calibre." *Contemporary Sociological Theories,* p. 298, footnote 162.

30. Hegel, Marx's pet philosopher, put Negroes on a par with animals.
Vorlesungen über die Philosophie der Geschichte, Stuttgart, 1971, pp. 137–
44. For Conrad's illumination of the dark crannies of the Negro psyche,
see *Heart of Darkness.* Schweitzer, who spent much of his life in Africa,
said the white man was the Negro's "elder brother." He considered the
average Negro a child, adding that "with children nothing can be done
without the use of authority." Putnam, *Race and Reason,* p. 76, and *Newsweek,* April 8, 1963, p. 21. Much as he liked and respected Negroes, Faulkner said that if antiwhite racial agitation increased he would be forced to
join his native state of Mississippi against the United States and shoot Negroes in the street. *Reporter,* March 22, 1956, pp. 18–19.

It would be superfluous to say that Negro intellectuals and their white partisans disagree with these hereditarian arguments. In rebuttal, however, they are not above retouching history. The stone ruins of Zimbabwe in Southern Rhodesia are held up as proof that an ancient and sophisticated Negro civilization was in full flower when Europeans were groping their way through the Dark Ages. A little later the "kingdoms" of Ghana, Mali and Songhai purportedly inaugurated a golden age in West Africa, where several new emerging nations have been named in their honor. That Zimbabwe was probably built by Arab traders in the eleventh century with Hottentot labor should not be permitted to spoil a good legend. In regard to Ghana, Mali and Songhai, the fact is they were founded by Hamitic Berbers and Semitic Arabs and were not in West Africa, but located further east.[31] Actually, the most articulated, all-Negro cultural complexes were in Western Nigeria and need no historical buildup from those who slavishly insist on measuring black accomplishments by white standards.

In an overzealous attempt to raise Negro pride to the boiling point, one Ghanaian historian has stated that Moses and Buddha were Egyptian Negroes, that Christianity originated in the Sudan and that the writings of Nietzsche, Bergson, Marx and the Existentialists were reflections of Bantu thought. In the same vein, the "original Hebrews" and St. Paul are described as black and Spinoza is called a "black Spanish Jew."[32] The Nubian or 25th dynasty, which appeared in the twilight of Egyptian history (730–663 B.C.), is taken as evidence that the brilliant Egyptian civilizations of the Old and Middle Kingdoms were the work of Negroes, which they indisputably were not.[33] To television audiences Cleopatra is sometimes depicted as a Negress,[34] and a black

31. R. Gayre, "Negrophile Falsification of Racial History," *The Mankind Quarterly*, Jan.–March, 1967, pp. 131–43. Also see "Zimbabwe" by the same author in the April–June, 1965 issue.
32. *Autobiography of Malcolm X*, pp. 180, 190.
33. The Old Kingdom constructed forts to repel Nubians and the Middle Kingdom prevented the entry of all but slaves from Nubia. Darlington, *op. cit.*, p. 121.
34. In reality, Cleopatra was not even an Egyptian, "being by descent half-Greek and half-Macedonian." John Buchan, *Augustus*, Houghton Mifflin Co., Boston, 1937, p. 77.

TV program informed its viewers that a West African king sent a hundred ships to South America 200 years before Columbus. This explains why the latter when he sailed to the New World had to stop at the Canary Islands to pick up a Negro pilot.[35] As for American history, Crispus Attucks, who may have been a Negro or may have been an Indian, has become a black hero, the first patriot to give his life in the cause of American independence.[36]

Perhaps the most far-fetched example of the new Negro historicism is a revised version of Genesis by Elijah Muhammad, the prophet of the Black Muslims. He asseverates that 6,600 years ago, when all men were Negroes, a black scientist named Yacub was exiled from Mecca with 59,999 followers. Embittered toward Allah, Yacub decided to create a devil race of "bleached-out whites." Scientifically bred for blondness, Yacub's followers became, in successive two-hundred-year stages, brown, red, yellow and finally "blond, pale-skinned, cold-blue-eyed devils—savages, nude and shameless; hairy, like animals [walking] on all fours and [living] in trees." Later these whites were rounded up by Negroes and sent to European caves where, after two thousand years, Moses went to tame and civilize them. They then set forth to rule the earth for six thousand years. The white interregnum was scheduled to end when a savior, Master W. D. Fard, a half-white, half-black silk salesman, brought Allah's message and divine guidance to Elijah Muhammad, which he did in Detroit in 1931.[37]

The gilding of the Negro past by religious and historical enthusiasts throws little constructive light on the great debate about Negro racial differences. If the environmentalists are correct, then Negroes ought to catch up to whites as soon as they are given equal political and legal rights and the same educational and economic opportunities. If, as Marshall McLuhan contends, the Negro is actually a superior being, the time lag should be very short.[38] Yet every day the Negro

---

35. From the program, *Soul,* WNET, New York, Aug. 21, 1969.

36. In the 1770 Boston massacre. *New York Times Magazine,* April 20, 1969, pp. 33, 109–10.

37. *Autobiography of Malcolm X,* pp. 164–7.

38. McLuhan's racial theories give first place to the Indian as well as to the Negro. Although not explaining how such gifted people could have

problem increases in gravity. The more Negroes are helped, the more they seem to need help, and the louder they demand it. The more they progress, the more America as a nation seems to retrogress.

If, on the other hand, those who advance the genetic argument are right, then all the short-term gains Negroes have made in the last several decades will add up to a long-term disaster. Instead of trying to be the equals of whites, Negroes should try to be better Negroes. Instead of playing the white man's game with dice that heredity has loaded against them, they should develop their own special talents in their own special ways. Negro frustrations, say the hereditarians, will only vanish when American Negroes lead a black rather than a white life.

Some of the most ardent support for the belief that Negro racial differences are so distinct as to make integration all but impossible has come from American Negroes themselves. Booker T. Washington warned his people to accept segregation and to remain well apart from the main currents of white civilization.[39] Marcus Garvey, who after World War I organized the first and so far the only important Negro mass movement, decided the solution was to return to Africa.[40] Father Divine, although Mother Divine was a Canadian blonde, insisted on moving his congregation into walled-off communities beyond the reach of white contamination.

The most recent advocates of black withdrawal are Black Muslims and other black nationalist groups, some Marxist-

---

fallen so far behind, the Canadian-born social critic has written that the "Negro and Indian . . . are actually psychically and socially superior to the fragmented, alienated and disassociated man of Western civilization. . . . It has been the sad fate of the Negro and the Indian to be : . . born ahead of rather than behind their time." Julius Lester, *Search for the New Land*, Dial Press, New York, 1969, pp. 57–8.

39. "In all things purely social," Washington said, "we can be separate as the fingers, yet one as the hand in all things essential to mutual progress." Putnam, *Race and Reason*, p. 90.

40. It is significant that Garvey was a full-blooded Negro who directed his appeal to the blacker elements of the Negro population. He was an exception to the doubtful rule that the leaders of black movements must be mulattoes, whose hybrid status makes them ideal mediators between whites and Negroes. See Richard Swartzbaugh, *The Mediator*, Howard Allen, Cape Canaveral, Florida.

oriented, who either demand a return to Africa or the establishment of independent Negro states on American soil. But in aligning themselves with white radicals and hostile foreign regimes, black leaders are only compounding their troubles.

The great deterrent to black separatism is not the integrationist aspiration of Negro "Uncle Toms," but the whole superstructure of modern liberal thought. If the notion of racial equality is surrendered to separatism, which recognizes and institutionalizes racial differences, environmentalism, behaviorism, economic determinism and even democracy itself would soon be called into question. The prevailing Western orthodoxies might then dissolve into thin air, and the occidental mind might have to set off on an entirely new path or find its way back to an old one.

Pragmatically, black separatism would be an overwhelming political loss to the liberal-minority coalition. Racial separation of any kind is not at all uncongenial to racially-minded whites and it is not inconceivable that hard-pressed Majority members, especially in the Deep South, together with harder-pressed Assimilable Minority members in the nation's largest cities, would join black separatists in a nonaggression pact to free themselves from an integrationist liberal administration in Washington. Also, if Negro separatism should ever become the order of the day, other Unassimilable Minorities might take the hint, leaving liberalism an ideology in search of a party. At the other extreme, total integration would deal an equally lethal blow to the liberal-minority axis by spelling the doom of all minorities and with them liberalism's *raison d'être*.[41] It is only in the boundary zone between the segregated and the integrated society, between reality and utopia, that the modern liberal feels at home.

Because there is so much more at stake than the fate of American Negroes, the liberal-minority coalition, abetted by a sizable contingent of so-called conservatives, presses forward with integration at all costs. As always, those who have the

---

41. "What we arrive at is that 'integration,' socially, is no good for either side. 'Integration,' ultimately, would destroy the white race . . . and destroy the black race." *Autobiography of Malcolm X*, p. 276.

courage to air opposing views are either ignored or subjected to instant character assassination.

But while liberalism still rules the country's thinking, it has little control over the organic processes of society. As a tribesman, the Negro was a member of the tribal family. As a slave, he had his master's family. As a sharecropper, he had his own family. As an industrial peon or hard-core unemployed, he is beginning to have no family at all, since the present welfare system provides extra financial assistance for fatherless households and for each illegitimate child. The upshot is that the urban Negro has now reached an impasse where he has little left but his color and sense of oppression. Having lost his hearth, his roots, his religion and his way, he is rapidly losing whatever social commitments he has left.

The worst having been done, the more dynamic elements of the Negro minority are demanding redress, somewhat as undisciplined children who have lost their innocence might seek redress from parents who abandoned them. To these demands, whites have a choice of four responses—oppression, which is immoral; [42] integration without intermarriage, which is impossible; integration with intermarriage, which is inconceivable; separation, which is impractical.

Of all these untenable courses of action the last, which would establish independent or semi-independent Negro communities tangential to white communities, is perhaps the most nearly tenable. Whichever is ultimately chosen, the American Negro will soon be out of his private wilderness. He will either return to his Old World homeland or be assigned a homeland in the New, or there will be no homeland for anyone, black or white, in urban America.

---

42. It is much too late for the tactics Tacitus put in the mouth of a Roman general endeavoring to suppress a revolt of the Gauls. "Nunc hostis, quia molle servitium; cum spoliati exutique fuerint, amicos fore." *Historiarum,* IV, lvii. "Now they are our enemies because the burden of their servitude is light; when we have despoiled and stripped them they will be our friends."

PART V

The Cultural Clash

Chapter 18

The Atomization of Art

THE MAJOR THEME of Parts I-IV was the decline of the Majority and the rise of the minorities. The minor theme was the Majority-minority conflict itself, including the origins, motivations and numbers of the combatants. The remainder of this study will examine the extension of this conflict into the realms of art, religion, education, politics, economics, law and foreign policy. This chapter, the first of three to deal with minority inroads into the nation's culture, will be concerned with the artistic phase of the struggle.[1] In the dispossession of the Majority, it is the Majority artist who so far has been the greatest casualty.

A basic assumption of contemporary Western thought is that democracy is the political form and liberalism the political ideology most generative of art. The more there is of both, it is generally agreed, the greater will be the artistic outpouring, both quantitatively and qualitatively. The corollary assumption is that once art has been liberated from the dead weight of caste, class and religious and racial bigotry, its horizon will become limitless.

---

1. Culture is "a pursuit of our total perfection by means of getting to know . . . the best which has been thought and said in the world; and through this knowledge, turning a stream of fresh and free thought upon our stock notions and habits, which we now follow staunchly but mechanically, vainly imagining that there is a virtue in following them staunchly which makes up for the mischief of following them mechanically." Matthew Arnold, *Culture and Anarchy*, Cambridge University Press, England, 1961, p. 6.

Of all modern myths, this is perhaps the most misleading. If anything, art, or at least great art,[2] seems to be contingent on two social phenomena poles apart from democracy and liberalism: (1) a dominant, homogeneous population group which has resided long enough in the land to raise up from its ranks a responsible and functioning aristocracy;[3] (2) one or more schools of writers, painters, sculptors, architects or composers who belong to this population group and whose creative impulses crystalize the tastes, tone and manners of the aristocratic leadership into a radiating cultural continuity.

Few will dispute that the societies of Homeric Greece, Augustan Rome, Medieval Western Europe, Elizabethan England, seventeenth-century Spain, Louis XIV's France, Goethe's Weimar, Mozart's Vienna and nineteenth-century Russia had an aristocratic base. Fewer will dispute that great art was produced in these societies. But what of Athens, scene of the most magnificent artistic efflorescence of all time, and of Florence, with the highest per capita genius of the Renaissance? Did they not as city states lack a nobility or formal aristocracy? Is it not true that neither Pericles nor Cosimo de' Medici was a prince?

Before any conclusions are reached, these two cities and their two greatest statesmen should be placed in a sharper historical focus. If Athens was the glory of Greece, the Age of Pericles—artistically speaking—was the glory of Athens. In 431 B.C., two years before Pericles' death, the adult male population of Athens consisted of 50,000 citizens, 25,000 metics or resident aliens and 55,000 slaves.[4] Since the slaves

---

2. Great art in this context is considered timeless, not dated; great artists to be creative, not interpretative geniuses.

3. Aristocracy is here meant to designate both the rule of the well-born and the well-born who rule. Its meaning is not restricted to families of high social standing or to the products of one or two generations of political or financial preeminence. Aristocrats of the latter sort can be found in all states, including proletarian and plutocratic societies. For those convinced there is an unbridgeable gap between aristocracy and freedom, de Tocqueville wrote the following words of caution: ". . . parmi toutes les sociétés du monde, celles qui auront toujours le plus de peine à échapper pendant longtemps au gouvernement absolu seront précisément ces sociétés où l'aristocratie n'est plus et ne peut plus être." *L'ancien régime et la révolution.* Michel Lévy Frères, Paris, 1856, p. xvi.

4. Cyril Robinson, *A History of Greece,* Barnes & Noble, New York, 1957, p. 83.

had no rights at all, since metics and women could not vote and since citizenship was limited to those with Athenian parents on both sides, one historian has described Athens as "an aristocracy of a half-leisured class."[5] This aristocracy, of which Pericles was a prominent member, traced its ancestry back to the Trojan War.[6]

In regard to Florence, one should not be surprised to learn that in 1494, when the city's most liberal constitution was in force, there were not more than 3,200 citizens out of a total population of 90,000.[7] From Dante's day until the rise of the Medici, except for a few brief attempts at popular government brought off by pressure from the merchants and guilds, Florence was largely the political plaything of two rival aristocratic factions, the Guelphs (pro-Pope) and the Ghibellines (pro-Emperor). As for Cosimo de' Medici, the patron of Donatello, Ghiberti, Brunelleschi and Luca della Robbia, he could pride himself on a lineage that stretched back through ten generations of Florentine history. Although Cosimo himself shunned titles, there were cardinals, princes, reigning dukes and even two Popes who later bore the Medici name.

If Florence and Athens are admitted to be semi-aristocracies, or at least aristocratic republics, it is evident that all the great artistic epochs of the West have taken place in aristocratic societies. There has been art in non-aristocratic societies, often good art, but never anything approaching Greek sculpture and drama, Gothic cathedrals, Renaissance painting, Shakespearean plays, German music or Russian novels.

The mere existence of an aristocracy, of course, does not guarantee great art. It has to be a vital aristocracy with its attitudes, manners and ways of life firmly imprinted on the society in which it functions. It need not be, in fact it should not be, too wealthy. More important is the possession of a cultural conscience, plus the leisure and will to express this

5. *Ibid.*, p. 82.
6. Pericles' mother was descended from an ancient Athenian family, the Alcmaeonidae, and his father was a victorious naval commander.
7. Villari, *Life and Times of Machiavelli*, trans. Linda Villari, Fisher, Unwin, London, 1892, p. 4.

conscience in the form of art. To the artist, an aristocracy is of immense practical value because it provides a cultivated and discriminating audience to keep him on the creative *qui vive,* as well as a sense of refinement and a set of critical standards that are both a model and an incentive for the highest quality of artistic craftsmanship.

Paradoxically, relations between artist and patron are generally more "democratic" in an aristocracy than they are in a democracy.[8] The aristocrat, having both by birth and upbringing acquired an easy familiarity with art, is quite at home in the company of artists, and generally makes a practice of seeking them out. The self-made man, on the other hand, no matter how high he climbs in politics or business, can never quite shed his native philistinism. He may take an interest in art, often surreptitiously to avoid accusations of effeminacy, but he will always have difficulty moving freely in artistic circles.

The close alliance between art and aristocracy has another advantage for the artist in that it facilitates personal acquaintance with many of the leading men of his day. According to Aristotle, tragedy only really succeeds when it concerns the fall of a great or noble man—a theory still uncontradicted by the most valiant efforts of liberal and Marxist dramatists. History or current events may provide names and plots, but only physical association with the great furnishes the playwright who tackles high tragedy with the meat and sinew of believable portrayal and characterization.

That great artists must belong to the dominant population group of a nation seems to be as unassailable as the law that

8. Pericles, Augustus and the Medici freely mixed with the great artists of their time. Virgil read Augustus his completed *Georgics* on the latter's return from Egypt in 30 B.C. The meeting was momentous because Virgil's lines may have revived Augustus' latent Italianism. Buchan, *Augustus,* p. 124. Lincoln, beyond a brief handshake at a White House reception, never met Melville. Raymond Weaver, *Herman Melville,* Pageant Books, N.Y., 1961, p. 375. Nor did Franklin D. Roosevelt ever meet Faulkner or T. S. Eliot. Kennedy may have bestowed a few minutes of friendship on Robert Frost, but this could hardly be compared to the attention Louis XIV lavished on Racine and Molière. At one time the Sun King acted as "advance man" for Racine's *Esther* and actually played a role in one of Molière's productions. Racine, *Theâtre Complet,* Edition Garnier Frères, Paris, 1960, p. 598; H. C. Chatfield-Taylor, *Molière,* Duffield, New York, 1906, pp. 189–90.

great art grows best in aristocratic soil. A racial and cultural background similar to that of his patron makes it possible for the artist to avoid the usual psychological and social hurdles that often slow or break down communication between members of racially and culturally differentiated human groups.

The fatal flaw which denies the minority artist a place among the artistic great is his inherent alienation. Because he does not really belong, because he is writing or painting or composing for "other people," he pushes a little too hard, raises his voice a little too high, makes his point a little too desperately. He is, inevitably, a bit *outré*—in the land, but not of the land. His art seems always encumbered by an artificial dimension—the proof of his belonging.[9]

In a non-aristocratic, heterogeneous, fragmented society which has become an arena of contending cultures or sub-cultures, the minority artist may concentrate on proving his "non-belonging." He now rejects instead of adopts the host culture in order to demonstrate his independence or his allegiance to the cultural traditions of his own group. In the process his art becomes a weapon. Having sacrificed his talent to immediacy and robbed it of the proportion and subtlety which make art art, the minority artist not only lowers his own artistic standards, but those of society as a whole. All that remains is the crude force of his stridency and his "message." [10]

Perhaps the clearest proof of the art-building and art-nourishing qualities of aristocracy and racial homogeneity can be found in the history of those nations which have passed through both aristocratic and democratic, homogeneous and heterogeneous cycles. It was not in the First,

9. A few examples that come quickly to mind are Heine's super-romantic German lieder, Mendelssohn's thumping Christian hymns, El Greco's hyperbolized Spanish landscapes and elongated holy men, Jakob Wasserman's souped-up *Christian Wahnschaffe*, Siegfried Sassoon's synthetic *Memoirs of a Fox-Hunting Man*, Grofé's outlandish *Grand Canyon Suite*, and Rodger and Hammerstein's totally counterfeit *Oklahoma*. For a better understanding of the difference between the authentic and the inauthentic in art, compare Goethe's *Faust* with Heine's *Doktor Faust*.

10. Examples of contemporary minority stridency are the music of Darius Milhaud, the sculpture of Jacques Lipchitz, the poetry of Allen Ginsberg and the plays of LeRoi Jones.

Second, Third or Fourth French Republics that the cathedrals of Chartres and Rheims were constructed, but in feudal France, when there was a dominant population group (the Teutonic) and the structure of society was aristocratic. The highest flights of English genius took place in the reigns of absolute, not constitutional, monarchs and before the English were absorbed in the enlarged and more heterogeneous citizenry of Great Britain and the United Kingdom. The Rome of Augustus, who favored and protected the patricians and heaped restrictions upon plebeians, non-Romans and slaves, produced the Golden Age of Latin literature. The Rome of Caracalla, who in 211 A.D. extended citizenship to all the free inhabitants of the Roman Empire, left little of artistic consequence. The Spain of Philip II, III and IV with all its religious bigotry and inquisitional zeal was the era of Cervantes and Calderón, artists of a calibre that were not to be found in more liberal eras of Spanish history. Dostoyevsky and Tolstoy, the culmination of Russian literary genius, flourished under the Czars, not minority commissars.

Liberal dogma to the contrary, such popular goals as universal literacy are not necessarily conducive to great literature. The England of Shakespeare, apart from a much smaller population, had a much higher illiteracy rate than present-day Britain.[11] Neither does universal suffrage seem to raise the quality of artistic output. When Bach was *Konzertmeister* in Weimar and composing a new cantata every month, no one could vote. Two hundred and twenty years later in the Weimar Republic there were millions of voters, but no Bachs.

Great drama, which usually incorporates great poetry, is the rarest form of great art. Art critics and historians have been at some loss to explain why great plays have appeared so infrequently in history and then only in clusters—fifth-century (B.C.) Athens, late sixteenth and early seventeenth-

---

11. Literacy here signifies the simple ability to read and write. The rich language of Elizabethan literature and drama would indicate that if fewer Englishmen could write at that period, those who did wrote much better than those who came later. It also indicates that the "illiterates" had a deeper appreciation and better understanding of literature than their more literate modern equivalents.

century England, seventeenth-century Spain and France. The answer may be that conditions for great drama are only ripe when artist and audience are in biological as well as linguistic rapport. Such rapport, unfortunately, is bound to be short-lived because the era of great drama is usually accompanied by large-scale economic and material advances which tend to soften national character, sharpen class divisions and attract extraneous racial and cultural elements from abroad. To the great playwright, a divided audience is no audience at all.

Not only great art, but all art seems to stagnate in an environment of brawling minorities, diverse religions, clashing traditions and contrasting habits. This is probably why, in spite of their vast wealth and power, such world cities as Alexandria and Antioch in ancient times and New York City and Buenos Aires in modern times have produced nothing that can compare to the art of municipalities one-hundredth their size. The artist needs an audience which understands him—an audience of his own people. The artist needs an audience to write up to, paint up to and compose up to—an aristocracy of his own people. These seem to be the two *sine qua nons* of great art. Whenever they are absent great art is absent.

How else can the timeless art of the "benighted" Middle Ages and the already dated art of the "advanced" twentieth century be explained? Why is it that all the cultural resources of a *dernier cri* superpower like the United States cannot produce one single musical work that can compare with a minor composition of Mozart? Why is it that the greatest contribution to twentieth-century English literature has been made not by the English, Americans, Australians or Canadians, but by the Irish—the most nationalistic, most tribal, most religious and most racially minded of all present-day English-speaking peoples. Modern England may have had its D. H. Lawrence and the United States its Faulkner. But only Ireland in recent times has assembled such a formidable literary array as Moore, Wilde, Yeats, Synge, Shaw, Joyce, O'Casey, Elizabeth Bowen, Paul Vincent Carroll, Joyce Carey and James Stephens. If, as modern opinion holds, liberal democracy, internationalism and cultural pluralism enrich the soil of art, then these artists bloomed in a very unlikely garden.

The historical sequence of large states seems to be race-building, nation-building, art-building and empire-building. In most cases, the great artistic moments have preceded rather than followed maximum territorial expansion. As the nation moves closer to imperialism, the people move farther apart. The binding forces of state are weakened by war, civil strife and entropy, and the cultural shell is penetrated by outsiders. The aristocracy withdraws into an isolated decadence, as its place is taken by a plutocracy. Members of the once dominant population group mix with the newcomers and in order to compete are forced to adopt many of their attitudes and habits. Art becomes multiracial, multi-national, multi-directional and multifarious.

Much of Western art, particularly in the United States, is now in such a stage of atomization. The surrealist painters, atonal jazz musicologists, prosaic poets, emetic novelists, crypto-pornographers and revanchist pamphleteers say they are searching for new forms because the old forms are exhausted. Actually, they are exhuming the most ancient forms of all—simple geometric shapes, color blobs, drum beats, genitalia, four-letter words and four-word sentences. The old forms are not exhausted. The minority artist simply has no feeling for them because they are not his forms. Since style is not a commodity that can be bought or invented, the avant-garde, having no style of its own, can only retreat to a styleless primitivism.

The atomization of art is characterized by the emergence of the fake artist [12]—the man without talent and training who becomes an artist by self-proclamation. He thrives in a fissiparous culture because it is child's play to bemuse the artistic sensibilities of the motley *nouveaux riches*, assorted culture vultures, sexually ambivalent art critics and minority

---

12. The fake artist is not unrelated to the anti-artist—the type of individual who blew up *The Thinker* outside the Cleveland Museum in the spring of 1970. It was one of the eleven castings made under the personal supervision of Rodin. *New York Times*, July 17, 1970.

art agents who dictate the levels of modern taste. It is not so easy to deceive standards of taste established in the course of generations.

In a homogeneous society the artist has to contend with fewer sets of prejudices. He does not have to weigh and balance his art in order to be "fair." He need not be so mortally afraid of wounding the religious and racial feelings of others. Though his instincts, opinions and judgments often add up to bias, to the artist himself they may be the driving forces of his creativity. What really limits and devitalizes art are not the artist's prejudices but his audience's prejudices, of which in a vast heterogeneous society like the United States there is an almost infinite variety. The artist has trouble enough with one censor. When he has twenty, his art becomes a day-to-day accomodation.

Aristocracies have been sharply criticized for freezing commoners into castes and classes. Yet the artist certainly stands a better chance in a state directed by a cultivated nobility than in one directed by a convention of Babbitts. By no means to the manor born, Homer, Virgil, Dante, Chaucer, Michelangelo, Shakespeare, Cervantes, Molière, Mozart, Beethoven, Wagner and Dostoyevsky managed to acquire enough social mobility in aristocratic societies to climb to the summit of artistic perfection. How many of these geniuses would have been flattened by the leveling pressures of mid-century America is an open question.

Aristocracies have also been attacked for stultifying art, even though artists working in a tradition-oriented environment have made many more artistic breakthroughs than *soi-disant* liberal or progressive artists. Aristophanes, who revolutionized comedy, Wagner, who revolutionized music, Dostoyevsky, who revolutionized the novel, and T. S. Eliot, who revolutionized modern poetry,[13] were in liberal eyes hidebound conservatives. The proletarian or Marxist artist, on the other hand, hardly goes beyond the boundaries of photographic and tape-recorded naturalism—i.e., the tractor

13. Compare the startlingly new effect of the poetry of Eliot, who declared himself a royalist and Anglo-Catholic, with the classical verse style of the French Communist poet, Louis Aragon.

art of the Soviet Union and the op art, pop art and cave art of the "free world." [14]

No great art ever emerged from isolation, and no great artists ever sprang full-blown from the forehead of Zeus. Great artists come from schools of art and their works are the peaks rising above a high cultural plateau. First families, whose attitudes and tastes have been shaped by centuries of participation in national life, are not merely content to collect old art. They keep the schools busy elaborating and improving on what has been done before—the surest approach to artistic evolution. Conversely, the present-day ragtag collection of semi-literate millionaires, who speculate in art as they would in copper futures,[15] spend their money on old masters and "name" artists whose works can be resold at a handsome profit or given away at a handsome tax deduction. With no more demand for a continuity of art, schools of artists disappear, to be replaced by artistic cliques.[16] The arbiter of taste is no longer the art lover, but the art dealer.[17] Art is transformed into artiness.

The historic patterns and processes of artistic growth and decline as outlined in the preceding paragraphs have already blacked out most of the creativity of the Majority artist. Today in the United States, the Jewish-American writes of

---

14. Andy Warhol's painting of a Campbell Soup can was sold for $60,000 at a New York City auction in 1970. The late British art critic, Herbert Read, had two paintings by chimpanzees who, he said, allowed "their brushes to be guided by instinctive gestures, just like the action painters of America." *Times Literary Supplement,* Aug. 28, 1970, p. 944.

15. Regarding Joseph Hirschhorn, the uranium king, James Yaffe has written, "When he likes the painter's work, he often buys it in bulk and insists on a reduction in the price, just like any garment manufacturer buying fabrics." Yaffe, *op. cit.,* p. 233.

16. Picasso, often considered the greatest twentieth-century painter, had this to say about his role in modern art, "I am only a public entertainer who has understood his times and has exhausted as best he could the imbecility, the vanity, the cupidity of his contemporaries. Mine is a bitter confession, more painful than it may appear, but it has the merit of being sincere." *Life,* Dec. 27, 1968, p. 134.

17. Frank Lloyd, a former oil entrepreneur from Vienna, now heads a chain of art galleries in London, Rome and New York, which in the art world stands out "like U.S. Steel [in] a community of blacksmiths." A competitor said of Mr. Lloyd, who does not collect pictures himself, "he might as well be in the used car business. . . ." *Wall Street Journal,* Dec. 31, 1968, pp. 1, 10.

the Jew and his heritage, the Negro-American of the Negro, the Italian-American of the Italian, and so on. But of whom does the American-American, the Majority writer, write? Of Nordics and Anglo-Saxons? If he did, he would be laughed out of modern literature. Consciousness of one's people, one of the great emotional reserves of mankind, one of the greatest of artistic stimulants, is denied the Majority artist at the very moment the minority artist feeds upon it so hungrily. Besides its other psychological implications, such a one-sided, selective censorship obviously builds a high wall of frustration around the free play of imagination.

Aware or unaware of the forces working against them, many Majority artists have fled abroad to seek the cultural kinship they miss at home. Eliot became an English citizen. Robert Frost was first discovered and published while living in England. Pound, who probably exercised more influence on modern literature than any other poet, settled down in Rapallo and engaged in European right-wing politics.[18] Hemingway moved to France, Italy, Spain, Africa, Cuba and then to suicide. Thomas Wolfe and F. Scott Fitzgerald spent many of their most creative years abroad and returned to gypsy-like, coast-to-coast peregrinations and, in the latter case, to alcoholic poisoning.[19]

Other Majority artists escaped the dilemma of deracination by a form of spiritual emigration, which sometimes took them as far as self-destruction. Poet Robert Lowell, of the Boston Lowells, became a Roman Catholic convert and a conscientious objector.[20] Hart Crane, a poet of even greater talent, jumped off a ship and drowned in the Caribbean.[21] Ross Lockridge, Jr. wrote a promising first novel, *Raintree County*, then shut his garage door, got in the car and started the engine.[22] Thomas Heggen, another young author who learned the hollowness of success in an alien society, wrote *Mister Roberts* and then took an overdose of sleeping pills

---

18. See p. 533.
19. Cinema director D. W. Griffith was another casualty of the bottle.
20. *Time*, June 17, 1965, p. 29.
21. *New York Times*, April 28, 1932, p. 4.
22. *New York Times*, March 8, 1948, p. 1. Other writers who took their own lives: poets John Berryman and Silvia Plath; Laird Goldsborough, *Time* foreign affairs writer; Parker Lloyd-Smith, genius of *Fortune*.

in a rented New York apartment.[23] F. O. Matthiesen, one of the most brilliant modern American literary critics, heard the siren wail of Communism and leaped to his death from a Boston hotel room.[24] W. J. Cash, a Carolina-born essayist with a fine intelligence, lambasted his native South to the delight of liberal critics and shortly afterward was found hanging by his necktie.[25] Other talented Majority writers retreat to the sterilities and barbarities of college campuses where they avoid the problem of content by concentrating on form, in a hopeless attempt to separate the inseparable.

All Majority artists necessarily experience the wrenching depression that comes from enforced cultural homelessness. Less than any other person is the artist capable of working in a vacuum. Prevented from exercising his own "people-hood," the Majority artist looks for substitutes in minority racism, in exotic religions and Oriental cults, in harebrained exploits of civil disobedience, in African and pre-Columbian art, psychoanalysis, narcotics and homosexuality.

The ban on displays of Majority ethnocentrism in art—a ban so well established that it is now a universally accepted pre-censorship—also reaches back to the Majority cultural past. Chaucer and Shakespeare have been cut and blue-penciled and some of their work put on the minority index.[26]

23. *New York Times,* May 20, 1949, p. 1.

24. *Time,* April 10, 1950, p. 43. Another who heard the same song and who perhaps symbolized better than anyone the tragic fate of the Majority artist in a minority-oriented society was Howard Rushmore. A tenth-generation American, born in South Dakota, Rushmore first wrote for the *Daily Worker,* eventually losing his job for refusing to inject Negrophile sentiments in his film reviews. He then switched to anti-Communist bombast for Hearst newspapers and finally was employed by the libelous gossip magazine, *Confidential,* for which, unbeknown to himself and to his publisher, he wrote some of the finest satire in American literature. In 1958, he shot and killed himself and his wife in the back seat of a taxicab. *Newsweek,* Jan. 13, 1958, pp. 19–20.

25. Joseph L. Morrison, *W. J. Cash,* Knopf, New York, 1967, p. 131.

26. The New York Board of Rabbis protested the television showing of the *Merchant of Venice* and it has been removed from the English curriculum of New York City high schools. *Time,* June 29, 1962, p. 32. A 1941 Simon and Schuster edition of Chaucer's *Canterbury Tales* appeared with a foreword by Mark Van Doren but without *The Prioresses Tale,* which tells of a murder committed by Jews. The Oberammergau passion play, a fixture of European culture since 1634, has been under constant attack by the American Jewish Congress for its "notoriously anti-Semitic text." *New York Times,* Nov. 12, 1969, p. 4.

The motion picture of Charles Dickens' *Oliver Twist* had a hard time being released in the United States because of the recognizably Jewish traits of Fagin.[27] The masterpiece of American silent films, *The Birth of a Nation,* can no longer be shown without the presence of picket lines, while films like *Mandingo* (1975) with the crudest racial slurs against white Southerners are shown everywhere. Mark Twain's Huckleberry Finn has been blackwashed and expurgated by liberal-minority watchdog organizations.[28] Henry Miller's *Tropic of Capricorn* has been attacked by millionaire novelist Leon Uris as "anti-Semitic."[29] Many newspapers and magazines won't even carry advertising for *The Dispossessed Majority,*[30] while anti-Majority books are reviewed extensively. Even nursery rhymes and Stephen Foster are being rewritten and bowdlerized.[31] Meanwhile, a tireless, clandestine literary vendetta is being waged against such towering modern writers, composers[32] and scholars,[33] both American and European, as Eliot,

27. *Saturday Review of Literature,* Feb. 26, 1949, pp. 9–10.

28. The Philadelphia Board of Education banished *Huckleberry Finn* from the public school system and replaced it by a version in which all derogatory references to Negroes were deleted. *San Francisco Chronicle, This World,* May 27, 1962, p. 16 and April 27, 1963, p. 8.

29. *Los Angeles Times,* Feb. 16, 1962, Letter Section. Uris' attack was particularly ungracious because he is the minority racist writer *par excellence,* his bestseller, *Exodus,* about the Israeli conquest of Palestine, being fifth-rate Kipling.

30. See Wilmot Robertson's *Ventilations,* Howard Allen, Cape Canaveral, Florida, Chapter 3.

31. In "My Old Kentucky Home," the state anthem of Kentucky, such expressions as *Massa, Darkies* and *Mammy* have been carefully deleted. The Virginia state anthem, "Carry Me Back to Old Virginny," has been attacked by a Negro State Senator as being "abhorrent to his race." One Southern Congressman has predicted, not altogether facetiously, that minority lobbying will eventually bring about the renaming of the White House. *U.S. News & World Report,* Aug. 9, 1957, p. 43 and *New York Times,* March 2, 1970, p. 28.

32. Practically all the leading conductors, musicians and operatic performers who remained in Europe during World War II were victims of American-Jewish boycotts after the war came to an end. The list includes: Wilhelm Furtwängler, Herbert von Karajan, Walter Gieseking, Kirsten Flagstad and Elisabeth Schwarzkopf. Yaffe, *op. cit.,* p. 58. Jewish racism has also been responsible for depriving American audiences of the Bolshoi Opera company, whose American tour was cancelled in 1970 after a series of Zionist attacks, including a bombing, against Soviet installations in the New York area.

33. Perhaps the most bigoted censorship was exercised by refugee academicians who for years successfully "shut out" the philosophy of Martin Heidegger, one of the most original and disturbing thinkers of

Dreiser, Pound,[34] Toynbee, Ernst Jünger, D. H. Lawrence, Céline, Roy Campbell, Wyndham Lewis, Kipling, Hamsun, Franz Lehar and Richard Strauss. Their crime has been to have let slip some chance remark, written some poem, novel or essay, joined, or at least not opposed, some political movement offensive to one or more minorities. There is, of course, no counter vendetta of Majority literary critics against artists who indulge in minority racism.

The power and sustenance that an artist derives from being part of a racially and culturally homogeneous community helps explain the success of William Faulkner, the one first-rate Majority writer who survived both as an individual and as an artist the nationwide uprooting of his cultural heritage. Faulkner was born, lived, flourished and died in Mississippi, the fourth most illiterate state [35] and in his time one of the few remaining bastions of Majority control. Because they totally ignore the communal nature of art, liberals and Marxists can only treat Faulkner as a paradox.[36] Environmentalist logic can no more explain why a supposedly backward state in the Deep South should produce America's greatest twentieth-century novelist than why the most literate nation in Europe succumbed to Hitler.

Outside the South, American art is overwhelmingly dominated by members of minorities. To lend substance to the allegation that the basic tone of American creative intellectual life has become Jewish, one has only to unroll the almost endless roster of artists of Jewish or part-Jewish origin.[37] The number of artists belonging to non-Jewish

---

the modern era, only permitting it to seep through in the thinned-down adaptations of Sartre.

34. Random House barred all works of Pound from a poetry anthology, even though Conrad Aiken, one of the editors, had specifically chosen twelve Pound poems for inclusion. Charles Norman, *Ezra Pound*, Macmillan, New York, 1960, p. 416.

35. 1960 estimate by Bureau of Census.

36. Just as they treat as a paradox the fact that a disproportionate number of all Majority writers are Southerners—Harper Lee, Carson Mc-Cullers, Robert Penn Warren, Eudora Welty, Allen Tate, to name a few.

37. Among those who have been active in the middle third of the century: *Writers:* Edna Ferber, Gertrude Stein, Fanny Hurst, Mary McCarthy, Nathanael West, Bruce Friedman, J. D. Salinger, Herbert Gold, Harvey Swadow, Bernard Malamud, Saul Bellow, Norman Mailer, Irving Stone, Jerome Weidman, Irwin Shaw, Howard Fast, Budd Schulberg, Ben Hecht,

minorities is also increasing, particularly in the Negro category.[38]

The minority domination of the contemporary art scene is complicated by the presence of another, as yet unmentioned minority, unique in that it is composed of both Majority and minority members. This is the homosexual sect. Homosexuals, as is well known, are one of the two principal props of the American theater, the second being the Jews.[39] Jews

Irving Wallace, Harold Robbins, Philip Roth, Joseph Heller, Herman Wouk, Meyer Levin, S. J. Perelman, Alexander King.

Poets: Louis Untermeyer, Dorothy Parker, Delmore Schwartz, Kenneth Fearing, Babette Deutsch, Karl Shapiro, Allen Ginsberg.

Playwrights: Elmer Rice, George S. Kaufman, Moss Hart, Lillian Hellman, Sidney Kingsley, Clifford Odets, Sam and Bella Spewack, Arthur Miller, J. Howard Lawson, Neil Simon, Jack Gerber, Arthur Kopit, Paddy Chayevsky, Abe Burrows, Murray Schisgal, S. N. Behrman.

Critics: Irving Kristol, William Goldman, Lionel Trilling, Leslie Fiedler, Paul Goodman, Paul Jacobs, William Philips, Irving Howe, Joseph Wechsberg, Clifton Fadiman, Leon Edel, Brad Darrach, Ernest Samuels.

Painters and Sculptors: George Gross, Saul Steinberg, Moses and Raphael Soyer, Leon Kroll, Saul Raskin, Jacques Lipschitz, Jacob Epstein, Larry Rivers, Chaim Gross, Helen Frankenthaler, Mark Rothko.

Composers and Librettists: Aaron Copland, Ernest Bloch, Darius Milhaud, Irving Berlin, Lorenz Hart, Richard Rodgers, George and Ira Gershwin, Leonard Bernstein, Lerner & Loewe, Oscar Hammerstein II, Jerome Kern, Sigmund Romberg, Harold Arlen, Otto Harburg, Jules Styne, Jerry Bock, Sheldon Harnick, David Amram, Jule Styne, Harold Rome, André Previn.

Orchestra Conductors, Virtuosos and Singers: Bruno Walter, Serge Koussevitsky, Pierre Monteux, Erich Leinsdorf, Eugene Ormandy, George Szell, Mischa Elman, Jascha Heifetz, Yehudi Menuhin, Rudolf Serkin, Artur Schnabel, Alexander Kipnis, Fritz Kreisler, Nathan Milstein, Arthur Rubinstein, Jan Peerce, George London, Robert Merrill, Vladimir Horowitz, Gregor Piatigorsky, Arthur Fiedler, George Solti, Richard Tucker.

38. Negro writers include: Ralph Ellison, Frank Yerby, Langston Hughes, Countee Cullen, Claude McKay, Richard Wright, James Baldwin, Lorraine Hansberry. Other minority writers: Russian-born Vladimir Nabokov (considered by *Time* as America's greatest living novelist), James T. Farrell and Edwin O'Connor (Irish-Americans), Pietro di Donato and Lawrence Ferlinghetti (Italian-Americans), William Saroyan (Armenian-American) and Jack Kerouac, of French-Canadian descent, the progenitor of the Beat Generation.

39. "Without either one of [these minority groups] Broadway would be desperately enfeebled; without both, it would be a clear case of evisceration." William Goldman, *The Season*, Harcourt, Brace & World, New York, 1969, p. 12. In his statistical analysis of the fifty-eight plays of the 1967–68 Broadway season, Goldman stated that homosexuals produced eighteen and directed twenty-two. *Ibid.*, p. 237. The Jewish share of Broadway was indicated by the fact that of the thirty members of the Dramatist's Guild Council at least two-thirds were Jews. *Ibid.*, p. 148. Regarding David Mer-

own almost all the theater houses, comprise most of the producers and almost half the directors, and furnish 50 percent of the audience and playwrights. The other 50 percent of the playwrights consists largely of well-known Majority homosexuals.[40] The artistic corruption of the theater, it need hardly be mentioned, is only exceeded by its financial corruption, which includes payroll padding, kickbacks, ticket scalping and union featherbedding. Add these unwholesome ingredients together and it is readily understandable why in New York, still the radiating nucleus of the American theater, the greatest of all art forms has degenerated into homosexual or heterosexual pornography,[41] liberal-minority message plays, foreign imports and musicals.[42] It is doubtful if a new Aeschylus, Shakespeare or Pirandello could survive for one minute on Broadway, frequently described as an example of the minority enrichment of American culture.

The minority penetration of the communications media hardens minority cultural domination because the press, magazines and TV are the transmission belts of art and, as such, its supreme arbiter. By praising, condemning, featuring,

---

rick and Hal Prince, the two Jewish producers who brought in 40 percent of the season's gross, Goldman wrote, "The point is this: neither of them has the least interest, time, taste, skill or knowledge to produce an original American play." *Ibid.,* p. 111.

40. The chief dramatic contribution of the homosexual playwright has been the sensitive heroine in an insensitive society and the bitchy heroine, the former representing how the author feels, the latter how he acts. Homosexuals have also devised most of the flashy sets and fancy dance routines of the musical extravanganzas.

41. *Che,* by minority "playwright" Lennox Raphael, was the first American play to present the act of copulation on stage.

42. "The American musical comedy . . . sometimes seem to be largely the invention of Jews." Yaffe, *op. cit.,* p. 225. Forty years ago Owen Wister felt free of any literary or social inhibition in speaking frankly about this influence, which was obvious even then. Describing the Boston musicals of the late 1870's and contrasting them with those of New York fifty years later, he wrote: "Pinafore had recently blazed its trail of tune and laughter all over our map, pretty and witty comic operas from Paris and Vienna drew crowded houses, not a musical show had yet been concocted by the Broadway Jew for the American moron, clean-cut muscular light music hadn't yet rotted into the fleshy pulp of jazz." Owen Wister, *Roosevelt, The Story of a Friendship,* Macmillan. New York, 1930, pp. 17–18. Ironically, it was Wister's novel, *The Virginian,* which served as the model for Hollywood and television Westerns.

underplaying or ignoring books,[43] paintings, sculpture, music and other artistic works the communications media decide, in effect, what will be distributed (and become known) and what will not be distributed (and remain unknown). A book not reviewed favorably or not reviewed at all in the influential, opinion-shaping columns of *The New York Times, The New York Times Book Review* and *Time*—together with several "higher-brow" weeklies and monthlies [44]—has little or no chance of getting into bookstores or libraries.

This effective winnowing process also extends to advertising. Books promoting minority racism are acceptable for advertising in most newspapers and magazines. Books promoting Majority racism are not. Press agentry in the form of praise from columnists and television personalities (i.e., the David Susskind show) are another tested means of lending a helping hand to minority artists or Majority artists who specialize in minority themes. Perhaps the most banal example of minority mutual admiration in the arts is the practice adopted by *The New York Times Book Review* of permitting books espousing Negro racism to be reviewed by Negro racists. For example, *Die Nigger Die!* by H. Rap Brown, a fugitive from justice recently rearrested after holding up a New York bar, received a generally favorable review, although Brown wrote that he "saw no sense in reading Shakespeare," who was a "racist" and a "faggot." [45]

Throughout his life and career the minority-conscious artist identifies with one group of Americans—his group. In so doing he inevitably attacks the Majority and Northern European cultural tradition because Majority America both

43. In speaking of books, it should be remembered that just under 50 percent of the major American publishing houses are Jewish. Yaffe, *op. cit.*, p. 225.
44. "American literary and political 'highbrow' magazines offer the clearest example we have of this [Jewish] predominance. Here a bias, oddly enough quite unconscious, selects the subject matter, the treatment, and the authors most appealing to the Jewish sensibility (or which can best be fitted into it). It can be fairly said that these magazines are dominated by what may be called the Jewish cultural establishment." Van den Haag, *op. cit.*, p. 129.
45. *New York Times Book Review,* June 15, 1969, pp. 6, 38. Brown, the reviewer also seemed happy to report, stole a few articles from the White House during a meeting with President Johnson. He wanted to steal a painting, but was unable to think of a way of concealing it under his coat.

in the historical and contemporary sense is not his America. The Puritans are reduced to witch hunters, reactionary pietists and holier-than-thou bigots. The antebellum and post-bellum South is turned into a vast concentration camp. The giants of industry are described as robber barons. The earliest pioneers and settlers are typecast as specialists in genocide. The police are pigs. Majority members are goys, rednecks, honkies or just plain beasts.

But it goes far beyond this. A principal theme of modern Negro writing is the rape or violation of Majority women. In his bestselling *Soul on Ice,* which is now required reading in the English curriculum of hundreds of colleges, Negro militant Eldridge Cleaver, who in 1972 was directing a Black Panther faction in Algiers, tells how he feels about "consciously, deliberately, willfully, methodically" despoiling white women. "It delighted me that I was defying and trampling upon the white man's law . . . that I was defiling his women . . . I felt I was getting revenge . . . I wanted to send waves of consternation through the white race."

Cleaver quotes approvingly from a work of Negro playwright LeRoi Jones. "Rape the white girls," Jones wrote. "Rape their fathers. Cut their mothers' throats." [46] Intercourse with Majority females, although on a much more sedate and controlled scale, is a theme that also appears frequently in the so-called Jewish literary renaissance. The heroes of Jewish fiction often seek out Gentile girls because there is "less need for respect, and thus more possibility . . . to do things that could not be done with a person one has to respect." [47]

When it centers on Majority history, the minority *Kulturkampf* moves out of bounds. A Broadway play turns Indians into a race of virtuous higher beings while whites are portrayed as ignoble savages, and the quondam heroic figure of Custer struts about the stage as a second-rate

---

46. Eldridge Cleaver, *Soul on Ice,* Dell, New York, 1968, p. 14.
47. Van den Haag, *op. cit.,* p. 217. The author refers in particular to Philip Roth's novel, *Portnoy's Complaint.* At one point Roth wrote: "But the shikses ah, the shikses are something else again . . . the sight of their fresh cold blond hair spilling out of their kerchiefs and caps . . . I am ecstatic. How do they get so gorgeous, so healthy, so blond!"

gangster.[48] A Hollywood film shows U.S. cavalrymen raping and mutilating Indian maidens on screen.[49] A television play set in the depression years of the 1930's puts the blame for America's ills squarely on the Majority and ends with a specific tirade against "Anglo-Saxons." [50]

Contemporary white artistic efforts are dismissed as "pimp art" by LeRoi Jones on the front page (second section) of the Sunday *New York Times.*[51] One Jewish author states, "The family is American fascism." A Jewish literary critic calls the late Thomas Wolfe, who had twice the talent of any minority novelist yet to appear in American literature, a "professional hillbilly." A leading Negro writer labels America, "the Fourth Reich." As mentioned previously, a literary Jewess describes the white race as "the cancer of history." [52]

But the ultimate objective goes beyond the destruction or upending of Majority institutions. There is an increasing frequency in minority art of subtle and not so subtle appeals for the physical molestation and even the outright massacre of whites. Such was the message of LeRoi Jones' play, *Slave Ship.*[53] With the same vitriolic splash, Eldridge Cleaver writes of "young blacks out there right now who are slitting white throats." [54] Julius Lester, another popular and well-received Negro writer, may have identified the minority artist's real grudge, the radiant Western artistry that seems forever beyond his reach. Ranging as far afield as Paris, he called for the destruction of Notre Dame "because it separated man from himself." [55]

The communications media and principal academic forums having been closed to him, the Majority artist has no adequate defense against the blistering minority assault on his culture. He must avoid praising his own people *as a people*—and he

---

48. Arthur Kopit's *Indians.*   49. *Soldier Blue.*
50. Millard Lampell's *Hard Travelin',* WNET, New York, Oct. 16, 1969.
51. *New York Times,* Nov. 16, 1969, Sec. 2, p. 1.
52. Originators of these quotations are in order: Paul Goodman, Alfred Kazin, James Baldwin and Susan Sontag. Benjamin De Mott, *Supergrow,* pp. 74–5. James Agee, a Truckler of considerable talent, preferred Chinese, Italians and Negroes to his own people and despised Irishmen, Poles and Germans. *Letters of James Agee to Father Flye,* Houghton Mifflin, p. 151.
53. See footnote 34, p. 88.   54. Cleaver, *op. cit.,* p. 15.
55. Lester, *Search for a New Land,* p. 144.

also must avoid castigating other peoples, particularly the more dynamic minorities. The minority artist, on the other hand, wears no such straitjacket. He freely praises whom he likes and freely damns whom he dislikes, both as individuals and as groups. The Majority artist with a narrower choice of heroes and a narrower choice of villains has a narrower choice of theme. Lacking the drive and brute force of minority racism, Majority art tends to become bland, innocuous, emotionless, sterile and boring.[56] Forbidden to explore the text and context of his collective consciousness, the Majority artist retreats to surrealism, science fiction, murder mysteries, fantasy, travel guides and pornography.[57] He refuses to resort to the minority practice of "seeing man's essential struggle as social, against other men, rather than the moral one against himself." [58]

Many potential Majority artists [59] probably sense well in

---

56. An art historian of the future, having only at his disposal lists of bestsellers, art expositions and musical recitals for the period 1950–1970, would be forced to conclude that there was hardly any such thing as the American Majority. As reported by *Time* (May 19, 1969, p. 12), the nation's five leading fiction bestsellers were: #1, *Portnoy's Complaint,* which has a Jewish hero or anti-hero; #2, *The Godfather,* an Italian-American novel about Italian-Americans and the Mafia; #3, *The Salzburg Connection,* a spy tale with stock Nazi villains by an Englishwoman; #4, *Slaughterhouse Five,* a World War II novel by a Majority Truckler; #5, *Sunday the Rabbi Came Home.*

57. Pornography assumes an ever greater place in eras of cultural breakdown, not, as some apostles of permissiveness like to pretend, because it expands artistic horizons but because it shrinks them. As bad money drives out good, the art of the private parts drives out the art of the heart and mind. Of all man's artistic activities, pornography requires the least amount of mental effort. Perhaps nothing has done more harm to the torn fabric of American civilization than the Supreme Court's 1957 ruling in *Roth vs. U.S.,* which defined obscenity as something "utterly without redeeming social importance." Since a sharp lawyer would be able to find at least a trace of "social importance" in any kind of trash, Pandora's box was opened, and the minority tycoons of Hollywood, Broadway and Publishers' Row were quick to seize the opportunity—and the profits.

58. John Leggett, "The Wasp Novel," *New York Times Book Review,* Nov. 30, 1969, p. 2.

59. The genius bathed in what Matthew Arnold has called "the national glow" has a less difficult row to hoe than the genius in a fragmenting culture, which forces partisanship of one kind or another on everyone. As Goethe put it, "Bedauert doch den ausserordentlichen Menschen, dass er in einer so erbärmlichen Zeit leben, dass er immerfort polemisch wirken musste."

advance the roadblocks in the way of a successful artistic career and turn to science, where their creativity is less hampered. Similar situations in the past may illustrate why in the life span of nations the artistic efflorescence has generally preceded the scientific—why Sophocles came before Archimedes, Dante before Galileo, Shakespeare before Newton and Faraday, Goethe before Planck. Mathematics, physics and chemistry, but not the life sciences, are less controversial than art [60] and in a divided, pluralistic society may be the last refuge of free expression and free inquiry. It has been said by Ortega y Gasset that "people read to pronounce judgment." The aphorism might be extended by saying that as nations become older and more divergent in politics, religion, class and race, people only read to soothe or excite their prejudices.

The glimmering of a great artistic era appeared in the United States in the first half of the nineteenth century. In New England, New York, Philadelphia and the South, a native American aristocracy was evolving out of generations of landowners, shipping magnates, army and navy officers, and government, church and educational leaders. At the same time, schools of Majority artists were emerging, their growth rate synchronized with that of the budding aristocracy. It was perhaps no coincidence that the Hudson River Valley, the stamping ground of the first American aristocrats, produced the first great American writer, Washington Irving, the greatest American writer, Herman Melville, and the first American school of painting. The Dutch patroons of New

---

60. The least controversial art is music and consequently the last to be devitalized by censorship. Properly speaking, the only art that still remains in Majority hands is "country music," and even this is falling under the triple assault of Negro jazz, the drug traffic and cynical show business promoters. Critic Richard Goldstein, writing for the young female readership of *Mademoiselle* (June 1973), charged that country music was "threatening" to Jewish sensibilities and recommended the lubricious lilt of Negro rhythms. The rock festivals, which have drawn such gigantic audiences and such gigantic attention from the media, are in part a confused attempt to rescue popular music from Tin Pan Alley. But they are by no means as impromptu as the press makes them appear. The Woodstock Festival had an advance ticket sale of $1,400,000, and its two Jewish producers, John Roberts and Mike Lang, spent $200,000 in local radio and newspaper advertising—one of the most concentrated spot campaigns in the history of Madison Avenue. *New York Times Magazine*, Sept. 7, 1969, pp. 122, 124.

Amsterdam had carved out their riverine estates decades before the founding of the Virginia plantations and while Boston was still a log-cabin theocracy.[61]

The traumatic experience of the Civil War was not entirely responsible for putting an end to America's great artistic promise. There was the overbrimming social fluidity which followed the war, and the settlement of the West. There were fortunes to be made—in commerce, in industry, in mining, in land—and as plutocracy waxed, art waned.[62] There was also the sudden arrival of the New Immigration, which played havoc with the normal, organic processes of artistic evolution.

In the last moment of the Republic, when Roman culture was displaying signs of rigor mortis, Augustus stopped the atomization of Roman art by halting the dispossession of the Roman Majority. The outcome was the Golden Age of Latin literature. It was not until Rome's decline properly began— according to Gibbon, with the accession of Commodus in A.D. 180—that the demise of Roman art and the Roman Majority could be considered official.

For the sake of the American Majority, and American art, it is to be hoped that the United States is now in its pre-Augustan, not its pre-Commodian period.[63]

---

61. Significantly, Melville's mother, Maria Gansevoort, a descendant of one of the oldest Dutch families, was a "cold, proud woman, arrogant in the sense of her name, her blood and the affluence of her forebears." Raymond M. Weaver, *Herman Melville*, p. 34. Also see Morison, *Oxford History of the American People*, pp. 177, 487 for a chronological comparison of the New York and New England aristocracies.

62. "The real revolution [in the U.S.] was not what is called the Revolution in history books, but is a consequence of the Civil War; after which arose a plutocratic elite." T. S. Eliot, *Notes Towards the Definition of Culture*, p. 44.

63. The ways and means adopted by Augustus in his rehabilitation of the "Old Romans" and Roman art should provide those interested in stopping the dispossession of the Majority with ample food for thought and with a fairly comprehensive blueprint for solving problems similar in many respects to those facing present-day Americans. Augustus' point of departure was "that the Italian race was immeasurably the superior of any other, and he did not wish to see it lost in a polyglot welter." Buchan, *Augustus*, pp. 16, 20, 124, 128, 130, 170–1, 206–9, 235, 244. "Considering it also of great importance to keep the people pure and unsullied by any taint of foreign or servile blood, he was most chary of conferring Roman citizenship and set a limit to manumission." Suetonius, *Divus Augustus*, trans. J. C. Rolfe, XL, 3.

Chapter 19

The Secularization of Religion

ART IS ONE OF the battlegrounds of the cultural clash now taking place in the United States. Religion is another. But the intention of this chapter is not to indulge in theological speculations or to question the truth or error of any particular faith. It is to examine the purely social and pragmatic side of religion and its relationship to the present tide of political, economic and social change.

God may be dead, as it was once announced that great Pan was dead and as many twentieth-century churchmen, echoing the wishful thinking of Nietzsche, presently proclaim. But the religious instinct is very much alive. Though science is a long way from confirming it, it almost seems that men are born with a religious gene. There may have been an alarming decrease in the spiritual magnetism and uplift of formal religion in recent times, but men have made up for it by shifting their innate religiosity to more mundane creeds—democracy, liberalism, capitalism, nationalism, fascism, socialism and communism. If an abundance of saints, devils, martyrs and prophets is a sign of religious zeal, the twentieth century ought to rank as the most religious of all centuries. Never since the days of Rome have so many heads of state, both living and dead, been deified or diabolized on such a grand scale. Belief in the old gods may be flickering, but belief in the more worldly deities of the present is burning laser hot.

A review of organized religion in America must concentrate on a discussion of Christianity. Until quite recently, the United States was called a Christian nation and statistically about 60 percent of all Americans still belong to a Christian church.[1] But what exactly is a Christian? The definition seems to depend on the religious denomination of the definer. In Roman Catholic eyes, St. Francis, one of the few who ever took Christ literally, and Boniface VIII, wearing his triple crown and announcing "I am Caesar, I am Pope," were both Christians. In Protestant eyes, so was Captain (later Reverend) John Newton, who composed the ever popular hymn, "How Sweet the Name of Jesus Sounds," while the vessel he commanded waited off the Guinea coast to pick up a new shipment of slaves from the interior.[2] Other Christians have included Syrian column-sitters, sword-wielding Northmen, cannibalistic blacks, lust-ridden empresses and piety-ridden nuns.

The difficulty of defining a Christian stems in part from the massive polarizations and cyclic sweeps of Christianity in the first nineteen centuries of its existence. No religion has been so many things to so many believers and so many theologians. None has provoked so many heresies and schisms . . . so much war and so much peace . . . so much animosity and so much love. Perhaps the only time that Christianity was truly unified and truly one religion was in its very beginnings, when it was a simple offshoot of Judaism— one of the many sects which flourished in the spiritual ferment stirred up by Roman encroachments on Jewish statehood.

1. The 1965 Census of U.S. Religious Bodies lists 253 separate denominations with a total membership of 120,965,234 or 64 percent of the population. Of these 66,854,200 were Protestants, 44,874,371 Roman Catholics, 3,260,835 Eastern Orthodox, 5,500,000 Jews, 100,000 Buddhists. No statistics were available for Moslems. The number of Roman Catholics and Jews is quite misleading, because the Catholic Church counts as members all who are baptized and the total given for the membership of Jewish congregations is equivalent to that of the entire Jewish population. The Protestant churches, on the other hand, include in most cases only practicing churchgoers and communicants. If Protestant churches used Jewish methods of statistical compilation, many could more than double their membership. The breakdown of the larger Protestant denominations is as follows: 23,252,644 Baptists, 12,824,109 Methodists, 8,569,194 Lutherans, 4,383,246 Presbyterians, 3,338,728 Episcopalians.
2. *Times Literary Supplement,* Jan. 9, 1964, p. 25.

The first great problem of Christianity was a purely racial one. Would it be a religion for Jews or for Gentiles? Jesus himself was a Galilean from "Galilee of the Gentiles." [3] There is no definite proof that he was a Jew, but it is almost certain he was brought up in a Jewish cultural ambiance. At first many Jews looked upon him as a possible Messiah come to satisfy their craving for a return to the long-departed temporal glories of Solomon. Later, when the ministry of Jesus began to include outsiders and when he demonstrated more interest in an otherworldly than in a worldly kingdom, the Jews quickly closed their hearts and their purses.[4] In the words of Toynbee, "this inspired Jewish scion of forcibly converted Galilean Gentiles was then rejected and done to death by the Judaean leaders of the Jewry of his age." [5]

The next problem facing Christianity, once it moved away from the Jews, was how much of its original Jewish background and tradition would or should be preserved. One faction, the Marcionites, attempted to purge the early church of all Jewish influence and went so far as to brand the Old Testament the work of the devil. The Petrine Church, on the other hand, accepted the Jewish Bible, a great deal of Jewish theology and law, and the special position of the Jews as midwives of Christianity—indeed almost everything Jewish except the Jews themselves. Eventually the Judaising party won, though remnants of Marcionite influence persisted until the Cathars of Southern France were liquidated by Papal auxiliaries in the twelfth century.[6] If the Marcionites had

---

3. "Galilee of the Gentiles" is found in Matthew (4:15). At the time of Jesus' birth, Galilee was a Roman province in Northern Palestine and had a mixed Jewish-Assyrian population, *Ency. Brit.*, Vol. 9, p. 978. Actually Galilee had been part of the Jewish state for less than a century before Jesus' birth. After throwing off the Macedonian rule, the Jews had extended their territory northward. Toynbee, *Study of History*, Vol. II, pp. 73–4. Both ultra- and anti-Semites have occasionally tried to make Jesus something other than a Jew. The Talmudic tradition of a part-Roman ancestry has been noted in footnote 137, p. 192. Certain Aryanizers of Jesus point to a descent from "blond Amorites" who once lived in and about Galilee.

4. The Spanish philosopher Miguel de Unamuno gave another reason why Jews turned their backs on Jesus: he was preaching immortality and Jews are not immortality minded. Unamuno, *Del Sentimiento Trágico de la Vida*, Las Americas Publishing Co., New York, 1966, Chapter III.

5. *A Study of History*, Vol. V, p. 658.

6. *Ency. Brit.*, Vol. 5, p. 72 and Vol. 14, p. 868.

prevailed, there would have been very little Judaeo in the Judaeo-Christian heritage of Western civilization.[7]

One of the principal themes of Gibbon's magnificent obituary of the Roman Empire was the important role of Christianity in its decay and dissolution.[8] If the great historian had explored the workings of the early church more penetratingly, he might have found the real culprit was not the Christian religion as such, but those who played up the equalitarian and insurrectionary elements of Christianity at the expense of the more fundamental Christian concept of otherworldliness. On the one side, the power and privilege of the dwindling Roman elite were undermined by the New Testament's accent on brotherhood and renunciation. On the other, the subject races were aroused to violence by the inflammatory sermons of the Early Fathers, whose strictures against Roman paganism demanded the destruction of everyone and everything connected with the old religion. In

---

7. Certain racial manifestations can be detected in this divided inheritance. Marcion, a native of Northern Asia Minor, was born outside the Semitic ecumene. Saints Peter and Paul and many other leaders of the Petrine Church were converted Jews. An important Jewish legacy to Christianity was the doctrine of original sin, strongly supported by St. Augustine, a North African, and strongly opposed by Pelagius, a native of the British Isles, during one of Christianity's most serious theological feuds. Alien to Hebrew thought and tradition, but too well established to be purged by the more fanatic Judaizers, were the New Testament's three wise men, the temptation on the mountain, baptism, paradise and the resurrection. This non-Jewish side of Christianity, according to one view, originated with the Persian prophet, Zoroaster, with whose teachings Jesus became familiar as a result of his association with the Amorites, who had close contacts with the Persians. C. G. Campbell, *Race and Religion*, Peter Nevill, London, pp. 24 ff. T. E. Lawrence had this to say in regard to the seemingly congenital differences in the religious sensibilities of Semites and non-Semites: "I had believed Semites unable to use love as a link between themselves and God. . . . Christianity had seemed to me the first creed to proclaim love in this upper world, from which the desert and the Semite (from Moses to Zeno) had shut it out. . . . Its birth in Galilee had saved it from being just one more of the innumerable revelations of the Semite. Galilee was Syria's non-Semitic province, contact with which was almost uncleanness for the perfect Jew. . . . Christ by choice passed his ministry in its intellectual freedom. . . ." T. E. Lawrence, *Seven Pillars of Wisdom*, Doubleday, Doran, Garden City, N.Y., 1935, p. 356. There might also have been a racial repulsion on the part of Gentiles for some Jewish religious practices, in particular that aspect of the circumcision ritual in which a "venerable and honored guest is asked to apply his mouth to the penis, and suck up the first drop of blood." Van den Haag, *op. cit.*, p. 160.

8. *Decline and Fall of the Roman Empire*, Chapters 15 and 16.

A.D. 310 there was one last flare-up of pagan repression when the Emperor Galerius poured molten lead down Christian throats and fed the lions a final meal of martyrs in the Coliseum. Two years later, Constantine saw the blazing cross and Rome soon had a Christian Emperor.

When Christianity became a state religion the bishops changed their tune. Instead of opposing the government the Church became its guardian. Instead of attacking military service it advocated it. Once the oppressed, Christians were now the oppressors and the flames of Greek and Roman temples lit the night sky of dying Rome. Although it was too late to prevent the Empire's collapse, the bishops did manage to convert, in a fashion, the conquering Teutons, who later saved Western Christianity from the Huns, Arabs, Turks and other heathen marauders.

By the time of the Crusades, Christianity had divided into the Roman Catholic and Greek Orthodox Churches. It divided again when Northern Europe, incited by princes with a covetous eye on the heavy gold exports to the Holy See, broke away from the spiritual absolutism and temporal *Realpolitik* of the Latinized Popes. The Reformation drew the religious frontiers which today separate Protestant from Catholic Europe and the racial frontiers which in many areas separate Nordic from Alpine Europe.

Professor Guignebert of the University of Paris, perhaps the most informed modern biblical scholar, has provided an interesting sidelight on the development of Christianity by noting the changing "appearance" of Jesus through the ages. The first depictions of Jesus made him hairy, ugly and abject. Later in Gothic rose windows and statuary and in Renaissance paintings and frescoes, Christ was endowed with Nordic features and at times looked more like Siegfried than the son of a Mediterranean carpenter. Many paintings of the Holy Family portrayed the Virgin and the Christ Child with blond hair and blue eyes. The Esthetic Prop was everywhere visible in the greatest masterpieces of Church-sponsored art.

Christianity was brought to the United States by members

9. Charles Guignebert, *Jésus*, Le Renaissance du Livre, Paris, 1933, pp. 189–96. In *The Everlasting Gospel*, Blake defined the extremes: "The Vision of Christ that thou dost see/ Is my vision's greatest enemy./ Thine has a great hooked nose like thine;/ Mine has a snub nose like to mine."

of practically every Christian denomination—Anglicans and Anabaptists, Catholics and Mennonites, Lutherans, Quakers and Shakers, Greek Orthodox and Doukhobors. The Episcopal Church—two-thirds of the signers of the Declaration of Independence were Episcopalians [10]—and the Calvinist churches (principally the Congregational and the Presbyterian) remained dominant until the rise of the revivalist and evangelical sects in the early nineteenth century. The slavery issue dissolved whatever Christian unity existed between North and South, turning many Yankees from the eye-for-an-eye morality and ironbound predestination of Calvinism [11] to Unitarianism and other less rigorous and less selective religious creeds. In the same years, Southern churches fastened a stratified, black-and-white Christianity on the slave states, justifying their actions by murky biblical passages on human bondage.[12]

Shortly before the Civil War, Roman Catholicism began to assume some prominence in national affairs. In addition to its religious function, the Church served as a vast social service organization for the mass influx of hungry, homesick Irish immigrants. Decades later, it became the spiritual and, on occasion, the political shepherd for the millions of Central and Southern European Catholics who furnished the bulk of the New Immigration. By the early 1930's, the Catholic Church was the largest and most powerful religious body in the United States. In 1928, Alfred E. Smith lost the presidential election partly because he was a Catholic. In 1960, John F. Kennedy won the presidency partly because he was a Catholic. In the 92nd Congress (1971–72), more Congressmen belonged to the Catholic Church than to any other religious denomination.

---

10. *Ency. Brit.*, Vol. 18, p. 612.

11. The earlier New England Calvinist was typified by Samuel Adams, who "was no revolutionist, but a racist, anti-Catholic—with no favor for minorities." Morison, *Oxford History of the American People*, p. 211.

12. The most quoted was Genesis (9:22–27). Ham, considered by some theologians to be the progenitor of the Negro race, sees his father, Noah, naked in his drunkenness. When Noah hears about it, he lays a curse on Canaan, the son of Ham, destining him to be a "servant of servants." Shem (the first Semite) and Japheth (the first non-Semite?), Ham's brothers, were thereafter to be served through all eternity by Canaan, according to pro-slavery interpreters of the Old Testament.

Today, Christianity in the United States has come full circle. Once again, it has turned its attention from God to man and become the champion of the minorities. Many Protestant ministers take the money from their collection plates and spend it on projects for blacks and chicanos, which are quite often more in the nature of political subsidies than charity.[13] They transform their churches into meeting places for black gangs. They record their "deep appreciation" to the black militant who stormed into Manhattan's Riverside Church and demanded $500 million in reparations.[14] Long tolerant of communism in its various Stalinist, Titoesque and Maoist guises,[15] many churchmen now openly endorse certain forms of revolution,[16] support civil disobedience, are jailed for unlawful picketing,[17] raise $100,000 bail for Black Panthers,[18] and frequently conspired against the American war effort in Vietnam.[19]

---

13. All in vain, as Nietzsche predicted a century ago: "There is nothing more terrible than a barbaric slave class, who have learned to regard their existence as an injustice, and now prepare to avenge, not only themselves, but all future generations. In the face of such threatening storms, who dares to appeal with any confidence to our pale and exhausted religions. . . ." *The Birth of Tragedy* from *The Philosophy of Nietzsche,* trans. Clifton Fadiman, Modern Library, New York, p. 1048.

14. *Time,* May 16, 1969, p. 94.

15. According to Congressional investigator J. B. Matthews, 7,000 clergymen once espoused the Communist party line. As Russian policy becomes more nationalistic, many of them have probably veered off to other, more popular brands of Marxism. For Matthews' estimate, see Walter Goodman, *The Committee,* Farrar Straus, New York, 1968, p. 335.

16. A London conference organized by the World Council of Churches (Protestant) produced a report which stated that "guerrilla fighters struggling against racist regimes must be given the support of the church if all else has been seen to fail." It also stated that in certain circumstances, "The church must support resistance movements, including revolutions, which are aimed at the elimination of political or economic tyranny that makes racism possible." The conference was under the chairmanship of Senator George McGovern, a Methodist lay delegate. *Time,* June 6, 1969, p. 88.

17. *Time,* Dec. 10, 1965, p. 96.

18. *New York Times,* Jan. 31, 1970, p. 9. In September 1970, black militant Angela Davis, while on the FBI's list of the ten most wanted criminals for owning the guns which killed a California judge, was honored by having her portrait prominently displayed in the annual Liberation Sunday of St. Stephen's Episcopal Church in St. Louis. *Miami Herald,* Sept. 27, 1970, p. 30-A. Miss Davis was later exonerated by an all-white jury.

19. Yale University Chaplain William Sloane Coffin, Jr., once married to the ballerina daughter of Arthur Rubinstein, was sentenced to two years in prison in 1968 along with pediatrician Dr. Benjamin Spock for conspiring

The Roman Catholic Church, though not so soft on communism, still has a large minority priesthood. Some Catholic priests have been active in inciting Mexican-American strikes against California farmers.[20] Others, notably the Berrigan brothers, have broken into Selective Service offices and destroyed draft records.[21] Still others have taken to the streets and led mass sit-ins in defiance of state and local laws. In only a very few cases were such activities censured or forbidden by the Catholic hierarchy.

Nevertheless, the present liberal-minority stance of Christianity in America lacks credibility and smacks of dilettantism. Jesus *was* an underdog and his poverty and minority status stimulated an honest concern for the oppressed and downtrodden. The well-fed, well-funded clergyman who walks a mile or two in a "freedom march" and drops in from time to time to see how his Negro friends are doing in the slums seems a little counterfeit. So does the "social conscience" of the Vatican ($5.6 billion stock portfolio and $1.5 billion annual income)[22] and of the U.S. religious establishment as a whole (property valued at $102 billion).[23] Such a vast hoarding of wealth, which is nothing new in church history, has always made Christianity suspect in the eyes of hardshell leftists. It helps explain why, despite all that Christian liberals did to prepare the way, in the three great revolutions of modern history—French, Russian

to counsel young Americans to evade the draft. The jury's verdict was later thrown out by a higher court. *1970 World Almanac*, p. 922.

20. *Time*, Dec. 10, 1965, p. 96.

21. *New York Times*, Aug. 9, 1970, Sec. 4, p. 7. In January 1971, the Berrigans were charged with plotting to blow up the heating systems of five government buildings in Washington and to kidnap Henry Kissinger. According to *Time*, the two brothers were "cradle rebels." Their father, Tom Berrigan, was a trade union organizer who had been brought to the U.S. by Irish immigrants fleeing the poverty of Tipperary. *Time*, Jan. 25, 1971, pp. 14–15. Eventually the kidnap charges were dropped against Daniel Berrigan and Philip was only found guilty of smuggling letters out of prison.

22. Nino Lo Bello, *The Vatican Empire*, Trident Press, New York, pp. 23, 135. Rome has formally denied these estimates. Yet the Holy See is so enmeshed in high finance that it has now established close relations with the Rothschild banking interests. *New York Times*, July 22, 1970, p. 8.

23. *Time*, May 18, 1970, p. 44. Of the $17.6 billion that American individuals or organizations contributed to charity in 1969, $7.9 billion (45 percent) was earmarked for religious purposes. *U.S. News & World Report*, July 13, 1970, p. 65.

and Chinese—Christianity was officially or unofficially proscribed.

Although Christians are still strong in numbers,[24] their faith is cooling. Popes no longer command armies, excommunicate kings and organize crusades. There are no more Sainte Chapelles abuilding and no artists with one iota of the religious intensity found in a Fra Angelico painting. The pens of Luther and Milton are still and the rousing Protestant hymns of yesteryear are gone out of style and increasingly unsung. Some revival meetings continue to draw large audiences, but more lips are converted than hearts. The old-time religion still exists in rural areas, but it no longer has much relevance. Catholic priests and Protestant ministers may get reams of favorable publicity in the press when they abandon their flocks to spread their "good works" abroad, but it gains them few points with their hometown congregations.

The deformation of religion in America, the shift from the Old Testament stamp of the original white settlers to the permissive social Christianity of the present, brings up the age-old question of how effectively religion shapes a people's character and how effectively a people's character shapes religion. According to modern standards the colonial American, his rifle in one hand and his Bible in the other, was a caricature of a Christian. He may have read the Good Book to his family once a week, but he seldom went to church. The Pilgrims, it is known, had no pastor for nine years after their arrival. In Virginia, fewer than one out of nineteen were church members. Among Massachusetts Bay colonists, only one-fifth were even professing Christians.[25] Joshua, though perhaps not the late Bishop Pike,[26] would

---

24. According to the *Osservatore Romano,* there are 1,027,000,000 Christians in the world, as against 509,000,000 Mohammedans, 444,000,000 Hindus, 1,300,000,000 assorted Buddhists, Shintoists and animists, and 13,900,000 Jews. *New York Times,* March 28, 1970.

25. William Warren Sweet, *The Story of Religion in America,* Harper, New York, 1950, pp. 5, 45, 48.

26. The public immorality of many modern church leaders is the best proof of the profound change that has taken place in American religion. Bishop Pike, for example, was almost the antithesis of the seventeenth-century Puritan divine. Born a Roman Catholic in Hollywood, Calif., Pike attended a Jesuit school and became a lawyer before being ordained an

have been proud of the Pilgrims. When they did go to
Plymouth Church, they marched in three abreast with their
muskets and firelocks at the ready, while other members of
the congregation manned six cannon on the roof, each
capable of shooting iron balls of four to five pounds.[27] Was
this a different kind of Christianity? Or was it a different kind
of Christian?

Many other aspects of early American Christianity are
equally abhorrent to modern church leaders. John Winthrop,
the first governor of the Massachusetts Bay Colony, probably spoke for all the Puritan elders when he said that
democracy "has always been counted the meanest and worst
of all forms of government." [28] In Connecticut and Massachusetts the right to vote was restricted to church members,
upsetting as this may be to those who believe that the
American political tradition is unalterably bound to the
separation of church and state.[29] Equally upsetting is the

Episcopal priest. An alcoholic when promoted to bishop, Pike was thrice
married and twice divorced. His son and a favorite secretary committed
suicide, and his daughter attempted suicide. Before he died in Israel, he
resigned his bishopric under fire and devoted himself to spiritualism. *Time*,
Nov. 11, 1966, pp. 56 ff. and *New York Times*, Sept. 8, 1969, p. 1. Two
prominent black churchmen set as poor an example as Pike. Adam Clayton
Powell with his padded payrolls and expense-account shenanigans, and
Martin Luther King, with his attempts to direct the course of American
foreign and domestic policy, behaved more like Renaissance cardinals than
Baptist ministers. *New York Times*, Jan. 4, 1969, p. 1 and *Time*, Aug. 17,
1970, p. 13. Even the "prophet" of the Black Muslims, Elijah Muhammad,
who served a three and one-half-year prison term for draft dodging,
scandalized his principal lieutenant by his dalliance with the office help.
Autobiography of Malcolm X, pp. 209–10, 299. Dean Moorehouse, a former
Methodist minister, went to jail for giving LSD to minors. He was the
friend of Charles Manson, leader of a West Coast cult that committed more
than nine murders. Moorehouse remained Manson's friend, even after the
latter "adopted" Moorehouse's fifteen-year-old daughter into his homicidal
band. *New York Times Magazine*, Jan. 4, 1970, p. 32. When Episcopal
Bishop Robert Hatch was informed that his daughter was appearing nude in
a San Francisco theater, he said, "I am glad she has a chance to express
herself." *Time*, June 8, 1970, p. 40. The California Methodist Church is
selling a $500 package of erotic, pornographic and obscene visual material
to groups of priests, ministers and doctors. Business has been so good that
the church decided to make its own pornographic films, rather than buy
them from suppliers. *Miami Herald*, Oct. 19, 1970, p. 2-B.
    27. Sweet, *op. cit.*, pp. 46–7.
    28. *Ibid.*, p. 51.
    29. *Ibid.*, p. 53.

fact that the New England church thrived on the slave and rum trade and that many well-known Congregational ministers owned slaves.[30]

The Protestant religion has passed through its Old Testament pioneering phase and its New Testament evangelical phase and has now entered its equalitarian phase. The Catholic religion is on a somewhat similar, but later-starting, timetable.[31] The burning faith brought over by immigrants from Ireland and Central Europe has gradually cooled. Their descendants now obey a less rigid and more tolerant code, which permits them to defy their church's ban on contraceptives, skip mass for golf and escape ever farther from the warm protection of their religious cocoon into the uncharted spaces of agnosticism.

Priests and even nuns are marrying, and not always within the church.[32] Parochial schools are shut down for lack of funds. Members of the hierarchy are challenging Papal infallibility. As the possibility of another great schism looms, the Church only manages to retain its ancient, unchallenged authority over the Unassimilable Latin Minorities—a predictable turn of events since what has become a primarily Mediterranean expression of Christianity could be expected to have the most enduring appeal to Mediterraneans.[33]

Judaism in America has followed the same hylotheistic route as Protestantism and Catholicism. Comparing the orthodox zealotry of the Sephardim of pre-revolutionary and revolutionary days to the more rational religious approach of contemporary Reform and Conservative Judaism is like comparing an acetylene torch to a candle. At present no more than ten percent of American Jewry observes dietary laws and surveys show that Jewish college students are con-

---

30. *Ibid.*, pp. 285–6. There were 6,000 slaves in Massachusetts in 1776.

31. The "Catholic" colony of Maryland was largely a fiction. During most of its existence Catholic immigrants were forbidden and Catholic worship prohibited. Beard, *op. cit.*, Vol. 1, p. 65.

32. Sister Jacqueline Grennan married Paul Wexler, a Jewish widower. Mrs. Wexler is now president of Hunter College. Philip Berrigan, the radicalized ex-priest, married a nun who was later arrested for shoplifting. *Time*, Sept. 18, 1973, p. 46.

33. This is not to say that American Catholics are decreasing numerically. According to the anti-Catholic historian Paul Blanshard, Catholics in America will outnumber Protestants by the year 2125. *American Freedom and Catholic Power*, Beacon, Boston, 1958, p. 298.

siderably less religious than non-Jewish students.[34] There are some 4,000 Jewish congregations in the United States, comprising approximately seventy percent of all Jewish families, but the majority of Jews affiliated with synagogues are by no means devout and only nineteen percent of all American Jews visit a temple once a week.[35]

The establishment of Israel has had its effect in reversing this rationalistic trend and drawing some Jews back to the religious fold by renewing their interest in Jewish history.[36] Judaism also continues to be attractive to many Jewish leaders for a reason that has nothing to do with religion and much to do with practical politics. As one prominent American Jew explained, "In fighting the cause of Jewish rights abroad, the religious approach is usually the one that Jewish leadership finds it most advisable to take." [37] He might have added that Judaism also serves as a useful camouflage for the Jewish engagement in domestic affairs. In the meantime, their old religious animus against Christianity has been mollified as Jews discover the advantages to be gained from the present Christian emphasis on selective tolerance.

The ecumenical movement, though successful in bringing Protestants and Catholics closer together than at any time since the Reformation, has been powerless to prevent the various Christian denominations from abandoning their moral ascendancy over American life. If secularization continues at its present pace, Christianity may soon have no deeper significance in the American scheme of things than sports. Protestantism, in fact, has become so lukewarm that even the issue of federal aid to education no longer secretes

---

34. Albert L. Gordon, *Intermarriage,* Beacon, Boston, 1964, pp. 42, 47–8, 50, 97.

35. Gallup Poll, Jan. 13, 1974.

36. Nevertheless, in respect to numbers, religious Jewry is barely holding its own. At best there are only 3,000 conversions a year—mostly Gentile women preparing to marry traditionally oriented Jewish males. Not many of them, however, convert to the Orthodox branch of Judaism, a process which includes sitting in a tub of water up to the neck while two learned elders discourse on the major and minor commandments, plus shaving the head and wearing a wig forever after. Litvinoff, *op. cit.,* p. 26 and Yaffe, *op. cit.,* pp. 46, 100, 102.

37. Dr. Israel Goldstein, *The American Jewish Community,* Block Publishing, New York, 1960.

undue amounts of adrenaline in Baptist or Methodist glands. Without regard to small, scattered voices of protest, national, state or local governments now subsidize parochial schools with free lunches and transportation and aid parochial institutions of higher learning with five- and six-figure monetary grants for the physical and social sciences. There is even less public outcry when liberal Protestant and Catholic clergymen, their white collars resplendent in television floodlights, run for public office.[38]

The most sensitive area of church-state relationship is no longer religion in politics, which presently serves liberal-minority interests, but the public observance of religion, which still has a faint Majority ring. Supreme Court rulings against prayers in public schools [39] and the display of religious symbols in public places,[40] as well as minority attacks on Christmas pageantry in the classroom,[41] and even on Christmas stamps with religious themes [42]—all these are the elements of what is essentially a new controversy.

Formerly, separation of church and state meant that churches were to stand alone without financial, legal or any other kind of assistance from government. Now it is coming to mean that religion must be isolated and even quarantined from public contact. This could be construed as more of a constriction than an extension of religious liberty. The free

---

38. But there is a public outcry when an anti-liberal clergyman like Carl McIntire takes the political stump.

39. In 1962, the Court decided that the recitation of the Lord's Prayer or Bible verses in public schools was unconstitutional, thereby, according to Senator Ervin of North Carolina, making God Himself unconstitutional. L. A. Huston, *Pathway to Judgment,* Chilton Press, Philadelphia, 1966, p. 4. The prayer on which the Court ruled said simply, "Almighty God, we acknowledge our dependence upon Thee and we beg Thy blessings upon us, our parents, our teachers and our country."

40. The Court ruled five to two in forbidding the erection of a cross in a city park in Eugene, Ore. *New York Times,* Oct. 5, 1969, p. 68.

41. The superintendent of the Marblehead, Mass., public school system banned all mention of Christmas in 1969, but finally reversed himself after a series of demonstrations by Majority children. *Washington Evening Star,* Dec. 1, 1969, p. 4.

42. The U.S. Post Office was bitterly condemned by the American Jewish Congress for issuing a stamp which contained a reproduction of Hans Memling's great Renaissance painting, *Madonna and Child. New York Times,* July 17, 1966.

exercise of religion is hardly possible without freedom of religious expression.

The campaign against public celebrations of the nation's religion,[43] in addition to its built-in iconoclasm, cannot avoid becoming a campaign against the nation's culture. Quite apart from its religious significance, Christmas—decorative tree, yule log, Santa Claus, elves, reindeer, sky-riding sleigh and all—is an exuberant manifestation, perhaps the most exuberant manifestation, of Majority folkways.

Already Majority members have permitted their biggest holiday to be transformed into an overcommercialized Oriental bazaar by the great department store chains, most of which are owned by non-Christians. Any further censorship or perversion of Christmas would be a further abridgement, not just of the Majority's religious freedom, but of its cultural freedom. Justice Potter Stewart, the lone dissenter in the Supreme Court's school prayer rulings, made this point clear when he said that the Court, instead of being neutral toward religion, was actually showing signs of hostility by denying students "the opportunity of sharing in the spiritual heritage of the nation." [44]

Eliot has written, "The culture of a people [is] an incarnation of its religion . . . no culture has appeared or developed except together with a religion. . . ." [45] This is tantamount to saying that religion and culture are indivisible, that one cannot be isolated from the other without severe damage to both. In Eliot's view, it was no coincidence

---

43. Christianity is designated the national religion of the U.S. in the sense that at most only 4 percent of the population belongs to a non-Christian church and that the remaining 96 percent either by religious affiliation, church attendance, birth, baptism, tradition or inclination exhibits some degree of attachment to Christianity. It is true that a 1968 Gallup Poll reported only 50,000,000 Americans attended church regularly. Nevertheless, most Americans who do not go to church still consider themselves Christians. *San Francisco Sunday Examiner & Chronicle, This World,* Dec. 29, 1968, p. 10.

44. *New York Times,* June 26, 1962, p. 16 and June 18, 1963, p. 28. In Boston, the *Jewish Advocate* in an editorial agreeing with the prayer decision suggested it might logically be extended to bar the traditional display at Christmas of the Nativity scene and other religious symbols at any public gathering or party. *Wall Street Journal,* July 6, 1962, p. 1.

45. *Notes Towards a Definition of Culture,* Harcourt, Brace, New York, 1949, pp. 13, 32.

that mankind's greatest artistic achievements occurred when church and state were working together, not apart.

Nine of the thirteen colonies had established churches, and so throughout almost all their history had England and the Scandinavian countries. Church disestablishment in America came about during the War of Independence, which disrupted colonial ties to the Church of England. It was made official by the First Amendment, which was chiefly the work of Franklin, Jefferson and Madison, many of whose religious (or irreligious) ideas had been taken from the French Enlightenment.

If the Greeks had been disestablishmentarians, there would have been no Parthenon, which was built with government funds. Nor any of the great plays of Aeschylus, Sophocles, Euripides and Aristophanes, which were staged in a government amphitheater, subsidized in part by the state treasury and offered to the public during state-sponsored religious festivities. If church and state had been separated in the Middle Ages and Renaissance, there would have been no St. Mark's, no Gothic cathedrals, no Florentine Baptistery, no Sistine Chapel and no *Last Supper*. Bach, it should be added, spent much of his musical life in state-supported churches. Finally, since the most ardent advocates of church-state separation are frequently those who consider every word of the Bible divine revelation, it might be recalled that the Old Testament was the book of the ancient Hebrews, who more than any other people believed that church and state were one.

It is ironic that the Supreme Court, presently the most powerful opponent of church-state unity, sits in an imitation Greek temple, the originals of which would never have been built without the subsidies of established churches.[46] Perhaps the very poverty and unoriginality of Washington architecture —with its highest monument copied from an Egyptian obelisk and its most famous landmarks slavishly duplicating Greek, Hellenistic and Roman building styles—has something to do with the circumstance that it is the only major

---

46. The anachronism of imitating ancient architectural styles in an age of magnificent new construction materials was made plain to all when the Corinthian columns of the Supreme Court building were installed after the roof had been put on.

world capital where church and state have been separated for more than a hundred years.

The greatest attraction of religion, according to Miguel de Unamuno, is the promise of immortality.[47] Equally as attractive, if endurance and survival are signs of attractiveness, are religious ceremonies, rites, sacraments, liturgies and feast days—the intersecting points between religion and folkways, between faith and art. The Northern gods have gone to Valhalla, but the yule log still blazes. In Russia, the Eastern Orthodox Church has been stripped of its primacy and its privileges, but the spectacular Russian Easter services continue to enthrall believers and non-believers alike. In Mexico, priests are forbidden to wear cassocks in the streets, yet each year hundreds of thousands of Mexicans go on pilgrimages, some even bloodying their heads with crowns of thorns in gruesome reenactments of the stations of the cross.

Unamuno to the contrary, most people want to live in the present as well as in the hereafter, and the more immediately understandable and enjoyable emanations of religion, its dramaturgy, seem as necessary to Western man and to

---

47. Unamuno, *op. cit.*, p. 42. In addition to its purely religious impact, the concept of an afterlife obviously has enormous social utility. It is easier for individuals and races to put up with the inequalities of earthly existence if they believe, or can be persuaded to believe, they will have another—and better—chance in the Great Beyond. In this context, the promise of immortality cannot help but exercise a calming and stabilizing effect on society. On the other hand, the effect may be too calming and too stabilizing, perhaps to the point of social stagnation. In the view of Martin Heidegger, whose teachings have been twisted beyond all comprehension by the so-called existentialist school of philosophy, immortality tends to devalue life. According to Heidegger, it is the awareness of death and its finality that intensifies human existence and gives it its deepest meaning. Just as the drama without a final curtain is hardly a drama, so endless immeasurable time is not time at all. Heidegger's philosophy increases man's individuality to where it becomes almost godlike and almost unbearable. It goes well, however, with the new anti-Copernican view. Man, sharply reduced in size when the earth was demoted from center of the universe to galactic speck, has now grown large again, perhaps larger than before. It is now remotely possible that he is the only intelligent being in all space—the exalted status accorded him until the Renaissance. If there are higher life forms in the cosmos, it is almost mathematically certain that some would be far enough ahead of man in the evolutionary process to send him simple signals that could be picked up on radio telescopes and other sophisticated electronic listening devices. But, at least for the moment, outer space is very still.

Western esthetics as its theology. As if sensing this, the liberal-minority coalition now attacks the manifestations of Christianity rather than Christianity itself. Those in the vanguard of the attack, however, are already finding it simpler to remove prayers from public schools than Christmas trees from public squares.

Many devout Christians, having taken note of the intelligentsia's open season on religion and religious observance, have concluded they are living in a profane age. They are right to the extent that the times are inauspicious for organized religion. But, as pointed out earlier, the reservoir of human faith is always full. It is not the amount of faith that changes, it is the direction. Religious ages do not yield to ages of skepticism, as some historians pretend. Old, established faiths simply give way to new, inchoate faiths. Much of the religious feeling loose in the world is in the hearts of those who would most object to being called religious.

The usual sequel to the decline of formal religion is the reappearance of the shaman or witch doctor, whose bag of magical potions and cure-alls is as old as humanity itself. In times of established churches, the shaman must work in the shadows. But in eras of religious "freedom" he is everywhere at once, gathering followers here, collecting donations there and spreading the tidings of his own peculiar metaphysics up and down the land. Sometimes the shaman operates on the outer fringes of a universal religion. Sometimes he leads his flock out of one universal religion into another, as did Elijah Muhammad of the Black Muslims. Frequently, he disassociates himself from all contemporary religious manifestations and goes back to the primeval bedrock of religion— to animism and anthropomorphism.

The phenomenal resurgence of astrology and soothsaying is one example of this trend.[48] But the most striking evidence of the descent of religion from the sublime to the subliminal is provided by that special and somewhat illegitimate branch of psychology known as psychoanalysis. Here in one beguiling package with a pseudo-scientific, mail-order appeal

---

48. So phenomenal it rated a cover story in *Time*, March 21, 1969.

is almost all the religious stock-in-trade of ancient man—interpretations of dreams, casting out of devils, incest myths, obsessive sexual teleologies, confessionals, and at the top of the totem poll the grand old shaman himself, Sigmund Freud.

As a scientific method for the investigation of man's being or as a therapeutic tool for mental illness, psychoanalysis can hardly be taken seriously by any rational person. Yet this half-sophisticated, half-crude masterwork of spiritual primitivism has been raised to such psychological, philosophical and even religious heights that it has exercised and continues to exercise a deeply corrosive effect on Western manners and morals. In the realm of art and esthetics, where it has probably done the most harm, psychoanalysis has taken man, once thought to be a little lower than the angels, and de-escalated him to the level of the brute.

To learn about the workings of the human brain it would have seemed wiser to investigate the neuron, a physiological fact, than the id, ego or superego, hardly more than psychological or, more accurately, *psychomantic* fancies. That Freud did not take the more difficult approach is one of the secrets of his popularity. Intuition and revelation, the scientific euphemism for which is synthesis, pack in a much bigger audience than long hours of controlled laboratory experiments.[49] To establish and preserve his professional status, Freud coated his teachings with just enough psychological lore to convince the unwary, the unstable and the untutored that he was not a humbug. His scientific pretensions notwithstanding, he operated more in the tradition of Joseph, Aaron and Daniel, his remote forebears, than in the footsteps of those who performed the plodding, painful research responsible for the real advances in the study of human behavior.[50]

49. The tendency of Jewish scientists to rely on mathematical instead of physical laws, on induction rather than deduction, is so pronounced that it can almost be described as a racial trait. Einstein is the most celebrated case. Spengler wrote that Hertz, a Jew, was the only important modern scientist to attempt to eliminate the concept of force from his physics. *The Decline of the West*, Vol. 1, p. 414.

50. While Freud was postulating about neuroses and psychoses, John Houghlings Jackson (1835–1911), the noted British neurologist, spent his life studying the function and development of the nervous system, making extensive clinical observations on epilepsy and other brain diseases. Jack-

After reading Freud one has difficulty in imagining how the world managed to get along until the advent of psychoanalysis. Either the pre-Freudian victims of neurosis never knew what they were suffering from, or the affliction was no older than the prognosis. Though only the rich can afford psychoanalysis—at rates presently ranging from $20 to $200 an hour—the man-in-the-street undergoes it daily at bargain prices through the massive Freudian backwash in the arts. The greatest writers in modern English literature—Eliot, Yeats and D. H. Lawrence, to name three—abhorred Freud, and Lawrence even went to the trouble of writing two anti-Freudian tracts, *Fantasia of the Unconscious* and *Psychoanalysis and the Unconscious*. But second-rate writers made Freudian theories and characters a central part of their work. James Joyce and Thomas Mann were two of the better novelists who borrowed from Freud, although the latter warned that there is an aspect of psychoanalysis which "maims life at its roots. . . ." [51]

One reason for the ready acceptance of psychoanalysis has been its timeliness. It meshes nicely, perhaps even designedly, with modern liberalism, which makes man the creature of environmental forces. Freud found the controlling forces of man to be internal, but so deeply buried in the "unconscious" as to be practically unreachable and uncontrollable. Consequently, both psychoanalysis and liberalism have bestowed extra credence and prestige on the school of behavioristic determinism, differing only as to the sources of such determinism. In either case, the human personality comes off second best.

Freud carried his attack on the freedom of the will even farther afield. He classified several important manifestations of individuality as repressions, describing them as harbingers of neuroses, psychoses or worse. One such repression was guilt, Freud's favorite *bête noire,* the elimination of which he set as one of the principal goals of psychotherapy. [52] But

---

son's epoch-making evolutionary theory of brain development is fundamental to the study of the function or malfunction of the human intellect. But how many have heard of John Houghlings Jackson?

51. *Ency. Brit.*, Vol. 18, p. 674.

52. When it is a question of the guilt of Majority members toward Negroes and other minorities, or of Germans toward Jews, most faithful

by getting rid of guilt, one also gets rid of a bulwark of social stability—the most practical, or at least the most inexpensive, of all crime deterrents. If it had the choice, which would society prefer, murderers who feel guilty or those who don't?

Freud's advocacy of compliant adjustment to one's surroundings is not unrelated to the widespread intellectual conformity which has descended on America. His cloacal approach to the roots of human thought and action has opened up a whole new dimension of vulgarity and tastelessness and helped smooth the way for the present Age of Pornography. The Freudian antidote for the mental imbalance caused by technology, deracination and the contemporary social centrifuge is to rummage around the events of one's childhood for sexual ghosts. Freud's seething concern for the bizarre, the banal and the perverse [53] has attracted many neurotic personalities to his camp, and it is often difficult to distinguish between patient and psychiatrist.

Frequently, the analyst seems to be in as much need of treatment as those he is treating. A case in point is Dr. Douglas Kelley, the court-appointed psychiatrist of the Nuremberg trials, who wrote a bestseller on the neurotic tendencies of the incarcerated Nazi leaders, much of the space being devoted to an analysis of Hermann Goering. Later Kelley, like Goering, committed suicide by swallowing cyanide.[54]

Freudians have convenient dogmatic lapses and turn from the teachings of psychoanalysis to the Old Testament.

53. Only a specialist in perversity could have taken such liberties with the beautiful Greek legends of the phoenix and Prometheus. Of the former, Freud wrote, "Probably the earliest significance of the phoenix was that of the revivified penis after its state of flaccidity, rather than that of the sun setting in the evening glow and rising again." Freud dismissed Prometheus as a "penis-symbol" and gave his own version of the discovery of fire. "Now I conjecture that, in order to possess himself of fire, it was necessary for man to renounce the homosexually-tinged desire to extinguish it by a stream of urine . . . to primeval man the attempt to extinguish fire by means of his own water signified a pleasurable struggle with another phallus." It was for these reasons, according to Freud, that primitive societies put women in charge of fire because their anatomy precluded yielding to the temptation faced by males. Freud, *Collected Papers* (Hogarth Press, London, 1950), Vol. 5, pp. 288, 291–2 and *Civilization and its Discontents,* trans. Joan Riviere, Jonathan Cape and Harrison Smith, New York, 1930, p. 50, footnote 1.

54. *New York Times,* Jan. 2, 1958 and *22 Cells in Nuremberg,* Greenberg, New York, 1947, pp. 76–77. Kelley described Goering, whose suicide was never satisfactorily explained, in unusually moderate terms. Could the author himself have slipped the Reich Marshal the pill?

Another Freudian doctor, Wilhelm Reich, who died in Lewisburg Federal Penitentiary in 1957 while serving a sentence for mail fraud, founded and directed a schismatic psychoanalytic cult dedicated to the knowledge, function and psychological ramifications of the orgasm.[55]

In its aberrant attempts to cure or control mental disorders, psychoanalysis has been able to obscure but not bury certain axiomatic truths. The mind breaks down permanently or temporarily from overwork or overleisure. Some minds are born with organic defects. Some develop them. If the mind lives alone, if the mind tries to survive on its own nourishment or on its own waste, it becomes disordered. Sanity is a function of purpose. Remove the spiritual props, the cultural reinforcements, the time-tested morale builders, the four-dimensional insurance of family, race, nation and church, and the delicate balance of the human mentality can easily crack. Even a brain as powerful as Nietzsche's could not stand the strain of continuous isolation.

Psychoanalysis recognizes rootlessness as a cause of mental disorder, but it avoids the subject of racelessness, the extreme case of rootlessness. It stresses the importance to mental health of the feeling of belonging, but it ignores race consciousness, the most intensive expression of the feeling of belonging. For such reasons, psychoanalysis totally misses the point when it tries to explain the origins of the most pernicious mental affliction of all—the state of mind which leads to suicide.

Suicide is the tenth cause of death in the United States among the general population, the third cause among the 15–19 age group and the second cause among college students.[56] Some of the lowest suicide rates are found in Mississippi and South Carolina, some of the highest in the Pacific states. A 1959 study revealed that the suicide rate of American whites (11.2 per 100,000) was more than twice as great as that of American nonwhites (4.5 per 100,000).[57]

---

55. Wilhelm Reich, *Selected Writings,* Noonday Press, New York, 1956, especially page 6. Reich established a thriving business selling "orgone boxes" to his band of true believers.

56. *Time,* Nov. 25, 1966, p. 48.

57. The low nonwhite rate was almost entirely due to Negroes, since the rate for American Indians was 11.5, for Japanese-Americans, 6.9 and for

The racial patterns that emerge from these statistics seem to be almost totally lost on psychoanalysts, who continue to explain suicide in terms of death wishes, depressive states and the turning inward of aggressive instincts. According to psychoanalytic theory, the downtrodden and the disadvantaged would be more likely candidates for suicide than those at the top of the social ladder, just as in Marxist theory the rich with their greater material blessings would be less apt to commit suicide than the poor.

It is, of course, the opposite that takes place. The greatest number of suicides occur not in the backward areas, but in the more advanced. It is among the rich and "successful" that the highest suicide rates are usually found, not among the poor. Where there is more racism, there is likely to be less suicide. Urbanism, loss of religion, career frustrations and intellectual exhaustion are contributing factors to suicide, but an all-important correlation remains the "racial morale" of a given population group at a given time.

Almost everyone who has studied the origins of psychoanalysis is aware that it is the product of the minority mind. Not only was Freud Jewish, but so were almost all his associates.[58] Few, however, are aware that psychoanalysis is

---

Chinese-Americans, 13.1. Louis Dublin, *Suicide,* Ronald Press, New York, 1963, pp. 33 ff.

58. Sachar, *op. cit.,* p. 400. The original Freudian circle included Kahane, Reitler, Heller, Graf, Sadger, Steiner, Sachs and Silberer. Among Freud's principal followers, though some have now strayed well beyond the doctrinal frontiers of the founder, were Adler, Rank, Abraham, Stekel, Federn, Klein, Reich, Horney and Fromm. Ruth L. Monroe, *School of Psychoanalytic Thought,* Dryden Press, New York, 1955, p. 14. The three most prominent non-Jewish psychoanalysts were Ernest Jones, the glib and gifted Welshman known as "Freud's apostle to the Anglo-Saxons," Harry S. Sullivan of Irish extraction, the one topranking American psychoanalyst, and Carl Jung, a Swiss. Freud was so interested in preventing psychoanalysis from being known as a "Jewish science" that he tolerated Jung as head of the International Psychoanalytic Society despite his basic disagreement with Freudian dogma. Jung eventually became interested in the collective rather than the individual unconscious and flirted with problems of racial memory and racial archetypes. For this and for making a few not too unfriendly remarks about National Socialist Germany, he was branded a Fascist. Weyl, *The Creative Elite in America,* p. 95 and the *Saturday Review of Literature,* Sept. 6, 1947, p. 21 and June 11, 1949, p. 10. Although he never quite escaped the Freudian taint, Jung's most important contributions may eventually prove to be in the fields of mythology and culture history.

also the product of minority animus. According to Howard Sachar, a chief motivation of the pioneer Freudians was "the unconscious desire of Jews to unmask the respectability of the European society which closed them out. There was no more effective way of doing this than by dredging up from the human psyche . . . sordid and infantile sexual aberrations. . . . Even Jews who were not psychiatrists must have taken pleasure in the feat of social equalization performed by Freud's 'new thinking.' The B'nai B'rith Lodge of Vienna, for example, delighted in listening to Freud air his theories. . . ." [59]

Freud can also count a large number of prominent social scientists among his following. Claude Lévi-Strauss, the "structural anthropologist," has injected the Freudian schematic into modern anthropology, writing in typical psychoanalytical fashion, "In the language . . . of myth vomit is the correlative and inverse term of coitus and defecation is the correlative and inverse term to auditory communication." [60]

Herbert Marcuse, the mentor of the New Left, has made a synthesis of Marx and Freud, modifying and rearranging the Oedipus Complex in such a way that the father stands for capitalism and the parricidal son, the proletariat. [61] Such fanciful nonsense would make interesting footnotes in a history of scholarly tomfoolery, if it were not taken seriously by so many liberal intellectuals.

It is to Freudianism and its basically hostile practitioners, with their near monopoly in psychiatry, that the disturbed Majority member habitually comes when seeking relief from mental illness. He is at once subjected to a sordid, demeaning, demoralizing and deracinating interrogatory which extinguishes whatever sparks of self-respect he may have retained. [62] The crux of his problem is not touched, and the

---

59. Sachar, *op. cit.,* pp. 400–1.
60. Edmund Leach, *Lévi-Strauss,* Fontana/Collins, London, 1970, p. 81.
61. Alasdair MacIntyre, *Marcuse,* Fontana/Collins, London, 1970, pp. 41–54 and *New York Times Book Review,* Oct. 26, 1969, p. 66.
62. Jewish patients have fared little better, even though their high racist quotient offers more resistance to deracination. As they turn from Judaism, Jews have taken to analysis in ever increasing numbers because "such concepts as equality, brotherhood and internationalism, have been differentially

problem itself is exacerbated. For the Majority patient, as he may or may not discover in time, the psychoanalyst's couch is the bed of Procrustes. There is no area of the cultural clash where the toll of the Majority spirit has been so heavy.[63]

Religious faith can be the great catalyst of human energy. But a pseudo-religious throwback like Freudianism, ministered by a minority priesthood to a congregation with which it has a minimum of empathy, can offer little constructive impetus in an age when human faculties if properly or improperly aroused seem capable of unlimited expansion or unlimited destruction. Nor is any genuine religious inspiration likely to be gathered from what Jung has called those "frightful gods [who] have only changed their names and now . . . rhyme with 'ism.' " [64]

Dr. Percival Bailey, Director of Research of the Illinois Psychiatric Institute, in perhaps the most devastating attack ever written on Freud and his works, has predicted that psychoanalysis in the long run will probably be remembered as something akin to animal magnetism.[65] As a means of

attractive to Jews." Weyl, *op. cit.*, p. 96. As for the psychoanalytic profession itself, Weyl states that it has been "attractive to Jews of East European origin . . . steeped in Talmudic traditions, because it involved a highly abstract manipulation of abstruse concepts and a minimum of scientific experimentation."

63. "Thus it is a quite unpardonable mistake," Carl Jung has written, "to accept the conclusions of a Jewish psychology as generally valid. Nobody would dream of taking Chinese or Indian psychology as binding upon ourselves. The cheap accusation of anti-Semitism that has been levelled at me on the ground of this criticism is about as intelligent as accusing me of an anti-Chinese prejudice. No doubt, on an earlier and deeper level of psychic development, where it is still impossible to distinguish between an Aryan, Semitic, Hamitic, or Mongolian mentality, all human races have a common collective psyche. But with the beginning of racial differentiation, essential differences are developed in the collective psyche as well. For this reason we cannot transplant the spirit of a foreign race *in globo* into our own mentality without sensible injury to the latter, a fact which does not, however, deter sundry natures of feeble instinct from affecting Indian philosophy and the like." *Collected Works*, trans. R. F. C. Hull, Pantheon Books, New York, 1953, Vol. 7, p. 149, footnote 8.

64. *Psychological Reflections*, Harper & Row, New York, 1961, p. 134.

65. Percival Bailey, "A Rigged Radio Interview—with Illustrations of Various Ego-Ideals," *Perspectives in Biology and Medicine,* The University of Chicago Press, Winter, 1961, pp. 199–265. Two other prominent anti-Freudians are Dr. Thomas Szasz and Dr. Ronald Laing, who consider

avoiding the Freudian cul-de-sac which he asserts has never kept a psychiatric patient out of an asylum,[66] as well as providing a cautionary guideline for the Majority member in search of a religion, Dr. Bailey invokes some memorable words of D. H. Lawrence:

"The soul is not to pile up defenses around herself. She is not to withdraw and seek out her heavens inwardly, in mystical ecstasies. She is not to cry to some God beyond, for salvation. She is to go down the open road, as the road opens, into the unknown, keeping company with those whose soul draws them near to her, accomplishing nothing save the journey, and the works incident to the journey, in the long life-travel into the unknown, the soul, in her subtle sympathies accomplishing herself by the way." [67]

---

mental illness not so much a disease as a form of role playing, where the patient deliberately employs a dramatic means of making a point and getting his own way. Laing says that every psychosis carries the seed of its own cure, and that some forms of madness are a vastly enriching human experience if allowed to run their course. Thomas Szasz, *The Myth of Mental Illness*, Hoeber-Harper, New York, 1961, Chapter 13. For more on Laing's theories, see *Time*, Feb. 7, 1969, p. 63. Philosopher Alfred North Whitehead found more fault with Freudians than with Freud himself. "The ideas of Freud were popularized by people who only imperfectly understood them, who were incapable of the great effort required to grasp them in their relationship to larger truths, and who therefore assigned to them a prominence out of all proportion to their true importance." *Dialogues of Alfred N. Whitehead*, Little, Brown, Boston, 1954, p. 211.

66. One prominent psychologist, Franz Winkler, has vaguely implied that Freudian psychoanalysis has never effected any cures at all. "Almost invariably an increasing indifference to other people's needs, a shifting of symptoms with serious psychosomatic ailments, and a deep-seated unhappiness replaced the emotional conflicts and struggles which had been 'cured.'" *Man: The Bridge Between Two Worlds*, Harper, New York, 1960, p. 2.

67. D. H. Lawrence, *Studies in Classical American Literature*, The Viking Press, New York, 1964, p. 173.

Chapter 20

The Atrophy of Education

EDUCATION, THE THIRD of the three principal battle zones in the cultural clash, is the process whereby man's most priceless possession, his culture, is passed on to posterity. If the process is tampered with, if the cultural testament of a people or race is altered, so to speak, while still in probate, the inheritance itself may waste away. It is the creeping atrophy of the traditional mechanics of cultural flow from one generation to another which characterizes the present state of American education.

In the terminal chapter of the *Decline and Fall of the Roman Empire*, Edward Gibbon said he had described the triumph of barbarism and religion. A future historian completing a survey of the deterioration of American education might say with equal oversimplification that he had described the triumph of John Dewey and Benjamin Spock. Dr. Spock has been singled out because his *Common Sense Book of Baby and Child Care* has sold more than nineteen million copies and except for the Bible is *the* bestseller of all time.[1] It has been estimated that one out of every four American children since World War II has been brought up according to Spockian precepts.[2] Since the home phase of education is as important as any of the later stages, Spock has probably

---

1. The exact figure is 19,076,822. Alice Hackett, *70 Years of Best Sellers,* Bowker, New York, 1967, p. 12.

2. *Current Biography,* 1956, pp. 599–601.

wielded more influence than any other person, living or dead, on American education.

As for the merits or demerits of such influence, one point should be made clear in advance: Dr. Spock is not only a pediatrician, but a psychiatrist, and a Freudian psychiatrist to boot. This means that his theories are grounded in such banal Freudiana as birth trauma, infantile sexuality, oral and anal stages and penis envy.[3] Spock, moreover, centered the child's pre-school education on the child himself instead of on parent and child as a unit—on the link rather than the chain of the human continuum. Self-expression, in Spock's *Weltblick*, is more important than discipline, and affection more important than guidance. Most important, although he never mentions it as such, is what might be called the economy of parental worry. Almost nothing will go wrong, according to Spock, if things are allowed to run their course. In this respect Spock's wildlife approach to pediatrics reduces to a gigantic nostrum to relieve parental anxiety. In appreciation for lightening their traditional burden of responsibility and pushing a great deal of it off on the child, millions of American mothers have made Spock a multimillionaire.[4]

It was obvious from the start that parents who followed Spock's teachings would pamper and spoil their children for fear of wounding their egos and implanting neuroses they might carry about with them for the rest of their lives. The fruits of such permissiveness were to be seen in the activities of the "flower children," hippie cultists and student insurrectionaries, all of whom belonged to the first Spock-trained generation of Americans.[5] The results are also to be found in

3. Spock began his career as a psychiatrist and only later became a pediatrician. Even after *Baby and Child Care* was first published in 1946, he served as Assoc. Prof. of Psychiatry at the University of Minnesota and then as a member of the Psychiatry Department of Western Reserve University, a post he held for almost two decades. Freud's daughter, Anna, who specializes in applying psychoanalysis to childhood disorders, has had almost as much influence on Spock as Freud himself.
4. Spock's popularity may be attributed in part to what Alexis Carrel has described as "la trahison des femmes." Carrel accused modern women of putting careers, sexual pleasures, bridge-playing and movie-going above child-rearing. He urged women "non seulement de faire des enfants, mais de les élever." *L'homme, cet inconnu,* pp. 372, 431.
5. One wonders how much of the speech of Jerry Rubin, one of the "Chicago 7" hooligans, to a gathering of Ohio college students could be

Spock's oldest son, Michael, a problem child and three-time college dropout who spent nine years in deep analysis.[6]

Too late and too half-heartedly, Spock came to see, at least dimly, the error of his ways. Admitting he had been "over-permissive," Spock recanted to the extent of drawing in some of the latitudinous boundaries he had placed on self-expression and in later editions of his book the word discipline is seen more frequently. In 1968, after shifting his sphere of interest from pediatrics to the Vietnamese war, Spock was sentenced to jail for conspiracy to counsel draft evasion. He had finally become a martyr, albeit a short-lived one because the verdict was later reversed.[7]

When Spock began to devote most of his time to protest movements and legal maneuvers to escape imprisonment, his place was filled in part by the Israeli-born Dr. Haim Ginott, described as the "Dr. Spock of the emotions." Ginott's principal thesis is that parents should become amateur psycologists in order to "decode" their children's behavior. Misbehavior may be tolerated but not sanctioned and a balance between strictness and indulgence is best achieved by a strategy of sympathy.[8]

The minority grip on the upbringing of Majority children has been further tightened by newspaper and magazine pundits whose readerships reach into the millions. The columnists who hold the most authoritative sway over parental and teenage attitudes are those who deal with personal

---

traced to Spock. Rubin's remarks included: "The first part of the Yippie program, you know, is kill your parents. And I mean that quite seriously, because unless you are prepared to kill your parents, you're not really prepared to change the country . . ." *Human Events,* May 16, 1970, p. 31.

6. Michael Spock, "My Father," *Ladies Home Journal,* May, 1968, p. 72. Michael also revealed—rather surprisingly considering the emphasis his father put on parental love—that his father never kissed him.

7. It should be pointed out that Spock is a selective pacifist. He has admitted, "If another Hitler came along, I would just as soon go to war and take the chance of being killed." But when he had the chance to do just that in World War II, he spent most of his time serving in a San Francisco Naval Medical Facility, writing his book in the evening. Jessica Mitford, *The Trial of Dr. Spock,* Knopf, New York, 1969, pp. 8, 10–12.

8. *Time,* May 30, 1969, pp. 62–63. Ginott adamantly refuses to say whether he is married and has children. His book, *Between Parent and Child,* has already been translated into thirteen languages and one and one-half million copies have been sold.

problems in the form of replies to letters, some of which are bona fide, some obviously planted. The two most widely read "sob sisters" of the 1960's were Abigail Van Buren ("Dear Abby") and Ann Landers ("Your Problems"), who are not only real sisters but identical Jewish twins.[9] The creator of Sesame Street, the network television program which teaches integration to children at the pre-school level, is Joan Ganz Cooney, also of Jewish extraction.

Once the child leaves home for school, the dogmatic lures of child psychiatrists, amateur and professional, are traded for those of formal educationists. Here, even in the first grade, children will fall under the long, quixotic shadow of the late John Dewey, the driving force of what has become known as progressive education. To Spock, the child was the senior partner of the parent. To Dewey, the student was the senior partner of the teacher.

The subject matter of education, in Dewey's view, was not as important as the method. Character forming and moral training yielded to problem solving and learning by doing. The use of religious and historical example to instill courage, loyalty, pride and good citizenship was discouraged. The true goal of education was determined to be the search for a better social order. The study of the classics and of Latin and Greek was dropped and replaced by the social sciences. Classroom discipline was relaxed in favor of teacher-student dialogues. The instructor himself became more concerned with the *how* of learning than the *what*.

Predictably, progressive education soon progressed into a state of educational anarchy. It was a noble attempt, as so many of the great ideals of liberalism and democracy are noble in theory before their indiscriminate application makes them ignoble in practice. Unhappily, man, who belongs to *Homo sapiens,* not to a race of gods, is neither mentally, morally nor physically self-sufficient. The most intelligent, the most advanced and the most responsible society in history could hardly have profited from such uncontrolled and un-coordinated experimental stabs at the learning process. Yet they were thrust upon increasing hordes of slum-dwelling,

---

9. They were born on July 4, 1918, to Mr. and Mrs. Abraham Friedman of Sioux City, Iowa. *Current Biography,* 1957, p. 315.

uprooted children, whose upbringing, surroundings and educational capacity were hardly above the Neanderthal level.
In no time, all the high hopes and good intentions were reduced to shibboleths of racial and class agitators, while in
large urban areas the lack of ethical indoctrination and the
incessant depreciation of tested societal values turned out a
whole generation of mentally anesthetized, morally disoriented hoodlums.

Even Dewey began to see the light in his latter days and,
like Spock, shortened his sails by advocating the reestablishment of a measure of educational discipline.[10] But it was much
too little and far too late. The blackboard jungle, student
assaults on teachers, campus violence and the seizure of
college facilities, the senseless destruction of laboratories
and libraries—all signaled the death agonies of a once great
educational system. If Dewey had lived, he would have been
forced, as an Old Believer and an honest pragmatist who
knew the proof of the theory was in the testing, to have
abandoned almost all his educational ideas.[11] *Si monumentum
requiris, circumspice.*

One extreme example of education failing completely to
equip young Americans to meet the trials and tribulations of
modern life was the mass murder of eight nurses in Chicago
in 1966. A ninth nurse, a Filipino girl, was the only one to
escape. It was no coincidence that she happened to be the
one who had been least exposed to contemporary educational
techniques. She hid under the bed while the others were led
off one by one to be knifed to death. The other nurses did
not resist because they felt they could reason with the
murderer. They thought they could calm him with procedures

---

10. *Ency. Brit.,* Vol. 7, p. 347.

11. It is unfortunate that the brilliant minds who so frequently attempt
to propel society up new educational byways have the habit of warning their
social guinea pigs of the obvious pitfalls *after* rather than *before* the event.
With all due allowance for Dewey's epistemological flair and contributions
to modern philosophy, there is simply no excuse for his avoidance of the
racial factor in education or stating, as he did, that any learning activity
"done under external constraint or dictation . . . has no significance for
the mind of him who performs it." How much of the chaos of modern
education flows from such a premise? *Intelligence in the Modern World,
John Dewey's Philosophy,* Modern Library, New York, 1939, pp. 607–8.

they had learned in class. According to newspaper reports, they "all had psych and they were pretty sharp." [12]

Although American education is *in extremis,* there have been few attempts to save it. One proposal has been to bring back the "great books" and let them stand as permanent guideposts for learning.[13] But the problems of American education are much too complex to be solved by the simple substitution of the very old for the very new. Another proposal has been put forward by the "essentialist" pedagogues who prescribe a common core of learning to be absorbed by everyone, regardless of ability or personal aims.[14] A few educators are turning back to Plato, who believed that education was the drawing out of innate ideas and who could not insist enough on the moral aspects of teaching. "But if you ask what is the good of education in general, the answer is easy—that education makes good men, and that good men act nobly. . . ." [15]

Aristotle, once considered the greatest of all authorities on education, has been largely abandoned by Western educationists. It is not hard to understand why. Aristotle asserted that the chief purpose of education was the molding of citizens to fit the form of government under which they lived, to develop in them a sense of affection for the state and to encourage the growth and unfolding of human intelligence.[16] Still widely prevalent, on the other hand, are the educational theories of Locke, who stressed the teaching of tolerance and civil liberty. Even more popular are the ideas of Rousseau, who abandoned his own five offspring, but whose *Émile* had more influence on child upbringing than any other work until Dr. Spock's *magnum opus.* Although

12. *San Francisco Chronicle,* July 23, 1966, p. 7.
13. S. E. Frost, Jr., *Introduction to American Education,* Doubleday, Garden City, N.Y., 1962, p. 42.   14. *Ibid.,* p. 26–7.
15. *Laws,* trans. Jowett, I, 641.
16. Plato was more favorable than Aristotle to the Spartan educational system which removed all male children from home at the age of seven and put them in state institutions where they received an eleven-year indoctrination course in such soldierly qualities as bravery and courage. Because ROTC began so early in Sparta, Spartans have been considered educationally backward, even though they were the only Greeks who provided for the education of women. For Aristotle's thoughts on education, see *Politics,* viii, 1, and *Ency. Brit.,* Vol. 7, pp. 983–4.

Rousseau declared that Negroes were intellectually inferior to Europeans,[17] he is a favorite theorist of those who press hardest for school desegregation. Whereas Plato suggested that goodness be implanted in the student by education, Rousseau decided that goodness was already there and that the teacher's job was to coax it to the surface.

In colonial times and in the early days of independence, American education was primarily a religious undertaking. It did not become public, secular, compulsory and "universal" until the last half of the nineteenth century. At present, religious control and sponsorship of education are limited to parochial schools, of which the Roman Catholic church has by far the largest number. As of 1967, slightly more than one-half of the eleven million American Catholics of school age were in parochial schools, a ratio that was expected to fall to one-third in the next generation. Catholic parochial education was made possible in large part by the fact that as many as 100,000 people—mostly members of religious orders—were willing to receive as little as twenty dollars a month in salary.[18] But the steady increase in living costs and the steady decrease in faith are serious threats to the future of the Catholic teaching profession.

As suggested previously, a decline in formal religion does not necessarily result in a nation of atheists. The religious instinct does not mortify. It flows into different channels in the search for different divinities. In the school system, as in so many other American institutions, Christianity is simply being phased out by the modern religious syncretism of democracy, equality and minority racism. Certainly anyone familiar with contemporary school and college curricula can hardly fail to detect a theological tone in much of the subject matter. Whatever else they may be, political science lectures are becoming increasingly difficult to distinguish from sermons.

No attack on American education—not even the bombings or the armed incursions of black students—has been as shattering as school desegregation. The 1954 Supreme Court

17. *Émile ou de l'éducation,* Editions Garnier Frères, Paris, 1964, p. 27.
18. John Leo, "The American Catholic is Changing," *Minorities in a Changing World,* Knopf, New York, 1967, p. 308.

ruling in *Brown vs. Board of Education of Topeka* may some day be ranked as the Fort Sumter of the second American Civil War. Although the Constitution says nothing about education, the Court ordered the desegregation of all public schools on the ground that segregation denies equal opportunities to minorities. Even if school facilities were equal—as some were, but most were not—the very fact of separation, in the Court's view, was generating in children "a feeling of inferiority as to their status in the community that may affect their hearts and minds in ways unlikely ever to be undone." The Court built its case on the equal protection clause of the 14th Amendment.[19]

In reaching its decision the Court took judicial notice of sociological evidence which had not been heard in the lower courts and which was introduced during its hearings by a legal technicality known as the "Brandeis brief." Normally, appeal courts did not permit the injection of new facts or new evidence. But Brandeis, when a Supreme Court Justice, broke this longtime precedent by encouraging the admission of briefs containing materials which he considered unquestionable and not openly prejudiced against either side of the dispute. As it turned out, the "Brandeis brief" heard by the Supreme Court in *Brown* was simply the repetition and elaboration of the liberal-minority thesis of racial equalitarianism. The genetic side of the argument and the effect of integration on the education of white children were totally ignored.[20] The defense was permitted no rebuttal.[21]

19. Frost, *op. cit.*, pp. 305–6.
20. In its opinion the Supreme Court mentioned the Swedish sociologist, Gunnar Myrdal, by name. Myrdal's tract, *An American Dilemma*, bears somewhat the same relationship to the contemporary black revolution in America as Diderot's *Encyclopédie* bore to the French Revolution. The author's significant misconception of current social trends in the U.S. is the subject of footnote 13, p. 211.
21. A later attempt to overturn *Brown* by introducing such evidence in another desegregation case, *Stell vs. Savannah Board of Education*, 220 Fed. Supp. 667 (S.D. Ga., 1963), failed when the Supreme Court refused to act on an appeal from the Fifth Circuit Court of Appeals. See also *Evers vs. Jackson School District*, 232 Fed. Supp. 241 (S.D. Miss., 1964) and *Brown vs. School District No. 20*, 226 Fed. Supp. 819 (E.D.S.C., 1963). For a detailed description of the *Stell* trial, as well as an analysis of certain factual errors in the testimony presented in *Brown*, see Putnam, *Race and Reality*, Chapter IV.

Because desegregation led to social mixing of whites and Negroes, resistance to the Supreme Court's ruling flared up immediately in the South.[22] It took longer to develop in the North, where *de facto* segregation in the ghetto areas gave authorities the chance to look the other way. In both the North and South, however, integration meant abandoning the concept of the neighborhood school, since it could only be accomplished by the educational gerrymandering of entire school districts and by busing.[23] Once such steps were undertaken or considered seriously by local school boards, resistance in the North often became as solid and intractable as in the South.

School desegregation, slowed by massive white noncompliance, has been further decelerated by the white exodus to the suburbs. In the birthplace of desegregation, Washington, D.C., the public school system is now 94.3 percent black. Although it might be expected that the government sponsors of desegregation would at least make a pretense of doing what they are trying to force others to do, there are only a few authenticated cases of highly placed white members of the executive, legislative or judicial branches sending their own children to desegregated public schools.

In the once all-white schools where almost half of all Negro pupils are now enrolled,[24] the results have been far from gratifying. Students of each race have tended to adopt the worst customs, habits, morals and speech of the other. Bright pupils, black and white, have either left or attempted to leave, and in many schools all social activities have had to be abandoned.[25] Classroom violence and vandalism have

22. The *Brown* ruling "crowned a generation's work by the American Jewish Congress in domestic affairs, consummating the alliance between the two minorities but incurring deep resentment among white conservatives." Litvinoff, *A Peculiar People*, p. 51.

23. The Nixon administration continued to implement busing although one Gallup Poll showed that the people opposed it by an eight to one margin. *New York Times*, April 5, 1970.

24. *New York Times*, Aug. 31, 1969, Sec. 4, p. 1. Integrationists know that there can never be total school desegregation until white children in the suburbs are bused to black inner city schools, and vice versa—which is why the educational establishment was so strongly for McGovern in 1972.

25. Edward Langerton, *The Busing Coverup*, Howard Allen, Cape Canaveral, Florida, 1975.

reduced the quality of education as much as they have raised its cost.[26]

As for the student record, the mixing of white children with blacks two to three years behind them in educational level and twenty points lower in I.Q. scores has not only substantially slowed the progress of students as a whole, but increased the number of dropouts by pressuring Negro students to perform beyond their ability.[27] The celebrated Jensen study, which found that heredity accounts for about eighty percent of individual I.Q. variations, concluded that Negro pupils, while as adept as whites in rote learning, are much less adept in cognitive learning.[28] Although these findings clearly call for different curricula for black students, the drive for nationwide educational conformity goes forward unabated.

---

26. In the 1968–69 school year, there were 205 assaults on teachers in the New York City public school system and the cost of vandalism was $3,266,025. *New York Times,* April 19, 1970, p. 40. In the same approximate period there were 61 arson or bomb incidents in schools and colleges throughout the nation, 200 sit-ins or building seizures and 4,000 arrests. *U.S. News & World Report,* Feb. 16, 1970, p. 55.

27. "In grade 12 the typical nonwhite lags up to three years behind the typical white in achievement test scores for reading." *Wall Street Journal,* July 8, 1968, p. 10. In the New York City public school system, where Negroes and Puerto Ricans outnumber whites 544,227 to 540,591, the reading level of Negro children is two years behind the white reading level. *San Francisco Sunday Examiner,* June 4, 1967, Sec. A., p. 26.

28. Dr. Arthur R. Jensen is director of the Institute of Human Learning at the University of California and vice-president of the American Educational Research Association. The *Harvard Educational Review* (Winter, 1969) was largely devoted to Jensen's statistics-studded examination of the inability of education to correct genetic differences in Negro and white intelligence. After publication, Jensen received an unprecedented amount of hate mail, including a few death threats. In Berkeley, the Students for a Democratic Society engaged a sound truck to demand Jensen's dismissal, later invading his classroom and forcing him to hold his classes in secret. He finally had to call on the police to protect his files and kept the lights burning in his office all night to discourage looters. A number of his liberal colleagues brought him before a specially organized investigatory board with all the trappings of a medieval witch trial—the first time in American academic history that a professor has had to defend a scholarly paper before an inquisitional proceeding that included videotape cameras. *New York Times Magazine,* Aug. 31, 1969, p. 11. In 1970, a group of Harvard students called on the *Harvard Educational Review* to turn over to the Black Panther legal fund all revenues from the sale or distribution of the Jensen article. They further demanded that all copies and reprints in circulation be destroyed and no further reproduction and distribution be permitted.

To help them "catch up," Negro students are frequently promoted on the basis of age, not achievement, with the result that some students with a third-grade reading level are found in the ninth and tenth grades.[29] As for higher learning, only about one-half of black high school graduates are fully capable of handling a college curriculum.[30] Once they get to college, Negroes may be given two grades higher than whites for the same work.[31] One professor has been known to pass everyone in his class because he will not ‘fail a Negro student.[32] This same two-tier grading system is applied by other teachers to forestall accusations of racial prejudice.[33] The envy, frustration, distrust and cynicism aroused by such practices are more noticeable in those universities and colleges which, in their race to enroll Negroes, have dropped their traditional entrance requirements.[34] Minorities are now insisting this practice become universal and actually closed down City College of New York to enforce their demands. Mayor John Lindsay and his Board of Education surrendered, and an open enrollment policy for City College was begun in 1970.[35] Any New Yorker who finished high school, no matter what his grades, was qualified to enter.

Admission to college without proper academic credits is a new idea in American education. If pursued, it could lead to certain complications, particularly in the area of scientific studies. If students can enter college with insufficient preparation, will they then be given degrees even though failing most of their courses? And if given such degrees, can they then use them to obtain employment designing skyscrapers,

---

29. *San Francisco Sunday Examiner,* May 20, 1967, p. 2.
30. According to Fred Crossland, a Ford Foundation education expert.
31. One such case, in New York University, was reported by James Burnham in his *Suicide of the West,* John Day, New York, 1964, p. 197.
32. *New York Times Magazine,* July 28, 1969, p. 49.
33. *Ibid.*
34. At the very height of the undergraduate riots in the spring of 1969 the eight leading Ivy League universities and the seven leading women's colleges announced an 89 percent and 120 percent increase, respectively, in the enrollment of black freshmen for the class of 1973. *New York Times,* April 20, 1969, p. 76. In 1964, there were 234,000 Negroes in college; in 1969, 492,000. *U.S. News & World Report,* June 1, 1970, p. 20.
35. *Time,* May 16, 1969, p. 59 and *New York Times,* Feb. 8, 1970, p. 25. In 1971, half of the City College students were on drugs. *New York Daily News,* Feb. 24, 1971, p. 4.

bridges and aircraft?[36] The answers have a direct bearing on national security, since Soviet engineers are still awarded degrees on the basis of their grades, not their race.

The Negro invasion of American education has brought with it Black Studies programs, which teach minority racism in classrooms where Majority racism is forbidden. But the injection of minority racism into college and high school curricula is not exclusively the work of Negro groups. There are just as many white as black organizations on the lookout for "racial slights" in courses and textbooks which do not elaborate fully on minority contributions to American history or persecutions of minorities abroad.[37] At their insistence, which often borders on outright coercion, many such textbooks have been rewritten, and more have been replaced.[38] Concurrently, public educational facilities have been put at the disposal of minority groups for research projects highly critical of Majority institutions.[39]

Although minorities generally supported the British or were neutral in the War of Independence,[40] a reading of recently published school and college texts would indicate that without minority assistance Americans might now be swearing allegiance to Queen Elizabeth II. Crispus Attucks has become an important figure in American history—so important that an illustrated child's history of colonial times, published in 1969, gives him more space than George Washington.[41] Haym Salomon, a Polish-born commission

36. One way to reverse this trend might be to force the professors and college administrators who hand out such degrees to live in the buildings, drive across the bridges and fly in the airplanes designed and built by these ersatz engineers.

37. In October 1960, the New York City Board of Education sent a letter to 100 textbook publishers asking for "substantial revisions" in history books to place a much sharper emphasis on German atrocities against minorities in World War II. *Overview*, October, 1961, p. 53.

38. In California, minority lobbies forced a resolution through the Oakland Board of Education to purchase textbooks which "accurately portray the contribution of minority groups in America." *San Francisco Chronicle*, Jan. 23, 1963, p. 30.

39. The B'nai B'rith Anti-Defamation League gave $500,000 to the University of California, a state university, to investigate the role Christian churches play in fostering anti-Semitism. *Look*, June 4, 1963, p. 78.

40. William H. Nelson, *The American Tory*, p. 89.

41. Review of *An Album of Colonial America* in the *New York Times Book Review*, July 6, 1969, p. 16.

merchant, is another recently discovered minority "hero" of American independence and has been awarded an article under his own name in the *Encyclopaedia Britannica,* although he was more than once welcomed behind the British lines.[42] On the other hand, those Negroes in the War of Independence who supplied British warships off the Southern coast and who remained on board as volunteers are seldom featured in the "new history." [43]

Whatever may be said about contemporary American education, its pyromaniac state is a far cry from the 1660's when the entire student body and faculty of Harvard conversed freely in Latin.[44] It is an even farther cry from the onetime disciplined earnestness of Western education as summed up by the Latin hexameter with which Winchester School in the Middle Ages greeted its new pupils, *Aut disce aut discede; manet sors tertia caedi.*[45] There was an air of Melville's *Benito Cereno* [46] about the armed band of black militants who occupied Cornell University's student union center for thirty-four hours and then marched out, guns at the ready, to receive a general amnesty from administration and faculty.[47] There was an air of surrealism about Princeton making Brent Henry a trustee after the twenty-one-year-old Negro senior distinguished himself in the seizure of a campus building.[48]

One can find, of course, much to protest in present-day American education—the soullessness, the mechanized

---

42. *Ency. Brit.,* Vol. 19, p. 890.   43. Nelson, *op. cit.,* p. 111.
44. *Ency. Brit.,* Vol. 5, p. 876.
45. "Learn or depart; a third alternative is to be flogged."
46. The character of Benito Cereno, a Spanish sea captain made prisoner on his own ship by blacks, is most nearly duplicated in the modern educational scene by Kingman Brewster, president of Yale University. Brewster banned George Wallace from the Yale campus in 1963, yet opened it wide to a 1970 May Day meeting of Black Panthers. *New York Times,* April 30, 1970, p. 38. Brewster, who claimed that blacks could not get a fair trial in the United States, took a large part in the nationwide mourning for the Kent State "4," who were presented by the press as typical American students, although three of them were Jewish and the girl kneeling beside the dead student in the widely distributed photograph was a fifteen-year-old runaway from Florida. But Brewster and his New Left constituency made no outcry when a Majority student was murdered and other Majority students wounded in the bombing of a University of Wisconsin physics and mathematics center. *Time,* Sept. 7, 1970, p. 9.
47. *Time,* May 2, 1969, pp. 37–8.
48. *New York Times,* June 8, 1969, p. 1.

mnemonics and the scandalously low salaries of teachers.[49] But such inequities can hardly be corrected by strutting Negro commandos or by the library and laboratory-burning Students for a Democratic Society. The minority underpinnings of the SDS can be surmised from the nationwide educational survey which found, "Almost half of the protest-prone students are Jewish. . . ."[50]

If the purpose of education is the transmission of culture, as the greatest modern poet has opined,[51] then the duty of educators is the safeguarding of culture. Here the failure of American education is most glaring. One of the many notable examples of this failure is the career of Dr. Hsue Shen-tsien. With the help of scholarships paid for in part by the American government, Dr. Hsue received his master's degree from the Massachusetts Institute of Technology and his Ph.D. from the California Institute of Technology. He then returned to his homeland where he was put in charge of the design and production of rocket systems for Red China's new H-bombs.[52]

The concept of American education as a denationalized data bank whose deposits belong to everyone, and should be passed on by everyone to everyone, is not very realistic—especially in a world where the nations most unfriendly toward the United States, one of the most unfriendly being Dr. Hsue's, have a totally different idea of the learning process. The Communist countries hold the old-fashioned view that the job of education is to strengthen the state and that all instruction, a euphemism for indoctrination, should ultimately be directed toward that end. This attitude is essentially Aristotelian, in spite of what the heirs of Lenin may say, and is shared by those members of American minorities

49. The average starting pay of a grade school teacher is $5,519 compared to the $8,000 starting pay of engineers, physicists and chemists. The average federal worker's pay is $8,500. The average grade school teacher's $7,077. Compare the annual $500,000, plus stock bonus, singer Barbra Streisand receives for four weeks' work at a Las Vegas gambling casino. *U.S. News & World Report*, Feb. 19, 1968, p. 85 and *Time*, Feb. 28, 1969 p. 84.

50. *Time*, May 3, 1968, p. 25 and May 23, 1969, p. 49.

51. Eliot, *Notes Towards a Definition of Culture*, p. 98.

52. *Life*, May 28, 1965, pp. 92, 94.

whose cry for equal educational opportunities is really a demand for power, not learning for learning's sake.

The Soviet Union coddles its minorities or nationality groups by giving them their own schools and universities where they may pursue the study of their own history and literature and where the language of instruction is their own.[53] No matter what his origin, however, every student must take the same required basic courses in Marxism-Leninism, in line with the dictum of the Eighth Party Congress (1919) that Russian schools be transformed into a "weapon of the Communist rebirth of society."[54] Aside from this political indoctrination, applied sciences and vocational training are given preference over academic subjects in the Soviet educational system. One consequence has been that in 1958 the USSR graduated 94,000 engineers as compared to 35,000 in the United States.[55] The teachings of Freud, which have assumed such importance in many aspects of American education, are hardly known in Russia.

There are some who ascribe the crisis in American education to the generation gap, a social phenomenon which has always existed to some extent in fragmenting societies. But in contemporary America the gap is more publicized than real. Those who do fit the description of belonging to an alienated younger generation have not so much turned, as *been turned,* against their parents—ironically by minority intellectuals often old enough to be their grandfathers. It has been the septuagenarian German refugee philosopher, Herbert Marcuse, who has given most of the ideological impetus to that segment of the teaching profession which seeks not only to set Majority students against their families, but also against their history, their institutions, their race and even themselves. Having decided that revolution is no longer

53. Nicholas Hans, *Comparative Education*, Routledge, London, 1949, pp. 28–31, 58.

54. *Encyclopedia of Russia and the Soviet Union*, p. 150.

55. *Ibid.*, p. 152. It is noteworthy that the Russians developed a special educational system for their *bezprizorny*, the great numbers of homeless children who lived by their wits and by crime during the tumult and chaos of the Revolution. For equally large numbers of homeless ghetto children, who are displaying similar criminal symptoms, American educators rather than give them special schools are trying to solve the problem by putting them in the same classroom with normal children.

possible according to the old Marxist formula of class war, Marcuse has proposed building a new revolutionary base on an alliance of students and blacks.[56] Two other prominent leaders of "revolutionary youth" are Harvard Professor George Wald (born in 1906) and M.I.T. Professor Noam Chomsky (born in 1928).

In spite of intensive brainwashing by their Marcusian-minded social science departments, a third of American students are still not afraid to identify themselves as "conservatives," even though the new masters of the educational process have succeeded in making the word an obscenity.[57] Moreover, it was not the conservative or even the liberal students who provoked most of the campus violence that has descended on the country. Students did not seize a New York University computer and threaten to destroy it unless $100,000 was given to the Black Panthers. It was, according to the New York District Attorney, the act of two minority professors, Robert Wolfe and Nicholas Unger.[58] A student shotgun did not shoot down a judge in San Rafael, California, in an abortive courtroom kidnapping. It had been bought two days previously by black philosophy instructor, Angela Davis, whom Marcuse has described as his "best" pupil.[59] It was not the student body which turned the University of California at Berkeley, once the pride of American higher education, into an intellectual skid row. It was a mindless clique of nonstudents, dropouts, minority students, radicalized faculty members and spineless administrators.

It is not difficult to find a better explanation than the generation gap for the change that has come over American education. In the year preceding the student deaths at Kent State, minority enrollment in Midwest colleges jumped 25 percent.[60] The faculty at Harvard, one of the greatest centers

56. MacIntyre, *Marcuse*, p. 88.
57. Gallup Poll, *New York Times*, May 11, 1970, p. 56. Considering the intellectual cowardice and vacuity of most professional conservatives, it is a wonder that any students at all, no matter how intense their feelings against the liberal-minority educational monopoly, were willing to flaunt the conservative label. It can only be explained as a protest vote, not as a vote of affirmation.
58. *New York Times*, July 30, 1970, p. 54.
59. *Life*, Sept. 11, 1970, pp. 22 ff.
60. *New York Times*, May 20, 1970, p. 1.

of unrest and agitation, is now "dominated by Jews" and 15 to 20 percent of the faculty of other leading universities are Jewish.[61] Younger Jews now compose 25 percent of the student body at Harvard, 18 percent at Yale, 15 percent at Princeton and 40 percent at Columbia.[62] At the same time, according to a visiting Israeli educational expert, at least half the nation's adults have now become functionally illiterate.[63]

By way of summarizing the present state of American learning, one point should be stressed. Like established institutions everywhere, the American system of education was the outgrowth of a specific concrescence of people, environment and history. To suppose this system would function efficiently, or at all, under different conditions and for different ethnic groups is asking man to construct timeless macrocosms out of ephemeral microcosms. A multiracial state, especially one which both permits and advocates cultural pluralism, would seem to require a multiracial educational program, not only because population groups differ in learning capacities but because they differ in learning goals. To force-feed minority and Majority students alike on a thin, curricular soup of one part liberal dogma, one part Majority belittlement and one part minority mythology is to provide little educational nourishment for anyone.

Some Negro separatists, to the confusion and dismay of black and white desegregationists, call for more, not less, educational segregation so they can more fully develop their racial and cultural identity. Acceding to this proposal could lead to the establishment of separate schools and colleges for all Unassimilable Minorities, who by definition can never be assimilated by education or by any other means. This would formalize the apartness of all such minorities, and at the

---

61. Yaffe, *op. cit.,* p. 51. The percentages are probably higher in the "mind-shaping" social science departments, in which Jewish educators congregate. It is this high concentration of Jews in the more sensitive areas of the educational process that lends support to van den Haag's comment, "The literate American mind has come in some measure to think Jewish, to respond Jewishly. It has been taught to, and it was ready to." *The Jewish Mystique,* p. 98.
62. Yaffe, *op. cit.,* p. 52.
63. *New York Times,* May 20, 1970, p. 1.

same time penetrate the assimilationist disguise of some. In any event, such a measure could not help but give Majority education a new lift by removing it from the control of its detractors and despoilers.

All in all, the great failure of a heterogeneous school system remains its inability to stress effectively the morale-building aspects of education. There is no higher incentive for learning than the self-esteem that flows spontaneously from the awareness of a great past—an awareness that does not come from guidelines published by the Department of Health, Education and Welfare or from textbooks censored or pre-censored by urban boards of education.

This is the kind of learning for which the only adequate preparation is centuries of common history and millennia of common ancestry. Desegregation kills it by robbing it of its principal ingredient—the homogeneity of teacher and pupil. The disappearance of this vital bond from the American classroom may prove to be the greatest educational tragedy of all.

PART VI

The Political Clash

Chapter 21

The Adaptability of Dogma

I F THE CULTURAL PHASE of the Majority's dispossession
may be described as the assault on the Majority soul, the
political phase is the assault on the Majority mind. Political
power may emanate from the barrel of a gun, as Chairman
Mao has proposed.[1] But a gun is quite ineffective without the
will to shoot, an ingredient supplied by that form of intellectual programming known as dogma.

The mind feeds voraciously on dogma because human
beings seem to need some system of thought, some frame
of reference, from which to view the world. Only a very few
lonely souls have the stamina, courage and wisdom to develop
their own beliefs from independent observation. And there
are fewer every day. The farther the frontiers of knowledge
are pushed outward, the more elusive this knowledge becomes and the farther it moves beyond the individual's grasp.
Desperate for truth, ravaged by doubt, even the best minds
home in on dogma, the great enemy of doubt, which is
always willing, but seldom qualified, to fill the intellectual
void. Pontius Pilate received no immediate response when
he posed his celebrated question.[2] When Christianity was
properly organized, the Church answered him—with dogma.

Of the major components of dogma—truth, falsehood,
opinion and authority—the greatest is authority. One of the
oldest human habits, a habit roundly encouraged by the

---

1. See Chapter 34 for other Nietzschean utterances by Chairman Mao.
2. *John* (18:38).

brain's immeasurable inertia, is to surrender one's mind to a
dogma, simply because of the dogma's ancient pedigree. It
was the authority of age which made it possible for readily
detectable falsehoods in the Old Testament and Aristotelian
natural philosophy to be held as truths for more than fifteen
hundred years.

Those few who accept dogma halfheartedly instead of
wholeheartedly do pick and choose to some extent. But the
dogma they finally light upon is usually selected not for its
relevancy or correspondence to the facts, but because it
coincides with their own particular set of prejudices, animosities and fears. Modern intellectuals continued to subscribe to Communist dogma long after they had recognized
its contradictions, its persiflage and its errors. Indeed, they
seemed to venerate it most at the very moment (the climax
of the great Stalinist purges of the 1930's) they were being
most deceived. They wanted to believe, so they did believe.
Credo quia absurdum.[3]

Unfortunately for the human race, the intellectual has a
near monopoly in the formulation and propagation of dogma
because of his verbal training and linguistic agility. The facile
tongue (or pen) and dogma seem mutually generative. It
was this close, almost predestined, connection between dogma
and intellectuals that led Brunetière, the French literary
critic, to define an intellectual as one who meddles dogmatically in matters about which he is ignorant.[4]

One would logically suppose that the more education one
has the less would be one's susceptibility to dogma. It is
quite the opposite. Education, apart from the physical
sciences, and even these are not always exempt, has always
been the most notorious example of organized indoctrination.
Indeed, the well-educated person or, more precisely, the

3. In more ways than one Tertullian strikes a modern note. A Carthaginian lawyer and the most dogmatic of the early church fathers, he advised Christians to refuse military service under the Roman Emperors and
not to obey laws they deemed unjust. Will Durant, *Caesar and Christ*,
p. 647. For Tertullian's exact words, see Toynbee, *Study of History*, Vol.
V, p. 56.
4. *Times Literary Supplement*, June 22, 1962, p. 462. The difference
between an intellectual and an intelligent man might be described as the
difference between one who uses his mind and one who uses his mind wisely.

"most educated" person is often the most dogmatized, as well as the most dogmatic of men. The teacher who spends his life teaching dogma has become, so to speak, dogmatically blind. He is quick to attack opposing dogma, but slow to condemn or even to recognize his own.

Only unsophisticated minds, whose number is legion, and great minds, *rarissimae aves,* seem to have developed some immunity to the dogma at the bottom of prevailing Western political and social ideology. The former are equipped by neither upbringing, training nor inclination to comprehend such dogma, while the latter are reluctant to swallow it because they comprehend it all too well.

Consequently, it should not come as a shock to say that the intellectual or "educated" man can be more harmful to society than the uneducated or unsophisticated man. The literate person has the ability to spread his ignorance abroad, to sell his dogma wholesale. The unlettered person can only pass on his beliefs to those in his immediate vicinity.

At times, political dogma becomes so firmly rooted in the social order that merely to question it is to put oneself beyond the pale. Often the entire intellectual establishment of civilization will draw in its head, turtle-fashion, at the slightest attempt to throw an objective light on the darker recesses of the dogma it has come to live by. The merest trace of criticism will be judged as a cynical, anti-social mixture of iconoclasm and desanctification. If the critic works in secret, he eventually begins to feel like a criminal. If he comes out in the open, he is regarded as one. In the words of Charles Peirce, "let it be known that you seriously hold a tabooed belief, and you may be perfectly sure of being treated with a cruelty less brutal but more refined than hunting you like a wolf." [5]

Political dogma, as all dogma, ultimately rests on opinion and feeling rather than on fact. It could only be tested objectively by the almost impossible method of placing similar population groups in similar environments over a period of generations while subjecting each to a different political system. Even then, the results of these lengthy and

---

5. *The Fixation of Belief, Collected Papers,* Harvard University Press, Cambridge, 1934, pp. 245–6.

complicated tests would have to be measured according to such dubious criteria as economic progress, cultural achievement, governmental stability and public security—all of which easily lend themselves to varying interpretations.

Not surprisingly, in view of man's incurable "dogmatitis," scientific dogma often receives the same uncritical acclaim and acceptance as political dogma. Einstein's Relativity theory, for example, has become a quasi-permanent fixture in modern physics although technology has been strained to produce even a few tentative and inconclusive proofs [6] and in spite of the increasingly high mortality rate in recent times of the most cherished scientific "laws." [7]

There is, however, one notable difference between scientific and political dogma. The former can often be put to the

6. Einstein's critics have had difficulty getting public attention. In 1967, physicist Robert Dicke stated he had found important discrepancies in the General Theory regarding the measurement of the orbit of Mercury. *Science News Letter,* Feb. 11, 1967, p. 144. Albert Eagle, Instructor of Mathematics at the University of Manchester in England, has had to confine his rather extensive rebuttal of Einstein to an obscure, but highly respected British journal. "Einstein's choice of [certain constants and values in the Special Theory] is so deliberately artificial, and so devoid of any known justification that it must be considered theoretically valueless." At another time Eagle wrote, "Thus we have seen that the three minute astronomical phenomena which are so often regarded as proof of the existence of some 'space-time continuum' and of 'curved space' can be explained in a perfectly rational manner by only a slight development of pre-Relativity electromagnetic theory." *Philosophical Magazine;* Nov. 1939, p. 697; Dec. 1939, p. 701. "[No] Jewish scientist has ever equalled Newton, Darwin, Pasteur, or Mendel. . . . such apparent exceptions as Ehrlich, Freud and Einstein are only apparent. Ehrlich, in fact, contributed less to biochemical fact than to biochemical theory, and most of his theory was dubious. Freud was nine-tenths quack, and there is sound reason for believing that Einstein will not hold up; in the long run his curved space may be classed with the psychosomatic bumps of Gall and Spurzheim." *H. L. Mencken's Notebooks,* pp. 273–4.

7. Before the supersonic jet, some scientists declared it would be impossible for an airplane to penetrate the sound barrier and survive. In his Special Theory of Relativity, Einstein created a light barrier by mathematically dogmatizing that nothing in the universe can move faster than the velocity of light (186,282 miles/sec). This taboo may hold for some time since modern technology has many problems to solve before an accelerator can be designed to produce such velocities. (Subatomic particles seem to increase in mass as they approach the velocity of light, but may obey a different set of physical laws.) In 1962, a theory more firmly ensconced in the scientific decalogue than Relativity was jettisoned when Professor Bartlett of the University of British Columbia made some xenon-platinum hexafluoride. Until then there had been an "immutable" law in chemistry that platinum and xenon, a noble metal and a noble gas, were totally resistant to chemical combination. *San Francisco Chronicle, This World,* Dec. 9, 1962, p. 25.

test under controlled laboratory conditions.[8] When validated, it becomes a law, an exalted status seldom achieved by a political dogma. When it is overturned, a mild wave of astonishment ripples through the scientific community, and that is that. But when a political dogma goes under—it may be whittled away by reason, but it can only be supplanted by another dogma—its demise is frequently accompanied by social chaos, revolution and the destruction of thousands or even millions of lives.

The most powerful dogmas are those which have a time-less, universal appeal to the hearts and minds of all men. Yet it is the very universality of the great dogmas which makes them so fickle and unpredictable, which allows them to play so fast and loose with the hopes and aspirations of their expounders. Dogmatic pronouncements concerning men's "inalienable rights" have a totally different political and social effect in monoracial than in multiracial societies. The same religious dogma which helped destroy the Roman Empire helped preserve the Holy Roman Empire. The same political dogma which inspired one people to put American society together now inspires other peoples to tear it apart.

It seems reasonable to suppose that the great dogmas have not survived for centuries and even millennia on content alone. Their vitality must also have depended heavily on their

---

8. Macaulay was one of the few politicians who favored applying the scientific method to politics: "How, then, are we to arrive at just conclusions on a subject so important to the happiness of mankind? Surely by that method which, in every experimental science to which it has been applied, has signally increased the power and knowledge of our species—by that method for which our new philosophers would substitute quibbles scarcely worthy of the barbarous respondents and opponents of the Middle Ages—by the method of Induction—by observing the present state of the world—by assiduously studying the history of past ages—by sifting the evidence of facts—by carefully combining and contrasting those which are authentic—by generalizing with judgment and diffidence—by perpetually bringing the theory which we have constructed to the test of new facts—by correcting, or altogether abandoning it, according as those new facts prove to be partially or fundamentally unsound. Proceeding thus—patiently, diligently, candidly —we may hope to form a system as far inferior in pretension to that which we have been examining, and as far superior to it in real utility, as the prescriptions of a great physician, varying with every stage of every malady and with the constitution of every patient, to the pill of the advertising quack which is to cure all human beings, in all climates, of all diseases." The Miscellaneous Works of Lord Macaulay, Universal Library Association, Philadelphia, Vol. 1, p. 399.

adaptability, on their capacity to alleviate so many conflicting human sorrows, to satisfy so many conflicting human goals. The gift of adapting dogma to one's advantage is surely one of the greatest a people can possess. A greater gift, however, is knowing when dogma is no longer working to one's advantage and rejecting it.

From the standpoint of the American Majority, the political dogma which served it so well during most of American history has now become one of the chief agents of its decline. From the standpoint of the minorities, it has become a powerful tool for their advancement. Almost every political act is now measured against the yardstick of minority interests. Almost every political event of the past and present is assigned to some way station along the March of Democracy. The current political struggle is falsely presented as a contest between liberalism and conservatism, exploited and exploiters, tolerance and intolerance, equality and inequality, freedom and oppression. Since it conceals the real nature of what is happening and the real intentions of the dogmatizers, dogmatic interpretation has become as powerful a force as dogma itself.

Chapter 22

The Three Phases of Democracy

Sociologist William Graham Sumner once said of democracy, "It is impossible to discuss or criticize it. . . . No one treats it with complete candor and sincerity." [1] In the sixty-five years since Sumner wrote these lines the climate for objectivity has not noticeably improved. Yet without some clearer understanding of democracy than exists in the popular mind there can be little comprehension of present-day American politics.

Most contemporary political scientists like to place democracy at the top of the ladder of political evolution. But traces of democracy have been found in the tribal organizations of the most backward and most ancient peoples. In the opinion of Robert Marrett, late Oxford don and noted anthropologist, "Where society is most primitive, it is most democratic. . . ." [2]

Historically, democracy did not appear as a recognized form of government until the flowering of the Greek city states, when it acquired enough status to be included among the five political orders of Plato. In order of precedence these were: (1) Aristocracy (rule of the best); (2) Timocracy (rule of the honorable); (3) Oligarchy (rule of the few); (4) Democracy (rule of the people); (5) Tyranny (rule of the despot or upstart). [3] Plato's classifications were five steps

---

1. *Folkways,* p. 77.
2. *Ency. Brit.,* Vol. 19, p. 105.
3. *Republic,* trans. Paul Shorey, VIII, 545.

of a descending staircase down which most Greek city states were doomed to travel. The stairs could be climbed again, either partly or all the way. But inevitably there would be another descent, even after the creation of the perfect state, that supreme feat of Platonic utopianism, where "either philosophers become kings . . . or those whom we now call our kings and rulers take to the pursuit of philosophy. . . ." [4]

Aristotle found a similar degenerative process at work in politics. He divided government into three good and three bad forms. The good forms were monarchy, aristocracy and constitutional government which, he explained, were "perverted" into tyranny, oligarchy and democracy, respectively.[5] In Aristotle's view there were five different varieties of democracy, but he had trouble delineating them. He did, however, make a sharp distinction between democracies where laws were above the people and democracies where the people were above the laws.[6]

Aristotle's politics were shaped in part by his faith in the middle class, to which he happened to belong. His preferred state was a middle-class republic not too dissimilar to the limited representative government of the United States in the early years of its independence.[7] But Aristotle was also a political relativist, allowing that the best government might be the one best suited to the people, time and circumstance. He was not a fanatic believer in the inherent superiority of any one political system.[8]

The aristocrat, Plato, was more hostile than Aristotle to democracy, whose end stages he described in terms which have a curiously modern ring: "In such a state of society the master fears and flatters his scholars, and the scholars despise their masters and tutors . . . the father grows accustomed to descend to the level of his sons and to fear them, and the son is on a level with his father, he having no respect or

---

4. *Ibid.*, V, 473 d.
5. *Politics*, trans. Jowett, III, 7.
6. *Ibid.*, IV, 4.
7. *Ibid.*, IV, 11.
8. *Ibid.*

reverence for either of his parents . . . the metic is equal with the citizen and the citizen with the metic, and the stranger is quite as good as either. . . . [Democratic leaders] seize upon the citadel of the young man's soul . . . and do not suffer a word to be said on the other side . . . all things are just ready to burst with liberty. . . . And so tyranny naturally arises out of democracy, and the most aggravated form of tyranny and slavery out of the most extreme form of liberty." [9]

It was shown in the earlier discussion of the aristocratic origins of great art that Greek democracy had very little in common with the kind of democracy affected by present-day democratic regimes. In their democratic phases, almost all Greek city states clung tenaciously to the institution of slavery and refused voting rights to women, foreigners and metics —even disenfranchising many of the native born by means of racial and property qualifications. On the other hand, some cities like Athens carried democracy to extremes by the practice of sortition, in which office holders were selected not by vote but by lot. Sortition, a kind of democratic bingo, is only conceivable where a small, homogeneous, highly intelligent citizenry possesses a high degree of political sophistication.

The Roman Republic exhibited occasional democratic trends or flashes. Some may have been the legacy of the ruggedly individualistic Italic tribesmen who founded Rome. Some undoubtedly had Greek origins. Most probably came from patrician concessions to the mounting demands of plebeians. But the Senate, the most enduring Roman political institution and the repository of aristocracy and privilege, was congenitally oligarchic and authoritarian. When the

---

9. *Republic*, trans. Jowett, VIII, 562–3. One of Plato's most telling complaints against democracy was its failure to encourage the emergence of virtuous statesmen: "[Except] in the case of some rarely gifted nature, there never will be a good man who has not from his childhood been used to play amid things of beauty and make of them a joy and a study—how grandly does she [democracy] trample all these fine notions of ours under her feet, never giving a thought to the pursuits which make a statesman, and promoting to honour any one who professes to be the people's friend." *Ibid.*, 558.

dim lamp of democracy was finally turned off by the Gracchites and dictators who buried the Republic,[10] it did not burn again until the seventeenth century.

During this long hiatus, however, there were some feeble democratic stirrings. In 930 A.D., Iceland's *Althing* had its first session and, as this parliamentary body still sits today, Icelanders can claim to be the founders of history's most enduring representative government.[11] Other libertarian manifestations can be detected in the early days of the English Parliament, in the Swiss cantons and in the medieval communes, "the chief parent of modern democracy." [12]

It is generally conceded that modern democracy was born during the popular reaction against the Stuart dynasty in England. Its midwife was John Locke, whose treatises on civil government contained many seminal democratic ideas. In phraseology that was later reworked and partly plagiarized by Jefferson in the Declaration of Independence, Locke asserted that men, all of whom had certain natural rights, were "free, equal and independent" and that "no one ought to harm another in his life, health, liberty or possessions." [13]

But then Locke took a dogmatic tack that alienated him forever from the oracles of modern democratic thought. The basic purpose of government, he declared, was the preservation of property.[14] He added that, if monarchs could not protect the material possessions of their subjects, people had the right to look elsewhere for protection, even if need be to themselves.[15]

In Locke's opinion, the preservation of property was tantamount to the preservation of human liberty, and to safeguard this liberty he called for the division of government into

---

10. Roman imperial rule was perhaps best summed up by Tiberius, who said it was the part of a good shepherd to shear his flock, not skin it. Suetonius, *Tiberius,* 32.

11. *Ency. Brit.,* Vol. 12, p. 45.

12. Durant, *The Age of Faith,* p. 641.

13. Locke, *Of Civil Government,* First Treatise, preface, p. 3. Also *Ency. Brit.,* Vol. 16, p. 172D and Vol. 7, p. 217. It might be noted that in the constitution he was asked to draw up for Carolina, Locke included such strange democratic bedfellows as hereditary serfdom and primogeniture. Beard, *Rise of American Civilization,* Vol. 1, p. 66.

14. Locke, *op. cit.,* Second Treatise, No. 94.

15. *Ibid.,* Nos. 228–9.

legislative and executive branches. Later, the French philosopher Montesquieu went beyond Locke in the separation of powers by adding a third branch of government, the judiciary.[16] Jean-Jacques Rousseau rounded out the basic structure of pre-Marxian democratic theory by making man inherently good, that is, capable and worthy of controlling his own destiny without outside interference or regimentation.[17] It was less of a mental strain for Rousseau, born in the relatively pure moral atmosphere of Geneva, to entertain such optimistic views than for philosophers brought up in the fleshpots of Paris or London.

English democracy, though it made important strides after the Stuarts had been sent packing a second and final time, did not lose its aristocratic flavor until the Reform Act of 1832. But across the Atlantic in some of the British colonies, more safely removed from the conservative restraint of king and lord, democracy had a freer hand. In New England, after the relaxation of Puritan theocracy, the right to intervene in government affairs, public accountability of magistrates, trial by jury of ordinary citizens, statutory guarantees of personal liberty and taxation initiated by taxpayers—reforms that made English democrats green with envy—came to be considered the birthright of every citizen.[18]

The democratic exuberance of the New England town meeting, however, did not spill over into the nation as a whole when the colonies obtained their independence.[19] Some of the intellectuals among the Founding Fathers, notably in

16. *L'esprit des lois*, XI, vi.
17. At least this is the impression gathered from reading the first pages of Rousseau's *Du contrat social*. In the latter part, the citizen is threatened with death if he does not believe in the articles of the religion of the state in which he happens to reside. Rousseau, parenthetically, considered a mixture of aristocracy and democracy the best form of government. He felt direct democracy was impossible and that people living in arctic or tropical zones might require absolute rule. Durant, *Rousseau and Revolution*, pp. 173–4.
18. De Tocqueville, *De la démocratie en Amérique*, Tome 1, p. 38, Tome 2, p. 298.
19. When the U.S. became a sovereign nation in 1776, the American popula‘ion numbered less than four million of which only 6 percent voted. *Time*, March 22, 1963, p. 96. Since citizen participation in government was much higher in New England than elsewhere, it must have been extremely low in most other colonies.

the South, subscribed to many of the ideas and platitudes that were giving birth to the French Revolution. But this doctrinaire brand of political and social leveling was in sharp contrast to the evolutionary and pragmatic democracy of most independence-minded American colonists. While it is true that Jefferson's clarion appeals to human liberty helped build up the colonists' inclination for war, they were mere rhetorical shadows compared to the substantial democratic achievements of Majority pioneers and settlers who had never heard of natural laws, social contracts or unalienable rights and to whom "the pursuit of happiness" would have seemed blasphemous and downright hedonistic.

Perhaps more than any other American, Jefferson must assume the responsibility for loading American democracy with the ambiguity and cant which have pursued it down to the present day. When one of the largest slave owners in Virginia solemnly writes, "all men are created equal," either his semantics or his integrity must be called into account. What Jefferson and most of the other signers of the Declaration of Independence meant by equality was that English colonists had the same natural right to self-government as the English in the mother country.[20] But that is not what they wrote or signed. And it is what they wrote or signed, carried forward to another century and used in another context, that has proved to be such an effective time bomb in the hands of those who advocate projects and policies totally antithetical to Jeffersonian democracy.

To obtain a clearer picture of Jefferson's interpretation of equality, one need only read the Declaration of Independence all the way through. In the beginning, the tone is equalitarian. But further on, Jefferson writes of "the merciless Indian Savages, whose known Rule of Warfare, is an un-

---

20. Richard Hofstadter, *The American Political Tradition*, p. 12. Stephen Douglas said (1858): "the signers of the Declaration had no reference to the Negro whatever . . . [they were referring to] white men, men of European birth and European descent . . . that such was their understanding, is to be found in the fact . . . everyone of the thirteen colonies was a slaveholding colony, every signer of the Declaration represented a slaveholding constituency . . . if they intended to declare that the Negro was the equal of the white man . . . they were bound, as honest men, that day and hour to have put their Negroes on an equality with themselves. . . ."

distinguished Destruction of all Ages, Sexes and Conditions." [21] Other signs of a basically anti-equalitarian disposition are provided by Jefferson's belief in "natural aristocracy" and by his insistence on the innate supremacy of the American yeoman or small farmer. In spite of his strong sympathies for the French Revolution, he wrote to Lafayette, "The yeomanry of the United States are not the *canaille* of Paris." [22]

Jefferson gave American democracy a chance of survival only so long as the country remained basically agricultural. He was convinced that members of the working class, merchants and speculators were corrupt, that cities were "pestilential" and city mobs "the panders of vice and the instruments by which the liberties of a country are generally overturned." [23] Paradoxically, it is this same Jefferson who is now, with Lincoln, the idol of the very sort of people he held in abomination. The paradox has been compounded by the Democratic party which, despite its power base in the big cities, has nominated itself Jefferson's political heir.

Jefferson was in France during the framing of the Constitution [24]—one good reason the word democracy appears nowhere in that document. The Founding Fathers, most of whom were of a conservative bent, determined to call the United States a republic, which in those days meant almost any government that was not a monarchy. [25] The few delegates to the Constitutional Convention who did profess democratic sentiments certainly held views closer to Greek and Roman concepts of democracy than to the leveling notions of utopian Parisian regicides. John Adams probably represented the

---

21. For Jefferson's remarks on Negroes, see p. 207.

22. Hofstadter, *op. cit.*, p. 22.

23. *Ibid.*, pp. 31–2.

24. "The men who put 'We, the People' into the Constitution, with a few exceptions perhaps, feared the rule of the people and would have been horrified if they could have foreseen all that was to happen under their Constitution in the next 150 years." Beard, *The Republic*, p. 4. The Constitution, it might be added, was even created in an undemocratic atmosphere, since all the Convention's sessions were secret.

25. Only recently have democratic shades of meaning been introduced into republic. *Webster's Third New International Dictionary* offers as an alternate definition of republic, "a community of beings . . . characterized by a general equality among members."

feelings of most of his colleagues when he expostulated, "Remember, democracy never lasts long. It soon wastes, exhausts, and murders itself. There never was a democracy yet that did not commit suicide." [26]

Such prophetic gloom was in no small measure responsible for the fear of democracy inherent in many of the laws and procedures which shaped the political stance and behavior of the nation during its childhood and adolescence. Senators were chosen by the legislatures of the various states, not by direct popular vote.[27] There were property, occasionally even religious, qualifications for voting in almost all the states. A Negro, for statistical purposes, was counted as three-fifths of a white man, and slavery was acknowledged and protected by the federal government and most states.[28] There was much interest in guarding the rights of citizens, as demonstrated by the Bill of Rights, but much less interest, as evidenced by the emergence of machine politics, in encouraging citizens to participate independently in the governmental process.

Nevertheless, the democratic seed had been planted, and the relentless drive to broaden and widen the voting base, to make everyone a citizen and every citizen a voter, is one of the most discernible threads in American history. It started rather slowly. The last of the states did not remove the last of their property requirements for voting until 1856.[29] The slaves were freed in 1863, but the Negro's right to vote was not specifically spelled out until 1870.[30] Senators were not elected directly until the 17th Amendment (1913), and women not given the ballot until the 19th Amendment (1919). The electoral process for selecting Presidents and Vice-Presidents is still retained, but is now almost wholly dependent on the popular vote. The poll tax was not prohibited until the 24th Amendment (1962). The "one man,

26. Hofstadter, *op cit.,* p. 13. Hamilton, who called the people a "great beast," was even more pessimistic about democracy than Adams. Beard, *The Republic,* p. 11.

27. Constitution, Art. I, Sec. 3, Par. 1.

28. Art. I, Sec. 2, Par. 3; Art. IV, Sec. 2, Par. 3. Slavery was forbidden in the Northwest Territory in 1787, and the last Northern state, New Jersey, abolished it or provided for its gradual abolition in 1804.

29. *Ency. Brit.,* Vol. 7, p. 218.

30. The 15th Amendment (1870) forbade denying the right to vote to any citizen on account of "race, color or previous condition of servitude."

one vote" Supreme Court decisions in 1962, 1964 and 1968 made it mandatory that districts electing representatives to legally constituted city, county and town governments be substantially equal in population.[31] If the constituencies of representatives to the same legislative body differed too greatly in population, they were to be brought into line by reapportionment. Only members of the United States Senate, some of whom now represent states with ten to twenty times the population of other states, are exempt from this rule.[32]

That universal suffrage and equal representation now exist in theory in the United States does not mean that everyone votes.[33] In the 1964 presidential election, for example, only 60 percent of the electorate went to the polls.[34] In off-year Congressional elections voter participation is sometimes as low as 10 or 15 percent.[35]

One explanation of these statistics lies in the political apathy of Southern Negroes, an apathy deliberately encouraged by white Southerners and now disappearing as the result of federal intervention and organized campaigns by liberals and minority groups to get out the Negro vote. Another reason for voter apathy has been the hopelessness of defeating political machines whose concept of universal suffrage extends to the registration of voters who are repeaters, deceased or fictional.[36]

Belgium, Australia and a few other nations force voters to the polls by fining absentees. Without going to such extremes, American politicians might accomplish the same purpose by presenting their constituents with clear-cut issues they can either support or oppose. When the object is to increase voter participation, there is nothing like increased

---

31. *Time*, July 4, 1969, pp. 62–3.

32. The exemption is provided by the 17th Amendment and Art. 1, Sec. 3, Par. 1 of the Constitution.

33. There are still restrictions on residence, voting age and literacy tests, where such tests do not imply racial discrimination.

34. *Time*, Nov. 23, 1964, p. 39.

35. Ferdinand Lundberg, *The Treason of the People*, pp. 9–10.

36. In the 1960 presidential election 150,000 "ghost" votes were turned in by 5,199 Cook County (Chicago) precincts. In the same election Texas judges threw out an estimated 100,000 ballots on technicalities. A shift of 23,117 votes in Texas and 4,430 votes in Illinois would have given Nixon the presidency. *Reader's Digest*, July, 1969, pp. 37–43.

voter interest. The candidates' long established habit of dividing on secondary rather than primary issues is one of the great failures of American democracy.

In the 1940 presidential election, when the overriding question was intervention or nonintervention in World War II, both major party candidates promised to keep the United States out of war, although both were interventionists at heart. In fact, while campaigning for his third term President Roosevelt was already implementing a policy of military aid to Britain that made American involvement inevitable.[37]

The situation was similar in the civil rights struggles of the 1950's and 1960's. All Republican and Democratic presidential candidates were in favor of practically every civil rights bill, although large segments of voters were opposed. In the early 1970's, seventy-five percent of Americans were against racial busing, but it went on, and on. Both parties supported military aid to Israel, even though it triggered the oil shortage in 1973 and may lead to nuclear war. Here again voters had no effective means of approving or disapproving policies of crucial importance.

In state and city elections, where voters were sometimes presented with a choice, the pluralities registered against civil rights were staggering—an indication that the federal government was actively pursuing policies to which most Americans were opposed. In 1964, in the very same election in which President Johnson, an ardent backer of civil rights, carried California by 1,200,000 votes, the people of California voted two to one to repeal an open housing statute in a statewide referendum.[38] In a few local elections, a proposal for the establishment of a police review board in New York

---

37. Beard, *President Roosevelt and the Coming of the War*, pp. 5, 413.
38. *Time*, Nov. 13, 1964, pp. 39, 43. The California courts later declared the results of the referendum unconstitutional. That the courts can overturn a referendum—the purest expression of democracy—raises questions about how democratic the American democratic process really is. Since open housing was almost universally supported by the news media, the referendum also served to demonstrate that editorial opinion is usually much closer to minority than Majority opinion. The popular vote was 2 to 1 against open housing, while the Jews voted 2 to 1 in favor. Yaffe, *The American Jews*, p. 258.

City in 1966 and in the 1969 Los Angeles and Minneapolis mayoralty races, voters also had the rare opportunity of voting pro or con on the civil rights issue, which by now had acquired a synonym, Black Power, and an antonym, law and order. Large pluralities expressed a sharp divergence from the national political "consensus."

Perhaps the greatest of all voter shutouts developed during the Vietnam War. In the 1968 presidential campaign, both major party candidates proposed a strategy of slow disengagement. Those who wanted to win the war or who wanted immediate withdrawal simply had no vote, or no vote that counted. The only candidate who promised a harder line on both the war and the race issue was George Wallace, whose American Independent party received 9,897,141 votes or 13.53 percent of the total cast, the largest percentage obtained by any third party since Senator La Follette ran on the Progressive ticket in 1924.[39]

Wallace performed this minor miracle although the entire American political establishment and communications network were solidly arrayed against him. Even in the South not one important newspaper came to his support.[40] If Wallace had had the political machine of a major party, if even 10 percent of the press had backed him, if Republicans had not tried to steal his thunder as the campaign progressed he might have won almost as many votes as Nixon or Humphrey.[41]

All of which goes to show that democracy, as it now operates in the United States, cannot genuinely reflect voter opinion. The voter is simply not given a real chance to make known his feelings on the critical issues. Even on the rare occasions he does have such a chance, his duly elected representatives will hedge on their most solemn campaign commitments once they feel the hot breath of the news media and the liberal-minority lobbies.

---

39. *1969 World Almanac*, p. 36 and *S. F. Chronicle*, Dec. 12, 1968, p. 11.
40. *Time*, Oct. 18, 1968, p. 70.
41. Wallace performed more spectacularly in the 1972 Democratic primaries, even carrying the state of Michigan. But the Alabama governor was immobilized physically by a bullet in the spine and politically by the McGovern steamroller at the Miami Democratic convention. Once again the wishes of the ordinary voter counted for nothing.

A principal cause of this powerful and pervasive anti-democratic element in modern American democracy is that elections come every two, four or six years, while the press and pressure groups grind out their propaganda every day. It is extremely difficult for any political figure to stand up for long against the combined onslaught of thousands of newspapers, hundreds of radio and television stations and scores of policy-making periodicals. To all but the hardiest politician, the partial betrayal of his constituency or even the loss of an election are preferable to the social Siberia reserved for the maverick who insists on putting the interests of society as a whole above special interests. The fate of James Forrestal and Senator Joseph McCarthy should be an unforgettable object lesson on the dangers inherent in promoting policies with broad appeal to the people, but with narrow appeal to the right people.[42]

Allowing the voter a limited choice or no choice at all has had the effect of moving government toward a corporate "democracy"—Mussolini would have called it a corporate state—in which professions, religions, regional economies, classes and races supplant the individual as the basic voting unit. Every politician is extremely sensitive to the labor vote, religious vote, farm vote and minority vote. His political reflexes, however, respond more slowly to the wishes of the individual voter who does not enjoy the bloc voter's ready access to the news media. It is this corporate system of representation—the organized vote or, more accurately, the fear of the organized vote—which inspires most of the policies and decisions of present-day elected officials.

---

42. An extraordinary series of personal attacks by press and radio helped drive the nation's first Secretary of Defense to suicide in 1949. One commentator, Ira Hirschman, went so far as to accuse Forrestal of preventing the bombing of the German I.G. Farben chemical plant in World War II because he owned stock in the company. Another, Walter Winchell, accused Forrestal of running away while his wife was being robbed. Forrestal had incurred the wrath of the press because he was opposed to American support of the Zionist occupation of Palestine and the stirring up of the Arab world against the U.S. Arnold Rogow, *Victim of Duty*, Rupert Hart-Davis, London, 1966, especially p. 24. The news media's vendetta against McCarthy, together with the almost unprecedented censure by the Senate, seemed to break him down physically as well as mentally, and certainly had much to do with his untimely death in 1957. *Time*, May 30, 1949, pp. 13–14 and *U.S. News & World Report*, June 7, 1957, p. 143.

The economic blocs which form within the framework of representative government are storm signals of the second stage of the democratic cycle, the progression from political to economic democracy.[43] Leading contributors to the development of political democracy—Locke, the eighteenth-century British Parliamentarians, a few philosophers of the French Enlightenment and the authors of the American Constitution—generally held economic democracy in contempt and dismissed it as the fantasy of disorderly and dangerous minds. But there are many who claim, and if the equalitarian premises of democracy are granted their logic can hardly be refuted, that without an "equitable" distribution of wealth there can be no democracy at all. The one great stumbling block to this line of reasoning is usually passed over in silence. To prevent the accumulation of vast amounts of property in individual hands and to effectively flatten out the highs and lows of the national income curve require a centralized control which is only a step removed from absolutism.

Economic democracy has haunted the halls of government almost as long as political democracy. The Levellers, founders of the first political party in modern history, were ardent supporters of Cromwell in the initial stages of the English Civil War. But their economic demands, which included the abolition of trading monopolies, finally caused Cromwell to turn against them.[44] Thereafter, both in England and on the Continent, there were few evidences of economic democracy until the French Revolution. What helped to keep it in check was the absence of any developed body of doctrine, any corpus like Locke's, to give it direction and coherence.

If Locke was the dean of political democracy, Marx was the midwife of economic democracy. Borrowing many of his ideas and methods from the hardline, "share-the-wealth" faction of French Jacobinism, Marx drew up an impassioned, encyclopedic agenda of utopian eschatology, obsessive materialism and crass economic leveling which clashed so violently with classical democratic theory that the latter has

43. The purely economic aspects of economic democracy will be taken up in Part VII.
44. *Ency. Brit.*, Vol. 13, p. 964.

not been the same since. "Passionately concerned with the achievement of economic democracy as he conceived it, he had no real interest in or comprehension of the problems of democratic politics." [45] The lack of this comprehension among his followers was made plain in the Bolshevik Revolution.

Economic democracy first became a permanent fixture on the American political scene with the advent of populism. Bryan may not have prevented mankind from being crucified on a cross of gold, but he and the Populist party which supported him firmly implanted an enduring awareness of economics in the American political consciousness. Theodore Roosevelt and his trust-busting, Senator La Follette and his Progressive party, Woodrow Wilson and his graduated income tax and, most important, the rise of Labor—all these set an economic tone to democracy culminating in the New Deal, which in its early years was concerned almost exclusively with democratic solutions to economic problems. Welfare in the form of security for the aged, minimum wages, and medical and unemployment insurance—in short the most significant dollars-and-cents legislation of recent administrations—were further examples of democracy's continuing accent on economic issues.

Lately the third phase of democracy, the social phase, has begun to materialize. Like political and economic democracy, social democracy is not new. But it seems to come last in the cycle of democratic growth (or decay). Because it capitalizes on the deeper, instinctive undercurrents of human behavior, its historical manifestations are not always easy to recognize and do not often penetrate conventional history books. Its theoretical genesis, however, is not difficult to trace, being a composite of the religious concept of the brotherhood of man, Lockean and Jeffersonian assertions about human rights, Marxist class agitation and the pronouncements of modern anthropologists and sociologists concerning human sameness.

Once political and economic democracy takes hold in a

----

45. Frederick M. Watkins in the article, "Democracy," *Ency. Brit.*, Vol. 7, p. 222.

society, the pressure for social democracy is certain to mount. This is especially true in a multiracial state. Inevitably, the unwashed, the disadvantaged and the envious will begin to ask, or will be asked to ask by ambitious politicians, "Why, if man is politically equal and getting to be economically equal, should he not be socially equal?" In the context of contemporary democratic politics, such a question has but one answer.

Social democracy is the thorniest stage of democracy in a multiracial state because more than any other phase it increases the area of contact, the social interface, of the various demographic elements—and the study of racial relations has shown that the greater the social interface, the greater the racial friction. Political democracy orders members of different population groups to vote together, legislate together and rule together. Economic democracy makes it necessary for them to work together. Social democracy, however, exponentially enlarges the area of contact by forcing the most diverse elements of the population to live together. At present this social mixing is restricted to neighborhoods, schools, playgrounds and clubs.[46] But there are forces at work to carry it into the last redoubt of individualism and privacy, the home.

The inner contradictions of the three phases of both ancient and modern democracy become apparent when it is remembered that political democracy begins as a means of protecting property, while economic democracy seeks to divide it up and social democracy encourages its theft. In the ironic chain of events that governs the democratic cycle, the same rights which were secured and recognized, often with great difficulty, in the political phase of democracy are de-emphasized and frequently revoked in the economic and social phases. It is hard to believe that the right to privacy,

---

46. Jews, who have proportionately a far greater number of clubs and organizations than any other population group, have waged a ten-year campaign under the leadership of the American Jewish Committee to force their admission into private clubs on the basis that exclusion discriminates against them financially as well as socially. Many prominent politicians and other public figures have already been forced to resign from such clubs in order to escape charges of anti-Semitism. *Los Angeles Times,* July 3, 1969, pp. 1, 19.

the right to choose friends, neighbors and schoolmates, the right to join fraternal or social organizations, the right to air one's opinions in public and *the right of access to one's own culture* are not as fundamental to human liberty or to the unfoldment of the human spirit as any other. Yet these are precisely the rights held in low esteem by the most ardent advocates of social democracy.

Hindsight and a certain amount of historical streamlining make it possible to view the three phases of democracy as three stages of Majority dispossession. Political democracy divided the Majority into parties representing various geographical, regional and sectional interests. Economic democracy divided the Majority into classes while the other population groups remained united.

But the Majority would not stay divided, either politically or economically. In mid-century, disaffected Majority Southerners and embattled Majority Northerners were beginning to find a common ground again. Also, in spite of its gruesome enclaves of poverty, America was still too rich and prosperous for permanent class divisions, either within the Majority or, equally as important, within the more affluent minorities.

So another, more effective strategy had to be adopted. The social democrats attacked the Majority in a way that pleased the Majority's opponents most—as a race. The basic plan was to raise minority racism to the boiling point while submitting Majority race consciousness to the numbing ideology of liberalism. The secondary plan was to develop a technique whereby the will of the many could be defeated and voted down by the few. This was to be accomplished in two ways: (1) controlling the vote by managed news, educational indoctrination and the nomination of carefully screened candidates; (2) going around the vote, when necessary, by Supreme Court edicts and secret foreign policy commitments. Meanwhile, whenever social democracy went too far, too fast, and a spark of resistance flared, it could be taken care of by shouting down the speakers, breaking up their meetings, occupying plants, government offices and centers of learning or, if worst came to worst, detonating a few well-placed sticks of dynamite.

But there was always the nagging fear that some day the

Majority might turn around and vote en bloc like the minorities. In this case, the cleverly constructed Potemkin village of social democracy would fall as flat as a house of cards. To prevent this, minority social scientists are today busy formulating doctrinal antidotes to any possible manifestation of what they nervously refer to as the "tyranny of the majority," a phrase dredged up from John Stuart Mill. One proposal would make minority votes count more than Majority votes by the simple expedient of permitting ethnic and economic groups to have their own representatives, in addition to representatives chosen in the traditional manner. This would permit delegates of minorities, urban conglomerations and welfare groups to wield as much power as delegates of the people at large.[47]

In the event of such minority gerrymandering, American democracy, even in its social or "depraved"[48] phase, could hardly survive much longer. Certainly, if the political phase is ever to be revived through the Herculean efforts of a united Majority party, it must be clearly remembered, as it was once so clearly understood, that democracy makes the highest demands of its participants and offers a measure of freedom only to those who can handle freedom. It is the rule of a people, not several peoples. The loftiest and most quixotic of all political ideals, it is even, perhaps, the expression of a racial trait. If so, modern political scientists have been the biggest prospectors of fool's gold in the history of human thought.

---

47. *New York Times Magazine*, Aug. 3, 1969, pp. 12 ff. That this proposal appeared in the form of a long article in America's most prestigious newspaper meant that it was to be taken seriously. The author was Herbert J. Gans, a prominent sociologist. In the course of his argument, Gans suggested that the approval of 25 percent of a legislative body would be sufficient for the introduction of minority-sponsored legislation while 76 percent would be necessary to prevent its passing. If the Majority took advantage of this situation to slip through legislation favorable to the Majority, the Supreme Court, leaning on a new "racial and economic Bill of Rights," would throw it out.

48. De Tocqueville used the word advisedly when he predicted that the political future of the U.S. "lay between two inevitable evils; that the question had ceased to be whether [it] would have an aristocracy or a democracy, and now lay between a democracy without poetry or elevation indeed, but with order and morality, and an undisciplined and depraved democracy." Letter to M. Stoffels, trans. Phillips Bradley, in *Democracy in America*, Knopf, New York, Vol. 1, pp. xx, xxi.

Chapter 23

The Metamorphosis of Liberalism

W HEN DISCUSSING democracy and liberalism in the same breath, it is hard to make a distinction between the two. One way to resolve the difficulty is to treat democracy as a political system rather than a political theology, as the expression of a dogma rather than the dogma itself. Then liberalism can be considered the democratic credo—the ideology that provides democracy's intellectual justification as well as its emotional drive.

Webster's Third New International Dictionary offers as one definition of liberalism, "a political philosophy based on belief in progress, the essential goodness of man, and the autonomy of the individual and standing for tolerance and freedom for the individual from arbitrary authority in all spheres of life. . . ." With less elaboration and bombast, and in better English, a popular dictionary describes the liberal as being "free from prejudice or bigotry." [1] If an historical reference will help nail down the elusiveness of liberalism, the first liberal, according to Walter Bagehot, was Jeroboam. [2]

---

1. *The American Everyday Dictionary*, Random House, New York, 1955.
2. Walter Bagehot, *Physics and Politics*, Knopf, New York, 1948, p. 31. Jeroboam was presumably classified as a liberal because he appointed "the lowest of the people priests of the high places" and asked King Rehoboam to "make the yoke which thy father did put upon us lighter." In reply, Rehoboam promised to chastise Jeroboam, not with whips but with scorpions. Jeroboam thereupon permanently split the Jewish state by setting up the northern kingdom of Israel, where he worshipped two golden calves. I Kings (12:4–19; 13:33).

In a more irreverent vein, a modern liberal might be defined as one who, while professing a horror of totalitarianism, favors one brand of totalitarianism over another;[3] who, professing a horror of racism, actively promotes minority racism; and who, professing a horror of big business, is an enthusiastic supporter of big labor. The intolerant champion of tolerance, the modern liberal is the bigoted enemy of bigotry. It is true he is willing to forge ahead, recklessly ahead, in the search for new ways of promoting equalitarianism in politics, education and intergroup relations. But he is not so progressive about space exploration,[4] political science (the only form of government he will hear of is democracy) and anthropology (except for the Boas and Lévi-Strauss schools). It is unnecessary to add that he is very suspicious of genetics and keeps his mind firmly closed on the subject of eugenics.

The sharp discrepancies between liberal pretensions and liberal behavior, between the liberal pose and the liberal performance, are relatively recent phenomena and not typical of the liberalism that existed two centuries or even two millennia ago. Like democracy, liberalism made a brief appearance in Greece and Rome, where Cynic and Stoic philosophers occasionally threw anti-establishment epigrams in the faces of kings and dictators. There were liberal sentiments in some of the sayings of Jesus[5] and a liberal outlook in some of the writings of Spinoza.[6] But liberalism never really found its voice until the time of John Locke—a

---

3. In August, 1939, the month of the signing of the Russo-German Non-aggression Pact which launched World War II, the names of 400 leading American liberals appeared on a manifesto affirming that Russia was a bulwark of peace and that Soviet citizens had as many civil liberties as Americans. *The Nation*, August 26, 1939, p. 228.

4. Nobel laureate Linus Pauling, a pillar of modern American liberalism, called the Apollo project, long before it got off the ground, a "pitiful demonstration." *Science*, Nov. 1, 1963, p. 560.

5. Both liberals and conservatives can quote scripture to their advantage, but the present accent of Christianity is decidedly liberal—on the radical, equalitarian Christ who "came to set a man at variance against his father," not on the apolitical Christ of "render unto Caesar."

6. "The political philosophy of Spinoza is the first statement in history of the standpoint of a democratic liberalism." Lewis Feuer, *Spinoza and the Rise of Liberalism*, Beacon Press, Boston, 1966, p. 65.

voice which swelled into a chorus when joined by such other liberal sages as Hume, Voltaire, Rousseau, Adam Smith and Thomas Jefferson. The word of liberalism became flesh with the eighteenth-century Whig governments in England, the founding of the United States and the outbreak of the French Revolution.

But the Old Liberalism of Locke and Jefferson was an entirely different breed of ideology from the New Liberalism of today. The Old Liberalism stressed individual not collective enterprise, less government not more, states' rights not federal control, laissez-faire not welfare, liberty not security, evolution not revolution. Moreover, very few of the great liberals of the past, in spite of their ringing appeals to equality, were willing to admit the equality of races.

Today, in the hands of those who call themselves modern liberals, the grand humanistic design of eighteenth- and nineteenth-century liberalism has been narrowed down to a mechanical catechism of "other caring." Contemporary liberal artists care more about what others think of their work than what they themselves think. Liberal statesmen and politicians do not act. They react. The liberal guardians of national security put defense above offense and even in a nuclear age base their strategy on retaliation, not attack. On the rare occasions their thoughts turn to God, liberal intellectuals prefer to blame Him for the evil in man rather than praise Him for the good.[7] Again and again, the focus shifts from the heart of the matter to the periphery.

Although the liberal's obsessive extroversion leaves him little opportunity to solve his own problems, he nevertheless feels obliged to tell the rest of the population how to solve theirs. Public figures whose private lives have been a shambles and who have proved utterly incapable of raising their own children presume to write copious newspaper columns and magazine articles on family life, marital problems and child upbringing. The mother with a delinquent daughter, instead of improving conditions in her own home, becomes a social

---

7. "God made my body, and if it is dirty, then the imperfection lies with the manufacturer, not the product." The quotation is from the late Lenny Bruce, a comedian whom many liberal writers are now trying to elevate to sainthood. *Holiday,* Nov. 1968, p. 74.

worker and attempts to help other families with delinquent daughters.[8]

In the liberal scheme of things there is a widening gulf between the person and the act, the thought and the deed. The politician who fights for school integration sends his own children to private schools. The criminal is not really guilty. He has merely committed an unfortunate act caused by an unfavorable environment. Someone else or something else is guilty. Millionaires of the liberal persuasion are often more interested in helping poor foreigners than poor Americans, and transfer much more money overseas than to the ghettos. The liberal loves everyone of every race, but he flees to the suburbs where he prefers to live among whites, even conservative whites.

It is no secret that liberals are fonder of mankind than men. The tragic view of life—the struggle of one man, not mass man, against the irreversibility of fate—does not fit easily into liberal thought. Nor does patriotism. While the average American looks upon the United States as *his* country—no more, no less—the liberal regards it chiefly as a repository of liberal principles.

It is this habit of reification, this fear of the personal touch in human affairs, which may explain why the modern liberal pantheon only has room for heroes who have displayed a noticeably anti-heroic streak. Woodrow Wilson and Franklin Roosevelt won two important wars, but lost two equally important peaces. Winston Churchill, who as a British Conservative was roughly equivalent to a liberal Republican, beat back the Germans, but presided over the liquidation of the British Empire.[9] Charles de Gaulle, hailed

---

8. Such a case was documented in the report, "Girls on the Run," by Jane Conant in the *San Francisco News-Call Bulletin*, Feb. 22, 1961, p. 1.

9. Churchill's phrasing and cadences may have sounded like Gibbon and Macaulay to those who like their oratory served with sonorous corn, but hero is hardly the word for a brilliant political opportunist who takes the helm of the ship of state during a storm and in spite of some gallant steersmanship leaves it a drifting hulk. In some of his most trying moments in World War II, for motives not too difficult to decipher, Churchill made much of his American ancestry. His mother, Jennie, was the daughter of Leonard Jerome, a New York City playboy promoter. But Churchill said little of the Indian blood which may have been transmitted to him through the Jerome family. Ralph Martin, *Jennie, the Life of Lady Randolph*

as a great liberal crusader when leading the Free French against Hitler, surrendered France's richest possession, Algeria. It was the deified liberal Democrat, President John Kennedy, who permitted Cuba, once an American economic outpost, to become a Russian client state.

To recapitulate, the metamorphosis of classical liberalism —the liberalism of Locke, Jefferson and Lincoln—into modern liberalism has been as miraculous and complete as the tadpole's transmogrification into the hoptoad. What was man-centered has become state-centered . . . what was dedicated to the protection of property now threatens it . . . what attempted to get the crushing load of absolutism off man's back now weighs him down with more regimentation than ever . . . what was once progressive in the truest sense of the word has now become the ideological crutch of nihilists, cranks and obscurantists.

How is this 180-degree shift in liberal orthodoxy, this total turnabout of the humanitarian party line, to be explained? How has this sophistic, schizophrenic, new-style, illiberal liberalism managed to fob itself off as the authentic product and not been argued or ridiculed out of existence? Above all, how does it keep such a firm hold on the American mind?

One answer has to do with the tenacity of tradition. As the credo of democracy, liberalism has gone down much the same path as democracy itself. Its articles of faith nourished and inspired the popular movements that freed Europeans in the Old World, and European colonists in the New, from the stifling authority of decadent monarchs. Its heuristic pronouncements on the nature of man produced some of the finest hours of the British Parliament and the American Congress. In its great days, classical liberalism transformed the political soul of the Western world.

. But as times changed, as the proprietor of forty acres and a mule moved into a rented coldwater flat, as financial and industrial monopoly passed beyond the bounds of reason, as the population doubled and redoubled, liberals began to concentrate on economic problems. Somewhat apologet-

Churchill, Prentice-Hall, Englewood Cliffs, N.J., pp. 2, 12. Also Darlington, *op. cit.*, p. 499.

ically, they explained that a decentralized government of checks and balances, the kind of government they had always upheld in the past, did not have the power to enact or enforce the economic legislation and controls which the injustices and the inanities of mass unemployment and boom-and-bust business cycles had demanded. Accused of neglecting property rights, they pointed to the blight of poverty and declared that human rights must now take precedence.

It was this new, economically oriented liberalism, hardly to be distinguished from the milder forms of socialism, which prepared the way for the welfare state. Its continuing popularity resides in the social services made possible by deficit spending. It is lotus-eating politics, and it might last forever were it not for the inflation and pacifism which leave the nations that adopt it fair game for hardier, more frugal and more belligerent peoples.

In its attachment to collectivism, modern liberalism has taken the same direction as socialism and communism, without going as far. Continually assailed and insulted by communists for their lukewarm attitude toward revolution, liberals have turned the other cheek and gone on lending their support and respectability to a variety of Marxist causes. When the twists and turns of Kremlin policy permitted, they joined communists in Popular Front governments. At one epoch in American history, the Roosevelt and Truman administrations, it became so difficult to differentiate between ultraliberals and communists that their opponents could be forgiven for considering them identical twins.

In recent years liberalism and communism have tended to drift apart, even though their hostility to laissez faire economics coincides as closely as ever. The reason has been liberalism's recent concentration on *social* democracy, on race leveling rather than economic leveling. In Europe this shift has not been so noticeable since the racial problem there is less acute. But the liberalism of social democracy has the status of a quasi-religion in the emerging nations of Africa and Asia and in the racially divided nations of the New World.

Within the last two decades in the United States, modern liberalism has become the party platform of minority racism.

With just a few changes in wording—*race* for *men, security* for *liberty, minority rights* for *inalienable rights*—the whole apparatus of Western liberal thought has moved bag and baggage into the minority camp. The enemy—always the most important figure in any ideology—is no longer dissolute European monarchs, Hamiltonian reactionaries, Southern slave owners, nineteenth century robber barons, twentieth century economic royalists, Italian and German fascists or Japanese militarists. It is now the corporate elite, the military-industrial complex, the white power structure, white racism, WASPs—in short, the American Majority.

Modern liberalism, of course, does not admit to being racist. In fact, it pretends to be anti-racist. But every word it speaks, every policy it supports, every program it publicizes, every cause it underwrites, every piece of legislation it introduces is likely to have some direct or tenuous racial connotation. Classical liberalism in America, in spite of its emphasis on mankind, was principally concerned with the interests and aspirations of the Majority at a time when Negroes, Indians and other minorities hardly counted. Modern liberalism, in spite of its bewitching ecumenical cliches, is also dedicated to one segment of the American population, this time the Unassimilable Minorities.

Its original purpose subverted, its original ideals redirected and reinterpreted, the liberalism of today has become a minority religion.[10] It has also become a grotesque masque in which the players will not and cannot suit the action to the word and where the platitudes of the script almost totally obscure the plot, which is the protagonists' thirst for power and ascendancy. This incessant clash of dialogue and motive lies at the root of the dramatic contradictions between modern liberal thought and modern liberal behavior. At the same time, the fustian soliloquies on humanitarianism serve an important purpose by concealing the close collaboration between liberalism and minority racism in major areas of political, economic, social and foreign policy.

---

10. "Liberalism is the American Jew's lay religion," writes James Yaffe, who also points out that half the membership of the Peace Corps, perhaps the most liberal agency of the U.S. government, is Jewish. Yaffe, *op. cit.*, pp. 245–6.

Modern liberalism is particularly useful to the minorities because it has the effect of dimming the Majority's racial perspective. Its ambiguous idealism and counterfeit Good Samaritanism permit Majority members to support the minority side without necessarily knowing or admitting they are working against the interests of their own people. It also allows those Majority members who are quite aware of what they are doing to rationalize their anti-Majority behavior.

One of the notable curiosities of modern liberalism is the striking variance between the Majority and the minority liberal—a variance of intent, not content. Majority and minority liberals not only have different motivations, but they are accorded strikingly different privileges. To the Majority liberal, his ideology is at best a warm faith in human goodness and human intelligence, at worst a dubious set of value judgments which it is wiser and safer to accept than reject. To the minority liberal, liberalism represents a package of solid accomplishments that has not only put money in his pocket, but has also put down or is putting down his old superiors and mentors, thereby satisfying his long-simmering, all-too-human desire for getting even. Liberalism, consequently, is to the minority member a pragmatic program of advancement, a chance for revenge and an idealistic crusade. It wraps him in a glittering robe of shining generalities, but conveniently accords him the privilege of being a racist and even encourages him to be one. The Majority liberal is permitted no such double standard. A minority racist can be a good liberal. A Majority racist cannot be a liberal at all and is anathematized as an incipient Nazi.

The question was previously raised as to how liberalism with its monumental inconsistencies and aberrations could survive in present-day America. It can now be answered in specific rather than general terms. Liberalism has survived and even prospered because it has become directly attached to the cause of minority racism, the most dynamic movement in contemporary American life. It will continue to survive and prosper until minority racism has no further use for it, until it is no longer able to function as the "emotional cover" of Majority liberals in their role as minority fellow travelers.

But as the years progress and the racial struggle in America hardens, the Majority liberal is bound to become increasingly suspect, not only to Majority members at large, but also to minority members who, as good racists, can only have contempt for racial renegades. As the Majority liberal continues to lose face, as he finds it ever more difficult and humiliating to tout other people's racism, he will probably have no choice but to retreat to conservatism, which in its present guise, as the next chapter will show, is simply a rehash of classical liberalism.

In the very largest and broadest sense, the metamorphosis of liberalism signifies the transformation of an *intra*racial struggle for individual rights and liberty into an *inter*racial struggle for power. The struggle is a total one. It encompasses every domain of human endeavor, particularly the highest levels of such endeavor—the realms of art, religion, education and philosophy. It was not Socrates—*pace* Nietzsche—who marked the end of Greek creativity. He was a sower and a reaper of the intraracial conflict, and the great works of Plato and Aristotle came later. What did mark the metamorphosis of liberalism in Greece was the establishment, still later, of the Cynic, Epicurean and Stoic schools of philosophy.[11] It should be no surprise to those familiar with the workings of racial dynamics to learn that the founding fathers of these schools did not come from Greece proper, but from Asia Minor.

Diogenes, the most cynical of the Cynics and the archetypal hippie, was a self-confessed forger from Sinope, a semi-Greek colony far up the Black Sea coast of Asia Minor. He fancied himself a "world citizen" and celebrated "freedom of speech" above all other freedoms. He also came out strongly for cannibalism and incest. Menippus, another prominent Cynic, was a native of Coele-Syria. Although starting out as a moneylender, he taught that the rich must share their wealth with the "virtuous" poor. Epicurus, the

11. Socrates died in 399 B.C.; Plato, 347 B.C.; Aristotle, 322 B.C. The Cynic, Epicurean and Stoic philosophies began to flourish after the death of Aristotle. The Stoics proposed, "one vast society in which there would be no nations, no classes, no rich or poor, no masters or slaves. . . ." Durant, *The Life of Greece*, pp. 506–7, 656.

pivot man of the Epicurean philosophy, was born in Samos, an island one mile off the Asia Minor shoreline. According to Will Durant, "He made no distinctions of station or race. . . ." Zeno, the first Stoic, came from Citium, a Phoenician city in Cyprus. One of the richest men of his time, he may have been the first man to say, "All men are by nature equal." In Will Durant's words, Stoicism derived from "Semitic pantheism, fatalism and resignation. . . ." Epictetus, the apostle of Stoicism to the Romans, was originally a Phrygian slave.[12]

Both as to content and timing, the latter-day schools of Greek philosophy are in many ways analogous to the latter-day "Western" doctrines of Marx, Freud and Boas. A strong equalitarian strain runs through all of them. But the end result is never equality. It is the casting up of new class or racial hierarchies. Distributed under a universal label, they are seemingly aimed at all men. Their special allure, however, is to those intent on realigning the social order. Predictably, leading proselytizers and leading proselytes are almost without exception aliens, outsiders and strangers.

The metamorphosis of liberalism takes place when and as the normal defenses of society are lowered, when the euphoria and exaltation of conquest, settlement and nation-building give way to the racelessness and mindlessness which are the bitter fruits of a job well done. Prosperity brings materialism and materialism brings what Gustave le Bon has described as the "enfeeblement of character."[13] The situation might be compared to that of an air foil, the pressure over which decreases as the wind velocity increases. As the winds of Babbittry blow harder, the minorities flow into the vacuum.

---

12. Biographical data from Diogenes Laertius, *The Lives and Opinions of the Eminent Philosophers,* trans. C. D. Yonge, Bohn's Classical Library, London, 1904. For Will Durant's remarks, see *The Life of Greece,* pp. 644–5.

13. "Or ce fût toujours par cet affaiblissement du caractère, et non par celui de l'intelligence, que de grands peuples disparurent de l'histoire." *Psychologie Politique,* Flammarion, Paris, 1919, p. 295.

Chapter 24

Conservatism Redefined

NOW THAT THE INDIAN no longer fits the label, the classical conservative has become the Vanishing American. Considering his beliefs—and considering the times—it is no wonder. The classical conservative upholds the mystique of authority and rank in society. He is an aristocrat by birth, an anti-democrat by nature and his principal concern is family, race and continuity. To him, the chain is more important than the links. He perceives the divine afflatus in man, but he also recognizes the odds against which it is working. He places the collective wisdom of the species (folkways and institutions) above the wisdom of governments and individuals (laws and politics).

The modern conservative has little in common with these views. He favors democracy up to a certain point, believes in racial equality—or says he does—and wants less government, not more. He is all for human rights, but he is all for property rights as well. He believes himself a rational, commonsensical being, and he takes his religion with a grain of salt. He is, in sum, a classical liberal[1] and has strayed as far from the fountainheads of classical conservatism—Plato, Dante and Hobbes—as the modern liberal has strayed from Locke. Where modern conservatism differs

---

1. "Classical liberalism, which took on its characteristic form in the eighteenth and nineteenth centuries, has with modification become the conservatism of our time." Henry Girvetz, *The Evolution of Liberalism*, Collier Books, New York, 1963.

from modern liberalism—in its concern for property, decentralized government and laissez faire—is precisely where classical liberalism parts company with modern liberalism.

Modern conservatism diverged from what might be described as the conservative world line under the direction of Edmund Burke at the end of the eighteenth century. Burke, an Irish Protestant who married a Roman Catholic and went to an English Quaker school, had somewhat surprising credentials for a leader of conservative thought. He belonged to the Whig party, was a conciliator and appeaser in the dispute with the American colonies and strongly opposed the policies of King George III and British imperialism. What propelled Burke into the rarified heights of political philosophy was the anarchism of the French Revolution. He was one of the first to realize that the Jacobin fury was deadly to the existing European social order. In his *Reflections on the Revolution in France,* Burke, like Locke before him, advocated individual responsibility, the sanctity of property, and minimal political and economic controls. Unlike Locke, he stressed religion, tradition and *prescription,* by which he meant the totality of a people's ancient rights, moral precepts and customs.[2]

In spite of the loss of the most aristocratic element of the American population—a hundred thousand Loyalists who were expelled or retired voluntarily to Canada or elsewhere during the War of Independence—American conservatism got off to a relatively good start. President Washington, the Federalist party, the party's leading intellectual, Alexander Hamilton, as well as most of the judiciary, were all conservative in the Burkean sense, while the Constitution was as conservative a document as could be expected from men who had recently established a representative government that seemed like a raging ochlocracy to horrified European autocrats. John Adams, the second president, was not as good a Christian as Burke but was, perhaps, a little farther to the right. Due to his high office, he was able on occasion to manifest his conservatism by executive order—something that Burke, in spite of his brilliant, oracular career in the House of

---

2. *Reflections on the Revolution in France,* Dolphin Books, New York. 1961, pp. 71, 167.

Commons and his powerful friends, was never able to do.

As the years passed, American conservatism followed the liberal drift of American history, though generally with a time lag of one or more decades. Jeffersonian and Jacksonian democracy dealt conservatism some hard blows, but the hardest blow was the Civil War, which divided Northern and Southern conservatives and cut short Southerner John Calhoun's dream of an aristocratic, racially oriented, slave-holding republic on the Periclean model.[3]

The great industrial expansion in the latter nineteenth century, together with the Winning of the West, helped conservatism indirectly by the political stability inherent in prosperity and economic growth. Conversely, the conservative cause was hurt by the tidal waves of the New Immigration, which brought in millions of liberal recruits. Despite certain liberal tendencies, Theodore Roosevelt's dynamic blend of enlightened patriotism, the strenuous life, trust-busting and an America First foreign policy was, perhaps, the last manifestation of an American conservatism with a high sense of national purpose.

The Great Depression was a setback of almost catastrophic proportions. As the champions of property, unrestricted capitalism and an unregulated stock market, conservatives were directly blamed for the financial chaos and misery of the depression years. Modern liberals, on the other hand, since they had long ago shaken off their Lockean anchor to property, were able to profit politically from the fear and confusion and claim all the credit for imposing the urgently needed economic measures.[4] As the New Deal wrestled boldly with the frightening problems of production and distribution in the world's most highly industrialized society,

---

3. In the postbellum period, after the battered South had sunk back into a hermetic nativism, such innately conservative Northerners as Herman Melville, Henry Adams and Brooks Adams, eventually turned their backs on the American dream altogether, the later Melville polarizing into a bleak pessimism (*Clarel*) and a high-pitched religious mysticism (*Billy Budd*). Henry Adams focused his attention and imagination on the Middle Ages (*Mont-Saint-Michel and Chartres*) and the dreadful future (*The Education of Henry Adams*), while brother Brooks threw in the sponge by predicting and even blueprinting the inevitable triumph of a cold, gutless, scientific determinism (*The Law of Civilization and Decay*).

4. The economic Achilles' heel of conservatism will be discussed more fully in Part VII, *The Economic Clash*.

conservatives made matters worse by their destructive criticism, their reactionary financial nostrums and their antiquated and pathetic appeals for the return of the "good old days."

The rise of European fascism provided liberals with another opportunity for demeaning and demoralizing the conservative opposition. There are, of course, vague bloodlines between certain aspects of conservatism and the Nietzschean attitudinizing of Hitler, just as there are historic links between certain aspects of liberalism and the demonic politicking of Lenin.[5] Both liberals and conservatives had often taken advantage of these tenuous analogies for purposes of mutual slander. But since liberals held the reins of power from the 1930's on, they were better able to make their calumnies stick.[6] These calumnies, given further credibility by the events of World War II, plus lingering memories of the depression, kept millions of normally conservative voters in the Democratic party. It was not until mid-century, after crucial liberal failures in foreign affairs and incredible liberal lapses in national security could no longer be concealed, that a resurgence of conservatism became noticeable. Conservatism expanded significantly in the 1960's, when excesses of minority racism generated a white backlash.[7]

But even the conservative resurgence was in part a lib-

---

5. It is also possible to argue that classical conservatism and modern liberalism in their high regard for governmental authority stand closer to each other and to Lenin and Hitler than to classical liberalism and modern conservatism.

6. ". . . to the Jewish mind, the *Gestalt* of the rightist requires anti-Semitism." Van den Haag, *op. cit.,* p. 139.

7. Conservatism had little intellectual leadership after the takeover of the New Deal. The works of the racial historians, Madison Grant and Lothrop Stoddard, fell into disrepute and the voices of two college professors, Paul Elmer More and Irving Babbitt, who advocated a return to the principles of Burke, were inaudible. After World War II the ideas of three Central European economists, Wilhelm Roepke, Ludwig von Mises and F. A. Hayek. who proposed the removal of economic controls and the reestablishment of a free market, were given some cursory attention. The monarchism and Anglo-Catholicism of expatriate T. S. Eliot had no discernible impact on American thought. Nor did the economic and racial theories of Ezra Pound. The two most influential conservative intellectuals of the 1950's and 1960's were William F. Buckley, Jr. and Russell Kirk, whose thinking was pure Burke and who shied desperately away from the race issue. Kirk, incidentally, attacked universal military training as adamantly as any liberal. *The Conservative Mind,* Henry Regnery, Chicago, 1960, p. 378.

eral victory. By now, modern liberalism was so entrenched
it was able to dictate the arguments and even the tactics of
its critics. Before he was allowed a nationwide platform, the
modern conservative had to demonstrate that he was a member of the loyal opposition, that on the "sensitive" issues he
was of one mind with the liberal himself. No public manifestation of classical conservatism—i.e., no forthright attack
against democracy and minority racism—was to be tolerated. If the fires of minority illiberalism and minority racism
could not be quenched by modest, hand-in-glove appeals for
decorum, they were to be left raging. The only notes of dis-
sension permitted the modern conservative were the safe
ones. He could be more reverent toward big business, property, patriotism, religion, states' rights, and law and order.
He could be more realistic toward Russia, Vietnam, big labor and school busing. But the permissible differences were
differences in degree, not in kind. On the larger issues, the
issues behind the issues, modern liberalism and modern conservatism were in many cases becoming synonomous.[8]

Such were and continue to be the liberal rules of the road,
the liberal-minority limitations on conservative political debate and inquiry. Not one prominent conservative politician
in recent memory has failed to observe them.[9] The three
most prominent—the late Senator Robert Taft, Senator
Barry Goldwater and Vice-President Spiro Agnew—were
each very careful to proclaim, throughout their criticism of
the liberal establishment, their total commitment to the
democratic process, to racial equality and to liberal dogma
in general.[10] As for such middle-of-the-roaders as Presidents

---

8. As conservatives were becoming liberals, so communists were becoming
conservatives. "Suslov is the leader of the party conservatives," wrote
Stalin's daughter, Svetlana Alliluyeva. *Only One Year,* Harper & Row, New
York, 1969, p. 47.

9. Even political maverick George Wallace complied with the ban on
open discussion of the race problem. In his campaign speeches Wallace
relied on inference rather than statement, allowing his listeners to draw
their own conclusions whenever he attacked busing.

10. It was not as great a mental leap as some imagined for Karl Hess, a
trusted Goldwater speechwriter and idea man, to later become a "radical
and philosophical anarchist" and supporter of the North Vietnamese and
the Students for a Democratic Society. *New York Times,* Sept. 28, 1969,
p. 62.

Eisenhower and Nixon, conservatives only in a comparative
sense, they both preached the fundamental tenets of modern
liberalism as loudly as any Americans in public life. Plato,
not to mention Locke and Jefferson, would probably have
judged all these political figures as little better than wild-
eyed radicals.

It is relatively simple to identify the modern conservative
intellectual, pundit and politician. But who are the members of the conservative rank and file? There must be a great
many because a 1970 Gallup Poll claimed there were more
American conservatives than liberals. Of those who agreed
to give themselves either a conservative or liberal label, the
former outnumbered the latter almost three to two.[11]

Occupationally, farmers, business executives, officers in
the armed forces, professional people and white-collar
workers are supposed to be conservatives. Clergymen, college professors, toilers in the news media, blue-collar workers and household help are usually categorized as liberals.
Property and a stock portfolio allegedly turn a man into a
conservative. Lack of property and a mass of unpaid bills
help keep him liberal.

Such generalizations, which have become articles of faith
to many sociologists, fit some but not all of the facts. The
richest population group in America—richest, that is, on a
per capita basis—is solidly liberal,[12] and the blue-collar

11. The exact breakdown was conservative, 52 percent; liberal, 34 percent; no opinion, 14 percent. Gallup Poll, *New York Times*, May 11, 1970,
p. 56. For the reverse proportion of student conservatives and student
liberals, see Chapter 20. In a 1964 Marvin Field Poll in California, 32 percent of the voters identified themselves as conservatives; 30 percent as
middle-of-the-roaders; 28 percent as liberals. In a similar 1969 Field Poll,
the percentages were 42, 27 and 24, respectively. *Time*, Sept. 26, 1969, p. 22.

12. "All the available evidence indicated that politically Jews remain
disproportionately on the left. They vote 75–85 percent Democratic. . . .
Jewish money supports much of the civil rights activity in this country. . . .
Radical movements in America . . . are again disproportionately Jewish in
composition." *Commentary*, July, 1961, p. 68. In the 1960 presidential election, the Jewish vote was 80 percent Democratic. James Yaffe, *The American
Jews*, p. 240. In the 1968 election, Jews voted better than 90 percent
Democratic. *Time*, Nov. 10, 1968, pp. 21–2. In 1968, the voters of Scars-
dale, N.Y., one of the richest suburbs in the U.S. and heavily Jewish, chose
Humphrey over Nixon. Phillips, *The Emerging Republican Majority*, p.
179. That many Jews voted for Nixon in 1972 did not mean a shift to
conservatism. They merely believed that Nixon was "better" for Israel.

workers, many of them unionized, are increasingly conserv--
ative. Whenever there is a direct political confrontation between the white and the nonwhite poor, the former become
less liberal in their voting habits.

Geographically, big cities are marked off as liberal territory; suburbia and the rural areas as conservative country.
The flight from the land to the cities, which began in World
War I, was accompanied by a great increase in the number
of liberals, just as the more recent flight from the cities to
suburbia swelled the number of conservatives. The Midwest,
the Deep South and the so-called "Sun Belt" are said to be
conservative, while the industrialized Middle Atlantic states,
the large manufacturing centers and the Northwest are liberal.

Here again there is much truth, but more half-truth. The
Deep South has its "liberal" Negroes, now casting ballots in
droves, and the Sun Belt its "liberal" Mexican-Americans,
also increasingly addicted to the bloc-voting habit. The
Northwest is still liberal, but more by tradition than conviction, and the old Democratic pluralities are dwindling. It
is one of the few regions in America that has remained relatively unscathed by minority violence because of its relatively
high degree of homogeneity. Without racial problems, as the
Scandinavians have discovered, liberalism wears better.

The racial correlation of liberalism and conservatism is
more clear-cut than geographical, economic or other environmental correlations. The American Majority is largely conservative. The Unassimilable Minorities are liberal, though
one or two Oriental population groups (in the continental
United States) vote Republican, and the Indians have so far
exhibited relatively few enduring political commitments of
any kind. Since conservatism in the United States is, among
other things, a function of assimilation, the Assimilable Minorities are moving from the liberal to the conservative side.

From the political standpoint, both liberalism and conservatism have probably been more hampered than helped
by the two-party system. Southern Democrats, the most conservative Americans, have long acted as a brake on the
ultra-liberalism of Northern Democrats. At the same time,
the liberal wing of the Republican party has consistently

stunted the growth of conservatism within Republican ranks.

If parties are supposed to represent basic differences in political attitudes and political thought, the Republican should be the party of conservatism and the Democratic the party of liberalism. To some extent this desideratum has already been accomplished by liberal Northern Democrats, who in the last several decades have outvoted, outmaneuvered and overpowered the party's Southern membership.

The Republican party, however, has a long way to go before it becomes the champion of conservatism. Its present attempt to enlarge its following in the South, the so-called Southern strategy, will have no more than limited success as long as Republican presidents enforce Supreme Court rulings on integration—and if they fail to enforce them they will lose the Republican Eastern establishment, still a desperately needed cornucopia of votes and campaign contributions. As for the hard-hat strategy, the Republican beguilement of Labor by siren promises of safer streets may win over many Assimilable Minority voters, but it may infuriate just as many oldline Republicans, who still associate unions with Red flags and street barricades.

Even if Republican conservatives did manage to assume undisputed control of their party, even if both the Southern and hard-hat strategies paid off handsomely, even if Republicans were able to dominate American politics as long and as effectively as the Democratic reign inaugurated by Roosevelt, they would still have little to offer the American Majority. By combining the humanistic abstractions of classical liberalism with modern liberal notions of equality and social democracy, the modern conservative's net effect on Majority members is to anesthetize them into dropping their racial guard at the very moment they need it most.

That is why, of all those who consciously or unconsciously oppose the Majority cause, the modern conservative is the most dangerous. Majority and minority liberals are always somewhat suspect to the average, uncommitted Majority member. The dissimilarity in racial or religious background of the minority liberal may affect his credibility, while the fake humanitarianism and special pleading of the professional Majority liberal may have a hollow and unconvincing ring. The modern conservative, on the other hand, is given a more attentive hearing. His ideas and arguments —less minority-oriented and less apocalyptic—are presented less abrasively and are not as likely to rub Majority instincts the wrong way. That the modern conservative leader usually belongs to the Majority also works to his advantage. People are more amenable to brainwashing by "one of their own" than by strangers.

The Old Believer,[13] who is the quintessential modern conservative because he is the quintessential classical liberal, is probably the most effective of all Americans in keeping the Majority in what might be called the deep freeze of racial apathy. The Old Believer has come by his political views honestly and he does not degrade them with ulterior motives. He sincerely feels that the principles of Locke and Burke are still operative in the United States of the 1970's. He still believes in the innate goodness of man and in the power of reason. Unlike the modern liberal, he is devoted to the advancement of all people, not just minorities, and he still finds a place in his heart for religion, though he prefers the social teachings of Christ to Christian theology. He does not realize that by publishing the tidings of equalitarianism and tolerance at this particular moment in time he is disarming the Majority in the very throes of its dispossession. Also, since he stands for all that was best in the American experience, the Old Believer's rationale is embellished by the appeal to tradition.

There are, of course, many less idealistic conservatives. There are the economic conservatives, the millionaires and centimillionaires who support conservatism in the hopes that it will keep their taxes down and their profits up. There are the members of the Ayn Rand cult who have actually gone so far as to deify capitalism and sanctify the dollar bill. There are the religionists of the fundamentalist or evangelistic variety, who are more interested in saving their church than their congregations. There are the fearful conservatives, who know that modern conservatism isn't enough, but

13. See Chapter 11.

also know it is as far right as they can go without losing their respectability or their livelihood.

There are the sunshine patriots and the professional patriots, who ease their consciences and fill their pocketbooks by specializing in a reactionary conservatism aimed principally at little old ladies and big old generals. There are the obsessive anti-Communists who avoid the racial issue by discovering bearded Bolsheviks under every mattress.[14] There are the reformed liberals, ashamed of their political myopia, and the bathetic ex-Communists, avidly aware of the pecuniary rewards of informing. Finally, there are the nostalgic Southerners who wistfully believe that the day will come when a loosening of government controls and a reaffirmation of states' rights will allow the South to work out its own destiny in peace.

It is probably unnecessary to explain that there are more than a few minority members in the above categories. After all, modern conservatism is now as safely equalitarian as modern liberalism and the presence of minority intellectuals in its higher echelons can only serve to keep it that way. Leading Jewish conservatives include: Ayn Rand, the Russian-born authoress of *Atlas Shrugged,* a wordy, hero-worshiping, capitalistic soap opera featuring a poltroonish industrial giant;[15] Barry Goldwater, whose quasi-minority status was mentioned earlier; the late David Lawrence of *U.S. News & World Report,* the mass-circulation conserva-

---

14. It is easier to understand and condone conservative and Catholic hypersensitivity to the handful of American Communists if it is remembered that there were only 10,000 card-carrying Communists in Spain at the beginning of the Spanish Civil War—during which the Republican side murdered 12 bishops, 283 nuns, 5,255 priests, 2,492 monks and 249 novices. The Bishop of Ciudad Real was killed while working on a history of Toledo and 1,200 irreplaceable filing cards destroyed. 10,000 priceless volumes were burnt to ashes in the Cathedral library at Cuenca. Hugh Thomas, *The Spanish Civil War,* Harper & Row, New York, 1961, pp. 99, 172–4. In 1917, the year of the successful November revolution, there was one Russian Bolshevik for every 2,777 Russians. In 1947, there was one American Communist for every 1,814 Americans. Goodman, *The Committee,* p. 196.

15. Poltroonish because when hounded to the breaking point by liberals and Communists, instead of fighting back, Miss Rand's hero "went on strike" and retreated to the safety of a Rocky Mountain fastness. Ayn Rand, *Atlas Shrugged,* Random House, New York, 1957, Part III.

tive weekly newsmagazine; Lionel Trilling (literary criticism); Herman Kahn (futurology); Ludwig von Mises and Milton Friedman (economics); Nathaniel Weyl (history and social criticism); Irving Kristol, Ralph de Toledano [16] and Victor Lasky (punditry); Fred Schwarz, the Australian-born head of the Christian Crusade; Arthur Burns, chairman of the Federal Reserve Board; [17] Lewis Strauss, former head of the Atomic Energy Commission and Lessing Rosenwald [18] of the American Council for Judaism.

Although many Unassimilable Minority intellectuals and politicians have infiltrated modern conservatism, the Unassimilable Minority masses keep their distance. They are not at all fearful of conservatism in its present-day anemic form, but they are afraid of what conservatism has been in the past and what it could be in the future. They can hardly forget the aristocratic, classical conservatism that kept their forebears "in their place" in the Old World for centuries. They are well acquainted—and some have had firsthand experience—with National Socialist racism in Germany, which they identify with conservatism, although Nazism had many radical facets. They quite understand that the quiescent racism of the Majority could one day be reawakened and turned against certain kinds of whites as well as all kinds of nonwhites.

In spite of their savage overreaction to the slightest sign of serious conservatism on the American political horizon, most minorities are generally far more conservative (old-style) than the Majority.[19] Minority members may be the liberals of the voting booth, but they are the reactionaries of

16. The "de" was added by Toledano himself in an act of self-ennoblement.
17. The news media insisted on calling Burns a conservative, although he was soft on Vietnam and even softer on equalitarianism.
18. Rosenwald, of the Sears, Roebuck Rosenwalds, leads the small, almost inaudible band of American Jews who feel that Zionism is detrimental to U.S. interests—as well as to Jewish interests.
19. Even Negroes, the most unconservative of all Americans because of their frail links to the past, are becoming more conservative as they search for bits and pieces of their African heritage and invent what they cannot find. But this should be of small comfort to Majority conservatives. An upsurge of Negro tribalism will strengthen rather than weaken the Black Power movement.

the living room. They rule their inner world according to rules and regulations they publicly decry in the outside world. Their family life is authoritarian, with the father still the paterfamilias and the children, when home from college, still filial. It is this fireside conservatism, this basically tribal psychology, which germinates the racism that has won so many minority victories in the ethnic scramble for power.

Modern conservatism, which lacks the racial drive of modern liberalism, has been and will continue to be of little help in unifying the Majority and rousing it to the high pitch of performance necessary to reverse its present decline. Stronger medicine is required for those who are trapped in a racial conflagration that is getting out of hand and who must fight fire with fire to avoid being consumed in the flames.

The only conservatism that can be useful to the Majority in its present state of siege is a conservatism stripped of the dead weight of outmoded political dogma, one that appeals to the young as well as the old, to the heart as well as the pocketbook, to the powers of imagination as well as the powers of reason—a conservatism, in short, which has to do with the care and feeding of the ethos, that intangible repository of beliefs, values and ideals that constitutes a people's tradition.

The business of conservatism is to preserve and to vitalize tradition. Without the past there is only the present. And when there is only the present, there is no future.

PART VII

The Economic Clash

Chapter 25

The Biology of Revolution

I F THERE WAS EVER a discipline that should be founded on reason, and on reason alone, it is economics. Yet, like politics, economics has now been so theorized and theologized, so supercharged with tendentiousness and unreason, as to be almost completely shrouded from the prying eye of objectivity.[1] Officiating as the priesthood of the various fiscal cults that dominate modern economic thought—some of which stray well beyond the boundaries of economics and meddle in practically every aspect of human behavior—is a mishmash of liberal historicists, doctrinaire materialists, bureaucratic statisticians and tax-happy plutocrats.

Any given economic system must prove to be false or inadequate over a period of time, for the obvious reason that no one economic system can effectively adjust to the wildly fluctuating economic conditions which harry and bedevil every nation during its life span. What is good economics for a country with unlimited natural resources and an industrious,

---

1. A course in comparative economy would be an extremely enlightening addition to the college curriculum. Equally enlightening would be a compulsory test on the scientific method to be taken and passed by every writer on economic subjects *before publication.* "The scientific method," according to one interpretation, "involves skillful handling of the material being studied, careful observations, controlled experiments, if possible, close attention to detail . . . intellectual honesty . . . open-mindedness . . . cautiousness in reaching conclusions . . . willingness to repeat experiments . . . vigilance for the occurence of possible flaws in hypotheses, theories, evidences and conclusions." Hegner and Stiles, *College Zoology,* Macmillan, New York, 1959, p. 11.

expanding population can be bad economics for a nation without resources and with a declining birthrate. Also, foreign or civil wars have a habit of overturning the best-laid economic plans, and in an ever more interdependent world even a small shift in the economy of one nation may produce a chain reaction in the economies of others.

One of history's most dismal sights is that of two political factions tearing a country apart in order to force a favorite economic dogma on the population at large. The best that can happen when two economic doctrines are in sharp opposition is that one of them is right, or at least better geared to serve the country at that particular moment in time. Often both are wrong and totally inappropriate. Nevertheless thousands, sometimes millions, of people have to die and the state apparatus has to be disrupted so that one side can make its point. Two physicists who fought a duel to the death over the outcome of a laboratory experiment before conducting the experiment would be considered hopelessly insane. But mass duels to the death between partisans of economic systems over unproven and unprovable economic assumptions have become increasingly common.

It seems almost impossible for modern man, as it was impossible for ancient man, to understand or accept the basic relativity of economics. By reducing economics to the common denominator of the pocketbook and by capitalizing on the economic breakdowns that affect living standards and sometimes even life itself, the political agitator manages to inject irrationality, emotion and fanaticism into a subject that requires the highest degree of rationality. Just as the demagogue attunes his politics to the fact that there are more *hoi polloi* than aristocrats, he attunes his economics to the fact that there are more paupers than millionaires. Consequently, the politician who promises to take from the rich and give to the poor has more votes in his pocket to begin with than his opponent. Except in those rare eras when a highly responsible and gifted people finds itself in the midst of an almost limitless expanse of fertile, undeveloped land and is too busy pioneering, exploring or acquiring worldly goods to hear the songs of economic Loreleis, Robin Hood is always a more popular figure than Horatio Alger.

If the two great rival economic systems of the twentieth century, capitalism and socialism, are judged on the basis of production, it is found that the former (in its American version) outproduces the latter (in its Russian version) by as much as twenty to one in consumer products.[2] In spite of its lower living standards, however, socialism is greatly outdistancing capitalism in gaining new converts, while capitalism itself continues to adopt more socialist controls.

Repetitious references to the successes of capitalism no longer evoke the Pollyanna responses they once did, even in that citadel of capitalism, America. Nor do they help to justify capitalism's cyclic booms and busts, creeping and galloping inflation, mass unemployment, vast pockets of desolation and poverty, and the monopolistic proclivities of the large producers. But the defects of socialism are also considerable. Socialist economies have their own inflationary periods and suffer from other severe economic dislocations. They have never solved the agricultural impasse created by taking the land away from the peasants. Socialism also stifles individual initiative by the formation of monstrous, bumbling bureaucracies whose heartlessness and spinelessness exceed those of capitalism.

The swing to socialism, which offers no real economic advantages to consumers (compare the economies of West and East Germany), must be explained by other than economic factors. The most important of these is that socialist economic doctrine—though not socialist economic practice—is tailored to the spirit of the age. In a time of equalitarianism and minority racism, economic policy concentrates on the sharing, not the creation of wealth, on job security, not job betterment. It is no longer a question of *making* a decent wage, but of being *guaranteed* a decent wage—no longer a matter of accumulating savings for retirement but of being given a retirement income. In psychological terms, as capitalism moves toward socialism,

2. In 1964, after nearly a half century of Marxist-Leninist economics, the average Moscow citizen still had to work 16 minutes for a loaf of bread, 315 minutes for a two-pound chicken, 71 minutes for a quart of milk. The average New Yorker, on the other hand, works only 8 minutes for his bread, 23 minutes for his chicken, 7 minutes for his milk. *San Francisco Chronicle*, Nov. 12, 1964, Financial Section.

344 The Economic Clash

proletarian feelings of insecurity supersede Yankee super-confidence.

Votes are still bought with economic promises, but the promises are now made to races and population groups as well as to religions, classes and individuals. The attack on private ownership grows fiercer, not because, as official socialist doctrine has it, state control of the means of production would bring about greater economic benefits, but because private property is one of the biggest stumbling blocks to the latter-day perversions of democracy and liberalism.[3] The liberal-minority coalition does not covet property solely to divide it more equitably among the citizenry. The affluent minorities and most Majority liberals have enough possessions and the poor minorities are as envious as they are needy. The prime motivation is an odd mix of compassion and revenge. The declining fortunes of those on the way down provide a kind of ghoulish satisfaction to those on the way up.

Similarly, Majority members are not merely defending private property for its own sake or for the power and physical comfort it affords. They are defending an institution handed down from the great days of Majority domination.[4] Property, particularly property in the form of farm land, was a fixation of the Majority settlers who transformed America into the cornucopia which now feeds populations whose rulers favor collective agriculture.

The non-economic foundations of most economic doctrine show up most clearly in times of revolution, which modern historians teach are wars between classes. This assumption

---

3. Private property is not dead in Russia. People can still own homes, have bank accounts and leave their possessions to heirs. But the elimination of the profit system has prevented the accumulation of great fortunes, even though the gulf between high and low wage scales is greater in Russia than in the U.S. See footnote 33, p. 351.

4. Max Weber has alleged that the great economic feats of nineteenth-century capitalism were inspired by the Protestant Ethic. He might have traced the inspiration back farther, to the Northern European peoples themselves, who were not only responsible for Protestantism but for capitalism and the industrial revolution which accompanied it. Weber, however, was careful to distinguish between Protestant capitalism, the "bourgeois organization of labour" and Jewish capitalism, a "speculative pariah-capitalism." Max Weber, *The Protestant Ethic and the Spirit of Capitalism*, trans, Talcott Parsons, Allen and Unwin, London, 1930, especially p. 271, footnote 58.

may have some relevance when confined to monoracial nations, but in most instances of class warfare the racial elements have probably outweighed the economic.[5] In the incessant clashes between the Roman patricians and plebeians and between the medieval peasantry and the Teutonic aristocracy, the contending parties differed racially as well as economically, and the racial differences preceded rather than followed the establishment of class and caste.[6]

Although the French Revolution is supposed to be the prototype of the modern class war, it might be profitable to heed what a leading British literary review recently had to say about the life and literary output of Restif de la Bretonne, whose eyewitness accounts of Paris in the heyday of the Terror provide an almost inexhaustible storehouse of background material for historians. "There are hints in Restif too of a class racialism, of the fears felt by the bourgeois and by the artisan for the pale men with dark ill-kempt hair, piercing eyes and shaggy mustaches. . . . His canaille is always dark and glowering. . . . The respectable, the men of property, the virtuous craftsmen, are fair and have good complexions. . . . Restif dwells on Charlotte Corday's essential innocence, for she is blonde and Norman. In the 1780's the population of Paris . . . was still predominantly fair. In the 1790's Royalist pamphleteers make much of the fact that the terrorists tended to be dark and from the Mediterranean area: Marat in particular served their purpose in this respect. And so too Restif's massacreurs would almost inevitably be depicted as men of the South." [7] Abbé Sièyes, who also happened to be from the South and who with perfect timing turned from Catholicism to Robespierre's Goddess of Reason and back again, revealed the racial motivations of the revolutionists when he urged returning the French aristocracy to the

---

5. Darlington finds that the makers of revolution have few economic motives. "Most [revolutionaries] came from groups denied their opportunities in society on national, racial or religious grounds: Irish in Britain, Poles in Russia, Jews in Germany and later in Russia, bastards (like Herzen) anywhere." *The Evolution of Man and Society*, p. 543.

6. "Indeed class differences ultimately all derive from genetic and, usually, racial differences . . . it is the inequalities which create advances in society rather than advances in society which create the inequalities." *Ibid.*, p. 547.

7. *Times Literary Supplement*, Oct. 27, 1961.

"German marshes" whence they had come.[8] Sièyes' racial line was echoed by thousands of more authentic sansculottes who insisted on portraying themselves as Gauls fighting for liberation from the barbarous Franks.[9]

If racial factors had something to do with the overthrow of the Bourbons,[10] they had much to do with the overthrow of the Romanovs. Almost to a man, the Bolshevik ruling clique was composed of members of Russian minorities.[11] The leading Bolshevik, Lenin, was a walking farrago of races. "Young Vladimir's slanted eyes and high cheekbones bore witness to his father's Tartar blood." [12] Lenin's grandmother "married a well-to-do retired Jewish physician, Alexander Blank. . . . Lenin's four grandparents were . . . of four different races and religions. . . ." [13]

Once the revolution was won and the expropriators expropriated, Marxist theory predicted that there would be no more cause for internal power struggles or Machiavellian horseplay, since such reactionary and internecine politics always had economic roots. Racial theory, on the other hand, predicted that once the minorities had driven out the Czar, the aristocracy, the Orthodox Church and lesser members of the Russian leadership, they would then direct their racism against each other. And this, of course, is what happened.

---

8. Ripley, *The Races of Europe*, p. 156.

9. Toynbee, *Study of History*, Vol. VI, p. 217.

10. The deracination of the French nobility and the higher strata of the Catholic hierarchy represented an aristocratic split in the ranks. The Third Estate by itself would never have been strong enough to bring about the French Revolution if it had not been joined by 50 nobles, 44 bishops and 200 parish priests in 1789. In 1792, the National Convention was composed of 782 members of which only two were workmen. Even Danton and Robespierre were so unproletarian that they originally wished to be known as d'Anton and de Robespierre. Darlington, *op. cit.*, p. 534.

11. ". . . with a population ratio of 1.77 percent, Jews in Lenin's Russia made up 5.2 percent of the total party membership, 25.7 percent of the party's Central Committee and from 36.8 percent to 42.9 percent of the ruling Politburo, while among Soviet diplomats and especially senior officials of the secret police the percentage of Jews was even greater." Geoffrey Bailey, *The Conspirators*, Harper, New York, 1960, p. 129, footnote.

12. *Look*, May 22, 1962, p. 36.

13. Darlington, *op. cit.*, p. 557. Darlington also points out the minority status of two other historic equalitarians—Engels, the English capitalist and cotton magnate who was a German of French Huguenot descent, and Rousseau, the French moralist from Switzerland. *Ibid.*, pp. 543, 545.

After the death of Lenin, Stalin, the Mediterranean from Georgia, began his tortuous rise to one-man rule, first by exiling his rival, Trotsky (whom he later had murdered in Mexico City), then by the sequential liquidation of Kamenev, Rykov, Zinoviev, Yagoda and Radek, all of whom happened to be Jews.[14]

During World War II, other minorities were brought to heel: 600,000 Volga Germans, as well as most members of the Tatar, Kalmyk, Karachai, Balkar and Chechen-Ingush nationality groups were deported to Siberia.[15] At the height of the German attack, when Russia was on the verge of collapse, the Russian Majority came back into favor, since it was called upon to do most of the fighting.[16] But the minorities still held the reins of power. Stalin was succeeded as Communist party leader by Malenkov, a Southern Russian with a "Mongolian admixture," [17] who in turn was followed by Khrushchev, the Ukrainian, and Brezhnev, born in the Ukraine.[18] It was Malenkov who deposed and ordered the shooting of Beria, Stalin's fellow Georgian and longtime Chief of the Secret Police, though he retained Mikoyan, the Armenian financial expert.[19] As for Soviet Jews, they eventually became the targets of an official anti-Zionist and a quasi-official anti-Semitic campaign—a turn of events which constituted a supreme act of ingratitude to Marx and other

---

14. Only a few high Jewish officials escaped judicial murder or Siberia. Among them were Litvinov and Kaganovich. In all, thousands of Jewish members of the Old Bolshevik hierarchy were purged. See article, "Jews," *Ency. of Russia and the Soviet Union,* as well as Chapter 33 of this study. The highest Soviet officer purged by Stalin, it might be noted, was Marshal Tukhachevsky, who was half Italian.

15. *Ency. of Russia and the Soviet Union,* p. 230.

16. "[Stalin] abolished . . . the extensive cultural autonomy which the minorities had enjoyed in the 1920's, leaving them in the end with little more than the right to use their language . . . and to enjoy folk art. Stalin . . . felt impelled to discriminate against the minorities, not only in the matter of state and party appointments, but also in cultural affairs. This discrimination was particularly intense in [his last 10 years.]" *Ibid.,* p. 380. For more concerning Stalin's latter-day support of Russian nationalism, see pp. 453–4.

17. Milovan Djilas, *Conversations with Stalin,* Harcourt Brace, New York, 1962, p. 108.

18. *Ibid.,* pp. 74–5, 274, 329.

19. *Ibid.,* pp. 329, 355.

Jewish prime movers of international communism and the Soviet Union.[20]

The commanding role played by minorities, particularly Jewish minorities, in the abortive or short-lived post-World War I revolutions in Hungary, Bavaria and Prussia has already been noted.[21] Marshal Tito, the architect of Communist Yugoslavia, belonged to the Croatian minority in his country. The original Communist leadership of the Polish and Czechoslovakian Communist parties was heavily Jewish and, accordingly, decimated by Stalin.[22] In China, the chief advisors to the Chinese revolutionaries in the 1920's were Blucher, a Russian, and Borodin, a Russian Jew.[23]

In the United States, minorities dominated the Communist party from its inception. The Irish-American Communist leaders, Foster and Flynn, have previously been mentioned,[24] and the proportion of Jews in the Party in the 1920's and 1930's was staggering.[25] When Jews began withdrawing from communism as a result of Stalin's purges and the 1939 Russo-German Nonaggression Pact, they did not necessarily abandon their traditional radical leanings, but channeled them into other non-Soviet or anti-Soviet forms of Marxism.[26]

---

20. See pp. 454–7.
21. See Chapter 15. Typical of the revolutionaries who peregrinated about Europe in the early part of the century was Parvus-Helphand, born in Hungary of Jewish parents, student of Marxism in Switzerland, leading ideologue of the German Socialist party's left wing, friend of Lenin, German spy, booster of the Russian revolution and finally a millionaire land speculator. Parvus-Helphand will probably be best remembered for his deathless words on first arriving in Germany: "I am looking for a fatherland. Where can I buy one cheap?" *Ich suche ein Vaterland, wo ist ein Vaterland zu haben für billiges Geld?* Winfried Scharlan and Zbynek Zeinan, *Freibeuter der Revolution,* Verlag Wissenschaft und Politik, Köln, 1964, especially p. 36.
22. Sachar, *The Course of Modern Jewish History,* p. 545.
23. *Ency. of Russia and the Soviet Union,* pp. 70, 72–3.
24. See p. 129.
25. Even as late as 1947 it was estimated that 39.3 percent of American Communist party activists were Jewish—approximately thirteen times more than the Jewish proportion of the population warranted. This figure, needless to say, did not include Jewish fellow travelers. Weyl, *The Creative Elite in America,* p. 103. Weyl speaks from some experience since he formerly belonged to the Communist party himself.
26. A few Jews became strident anti-Communists, but their anti-Communism was dialectical, polemical and largely uninspiring. Some remained in the party in spite of the shabby treatment accorded Russian Jews. Herbert

At last report (1969), American Jews composed "at least half of the active protestors among the New Left," [27] and "the nonpopulist brand of radicalism is noisy, intellectual, ideological, and primarily Jewish." [28]

In the mind's eye of Marx,[29] the proletarian revolution, the

---

Aptheker, for example, is presently the chief theoretician of the U.S. Communist party. Other Jews combined a lingering sympathy for communism with a new sympathy for Israel. An example of such mixed feelings, if it were not taken from the *Wall Street Journal* (July 3, 1962), would seem appropriate to the wilder pages of the *Protocols of Zion*. It concerned the convicted Communist spy, Robert Soblen, who jumped $100,000 bail and sought refuge, not in Russia, but in Israel. Part of the bail was raised by Mrs. Benjamin Buttenwieser, the wife of a Kuhn, Loeb partner, who lent Mrs. Soblen $60,000 with the understanding that George Kirstein, publisher of *The Nation*, would reimburse half of the amount in case of a loss. Soblen, a psychiatrist, later committed suicide in England while being returned to the U.S.

27. According to an estimate by Nathan Glazer, Professor of Sociology at the University of California. *New York Times*, May 4, 1969, p. 80. Another sociology professor phrased his estimate differently: "Out of ten radicals, five are likely to be Jewish." Van den Haag, *op. cit.*, p. 118.

28. Yaffe, *op. cit.*, p. 255.

29. One sign that human evolution has just begun or is already at an end is the seriousness and respect which generations of Western minds have bestowed upon the "thinking" of Marx and Engels. Both of them were Lamarckians, that is to say, they were as knowledgeable in biology and genetics as a present-day "flat-worlder" is in celestial mechanics and astrophysics. The two founders of Communism also believed in inferior races and sneered at the 'tartarized and mongolized" Slavs. Darlington, *op. cit.*, p. 546. They even made disparaging remarks about "niggers." Weyl and Possony, *Geography of Intellect*, p. 20. But they were convinced that all evidences of racial inferiority would be quickly eradicated and all inferior beings quickly raised to the level of the advanced races once the proletariat took over the direction of human society. Engels was particularly noted for a perverted brand of Hegelian gibberish that would be utterly ludicrous if it were not now considered Holy Writ by a large segment of mankind. "Butterflies, for example, spring from the egg through a negation of the egg. . . ." wrote Engels in his *Anti-Dühring* (p. 154). "But if we take . . . a dahlia or an orchid: if we treat the seed and the plant which grows from it as a gardener does, we get as the result of this negation of the negation not only more seeds, but also qualitatively better seeds [and] each repeated negation of the negation increases this improvement" (p. 154). Like the cave men of the Stone Age, who saw the world as a battleground of rival supernatural powers, Engels had an equally simplistic view—a world struggle between exploiters and exploited, capitalists and workers. "All past history was the history of class struggles . . . the warring classes of society are always the product of the modes of production and exchange. . . ." (p. 33). There was, of course, no possibility of rational debate with Marx, Engels and company since "their adversaries could only be either bourgeois idiots or proletarian traitors." Ludwig von Mises, *Theory and History*, Ar-

ultimate extension of class war, would first occur in the highly industrialized nations, which in his time were England and Germany.[30] He put Russia toward the end of the revolutionary timetable and China at the very end. He paid little or no attention to the influences that racial homogeneity or heterogeneity might have in provoking or dampening the revolution. Marx's predictions might not have been so absurdly wrong if he had stopped to consider that just as some races are more prone to industrialization than others, some are more resistant to revolution than others, particularly revolution in its proletarian form.[31]

Why have there been no successful proletarian revolutions and very few attempts at any kind of revolution in Northern European nations or in nations with predominantly Northern European populations? Is it unreasonable to assume that the genetic composition of the Northern European peoples

lington House, New Rochelle, N.Y., 1969, p. 131. As time went on, Marxists "no longer based their hopes upon the power of their arguments but upon the resentment, envy, and hatred of the masses." *Ibid.*, p. 65. In his *Address on the Civil War in France* (1871), the "philosopher" Marx displayed his detachment by accusing Vice-President Jules Favre, of "living in concubinage with the wife of a dipsomaniac." *Ibid.*, p. 134. "As far as the originality and content of the theory of Marx's materialistic conception of history is concerned . . . there seems to be no possibility to claim that Marx added any single new idea in this field or gave a new and scientifically better synthesis of the ideas which existed before him." Pitirim Sorokin, *Contemporary Sociological Theories,* p. 520, footnote 24. Sorokin added that a little known Prussian economist, Georg Wilhelm von Raumer, formulated an economic theory of history almost identical to Marx's. *Ibid.*, pp. 521–22.

30. The despised "racist" de Gobineau was a much better prophet of European events than Marx. In an 1866 letter, de Gobineau wrote that if present trends in German politics continued, "power will fall to the first corporal who, in passing, will seize it." Dostoyevsky in his novel *The Possessed* gave an almost exact picture of events in twentieth century Russia. The most uncanny forecaster of the future was the French anthropologist Vacher de Lapouge, who predicted in 1899: (1) the meteoric rise and fall of the Third Reich; (2) absolute socialism in Russia; (3) a contest for world supremacy between Russia and the U.S., with the latter being favored because it had 15 percent of the world's Nordic population as against Russia's 9 percent; (4) the Jewish ascendancy, which he said could only be broken by socialism. An anti-Semite himself, Lapouge was opposed to the French anti-Semitism of his day, which he characterized as favoring France's Gallic element over the Germanic element and as being a weird compost of economic protectionism and liberal clericalism. *L'Aryen, son rôle social,* Fontemoing, Paris, 1899, pp. 345, 371, 464, 469, 482, 510.

31. Revolution is here defined as the overthrow of the greater part of a state's political, economic and religious institutions.

has something to do with this record? Why is Japan, in spite of a defeat in World War II that involved atomic devastation, the most stable great power in Asia and the least susceptible to revolution? Is not part of the answer that Japan is the most racially homogeneous of the large Asian nations? Why is Costa Rica the most prosperous and progressive country in Central America? The fact that it is the one Central American state with a dominant and homogeneous white population (only 2 percent Negro, 0.4 percent Indian) may provide a clue. Why did Germany almost succumb to revolution after defeat in World War I, yet become the most affluent and most stable nation in Europe after its much worse defeat in World War II? Could it be because the dynamic minority which was present in large numbers after the First World War could hardly be said to exist after the Second? [32]

And was not this same minority, hyperactive in stirring up the revolutionary chaos that helped bring about Russia's defeat in World War I, mute, restricted and oppressed in Russia at the end of World War II? From the latter war, although having suffered much greater destruction and casualties, Russia emerged victorious and was stronger and more united than ever before in its history.[33] Also, is it sheer coincidence that the two great Communist powers, which Marxist theory predicts should be the warmest and closest of allies, are now at each other's throats? [34]

---

32. There were 600,000 Jews in Germany at the end of World War I—only 25,000 in West Germany at the end of World War II. Sachar, *op. cit.*, pp. 425, 489. Jews, however, have recently been returning in some numbers.

33. In some respects there was as much reason for a revolution in Russia during World War II as during World War I. The military situation was as hopeless in 1941–42 as it was in 1917. Moreover, the Communist hierarchy had formed a new upper class which was almost as far removed politically, socially and economically from the mass of the people as was the old Russian aristocracy and capitalist and merchant class. By the middle 1950's, the average Russian industrial worker earned 10,000 rubles a year, the average member of the intelligentsia 50,000 rubles, while the heads of the major ministries and government committees were given annual stipends of hundreds of thousands of rubles. The salaries of the highest political officials are a state secret. *Ency. of Russia and the Soviet Union*, pp. 522–3.

34. At present the Chinese are calling Russian leaders "the new Czars" and Russian troops "the new Cossacks." The quotations are from an article by a *New York Times* reporter, who was told by a Soviet colonel, "It's time to teach those yellow bastards a lesson." *New York Times Magazine*, July 27, 1969, p. 55.

352

The Economic Clash

This long interrogatory is not meant to lay the foundation for a racial theory of history. It merely suggests that race may often provide a better explanation of events than class.[35] Perhaps this is why, in the vernacular of modern liberalism, class has become a euphemism, if not a code word, for race. Race has an ugly ring and tends to reduce all arguments to the personal equation. Class, on the other hand, is well-suited to current political and economic semantics. Minorities know at first hand the racial background of most class antagonisms. But the more subtle of their leaders also know that by bringing race out in the open they may awaken the race consciousness of those who have been so effectively divided and disarmed by class propaganda. Also, since a coalition of minorities is necessary for a successful revolutionary struggle, too much talk about race might set one minority against another.

If the Marxists' long-predicted proletarian revolution ever takes place in the United States, the principal causes will not be the hardening of class divisions or capitalist exploitations.[36]

---

35. The *reductio ad absurdum* of Marxism is the case of Marx himself. If the Marxist diagnosis of the economic motivation of human behavior is correct, then Marx's own career must be the exception that proves the rule. The middle-class son of an affluent Jewish lawyer who converted to Protestantism, Marx had aspirations toward the aristocracy, as evidenced by his marriage to Jenny von Westphalen, the daughter of a high government official who was a member of the petty nobility. What class motivations could possibly have influenced Marx to take up the cause of the proletariat? As a member of a minority, however, his social climbing, his self-serving dogmatism and his hatred of nineteenth-century European civilization become more understandable. What is more, like all professional dogmatists, Marx was loathe to practice what he preached. At the very time he was finishing his masterwork, *Das Kapital,* he invested heavily and foolishly in the London stock market and had to call on his banker uncle, Philips, whose descendants founded the giant Dutch electronics firm of the same name, to bail him out. See the German periodical, *Capital,* Hamburg, June 1970, p. 166.

36. It is interesting to note that Negro militancy in the U.S. is increasing in direct proportion to Negro income—in total contradiction to Marxist theory. In 1960, Negro income was 55 percent of white income. By 1967, it had climbed to 63 percent. In 1960, 48 percent of the Negro population lived at the poverty level. In 1967, 29 percent. The median increase of Negro family income during these years was 47 percent, as against a white increase of 30 percent. In 1960, one-twelfth of Negro families earned $10,000 a year; in 1967, one-fifth. Living habits, on the other hand, provide a better indication of Negro unrest than economics. In 1960, 22.4 percent of Negro families were headed by a woman. By 1967, the number of female-

They will be the heterogeneity of the American population, the racial dynamism of minority elements within this population and the deracination of the American Majority. The order of battle is already drawn up. On the revolutionary side of the barricades will be the fire-breathing militants of the Unassimilable Minorities, the less assimilated leaders of some Assimilable Minorities and the more desperate and more compromised Majority liberals. On the counterrevolutionary side [37] will be the Majority activists and the more assimilated leaders of the Assimilable Minorities. As in all revolutions, most of the population will assume, or try to assume, a lethargic neutrality.

A proletarian revolution would obviously put the finishing touches on the dispossession of the Majority. But the present round of skirmishing and armed reconnoitering, the virtual guerrilla war which the electronic media still prefer to call a crime wave, is achieving revolutionary objectives so fast, is putting so many Americans in such a revolutionary state of mind, that there is hardly any need for escalation. A few more decades of this softening up, this preparation for the kill, will be as damaging to the Majority as an all-out Red putsch.

Meanwhile, many of the richest and most influential Majority members continue to lend substance to the notion of class war by their stiff-necked subservience to nineteenth-century economic dogma. Their voting record, their reading matter and their speeches often give the impression that they are more interested in saving an economic system than in saving their people, their country or themselves. The Marxists, who also believe in associating economic doctrine with the

---

headed families had climbed to 27.3 percent. In 1960, 21.6 percent of Negro births were illegitimate; in 1967, 29.4 percent. In the same year, the white rate of illegitimacy was only 4.9 percent. *U.S. News & World Report*, March 30, 1970, p. 30. Later figures showed that the proportion of Negroes earning $7,000 a year or more went from 22 percent in 1960 to 44 percent in 1970. *U.S. News & World Report*, June 1, 1970, p. 19. The most disturbing statistics were those which revealed there were 2,241,000 Negro children in female-headed homes, as against 1,947,000 in families with both parents present.

37. The terms revolutionary and counterrevolutionary can be misleading when applied to the proponents and opponents of revolution. In the long run, the successful counterrevolution may overturn more institutions and change society more radically than the revolution which inspired it.

destiny of nations and races, rejoice at the paranoid materialism of the Majority Old Guard.

When economics becomes a sacred cow, it also becomes a Trojan Horse. The only true measure of any given economic system at any given moment in a nation's history is its ability to prime the environment for the maximum expansion of the people's creativity. To measure economics any other way, to allow economics to degenerate into the peevish little dogmas which presently disarm Majority resistance, is to hasten the economic breakdown that the liberal-minority coalition awaits with bated breath.

Chapter 26

The Proletarian Syndrome

A BRIEF SURVEY of American unionism will furnish additional evidence of the racial nature of the class struggle. Whatever form labor unions have taken in the United States—the paternalistic craft unions, the revolutionary Industrial Workers of the World, the dynamic industrial unions of the thirties, the huge million-membered union conglomerates of the present—almost all have had one thing in common. Their leadership has not been drawn from the ranks of the Majority.

It is not news to say that there is little of the medieval guild in modern unions. The religious ties of the guild, the oaths of brotherhood, the emphasis on quality instead of quantity, the personal pride in the finished work—all these are far removed from the practice and philosophy of today's giant unions. The guildsman worried about what he received for his labor. But he also cared about the product of his labor. In comparison, the typical member of the large industrial union is concerned almost exclusively with his pay and his fringe benefits.

Unions had a spotty and somewhat violent history in nineteenth-century America.[1] Often their very existence was

---

1. The most dramatic example of a nineteenth-century racial labor union was the Molly Maguires, a secret group of Irish coal workers who committed murder and mayhem in Pennsylvania coal-producing counties during the years 1862–1876. Nineteen members of the group were hanged and many others imprisoned. *Ency. Brit.*, Vol. 15, p. 678.

pronounced illegal, and well into the twentieth century courts were liberally handing out anti-strike injunctions. Then came the economic troubles of the early 1930's, when the weight of the law shifted to the union side. Instead of the employee being punished for union activities, it was now the employer who was penalized for anti-union activities. The closed shop became a hallowed institution and yellow dog contracts (prohibiting workers from joining a union) were forbidden.

It was not until mid-century that the seemingly irresistible force acquired by Labor in the New Deal era was challenged. The Taft-Hartley Act (1947), passed over President Truman's veto, curbed certain union abuses by providing a cooling-off period in strikes affecting the national interest and by permitting states to outlaw the union shop with "right-to-work" laws. The economic determinists who automatically deny any connection between unionism and race might take note that the nineteen states which had "right-to-work" laws in 1966 were precisely those states which could still be called Majority strongholds.[2]

The minority vise on the American labor movement was apparent from the very start. The Knights of Labor became the first important national labor organization, thanks largely to Terence Powderly, the lawyer son of immigrants from Ireland.[3] The Knights of Labor later evolved into the American Federation of Labor, whose first and foremost president was cigarmaker Samuel Gompers, born in Britain of Dutch-Jewish parentage. Eugene Debs, organizer of the first large railway union and perennial Socialist candidate for president, was the son of French-Alsatian immigrants.[4]

---

2. The states were: Alabama, Arizona, Arkansas, Florida, Georgia, Iowa, Kansas, Mississippi, Nebraska, Nevada, North Carolina, North Dakota, South Carolina, South Dakota, Tennessee, Texas, Utah, Virginia and Wyoming.

3. For a roster of Irish-American labor leaders, see p. 130.

4. Assimilable Minority members, some of whom are themselves descended from minorities in their Old World homelands, have as labor leaders both a professional and personal stake in resisting assimilation. In a multiracial state like the U.S., unions can hardly avoid a certain amount of pandering to minorities, and a minority background is a helpful and often a necessary qualification for union leadership, especially for those labor leaders who specialize in playing class against class. The carefully cultivated

The huge needle trades unions were almost solidly minority in composition from the Jewish leadership at the top to the Jewish and Italian rank and file at the bottom. Both David Dubinsky and Sidney Hillman, who headed, respectively, the International Ladies Garment Workers and the Amalgamated Clothing Workers, were born abroad of Jewish parents. Hillman played a principal part with John L. Lewis, the colorful son of a Welsh miner,[5] in the formation of the CIO (Congress of Industrial Organizations), and personified the apogee of union power in the 1944 Democratic Convention when President Roosevelt gave instructions that anyone wishing to make proposals concerning the party platform or political strategy first had to "clear it with Sidney."[6]

Other high-ranking labor leaders with minority backgrounds were or are: William Green, the second president of the American Federation of Labor, like Lewis the son of a Welsh miner; George Meany, present president of the AFL-CIO, an Irish-American; Ike Gold of the United Rubber Workers; Sol Stetin of the Textile Workers; Caesar Petrillo of the American Federation of Musicians; Philip Murray of the United Steelworkers, born in Scotland of Irish parents; Joseph Curran of the National Maritime Union; Mike Quill of the Transport Workers; Walter Reuther of the United Auto Workers, son of a German Socialist and married to a Jewish social worker; Harry Bridges, an Australian, chief of the International Longshoremen, married to a Japanese; Albert Shanker of the American Federation of Teachers; Jerry Wurf of the American Federation of State, County and Municipal Employees; and Cesar Chavez of the United Farm Workers.

There are, of course, millions of Majority members in the

"minority pose" of many union officials who belong to Assimilable Minorities cannot help but rub off on their private attitudes and feelings and strew many psychological roadblocks in the path of their assimilation.

5. Lewis' father was a member of a British minority. His son must have allowed his inherited minority sentiments and his unionism to delay the assimilation process usually completed by a second-generation citizen of British descent. It is extremely doubtful if a fully assimilated American would have called a nationwide coal strike in 1944 while his country was engaged in a world war.

6. The story is related as an historic fact by Adrian A. Paradis in *Labor in Action*, Julian Messner, New York, 1963, p. 119.

rank and file of American unions, but they are not often found in the top echelons of union management. It is the high concentration of minority members in Labor's ruling circles that has given the "minority tone" to unionism. It explains the expenditure of vast amounts of union funds on minority-oriented projects and minority-oriented politics which have little to do with, and are often opposed to, the interests of the membership at large.[7] Certainly school desegregation, appeasement of black militants, sanctions against South Africa and Rhodesia, interventionist policies in the Middle East and monetary grants to anti-American European labor organizations cannot be said to represent the wishes of the typical union member.

American labor in conjunction with American business has been responsible for the greatest outpouring of goods and services in history. But while achieving notable success in raising the income of working people and in ending some of the worst abuses of pre-depression, tooth-and-claw capitalism, unionism has not had a spotless record. The loss in production caused by featherbedding and strikes has been one of the greatest economic wastes in history.[8]

Unions still like to assign themselves to the progressive side of the political balance sheet, but their selfish and fearful attitude toward automation has now made unionism one of the most retrogressive and reactionary forces in American life.[9] In the communications field, unions have succeeded in accomplishing what the press lords were never able to do—

7. Both unions and corporations are prevented by law from contributing to political campaigns. Unions, however, can sponsor "political action committees" whose funds come from compulsory union dues. The committees may then contribute as much as they like to any political candidate. The result is that a part or often a majority of the union membership is forced to give money to a party, issue or candidate which it may strongly oppose. In the 1968 presidential race, unions donated $60 million to the campaign of Hubert Humphrey, although 44 percent of the labor vote went to Nixon. The union contribution to Nixon's campaign was minuscule. See Victor Riesel's newspaper column, Nov. 11, 1968. The Teamsters' Union supported Nixon in 1972 after the President commuted Hoffa's prison term.

8. In 1970, 66,414,000 man hours were lost in 5,716 work stoppages.

9. Labor's fear of technological progress might be described as Vespasian-like. When offered a machine that would eliminate the use of manpower in transporting heavy stone columns, Roman Emperor Vespasian refused, saying, "Let me feed my poor commons."

reduce some of the largest metropolitan areas to a diet of two or three daily newspapers. In the cultural field, union influence has been catastrophic. Fantastic wage scales and the forced hiring of superfluous stage hands and musicians have transformed the theater, opera and concert hall into a big business operation, where the art of financing has become more important than art itself.

The Majority has nothing to fear from American labor, male or female, union or non-union. Most working people are either bona fide Majority members or are rapidly being assimilated into the Majority. What the Majority has to fear are the Unassimilable or half-assimilated union leaders who call strikes during national emergencies, who use their stranglehold on various sectors of the economy to blackmail employers, non-union employees and the public alike, who divert union dues to non-union causes, and who are more concerned with what is happening abroad or in Washington than in their own unions. All such are the grey eminences of the liberal-minority coalition.

In a relatively homogeneous country like Britain, unionism is the incarnation of the class struggle and not to be viewed as the outgrowth of a racial conflict, even though the minority component of the British population is almost always found on the union side. The success of the British trade union movement, which helped turn an empire into a welfare state, can be more accurately attributed to an aging process, in which the aristocracy, landed gentry and civil service, thinned out to the point of extinction by centuries of imperial swashbuckling and two genocidal world wars, lost their grip. In other words, the class war in Britain is not being won by British unionism. It is being lost by the entropy of the British ruling class. And since the institutions of a nation can survive the surrender of power to another class, but not to another race, Britain in recent years has been spared widespread violence.[10]

----

10. There is a growing colored population in Britain and a very rich, though small, Jewish minority—the two chief ingredients of minority racism in the U.S. It is possible, though highly improbable, that these minority elements will be able to turn Britons from evolutionary socialism to revolutionary Leninism. It need not be noted that I.R.A. terrorism has been the work of outsiders.

In a multiracial state, on the other hand, unionism cannot avoid becoming a prop of minority racism. Fortunately for the American Majority, it is a weak prop because of the racial differences which open such a broad gap between union leadership and union membership. As long as labor leaders produce higher wages and greater fringe benefits for the union rank and file, all is well.[11] But when union policies clash too sharply with the social attitudes of a considerable part of the union membership, the delicate alliance begins to crumble.

It is precisely from the labor movement itself that has come the most militant stand against the encroachments of Black Power—encroachments fostered and in part subsidized by the bosses of the labor movement. While most Majority members remain cowed by minority violence or hopefully removed from it in their pleasant suburbs, the hard-hats of the craft unions, many of them Assimilable Minority members, have dared fight Marxist and New Left street gangs with their own weapons on their own ground. The aggressiveness of the construction workers in attacking "peace" demonstrators on Wall Street in 1970 not only dealt another mortal blow to Marxist theory, but revealed that the American Legion and the DAR no longer have a corner on patriotism.

On the debit side, these same hard-hats are staunchly committed, as are most other union members, to the wage-price spiral which has made big business and big labor synonomous with inflation and monopoly. Only the most affluent corporations are now able to afford the ballooning wages, free medical care, accident insurance, retirement pensions, long vacations, multiple rest periods, as well as the increasing incidence of absenteeism, slowdowns and walkouts, which seem to be inexorably associated with union contracts.

Because they cannot possibly meet these rising costs, small business and small agriculture are being driven out of the

---

11. It is logical for American labor organizations to strive for higher living standards and better working conditions for their members. But if the end result is a labor force working 25 hours or less a week, while the labor force of an aggressive superpower—where piecework and production quotas flourish, strikes are forbidden and all workers must carry internal passports —is averaging 40 to 50 hours a week, the national security of the country with the better working conditions may well be threatened.

economy.[12] The small-time American entrepreneur, the small-town store owner, the wildcatter, the prospector, the rancher with a small cattle spread, the dirt farmer [13]—all those engaged in the traditional Majority occupations—are joining, or facing the prospect of being forced to join, the ranks of the proletariat.

"The true hallmark of the proletarian," Toynbee has written, "is neither poverty nor humble birth but a consciousness—and the resentment which this consciousness inspires—of being disinherited from his ancestral place in Society and being unwanted in a community which is his rightful home; and this subjective proletarianism is not incompatible with the possession of material assets." [14] To apply Toynbee's words to the United States of 1970, the proletarian is a casualty in the struggle for Majority survival. His body may be unscarred, but his mind and his will have been temporarily or permanently wounded. And as a proletarian, as one who has been racially neutralized, he may be easily persuaded to enlist in the liberal-minority forces.

Proletarianization often reaches as high as the skyscraper offices of corporate management, where Majority executives caught up in an octopean mass of government regulations, labor codes and administrative red tape, have become as much the faceless cogs of a soulless economy as the lowliest production worker. Their six-figure incomes, their over-generous expense accounts and their imposing titles hardly compensate for the frustration of losing command, of giving fewer orders and taking more, of bowing and bending incessantly to the demands of troublesome shareholders and greedy union shop stewards. They have lost or are losing the authority to fire, and are beginning to lose the authority to hire. The union shop has abrogated the former power and union rules are abrogating the latter. In fact, the latest

12. In 1960, there were 2,707,519 business concerns in the U.S., as compared to 2,518,664 in 1967—a loss of some 190,000 within seven years. *Statistical Abstract of the U.S.*, 89th Edition, p. 491.
13. In 1940, there were 6,097,799 farms in the U.S., as compared to 3,157,837 in 1964—a drop of almost 50 percent in twenty-four years. The number of Negro farms dropped almost 75 percent in the same period. *Ibid.*, p. 602.
14. *A Study of History,* Vol. V, p. 63.

federal regulations have put the government in the corporate personnel field by making the award of defense contracts contingent on the hiring of minority members, many of them totally unqualified.[15]

The separation of ownership from management in big business and the growing impossibility of ownership in small business have transformed once hardworking Majority executives into a soulless mobile bureaucratic caste that moves from company to company in an unending, nonsensical circular migration. In many corporations, the driving, corner-cutting chief executive—in some cases the man who built the company from scratch, in every case the only man who could get things moving—has been replaced by an accountant, with the result that quality mass production, the great invention of Majority business genius, has been made subservient to finance.[16] Even more humiliating to old school Majority decision-makers is the fact that many critical company policies are no longer formulated by management, but by "public opinion," and as such can only be described as concessions to outside pressures.[17]

In its day-in, day-out attack on the Majority business community, the liberal-minority intelligentsia adds insult to injury by constantly raising the specter of a "military-industrial complex," which is depicted as a sort of wholesale conspiracy against the American people by WASP military brass and WASP industrial leaders.[18] Since all it takes is a

15. The so-called Philadelphia Plan initiated by the Nixon administration in 1969 sets minimum quotas for nonwhites in large, government-financed construction projects.

16. Robert McNamara, president of the Ford Motor Company and later Secretary of Defense, began his business career as an accountant, not joining Ford until he was thirty. *Current Biography*, 1961, p. 292.

17. Monroe J. Rathbone, president of Standard Oil of New Jersey, stated, "We never do anything of importance without first considering in great detail the public relations aspects." *Wall Street Journal*, Vol. LXVII, No. 99, p. 1.

18. The phrase first appeared in President Eisenhower's valedictory address at the end of his second term, and was supplied by Dr. Malcolm Moos. *Nation*, April 28, 1969, p. 525 and *U.S. News & World Report*, Sept. 19, 1958, p. 17. As head of the University of Minnesota in 1969, Moos preferred no disciplinary charges against 70 Negro students who seized a building for 24 hours and did $5,000 damage. *New York Times*, Oct. 26, 1969, p. 59. The closest thing to a military-industrial complex first made its appearance during World War I, when Bernard Baruch regimented Ameri-

stroke of the presidential pen to remove any officer from the armed services, the presidents themselves must have been privy to the plot and, as the complex supposedly feeds on war, it must have been much better nourished under the Democratic administrations which engaged the U.S. in World Wars I and II and the Korean and Vietnam conflicts than under Republican administrations. To put it another way, the military-industrial complex, if it exists, must be the brain-child of its critics. The fact that such an all-powerful conspiracy gets such a bad press and that any topflight television commentator, newspaper editor or columnist wields ten times the influence of a big corporation executive or high-ranking staff officer would also seem to militate against the danger of such a conspiracy.

The military-industrial complex is merely one of many semantical bugbears—an updated version of bourgeois exploiter, capitalist monster, economic royalist, Zurich gnome, Wall Street bloodsucker, fascist and other favorite liberal and Marxist pejoratives of days past—by which the Majority is divided into classes, into rich and poor, business and labor, advantaged and disadvantaged. It is again part of the grand strategy of attempting to assign man to economic instead of genetic categories, and it is a very useful and effective weapon for minorities who wish to overcome majorities.

Labor leaders know better than anyone else that the most direct route to the human heart is via the appeal to self-interest, which in the best union tradition includes both the carrot of the pay raise and the stick of joblessness. They also know that there is a bit of the proletarian in everyone and that their job is to maximize it and bring it to the surface. What they do not know, or pretend not to know, is that when man is turned into economic man he becomes an animal that preys on his own kind.

---

can industry to meet the requirements of total warfare. It was revived in World War II as part of the Industrial Mobilization Plan developed by Louis Johnson, Assistant Secretary of War, and approved by President Roosevelt. *New York Times,* March 22, 1970.

Chapter 27

The Fiscal Battlefront

O N THE SURFACE, taxation is a means of defraying the cost of government and—in this Keynesian age—of regulating the economy. Beneath the surface, taxation is a means of capturing and keeping control of the state, of choosing those who sit in the seats of power. In the past, it was the habit of the conquerors of a nation to exempt themselves from taxation and place the tax burden entirely on the subjugated population. Taxation, consequently, was the price of defeat. With the coming of economic and social democracy, little has changed. The purpose of taxation has been extended from the tapping of wealth to its equalization and redistribution. Not surprisingly, these new tax functions, which under the name of "tax reform" have presented Americans with a soaring income tax bill, have had a peculiar attraction for the liberal-minority coalition.

The taxes that lend themselves most readily to the art of fiscal warfare are individual and corporate income taxes and inheritance and gift taxes. Unlike property, excise and sales taxes, these "selective" taxes have a sliding scale, which varies, as the case may be, with income, profits and amount of bequest or gift. Eighty-two percent of all federal tax revenue now comes from the individual and corporate income tax, taxes which did not even exist at the turn of the century.[1]

---

1. In 1966, the federal individual income tax amounted to $55.4 billion; corporation income tax $30.1 billion; sales taxes, customs duties and fuel,

It was the Democratic administration of Woodrow Wilson which inaugurated the federal income tax in 1913, the same year the 16th Amendment became law.[2] The rate was a flat 1 percent on income above $3,000 (single) and $4,000 (married) with surtaxes of from 1 percent to 6 percent on taxable income above $20,000. By World War I, income taxes had risen to 6 percent to 12 percent with surtaxes of up to 65 percent.[3]

It was another Democratic administration, that of Franklin Roosevelt, which raised individual income taxes to the semi-confiscatory rate of from 23 percent minimum to 94 percent maximum, and the corporation tax, which was 1 percent in Wilson's day, to 52 percent.[4] Since World War II there have been some reductions of the individual and corporate income tax, but few of any significance. Meanwhile, thirty-six states now have their own income tax.[5]

In its present form, the income tax discriminates against the American Majority for many subtle and many not so subtle reasons. First of all, the income tax is a Northern European fiscal institution [6] and the historical record shows that it only functions properly in countries where Northern Europeans or descendants of Northern Europeans predominate. In Latin nations, for example, cheating on income tax is so widespread that the tax is hardly enforceable.[7] And the tax-paying habits of Old World peoples have not been radically altered by their descendants in the New.

A review of the tax fraud cases in the United States in recent years reveals an unusually high proportion of minority

---

alcohol, tobacco and miscellaneous taxes $15.5 billion; death and gift taxes $3 billion. *Statistical Abstract of the U.S.*, 89th Edition, p. 409.

2. There was a federal income tax for ten years during and after the Civil War and another in 1894, which was found to be unconstitutional by the Supreme Court.

3. *Ency. Brit.*, Vol. 12, p. 136.

4. *Ibid.*

5. *Statistical Abstract of the U.S.*, 89th edition, p. 423.

6. "Credit for the establishment of the first major successful income tax in the world is usually given to Great Britain. The British tax was first introduced in 1799. . . ." *Ency. Brit.*, Vol. 12, p. 136.

7. In Italy people are often taxed for their "apparent" rather than their real income. For this reason they keep their sports cars in their garages in the days preceding income tax assessment.

366 *The Economic Clash*

names.[8] The days of the medieval burghers of Bremen who, without benefit of tax collectors or tax laws, paid their taxes "in honest assessment of one's ability to pay and in voluntary fulfillment of an honorary duty" have long passed.[9] But it is fair to say that the Majority is still underrepresented in the list of tax dodgers who, according to an Internal Revenue Service estimate, annually bilk the United States Treasury of $4 billion.[10] The Mafia, of course, pays little or no taxes on its annual $30 billion "take." [11]

Since it is precisely at either end of the American wealth spectrum that the minorities are concentrated, the tax load has fallen oppressively on the middle of the spectrum, the Majority center. Tax loopholes and exemptions help the very rich and the very poor, but not the white-collar and blue-collar worker, the junior executive and the engineer. Withholding taxes make it impossible for salaried people to escape the tax collector, but medical and legal fees, the emoluments received by the minority-crowded professions, are more difficult to trace. As for tax revision, which all politicians insist is an absolute necessity, it usually takes the form of a hue and cry against the oil depletion allowance, oil being a Majority-dominated industry, while nothing is said about the tax-deductible contributions that are financing Israeli expansion in the Middle East. The most recent tax proposal is a "negative" income tax, whereby the poor are to receive an annual cash subsidy proportionate to their family requirements.

In addition to being weighted against the Majority's pocketbook, the graduated income tax (state and federal) is also weighted against the Majority's work habits. When taxes get too high, they destroy incentive, discourage saving, encourage spending—all of which amounts to a repudiation of the Puritan Ethic, the traditional guideline of Majority economic behavior. Centuries of religious indoctrination plus some possible genetic influences make it more difficult for Majority

---

8. See Chapter 30.
9. Roepke, *A Humane Economy*, p. 133.
10. Internal Revenue estimate from *New York Times Magazine*, April 15, 1962, p. 70.
11. If the Mafia paid taxes on its illegal profits, there could be a 10 percent tax reduction for everyone. *Reader's Digest*, Jan., 1969, p. 225.

than minority members to adjust to the new Prodigal Ethic of expense accounts, credit cards and limitless installment buying—the fly-now, pay-later mores of a spendthrift economy. Perhaps the hardest hit by this turn of events is the Majority entrepreneur who can no longer build up a business out of profits and who even at the earliest stages of business growth is forced by high taxation to find outside capital in order to survive. The more successful a company becomes, the more quickly its creator loses his independence. But investors and speculators—the Internal Revenue Service makes no grand distinction between the two—have only to pay a 25 percent capital gains tax (1969).

The heirs of those Majority fortunes which have not yet been squandered still keep most of their holdings in the large corporations founded by their forebears. The income from these fortunes has now become the target of a double taxation system, whereby corporation profits are taxed at 52.8 percent (1969) and the dividends paid out of the remaining profits again taxed as individual income. Even more detrimental to conserving Majority capital are the steadily rising inheritance, estate, death and gift taxes (federal or state). These, together with soaring probate costs, are approaching a confiscatory level [12] and are chiefly responsible for the creation of the monumental tax dodge known as the tax-exempt foundation.

Today there are 6,803 tax-exempt foundations in the United States with assets of $19.9 billion and annual disbursements of some $1.5 billion.[13] The six largest foundations (as of 1967) were (in hundreds of millions): Ford, $3,050; Rockefeller, $854; Duke Endowment, $692; Kellogg, $492; Mott, $424; Hartford, $342.[14] By establishing these huge institutions, Majority millionaires have managed to keep their wealth out of the reach of the Internal Revenue Service, but they have not prevented it from falling into the hands of

12. Federal estate taxes go as high as 77 percent and state taxes raise the federal rate by several percentage points.
13. *Statistical Abstract of the United States,* 89th edition, p. 307 and *Wall Street Journal,* Feb. 18, 1969, p. 16.
14. *The Foundation Directory,* Russell Sage Foundation, New York, 1967, p. 16.

those whose political and economic philosophies are far removed from their own.

Practically all the large foundations are now administered by liberals and are generally slanted toward liberal and minority causes.[15] One might well imagine Henry Ford's reaction if he discovered that his Ford Foundation gave $175,000 to the Congress of Racial Equality in 1967 to elect Cleveland's first Negro mayor, Carl Stokes,[16] or that his money was being used to subsidize the writing and production of Black Power melodramas, many of whose characters do nothing but mouth imprecations against everything white.[17] As a onetime anti-Semite, however, Ford might have been amused when his Ford Foundation financed a New York City school decentralization experiment which precipitated a bitter racial split between Negro parents and Jewish teachers.[18]

Small foundations are likely to have an even more pronounced minority slant than the larger ones. An increasing number are being set up by minority millionaires who are more specific about the future use of their money. The minority rich are also more apt to take the alternate path of avoiding inheritance taxes by leaving their estates directly to "charitable organizations"—organizations strictly devoted to the domestic or overseas interests of their own minority.[19]

---

15. The present head of the Ford Foundation is the liberal intellectual, McGeorge Bundy, long-time assistant to Presidents Kennedy and Johnson. Alger Hiss once headed the Carnegie Endowment for International Peace. Another Carnegie foundation, the Carnegie Corp., financed Gunnar Myrdal's *An American Dilemma.*

16. *Time,* Jan. 19, 1968, p. 16.

17. The plays sponsored by the Ford Foundation were not quite as bad as those put on by the Black Arts Theater School with $44,000 of federal anti-poverty funds. Even Sargent Shriver, a brother-in-law of the late President Kennedy, who was ultimately responsible for the allocation of such funds, had to admit that they were "vile, racist plays." *New York Times,* Feb. 28, 1966, p. 11 and March 9, 1966, p. 24. In 1951, the Ford Foundation set up the Fund for the Republic, which among its other projects has spent $15,000,000 attacking the House Committee on Un-American Activities. Goodman, *The Committee,* p. 379.

18. *Wall Street Journal,* Feb. 18, 1969, p. 16.

19. Of the 107 tax-exempt foundations in Maryland in 1967, 57 were Jewish, almost all with specifically Jewish objectives. *The Foundation Directory,* pp. 315–28. The Jewish proportion of the Maryland population is less than 3 percent.

It is ironic that Majority members, whose ancestors were the first to develop the revolutionary concept that taxation should derive from the consent of the taxpayer and whose war cry in the struggle against King George III was "no taxation without representation," should have given up their tax prerogatives so easily. Theoretically, members of Congress still determine the national tax structure. Practically, government spending has become so enormous that, when tax bills are rushed through to meet it, there is little that Congress can do but rubberstamp them.[20] Also, as in other areas of legislation, Majority representatives are so sensitive to liberal-minority lobbying that they frequently vote for taxes which discriminate directly against their own constituents.

Taxation, however, is only one aspect of the fiscal war being waged against the Majority. Welfare is another. The duties and obligations of society to the destitute, sick, aged and unemployed were once assumed by the family, the village, private charity and the church. Today these functions are being taken over by federal, state and local governments. Here again, the benefits are not distributed proportionately. The poor, who are disproportionately nonwhite, can have as many children as they want, since they receive free medical and hospital care, as well as bigger welfare checks for each additional child. The middle-income American, who insists on paying his own way, cannot afford large families.

Now that charity no longer begins at home, national, state and local governments are spending some $19 billion a year on direct aid to the poor.[21] Relief recipients number almost ten million,[22] most of them minority mothers and their dependent children. Some of the dependent daughters already have their own children, thereby putting three generations of the same family on welfare.[23] In one New York City tenement, "Every girl . . . over the age of 13 was pregnant, or had delivered a baby. [At] 18 they could expect to receive their own crisp, IBM-processed public-assistance check." [24]

20. The federal government spent $206 billion in fiscal 1969.
21. *U.S. News & World Report,* Sept. 1, 1969, p. 55.
22. *Statistical Abstract of the U.S.,* 89th edition, p. 299.
23. *Wall Street Journal,* Feb. 7, 1964, p. 1.
24. *Ibid.* As quoted from a magazine article by a consultant to the New York State Senate on public welfare.

In all, about 40 percent of the two hundred thousand welfare children in New York are illegitimate and 80 percent of these are in "repeater" families, where the mother has two or more illegitimate children.[25] Ninety percent of the one million New Yorkers presently on relief are Negroes or Puerto Ricans, and the relief rolls are swelling at the rate of twenty thousand a month.[26] Half of the annual New York City welfare bill—$1.7 billion in 1968—is paid by taxpayers in other cities and states through federal contributions.[27]

Relief is made more difficult by the work attitudes of America's proliferating indigent class. An unemployed person can consider a job "menial," refuse it and still qualify for unemployment insurance. Yet these so-called menial positions are the only ones for which most of the jobless are qualified.[28] The unemployment problem, consequently, has social as well as economic roots. It may also have genetic roots. The "disadvantaged" population groups in America have always been "disadvantaged" in whatever countries they happened to live, including their native countries. To permit and even to encourage this indigent class to reproduce at a much faster rate than the rest of the population [29] is simply to compound the relief crisis and force the allocation of an ever greater share of the gross national product to non-producers.[30]

At present, welfare wears the dress of humanitarianism, but its political slip is showing. The basic purpose of welfare, it is reasonable to assume, is to insure a decent standard of

25. *Ibid.* At last report, women on welfare accounted for 60 percent of New York City's illegitimate births. *New York Times,* Nov. 30, 1970, p. 26.

26. *U.S. News & World Report,* March 31, 1969, p. 36.

27. *Ibid.* According to Nicholas Kisburg, a Teamsters Union research director, New York City welfare agencies were giving as much as $250 million a year to cheaters. *New York Times,* Oct. 1, 1969, p. 22.

28. In 1964, the nation lost $2.5 to $5.7 billion for 75.6 million lost work weeks for the unemployed, even though there were two thousand state-supported employment offices to help them find work. In the same year, California had to import tens of thousands of Mexicans to harvest the crops. George Pettitt, *Prisoners of Culture,* Scribner's, New York, 1970, pp. 140, 142.

29. A cretin class is also being reproduced. In 1965, there were 1,117,800 mentally retarded children, 972,000 mentally disturbed children and 486,-000 children with major learning difficulties in the U.S. Pettitt, *op. cit.,* p. 221.

30. In 1950, the total cost of federal, state and local social welfare programs was $23.5 billion. In 1967, it was $100.2 billion. *Statistical Abstract of U.S.,* 89th edition, p. 276. Social welfare includes aid to education.

living and a decent life to those incapacitated by age, ill health or accidents. But the most active proponents of the welfare state talk about cradle-to-grave security, minimum $5,000-a-year incomes for every adult and, occasionally, capital levies to redistribute the wealth. They go far, but often in the wrong direction. They look for the economic and social causes of poverty, but shun the genetic causes. They demand slum clearance, but will do nothing to control the breeding populations that create the slums.

The political nature of welfare and the inherent anti-humanitarianism of prominent welfare advocates are best revealed by the black minority's rejection—both in practice and in theory—of birth control as one solution of the poverty problem. As a high-ranking NAACP official stated, blacks "need to produce more babies, not less" for added political power.[31]

The welfare state contains the seeds of its own destruction in the underwriting of inflation as a means of meeting ever increasing government expenditures. In order to keep the votes rolling in and make good on their campaign promises of more sizable and more frequent federal subsidies, the politicians of welfare—a category which now includes major political figures in both parties—must resort to the device of deficit spending.[32] As the public debt goes up (more than twenty times since 1930), the value of the dollar goes down (62.1 percent since 1939) and so do the nation's gold reserves ($11.2 billion or 50 percent since 1949).[33] As unions force business to pay higher wages, business forces consumers to pay higher prices.[34]

It is all very Keynesian and very clever and, predictably,

---

31. *Time*, July 25, 1969, p. 21.
32. In the 1937–1968 period there were deficits in every year but five. *1969 World Almanac*, p. 132.
33. *U.S. News & World Report*, Sept. 1, 1969, pp. 19–21.
34. The wage-price spiral raised factory wages 42 percent between 1958 and 1968, while consumer prices went up approximately 20 percent. Despite the Nixon administration's all-out drive against inflation, wage increases in the first half of 1969 ranged from 19.4 cents an hour in the manufacturing industries to 69.5 cents an hour in the construction trades. At the present rate of inflation, the dollar, now worth 37.9 cents compared to the 1939 dollar, will be worth less than a dime before the end of the century. *Time*, Jan. 26, 1968, p. 20 and *U.S. News & World Report*, June 3, 1969, p. 54 and July 28, 1969, p. 69.

hurts the Majority, the most stable element of the population, more than any other group. It is the Majority, which out of habit and tradition—sometimes even out of patriotism—prefers savings accounts, life insurance and government bonds, the "safe" investments that depreciate most during inflation, to the speculations and peculations which make fortunes for the financial plungers in times of currency debasement. And it will be the Majority, clinging forlornly to the last shreds of the Puritan Ethic, who will doubtless continue to take this economic drubbing until the American dollar, presently decreasing at the rate of 6.4 percent per annum (July 1969), starts imitating the German mark, which in late 1923 was collapsing at the rate of 50 percent an hour.[35]

The poison of inflation is slow-acting. It does not destroy an economy as swiftly and dramatically as the ravaging venom of a stock market debacle or a military occupation. But in the long run it is just as deadly. That a day of judgment will eventually come for the liberal-minority inflationists should offer the Majority scant comfort. By then it will be too late—just as it was too late for Aesop's grasshopper when winter came.

Inflation can be stopped by making every increase in wages contingent upon an increase in production. But this must be preceded by far-reaching changes in the thinking and composition of the present-day union hierarchy. The welfare system, which now starves the spirit as it feeds the body, can be redeemed by continuing to assist the needy, but ceasing to reward the idlers, the delinquents and the brood mares of the ghetto. The power of taxation can be reclaimed by restricting it to defraying the costs of government. Tax laws should have a higher purpose than establishing a collection agency for lobbyists,[36] or providing the legal

---

35. Postage for a local letter in Germany cost 100 billion marks at the end of 1923. Salaries were often paid daily so wage earners could purchase their necessities instanter. If they kept their money overnight, they might only be able to buy half as much the next day.

36. A. Philip Randolph, the influential Negro head of the Brotherhood of Sleeping Car Porters, has demanded that the federal government earmark $185 billion over the next ten years for the elimination of poverty. *Facts on File*, 1966, p. 508.

cover for arbitrary and selective assessments which encourage one population group to live off another. If there are to be tax loopholes, let them benefit the farmer, the manufacturer, the production worker, the engineer and the artist—the makers of civilization, not the freeloaders.

But none of these vital reforms will be accomplished as long as they are regarded as purely fiscal matters. Fiscal policies are not the expressions or trademarks of an economic system. They are the expressions of how different peoples measure the input they expect to give society and the output they expect to receive from it.

The question boils down not to economics, but to character. There are those who view work as an end in itself, who conceive of America, the world and even the cosmos as an infinite series of frontiers offering infinite possibilities of work. Let them feel that the frontiers are numbered, that the last ones are coming into sight, and their incentive and initiative will all but vanish.

Then there are those who think of work as a means, as a hardship, often as a curse. Their America is a closed circle, an economic project that can and must be completed so that all human labor will be reduced to the barest minimum. Their world and their imagination are finite.[37] Even their universe is circumscribed by the Einsteinian curvature of space.

The latter, the new rulers of the American economy, are not moving the nation into the future. They are simply marching it backward to conform to an age-old philosophy of work that is not the Majority's.

---

37. "The more important fundamental laws and facts of physical science have all been discovered and these are now so firmly established that the possibility of their ever being supplanted in consequence of new discoveries must be looked for in the sixth place of decimals." Albert A. Michelson, 1894, in the dedication of the Ryerson Physical Laboratory, University of Chicago. Another example of the static mind is the argument of the Boas school of anthropology, voiced most loudly by Margaret Mead, that no one should waste his time searching for the origins of culture, a question upon which "there is not and cannot be any valid evidence." Leslie A. White, *The Evolution of Culture,* McGraw-Hill, New York, 1959, p. 71.

PART VIII

The Legal Clash

Chapter 28

The Adulteration of the Law

MUCH ATTENTION has been paid in this study to the adroitness the Unassimilable Minorities have shown in adapting Majority institutions to their own advantage. Nowhere has this talent been more dramatically displayed than in the field of jurisprudence. The effect has been so shattering on the text and context of American life that a few preliminary words on the nature and origin of law may help present a clearer picture of what has taken place.

Laws have their origins in the customs of the tribe. The first laws probably arose from crude attempts to formalize the social norms of primitive living. They were probably a simple list of things not to be done. In time, certain knowing tribal members, all too aware of their kinsmen's fear of the supernatural, received direct instructions from otherworldly voices concerning rules of behavior. Accordingly, laws were given a religious sanction. Even when the lawgiver claimed no heavenly connection, as in the cases of Lycurgus and Hammurabi, he was quickly elevated to semi-divine status. The canon law was the best proof of the early and persistent relationship between lawyer and priest.

As social systems grew more complex, laws were codified and began to spin their web throughout the length and breadth of human activity. In more sophisticated societies laws became the rules of the game of civilization. As respect for the law diminished, laws proliferated or rather degenerated into masses of contradictory regulations. Tacitus described the cause and effect relationship in one of his neater epigrams: "The more corrupt the government, the greater the number of laws." [1]

Nevertheless, an established body of law has a conservative influence on society. The older laws are, the more inertia they acquire and the more difficult they are to change, particularly when they have the combined support of custom, religion and practicality. It is a truism that these triple foundations of an effective legal system are far more common in homogeneous than in heterogeneous societies. A diversity of peoples means a diversity of customs, which create basic contradictions in the fabric of the law from the very beginning. As Matthew Arnold once noted: ". . . the mixture of persons of different race in the same commonwealth unless one race had a complete ascendancy, tended to confuse all the relations of human life, and all men's notions of right and wrong. . . ." [2]

In its article on English Law, the *Encyclopaedia Britannica* takes a similar approach to the subject by stating, "Law was a matter of race." [3] The law of Northern Europeans was in fact the Germanic law, which later evolved into the Anglo-Saxon or common law and is still being practiced in Britain, the British Dominions and the United States. It was unique among sophisticated legal systems because it was based on precedent rather than on written codes. It held that the accused was innocent until proven guilty and relied on a jury of his peers in most criminal actions to produce a fair verdict. [4]

The relationship of the law to the other symbols of state authority is as important as the law itself. De Tocqueville said that the stability of England had been largely due to the alliance between the aristocracy and the bar. He attributed the instability of France to the fact that French monarchs had

---

1. "et corruptissima re publica plurimae leges." *Ab Excessu Divi Augusti,* 3, 27.

2. As quoted by Walter Bagehot, *Physics and Politics,* pp. 29–30.

3. Volume 8, p. 547. The author was Frederic Maitland, a Cambridge University don.

4. Trial by jury of one's peers was brought to England by the Normans and probably originated in Scandinavia, where the judicial number of 12 was always held in great veneration. William Forsyth, *History of Trial by Jury,* John Parker, London, 1852, p. 4.

snubbed the lawyers as a class, thereby provoking their enduring resentment.[5] Edmund Burke agreed with de Tocqueville when he criticized the French Revolutionary Assembly for being composed, "not of distinguished magistrates but of the inferior, unlearned, mechanical, merely instrumental members of the legal profession . . . the whole train of the ministers of municipal litigation. . . ." [6]

In the United States, according to de Tocqueville, there was no aristocracy for the lawyers to either oppose or join, so they created their own and became a *"rang à part,"* a veritable *"noblesse de robe."* Describing the American legal profession as a powerful barrier against the vagaries of democracy, de Tocqueville came to the conclusion that it represented a power which was scarcely noticed, caused no great fear, bent quietly to the needs of the time and took a willing part in all the movements of the body politic, all the while penetrating deeply into every economic class, working in secret and acting unceasingly to mold society according to its wishes.[7]

De Tocqueville's somewhat ethereal, somewhat conspiratorial view of American lawyers had a certain relevancy in the days of Patrick Henry, Thomas Jefferson and even Abraham Lincoln—attorneys one and all. Today, any such idealization of the legal profession would seem absurd. There still remains, however, de Tocqueville's conspiratorial component—conspiratorial not in the manner of soldier lawyers Alexander Hamilton and John Marshall, who conspired with pen and gun to free the colonies from their British overlords,[8] but in the manner of union lawyer (and later Supreme Court Justice) Arthur Goldberg, who has specialized in pitting labor against business, and of demagogue lawyer Saul Alinsky,[9] who has specialized in pitting blacks against whites. As for those other contemporary members of the legal profession—including the swarms of divorce attorneys,

---

5. *De la démocratie en Amérique*, Tome I, pp. 275–6.

6. *Reflections on the Revolution in France*, p. 54.

7. This paragraph loosely summarizes the chapter, "De l'esprit légiste aux États-Unis," in de Tocqueville's work cited above.

8. The ratio of lawyers to non-lawyers in the First Continental Congress was 24/45; in the Second, 26/56; in the Constitutional Convention, 33/55. Beard, *The Rise of American Civilization*, Vol. 1, p. 101.

9. *Time*, March 2, 1970, pp. 56–7.

ambulance chasers, Mafia mouthpieces and other assorted shysters whose principal functions are breaking up families for extortionate fees, filing million-dollar damage suits or making certain the guilty go free—they have by and large reduced a once great body of law to mere word games and litigious byplay.[10] Meanwhile, the few Majority lawyers who still cling to the tradition of a *noblesse de robe* have for the most part walled themselves up in walnut-paneled skyscraper suites where they toil for the giant corporations.

Present-day legal statistics show there are 375,475 lawyers in the United States, 288 of them in Congress.[11] Twenty-five attorneys were found guilty of Watergate-related crimes. Britain, with one-quarter of the population of the United States, has one-tenth as many lawyers. Nationwide, 20 percent of all lawyers are Jewish—in New York City, 60 percent. In the top law schools, Jews now account for almost a third of the entering class. At Harvard, the most influential law school of all (25 percent of the nation's law professors are Harvard alumni), almost half the faculty is Jewish.

The more minority influence has been brought to bear on the American legal system, the more its breakdown is becoming apparent. The English common law, which derived from Northern European folk law,[12] functioned adequately,

---

10. If these are harsh words, it should be recalled that even Jesus Christ lost his equanimity when discussing the legal profession, saying, "Woe unto you also, ye lawyers! for ye lade men with burdens grievous to be borne, and ye yourselves touch not the burdens with one of your fingers . . . ye have taken away the key of knowledge:" (Luke 11:46,52). Shakespeare was probably venting his own personal feelings when Dick the Butcher advises Jack Cade that come the revolution, "The first thing we do, let's kill all the lawyers." Cade readily agreed, wondering why it was "that parchment being scribbled o'er, should undo a man?" (*Henry VI*, Second Part, Act 4, Scene 1). Harold Laski, who qualifies as an expert on the subject, has said that in every revolution the lawyers lead the way to the guillotine or the firing squad. Fred Rodell, *Woe Unto You, Lawyers!*, New York, 1939, p. 17.

11. Facts and figures in this paragraph are taken from Martin Mayer, *The Lawyers*, Harper & Row, New York, 1967, pp. 11–16, 84, 87, 93, 97–8 and the *U.S. News and World Report*, Mar. 25, 1974, pp. 23–24. Perhaps the most ominous statistic of all is the rapid rate of lawyer proliferation. In 1960–61, there were 43,000 law students—in 1966–67, 70,000. Twelve percent of all lawyers are in government service.

12. Hardly any Welsh, Irish or Roman traces can be found in the old Anglo-Saxon laws, which seem to have predominately Frankish (Teutonic) origins. *Ency. Brit.*, Vol. 8, pp. 546, 548.

at times superbly, in the United States as long as the nation was dominated by people of English and Northern European descent. But when minorities became an important element in both the law-making and the law-breaking process, American law underwent a deep transformation. The legal system which used to be principally concerned with the *intra*group relations of Majority members was now being forced to turn its attention to the *inter*group relations of increasingly alien elements.

Theories of legal absolutism to the contrary, the law is not an abstract set of principles equally applicable to all men, but an organic part of a people's culture, with a style and form uniquely its own. The English and American common law eventually came to rest on the axiom of individual responsibility and on commonly held moral attitudes and commonly shared ideas concerning life and property. The idea of collective rather than personal guilt and the habit of blaming society rather than the individual for criminal acts rub sharply against the grain of both the substance and practice of American jurisprudence. Neither Jewish, Oriental nor Negro law ever developed any substantial protection for the individual, whose interests were always put below those of the nation or tribe. This collective approach is clearly evident in contemporary legal patterns where the question is no longer that of the rights of individual Negroes or Jews, but of the rights of Jews and Negroes as groups.

The liberal-minority dilution of the bloodlines of Anglo-Saxon law was demonstrated in the Nuremberg trials (1945–46), which the late Senator Robert Taft characterized as "a blot on the American record that we shall long regret." The verdicts, Taft stated, "violate that fundamental principle of American law that a man cannot be tried under an *ex post facto* statute." He added that the purpose of the trials was to "clothe vengeance in the form of legal procedure." [13]

The news media, it goes without saying, gave the Nurem-

---

13. *New York Times*, Oct. 6, 1946, p. 1. It might be noted that one of the presiding judges at the Nuremberg trials was a Russian general, who represented a country which also had had some experience with genocide—i.e., the Katyn massacre of 14,300 Polish officers after the Soviet invasion of Poland in 1939. *Ency. Brit.*, Vol. 18, p. 150.

berg trials almost unanimous support, as it did the Eichmann trial in 1960, in which the accused was condemned to death without benefit of jury or impartial judges for a crime which existed in no recognized body of international law when he allegedly committed it. Eichmann, who was kidnapped from Argentina by Israeli agents, had to stand trial without his most important defense witness, to whom the Israeli government had refused to issue a "safe conduct." [14]

Of all American legal institutions, the one which has suffered the most in recent years has been trial by jury. It is one thing to be judged by one's neighbors and peers. It is quite another to get a unanimous verdict out of twelve people of widely varying intelligence levels, economic status, and racial and cultural backgrounds. It is even more difficult when racially mixed juries sit in cases that already have racial implications or into which unscrupulous attorneys can inject such implications. In a San Francisco trial, for example, ten white jurors who voted to convict a Negro "sit-in" demonstrator were actually threatened with violence by the predominantly Negro audience in the courtroom, while the two Negro jurors who voted to acquit were applauded as heroes.[15] In a murder trial in Los Angeles, no verdict could be obtained because two minority jurors (a Negro and a Mexican) felt they had been victims of racial slurs from white jurors.[16] In the murder and conspiracy trials that arose from Black Panther violence and from the 1968 Chicago riots, civil rights lawyers managed to make race the major issue and justice the minor.[17]

14. Yosal Rogal, *The Eichmann Trial*, Center for Study of Democratic Institutions, Santa Barbara, Calif., 1961, p. 28. The pamphlet contrasts retroactive laws with the traditional Western attitude of *nullum crimen sine lege, nulla poena sine lege. Ibid.*, p. 25.

15. *San Francisco Chronicle*, May 21, 1964, p. 16.

16. *Life*, March 28, 1960, p. 76. The admission of Negroes to Southern juries has produced another strange legal perversion—the illiterate juror. The foreman of one all-Negro jury signed a statement declaring the defendant innocent although he and the rest of the jury had actually found him guilty. *Time*, Aug. 27, 1965, p. 40.

17. William Kunstler, who is Jewish, is probably the foremost civil rights lawyer. It was he who led the defense in the so-called "Chicago 7" trial in 1970, in which the defendants, their lawyers and the judge, almost all minority members, nearly succeeded in wrecking the legal process. After being sentenced to four years in prison for contempt, Kunstler went on a

In the past, the presence of different racial and cultural elements within the same society was solved by the establishment of several legal systems. The ancient Jews had one set of laws for themselves and another for the Gentiles in their midst.[18] The Romans reserved the *jus civile* for Roman citizens and used the *jus gentium* for disputes between non-Romans of different provinces. Local statutes were only preempted by Roman law and imperial edict when the security of the empire was at stake.[19] In the Middle Ages, England had its common law, but it also had a special law for its Jews and for its merchants, most of whom were foreigners.

The United States, although it has never formally recognized separate legal systems for its minorities, has not interfered too violently when Indians settled internal problems according to old tribal laws. Since slaves did not come under the common law, a whole corpus of special codes, some originating from the judicial fiats of plantation owners, grew hand in hand with slavery and reflected not only white attitudes, but Negro customs brought over from Africa. Even after Negroes were officially included in the American legal system by the 13th, 14th and 15th Amendments, even after the full legal equality given them in recent decades, the law is still geared to Negro "differences." In the South, minor violations committed by Negroes against each other are frequently overlooked.[20] In the North, overtly seditious appeals by Negro militants for arson, the shooting down of "white pig cops" and armed insurrection are simply ignored.

If the United States has the legal flexibility to acknowledge the *Code Napoléon* as the state law of Louisiana, might it not be stretched a little farther to include separate legal systems

---

nationwide lecture tour. When he finished a wildly irresponsible speech at the University of California at Santa Barbara, some of his listeners staged a one-night insurrection, during which they burned down the $300,000 local branch of the Bank of America. *New York Times,* Oct. 1, 1969, p. 30 and Feb. 27, 1970, p. 1.

18. Deuteronomy, 15:3 and 23:6-20. Perhaps the most celebrated example of this legal double standard is the law which permitted Jews to lend money at usurious rates to strangers, but not to each other.

19. *Ency. Brit.,* Vol. 19, pp. 447–8.

20. A Georgia businessman who had given a lifetime to jury duty, once said: "In all my experience in the courts I have never seen a Negro get justice. What he got was mercy." Putnam, *Race and Reality,* p. 168.

for the Unassimilable Minorities—bodies of law patterned specifically to the different attitudes these groups have always displayed toward property, family relationships, business procedures and citizenship? Apart from ending the impracticality, and the injustice, of imposing the law of one people on another, the purpose should be twofold—to preserve the racial and cultural identity of *all* Americans, and to stop the immense psychological damage being wrought by aggressive forms of cultural overlap. Certainly, protecting one population group against the cultural monopoly of another is as basic a human right as protecting it against financial monopoly.

The point is that the present pluralistic society in the United States should be legalized and institutionalized. Every population group, including the Majority, should have as much cultural, political and social autonomy as is consistent with national security. To allow the law in America to continue to follow present trends is simply to put the law abiders increasingly at the mercy of the law breakers.

Even the most obtuse American is beginning to understand that no system of law is big enough or broad enough to encompass the urban militant who considers "the law" his mortal enemy, and the Pennsylvania farmer who, working the same land his forebears cleared eight generations ago, has an almost genetic affinity for Anglo-Saxon jurisprudence. Herding widely different population groups into one mammoth legal supersystem, one vast noetic corral of incomprehensible statutes, incoherent regulations and unobservable rules, is as unrewarding and dangerous a task as any other kind of forced integration. The way out of the impasse is in precisely the opposite direction—minority laws for minorities and Majority law for the Majority.

Such a departmentalization of the law would return to the minorities the laws they lived by for thousands of years. From them it would take the laws they never learned to live by. The national law would be the *Salus populi suprema est lex* [21] of the Romans, which would take precedence in disputes *between* not *within* population groups. It would not

---

21. The supreme law is the safety of the state.

be Majority law as such, but it would be administered by the Majority, the *national* population group. Majority law would be the common law restored to a climate of reason, respect and responsibility and again able to focus on its primary and original concern—guarding and expanding the freedom of action of its inheritors.

Chapter 29

The Legislating Judiciary

IT WAS FORESEEABLE that the main wave of the legal attack against the Majority would be launched from the judicial branch of government. Overriding the will of the greatest number of Americans is more easily accomplished by nine men appointed to office and responsible to no one, not even to each other, than by legislators who are subject to periodic electoral review. The rulings of the liberal and minority Justices of the Supreme Court offered anti-Majority factions a quasi-legal means of achieving societal goals that could never have been obtained through the normal legislative process.

The charter of the Supreme Court is the Constitution, a document whose very existence violated Anglo-Saxon legal tradition. The Founding Fathers' English ancestors had become quite skeptical toward written recipes for government and had decided, according to Walter Bagehot, that "most of them contain many errors . . . the best of them are remarkable for strange omissions . . . all of them will fail utterly when applied to a state of things different from any which its authors ever imagined." [1] That the American Constitution did not remain unwritten, as did its British counterpart, was partially due to the influence of such Francophiles as Franklin and Jefferson who, during their stay in Paris, had caught the contractual fever of the French Enlighten-

---

1. *Bagehot's Historical Essays,* Anchor Books, New York, 1965, pp. 348–9.

ment.² Fortunately the Constitution, despite its massive institutional inertia, can be amended, and has been—twenty-six times. It can also be changed by the Supreme Court's interpretative function, which in itself is a form of legislation, as former Chief Justice Earl Warren has freely admitted.³

Today, the Constitution has become an object of special veneration to conservatives, who look upon it as a stumbling block to modern liberalism, concentrating their wrath on what the Supreme Court has tried to make of the Constitution rather than on the document itself. They have apparently forgotten that some of the great American conservatives of the past were very unhappy about the Constitution. Alexander Hamilton, who did as much as anyone to get it adopted, called it a "frail and worthless fabric." ⁴ Patrick Henry was even more pessimistic. "I look upon that paper as the most fatal plan that could possibly be conceived to enslave a free people." ⁵

In their often quoted written and verbal debates, the framers of the Constitution refused to let their thoughts be dominated by racial issues. Reading John Jay, one would hardly think that minorities of any kind existed in the new nation. "Providence," he wrote in the second *Federalist* paper, "has been pleased to give this one connected country to one united people—a people descended from the same ancestors, speaking the same language, professing the same religion, attached to the same principles of government, very similar in their manners and customs. . . ." ⁶

Even though Indians and Negroes composed a somewhat higher proportion of the total population than today, the Constitution treated them with studied indifference. Slaves were described as "other persons" and for purposes of apportionment were counted as three-fifths of a white man,

2. One Frenchman, who was not of the Enlightenment, had an English view of constitutions, "Dès que l'on écrit une constitution," wrote Joseph de Maistre, "elle est morte."
3. As stated in a television interview on WNET, Sept. 8, 1969.
4. Frank Donovan, *Mr. Madison's Constitution,* Dodd, Mead, New York, 1965, p. 1.
5. *Ibid.,* p. 2.
6. *The Federalist Papers,* Mentor Books, New York, 1961, p. 38.

while untaxed Indians were treated as non-persons and not counted at all.[7] The troublesome issue of slavery itself was carefully bypassed—with two exceptions. The slave trade was permitted until 1808, and the return of fugitive slaves was made mandatory.[8]

The Constitution's "neutrality" on slavery provoked Abolitionists to the limits of invective. William Lloyd Garrison stumped the North, demanding nothing less than the annulment of this "covenant with death," "agreement with hell" and "refuge of lies." [9] Southerners slowly rallied to its defense. Chief Justice Taney, a Maryland planter's son, climaxed the verbal stage of the controversy by his ruling in the Dred Scott case (1857) that Negroes were "beings of an inferior order and altogether unfit to associate with the white race . . . so far inferior that they had no rights which the white man was bound to respect. . . ." [10]

The Constitution took on an entirely different aspect after the Civil War when it was updated to conform to the vengeful mood of the Northern victors. The 13th, 14th and 15th Amendments abolished slavery and guaranteed citizenship rights to Negroes although reiterating that "Indians not taxed" were not to be counted in the apportionment of representatives to Congress. That these amendments were necessary at all—theoretically they were already spelled out in the Bill of Rights—again proved that the Constitution in its original form was never intended to apply to nonwhites. After Reconstruction came to an end and Northern occupation troops were withdrawn, none of these amendments was seriously enforced in the South until well into the twentieth century. Meanwhile, once again reversing itself, the Supreme Court produced two landmark decisions which seemed to sanction non-enforcement: *Civil Rights* (1883), in which it ruled that Congress could not stop whites from discriminating against Negroes in public places, and *Plessy vs. Ferguson*

---

7. Art. I, Sec. 2, Par. 3.
8. Art. I, Sec. 9, Par. 1 and Art. IV, Sec. 2, Par. 3.
9. Carl Becker, *The Declaration of Independence*, Knopf, New York, 1956, p. 242. The parents of Garrison, an apprentice shoemaker, came from the British province of New Brunswick.
10. Bernard Steiner, *Roger B. Taney*, Williams and Wilkins, Baltimore, 1922, p. 347.

(1896), which set forth the historic "separate but equal" doctrine.

The Court welcomed its first minority member with Woodrow Wilson's appointment of Louis Brandeis in 1916. Together with Oliver Wendell Holmes, a constitutional and legal relativist, Brandeis racked up the all-time Court record for dissents. Though a millionaire several times over, he fought hard against the "curse of bigness," by which he meant the Majority corporations. He fought equally hard for what he called "his brethren," going to great anthropological lengths to establish their biological distinctiveness. "The percentage of foreign blood in Jews today is very low," he stated. "Probably no important European race is so pure." Brandeis, now acclaimed as one of the Supreme Court greats, used the prestige of his high office to urge young American Jews "to be trained in Zionism . . . to know their ancestors' great past [so that] when they grow up, they, too, shall be equipped for the harder task of Palestine building. . . ." [11]

After the appointment of Brandeis broke the cake of custom, the concept of a permanent "Jewish seat" on the Supreme Court began to capture the imagination of editorial writers. When Justice Holmes resigned in 1932, Herbert Hoover, a Republican president, named Benjamin Cardozo, a liberal Democrat, to fill the vacancy. Cardozo, who made his mark as a negligence case lawyer, had no difficulty winning Senate confirmation because the press unanimously agreed to suppress the unpleasant fact that his father had been a member of the corrupt Tweed Ring and had been forced to resign as a New York Supreme Court Justice during one of New York City's perennial political scandals. [12]

Cardozo died in 1938, and a year later Felix Frankfurter was appointed to the Court. Frankfurter was the Vienna-born Harvard law professor who managed to get his first big publicity break as the result of his zealous agitation on behalf

---

11. *Brandeis on Zionism*, Zionist Organization of America, Washington, D.C., 1942, p. 77.

12. *Dictionary of American Biography*, Vol. XXII, Supplement Two, Scribner's, New York, 1958, p. 94.

of Sacco and Vanzetti, two hoodlums who were canonized by the liberal press and executed by the State of Massachusetts for their part in a 1920 Boston murder-holdup.[13] Frankfurter, one of the founders of the American Civil Liberties Union, aspired to the label of conservative in his later years.[14] He quit the Court in 1962 at age eighty, making way for Arthur Goldberg, a labor lawyer for the CIO. Goldberg resigned in 1965 to become United States Ambassador to the United Nations, whereupon President Johnson appointed his friend, Abe Fortas, to succeed him.

Later, when Johnson tried to promote Fortas to the post of Chief Justice, the Senate refused confirmation. Although the news media raged, the Senators were well advised. In 1969, after the truth came out about his financial dealings with swindler Louis Wolfson, Fortas resigned as Associate Justice.[15] Thurgood Marshall, the first Negro member of the Court, was nominated and confirmed in 1967.

The votes of these Unassimilable Minority members, when added to those of the liberal Justices, were sufficient to generate the far-reaching decisions which have so drastically reordered the racial and cultural balance of American society.[16] The three Majority members most responsible for

---

13. In an article he wrote for the *Atlantic Monthly*, March 1924, Frankfurter called Judge Thayer's ruling in the case "a farrago of misquotations, misrepresentations, suppressions and mutilations." If a professor of law had made such a statement in England concerning a case on appeal, he would not only have lost his position but would have been sent to jail. *Times Literary Supplement*, July 26, 1963, p. 546. The quotation was taken from Francis Russell's *Tragedy in Dedham*, McGraw-Hill, New York, 1962, p. 343. Twelve months before Pearl Harbor, Frankfurter, when a Supreme Court Justice, sent a "Personal Secret" cable to Winston Churchill urging him to "butter up" Roosevelt as a means of bringing the United States into World War II. Jack Anderson column, Oct. 19, 1973.

14. One authentically conservative Supreme Court Justice, James McReynolds, was accused by Frankfurter of "primitive anti-Semitism." *Felix Frankfurter Reminisces*, Reynal, New York, 1960, p. 101.

15. See p. 418.

16. The Court's impact on crime and the rights of criminals will be examined in Chapter 30. According to Warren, his and his colleagues' most important decision was *Baker vs. Carr* (one man, one vote). Next was *Brown vs. Board of Education* (school desegregation). Then came *Gideon vs. Wainwright* (free legal counsel for the indigent accused), *Mapp vs. Ohio* (inadmissibility of illegally seized evidence), *Escobedo vs. Illinois* (suspect's right to legal counsel during interrogation) and *Miranda vs. Arizona* (duty of police to warn the accused of his rights). Warren apparently did

the Court's transmogrification of the American way, the three leading instigators of the transvaluation process were: Chief Justice Warren and Associate Justices Black and Douglas. Some clues as to the motivations of these men have already been given;[17] others may be pieced together by scanning certain of the darker paragraphs of their voluminous biographies.

Earl Warren was a second-generation American, both of his parents having been born abroad. His Norwegian father, Erik Methias Varran, whose education ended in the seventh grade, was an impecunious mechanic, who later became a prosperous California landlord. In 1938, he was bludgeoned to death with an iron pipe—a murder that was never solved.[18] Earl, a local district attorney at the time, is said to have shared a $177,653 estate with his sister.[19]

In 1942, as Attorney General of California, Warren advocated one of the most unconstitutional acts in American history—the forced transportation of 70,000 American citizens of Japanese ancestry from the West Coast to "relocation centers" in Colorado.[20] Two years later this Czarist approach to internal security was given the official approval of the Supreme Court in *Korematsu vs. United States,* Justice Black writing the majority opinion and Justice Douglas concurring.[21] In 1952, having progressed to the governorship

---

not consider the following decisions to be significant enough for comment: the 1963 decision barring prayers and Bible readings from public schools, the pornography rulings, the unconstitutionality of compulsory registration of Communist party members, the overturning of Virginia's miscegenation law, the definition of libel as malice and recklessness rather than untruth. For a thumbnail epitome of the Warren Court's record, see *Time,* July 14, 1969, pp. 62–3.

17. See Chapter 11.

18. Luther A. Huston, *Pathway to Judgment,* Chilton, Philadelphia, 1966, pp. 13, 15.

19. John D. Weaver, *Warren,* Little, Brown, Boston, 1967, p. 50. Another Warren biographer says he only inherited $6,000. Huston, *op. cit.,* p. 17.

20. See p. 198.

21. Weaver, *op. cit.,* pp. 105–6. Robert Jackson was one of the three Justices who could not stomach *Korematsu,* although he later took a leave of absence to become chief prosecutor in the Nuremberg trials. Another Supreme Court Justice, Tom Clark, who in 1942 as a Department of Justice official helped direct the roundup of Japanese-Americans, said in 1966: "I have made a lot of mistakes in my life, but there are two that I acknowledge publicly. One is my part in the evacuation of the Japanese from Cali-

of California and having failed to secure the nomination himself, Warren swung his delegation to Eisenhower at a critical moment in the Republican presidential convention. A year later, when Chief Justice Vinson died, Warren received his reward, although Eisenhower never admitted there had been a political payoff.

On being notified of the assassination of President Kennedy in 1963, Warren in a national news release described the murderer, in so many words, as a right-wing bigot.[22] In spite of prejudging the case—and prejudging it incorrectly— Warren was put in charge of the commission appointed by President Johnson to investigate Kennedy's murder. When asked by a reporter if all the facts would ever be made public, Warren replied, "Yes . . . But it might not be in your lifetime." [23]

The *Warren Report*, despite its length, had gaps. The investigation seemed to cool down perceptibly when it came to Jack Ruby's gangster background and the strange coincidence of his Cuban trip, to the part played by high government officials in arranging for the defector Oswald's return to America and to the connections of Marina Oswald's family with the Russian Secret Police.[24] The Commission ignored Ruby's confession that he had murdered Oswald

---

fornia . . . and the other is the Nuremberg Trials. I don't think they served any purpose at all. . . ." *Ibid.*, p. 113.

22. *New York Times*, Nov. 23, 1963, p. 8. The news media's attempt to make the Kennedy assassination a white supremacist plot failed lamentably when Warren's own commission conceded that, prior to gunning down the President, Oswald had taken a shot at right-wing General Edwin Walker. *Report of the President's Committee on the Assassination of President John F. Kennedy*, U.S. Government Printing Office, Washington, D.C., 1964, pp. 13–14.

23. Leo Katcher, *Earl Warren*, McGraw-Hill, New York, 1967, p. 458. A prominent member of the Warren Commission, Senator Richard Russell of Georgia, was convinced that more than one person was involved in the assassination. "There were too many things—the fact that he [Oswald] was at Minsk, and that was the principal center for educating Cuban students . . . some of the trips he made to Mexico City and a number of discrepancies in the evidence . . . caused me to doubt that he planned it all by himself." *Human Events*, Jan. 31, 1970, p. 2.

24. *Hearings Before the President's Commission on the Assassination of President Kennedy*, Vol. 1, p. 278. Marina Oswald's uncle. with whom she had lived for many years, was an officer in the MVD.

because "he wanted the whole world to know that the Jews had guts." [25]

Even Warren's most ardent supporters have had to agree he has displayed a broad streak of inconsistency. He was more responsible for school desegregation than any other American, yet he never sent any of his own four children (one adopted) to an integrated school. He climbed to the political heights as a Republican, yet always acted like a Democrat and was even described as one by President Truman.[26] Certain decisions of the Warren Court should have rested at least partly on the scientific evidence, but Warren was exceedingly reluctant to consider such evidence, perhaps because he had almost failed science in high school.[27]

Never one to be hamstrung by precedent, legal or otherwise, Warren did not become a crusader for the rights of the accused until he had taken his seat on the high bench. In his early days as a headline-making California District and State Attorney, he had achieved a certain notoriety for his arbitrary handling of suspects, occasionally holding them overnight without bail.[28] Today, however, Warren stands as the prophet emeritus of that school of criminal procedure that believes the accused should not only be given every benefit of the doubt, but every technicality of the law. Only in the area of religion did Warren, who may be fairly described as a latitudinarian, maintain a certain consistency. As one of his biographers stated: "Warren, a quondam Methodist married to a devout Baptist whose children . . . have drawn no

---

25. Melvin Belli, *Dallas Justice,* David McKay, New York, 1964, p. 167. Belli was Ruby's chief counsel in the murder trial. After losing the case for his client, Belli blamed his failure in part on the fact that Dallas was "anti-Semitic." *New York Times,* March 16, 1964, p. 23.

26. WNET television interview, Sept. 8, 1969.

27. Huston, *op. cit.,* p. 25. Warren did admit some "evidence" from social scientists in the all-important school desegregation case, but it was one-sided in favor of the plaintiffs. Later, he would not hear opposing evidence from more qualified scientists. See footnote 21, p. 279, of this study and Putnam, *Race and Reality,* Chapter IV.

28. Huston, *op. cit.,* p. 47. When the Senate Judiciary Committee was debating Warren's appointment as Chief Justice, the person who produced the most charges against him, a certain R. J. Wilson, was arrested after leaving an executive session of the committee at the telegraphed request of the San Francisco police chief. He was later released for lack of evidence. *Ibid.,* p. 99.

line in their marriages between Catholic and Protestant, Gentile and Jew, has never been one to make a public display of piety." [29]

Warren's rationale for his legal philosophy and his Supreme Court record is the same as that of his other liberal colleagues. He insists he is simply spelling out the Bill of Rights for all Americans, instead of some. His plan would be understandable if the legal institutions laboriously developed by one people could be moved bag and baggage across the centuries and made to function efficiently for a population mix of many peoples without undotting an "i" or deleting a comma. Unfortunately, they cannot. It turns out that one people's right to life, liberty and the pursuit of happiness is another people's right to crime, that rights which have been *earned* by one group become curiously transformed in text and context when they are *donated* to another group. It also turns out that the alteration of custom by judicial fiat is one of the more noxious forms of tyranny.

Warren is the classic example of the political operator who surfaces at the highest levels of government in a time of decline and disintegration—who is clever enough to swim beautifully with the political tides, but not intelligent enough to probe the deepwater evolutionary currents. The secret of his success is a delicate blend of ignorance, overweening ambition and an acute sensitivity to the wishes and moods of those who control public opinion. In one of the most ironic twists in the saga of human endeavor, Warren's fame rests on his almost total misconception of the one-to-one relationship between law and culture.[30]

Although it violates the bounds of permissible caricature both with respect to the Warren Court and to Warren's role, the late Justice Hugo Black may be categorized as the Warren Court's John the Baptist. Black, who "went to law

---

29. Weaver, *op. cit.,* p. 268.
30. Other Warren misconceptions were equally appalling. In an extreme example of illiteracy in high places, aired over a public television station, he gave his unstinting approval to the "Roman democracy" which, he explained, lasted "one thousand years" because of Roman proficiency in self-government—a statement, needless to say, that would be news to Marius, Sulla, Julius Caesar and Elagabalus. WNET television broadcast, Sept. 8, 1969.

school . . . because he was too poorly educated to go anywhere else," [31] was not born a liberal. Like Warren, he accumulated liberalism as he accumulated power. In 1923–24, he was a dues-paying member of the Georgia Ku Klux Klan, a stern prohibitionist and an affluent attorney who specialized in personal injury cases. When he ran for the United States Senate in 1926, Black felt it politic to drop his Klan membership. But after winning his Senatorial seat, he was given the Klan's Grand Passport, which he gratefully accepted in a public ceremony.[32]

Black was appointed to the Supreme Court in 1937, having convinced Roosevelt that he was an authentic, un-Klannish New Dealer. How as a Supreme Court Justice he dispensed his newly acquired liberalism has been noted in the discussion of the *Korematsu* decision. He went even further in *Yamashita* (1946), when he upheld the death sentence for a Japanese general handed down in a "war crimes" trial which had violated almost every article and paragraph of the Bill of Rights, the very document on which Black had built his legal philosophy.[33] In 1967, Black, who in his metaphysical exaltation of due process and social permissiveness had helped to push the law of the land to the threshhold of anarchy, dismayed his liberal-minority claque by upholding the sentences of street demonstrators found guilty of underscoring their protests with violence.[34] At the closing hours of his judicial career, he seemed dimly aware of what he had done to the law, and what had to be undone to prevent it from collapsing entirely.

Associate Justice William Douglas, like Black, is a product of the Majority Split in the Ranks. Douglas, a vigorous mountain climber, long-distance hiker, world traveler, conservationist and *bon vivant,* often out-liberaled Black himself. As much of a libertine as a liberal, at the age of sixty-seven he married his fourth wife, a twenty-two-year-old

31. John P. Frank, *The Warren Court,* Macmillan, New York, 1964, p. 42.
32. Leo Pfeffer, *This Honorable Court,* Beacon, Boston, 1965, pp. 326–27.
33. Rocco J. Tresolini, *Justice and the Supreme Court,* Lippincott, Philadelphia, 1963, Chapter VIII.
34. Weaver, *op. cit.,* pp. 337–40.

college coed.[35] A few months later it was discovered that Douglas was receiving $12,000 annually from something called the Albert Parvin Foundation, the income of which derived principally from mortgages on a Las Vegas hotel and gambling casino.[36] Douglas refused to give up this annual addition to his regular $39,500 salary (plus expenses, lecture fees, book royalties) until it was further discovered that Albert Parvin had once been named as a co-conspirator with Wolfson in one of the latter's many sordid financial dealings.[37] Though Douglas' relationship with Wolfson's friend was just as unethical as Fortas' relationship with Wolfson, Douglas refused to resign his seat.[38] In 1970, after the Senate Judiciary Committee's hearings to determine whether impeachment proceedings should be initiated against him, Douglas was given the expected whitewash by eighty-two-year-old Committee Chairman Emanuel Celler. The liberal-minority coalition protects its own.

Whatever the cause of Douglas' extreme strenuosity, whether glandular or compensation for a childhood attack of infantile paralysis, he is without doubt the most energetic of the 101 Supreme Court Justices. He was also one of the most dissenting Justices until he was able to join the liberal majority which emerged after Warren's appointment. In the *Cramer* decision (1945), which had its roots in an abortive wartime German sabotage operation, the Supreme Court threw out a death sentence for treason, since the Constitution specifically provides that "no person shall be convicted of treason unless on the testimony of two witnesses to the

---

35. *Time,* July 29, 1966, p. 17.

36. *San Francisco Examiner,* Oct. 16, 1966, p. 1.

37. *Time,* June 6, 1969, p. 23. So far, Parvin has not been brought to trial.

38. Among his other peccadilloes, Douglas sold an article in 1969 for $350 to the magazine, *Avant Garde,* whose publisher, Ralph Ginzburg had been given a five-year sentence on a charge of pornography. Three years earlier when Ginzburg's case had come before the Supreme Court and the verdict upheld, Douglas had been the lone dissenter. When Douglas' *Avant Garde* article appeared it was hard to find amid the collections of dreary, nude photographs. In 1970, Douglas' book, *Points of Rebellion,* was published. In it he warmly encouraged law-breaking demonstrations and wrote that "violence may be the only effective response" to present-day American problems. *Human Events,* Feb. 14, 1970, p. 4 and March 14, 1970, p. 3.

same overt act." [39] Though there were two witnesses, neither gave evidence of any overt act. Nevertheless, Douglas dissented sharply by insisting that the mere presence of Cramer in the company of two German saboteurs was sufficient to warrant conviction.[40]

Having failed to get a pro-German electrocuted, Douglas, who now poses as the arch enemy of capital punishment, failed in another dissent to save a pro-Russian from prison. In *Dennis vs. United States* (1950), his minority opinion defined Communist appeals to revolution as strictly within the law.[41] In view of his libertarian tilt, it came as no surprise that, when the Court refused to review the Rosenberg atomic spy case in 1953, the defense attorneys turned directly to Douglas, who at the last minute took it upon himself to stay the Rosenbergs' execution.[42] Douglas again exhibited his partiality for the totalitarian left when, swept up in the anti-McCarthy hysteria, he enthusiastically joined the Court majority in *Watkins* (1957), which attempted to curb the power of Congressional investigations by freeing a close-mouthed fellow traveler from a contempt citation issued by the House Un-American Activities Committee.[43]

Other members of the Warren Court included William Brennan, whose father was born in Ireland and who worked his way up from coal shoveler to union agent before becoming a lawyer; Byron White, a devoted Kennedy backer, who was the highest-paid professional football player in the nation in 1938; and John M. Harlan, a Wall Street corporation lawyer, whose grandfather when serving on the Supreme Court uttered the celebrated aphorism, "The Constitution is color blind." Of all the Warren Court Justices, only Potter Stewart demonstrated a direct concern for the Majority. He was the lone dissenter in the school prayer decision and the only one to recognize the real issue when he stated that the ruling was just as much an assault on the "religious traditions of our people" as it was on religion itself.[44]

---

39. Art. III, Sec. 3, Par. 1.
40. Frank, *op. cit.*, pp. 60–1.
41. *Ibid.*, pp. 58–9.
42. Pfeffer, *op. cit.*, pp. 374–6.
43. Katcher, *op. cit.*, pp. 365–8.
44. Most of the biographical items in this paragraph were taken from

The dearth of dignity which has surrounded the Supreme Court in recent decades was glaringly obvious in 1949 when Justices Frankfurter and Reed appeared in Federal Court in New York City as character witnesses for Alger Hiss.[45] Since then, the internal squabbling of Court members, their lecture-circuit moonlighting, their ward-heeling political partisanship, their conflicts of interest, the pettifoggery of Fortas, and the goatish marital exploits and gangster associations of Douglas have done little to restore the public's waning confidence in what used to be the most prestigious branch of American government.[46]

Wallowing in the deceptive glow of the liberal-minority *Weltanschauung,* the Court attempted to transform the organic law of Majority America into a code of abstract moral imperatives as unapplicable to the crucial issues of the day as they were unenforceable. By its ill-timed and ill-conceived reinterpretation of the Bill of Rights and other Constitutional guarantees, the Court in effect usurped the legislative function of Congress—a gross abuse of the judicial power as defined by the Constitution. Before they addressed themselves to the impractical task of changing men by changing laws, the Justices might have pondered the words

---

the chapter-length profiles of the Justices in John Frank's *The Warren Court.* For other remarks of Justice Stewart on the school prayer case, see p. 260 of this study.

45. *New York Times,* June 23, 1949, p. 1. Hiss started out as one of Frankfurter's Happy Hot Dogs at the Harvard Law School. Before going on to the State Department he had been a law clerk for Justice Reed, who himself had been a law clerk for Brandeis.

46. President Nixon's appointment of a middle-of-the-road judge, Warren Burger, to replace Warren offered a modicum of hope for a basic change in the Court's thought processes. The old liberal-minority clique is not as dominant as it used to be. But the Warren Court, even without Warren, is likely to endure for some time. The Senate's rejection of Nixon's second and third Court nominations, Judges Haynsworth and Carswell, demonstrated how far Democrats and liberal Republicans were prepared to go to preserve the high bench from a "conservative taint," although a 1970 Gallup Poll indicated the American people were five to three against appointing any more liberals to the Court. *New York Times,* April 19, 1970, p. 58. It is noteworthy that the Senators most in favor of promoting Fortas from Associate Justice to Chief Justice were those most active in turning down Haynsworth for his "conflict-of-interest" record and Carswell for his "mediocrity." Compared to the ethics of Douglas, Haynsworth's were as pure as the driven snow.

of Savigny (1779–1861), who wrote in his *Theory of Organic and Natural Law:* "Law is no more made by lawyers than language by grammarians. Law is the natural moral product of a people . . . the persistent customs of a nation, springing organically from its past and present. Even statute law lives in the general consensus of the people." [47]

Some have proposed that the best means of bringing a runaway Supreme Court to heel is by the complicated and little-used process of impeachment. But this would not eliminate the disease—only one or two of the carriers. If the Supreme Court is to be fought seriously, it should be fought with its own weapons and on its own ground. That which perverts the law can be controverted by the law. The Court, one need not point out, exists and acts on the sufferance of the Constitution. One simple amendment could limit its power, narrow its functions, transfer its authority to state courts,[48] or abolish it altogether.

When history hands down its final verdict on the Warren Court, it will be found guilty on many counts, none more serious than its tampering with the criminal law. Criminal procedure was originally intended to protect society from the lawbreaker. By the time the Warren Court had finished with it, its purpose was to protect the lawbreaker from society. On the surface, there were no racial implications in the Court's exaggerated magnification of criminal rights. But such rights worked directly to the advantage of the minorities that shelter criminal castes within their ranks. With batteries of expensive lawyers at their beck and call, organized criminals, whether they belong to the Mafia, black revolutionary cadres, anti-Soviet Jewish terrorist units, priest-ridden sabotage societies or bomb-planting student gangs, stand to gain much greater benefits from legal permissiveness than the criminal loner. Also, by stimulating minority racism the Court gave an added incentive to racially motivated crimes, particularly the mass outbreaks of vandalism and

---

47. As quoted from Carl Becker, *The Declaration of Independence* Knopf, New York, 1942, p. 264.

48. One such proposed amendment is now making the rounds of state legislatures. It provides that a majority of state Supreme Courts can overturn Supreme Court rulings. Katcher, *op. cit.,* pp. 450–1.

looting with which Negroes have celebrated their improved legal status.

As will be seen in the next chapter, the Supreme Court has opened a Pandora's box which may not be closed again without repressive measures that will put criminal procedure, and much else of what remains of American jurisprudence, back several centuries. Only the complete repudiation and reversal of the Warren Court's major rulings on criminal justice will provide the necessary legal machinery for weeding out the blight that has all but ended Western civilization in wide areas of America's largest cities. Meanwhile, as crime grows beyond all endurance, so does the catalog of criminals and of those who work hand in hand with criminals. This catalog is now so large and so replete with famous names that it is beginning to resemble *Who's Who in America.*

Chapter 30

The Minority Underground

T HE LEAST SAVORY dimension of the conflict being waged against the Majority is the underground war, which in the news media goes by the name of "crime wave." Its extent and ferocity is revealed by the number of its casualties, as given periodically by the Federal Bureau of Investigation in the form of crime statistics. Part of this crime is the work of the criminal elements present in every society and in every race. But more and more of it is the calculated effort of minority militants and their liberal paymasters.

In the period 1960–72, crime in the United States went up 191.7 percent while the population only increased about 14 percent. In 1972, there were 5,891,900 serious crimes, including 18,520 murders, 46,430 forcible rapes and 388,650 aggravated assaults. More than $1.1 billion was stolen as a result of 374,800 robberies, 2,345,000 burglaries, 1,837,800 larcenies and 881,000 auto thefts.[1] To make matters worse, a presidential crime commission has indicated that such figures should be doubled because less than half of all criminal offenses are reported.[2] But merely on the basis of reported

1. *Uniform Crime Reports for the United States (1972)*, Federal Bureau of Investigation, Washington, D.C., 1973, pp. 1–25. Predictably, in the most recent period (1971–72), forcible rape, aggravated assault and murder increased faster than any other type of crime.

2. *San Francisco Examiner,* June 4, 1963, p. 1. Only about one-tenth of shoplifting incidents are reported. Retailers say they could lower prices 15 percent across the board if shoplifting was halted. *New York Times Magazine,* March 15, 1970.

crimes, it is a mathematical probability that a criminal act will be committed against one out of every five American families every year.[3] According to former Senator Kenneth Keating of New York, "Every one in this land can expect to be a victim of a major crime at least once in his lifetime if he lives to be sixty years old." [4]

Correlated with the crime explosion, and a major contributory factor, were several Supreme Court rulings against standardized methods and practices of bringing criminals to judgment. In *Gideon vs. Wainwright* (1963), the Court upheld the right of the accused to counsel, if necessary at the taxpayers' expense. In *Escobedo vs. Illinois* (1964), it held that a suspect may not be prevented from seeing his lawyer during police interrogation. In *Miranda vs. Arizona* (1966), the Court stated that police must warn the suspect of his right to remain silent and to be represented by counsel before being questioned.[5] Since all these decisions were retroactive, their effect on already crowded court calendars and on already overburdened law enforcement officers was disastrous. After *Gideon,* in Florida alone 976 prisoners were set free and excused from retrial, while 500 more had to be arraigned a second time.[6]

For the Court to indulge in such a sweeping extension of due process at the very moment it was becoming impossible for millions of American citizens to walk the streets of their own cities at night was sheer judicial irresponsibility. Again, as it had in the miscegenation, school desegregation and school prayer rulings, the Court was playing favorites. Again, as in nearly all its landmark decisions, it ruled in favor of plaintiffs represented by minority lawyers in appeals financed largely by minority organizations.

Although the marked increase in crime could be attributed

---

3. As stated by Earl Morris, president of the American Bar Association. *U.S. News & World Report,* Feb. 5, 1968, p. 50.

4. *Wall Street Journal,* Vol. LXV, No. 68, p. 1.

5. *Time,* July 4, 1969, p. 63. Escobedo, who was freed while serving a murder sentence as a result of the Supreme Court's ruling that bears his name, was later re-arrested for selling 11 grams of heroin. *San Francisco Chronicle,* Aug. 4, 1967, p. 2.

6. Anthony Lewis, *Gideon's Trumpet,* Random House, New York, 1964, p. 205.

in part to the breakdown of law enforcement caused by the Court's coddling of criminals, it was due in larger part to the appearance of a new criminal type. Not that there was anything new about minority crime in America. As Samuel Eliot Morison wrote, the "alliance between urban politicians, the underworld of gambling and prostitution, and the foreign vote was already established in 1850." [7] But the invasion of the cities by an army of Negro looters, arsonists and snipers a century later raised minority crime to the level of urban warfare.

The property loss and death toll caused by Negro insurrections in major cities in 1964–68 have been given previously.[8] In 1969, while white businesses were still counting their losses in the larger metropolitan slums, Negroes turned their attention to the ghetto commercial areas in the middle-sized cities. Concurrently, there was a mounting incidence of attacks on white policemen, who were being murdered at the rate of two a week in mid-1972. And now that he is no longer a common thief or mugger but a self-appointed revolutionary, the Negro criminal is treated by his own people, and by more than a few whites, as a kind of twentieth-century Robin Hood.[9] The armed takeover of college buildings by black students and the armed invasion of a state legislature by swaggering black commandos were greeted as acts of liberation.[10] There remained, of course,

---

7. Morison, *The Oxford History of the American People*, p. 487.

8. See p. 211.

9. Most leading Negro militants acquired a criminal record long before they became revolutionaries. Malcolm X was a convicted pimp, dope peddler and robber; Eldridge Cleaver, a convicted rapist; H. Rap Brown, a convicted burglar. The crimes committed by Bobby Seale and others in the line of their revolutionary services for the Black Panthers overshadowed their earlier lawbreaking. The hero worship of these individuals by the Negro community and by many white liberals and white minority leaders was probably as great an incentive to Negro crime as the orders of white mayors forbidding the police to shoot looters. Summing up the attitude of Negro slum dwellers, a weekly news magazine reported, they "not only passively accept crime, but also actively admire the criminals—especially if their victims are white." *Time*, Feb. 14, 1969, p. 60.

10. In 1967, a group of Negroes with loaded rifles marched into the state capitol at Sacramento, Calif., while the legislature was in session. Punishment was meted out lightly or not at all. *New York Times*, May 3, 1967, p. 24.

considerable Negro crime against Negroes, but as white city dwellers were learning firsthand, the crimes of violence were being turned against "whitey." [11]

Negro lawbreaking has been militarized in the sense that much of it is committed against "the enemy," that many of its victims do not bother to report offenses to the police but simply become "casualties," [12] and that the criminals go foraging in bands from the inviolate sanctuaries of metropolitan ghettos, where white Americans are no safer than they would be in a Viet Cong stronghold. Negro crime has also been tribalized in that it is becoming an initiation rite and a proof of bravery. [13]

Conversely, the other minority criminal caste, [14] the Cosa

---

11. A 1970 government report stated that urban blacks are arrested eight to twenty times more often than whites for homicide, rape, aggravated assault and robbery. The report also said that 60 to 70 percent of the victims of black crime were blacks and therefore concluded that no racial factors were involved. *New York Times,* Sept. 8, 1970, p. 1. That one particular race has a crime rate eight to twenty times higher than other races may not have any racial connotations to government bureaucrats, but it has many such connotations to whites attacked by Negro muggers. The report, however, did admit that robbery was the one crime that was specifically directed by Negroes against whites. There is also the question of simple mathematics. If one race commits crimes at a rate eight to twenty times higher than that of another race, even though 60 to 70 percent of such acts are confined within the race, that leaves many thousands of crimes to be committed by blacks against whites. In Washington, D.C., for example, there is a direct relationship between crime and race. Of the rapes committed in the 1959–65 period, Negroes were responsible for nine out of ten, and 59 percent of the white women attacked were victims of Negroes. *San Francisco Chronicle,* Jan. 4, 1967, p. 2. The kidnapping of young white women, such as the recent abduction of Kathy Morris in Florida, indicated an ominous new trend in black crime.

12. A case in point: television network correspondent Hughes Rudd, after being mugged, robbed and left unconscious in a New York City street, came to four hours later when a passing patrolman wanted to know what happened and whether he should send for an ambulance. Rudd disclosed no details and limped home. "What was the use?" he said. *Time,* Feb. 14, 1969, p. 60.

13. The leader of a gang of young Negroes in Michigan told a twenty-two-year-old member: "Prove yourself a black warrior. Bring in the ears of a white man." The young black did just that, leaving a sixteen-year-old white boy not only earless, but dead. The youth group, it might be added, had received financial support from the Rockefeller-financed Urban League. *New York Times,* March 4, 1970, p. 31.

14. There are smaller hereditary minority bands who also may merit the status of criminal caste: Gypsies; the Cuban families who have taken over 20 percent of the $200 million annual take of the New York City numbers

Nostra, has grown less militant and even semi-respectable as it has scaled new heights of prosperity, its members having given up their white neckties and broad-brimmed hats for conservative Brooks Brothers styles.[15] Besides the blood oaths, paper burnings and other ceremonial claptrap, however, the basic requirement for membership remains the racial test of Southern Italian or Sicilian parentage.[16]

This racial test has only been suspended for Jews, who supply the Cosa Nostra with most of its legal and financial brains.[17] In fact, the Cosa Nostra leadership, according to Ralph Salerno, former New York City Police Department crime expert, has always been a "happy marriage of Italians and Jews." [18] Meyer Lansky, for many decades the Cosa Nostra's financial director, said with some understatement, "We're bigger than U.S. Steel." Since Cosa Nostra gross revenues are estimated at over $30 billion a year with annual profits of from $7 billion to $10 billion, he could have included a few more corporations.[19] Some idea of the individual wealth of Mafia members can be obtained from such news items as: $521,020 in cash was found in a suitcase belonging to the son of Buffalo's Boss Magaddino . . . New York's Boss Gambino and his adopted family had real estate holdings valued at $300 million . . . Philadelphia's Boss Bruno when asked to produce collateral for a business venture came up with a certified check for $50 million.[20]

The Cosa Nostra flourishes because of what might be described as political protection in depth. It exercises varying degrees of control over some twenty-five Congressmen as well as thousands of lesser political figures at state and local levels.[21] The servile relationships of certain New York City

---

game (*New York Times*, Feb. 22, 1970, p. 36); and certain Hasidic Jews who traditionally engage in jewel smuggling but do not consider it a crime because it is "Gentile law." (Yaffe, *op. cit.*, p. 120). In regard to Jewish crime in general, Yaffe has written, "Nobody, no matter how reprehensible, ever gets completely read out of the Jewish community." *Ibid.*, p. 277.

15. *Time*, Aug. 22, 1969, p. 21.   16. *Ibid.*, p. 19.   17. *Ibid.*, p. 18. 18. *Ibid.*   19. *Ibid.*   20. *Ibid.*, p. 21.

21. *Ibid.*, p. 19. As excerpted by *Time* from the book, *The Crime Federation* by Ralph Salerno. New Jersey Cosa Nostra leader Joe Zicarelli, according to Salerno, wields such power over Congressman Cornelius Gallagher that he can summon him from the floor of the House of Representatives to answer his phone calls. Gallagher is a member of the House Government

and Chicago judges to Mafia leaders are too well known to be documented. According to *Look* magazine, Mayor Alioto of San Francisco had direct connections with the underworld and even arranged a series of loans totaling $105,000 for notorious Cosa Nostra killer, Jimmy Fratianno.[22] Frank Sinatra, an associate of leading mob figures,[23] was for years one of the chief fund raisers of the Democratic party. For his work in organizing and directing the 1961 pre-Inaugural Ball in Washington, Sinatra received the profuse thanks of President Kennedy and the first dance with the First Lady.[24] Even Barry Goldwater, who despite his many failings was at least considered one of the most honest presidential candidates in decades, was quite close to two important underworld members. Of gangster Gus Greenbaum, who died with his wife in a macabre gangland double murder in Phoenix on Dec. 3, 1958, Goldwater said, "I knew him all my life." Goldwater was also a good friend of Willie Bioff, another noted gangster and a convicted panderer and extortionist, and piloted him back from Las Vegas to Phoenix in his own plane only two weeks before Bioff was blown to fragments when he tried to start his car.[25]

Although the Cosa Nostra buys most of its protection, some of it is furnished free of charge in the form of Italian-American solidarity. After the confessions of Joseph Valachi, a renegade Mafioso, had been written at the request of the Department of Justice, twelve prominent Italian-Americans, including four Congressmen, met with Attorney General Katzenbach and demanded that their publication be stopped. The Justice Department obediently started action to prevent

Operations Committee, which watches over the federal agencies which in turn watch over the Mafia. In 1972 he pleaded guilty to evading $74,000 in income taxes. *Miami Herald*, Dec. 22, 1972, p. 36-A.

22. *Look*, Sept. 23, 1969, p. 17. Alioto's libel action as a result of *Look*'s article ended in a hung jury.

23. Sinatra was a personal friend of Lucky Luciano, once the nation's top-ranking gangster, and owned 9 percent of the Mafia-controlled Sands Hotel in Las Vegas, before Howard Hughes bought it. Ed Reid and Ovid Demaris, *The Green Felt Jungle*, Pocket Books, New York, 1964, pp. 56, 74–76, 198. In the Nixon years Sinatra turned Republican, and Spiro Agnew became a perennial house guest at the crooner's Palm Springs hacienda.

24. Kennedy's exact words were: "I know we are all indebted to a great friend, Frank Sinatra." Victor Lasky, *JFK, The Man and the Myth*, Macmillan, New York, 1963, p. 14.

25. Reid and Demaris, *op. cit.*, pp. 43, 144, 202.

Peter Maas, a writer working with Valachi, from "disseminating or publishing" the manuscript.[26]

Mario Procaccino, the Democratic candidate in the 1969 New York City mayoralty race, was equally sensitive about the Mafia. Although Procaccino was not known to have any direct ties to gangsters, he nevertheless repeatedly refused to condemn the Cosa Nostra, even while going to great pains to stress the "law and order" theme in his campaign. "I don't know any Mafias," he declared. "I never have and I never will. Don't talk about the Mafia to me because I think it's insulting. . . ."[27] The Italian-American Civil Rights League, founded by Joseph Colombo, Sr., the head of a Mafia family, also denied the Mafia's existence and persuaded the Justice Department to stop referring to the Mafia or Cosa Nostra by name.[28] Since both Procaccino and the League are based in New York City, it would seem incredible that the Mafia had escaped their attention, particularly after a well-known New York political figure, James L. Marcus, was sentenced to jail for dividing a kickback from a municipal reservoir project with a leading Cosa Nostra gangster.[29]

Other Mafia links with the highest levels of government can be detected in the executive pardons issued frequently to important gangsters. Lucky Luciano, who succeeded Al Capone at the top of the Mafia hierarchy and who was a specialist in narcotics, murder and prostitution, was given a

26. It took a long court battle to get permission to publish the material, finally entitled *The Valachi Papers*. In the interim Valachi tried to commit suicide. *Reader's Digest*, January 1969, pp. 224–5.

27. *New York Times Magazine*, Aug. 10, 1969, p. 62. Many years earlier, Frank McGee, the noted TV commentator, had taken the same line as Procaccino by asserting on Aug. 29, 1958, "we have come to the conclusion that the Mafia in this country is a foolish and distracting myth." Musmanno, *The Story of the Italians*, p. 202. In spite of, or perhaps because of, his Mafia blindness, McGee remained at his influential job until his death in 1974.

28. *Time*, July 12, 1971, pp. 14–15.

29. It was the Cosa Nostra's loan shark operations which drew Marcus, whose wife was the daughter of former Connecticut Governor John Cabot Lodge, into the net. He could not afford the 104 percent yearly interest, so he tried to repay gangster Anthony Corallo in other ways. *Time*, Aug. 22, 1969, p. 20. The Cosa Nostra, it might be added, is also in the loan *receiving* business. The U.S. Small Business Administration admitted in 1969 that it had loaned more than $1,000,000 to the ANR Leasing Corp., a Mafia-controlled trucking concern in the Bronx. *New York Times*, April 27, 1969 p. 1.

full pardon by New York Governor Thomas Dewey in 1946.[30] Luciano's influence was so intercontinental that working through the American army in World War II he actually helped reestablish the Mafia in its original Sicilian homeland where it had been denuded of power during the Mussolini era. At his direction American planes dropped special packages to the world Mafia chieftain, Don Calo Vizzini, in the town of Villaba.[31]

President Kennedy gave a presidential pardon to another gangster, Jake (the Barber) Factor, who was scheduled for deportation by the Department of Justice but made a citizen after he contributed $10,000 to the Democratic party.[32] Factor repaid the favor by increasing his donations, and in 1968 he was revealed to be the largest financial contributor to the Democratic party's presidential campaign.[33] Another questionable pardon was given by President Truman to movie mogul Joseph Schenck, after he had been sent to prison for lying about his Mafia associations.[34]

There is no more visible sign of national decay than the continuing success story of the Cosa Nostra, an organization which, among other things, does a $350 million annual gross business in heroin.[35] Majority and minority politicians and public figures are still horrified by Nazi atrocities twenty-five years after the fact, but neither they nor the news media are half so upset about even worse atrocities practiced by Mafia thugs upon thousands of Americans. Though many Cosa Nostra leaders have moved to exclusive suburbs and now greet each other in public with handshakes instead of kisses, they still boast about sending some of their victims to Mafia-owned wholesale meat houses, from which they are

---

30. *New York Times*, Feb. 9, 1946, p. 19.
31. *Times Literary Supplement*, June 18, 1964, p. 534.
32. *New York Times*, Dec. 29, 1963, p. 4.
33. *San Francisco Sunday Examiner and Chronicle, This World*, Jan. 12, 1969. Factor and his wife allegedly donated or loaned $350,000 to various Humphrey-Muskie organizations.
34. *San Francisco Chronicle, This World*, Oct. 25, 1961, p. 22. Schenck died a multimillionaire in his penthouse suite at the Beverly Wilshire Hotel.
35. Donald Cressey, *Theft of the Nation*, Harper & Row, New York, 1969, pp. 91–2.

distributed to restaurants in the form of "manburgers." [36]
While the media still concentrate on Nazi brutality, the Mafia
has refined a particularly painful murder technique in which
death is accomplished by inserting the end of a home fire
extinguisher in the condemned man's ears.[37] Police tapped
and taped one Mafia telephone conversation in which a gig-
gling gangland executioner described in minute detail the last
three days of a man who had been hung on a meat hook and
who "flopped around . . . screaming" when tortured with
an electric prod.[38]

As two veteran crime reporters have summed it up:
"Slowly, but inexorably, the Mafia has assumed a position of
supremacy that is total and absolute. . . . Every Mafioso,
young or old, truly believes that he has an inalienable right to
traffic in dope and prostitution, to plunder and murder. The
laws of organized society do not bind him." [39]

Collective cr organized crime having become a minority
monopoly, one would expect to find the ranks of individual
criminals filled by Majority members. But such is not the
case. Here again, the minority disproportion is incontestable.
In fact, whenever a Majority member, particularly a well-
known Majority public figure, is haled into court, it is
surprising how often his partner or associate is a minority
member.

The following roster of peculations, embezzlements, tax
evasions, serious crimes, petty thieveries, conflicts of interest
or betrayals of public trust is restricted to people of national
or local importance. Occasionally, the catalog of wrongdoing
will list crimes in which the minority connection is tenuous
or nonexistent. In such cases, the intention is to demonstrate
the moral degradation of Majority leaders in an era of

36. *Saturday Evening Post,* Nov. 9, 1963, p. 21.
37. *Ibid.*
38. *Time,* Aug. 22, 1969, p. 22.
39. Reid and Demaris, *op. cit.,* pp. 186–7. Members of the Mafia, according to C. D. Darlington, are prisoners of their genes, "people for whom
there is no possibility of coercion, correction or conversion. Nothing on
earth will make them come to terms with the general body of society. They
are a race apart." *The Evolution of Man and Society,* p. 611.

minority domination—a degradation that has been both a cause and an effect of such domination.[40]

To begin at the top, one of the ugliest aspects of American crime has been its frequent appearance in the ambit of the presidency. Not one administration in recent decades has remained unscathed. Most, if not all, presidents or presidential candidates have engaged at one time or another in highly questionable conduct or have had known lawbreakers as friends, advisers or fund raisers. A typical example was President Truman's close association with the flamboyantly corrupt Pendergast organization, a Missouri version of the Irish-Catholic machines in Chicago and the big Eastern cities, which sponsored his entry into politics. In 1939, Boss Tom Pendergast, one of Truman's closest friends, went to jail for income tax evasion. In 1945, when Truman was Vice-President, Pendergast died. Truman immediately flew to St. Louis and lent the dignity of the second highest office in the land to the last rites of a convicted felon. A few months later, when he became President, Truman pardoned fifteen Pendergast henchmen who had been jailed for vote fraud.[41]

It was Truman who pardoned Mayor Curley of Boston for a previous criminal conviction and reduced Curley's jail sentence for mail fraud.[42] It was Truman who appointed Mayor O'Dwyer of New York, a friend of gangster Frank Costello, Ambassador to Mexico, and spirited him out of the country just in time to escape being arrested on charges of graft.[43] Truman made a further attempt to obstruct the course of justice, when he called the Alger Hiss case, months before it came to trial, a "red herring." [44]

---

40. Different races and population groups seem to have different propensities for crime—the Negro for crimes of violence, the Mediterranean for crimes of passion, the Jew for financial crimes. Also, unassimilated or partly assimilated peoples have an added incentive to crime in the hostility that newcomers often feel for the society around them. Or, to put it the other way around, they have less of a built-in crime deterrent because they have fewer emotional and personal attachments to the state and to the law of the state.

41. Jules Abels, *The Truman Scandals,* Henry Regnery, Chicago, 1956, pp. 22–3.

42. *Ibid.,* p. 32.

43. *Ibid.,* p. 36.

44. Although he later changed his mind about Communists, Truman,

The mink coat and deep freeze payoffs to Truman cronies made many headlines during the Truman administration. But it was not known until after Truman had left office that his Commissioner of Internal Revenue, Joseph Nunan, Jr., had been evading income taxes as well as collecting them, and that his Assistant Attorney General in charge of the Justice Department's Tax Division, T. Lamar Caudle, had been conspiring with men like Abraham Teitlebaum, a former lawyer for Al Capone, to avoid tax payments.[45] Nunan went to jail in 1957 and Caudle, who served only six months of his three-year sentence, was imprisoned in 1960.[46] Even J. Howard McGrath, Truman's Attorney General, had a brush with the law as the result of mail fraud charges against the International Guaranty and Insurance Co., of which he and Jake Ehrlich, the headline-hunting criminal lawyer, were trustees.[47]

President Eisenhower's administration produced little to compare with the scandals of the Truman era, although Sherman Adams, Eisenhower's chief assistant, was forced to resign when it was discovered he had received various gifts and subsidies from Bernard Goldfine. Jailed in 1961 for dodging taxes to the amount of $7,838,298,[48] Goldfine was paroled in less than two years after serving a good part of his sentence in a hospital.[49] Eisenhower himself accepted expensive gifts from well wishers, but unlike Adams did not exert any influence on their behalf with federal agencies. Senator Payne of Maine, who received more of Goldfine's largesse than Adams, was resoundingly defeated in his try for reelection in 1958.[50]

---

following the pattern established by Franklin Roosevelt, retained in office several key bureaucrats whom the FBI had certified as bona fide Soviet agents, among them Harry Dexter White, Assistant Secretary of the Treasury. Chambers, *Witness*, pp. 68, 510.

45. *New York Times*, May 24, 1957, p. 17 and May 5, 1960, p. 29.
46. *New York Times*, Oct. 30, 1960, p. 81.
47. *New York Times*, Nov. 25, 1961, p. 1 and March 30, 1963, p. 7. Both McGrath and Ehrlich signed their names to the very brochure for which Stewart Hopps, the promoter of the insurance company, was convicted of mail fraud. Both McGrath and Ehrlich got off scot-free.
48. *New York Times*, Jan. 30, 1962, p. 12 and June 6, 1961, p. 20.
49. *New York Times*, Feb. 21, 1963, p. 10.
50. *New York Times*, Sept. 9, 1958, p. 1.

The enormous Billie Sol Estes swindle began in the Eisenhower years, but climaxed in the Kennedy administration.
Estes, with high connections in Texan and national politics,
managed to defraud the Department of Agriculture of
$500,000 by falsifying inventory records. He was finally sent
to prison, but no one has yet been able to discover how he
managed to bilk so many important government officials, not
just once but again and again. When the investigation
started, the ranking Department of Agriculture official in
Texas, Hilton Bates, "committed suicide" by the astonishing
feat of shooting himself five times with a bolt action rifle.
The Department of Agriculture official who bore the chief
responsibility for the payments to Estes turned out to be
Under Secretary Thomas Murphy, who had been appointed
through the efforts of Estes' friend, Lyndon Johnson, at that
time Senator from Texas.[51]

President Kennedy's administration, aside from the Estes
affair, was relatively clean, perhaps because it was relatively
short. But Kennedy, as remarked earlier, was politically and
financially beholden to people like Frank Sinatra, a close
friend of Patricia Kennedy, the President's sister, who was
married to Peter Lawford, a British-born, Hollywood star,
whom she later divorced despite her Roman Catholic religion. Mr. and Mrs. Lawford were charter members of the
Sinatra clan, a high-living show business coterie which included Sammy Davis, Jr., the Negro song-and-dance man,
his Swedish wife (now divorced) and television comic Dino
Crocetti, otherwise known as Dean Martin.

The black sheep of the Kennedy family, excluding father
Joseph Kennedy who made millions in Wall Street by selling
short at the start of the depression,[52] is Senator Ted. Ted was
expelled from Harvard in 1951 for cheating, after persuading

---

51. Clark Mollenhoff, *Despoilers of Democracy*, Doubleday, New York,
1965, Chapters 7–9.
52. A typical Kennedy operation was the Libbey-Owens-Ford pool, in
which he and the banking house of Kuhn, Loeb had the biggest interest. The
group got control of 1,000,000 shares of the company's stock, forced down
the price by short sales and then bought in before the shares went up. Kennedy got $60,805 for his part in the transaction. No one invested a penny.
Frank Cormier, *Wall Street's Shady Side*, Public Affairs Press, Washington,
D.C., 1962, pp. 3, 9.

a fellow student to take a Spanish exam for him.[53] Family influence got him reinstated two years later, though students who had committed lesser offenses were expelled permanently. In the summer of 1969, on the night before two Americans landed on the moon, Kennedy drove his car off a bridge, drowning his young female passenger, Mary Jo Kopechne. A few days later Kennedy, who had waited ten hours before notifying the police, was given a two-month prison sentence (suspended) for leaving the scene of an accident. After the inquest, which was held in secret, Judge James Boyle accused Kennedy of driving "negligently," thus having "contributed to the death" of Miss Kopechne.[54]

While her husband was President, Jacqueline Kennedy, whose mechanical charm and artistic affectations, however galling, were at least an improvement on the dowdiness of her immediate predecessors, took an extended Mediterranean cruise on the yacht of Aristotle Onassis, the Greek shipping magnate indicted in 1953 for conspiracy to defraud the United States government. To escape being arrested the next time he visited his New York office, Onassis had to pay a $7 million fine.[55] Even in Nero's time it would have been difficult to believe that the first lady of Rome would consort publicly with a man who had admittedly defrauded the empire. It would have been unthinkable that, when she became a widow, she would marry him. The Kennedy-Onassis wedding in 1967, however, was not too surprising from a racial perspective. Jacqueline's paternal great grand-father was a carpenter from Southern France. Her father, who had a darker Mediterranean coloration than Onassis, had been nicknamed "Black Jack." [56]

The Kennedy administration ended with the crime double-header of the century, the assassination of the President by Lee Harvey Oswald and the subsequent gunning down of

---

53. *New York Times,* March 31, 1962, p. 1.
54. *The Inquest,* EVR Production, Inc., New York, 1970, p. 126.
55. Using dummy corporations, Onassis bought wartime Liberty ships, which by federal law were reserved for sale to American citizens in order to build up the post-war American merchant marine. The ships are now part of the Onassis merchant marine. *New York Times,* Feb. 26, 1963, p. 2, Feb. 9, 1954, p. 1 and Dec. 22, 1955, p. 47.
56. *Time,* May 16, 1969, p. E7.

the assassin in front of millions of television viewers by Jack Ruby (Rubenstein), a petty mobster and strip-tease entrepreneur. The racial motivations of Ruby's act have already been touched upon,[57] but Oswald's motives have never been properly established. Many minority intellectuals have struggled heroically to make the assassination the deed of a cowardly Southern white supremacist against a heroic minority President. Barbara Garson, a minority playwright, went so far as to compose a play, *MacBird,* which proposed that Johnson arranged Kennedy's death so he could succeed him in the presidency.[58] But the thesis of a Ku Klux Klannish plot was ludicrous in view of Oswald's communist affiliations and his minority background.[59]

The assassination in 1968 of Kennedy's brother, Robert, had explicit instead of implicit minority connotations. In his delayed candidacy for the Democratic presidential nomination, Kennedy demanded the reduction of the American commitment in Vietnam, but insisted on maintaining the American commitment to Israel. It was after he emphasized this point on a television broadcast that a first-generation Arab-American from Palestine was sufficiently aroused to shoot him down the next evening in the basement of a Los Angeles hotel. If Kennedy had concentrated more on problems affecting Majority interests and less on an issue of special interest to a minority that was not even his own, he might have become the 37th President.

57. See pp. 392–3.
58. It ran nearly a year in an off-Broadway theater. In 1972, a movie called "Executive Action" attributed the assassination to the machinations of a rightwing Texas plutocrat.
59. Little is known about Oswald's father, who died before his son was born. Oswald's mother (née Claverie) may have come from a Cajun family since she said her father was French and spoke French in his home. *Hearings Before the President's Commission on the Assassination of President Kennedy,* Vol. 1, pp. 252, 437. The conspiracy weavers had an easier time with the assassination of Martin Luther King in 1967. Nevertheless James Earl Ray, the guilty party, had minority as well as Majority connections. He was born north of the Mason-Dixon line and his mother "came from a devout Irish-Catholic family." *New York Daily News,* March 11, 1969, p. 4. Not many people, however, found any plot in the slaying of George Lincoln Rockwell, American Nazi leader, by John Patsalos, a Greek-American. *New York Times,* May 31, 1970, p. 8. The family origins and political connections of Arthur Bremer, the would-be assassin of George Wallace, are extremely obscure. The FBI duly certified that he was not a part of any conspiracy, though millions of Americans disagreed.

As Attorney General in his brother's administration, Robert Kennedy had shown some commendable zeal for law enforcement and had instituted the legal proceedings against Teamster James Hoffa, which ultimately sent the boss of the nation's biggest union to jail for eight years for jury tampering.[60] Robert's refusal to pamper criminals, however, did not prevent brother John from giving a presidential pardon to convicted arms smuggler Hank Greenspun, a Las Vegas publisher and former publicity agent for gangster Bugsy Siegel.[61] Greenspun took advantage of his restored civil rights to run unsuccessfully for the Republican nomination for Governor of Nevada.[62]

No presidential career has been as tainted with minority-related malfeasance and scandal as President Johnson's. The most fateful and agonizing moments in Johnson's political life came in the 1948 Texas senatorial primary when he ran what almost amounted to a dead heat with his opponent, Coke Stevenson. At the very last minute, when it appeared that Stevenson was winning by 100 votes, 203 votes for Johnson were suddenly discovered, after the official counting had come to an end, in a South Texas district run by a political boss named George Parr. These 203 votes gave Johnson an 87-vote edge, the final count being 494,191 to 494,104.[63]

A preliminary investigation showed that most of these votes came from Mexican-Americans, many of whom had been so inspired by Johnson's senatorial qualifications that they had actually risen from their graves to vote for him. When an official inquiry began, the 203 ballots suddenly disappeared in an "accidental" fire.[64] In the end, Johnson's political career was assured when the state investigation was quashed and when Associate Justice Hugo Black blocked a Court order to reopen it. It is noteworthy that during this crucial time in

---

60. *Facts on File*, 1967, p. 78. Also see footnote 7, p. 358, of this study.
61. The nature of Greenspun's criminal activities may explain Kennedy's leniency. See footnote 25, p. 483.
62. *Time*, Aug. 31, 1962, p. 18.
63. Harry Provence, *Lyndon B. Johnson*, Fleet, New York, 1964, pp. 81, 83–4, 86.
64. Robert Sherrill, *The Accidental President*, Grossman, New York, pp. 28–9, 114.

Johnson's life, Abe Fortas was his chief trouble shooter in Washington.[65]

Johnson overcame another embarrassing crisis when the Bobby Baker case came under the halfhearted scrutiny of a Senate investigating committee. Baker, while Secretary to the Senate Democratic Majority, had been a business associate of such men as Las Vegas casino operator Ed Levinson and Miami gambler Benny Siegelbaum.[66] Baker had also been a political protege of Johnson, who called him "my strong right arm," and "the last man I see at night, the first one I see in the morning." It was no surprise that Fortas quickly materialized as Baker's legal counsel.[67] Finally in 1967, after Fortas had withdrawn from the case, Baker was given a one to three-year jail sentence for income tax evasion, theft and conspiracy.[68]

In his role of perennial political fixer, Fortas had previously been ordered by the President to suppress the Jenkins' scandal, which cropped up in the middle of the 1964 presidential campaign. Walter Jenkins, Johnson's most trusted and most enduring assistant, who as Secretary of the National Security Council had access to almost every important classified document in Washington, was arrested for perversion in a YMCA men's room. Even though Jenkins, a Baptist who converted to Catholicism, had been arrested once before for similar activities, Johnson kept him on. Fortas, together with Clark Clifford, later Secretary of Defense, called on various newspaper editors to blue-pencil the story. Some agreed, but when the United Press broke the news, the censorship plot miscarried.[69]

In the matter of the probity and the close minority relationships of recent also-ran presidential candidates, Goldwater's close friendship with gangsters Gus Greenbaum and Willie Bioff has already been mentioned. Adlai Stevenson, the Democratic presidential candidate who lost to Eisenhower

65. Roland Evans and Robert Novak, *Lyndon B. Johnson,* New American Library, New York, 1966, p. 25.
66. *New York Times,* Jan. 14 and 15, 1964, p. 1.
67. *Esquire,* June 1965, p. 86.
68. *New York Times,* April 8, 1967, p. 1.
69. *Life,* May 9, 1969, p. 34 and *Time,* Oct. 23, 1964, pp. 19–23.

in 1952 and 1956, was the "political find" of lawyer Louis Kohn and the special protege of Jacob Arvey, retired boss of the venal Chicago Democratic machine.[70] The principal financial backer· of Hubert Humphrey's 1968 presidential bid, as previously related, was an ex-gangster.

Despite the financial backing of Majority corporations, President Nixon went begging for campaign money from minority peculators like Robert Vesco, whose $200,000 cash contribution led to the criminal trials of former cabinet members John Mitchell and Maurice Stans. Both were leading actors in the Watergate affair, which unloosed the greatest wave of media paranoia since the attack on McCarthy.[71] In an effort to make the Nixon administration a sinkhole of Majority corruption, the press carefully emphasized the German and WASP origins of some participants, while ignoring the minority background of other important wire-pullers.[72] Henry Kissinger, it is unnecessary to point out, came through unscathed.

Strong minority influences were brought to bear on the members of another famous American political dynasty—the four sons of Franklin D. Roosevelt. James Roosevelt, a Congressman from Los Angeles, the city with the second highest concentration of Jews in the United States, served as a kind of "minority spokesman" in Washington and after a succession of marital mishaps moved to Switzerland as an executive of a minority-owned overseas investment company.[73] Franklin D. Roosevelt, Jr., delinquent in his 1958 income taxes to the amount of $38,736, served as an attorney to

---

70. Kenneth S. Davis, *The Politics of Honor,* Putnam, New York, 1967, pp. 178 ff. Stevenson, who was as hero-worshipped by the liberal-minority coalition as was Ted Kennedy some fifteen years later, was also involved in a death incident. As a boy, he unwittingly shot and killed Ruth Merwin, a young girl who was visiting his family during the Christmas holidays. Eleanor Ives Stevenson and Hildegarde Dolson, *My Brother Adlai,* Morrow, New York, 1956, p. 72.

71. One phase of Watergate, the operation of the White House plumbers, was triggered by the late J. Edgar Hoover, who would not permit a full-scale investigation of Ellsberg, the purloiner of the Pentagon Papers, in deference to his friendship for Louis Marx, Ellsberg's millionaire father-in-law.

72. *The Washington Post,* so bitter about the Watergate coverup, had willingly participated in the Jenkins' coverup during the Johnson era.

73. It was in Switzerland, while working for Bernard Cornfeld, that Roosevelt was stabbed by his third wife as he was preparing to undertake his fourth marriage. *Time,* Oct. 10, 1969, p. 98.

dictator Trujillo of the Dominican Republic.[74] John Roosevelt, the youngest brother, spoke at a 1961 Miami Beach Teamsters' Convention in support of the reelection of President James Hoffa, even then in deep difficulty with the law.[75] Elliott Roosevelt, whose five wives had made him the most married and divorced of all FDR's sons, was hand-picked for Mayor of Miami Beach by Louis Wolfson,[76] the celebrated corporate raider and former inmate of the federal penitentiary at Atlanta, Georgia.[77] It was this same Wolfson who, when under government investigation for stock fraud, arranged to have his tax-exempt foundation pay Associate Supreme Court Justice Fortas $20,000 a year for life.[78]

Lesser minority political fry or influence peddlers who have done little to help the country that gave their immigrant forebears the first taste of freedom they had ever known include: Morris Shenker, one of Hoffa's lawyers, who paid Senator Edward Long of Missouri $48,000 while the latter's Senate subcommittee was investigating wiretapping, a method of criminal sleuthing abhorrent to Hoffa;[79] Marvin L. Kline, former Mayor of Minneapolis, given a ten-year sentence for grand larceny for stealing from the Sister Kenny Foundation, a charitable organization for infantile paralysis victims;[80] Victor Orsinger, Washington lawyer, found guilty of stealing

---

74. *New York Times*, May 23, 1963, p. 1. Franklin's third wife was Felicia Sarnoff, granddaughter of Jacob Schiff.

75. John Roosevelt was a partner in an investment counseling firm which handled a considerable amount of Teamsters Union pension funds. Clark Mollenhoff, *Tentacles of Power*, World Publishing, Cleveland, 1965, pp. 345–6.

76. Patricia Roosevelt, *I Love a Roosevelt*, pp. 134, 251, 328, 377, 379.

77. *San Francisco Sunday Examiner and Chronicle, This World*, Dec. 15, 1968, p. 5.

78. See Chapter 29. Fortas kept the first $20,000 installment for almost a year, long after Wolfson was formally indicted. In the meantime, he received $15,000 for a few lectures at American University's Washington College of Law. Later it was discovered the fee had not been paid by the University, but by such personages as Maurice Lazarus, department store magnate, and Gustave Levy and John Loeb, two of the world's richest private bankers. The money could be interpreted as the gift of friends or as the means by which the international banking community is able to keep a Supreme Court Justice on the payroll. *Time*, May 23, 1969, p. 23 and *Life*, May 23, 1969, pp. 38–9.

79. *Facts on File*, 1967, p. 460.

80. *New York Times*, Sept. 14, 1963, p. 10.

$1,500,000 from an order of Catholic nuns;[81] John Houlihan, former Mayor of Oakland, Calif., convicted of stealing $95,000 from a trust fund of which he was the executor;[82] Hugh Addonizio of Newark, N.J., another ex-Mayor, sentenced to ten years in prison for receiving kickbacks while in office.[83] Perhaps the worst case of influence peddling involved House Speaker John McCormack, in whose office two political fixers, Nathan Voloshen and Martin Sweig, operated for years, sometimes even using the Speaker's name. When Sweig and Voloshen were brought to trial McCormack, one of the canniest politicians in Washington, claimed he was unaware of his friends' actions.[84]

With the exception of Lowell Birrell, whose father was a Protestant minister, and Estes, Baker and a few others, every notorious financial con man since World War II has been a minority member. The biggest swindler of them all, Anthony De Angelis, incredibly cheated his friends, business associates and the United States Government out of some $219 million in a soy bean fraud.[85] Compared to De Angelis, Eddie Gilbert, who fleeced his stockholders out of $1.9 million and then ran off to Brazil, was a piker.[86] Another stock manipulator was Morris Schwebel who, with a few other operators, kited the price of Canadian penny stocks to five dollars a

---

81. *Washington Post,* June 4, 1970, p. B4.

82. After being indicted, but before going to jail, Houlihan served a three-month stint as consultant to the Center for Study of Democratic Institutions, Santa Barbara, Calif. *New York Times,* April 30, 1966, p. 28 and Sept. 8, 1968, p. 21, and *Oakland Tribune,* June 3, 1966, p. 22.

83. Associated Press report, Sept. 23, 1970.

84. *Life,* Oct. 31, 1969, pp. 52 ff and *New York Times,* Jan. 13, 1970, p. 1. John Dowdy and Daniel Brewster were two other Congressmen involved with minority criminals. Dowdy was jailed for perjury after he allegedly received a bribe from Nathan Cohen to block a gov't investigation. Brewster was given 2–6 years for taking money from Spiegel, a mail order house. The minority bribers, having been assured of immunity, went free.

85. *Time,* June 4, 1965, p. 20. The biggest tax dodger of them all was Samuel Cohen of Miami Beach, who, according to the Internal Revenue Service, neglected to report $25,578,000 taxable income for the single year of 1967. *Gannett News Service* report, July 11, 1971.

86. *New York Times,* April 24, 1964, p. 1 and April 28, 1967, p. 1. Gilbert later came back and surrendered. Although Benjamin Javits, the brother of New York Senator Jacob Javits, represented him, Gilbert was sent to jail. Gilbert's rich mother then paid a large sum of money to Speaker John McCormack's fixer co-worker, Voloshen, to get her son out of jail.

share. Later the shares turned out to be almost worthless and the public lost $16 million.[87] A more vicious type of financial predator was international banker Serge Rubinstein, who supplemented his monetary operations with draft dodging and was later murdered in gangland style.[88]

Louis Wolfson was relatively subtle in his financial dealings and leaned heavily on high government officials for support. With the help of ultraliberal Senator (now Representative) Claude Pepper of Florida and millionaire contractor Matt McCloskey, both high in Democratic party councils, Wolfson made his first killing by buying an American naval shipyard, which cost the taxpayers $19,262,725, for $1,926,500.[89] Like Wolfson, Leopold Silberstein went to jail for violating the rules of the Securities and Exchange Commission. Even the assistance of former Secretary of the Interior Oscar Chapman was unable to save him.[90] Other notorious Wolfson-type wheeler-dealers were: Leo and David Bakalar, who received $75 million for less than one third of their stock in Transitron Corp., which then dropped from $35 to $1 a share;[91] and Stanley Goldblum of Equity Funding, which forged $200,000,000 worth of insurance policies.[92]

Last, but not least, there is Roy Cohn, who has recently spent a great deal of his life in court defending himself—so far successfully—against a seemingly never-ending series of charges ranging from conspiracy and mail fraud to bribery, extortion and blackmail.[93] If Jewish lawyer Abe Fortas symbolizes the corruption of the liberal-minority coalition, Jewish lawyer Cohn, the former aide to the late Senator

---

87. In his trial, Schwebel was represented by former Federal Judge Simon Rifkind who explained that the defendant was a philanthropist and a religious and community leader, adding that both Schwebel and his wife had recently had heart attacks. Schwebel was fined $15,000 and sentenced to a year and a day in prison. The sentence was later suspended. *New York Times*, June 7, 1964, p. 60 and Aug. 26, 1964, p. 24.

88. *Time*, May 6, 1946, p. 84 and Feb. 7, 1955, pp. 16–7.

89. Leslie Gould, *The Manipulators*, David McKay, New York, 1966, pp. 5–6.

90. Benjamin Javits was also Silberstein's lawyer. *Ibid.*, p. 53.

91. *Ibid.*, pp. 175–6.

92. *Miami Herald*, April 22, 1973, p. 7E.

93. *New York Times*, Dec. 14, 1969, p. 74.

Joseph McCarthy, is the symbol of the spiritual desiccation of so-called American conservatism. In 1964, after Cohn had won acquittal in one trial, he received congratulations from Cardinal Spellman, Senator Dirksen and Senator Eastland.[94] Among Cohn's other friends are Senator Edward Long of Missouri, whose relationship with Hoffa was mentioned previously, and William F. Buckley, Jr.[95]

But Cohn's most important connections are Lewis Rosenstiel, the multimillionaire founder of Schenley Industries, and Louis Nichols, former Assistant to the Director of the FBI. Both men were extremely close to FBI head J. Edgar Hoover. Rosenstiel was the largest single contributor to the J. Edgar Hoover Foundation and Rosenstiel's own foundation helped subsidize two books on the FBI, one of which was authored by Hoover.[96] Cohn is also known to have been friendly with Congressman Emanuel Celler, Chairman of the House Judiciary Committee, Congressman Cornelius Gallagher, who has been openly accused of close association with the Cosa Nostra, and Edwin Weisl, President Johnson's financial advisor and hand-picked ambassador to New York's Democratic party.[97] It was on Cohn's yacht that ex-Tammany boss and convicted extortioner Carmine DeSapio and other Democratic bigwigs chose a slate of judges for the 1969 New York City election.

A month before the 1968 presidential race, Cohn gave the grateful Maurice Stans, later Secretary of Commerce, three checks amounting to $9,000 for the Republican campaign. In return he was allegedly assured that Chairman Manuel Cohen of the Securities and Exchange Commission and Robert Morgenthau, U.S. Attorney for the Southern District of New York, his alleged "persecutors," would be

---

94. *Life*, Sept. 5, 1969, p. 28.
95. Cohn arranged for a Chicago bank in which he had an interest to give Senator Long a $100,000 unsecured loan. Cohn also got a $60,000 loan for Buckley, who used it to buy a 60-foot sloop. *Life*, Sept. 5, 1969, p. 28–9.
96. *Life*, Sept. 5, 1969, pp. 29–30.
97. *Ibid.*, pp. 28–9. Weisl was also a director of Cenco Instruments Corp., controlled by Alfred E. Strelsin, one of the country's wealthiest and most dedicated Zionists.

removed if Nixon won. After the election Cohen was replaced
forthwith, and Morgenthau fired a few months later.[98] The
involvement of the Nixon administration with such shabby
promoters as Cohn was not an isolated incident. Later, Walter
Annenberg, the Philadelphia publisher who was once indicted
for income tax evasion, was appointed Ambassador to
England.[99]

Crime has penetrated so deeply into the minority-dominated
entertainment industry that it has become an underworld
jungle. Gangsters control the juke boxes, own many of the
nation's nightclubs, and put up much of the money for
Broadway productions. As the result of the gangster hold
over gambling, at least until the advent of Howard Hughes,
practically every big name in the entertainment world has at
one time or another received Mafia money for appearing in
Las Vegas. Several leading show business and television
personalities have even established criminal records of their
own. Jack Benny, one of the nation's highest-paid comedians,
was convicted of diamond smuggling in New York in 1939,
but it never seemed to hurt his ratings.[100] Winston Burdett,
a smooth-talking television news reporter, was a spy for the
Red Army in Finland when Russia was trying to overrun
that small nation in the winter of 1939–1940. After
Burdett had confessed all to a Congressional Committee, his
employers, William Paley's Columbia Broadcasting System,
kept him on as if nothing had happened.[101]

In the world of print, obscenity is now so much the thing
that when magazine publishers have been arrested for pornography, as have Hugh Hefner of *Playboy* and Ralph
Ginzburg of *Eros,* their reputations have been enhanced.
After Ginzburg received a five-year prison sentence, he
managed to solicit contributions for a new magazine, *Fact,*

98. *Ibid.,* p. 26. Cohn's three checks bounced for some time before they
were finally covered. He once wrote $50,000 worth of checks against a
non-existent account. *Ibid.,* p. 30.

99. Annenberg's father, Moses, went to jail for two years for evading $1.2
million in income taxes. Walter was never brought to trial. *Washington
Evening Star,* Jan. 7, 1969, p. 1.

100. *New York Times,* Oct. 12, 1940, p. 19.

101. *New York Times,* June 30, 1955, p. 1.

from such notables as Bertrand Russell, Mary McCarthy, Linus Pauling and Robert Hutchins.[102]

Other writers, almost all belonging to minorities, were not only involved with criminals but were criminals in their own right. The dean of this literary breed is Harry Golden, who, before becoming the best-selling author of anti-Southern homilies and the owner-publisher of the influential *Carolina Israelite,* served almost five years in Sing Sing under his real name, Herschel Goldhurst.[103] Norman Mailer, who received $400,000 for his denigrating series of essays on the moon landing, was arrested in New York in 1961 for stabbing his wife.[104] A less scatological author, literary critic Leslie Fiedler, aged fifty, was picked up by police with Mrs. Fiedler, his son and two teenagers in 1967 for maintaining premises where narcotics were used.[105] Timothy Leary, former Harvard instructor, writer and guru, was found guilty and given a thirty-year sentence (later reversed) for smuggling drugs into the country from Mexico.[106] Pearl Buck, the noted liberal who was born in China and won the Nobel prize in literature, was forbidden by the State of Pennsylvania to solicit any more money for her foundation because of its mishandling of charitable funds.[107] Topping them all was literary forger Clifford Irving.

102. *Time,* April 3, 1964, p. 59 and *New York Times,* June 26, 1963, p. 26. Although convicted in June 1963, Ginzburg never spent a day in jail until 1972. An equally adept prison dodger was Saul Birnbaum, an accountant convicted of bribing an Internal Revenue Agent in 1961. Birnbaum did not go to jail until May 1970, and then only as the result of some unfavorable publicity. *New York Times,* May 27, 1970, p. 26.

103. Nixon restored Golden's civil rights in 1973, whereupon he said he would run as a Democrat for a seat in the Charlotte (N.C.) city council.

104. *New York Times,* Jan. 13, 1961, p. 58; Jan. 31, 1961, p. 13; Nov. 14, 1961, p. 45.

105. *New York Times,* April 30, 1967, p. 78.

106. *New York Times,* March 12, 1966, p. 1 and Oct. 21, 1966, p. 1. Leary, who was later jailed on another drug charge and then broke out of prison, is probably as responsible as anyone for influencing a considerable portion of an entire generation of Americans to experiment with or take up drugs. The last time that drug addiction reached similar proportions was in early twentieth-century China. The New Left in the United States either favors or is tolerant of narcotics, yet Mao Tse-tung, the Chinese Communist boss and one of the New Left's heroes, has made even the use of drugs a severe crime, and the drug scourge has all but disappeared from China.

107. *Time,* July 25, 1969, p. 60. In 1965, the foundation's board of governors included Art Buchwald and Sargent Shriver.

The police records of leading black militant writers have already been referred to, but it is appropriate to mention that LeRoi Jones, the most prominent contemporary Negro playwright, was arrested in New York in 1966 for assault and robbery.[108] Arthur Miller, the most honored contemporary Jewish playwright, was cited for contempt of Congress in 1956.[109] Ten leading Hollywood film writers, minority members with one or two exceptions, had been previously jailed for the same offense.[110]

The emphasis on minority criminals in this chapter has not been intended to imply that there is no crime where there are no minorities. It is worth repeating that every race and every society have their criminals. But multiracial societies have more crime, and the multiracial society in which the struggle for power becomes an openly racial struggle has the most crime. Furthermore, there are some offenses, particularly certain kinds of sex offenses, which could only occur in heterogeneous societies. In 1964, thirty-eight people in a New York suburb watched for one hour and a half out of apartment windows as a young woman, repeatedly calling for help, was slowly murdered in the courtyard beneath them. The murderer, a Negro necrophile, climaxed the gruesome exhibition by raping her when she was dead. Still, not a single person lifted a finger to stop him, or raised his voice, or picked up the telephone to call the police.[111]

Such an event could never have happened in a homogeneous society. A sense of community and kinship, not to speak of the moral commands of a commonly shared religion, would have forced the onlookers to intervene. Also, in

---

108. Allen Ginsberg, the poet, put up the $500 bail. *New York Times,* July 31, 1966, p. 55.

109. *Facts on File,* 1956, p. 441 and *New York Times,* June 10, 1950, p. 3; June 30, 1950, p. 1; Sept. 28, 1950, p. 20. Miller probably escaped jail because he was married at the time to actress Marilyn Monroe, whose over-exploitation by Hollywood led to a pathetic suicide.

110. The most serious offenses committed by these movie trenchermen were the treacly, moronic potboilers they cranked out for salaries of up to $1,000 a week.

111. *Time,* June 26, 1964, pp. 21–2. A similar occurrence took place in Rochester, N.Y. Hundreds of cars passed a 10-year-old girl being assaulted beside a freeway. Not one car stopped, even though the girl momentarily escaped from her attacker and waved frantically for help. Her body was found two days later in a ditch. Associated Press report, Nov. 28, 1971.

a homogeneous society the chances of the occasional minority criminal being present would have been less, and even if he had contemplated such an act, he would have been aware of the fierce community reaction it would have aroused—an awareness which alone might have proved a decisive deterrent. For example, it is doubtful that the Boston Strangler, Albert DeSalvo, would have been able to murder eleven women in the closely-knit society of Southern Italy, where his family originated.[112] For one thing, he would not have been tempted by the presence of women of other races. Predictably, there was not one Italian name in the roster of his butchered victims.

Racial crime is becoming the most common type of crime in America, yet American law refuses to distinguish it from any other kind of crime. Every one is still equal before the law and entitled to the same legal safeguards, although the racially-motivated criminal no more deserves the protection and benefits of due process than an enemy soldier captured in battle. Both the enemy soldier and, increasingly, the minority lawbreaker feel their crimes are not crimes in the real sense, but simply acts of justifiable violence against an oppressor. This is why the odds against the racial criminal's rehabilitation in prison are so high. To most minority prisoners, the modern American prison is little more than a prisoner-of-war camp—albeit a strange and incomprehensible one from which prisoners are released while the war is still in progress and where the troops of both sides are incarcerated together, as they continue at close quarters the racial conflict being waged outside.[113]

Humanitarianism, which is the extension of familial love to all mankind,[114] was the chief architect of the present-day

112. Gerold Frank, *The Boston Strangler*, New American Library, New York, 1966, pp. 157–8. Twenty-four of the twenty-five victims of Mexican-American mass murderer Juan Corona were Americans of Anglo-Saxon background. The one Negro victim was buried in a separate grave. It is possible more graves will be discovered. *Miami Herald*, Oct. 12, 1973, p. 15A.

113. The U.S. has a higher proportion of its population in jail than any other country—178 per 100,000, as against Japan's 89 per 100,000 and Britain's 65. Simpson and Yinger, *Racial and Cultural Minorities*, p. 217.

114. Arnold Gehlen, *Moral und Hypermoral*, Athenaum Verlag, Bonn, 1969, pp. 79 ff, 123 ff, 142 ff.

prison system. Until recently, most civilized countries fined, branded, mutilated, enslaved or killed their criminals, when they did not exile them or organize them into large work gangs. The herding of large numbers of men into vast prison complexes is a relatively new development in criminology. Long prison sentences cause immeasurable psychological damage to inmates by wasting their lives away in useless and profitless pursuits, while the soaring costs of prison upkeep place a heavy financial penalty on those who observe the law. And as jails become more crowded, they become more insufferable. In most big-city prisons, white inmates are now almost totally at the mercy of black criminals, since the latter make up most of the prison population. The homosexual acts and terrorism to which youthful Majority prisoners are forced to submit represent one of the most cruel and hideous ordeals in the history of punishment.[115]

But the answer to the prison system is not the legal permissiveness which has clogged the courts to such a degree that many criminals commit two or three more offenses while free on bail awaiting trial for earlier crimes. This is merely a vicious circle which promotes rather than diminishes crime, as noted more than a half century ago by Vilfredo Pareto, the Italian sociologist:

"The effect of the probation law extends beyond the criminal whom it protects. The population at large grows accustomed to thinking that a first crime may be committed with impunity; and if that manner of thinking becomes ingrained in sentiment, diminishing the aversion for crime that the civilized human being instinctively feels, criminality may increase in general. . . . The whole-hearted punishment of crimes that took place over long periods of time in centuries past has contributed to the maintenance of

---

115. In three Pennsylvania jails, in which Negroes made up 80 percent of the inmates, there were 2,000 sexual assaults over a two-year period. Half of these assaults were directed against whites. *Time,* Sept. 20, 1968, p. 48. Often the only way a young Majority member can get by in jail is to debase himself by becoming the "punk" of a hardened minority criminal, who then protects him against gang assaults. In spite of this appalling situation, the Supreme Court upheld a lower court decision forbidding the segregation of prisoners by race to avoid violence. *1969 World Almanac,* p. 49.

certain sentiments of aversion to crime. . . . Those nations which are nowadays indulging in an orgy of humanitarianism are acting like the prodigal son in frittering away the fortune he had inherited from his father.

"Mild laws in general . . . the extreme mercifulness of courts and juries; the kind-hearted patience of magistrates who allow criminals to show contempt for them in public court, and sometimes to utter personal insults and ridicule the penalties with which they are threatened . . . the mitigation of penalties already mild; frequent commutations and pardons—all such things allow a large number of individuals to think lightly of crime and punishment of crime. . . ." [116]

Crime in America will almost certainly go on increasing until criminologists and social scientists are willing to consider the genetic ramifications of the problem. So far only one prominent American anthropologist has had the courage to assert that crime is largely the result of physical and racial factors. After conducting an anthropological study of 13,873 male prisoners in ten states, the late Earnest Hooton declared that the country's "criminal stock" must be eliminated. He further observed that the only way to check the growth of criminality was to breed a better race. [117]

As expected, the equalitarian prejudices of Boas and Ashley Montagu have provided most of the anthropological guidelines for contemporary criminology. Montagu himself has stated, "There is not the slightest evidence to believe that anyone ever inherits a tendency to commit criminal acts." [118] There is, of course, in addition to Hooton's work, a wealth of such evidence. Studies of glandular disorders and chromosome defects and the correlation of body types to delinquency all indicate the indisputable biological origin of certain criminal tendencies. [119]

116. *The Mind and Society,* trans. Andrew Bongiorno and Arthur Livingston, Harcourt Brace, New York, 1935, Vol. 3, pp. 1284–5.

117. Harry Elmer Barnes and Negley K. Teeters, *New Horizons in Criminology,* Prentice-Hall, Englewood Cliffs, N.J., 1959, pp. 131–2.

118. Ashley Montagu, "The Biologist Looks at Crime," *The Annals of the American Academy of Political and Social Sciences,* Vol. 217, p. 55.

119. The work of Cesare Lombroso, who linked crime to physical defects and stigmata, is not to be discounted because it has been attacked by equalitarian criminologists. The history of the Jukes family, which pro-

Because of the genetic link, crime prevention should start in the home or, more properly, in the bedroom. There are already too many Americans, and many too many criminal Americans. For those criminal elements who not only insist on multiplying, but multiplying much faster than non-criminal elements, the only alternative is sterilization. According to Professor H. S. Jennings, denying the right of reproduction to habitual criminal offenders would eliminate some 11 percent of the mental defectives (including the criminally insane) in each successive generation.[120] Professor Samuel J. Holmes has stated that the sterilization of 10 percent of the American population would get rid of most hereditary defectives.[121]

The psychic backwash of crime, its deadening and cynical effect on reciprocity, self-denial and other moral prerequisites of civilized man, are beyond the scope of this study. Here, in conclusion, it will merely be pointed out that a citizenry which must devote an ever larger portion of its time and resources to its personal security is neither in the mood nor in the position to care much about national security. The upshot is that crime has a direct bearing on America's defense capability. The stark, humiliating, daily record of the ongoing orgy of American crime is a searing proof of national division and disunity. As such, it stimulates the neutralist propensities of allies, while encouraging the aggressive instincts of enemies.

In ways too subtle for most historians or political analysts to grasp, one of the principal products of the minority underground has been the etiolation of American foreign policy.

---

duced hundreds of criminals in six generations, is further evidence of the genetic basis of much crime. Lothrop Stoddard, *Revolt Against Civilization,* pp. 95–6. More recently, the inherited XYY chromosomal defect has been shown to be a direct cause of criminal and anti-social behavior.

120. Barnes and Teeters, *op. cit.,* p. 137. As of 1958, twenty-seven states permitted some form of sterilization. In 1952, fifty thousand people were sterilized in the United States, only some for eugenic reasons.

121. *Ibid.*

PART IX

The Foreign Policy Clash

Chapter 31

The Denationalization of Foreign Policy

THE FOREIGN POLICY of the United States or of any nation is the vector addition of the internal forces which shape its domestic policy and the external forces brought to bear by the foreign policies of other nations. Since present-day American domestic policy reflects a liberal-minority bias, American foreign policy is bent in the same direction. As a consequence, it tends to favor those states and governments which appeal to the taste of modern liberalism and to the emotions of its more powerful minorities. As a further consequence, contemporary American foreign policy does not serve the interests of the nation as a whole, but rather of certain segments of the nation.

Democratic theory assumes that the foreign policy of a democracy is a truer and more faithful image of the people's attitudes, needs and desires than that of a monarchy, aristocracy or dictatorship. This might be true of a democratic country with a relatively homogeneous demographic base. But the theory can hardly be applied to large multiracial states where there is no "people" but a conglomerate of separate peoples, each with its own divergent and often divisive demands upon foreign relations.[1]

---

1. De Tocqueville, the great analyst and friend of American democracy, exhibited grave doubts about the ability of democratic governments in the field of foreign affairs, believing that the qualities which distinguish democracies in the conduct of domestic affairs were the opposite of those needed for the proper handling of foreign affairs. "La politique extérieure n'exige l'usage de presque aucune des qualités qui sont propres à la démocratie

American foreign policy was born and nurtured in the isolationism so ineluctably appropriate to the new nation's remoteness and limited resources and so succinctly set forth in Washington's Farewell Address.[2] The young country, although bursting at the seams with an energy that anywhere else would have been sublimated into a riotous imperialism, was at first forced by the demands of geography to turn the martial instincts it had not allocated to the preservation of its liberties to the more humble pursuits of wilderness clearing and land reclamation.

But once the crisis of independence had been surmounted and the War of 1812 had ended in a draw, America dropped its isolationist mask and embraced the entire Western Hemisphere with the pronouncements of the Monroe Doctrine. As most Europeans and Latin Americans correctly diagnosed it, the Monroe Doctrine was only a diplomatic euphemism for infectuous American expansionism. Another word for it was Manifest Destiny, which, though it did not become an article of faith until somewhat later, was in the wind from the time of the original settlements along the Eastern seaboard.

It is hard to estimate when and where the territorial aggrandizement would have stopped had American energies not been dissipated in the Civil War. If there had been no slavery issue, it is quite possible that Canada, Mexico, Central America and the Caribbean islands would now be additional stars in the American flag. After Appomattox, after the wounds had been bound (but before they had healed), the imperialistic *Drang* was renewed. In 1898–99, Cuba was "liberated" from Spain and America took over the Philippines. Then came Theodore Roosevelt, the last of a breed, the last of the *admitted* imperialists, with his big stick, his world-circumnavigating fleet, his Panama blitz and his aggressive arbitration of the Russo-Japanese War.

The twin forces of liberalism and minority racism did not secure a firm foothold in the formulation of American

---

. . . c'est dans la direction des intérêts extérieurs de la société que les gouvernements démocratiques me paraissent décidément inférieurs aux autres." *De la démocratie en Amérique,* Tome I, p. 238.

2. Washington, it should be emphasized, was not against expansion and empire. He was simply opposed to meddling in European politics and taking sides in European wars.

foreign policy until the Wilson administration. America's greatest classical liberal, Thomas Jefferson, had been as isolationist as Washington and, against his will, as expansionist as Theodore Roosevelt.[3] It had been the extreme elements among Jefferson's followers who tried to sweep the United States into a European war on the side of revolutionary France. Later the Abolitionists, another faction that put ideology above country, sabotaged the national interest wherever it meant an increase in slaveholding territory.[4] But by and large, until the inauguration in 1913 of Woodrow Wilson, the first modern liberal to win the presidency, American foreign policy remained unresponsive to the machinations of the liberal-minority coalition in its early phases. Washington's advice, although frequently ignored, was never repudiated.

The grand turnabout in American foreign policy was signaled by America's entry into World War I. At the war's outbreak, the Majority was neutral or mildly favorable to England, the less assimilated Germans and most German Jews mildly pro-German, the Eastern European Jews strongly anti-Russian (due to Czarist anti-Semitism) and the more unassimilated Irish vehemently anti-British. The other white minorities, although some of their homelands were directly involved, were either unconcerned or were unable to drum up nationwide sympathy. The nonwhite minorities were generally mute and dormant.

Since minority pressures more or less canceled each other out during the initial stages of World War I, the forces of intervention came from three quarters: (1) those who were still conscious of their Anglo-Saxon ancestry or were induced

---

3. De Tocqueville, *op. cit.,* Tome I, p. 239. Jefferson himself, although he always exhibited a noticeable French bias, called for, in his First Inaugural Address, "entangling alliances with none . . . absolute acquiescence in the decision of the majority." It was the southern and trans-Appalachian farmers, Jefferson's cherished yeomen, who furnished most of the support for American expansion. Much to Jefferson's consternation, his negotiation of the Louisiana Purchase transformed him, willy-nilly, into America's foremost imperialist. Beard, *The Rise of American Civilization,* Vol. 1, Chapter IX.

4. The Abolitionists favored seceding from the Union if there was no other way of ending slavery. They were most fanatic in their opposition to the annexation of Texas. Beard, *op. cit.,* pp. 581, 595.

to become conscious of it by pro-British newspapers; (2) those who believed in the superiority of Anglo-American political institutions and felt they were being threatened by goose-stepping militarists; (3) those who had a direct economic interest in a British victory, as the result of the close financial alliance which had sprung up between Wall and Threadneedle Streets after the British blockade of Germany.

To make their case, the interventionists embellished the British-French-Russian cause with favorite liberal shibboleths —democracy, human rights, self-determination of peoples— and blackened the German cause with favorite liberal pejoratives—tyranny, man's inhumanity to man, Teutonic supremacy. But despite the 1915 sinking of the *Lusitania,* the propaganda campaign was failing. There was hardly a modicum of truth in the allegorization of the war as a battle between Good and Evil, democracy and absolutism, unless the Czar was to be accepted as a good democrat. The Anglo-Saxon and financial connections, while admittedly there, were not considered worth dying for. Britain, on the brink of defeat in 1916, had to look for a more powerful loadstone to draw the United States into war.

One such magnet had been taking shape in America since the beginning of the New Immigration. British Ambassador to Washington, Cecil Spring-Rice, had unwittingly discovered it when he reported to his government on the increasing influence of American Jews. He wrote in one dispatch, "a Jewish deputation came down from New York and in two days 'fixed' the two houses so that the President had to renounce the idea of making a new treaty with Russia." [5] At almost the same time in England, Chaim Weizmann, the leader of the world Zionist movement, had been expounding on the strength of world Jewry and promising its full support to Britain in return for the British endorsement of a Jewish homeland in Palestine.[6] The British government paid particular heed to Weizmann's proposal because as a promi-

5. William Yale, *The Near East,* University of Michigan Press, Ann Arbor, 1958, p. 267. Yale, an American university professor, spent several years in the Near East on U.S. State Department assignments.
6. *Ibid.,* Also see Sachar, *The Course of Modern Jewish History,* pp. 372–3.

nent chemist he had greatly aided the British war effort by developing a process for the synthesis of acetone, a vital ingredient in the production of explosives.[7]

The British and French apparently decided to proceed with Weizmann's homeland idea in 1916. Samuel Landman, an influential British Zionist who had been transferred to the British Propaganda Ministry in accordance with Weizmann's wishes, has written that Mark Sykes, Under-Secretary to the British War Cabinet, and Georges Picot and Jean Gout of the French Foreign Office were convinced by 1916 "that the best and perhaps the only way (which proved so to be) to induce the American President to come into the war was to secure the cooperation of Zionist Jews by promising them Palestine, and thus enlist and mobilize the hitherto un-suspectedly powerful forces of Zionist Jews in America and elsewhere in favor of the Allies on a *quid pro quo* contract basis. Thus, as will be seen, the Zionists, having carried out their part, and greatly helped to bring America in, the Balfour Declaration of 1917 was but the public confirmation of the necessarily secret 'gentlemen's' agreement of 1916. . . ."[8]

In March 1917, the last formidable obstacle to enlisting the support of American Jews for the Allies was removed when a revolution overthrew the Czar and brought a pro-visional government to power in Russia. One of the new regime's first acts was to assure the world that Czarist anti-Semitism was a thing of the past and that Russian Jews would now have the same rights as all other Russians.[9] On April 2, Woodrow Wilson, who had been reelected President the preceding November on the campaign slogan, "He kept us out of war," asked Congress to declare war on Germany.[10]

---

7. Sachar, *op. cit.*, p. 372. Jewish work on high explosives and the tangible rewards accruing to Jewish causes therefrom are a recurring theme of modern Jewish history. See Chapter 38 of this study for the Jewish role in the development of the fission and fusion bombs.

8. Yale, *op. cit.*, p. 267. The quotation and reference are from Samuel Landman's book, *Great Britain, the Jews and Palestine*, New Zionist Press, London, 1936.

9. *New York Times*, March 21, 1917, p. 1 and April 3, 1917, p. 9.

10. American Zionists then held a convention and sent their formal con-gratulations to Wilson. *New York Times*, April 11, 1917, p. 8.

Within weeks, British Foreign Minister Arthur Balfour arrived in the United States. Almost immediately after seeing Wilson, he had a long conference with Justice Louis Brandeis, the leading American Zionist.

A few months later, Henry Morgenthau, Sr., and Felix Frankfurter, who were slightly below Brandeis in the American Zionist hierarchy, persuaded the State Department to send them on a secret mission to Europe to try and obtain a separate peace from Turkey. Chaim Weizmann headed them off at Gibraltar, convincing them that an early end to hostilities with Turkey would damage the Zionist cause. Palestine was then a Turkish possession, and presumably a thoroughly defeated Turkey would not be able to offer much resistance to the foundation of a Zionist state. Morgenthau and Frankfurter agreed and returned to the United States, their mission uncompleted.[11]

It will probably never be ascertained if Zionism was the blast of wind that knocked the already teetering United States off the tightrope of neutrality. Although the evidence is sketchy and circumstantial, it is not altogether unconvincing. The matter certainly deserves further study and should be rescued from the historical deep freeze in which overcautious historians have deposited it.[12] If nothing else,

---

11. Yale, *op. cit.*, p. 241 and Louis Gerson, *The Hyphenate in Recent American Politics and Diplomacy*, University of Kansas Press, Lawrence, 1964, pp. 91–2.

12. There are many other bits and pieces of historical evidence to strengthen the case that Zionism was an important cog in the wheel of American intervention in World War I. Lloyd George went on record as stating that the Balfour Declaration would have an important influence on world Jewry outside Russia and be in the best interests of Jewish financial circles. Leonard Stein, *The Balfour Declaration*, Simon and Schuster, New York, 1961, p. 575. In America, Lloyd George pointed out, the Declaration would have a special value when the Allies had exhausted their gold reserves and negotiable securities. *Ibid.*, p. 575. There was a French government mission to American Jews in 1915, and the British Foreign Office urged British Jews to help get American Jews interested in the Allied cause in 1916. *Ibid.*, pp. 218–9. French Zionists openly admitted attempts to influence public opinion in France, even to the extent of using government channels of information. *Ibid.*, p. 375. It is possible that Wilson assured prominent New York City Zionists of his true intentions toward intervention in return for support in the 1916 presidential election. *Ibid.*, p. 227. Brandeis at the time was receiving Zionist communications by British diplomatic courier. *Ibid.*, p. 377. He publicly agreed

the diplomatic attention given Palestine proved that minority racism was beginning to exert a dominating and self-serving influence in some sectors of American foreign policy and, in the case of the Morgenthau-Frankfurter mission, that Zionists were conducting a separate American foreign policy in their own interest.

After an outpouring of treasure such as only the world's most opulent nation could afford, the United States ended its first military incursion into Europe by retreating pell-mell to the New World, where American foreign relations again deflated to their traditional hemispheric range. At the inglorious peace conference at Versailles, Wilson's utopian hopes of a liberal world community had gone up in the

---

that Zionists stood to benefit from the Russian revolution. *Ibid.,* p. 382. After Wilson had endorsed the Balfour Declaration in a letter dated August 31, 1918, Brandeis "declared that opposition to Zionism could henceforth be considered disloyalty to the United States." Gerson, *op. cit.,* p. 94. Almost the very moment the revolution in Russia began, the Rothschilds, who had refused to loan money to the Czarist regime, telegraphed one million rubles to the new government. Frederic Morton, *The Rothschilds,* Atheneum, New York, 1962, p. 175. The Turkish revolution (1908–1909), which helped weaken Turkey's hold over Palestine, "had been organized from Salonica, where the Jews, together with crypto-Jews known as Dönmeh, formed a majority of the population. Stein, *op. cit.,* p. 35. British Prime Minister Asquith wrote in 1914, "it is a curious illustration of [Disraeli's] favourite maxim that 'race is everything' to find this almost lyrical [Zionist] outburst proceeding from the well-ordered, methodical brain of H.S." Stein, *op. cit.,* p. 112. He was referring to Herbert Samuel, one of Britain's most powerful Jews and a member of the British Cabinet. Later, a still more powerful Jew, Lord Reading (Rufus Isaacs), who had been a bankrupt stock speculator and the subject of Kipling's vitriolic poem *Gehazi,* was sent to America, first as chief of a British financial mission, then as British Ambassador. H. Montgomery Hyde, *Lord Reading,* Farrar, Straus and Giroux, New York, 1967, pp. 188 ff. Reading was a good friend of Colonel House, Wilson's closest adviser, and his "influence with Lloyd George [was] greater perhaps than any other man's in England." Hyde, *op. cit.,* p. 229. Samuel Gompers, a Jew and the head of the American Federation of Labor, seemed to synchronize his changing attitude toward the war with the shift in the Zionist position. In 1914, Gompers was all for neutrality. But in February 1917, he called a meeting of the AFL Executive Council and came out with a strong declaration against Germany. Ronald Radosh, *American Labor and U.S. Foreign Policy,* Random House, New York, 1969, p. 8. As for the average American's real desire to enter the war, Senator La Follette declared that if the issue had been submitted to a referendum the vote would have been ten to one for non-intervention. Beard, *op. cit.,* Vol. 2, p. 635. It might be noted that the Sedition Act of May 1918 made most criticism of intervention illegal. *Ibid.,* p. 640.

smoke of nationalism, irredentism and revolution. The President had even to suffer the final humiliation of having his own brainchild, the League of Nations, repudiated by the United States Senate. By the time of his death in 1924, it was generally conceded that, in direct contradiction to America's most trumpeted war aim, World War I had imperiled democracy everywhere by piling the Ossa of fascism on the Pelion of communism. Almost every thoughtful American, no matter what his politics, was ready to agree that intervention in Europe had been a disaster and must never happen again.

It happened again in less than a quarter century. This time the interventionists, despite the embarrassment of having to recant their most solemn promises and renege on their most repeated resolutions, had a much easier task. Before World War II, Hitler had established himself as the arch enemy of liberalism, Marxism and Jewry—precisely the three driving forces of the liberal-minority coalition that had ridden into power with Franklin Roosevelt's New Deal. In no time, the news media became rabid. By 1940, it was hard to find a liberal or minority intellectual—give or take a few Old Believers—who was not a raging interventionist.[13] The few Majority leaders who tried to make their voices heard above the martial clangor were quickly silenced or discredited by the tarbrush of anti-Semitism.[14]

---

13. Sidney Hillman, the minority labor chieftain, was so incensed at Hitler that he personally directed the breaking of a 1940 strike at North American Aviation in Inglewood, Calif. Radosh, *op. cit.*, p. 19. The man who had made a career out of the union movement wanted no slowdown in the production of war materials, even though it meant betraying a union local.

14. After he had made a brief mention of the specifically Jewish agitation for intervention, the press reduced Charles Lindbergh from the status of epic hero to Nazi hireling. Lindbergh remained a non-person for many years thereafter. *New Republic*, Sept. 22, 1941, pp. 360–1 and *Time*, Sept. 22, 1941, p. 17. In 1970, Lindbergh published his *Wartime Journals*, in which he insisted that his non-interventionist stand had been fundamentally correct and that the U.S. had actually lost the war, since it had merely destroyed a lesser menace to help establish a greater one. He particularly stressed the irreparable genetic loss suffered during the war by the Northern European peoples. Lindbergh's written words repeated, and did not modify, his 1941 accusation that Jews had been a major force in involving the U.S. in World War II. See footnote 34, p. 160 of this study and *The Wartime*

As Charles Beard ably demonstrated by a mass of documentation, America entered World War II long before Pearl Harbor and the Axis declaration of war.[15] It had, in fact, been unofficially committed by November 1940, when Roosevelt, repeating Wilson's feat, was reelected after solemnly promising to keep the United States out of war.[16] Even before his reelection, Roosevelt had transferred fifty American destroyers to Britain. After reelection, he persuaded Congress to adopt the Lend-Lease Act, which placed a large part of the war's financial burden on the American taxpayer. He then ordered in quick succession: (1) American naval escort of British convoys; (2) open warfare on German naval vessels; (3) the occupation of Iceland; (4) the drawing up of secret defensive agreements with Britain; (5) an ultimatum to Japan which demanded the removal of Japanese troops from China and tightened the American steel and oil embargo.[17] The official entry of the United States into the war came almost as an anticlimax.

If there was some difficulty in identifying the forces of intervention in the initial stages of American embroilment in World War II,[18] there was none in the end stages of the fighting itself. The policy of unconditional surrender, the Morgenthau Plan,[19] the abandonment of Eastern Europe to

---

Journals of Charles A. Lindbergh, Harcourt Brace Jovanovich, New York, 1970, pp. xv, 218, 245, 404, 481, 538–9, 541, 545.

15. Beard, *President Roosevelt and the Coming of the War 1941.*

16. In his celebrated campaign address in Boston (Oct. 30, 1940), Roosevelt stated: "I have said this before, but I shall say it again and again and again: Your boys are not going to be sent into any foreign wars."

17. Beard, *op. cit.,* pp. 68, 97 ff, 108 ff, 134, 140 ff, 239, 241, 356, 435 ff, 453 ff.

18. British Prime Minister Neville Chamberlain apparently shared some of Lindbergh's views as to the origins of the conflict. According to Ambassador Joseph Kennedy, Chamberlain told him, "America and the world Jews had forced England into the war." But Chamberlain's statement was not made known until 1951. *The Forrestal Diaries,* edited by Walter Millis, Viking, New York, 1951, p. 122.

19. Introduced at the Second Quebec conference (1944) by Secretary of the Treasury Morgenthau and authored by Harry Dexter White, Assistant Secretary of the Treasury (later identified as a Soviet agent), the plan called for the dismantling of all German industry and the reduction of Germany to an agrarian state. Churchill originally agreed to the plan in return for an extension of Lend-Lease. *Current Biography,* 1944, p. 724; *Time,* August 9,

Russia, the German war crimes trials and the denazification purges clearly proved that the United States had not been by any stretch of the imagination engaged in a war of survival, as newspaper editorials proclaimed, but rather in a war to destroy Hitler.[20]

There was no American retreat from Europe when World War II ended. Had there been, Western Europe would have followed Eastern Europe into the Soviet orbit. By force of circumstance, American foreign policy was now converted into an impromptu defense mechanism on the grand scale, an infinite series of on-the-spot reactions and counteractions to Communist acts of aggression, both in Europe and Asia. This containment policy, as it came to be called, made it necessary for Americans to pay for the rebuilding of the very same industries they had recently destroyed, and for American soldiers to join forces with the very enemy they had recently been ordered to kill. The West was saved, at least temporarily, but at the cost of another fearful outpouring of American human and industrial resources.[21] The East, or at least the greater part of the East, was lost.

1948, p. 15 and John M. Blum, *From the Morgenthau Diaries,* Houghton Mifflin, Boston, 1967, Vol. III, p. 373.

20. To some it was purely and simply a war of racial revenge. Secretary Morgenthau, in discussing the postwar treatment of Germany, said: "The only thing . . . I will have any part of, is the complete shut-down of the Ruhr. . . . Just strip it. I don't care what happens to the population. . . . I would take every mine, every mill and factory and wreck it . . . why the hell should I worry what happens to [the] people?" That such a policy would have starved thirty million Germans to death was beside the point. Morgenthau persisted in his plan even though New York Governor Thomas Dewey stated that the Morgenthau Plan brought about a sharp increase in German resistance. How many needless deaths and casualties on both sides were caused by Morgenthau's Old Testament vengeance can never be known. Blum, *op. cit.,* pp. 354 ff, 378.

21. The U.S. (as of June 30, 1964) is still owed $13,869,641,935 from unpaid World War I loans. In World War II, American Lend-Lease to the Allies amounted to $49,100,000,000, of which only a fraction has been repaid. In the postwar period (July 1, 1945 to June 30, 1964) the United States distributed $110,400,000,000 to 110 nations and territories. One-third of this was military aid, the remainder grants and loans. United States subscriptions to the International Monetary Fund, the International Bank and the Inter-American Development Bank and other international pools accounted for $11 billion more. Additional billions were given to the United Nations, the Organization of American States and to private organizations

During and after World War II, American foreign policy alternately went far beyond and fell far short of the national interest. As if in penance for not joining the League of Nations, the United States became the founder and principal shareholder of the United Nations.[22] But the UN was no better at keeping the peace than the League. Almost single-handedly, the United States assumed the defense of the West.

In Asia, America was on the losing side in China and then was drawn, in defiance of all military common sense, into Asiatic land wars it could only have won with the help of nuclear weapons or dedicated allies. In the Middle East, the once friendly Arab world turned against the United States and toward Russia after America's sponsorship of Israel. In Africa, the emerging black nations were given lavish financial and ideological support, while the white governments of South Africa and Rhodesia were condemned, and sanctions imposed on the latter. In Latin America, the blindness of one American president helped install Castro and the blindness of a second allowed the Pearl of the Antilles to become a Russian military base.

Prestige and power, the twin sources of respect, are an invincible combination in winning the friendship and support of foreign peoples and governments. Not so long ago America and Americans had the respect of most of the world and this universal esteem made the formulation and implementation of foreign policy relatively easy. Today the nation which is still on paper the richest and most powerful on earth is so shorn of respect that any fifth-rate banana dictatorship, Communist client state or tribal military junta is able to humble or humiliate America and Americans at will.

The nation that went to war with Spain over the sinking of

---

for use abroad. Above figures are from the *Congressional Digest,* June–July, 1965, pp. 164–170, 192 and *Ency. Brit.,* Vol. 4, p. 834. Many of the loans extended for forty years with no repayment for the first ten, after which there was a service charge of 0.75 percent, but still no interest. By the middle of 1964, less than 10 percent of the foreign aid loans had been repaid. As of mid-1970, foreign aid had climbed to $119 billion.

22. The U.S. pays one-third of the UN's operating budget and 70 percent of its total expenditures. Russia has three votes in the General Assembly, as against one for the U.S. Nations representing 153,000,000 of the earth's 3,000,000,000 population control a majority of votes in the General Assembly.

the battleship *Maine* now makes no military response at all
when Israeli torpedo boats and bombers kill thirty-four
navy crewmen on the communications ship *Liberty;* [23] when
North Korea captures the naval ship *Pueblo* with its entire
crew; when Guatemalan gunmen murder the American Ambassador in broad daylight; when Venezuelans stone the
American Vice-President; when hijacking terrorists com-
mandeer American airliners to Cuba with impunity; [24]
when American airplanes are blown up in Egypt and American airplane passengers held as hostages in Jordan; when
American prisoners of war in Asia are brainwashed, tortured and shot; when American citizens in the Congo are
raped and cannibalized; [25] when American embassies are besieged and invaded by mobs and their personnel kidnapped;
when American libraries are looted and gutted; and finally
when the nation which once proclaimed "Millions for defense, but not one cent for tribute" [26] pays $53 million ran-
som to a posturing Caribbean Mussolini for the release of
1,113 prisoners captured in the Bay of Pigs landing. [27]

As the above incidents illustrate, the new-style American
diplomacy in which the strong surrender to the weak—or
buy protection from the weak in the form of foreign aid—
has not produced many stirring successes. [28] In fact, whatever solid gains American foreign policy has achieved since
World War II must be largely attributed to two crucially important factors for which U.S. policy makers can take no

23. See p. 489.
24. Fifty-four American planes were hijacked between July 1, 1968 and
June 1, 1970, *U.S. News & World Report,* June 15, 1970, p. 31.
25. See p. 500.
26. Spoken by Charles Pinckney in 1797, when American Minister to
France.
27. *1965 World Almanac,* p. 371.
28. George Kennan, one of the few creative minds in the diplomatic
corps, has been highly critical of what he calls the "histrionic futility" of
American statesmanship. The addiction of American politicians to inject-
ing extraneous considerations into American foreign policy makes it, according to Mr. Kennan, "ineffective in the pursuit of real objectives in the
national interest, allowing it to degenerate into a mere striking of attitudes
before the mirror of domestic political opinion. Until the American press
and public learn to detect and repudiate such behavior, the country will not
have a mature and effective foreign policy worthy of a great power."
Memoirs, 1925–1950, Little, Brown, Boston, 1967, p. 54.

credit at all. These are America's nuclear preponderance, now rapidly diminishing, and the internal breakup of the communist world. That the movers and shakers of American foreign policy did not sufficiently exploit either of these two unique advantages is a diplomatic failure of the first magnitude, one that will weigh heavily on future generations.

But what else could be expected from a foreign policy that has been put through the grinder of denationalization? When the safety and security of the country come second, diplomacy becomes the shuttlecock of every lobby and pressure group in the liberal-minority coalition. Allies and friends of long standing are neutralized or turned into enemies, while professional diplomats, forced to sit on the sidelines, grow more cynical and more impotent than ever. The State Department may pretend to be the agency that directs or implements American foreign policy, but it is little better than a vast messenger service. One single editorial in *The New York Times* carries more weight than the dispatches of twenty ambassadors.

A denationalized foreign policy has many heads and hearts, but no soul. It supports imperialism in one part of the world and opposes it in another. It upholds democratic principles in some areas and violates them in others. It gives money and arms to anti-American regimes and boycotts pro-American governments. It is against Russian aggression in the Middle East, but tolerates it ninety miles from Florida.

Not only America but most of the world has lived to regret the day the Majority lost control of American foreign policy.[29] There is nothing more dangerous in international relations than misdirected energy, nothing more tragic than a great nation that expends its greatness blindly. Until the special interests of the minorities and the special enthusiasms of liberals are again made subservient to the national interest, American foreign relations will stagger from crisis to crisis and from war to war.

---

29. June 8, 1915, when William Jennings Bryan resigned as Secretary of State in protest against the first real signs of the Wilson administration's bristling interventionism, is as good a date as any to mark the end of nationalism as the guiding light of American foreign affairs.

Chapter 32

The United States and Western Europe

NOTHING POINTS UP the impermanency of the human condition so poignantly as the tragic deterioration of Western Europe in the twentieth century.[1] As the century began, Western Europe was the lord of the earth, the fountainhead of world industry, technology and military power, the headquarters of nine empires.[2] In 1970, Western Europe was a power vacuum, a buffer zone between Russia and the United States, relatively rich and prosperous after another quick recovery from another devastating war, but now almost totally defenseless. Slavic troops stood on the Elbe, from which they had been driven more than a millennium before by Charlemagne.[3] The Western European land space, a peninsula of a peninsula, beckoned the Russians as a divided, strife-torn Greece had once beckoned Alexander, while Western Euro-

---

1. Western Europe is here designated as that part of Europe west of the Slavic lands and the Balkans.

2. British, French, German, Austro-Hungarian, Italian, Dutch, Belgian, Spanish and Portuguese.

3. Describing conditions in Europe in the seventh century A.D., a modern Scandinavian historian has written: "In these dark centuries, the center of Europe's cultural life shifted so far west that the once-vital barter between Scandinavia and the South could take place only on the Rhine and along the Atlantic coast. The 'West' had been just as menacingly reduced and narrowed down as it is today." Eric Oxenstierna, *The Norsemen*, New York Graphic Society, Greenwich, Conn., 1965, p. 26.

peans themselves felt less and less comforted by America's protective nuclear canopy.

America and Russia are children of Western Europe, in the sense that both countries have depended on it for most of their cultural nourishment and both were founded by the race that has been dominant in Western Europe since the fall of Rome.[4] A great, unresolved question of the future is whether one of these unruly offspring, semi-barbaric Russia, will attempt to claim the patrimony defended by the other sibling, America, itself now sinking into semi-barbarism. Or will the parent revive, mend his self-destructive ways and re-assert his authority?

As yet, there are few signs of the latter possibility. Only the Germans still exhibit the perennial Northern European dyna-mism. But the West German defense forces, armed with for-eign weapons, their numbers restricted by law, their ranks demoralized by heavy doses of defeatism and modern liberal-ism, could hardly, even with the help of their American and NATO allies, roll back a conventional military attack by the Russians and would have no chance at all of resisting a nuclear one. It is true that the West German economy is now as healthy as any in the world. But if not used to shore up German defenses, economic prosperity can only make West Germany more attractive to the foreign predator.

Today, Western Europe is wracked by many of the same diseases that are tearing at the vitals of America. Western European nations have their own minority problems, their own liberal "public opinion" mills,[5] and their own insurrec-tionary Marxist cabals, both pro- and anti-Russian. There are not as many Jews as there are in the United States. But there are many extremely rich Jews and, when the overflow from New York and Beverly Hills is added, probably the same disproportionate Jewish influence in the arts, news media and government.[6] The nonwhite population of Britain

4. See pp. 72–3.

5. "If all the books written about the European Left were laid end to end, they might well stretch halfway around the globe. Books on the European Right would more likely not stretch a mile. . . ." *Times Literary Supplement,* May 14, 1970, p. 1.

6. Beside the century-old Jewish wealth represented by the Montagus, Mocattas and Rothschilds in England stand such pound millionaires as

now numbers 1,200,000 and is expected to rise to 2,200,000 in a few years.[7] Yet those who call for greater safeguards for the British gene pool are excoriated as mercilessly as their American counterparts. Britain's foremost opponent of black and Asian immigration, Enoch Powell, a professor of Greek before he worked his way up in the Conservative party, has been treated as an illiterate blackguard.[8]

Only in the matter of crime does Western Europe have a distinct advantage over the United States. The Southern Italian migration northward over the Alps did not begin until the 1950's, and apparently did not include the Mafia. The very much smaller proportion of Negroes also tends to keep the crime rate much lower than America's. Culturally, how-

---

Samuel Clore, Isaac Wolfson and Simon Marks (department stores); Sir Samuel Salmon and Isidore Gluckstein (restaurants and hotels); Siegmund Warburg and Baron Swaythling (banking); Baron Melchett (chemicals); The Marquess of Reading (steel); Viscount Bearsted (oil); Sir Louis Sterling (record players). Sachar, *The Course of Modern Jewish History*, pp. 497-8 and the British *Who's Who*. Arnold Weinstock heads the British equivalent of General Electric. There are forty Jewish Members of Parliament and a few Jewish Privy Councillors. Jewish academicians include Sir Isaiah Berlin, Max Beloff and David Daiches. At least half the leading British playwrights are Jewish—Bernard Kops, Arnold Wesker, Harold Pinter and Peter Shaffer. Stephen Spender leads the contingent of Jewish poets. Chaim Bermant, *Troubled Eden, an Anatomy of British Jewry*, Valentine, Mitchell, London, 1969, pp. 145, 169 ff, 254 ff, 258, 262. In France, the French branch of the Rothschild family still holds a large share of the nation's purse strings. Prominent Jewish publishers and pundits include Jacques Servan-Schreiber, Raymond Aron and Pierre Lazareff. Pierre Mendès-France, René Mayer, Michel Debré and Maurice Schumann are, or were, among the most influential politicians. The current president of France, Georges Pompidou, was once an employee of the Rothschilds. Leading intellectuals and literary lights like André Malraux, Jacques Maritain and Louis Aragon have or had Jewish wives. In Italy, the richest man is probably Arrigo Olivetti, the Jewish typewriter magnate. Litvinoff, *A Peculiar People*, pp. 113-38, 142. The West German government is so nervous about anti-Semitism that it pays huge annual reparations to Jews (see Chapter 35). In April 1958, a German school teacher was sentenced to a year in prison and the loss of his job merely for making a few anti-Semitic remarks in a bar. William Schlamm, *Die Grenzen des Wunders*, Europa Verlag, Zurich, 1959, p. 69.

7. *New York Times*, June 1, 1970, p. 3.
8. A Gallup Poll showed 74 percent of the British population supporting Powell's opposition to colored immigration. *San Francisco Chronicle*, May 8, 1968, p. 14. Powell predicts there will be 5 to 7 million Afro-Asians in Britain by the year 2000, if his country's new immigration restrictions are not tightened.

ever, there is little difference between Western Europe and the United States. The same Stone Age pop art dominates the exhibitions. The same Ziegfeld tinsel and hardcore pornography exercise their depredations on the theater. The same minority racial themes obsess the literati. The same African syncopations echo through the dance halls and rock concerts. In fact, the more influential culture vultures now feather their nests on both sides of the Atlantic.

In World War I, the United States assumed Britain's traditional role of preventing European unification by calling into play the "balance of power." In organizing coalitions against the strongest and most aggressive European nations, this policy was simply the politics of Polycrates on the grand scale. As a long-range strategy, it was not too destructive as long as Western Europe was so strong that even divided it could dominate the world. But carried to its ultimate conclusion in 1939–45, it demolished Western European military primacy, perhaps for all time, leaving the entire region a client state of the United States and the helpless target, if American forces should withdraw, of Soviet imperialism.

It is unlikely that any single Western European nation will soon again be able to qualify as a world power. Only a unified Western Europe would have the capability of equaling or surpassing the American or Russian military machines, and the keystone of any such European confederation would have to be West Germany or a reunited Germany. France and Italy proved conclusively in World War II that they can no longer fulfill any important military task beyond serving as a theater of operations and a source of supplies and auxiliary troops for allies. The smaller Western European nations have developed a tradition of neutrality or instant surrender which, with the possible exception of Sweden and Switzerland, would make their military contributions meaningless. The Spanish soldier is brave, but has few weapons and little European consciousness. Even the fighting ability of the British is currently open to question. No great people ever gave up so great an empire so effortlessly.[9]

___

9. In 1921, the British Empire had 524,000,000 inhabitants. In 1966, when the Colonial Office was closed down, Britain had only twenty-one overseas

Building Western European unity around a German nucleus would seem to be the only long-range assurance of keeping the Russians quarantined in Eastern Europe. In a united Western Europe, the Germans and other Northern Europeans would perform the same function as a resurrected American Majority in the United States and the present Great Russian Majority in the Soviet Union. They would supply the racial backbone, the physical stamina, the dynamism and organizational drive that a modern superpower must require of its dominant population group.

The unification of Western Europe would relieve the United States of furnishing most of the money, arms and men for repelling a Russian attack, a burden so heavy that it might well result in an American military and economic collapse. American troops could be withdrawn from Europe, as well as most of the American nuclear deterrent. Advanced rocket technology now makes it almost as simple to mount a nuclear counterstrike from New World installations and ocean-ranging submarines as from Old World land bases. Also disbanded would be the North Atlantic Treaty Organization, which makes its Western European military contingents seem like American mercenaries. A Western European defense force under a single flag and a single command would attract the best soldiers from those other European nations whose own armies no longer have any real fighting potential. From a military standpoint, it is certain that the whole would prove to be greater than the sum of its parts.

As a final step, the United States of America and the United States of Europe would join in an alliance based not on shifting political and economic dogmas, tactical opportunism or extraneous minority pressures, but on the more enduring foundation of a common race, a common culture and a common desire to raise Western civilization to new summits of achievement. Such an alliance, attuned to the true interests of Northern Europeans and their descendants across the Atlantic, would help prevent the recurrence of the political, economic and social failures brought about by centuries

---

possessions left, most of them remote islands, and the total number of people living under the British flag was 56,000,000.

of "balance-of-power" diplomacy. America can hardly afford another $350 billion war ($700–$800 billion at current prices).[10] Western Europe can scarcely survive a deeper Soviet penetration of its frontiers, another nine million dispossessed refugees from the East and another genocidal round of class and racial confrontations and saturation bombings.[11]

Most important, a formal acknowledgement of the racial and cultural basis of the alliance might stifle any renewed outbreak of the brutalized statesmanship which reduced the peacemaking of two wars to the level of a lynching bee. The unconscionable Allied demand of unconditional surrender prolonged World War II, perhaps as long as eighteen months, by playing directly into Hitler's immolation tactics and by cutting away popular support for an anti-Nazi uprising.[12] It also gave Stalin time to seize all of Eastern Europe, most of the Balkans and a large part of Germany.

A child seeing two school bullies locked in a knock-down, drag-out fight would know better than to help one bully overcome the other. But America, whose armed forces never even landed in Europe until after the battle of Stalingrad, the turning point of the war, devoted the major share of its military effort to the annihilation of an enemy that was already beaten.[13] Hitler, who had never been able to defeat Russia

10. *Ency. Brit.*, Vol. 23, p. 793R. The $350 billion figure is the estimated amount the U.S. spent between 1939 and 1946 on its own armed forces and on war materiel sent to the Allies.

11. *1969 World Almanac*, p. 752. According to one historian, the total cost of World War II to all nations was $4 trillion and the total number of dead, forty million. Martha Byrd Hoyle, *A World in Flames*, Atheneum, New York, 1970, pp. 323–4.

12. Major General J. F. C. Fuller, *A Military History of the Western World*, Minerva Press, 1956, Vol. 3, pp. 506–9, 538–9. The type of mentality directing the American war effort can be judged by the following remarks of President Roosevelt at the 1943 Casablanca conference. When he first uttered the phrase, "unconditional surrender," Roosevelt congratulated himself by saying, "Of course it's just the thing for the Russians. They couldn't want anything better. Unconditional surrender! Uncle Joe might have made it up himself." *Ibid.*, pp. 506–7. In the final pages of his book, General Fuller asked, "What persuaded them to adopt so fatal a policy?" The only explanation he could give was "blind hatred." *Ibid.*, p. 631.

13. The battle of Stalingrad, the greatest and most crucial battle of the war, ended in February 1943, with the surrender of an entire German army. American troops did not land in Italy until September 1943, and in France until June 1944.

and Britain, was replaced by a rocket-rattling Stalin with only America's nuclear might standing between him and an easy march to the Atlantic. If this march ever takes place, the United States will go down in history as the gravedigger rather than the liberator of Western Europe.[14]

---

14. It should be pointed out that the unification of Western Europe stressed in this chapter is limited to military and economic unification, without which no effective defense can be mounted against Russian expansionism. While advocating more organization at the top of the European community, the author at the same time urges less organization in the middle and much more at the bottom. By this is meant a deemphasis on the nationalism which has kept Europe divided for so many centuries and a reemphasis on the regional and provincial divisions, the seedbeds of the great flowerings of Western civilization. For example, France might be restructured to give full cultural and partial political autonomy to Normandy, Brittany, Provence, Lorraine; Germany to give the same to Bavaria, Saxony, Prussia and the Rhineland; the United Kingdom to England, Wales, Scotland, Ulster. Denationalization might also revive the glories of the great city states, Weimar, Florence, Venice, etc. The same process is recommended for the U.S. See "The Utopian States of America," in Wilmot Robertson's *Ventilations,* Howard Allen, Cape Canaveral.

Chapter 33

The United States and Russia

MOST AMERICANS are aware of the differences, especially the ideological differences, between their country and the Soviet Union. They are also aware of some of the similarities—the extended land mass, the advanced space technology, the vast industrial and natural resources. But there is one striking resemblance which is not so well known and which should be clearly comprehended before undertaking any serious discussion of Russian-American relations. This is the analogous fate the twentieth century had in store for both the American Majority and the Russian Majority.[1]

1. As shown in Table V, page 60, the American Majority represents 63.12 percent of the U.S. population. The Great Russian proportion of the Soviet population is indicated below:

THE POPULATION OF THE SOVIET UNION BY NATIONALITY GROUP

	Population	% of total		Population	% of total
Great Russians	129,015	53.37	Tatars	5,931	2.45
Ukrainians	40,753	16.86	Cossacks	5,299	2.19
Byelo-Russians	9,052	3.74	Azerbaijanians	4,380	1.81
Poles	1,167	.48	Chirvashians	1,694	.70
Lithuanians	2,665	1.10	Tajiks	2,136	.88
Latvians	1,430	.59	Turkomans	1,525	.63
Moldavians	2,698	1.11	Kirghis	1,452	.60
Rumanians	119	.05	Bashkirs	1,240	.51
Germans	1,846	.76	Georgians	3,245	1.34
Estonians	1,007	.42	Chechen-Ingush	613	.25
Karelians	146	.06	Armenians	3,559	1.47
Finns	85	.03	Others	6,899	2.86
Jews	2,151	.89			
Uzbeks	9,915	4.10	**TOTAL**	241,720	100.00

Note: Population figures (in thousands) taken from 1970 Soviet Census.

The Russian Majority is composed of Great Russians, the Russians proper, who as Slavs were originally Nordic in race, but centuries ago were inexplicably brachycephalized into Alpines.[2] While this racial transmutation was taking place, small quantities of Nordic genes were added back by the Scandinavian Varangians who founded the Russian state,[3] by the intermingling of the Russian and Teutonic aristocracies and by the agents of the 1000-year German commercial, technical and cultural penetration of Russia. For all these reasons, the Russian Majority, like the American Majority, belongs to the lighter-complexioned segment of the white race, with members of the American Majority tending on the average to be somewhat blonder, taller and longer-headed due to their higher incidence of Nordicism.

From the racial standpoint, the differences between the Slavic-speaking Russian Majority and the Slavic-speaking minorities (Ukrainians, Byelo-Russians, Poles) are minor. They are less than those which set the American Majority apart from the Assimilable Minorities and much less than those that set it apart from the white Unassimilable Minorities. The great separator of the Soviet Union's Slavic population groups is not race but culture. Each speaks its own particular Slavic language, has its own distinct brand of nationalism and inhabits its own particular territory. The non-Slavic minorities are equally regionalized—the blond East Baltic peoples in the northwest, the Mediterranean and part-Mediterranean Georgians, Armenians and Rumanians in the south, and the Mongolian Turkics and Tajiks in the east and southeast.[4]

In comparison with the American population, the Russian population has a smaller Mediterranean component and a larger proportion of Mongolians. Russia has fewer Jews than the United States, but, as in America, they are concentrated in large urban centers and in white-collar occupations. The one

---

2. See p. 74.
3. See pp. 72–3.
4. Only in some Siberian areas and perhaps in Moscow are the various Soviet peoples mixed together on the same scale as population groups in the United States.

overwhelming difference in the racial makeup of the two countries is that Russia has no Negroes.

The Russian and American Majorities are somewhat similar in racial composition. They are more similar in number and in their proportion to the total population of their respective countries. They are very similar in their recent historical experience. Both have known the humiliation of dispossession, the endless bowing and scraping to new control groups, the self-abasement and frustration of working for the greater good of one's detractors. In contrast to the slow decomposition of the American Majority, however, the Russian Majority was dispossessed all at once in the 1917 revolutionary holocaust.

The racial factors underlying the Bolshevik uprising have already been discussed,[5] but not the Russian Majority's return to favor, which began after the German attack on the Soviet Union in the summer of 1941. Since no country can long survive a massive invasion when its strongest and most numerous population group has been alienated and proletarianized, the Soviet government was quickly forced to renounce many of the key assumptions of communist dogma or face the prospect of total collapse.

On November 6, 1941, as the German *Wehrmacht* stood before the gates of Moscow, Stalin tore up the Marxist-Leninist rule book by describing Hitler's onslaught, not as an assault on the citadel of world communism, the Holy Land of Marxism, but as a war of extermination against the Slavs. No more were the German invaders portrayed as last-ditch capitalists trying to root out socialism from the face of the earth. Historical materialism, economic determinism, the class struggle, all the sacred pillars of communist ideology crumbled into dust as the Soviet news media revived the racial glories of Mother Russia, even going so far as to invoke the ghosts of long-departed Czarist heroes and Orthodox saints.[6]

---

5. See p. 346.
6. Hans Kohn, *Pan-Slavism*, Vintage Books, New York, 1960, p. 292. "Stalin understood intuitively that his government and his social system could not withstand the blows of the German Army unless they leaned for support on the age-old aspirations and ethos of the Russian people." Djilas, *Conversations with Stalin*, p. 48.

The result is history. On May 24, 1945, seventeen days after Germany had been defeated, Stalin proposed an almost heretical toast at a Kremlin banquet of Red Army commanders: "I should like to drink to the health of our Soviet people . . . and first of all to the health of the Russian people [Great Russians] . . . because it is the most outstanding nation of all the nations forming the Soviet Union. . . . It has won in this war universal recognition as the leading force in the Soviet Union among all the peoples of our country. . . ." [7]

On March 15, 1954, in a leading article, *Izvestia* stated: "Every people in the Soviet Union understands perfectly well that the main decisive role in the achievement of victory over the enemy in the Great Patriotic War . . . was played by the Great Russian people. For this reason the prestige of the Russian people is so immeasurably high among the other peoples; for this reason the peoples of the USSR bear toward it boundless confidence and a feeling of tremendous love and gratitude." [8] It is not necessary to point out that the American Majority received no such glowing tribute, either from the American government or the American press, for its overwhelming share in America's military victory.

The rehabilitation of the Russian Majority was accompanied by a revival of anti-Semitism. The Russian people had never been happy about the disproportionate number of Jews in the revolution. [9] The more nationalistic elements of the population had been even less pleased about Jewish responsibility for the murder of the Romanovs. It had been the Secret Police official, Yurovsky, a Jew, working under the orders of the Secretary of the Communist Party Central Committee, Sverdlov, another Jew, who had directed the massacre of the Czar, the Czarina, the Czarevitch Alexis (thirteen) and their four daughters, Olga (twenty-two), Tatiana (twenty), Maria (seventeen) and Anastasia (fifteen). [10]

---

7. Kohn, *op. cit.*, p. 297.
8. *Ibid.*, p. 299.
9. Russian anti-Semitism, it must be remembered, had a long and uninterrupted history and was never considered as "unrespectable" as it was in the West. Dostoyevsky, for example, had proudly proclaimed and elaborated his anti-Semitism, as had many other famous Russians.
10. The murders took place in an Ekaterinburg cellar in 1918. Yurovsky

Although anti-Semitism was made a capital crime when communists took over the government, it still remained in evidence among non-Jewish party cadres, flaring up sharply when Dora Kaplañ tried to assassinate Lenin, an event from which he never fully recovered.[11] But rather than taking the classical form of pogroms, anti-Semitism, as it developed and grew under Stalin, became an important tool in the struggle for control of the Communist party. In the 1930's, Stalin killed off many more important Jews than Hitler, who had been unable or unwilling to prevent many thousands of top-ranking German Jews from escaping before instituting his wartime anti-Semitic measures. But the Jewish aspect of the Great Terror, as Stalin's pre-World War II purges have come to be called, was never stressed by the Soviet government.[12]

It was not until a few years after the war that Stalin decided to bring his sub-rosa anti-Semitism out into the open.[13] In 1948, he closed down all Jewish cultural enterprises, prohibited the teaching of Hebrew and halted the construction of new synagogues. He imprisoned and shot hundreds of

---

shot some of the Romanovs himself. Also shot were the family doctor, three servants and Anastasia's dog. Nobel Franklin, *Imperial Tragedy*, Coward-McCann, New York, 1961, pp. 156 ff and Gleb Botkin, *The Real Romanovs*, Fleming Revell, New York, 1931, p. 236. A recent, meticulously documented bestseller on the Romanov tragedy has neglected to mention the Jewish origin of Sverdlov and Yurovsky, even though the non-Russian origin of the soldiers who helped carry out the murders was carefully noted. Robert Massie, *Nicholas and Alexandra*, Dell, New York, 1967, pp. 511–15.

11. Litvinoff, *A Peculiar People*, p. 74. Although a Jewess nearly killed Lenin, "Jewish revolutionaries were to be found in every branch of [his] administration." *Ibid.*, p. 73. Litvinoff also points out that Emelian Yaroslavski, the head of the Soviet League of Militant Atheists, was Jewish. *Ibid.*, p. 76.

12. For some Jewish victims of Stalin's purges, see Robert Conquest, *The Great Terror*, Macmillan, New York, 1968, pp. 76–7, 430, 498, 512, 538–9.

13. Stalin's daughter, Svetlana Alliluyeva, has made several pointed references to her father's chronic antipathy toward Jews. "To this [the rebirth of Russian anti-Semitism] my father not only gave his support; he even propagated a good deal of it himself." She said it developed from her father's fight with Trotsky. When she married her first Jewish husband— of her five husbands two were Jewish—her father told her, "The Zionists put him over on you." In regard to Rosa Kaganovich, widely heralded as Stalin's third wife by the Western press, Svetlana said that no such person existed. *Twenty Letters to a Friend*, Harper & Row, New York, 1967, pp. 68, 159, 181, 186, 196 and *Only One Year*, Harper & Row, New York, 1969, pp. 152–5, 168, 382.

456   *The Foreign Policy Clash*

Jewish writers and artists, all the while raising a great hue and cry against "cosmopolitans," who were invariably identified in the Soviet press as Jews.[14] The campaign climaxed in 1953, when nine top-ranking doctors, at least six of them Jewish, "confessed" to the murder of an important Soviet official, A. A. Zhdanov, and to plotting the elimination of high-level army officers.[15]

Stalin died as the plot was being unraveled and his successors, perhaps in response to the stentorian reaction from abroad, swept the whole affair under the rug. But as no Jew has been a member of the Presidium of the Central Committee, the inner sanctum of Soviet officialdom, since the expulsion of Kaganovich in 1957,[16] it can be assumed that present-day Russian policy toward Jews has not deviated too far from the established Stalinist line.[17] Zionism is still a crime

---

14. *The Saturday Evening Post,* June 16, 1962, pp. 15–7. Also see *Ency. of Russia and the Soviet Union,* p. 259.

15. They also "admitted" belonging to an American intelligence agency and working through an American-Jewish charity organization. *Ibid.,* p. 133. The Doctors' Plot was faintly reminiscent of the Lopez affair in which a Portuguese-Jewish physician was hanged for allegedly trying to poison Queen Elizabeth in 1597.

16. According to the *American Jewish Yearbook* (1967), pp. 383–4, the only Jew to retain an important government post was Benjamin Dimschitz, one of the several Deputy Premiers, and only five Jews were to be found among the 1,517 members of the two chambers of the Supreme Soviet. No Jews held an important position in the army or diplomatic corps. A report published in the *Richmond Times Dispatch* (Oct. 4, 1965, p. 19), stated 41.1 percent of the Deputies of the Supreme Soviet were Jewish before World War II, but by 1958 the figure had dropped to 0.25 percent. As to Jewish personalities, Molotov's wife was Jewish, but her husband could not or would not save her from arrest and transportation to Siberia. Khrushchev had a Jewish daughter-in-law, and there were well-known Jewish names in artistic, literary and scientific circles—ballerina Maria Plissetskaya, violinist David Oistrakh, some writers, a few of whom had been in and out of prison for years, and one or two noted physicists and economists. Litvinoff, *A Peculiar People,* pp. 91 ff.

17. Anti-Semitism hit the satellite countries particularly hard in the Stalin era. East Germany was forbidden to make any reparations to Israel for confiscation of Jewish property by Nazis. *New York Herald-Tribune,* Nov. 11, 1962, p. 25. Of the fourteen prominent Czechoslovak Communists whom Stalin brought to trial in Prague in 1952, eleven were Jews. It was at this trial that a wife denounced her husband as a "traitor to his party and his country" and a son demanded the death penalty for his father. The son wrote the presiding judge: "Only now do I see that this creature, whom one cannot call a man . . . was my greatest and vilest enemy . . . hatred

against the state. Jews are still listed as Jews in Soviet passports. One unreservedly anti-Semitic book has been published by the Ukrainian Academy of Sciences.[18] In the early 1970's Soviet trials of Jewish hijackers, Russian commitments to the Arab nations and Russian restrictions on exit visas to Israel triggered Jewish counterattacks that ranged from the bombing of Soviet agencies in New York and Washington to the personal harassment of the wives of Soviet officials as they shopped in American supermarkets.[19]

The tottering position of Russian Jewry and the reappearance of a member of the Russian Majority in the higher reaches of the Soviet hierarchy [20] are signs that the fifth and final stage of the Russian revolution is now running its course. These five stages, which bear certain resemblances to other revolutions, can be characterized as follows:

1. The Majority, divided and anesthetized by massive injections of liberalism, partially proletarianized by class agitation and left helpless by its own decadent leadership, is dispossessed by a coalition of minorities.

2. The triumphant minorities and their Messianic Leader, so talented in undermining the old state, find their revolutionary gifts of little avail in organizing a new state and turn their frustrations and failures on themselves.

3. The Minority Strongman [21] emerges, establishes the Terror and liquidates the dissident and discordant minority leaders, once his partners and political allies, but now his most effective and most dangerous opponents.

4. His regime in shambles, under military attack from abroad and pushed to extremes by increasing social and eco-

---

toward my father will always strengthen me in my struggle for the Communist future of my people." Edward Taborsky, *Communism in Czechoslovakia,* Princeton University Press, Princeton, N.J., 1961, pp. 95, 106.

18. It was entitled *Judaism without Embellishment* and contained the following statement, "They [the Jews] think above all of money and they despise productive work." After worldwide repercussions, the Soviet government withdrew the book. *Richmond Times Dispatch,* Oct. 4, 1965, p. 19.

19. *Time,* Jan. 25, 1971, p. 18.

20. Premier Aleksei Kosygin, an authentic Great Russian, was born in Leningrad.

21. It is possible that if Lenin, the Messianic Leader, had lived he would have forestalled Stalin by himself becoming the Minority Strongman.

nomic anarchy at home, the Strongman initiates the counterrevolution by abandoning proletarian dogma and building
a new power base on the Dispossessed Majority whom he
woos with appeals to patriotism, racism and tradition.

5. In his latter years, the Strongman identifies himself almost totally with the Majority [22] and at his death the state
slowly reverts to Majority control.[23]

Expansionism, which seems to be a common obsession of
Czars and Commissars, has been one of the two principal
determinants of Russo-American relations. America first felt
the hot breath of Russian imperialism in the middle of the
nineteenth century, when the Russians, who had occupied
Alaska, extended their fur-trading empire as far south as
Fort Ross in Northern California, seventy miles above San
Francisco. But Russia's unfortunate experience in the Cri-
mean War (1854–1856) led to a worldwide retrenchment.
The Russians first pulled back to Alaska, then in 1867 sold
"Seward's Icebox" to the United States for $7,200,000. There
were no other significant contacts between the two nations
until 1905, when President Theodore Roosevelt indulged his
passion for high politics by becoming the mediator of the
Russo-Japanese war. The lesson of this conflict, the first in
modern times in which a nonwhite country defeated a white
country, was not lost on the world's colonial peoples.

---

22. Stalin's daughter had this to say concerning her father's Russification.
"I have no idea whether or not my mother could sing, but it is said that
once in a long, long while she would dance a graceful Georgian *lezghinka*.
Otherwise, however, we paid no special attention to anything Georgian—
my father had become completely Russian." Svetlana Alliluyeva, *Twenty
Letters to a Friend*, p. 31.

23. When the above timetable is applied to other countries, fascist or
military counterrevolutions may upset it by entering it at stage 2, before the
proletarian forces have been able to consolidate their victory. In this case,
the role of Minority Strongman is usurped by a Majority Strongman, whose
Majority pedigree, however, may leave a lot to be desired. Hitler was
an Austrian and Napoleon a Corsican. Since Stalin was a Georgian, the
three leading revolutionary or counterrevolutionary figures of modern
European history all came from their country's southernmost periphery. If
this should prove to be a law of history, the future American Strongman
will be a Southerner—an hypothesis given some credibility by Huey Long
and Wallace. In Mediterranean countries the Strongman seems to come
from the North. Mussolini and Franco were born in the septentrional
regions of their countries. Castro is the illegitimate son of a Spaniard from
Galicia in Northern Spain.

The second principal determinant of Russo-American relations has been Russian anti-Semitism. The public outcry against the pogroms and other anti-Semitic acts of Czarist governments was first raised in the heyday of the New Immigration, as hundreds of thousands of Russian and Polish Jews were introduced into the American body politic.[24] Almost from the moment they landed, they joined with the more established and more restrained German and Sephardic Jews in demanding that the American government take official steps to protect the millions of other Jews still remaining in the Russian Empire. As a result, American relations with Russia became so strained that in the summer of 1915, when British and French officials approached Wall Street bankers for a war loan, Jacob Schiff, senior partner of Kuhn, Loeb, refused to let his firm participate unless the British and French Finance Ministers gave their assurance in writing that "not one cent of the proceeds of the loan would be given to Russia."[25]

The overthrow of Czar Nicholas II in 1917 completely reversed the attitude of American Jews toward Russia. As the chaos within Russia increased, Russo-American relations grew proportionately warmer, so warm that Woodrow Wilson hailed the Menshevik revolution in March as a kind of political second coming and used it as a justification for American intervention in World War I. That part of Wilson's war message to Congress dealing with the Russian situation can be considered as the first high-level outpouring of the blind

---

24. Total number of Jewish immigrants (to 1930) was 2,400,000, of which perhaps 5 to 7 percent arrived before 1880 and were largely of German and Sephardic origin. Davie, *World Immigration*, pp. 144–5.

25. This was not the first time that Jacob Schiff brought minority racism to bear on the fate of Russia. During the Russo-Japanese war, when London banking circles were skeptical of Japan's chances, Jacob Schiff raised $30 million for the Japanese. As his daughter, Frieda, later wrote, it was "his hatred of Imperial Russia and its anti-Semitic policies that prompted him to take this great financial risk." Later J. P. Morgan, George F. Baker and the Rockefeller-Stillman interests joined Schiff in three massive loans to the Japanese and the door was opened for Japanese conquests in Asia and the Pacific. In 1905, after a series of anti-Semitic outbursts in Odessa, Schiff went directly to Theodore Roosevelt and demanded presidential action against the Czarist government. Roosevelt obediently wrote a personal letter to the Czar. Stephen Birmingham, *Our Crowd,* Harper & Row, New York, 1967, pp. 282, 317.

mendacity, blind stupidity and blind idealism which poisoned the wells of information about Russia for the next half century.

"Does not every American feel," Wilson said, "that assurance has been added to our hope for the future peace of the world by the wonderful and heartening things that have been happening within the last few weeks to Russia? Russia was known by those who knew it best to have been always in fact democratic at heart. . . . The autocracy . . . was not in fact Russian in origin, character or purpose; and now it has been shaken off and the great, generous Russian people have been added in all their naive majesty and might to the forces that are fighting for freedom in the world, for justice, and for peace. Here is a fit partner for a league of honor." [26]

After the war, the "league of honor" was quickly dissolved. Totalitarian ukases outraged traditional American attitudes toward individual freedom and private property. Conversely, the arrival of American troops in Archangel and Vladivostok to aid the anti-Bolshevik forces offended as many non-Communist as Communist Russians. During the 1921–22 famine in the Ukraine, one of the world's most fertile areas, American financial aid and food shipments saved perhaps ten million lives. But since the Communist party did its best to keep the news secret, relations were not much improved. [27]

Until the coming of the New Deal, the Soviet Union remained unrecognized by the United States, although the appeal of communism to American minorities and to the more dogmatically inclined liberals made Russia, the most backward of the great powers, an intellectual Mecca for wayward American minds. In the 1930's a strong conspiratorial streak developed in Russo-American relations as the Comintern intensified its intercontinental espionage and as numerous American Communists and crypto-Communists covertly organized a formidable pro-Russian lobby. Ultimately, due to the fears aroused by the Spanish Civil War and Hitler's lengthening shadow, pro-communist bias reached a fever pitch of religiosity among liberal and minority intellectuals,

---

26. George Kennan, *Russia and the West Under Lenin and Stalin,* Little, Brown, Boston, 1961, p. 19.
27. *Ibid.,* p. 180.

who came to look upon Stalin as an anti-fascist Gabriel sent to destroy the Arch Fiend. It was both tragic and comic that at the very moment this idolatry reached its peak, the Russian dictator by his purges, massacres, institutionalized torture, show trials and slave labor camps was busy destroying almost the entire Communist hierarchy and state apparatus.[28] No political leader in history had so ruthlessly exploited and so cleverly duped his following.

The Russo-German Nonaggression Pact (1939) came as a traumatic shock to those who received their intellectual nourishment from the Communist party line. Bewildered, benumbed and betrayed, liberals and minority members, particularly Jews, began to desert the Communist cause in droves. But the German invasion of Russia two years later drove some of the recreants, at least temporarily, back into the corral. While there, they helped restore the Communist party to its prewar level of prestige and influence. Party members and fellow travelers were again appointed to several key posts in gov-

---

28. Of the 1,966 delegates to the XVIIth Party Congress (January 1934), 1,108 were shot on Stalin's orders within the next few years. Of the 139 members and candidate members of the Central Committee, 98 persons or 70 percent were to be arrested and shot (mostly in 1937–38). From the army Stalin purged three out of five marshals, thirteen out of 15 army commanders, 57 out of 87 corps commanders, 110 out of 195 division commanders, 220 out of 406 brigade commanders. In all, there were some 700,000 "legal" executions, about 1,000,000 secret executions and some 12,000,000 deaths in the prison camps themselves. Counting the 5,500,000 who died in the forced collectivization of agriculture in the early 30's and the man-made famine which accompanied it, Stalin can be credited with a grand total of 20,000,000 dead victims. According to some commentators, this figure is 50 percent too low. It only includes the period 1930–1950. It does not include the last years of Stalin's activities during which the slave labor camp population numbered at least 10,000,000. Conquest, *The Great Terror,* pp. 36–8, 527–8, 533; Hugh Seton-Watson, *From Lenin to Malenkov,* Praeger, New York, 1955, p. 170. It might be noted that during the Stalin purges, the worst of which took place before the outbreak of World War II, the communications media in the West gave Stalin a much better press than Hitler. Very little news of the mass liquidation of a sizable fraction of the Russian population was ever published and, when it was, it was attacked as false and unfounded by many of the West's leading intellectuals. This almost complete blackout for two decades of one of the greatest crimes in history lends substance to those who claim the near total corruption and venality of the world press. Typical was the observation of Professor Harold Laski: "Basically I did not observe much difference between the general character of a trial in Russia and in this country [England]." Conquest, *op. cit.,* p. 506. Sartre once said the evidence about the Soviet forced labor camps should be ignored. *Ibid.,* p. 509.

ernment departments and agencies.[29] In fact, if Roosevelt had not had a last-minute change of heart in the 1944 Democratic convention and replaced his Vice-President, Henry Wallace, with Harry Truman, a fellow traveler would have become President on Roosevelt's death in 1945.[30] It is true that Wallace finally recanted and admitted the error of his ways. But even as late as 1948 he was the presidential candidate of the Progressive party, which was almost totally dominated by Communists and Communist appeasers.[31]

As the cold war progressed, however, and as communist inroads into various sectors of American life were made public, America's close wartime associations with Russia were severed and dealings between the two countries took on an icy formality—interrupted by occasional hot flashes of hostility (Berlin airlift, U-2 incident, Cuba) and one joint peace-keeping venture (the halting of the 1956 British-French-Israeli blitz on Egypt). At a slower pace, the Soviet defense of the Arab world against Israeli aggression and continuing revelations of Soviet anti-Semitism were reducing the once overwhelming Jewish enthusiasm for Russia to the vanishing point.

Toward the middle of the 1950's, after the hysterical

29. The most important Communist concentrations were in the Departments of State, Agriculture and the Treasury. The roster of names includes Hiss, Currie, Ware, Pressman, Abt, Silverman, Collins, Duggan, Witt, Perlo, Reno, White, Remington, Wadleigh, Field and Gompertz. Chambers, *Witness,* especially pp. 466–9.

30. In 1944 Henry Wallace and Professor Owen Lattimore visited a Russian slave labor camp at Magadan, Siberia. This was part of a complex in which the death rate among prisoners was about 30 percent per annum, where outside work was compulsory until the temperature reached −50°C, where it was difficult to live on camp rations for more than two years and where the fate of most inmates followed the inexorable pattern of "sickness, self-mutilation, suicide." The food rations of prisoners were reduced to the starvation level when they did not fulfill norms. Yet Wallace found the camp idyllic and Lattimore considered it a great improvement over the Czarist system. By temporarily removing watch towers, segregating the prisoners in huts and peopling a model farm with girl swineherds who belonged to the Secret Police, the camp commandant duplicated the feat of Potemkin. Conquest, *op. cit.,* pp. 350 ff.

31. Wallace's apologia was issued in the form of a magazine article in *Life,* May 14, 1956. He admitted that he had misunderstood Russian intentions and that Communists had exerted a commanding and deleterious influence on his presidential campaign. Senator McGovern, it might be noted, was a delegate to the 1948 Progressive party convention.

liberal-minority reaction to Senator Joseph McCarthy's flail-
ing attack against the Red apparatus had subsided,[32] anti-
communism, at long last, became respectable in the United
States. But the respectability was assumed in large part by
the very intellectuals who had been most distinguished for
their apodictic communism in the past and who, as unreconstructed Marxists, had shown their true colors by blaming
the failures of communism not on the animadversions of
Lenin but on the perversions of Stalin. As for the non-liberal
and anti-liberal Americans who had known what had been
happening in Russia all along, they were given scant credit
for their prescience and were still beyond the intellectual
pale. Many of the conservatives among them deserved their
fate because they insisted on confusing the external Russian
threat with an internal Communist threat that had long since
passed. Their dogmatic obtuseness prevented them from understanding that those who represented the real internal
threat—the coalition of liberals and minority racists—had
now become as anti-Russian, though by no means as anti-
Marxist, as themselves.

By the end of the 1960's, it was safe to say that Russian
nationalism, militarism, imperialism and Great Russian racism, not Russian communism, comprised the greatest external menace to American national security. Internally, the
United States was becoming more revolutionary than Russia.
Now more than half a century old, the Russian revolution
had destroyed its creators and produced a bureaucratic-
military-managerial caste that was probably the most conservative ruling group of any great power. The present
masters of Russia, unlike the Old Bolsheviks, were no longer
interested in revolution for revolution's sake, but only as a
means of advancing their own and Russia's interests.

From the standpoint of numbers, there were still many
Communists spread over the face of the earth—a grand total
of 45,200,000 members in eighty-eight parties (as of
1969).[33] But as their recent divisions, revolts and defections

---

32. McCarthyism, the media intoned, had made America a land of fear
and trembling. But just who was fearful? It always took much more courage to say a good word for McCarthy than to denounce him.
33. *Time*, June 13, 1969, p. 28.

had shown, the hearts and minds of most Communists no longer belonged to Moscow. Some Communist parties, such as the Chinese, were more frantically anti-Russian than the most rabidly reactionary parties of the West. It is not overstating the case to say that the chief binding force of the Russian branch of world communism was nothing more or less than the presence or potential presence of the Red Army.

So far, the United States has had little to fear from Russia economically. With more people, land and resources than America, the Soviet Union has a Gross National Product only 48 percent of America's.[34] One American farmer still works four times the land that a Russian works on a collective farm, uses five and a half times more power and gets twice as much yield for five to sixteen times less labor.[35] As for consumer products and services such as public utilities and telephones, Russia is still in the pre-World War II stage. But since America's economic and technical superiority over Russia is due to the American Majority's superior capabilities in these fields, America's lead will narrow as the dispossession of the American Majority continues and as the Russian Majority, its dispossession ended, comes into its own.

If Americans should ever adopt a policy of self-interest in their dealings with Russia, they might start by doing unto the Russians as the latter have long been doing to the West. With lavish outpourings of Communist propaganda and subversion, Russia has sought, often only too successfully, to weaken Western nations from within by divisive appeals to class and race, and from without by jingoistic appeals to the nationalism and anti-colonialism of countries which have felt threatened by America's economic might. The United States has a fertile field for similar activities within the Soviet Union, whose minorities have never forgiven or forgotten Czarist and Bolshevik tyranny,[36] and within the Soviet satellite states,

---

34. *Wall Street Journal*, Dec. 31, 1968, p. 18.

35. *Ency. of Russia and the Soviet Union*, pp. 10–12. The U.S. has 6,000,000 people engaged in agriculture—Russia, 45,000,000.

36. Hitler could probably have defeated Russia if he had handled the Russian minorities less roughly. Until they came to know them better, the Ukrainians treated the German invaders as liberators. J. F. C. Fuller, *A Military History of the Western World*, Vol. 3, p. 447.

whose peoples, if given the chance, would break away from Russian domination with only the slightest regrets.

Although Russia must never be allowed to grow so strong that it can engulf Western Europe, it must never be permitted to become so weak that it cannot guard Europe against Mongolian inroads from the Asiatic steppes. To obviate the real possibility of the Russification of Europe, Russian nationalism must be prevented from coalescing into Pan-Slavism. There are, as mentioned in the beginning of this chapter, almost 130,000,000 Great Russians. But, including the Great Russians, there are some 200,000,000 Slavs.[37] The emergence of a latter-day Ivan the Terrible at the helm of a race-conscious Slavic imperium—in which the Slavic minorities in Russia and the Slavic populations in the Russian satellite states are raised to first-class citizenship and inspired with a common racial fervor—would present the West with an almost irresistible concentration of military strength. In such an event, in the words of Stalin, "No one in the future will be able to move a finger. Not even a finger!" [38]

It is, in brief, not the Russia of Lenin that the United States has to fear. It is the Russia of the Pan-Slav Dostoyevsky, a far greater genius with a much sharper eye for the shape of tomorrow.[39]

---

37. Hans Kohn, *Pan-Slavism,* p. 328. Kohn's tally, although partially based on figures from an earlier Russian census, is worth listing for the information it sheds on Slavic demography. Kohn finds a total Slav population of 195,000,000 divided as follows: Great Russians, 95,000,000; Ukrainians, 36,000,000; Byelo-Russians, 8,000,000; Poles, 24,000,000; Czechs, 8,000,000; Slovaks, 3,000,000; Serbs, 7,500,000; Croats, 4,500,000; Slovenes, 1,400,000; Macedonians, 1,000,000; Bulgarians, 6,500,000.
38. Djilas, *Conversations with Stalin,* p. 114.
39. The ban on Dostoyevsky, whose novel *The Possessed* (published in 1871) was an uncanny preview of twentieth-century Russian history, has now been lifted in the Soviet Union—one more proof of the resurgence of the Russian Majority.

Chapter 34

The United States and the Far East

NOWHERE IN RECENT decades has American foreign policy suffered more serious reverses than in China. At the
start of the twentieth century, Americans stood considerably
higher in Chinese esteem than the other foreign devils who
had been beleaguering the moribund Celestial kingdom. The
United States, though committed to extraterritorial rights and
the conversion of the heathen, was probably the least active
of all Western nations in concession hunting, lease grabbing,
opium smuggling and similar manifestations of Western financial privateering.[1] It was Secretary of State John Hay's
Open Door Policy in 1899 which helped tone down some of
the bolder forms of plundering China by insisting on equal
treatment for all nations. After the collapse of the Manchu
dynasty in 1911–12, American ideas and practices of constitutional government inspired Sun Yat-sen, China's first
modern hero, to set up a republic. When the Japanese attacked Manchuria in 1931, the United States protested louder
than any other Western nation.

China was an ally of the United States in World Wars I and
II. In the latter conflict, American military aid to Chiang
Kai-shek played a considerable part in preventing Japanese

---

1. One nineteenth-century lapse in American neutrality was Commander
Josiah Tattnall's rescue (1859) of a badly battered British naval force off
the Chinese coast. His excuse was the now almost forbidden proposition
that "blood is thicker than water." Tattnall later skippered the Confederate
ironclad *Virginia* (formerly *Merrimack*) after her battle with the *Monitor*.
Webster's Biographical Dictionary, Merriam, Springfield, Mass., 1966, p.
1448.

armies from overrunning all China. When World War II ended, the Chinese were particularly grateful for United States support since no territorial or financial favors were asked in return. But while the Nationalist Chinese and the Chinese Communists had been fighting the Japanese, they were both preparing for a renewal of the bitter civil strife which had begun in the 1920's and which had been temporarily postponed by the Japanese invasion. As expected, the Carthaginian struggle between the Communists and Nationalists reignited almost as soon as the war against Japan ended.

In 1949, Chiang Kai-shek and the rags and tatters of his Nationalist forces ignominiously fled to Formosa where they were sheltered from the triumphant Communists by the United States Navy. American aid to Chiang had not been sufficient to prevent his defeat, but more than sufficient to embitter the victors, who proceeded to make the United States the chief scapegoat for all China's ills, past and present, foreign and domestic, real and illusory. United States relations with China reached their low point in 1950 when American troops in the Korean war, having forced the North Koreans to retreat to the Chinese border, were in turn surprised, mauled and driven back to South Korea by 200,000 Chinese "volunteers." The Korean war ended with the reestablishment of the tenuous *status quo ante*. In spite of 57,000 American casualties, it was the second war in United States history to end in a stalemate.

One of the principal reasons for the collapse of Sino-American relations has been America's refusal to consider and understand the racial factors which have been shaping the momentous changes in modern China. For one thing, China is fundamentally a monoracial state. While the Northern Chinese are taller and have larger heads than the brachycephalic Southern Chinese, almost all Chinese are Mongoloids and belong to a race that is less differentiated than the Caucasian.[2]

Although American liberals have made much of the in-

---

2. Coon, *The Living Races of Man*. pp. 148–50. Only about 6 percent of the 760,000,000 inhabitants of China (1966 estimate) can be properly described as belonging to minorities, and most of these are situated in China's periphery. Amrit Lal, "Ethnic Minorities of Mainland China," *Mankind Quarterly*, April–June, 1968.

dignities heaped upon Chinese immigrants in California, the Chinese themselves have a long history of racism. Even the highest foreign dignitaries, classified by imperial edict as "outside barbarians," had to perform the kowtow in the Emperor's presence. In a formal communication to King George III in 1807, the Chinese Emperor employed slurs that would have been insulting to the denizens of skid row.[3]

The intensity of Chinese racism, however, does not mean that Western influences are no longer at work in China nor that divisions do not exist within the Communist regime. The cultural distinctions between Chinese provinces are often pronounced and there is such a variety of languages and dialects that some Chinese have been known to communicate with each other in English. Ironically, the anti-Western and anti-white Mao Tse-tung, in his grandiose attempt to transform China into an oriental national socialist state, has made Holy Writ of the teachings of the Western Jew, Karl Marx. But China's ancient ways, its ancestor worship and its family-centered provincial life still place massive inertial roadblocks in the way of proletarian revolution.

The racial influences active in modern China have been external rather than internal. The principal Chinese Communist dynamic has not been Marxism but xenophobia. The hated white had to be expelled from Chinese territory, and he was. Even the Russians, who were supposed to be permanently joined to the Chinese in the fraternal embrace of international communism, were driven out and damned as heretics.[4] The anti-white racial theme will probably continue until all the lost territories of the Celestial empire have been recovered, including Formosa, which is now occupied by an American puppet regime.

As to the future, Mao envisions a new kind of class war —the countryside, with the peasantry in the role of the proletariat, versus the city. Ruralized Africa, Asia and Latin

---

3. For a summary of China's snobbish attitudes toward the West, see Nathaniel Peffer, *The Far East,* University of Michigan Press, Ann Arbor, 1958, pp. 51–4.
4. The last Russians left in 1960. All that remains of white rule in China are the small and precarious enclaves of British Hong Kong and Portuguese Macao.

America will surround and strangle urbanized North America and Western Europe, the last stronghold of the moneygrubbing capitalists and bourgeoisie, corrupt labor unions and decadent Communist revisionists. The war will be won by guerrilla tactics à la Vietnam, though by the time it starts China will have accumulated a considerable nuclear arsenal.[5]

Mao's deeds will probably never match his threats or live up to his aphorisms.[6] Nevertheless, American foreign policy gained little by cultivating the Formosan nettle in China's eastern flank. American backing of Taiwan only strengthens the Communist position in China. The United States Seventh Fleet patrolling the Chinese coast and 600,000 Nationalist troops in training one hundred miles off the Chinese mainland fit neatly into the Communist propaganda picture of bloodthirsty imperialists readying a mass assault to recapture their lost financial hegemony. Also, there is nothing like a good invasion scare to take Chinese minds off the monumental problems besetting the home front.

Totally misunderstanding the nature of the Chinese Revolution, which in spite of its Marxist apologetics was more of an uprising against foreigners than against warlords and landlords, American foreign policy experts were convinced that any Communist state would *ipso facto* become a Russian ally. The truth is, as has been pointed out repeatedly, that in revolutions race takes precedence over class. As Yugoslavia and China itself have amply demonstrated, Communist states are just as proficient as anti-Communist states in developing and promoting an anti-Russian foreign policy. Reds, it has come to pass, have no greater enemies than other Reds.

The best means of preventing any further sacrifice of American lives in pointless Asiatic wars would be for

---

5. A. Doak Barnett, *China After Mao*, Princeton University Press, Princeton, N.J., 1967, pp. 59–60, 75, 77.

6. "Politics is war without bloodshed while war is politics with bloodshed . . . war can only be abolished through war, and in order to get rid of the gun it is necessary to take up the gun . . . the more books a person reads the more stupid he becomes. . . . I do not mean to close down the schools. What I mean is that it is not absolutely necessary to go to school . . . not to have a correct political point of view is like having no soul. . . ." *Quotations from Chairman Mao Tse-tung*, Bantam Books, New York, 1967, pp. 32, 35, 69, 78. Also see *New York Times*, March 1, 1970, p. 26.

America to continue to mend its diplomatic fences with China. Only by this policy can the United States restore its traditional friendship with the world's most populous nation. Renewed American neutrality in Far Eastern affairs might begin with an attempt to effect the reunification of Formosa with mainland China. Since Chiang Kai-shek and Chairman Mao were born in 1887 and 1893, respectively, their imminent demise may create the right moment for this all-important step towards Sino-American rapprochement.

In one sense, American foreign policy in the Far East has an easier task than anywhere else. In Eastern Asia, the United States does not need to establish a military counterweight against Russia. The counterweight already exists in the form of the one nation in the world that has the will, the manpower and the resources to fight Russia alone in a conventional war and perhaps soon in a nuclear war. That the United States should pursue a hostile policy toward China, the only possible bulwark against Russian expansion in the Far East, is schizoid diplomacy at its worst. History, geography, culture, race—all indicate an eventual clash between China and Russia.

This is not to say the United States should enter such a war, as no doubt will be proposed by anti-Russian minorities here and abroad. America helped destroy Germany, the Western bastion against Slavdom, in 1945. It would be a worse tragedy if America helped China destroy Russia, the white bastion against the yellow race.

Moving the discussion to Japan, one might begin by saying it would have been better for all concerned, especially the Japanese, if Commodore Perry had never landed in Yedo Bay in 1854. By forcing Japan to give up its 400-year isolation, the United States was unwittingly sowing the dragon's teeth which sprouted into the fanatic and dedicated military machine it would meet eighty-seven years later at Pearl Harbor. Since Japanese geography precluded regional and cultural fractionation on the Chinese model, Japan was able to convert to Western technology much faster and more efficiently, and without China's revolutionary turmoil.

Racially, the Japanese are a Mongolian people from the Asiatic mainland with an admixture of prehistoric migrants from Southeast Asia. Having experienced little immigration in the last thousand years, Japan boasts one of the most homogeneous populations on earth, which helps to account for its citizenry's fierce sense of race. Like the Chinese, the Japanese were outraged by American immigration restrictions against Orientals, although Japan itself had practiced racial exclusiveness for centuries. The original inhabitants of Japan were the Ainus, a Caucasoid stock, perhaps the remnants of a white race which once dominated Northern Asia. The Ainus have now been pushed back to the northernmost areas of Japan, where they have been undergoing a process of biological and cultural absorption that is rapidly destroying their racial identity. Another important minority in Japan has not fared much better. During the 1923 earthquake, there was an actual pogrom of Koreans in Tokyo.[7]

Article IX of Japan's postwar constitution contains the widely acclaimed clause renouncing war as a "sovereign right of the nation" and stating that "land, sea and air forces, as well as other war potentials, will never be maintained." This is a rather startling reversal for a country which had developed the military way of life to a fine art (Bushido) and whose social hierarchy consisted of the soldier, artisan, peasant and merchant in that order.[8] No other nation, not even Sparta, has ever produced anything like the incredible heroics of the Kamikaze pilots of World War II.

But America, which imposed pacifism on Japan as part of the peace settlement, paid much of the bill for the rebuilding of the Japanese armed forces. The constitution notwithstanding, Japan now has a "Self-Defense Force" of 260,000 men that includes 1,000 military aircraft, 40 destroyers and 11 submarines.[9] With American disengagement from the war in Indochina, with an increasingly militarized China a few rocket minutes away, with Russia poised on the southern half of Sakhalin Island (Stalin's prize for entering the Pacific war five days before it ended), Japan has little reason not to abandon altogether its uncharacteristic experiment in disarmament.

7. Peffer, *The Far East,* p. 341.
8. *Ibid.,* p. 34.
9. *1974 World Almanac,* p. 579.

A population of ninety-eight million packed in an area slightly smaller than California, only one-sixth of it arable,[10] means that Japan is running out of living space. Other troublesome factors are the continued presence of the American armed forces and incessant demands for the recovery of island territories lost in World War II.

American troops should be withdrawn from Japan, not because they are a growing source of friction in Japanese-American relations, but because they are no longer needed. An economic and industrial complex of vast power, Japan has all the strength and resources it needs to defend itself against a conventional military attack from Russia or China, the only conceivable aggressors.[11] Although it is not in the interest of the United States for Japanese rearmament to exceed a strong defensive capability, it is in the interest of hundreds of millions of impoverished East Asians that the Japanese economy produce enough low-cost consumer goods to raise them from their neolithic living standards. Such a project would be worthy of Japanese technical proficiency and an assurance of Japan's continuing prosperity. The pursuit of peace and uninvolvement in global power politics might also provide the proper stimulant for a revival of the glories of Japanese esthetics.

If an American withdrawal from Japan endangers the independence of South Korea, so be it. The United States cannot overextend itself indefinitely guaranteeing the freedom of small, Far Eastern client states. All such countries have been occupied so long by other nations that they have forgotten the meaning of independence. The moment it is thrust upon them, they usually lapse into civil war.

Elsewhere in the Far East, the Southeast Asia Treaty Organization would probably be as dubiously effective, if put to the test, as the North Atlantic Treaty Organization in Europe. The fundamental principle of SEATO seems to be the protection of the unprotectable. American intervention in Vietnam has already demonstrated what happens to a hamstrung, unmotivated, magnificently equipped modern military ma-

---

10. Peffer, *op. cit.*, p. 40.
11. Japan's nuclear defense, however, must rest in American hands. A Samurai with a hydrogen bomb is not a reassuring sight. See Chapter 38.

chine when it meets a determined, highly motivated, poorly equipped fighting force of guerrillas and regulars. If the makers of American foreign policy had understood that the anti-white feelings of the Vietnamese were so intense that the mere presence of American troops on one side would immeasurably boost the morale and will to fight of the other side, they might not have been so eager to send more than half a million Americans to replace the departed and defeated French.[12]

The worst mistake of those responsible for America's military involvement in Vietnam was to send American armed forces into a war which from the very first they were not permitted to win. Recent history has proved that the United States can only be aroused to a proper fighting pitch when the war objectives correspond to the goals of the liberal-minority coalition. Unless such "objectives" can be established or invented, the news media are likely to remain indifferent or even hostile. If North Vietnam had had a fascist dictator instead of the patriarchal "Uncle Ho," [13] if it had mistreated Jews and Negroes [14] instead of Vietnamese peasants, the theater of

---

12. Americans themselves would not be likely to hold any party or faction in high respect that invited the Vietnamese army into the United States to help defend it from an attack by other Americans. The appearance of foreign troops on either side in the Civil War would certainly have stiffened the resistance of the other. One reason Americans were able to escape defeat in Korea was that there were many fewer North Koreans than South Koreans, a proportion which does not prevail in Vietnam. The North Koreans had to call in the Chinese to save them, thereby robbing their propaganda of some of its nationalist, anti-foreign appeal. South Korea's population is 29,000,000; North Korea's 12,000,000. In contrast, North Vietnam's population is 20,000,000; South Vietnam's 16,000,000. The ethnic differences of the two nations should also be kept in mind. According to Darlington, the frontier between North and South Vietnam is "one of the great racial boundaries of the world." *The Evolution of Society*, p. 615.

13. The late Drew Pearson, who was syndicated in 650 papers, twice as many as any other columnist, compared Ho Chi Minh to George Washington. *San Francisco Chronicle*, June 2, 1965 and *Time*, Sept. 12, 1969, p. 82.

14. Many Negro soldiers in Vietnam had special war aims of their own. Almost half of those questioned said they would use arms to gain their rights when they returned to the States. There were several military skirmishes between white and black troops during the course of the war, and 305 attacks on whites with fragmentation grenades, resulting in 101 deaths, *Miami Herald*, Nov. 10, 1972, p. 2A, and *Time*, Sept. 19, 1969, p. 22 and Jan. 23, 1971, p. 34.

operations would have been extended to North Vietnam and the war quickly won. The American experience in Korea had already demonstrated the coldness and opposition of liberal and minority intellectuals to a conflict which did not have the right ideological ingredients to attract their support.

The most and the best that America can do for the nations of Asia is to leave them alone. For many of the smaller countries neutrality is the surest protection against invasion or revolution. Without the slightest assistance from the United States, the Indonesians rose up in 1965, liquidated 400,000 Communists and their supporters and established a relatively stable government.[15] The chances are that the same process, when and if communist agitation becomes intolerable, will succeed in the Philippine Islands. The Indonesian experience may even be repeated in Malaysia, Thailand and Burma. If, on the other hand, America's retirement from the Far East should produce a new surge of Communist infiltration, then it must be hoped—and it is a well-founded hope—that those nations which succumb will soon be as anti-Chinese as Communist Russia or as anti-Russian as Communist China or as neutral as Communist Yugoslavia.

There are only two countries in the Far East—or more correctly in Australasia—with which the United States should maintain the firmest military ties. These are Australia and New Zealand. Here the American commitment should transcend the usual materialistic and ideological considerations of strategy, anti-communism, self-determination and democracy, and rest on the more permanent and solid foundations of biological and cultural affinity. Australia and New Zealand, inhabited by fourteen million people of largely British descent, are the last frontier of the Northern European, who is never really happy unless he has a frontier. Since there were no Asians, only a few Stone Age aborigines, on the Australian continent when the whites arrived, Chinese, Japanese and

15. Indonesia, like some other Asian nations, is a Moslem country and, unlike some Christian nations, no Moslem country has ever turned Communist. It might also be noted that there are large, acquisitive and economically dominant Chinese minorities spread throughout most of Southeast Asia. Much as the economic success of Jews gives rise to anti-Semitism in the West, the affluence of the Chinese minorities provokes outbursts of anti-Sinicism in the East.

other Orientals can hardly accuse Australians of being white exploiters of the yellow man.[16]

Australia has a selective immigration policy that is intended to double or triple the country's population in the next several decades without, however, altering its basic racial composition.[17] Unless this policy is changed, Australia may eventually be the center of the most advanced and authentic expression of Western life, and a final port of call for those North Americans and Northern Europeans who allowed their own countries to become minority-ridden bedlams.

There is even a distinct possibility that Australia, the last great nation to be founded by Northern Europeans, may survive the longest by having learned in time the causes of the others' decline.[18]

---

16. Australia's aboriginal minority now totals 40,000, plus 30,000 half-castes. The aborigines belong to the separate Australoid race, have a coloration that ranges from sooty black to brown and are distinguished by their beetling brows, sloping foreheads and projecting jaws. Coon, *The Living Races of Man*, pp. 12, 310. Their low place on the human evolutionary scale makes it difficult for even the most equalitarian-minded anthropologist to credit them with the same mental abilities as whites or Mongoloids.

17. The 1966 Australian census showed a total population of 11,550,462, which included 11,039,387 Australians of British descent and 229,191 whites of other than British descent. There were 31,970 Australians who described themselves as Hebrews.

18. The Labour party victory in the 1972 election brought in a new welfare-oriented, equalitarian-minded government replete with high-level minority advisers, pornography, permissiveness and many other trappings of the typical Western democracy. Worst of all, the government immediately set about to "unwhiten" Australia's traditional immigration policy. Let this trend continue and Australia, in the words of poet A. D. Hope, may in fact become "the last of lands, the emptiest . . . where second-hand Europeans pullulate timidly on the edge of alien shores." In 1975, however, the Labour government was thrown out by an anti-Whitlam landslide.

Chapter 35

The United States and the Middle East

T̲HE EXACT GEOGRAPHICAL makeup of the Middle East has never been authoritatively defined or agreed upon by mapmakers, historians or experts in foreign affairs. Here it will be demarcated, perhaps too inclusively, as Persia, Iraq, Jordan, the Arabian peninsula and those countries contiguous to the Eastern Mediterranean ranging clockwise from Turkey through Algeria. It was in the Middle East that man first brought forth the phenomenon of civilization. It is in the Middle East, if the Arab-Israeli war grinds on much longer, that a nuclear confrontation may bring much of civilization to an end.

The United States was involved in Middle Eastern matters as far back as 1805 when Captain William Eaton, directing a land attack on the ports of the Barbary Pirates, marched a handful of American marines—and a few hundred Greeks, Bedouins and Arab camel drivers—five hundred miles across the desert from Egypt to the eastern edge of present-day Libya, where he captured the city of Derna.[1] Ten years later, Stephen Decatur with the help of an American naval squadron forced the Dey of Algiers to stop levying tribute on American vessels and holding American seamen for ransom.[2]

---

1. Henry Adams, *History of the U.S. during the First Administration of Thomas Jefferson,* Boni and Liveright, N.Y., 1930, Book II, pp. 432, 488.
2. Kendrick Babcock, "The Rise of American Nationality," *The Historians' History of the United States,* Putnam, New York, 1966, p. 458.

For more than a century thereafter, American relations with Middle Eastern nations were, on the whole, economic in nature, of small historical import, and friendly. It was only after World War II, when the United States was drawn into the void left by the imploding British Empire, that the Middle East drew the serious attention of American diplomacy. The Truman Doctrine (1947), in response to Stalin's resurrection of old Czarist designs on Constantinople, allocated part of a $400 million aid program to Turkey. In return for arms, money and full-scale military assistance in the event of a Russian invasion, Turkey gave the United States the right to construct air bases and became an American ally.

Then, in 1948, the liberal-minority coalition succeeded in shifting the fulcrum of America's Middle Eastern policy from Turkey to Israel, where it has remained ever since. The Balfour Declaration, by means of which the British government bought the support of world Jewry in World War I, has been mentioned earlier.[3] It must now be added that, while promising British backing for a Jewish homeland in Palestine, Britain had two years earlier, in 1915, made similar promises to the Arabs to enlist them in the fight against Turkey, Germany's ally in the Middle East.[4] The Palestinian Arabs, whose country had been ruled by Turkey for four hundred years, did not need much urging. But when the war had come to an end, when Turkey had lost all its Arab lands, when the League of Nations had given Britain the Palestinian mandate, the British government made no effort to make good its word to either side beyond allowing an ominous increase in Zionist immigration. Britain had in effect sold a house it did not own to two different buyers, the prior sale having been to its Arab occupants.

The size and rate of Zionist immigration is the key to all that followed. In World War I, Jews comprised 10 percent of

---

3. See p. 435.
4. Britain's High Commissioner to Egypt gave formal assurances regarding Arab independence in the Middle East to the Emir of Mecca, later the King of Hejaz, in what has come to be known as the McMahon-Hussein correspondence. It might be noted that World War I hero and desert fighter T. E. Lawrence was deeply indignant at his country for what he considered its later betrayal of the Arab cause. Sachar, *The Course of Modern Jewish History*, pp. 370–1 and Yale, *The Near East*, pp. 243–4, 320.

the Palestine population. By 1940, there were 456,743 Jews in Palestine—one-third of the population. The remaining two-thirds consisted of 145,063 Christians and 1,143,336 Moslems.[5] The ancestors of the latter had lived in Palestine for a hundred generations. After an absence of nearly two thousand years, it was the Jews who were the newcomers.

The Nazi persecution of European Jewry stimulated a worldwide Zionist effort to make the glowing dream of Israel an immediate reality. An unprecedented, intercontinental lobbying campaign, seasoned with mounting acts of Jewish terrorism,[6] finally drove the British to hand Palestine over to the United Nations and withdraw. The Zionists were ready. On the very day the last British High Commissioner left Palestine (May 14, 1948), the Republic of Israel was proclaimed. President Truman recognized it exactly ten minutes later,[7] despite President Roosevelt's written pledge to King Ibn Saud of Saudi Arabia (April 5, 1945) that as head of the United States government he would take no action which might prove hostile to the Arab people.[8]

Russia also hastened to recognize Israel, knowing that turmoil between Arab and Jew would smooth the entrance of Soviet communism into a sun-drenched, oil-rich southland long coveted by the Czars. Even the United Nations ultimately welcomed Israel as its fifty-ninth member (1949), although the Israelis had assassinated the UN mediator, Count Bernadotte, and although the creation of Israel by military might was in total violation of the letter and spirit of the UN charter.

Even before the establishment of Israel, war had broken out between the Jews and Arabs. The Jewish terrorist attack on Dair Yasin in April, 1948, in which 250 Arab villagers were indiscriminately slaughtered, half of them women and children,[9] precipitated an Arab exodus which eventually to-

---

5. Population statistics from *Ency. Brit.*, Vol. 17, pp. 133–4.
6. The Stern and Irgun terrorist gangs, armed with American Lend-Lease weapons stolen by the truckload, ran wild through Palestine, shooting down British soldiers. In July 1946, they set off a bomb in a Jerusalem hotel, killing ninety-one people, mostly civilians. *Ency. Brit.*, Vol. 17, p. 136.
7. Sachar, *The Course of Modern Jewish History*, p. 479.
8. Yale, *op. cit.*, p. 402.
9. *Ency. Brit.*, Vol. 17, p. 136. It is not known if the soldiers who com-

taled 2,700,000 displaced persons (the original refugees, their children born in exile and the latest refugees from the 1967 war).[10] Since most Palestinian Arabs and Arabs of neighboring states had barely progressed beyond the feudal stages of society, they were no match for the Westernized Jews—whose highest-ranking officers were mentally and physically often closer to the Northern European than to any Jewish stereotype.[11] Not surprisingly, the history of Arab-

---

mitted this massacre was ever punished. Most soldiers who took part in another atrocity—the machine-gunning of forty-nine Arab villagers returning to the hamlet of Kafr Kassim (Oct. 29, 1956), fourteen of them women with children in their arms—went scot-free after standing trial. A few, however, were given a one-year prison sentence. These sentences, were somewhat lighter than those given Nazi perpetrators of atrocities against Jews. Moreover, there was not the slightest outcry from the news media against the Israeli war criminals. *San Francisco Chronicle,* Jan 10, 1962 and Alfred Lilienthal, *The Other Side of the Coin,* Devin-Adair, New York, 1965, pp. 219–20. Within Israel, however, there has been some distress over the eventual repercussions of military adventurism. After an Israeli terrorist attack on Jordan in February 1951, four Hebrew University professors asked: "Is this the Jewish tradition on which we believe the state of Israel was founded? Is this the regard for human life on which the Jewish people stood when they were not yet a political nation? Is this the way of proving to the world that our nation upholds the principle of justice?" See William Ernest Hocking's article on Israel in *Christian Century,* Sept. 19, 1951. One of the worst and most incomprehensible acts of the Israelis was the looting of the Old City of Jerusalem in the 1967 war, described by Evan Wilson, the U.S. Consul General and Minister at Jerusalem, in his book, *Key to Peace,* The Middle East Institute, Washington, D.C., 1970, p. 111. A complete list of atrocities can be found in the UN *Report of Special Committee to Investigate Israeli Practices.*

10. In 1970 there were 3,000,000 people known as Palestinians. Half of them were refugees located in filthy tent camps in the Middle East; 300,000 remained in Israel; 700,000 were working in Jordan and other Arab countries. The remaining 500,000 are dispersed around the world in their own *diaspora. Life,* June 12, 1970, p. 28. In a rather exhaustive investigation of the present Palestinian refugee situation, James Michener said that the 1967 UN estimate of the number living in the refugee camps, 1,317,749, was too high, but admitted that 357,000 more Arabs fled Palestine during the 1967 reprise of the war. *New York Times Magazine,* Sept. 27, 1970, pp. 23, 25, 118.

11. Without question, the toughest stratum of European Jewry went to Palestine in the turn-of-the-century pioneering days, when most Jews were going to New York. Sabras, native-born Jewish Palestinians, evince their own particular "inside racism" by insisting that they are Israelis, not Jews. The lack of a Jewish stereotype in Israel is underlined by the popularity of a favorite Israeli anecdote—the reply of the tourist when asked how he liked Israel. "Fine," he said, "but where are the Jews?" Robert Ardrey, *The Territorial Imperative,* Atheneum, New York, 1966, p. 310.

Jewish military operations has been that of one Arab defeat after another—until the 1973 war. Even after adopting the hit-and-run commando tactics more suitable to the traditional fighting style of the desert raider, the Arabs never did any real damage to the Israelis. But in 1973 the picture changed. Israel's myth of invincibility faded with Egypt's successful crossing of the Suez and the deadly havoc wrought by Russian missiles on the Israeli air force. Only massive American aid saved the situation.

Today, the Palestinian and Jewish proportions of the population of Israel are almost the exact reverse of what they were in the same area fifty years ago. Half of the 2,389,000 Israeli Jews are *Schwarzim,* dark Jews from North Africa and Asia, who are rapidly outbreeding the lighter European elements.[12] Immigration is not helping to redress this racial imbalance nor doing much to build up the population as a whole. In 1961, 3,774 Jewish immigrants entered the United States *from* Israel.[13] In 1966, almost as many Jews left Israel as arrived,[14] some even going to Germany. Most of the emigrants were Western Jews. If the present demographic trend does not drastically change, European-descended Israelis will eventually become a minority.[15]

Almost totally dedicated to Israel in spirit, American Jews have nevertheless preferred to support the Jewish homeland by opening their purses rather than by dodging Arab bullets. Only one hundred American Jews (as of 1969) were serving in the Israeli armed forces.[16] Financially, however, the con-

---

12. J. Robert Moskin, "Prejudice in Israel," *Look,* Oct. 5, 1965, pp. 67 ff. According to Moskin, the *Schwarzim* have charged European Jews with discrimination because the latter hold on to all the important state jobs. As in America, the darker-skinned portion of the population has started a few riots to emphasize its displeasure and frustration.

13. *American Jewish Yearbook,* 1963, p. 77.

14. The exact number was 19,700 immigrants and 19,000 emigrants. In 1960 there were 40,000 immigrants, one-third from Western countries. By 1975, despite intense pressure from American Jewry, immigration to Israel from Russia was down to 8,518 (*Time,* Jan. 12, 1976, p. 24). Nevertheless, Congress appropriated $100 million to pay Russian Jews' traveling expenses and continued to withhold most-favored nation status for Russian trade.

15. The orientalization of Israel does not disturb Foreign Minister Abba Eban. "[Our] cultural future," he stated, "lies in the victory of the existing culture, which is European in its roots and Hebrew in its garb." *Look,* Oct. 1965, p. 72.

16. World Press Review, WNET, New York, Nov. 3, 1969. Among their other special privileges, American Jews are allowed dual citizenship.

tribution of American Jews to Israel has been staggering. So
has the contribution of others. Some have estimated the total
to be as high as $32 billion.[17] In 1973 alone, Congress author-
ized grants of $2.6 billion. The United Jewish Appeal
and the sale of Israeli bonds have recently been producing
more than $1 billion a year for Israel. German reparations to
the Jewish state now amount to nearly $1 billion and settle-
ments to individual Israelis have reached the multibillion figure. Help from other countries has also been astronomical.
Never has there been such an outpouring of funds—and all
to a nation of only 3,000,000.

Thirty-five percent of the Israeli budget is covered by foreign contributions. Since the nation runs an annual trade
deficit that ranges from $420 million (1963) to $674 million
(1970), Jewish charity and American and German government subsidies keep it from bankruptcy.[18] An equivalent
American trade deficit for 1970, based on the Israeli-
American population ratio, would be more than $47 billion.

American financial assistance to Israel is the highest per
capita aid given any nation.[19] In 1959, the American taxpayer contributed more to the social security of each Israeli
citizen than to the social security of each American citizen.[20]
In the matter of financing Israel arms purchases, the Department of Defense has a special deal with the Export-
Import Bank whereby it pays only 3.5 percent interest on
money for Israel arms credits, while for arms credits to other
nations it must pay 4 to 5.5 percent.[21] In 1969, when American scientists in Florida were driving taxis as a result of
space cutbacks, federal agencies were giving $23 million a
year in grants to Israeli scientists.[22]

17. Benjamin Friedman, *Borger News-Herald*, Borger, Texas, Jan. 7,
1974, p. 2. Much of the aid has been involuntary. Most American taxpayers
would never have approved the tax deductibility of financial gifts to Israel
or many of the Congressional grants. Quite a few members of the United
Auto Workers and the Teamsters disagree with the huge purchases of Israeli
bonds (paying only 5½%) by the directors of union pension funds.
18. Lilienthal, *The Other Side of the Coin*, p. 348, and *Time*, Nov. 19,
1956, p. 27 and Oct. 25, 1968, p. 63.
19. *S. F. Sunday Examiner & Chronicle*, July 2, 1967, Sec. A, p. 6.
20. Lilienthal, *op. cit.*, p. 346.
21. *New York Times*, July 31, 1967, p. 12.
22. *Report of the Select Subcommittee on Education*, p. 91. The Weizmann Institute and several other Israeli institutions are chartered by the

A great deal of the fantastic outpouring of American wealth to Israel has been made possible by an outright tax dodge. The Internal Revenue Service has ruled that contributions to Jewish "charitable organizations" that funnel money to Israel are tax deductible. When the Senate Foreign Relations Committee questioned the tax-deductible status of funds which are eventually used to purchase war materials for a foreign nation or to replace funds used for such purposes, members were accused of starting an inquisition and the matter was quickly dropped.[23] If Americans bought foreign securities (until 1974), they ordinarily had to pay an equalization tax. If they bought Israeli bonds, they did not have to pay such a tax, because Israel had been designated by the United States as a "less developed" nation. Compared to "less developed" countries like Afghanistan, San Salvador and Haiti, Israel is a plutocrat among nations. It has more money in circulation per capita than all but fourteen of the world's richest states.[24]

In all the recent discussions about "stopping the dollar drain" and plugging up loopholes in the income tax, not a single public figure has mentioned American financial aid to Israel, one of the most important sources of the dollar drain and one of the widest of the tax loopholes. The purchases of American tourists abroad are limited and the oil depletion allowance is reduced. The foundations are attacked. But tax-free money still flows in torrents to Israel—money that not only escapes the United States Treasury, so that every American is taxed a little more, but money that escapes the country altogether, so that the dollar is weakened and the balance of payments worsened.

The Internal Revenue Service is not the only government agency that has exceeded the bounds of its authority in helping the cause of Zionism. In the hectic days just preceding Israel's creation, the FBI winked at the establishment of a

---

Board of Regents of the State of New York, which qualifies them for additional U.S. Government support. *Ibid.*, p. 222.

23. Max Freedman, *Arizona Daily Star,* Aug. 8, 1963 and *San Francisco Chronicle,* Aug. 2, 1963, p. 10.

24. Associated Press report, Sept. 11, 1971. In Israeli elections political parties use American tax-deductible dollars for campaign expenses.

clandestine Zionist radio station on the Eastern seaboard and at the rash of gunrunning and other violations of American neutrality laws.[25] Rudolph Sonneborn, the millionaire head of Witco Chemical, set up in New York City what amounted to the American branch of Hagannah, the Zionist underground organization.[26] Five hundred American and Canadian flyers, many of them non-Jews, pieced together the Israeli Air Force while Palestine was still under British rule.[27] Three United States Army officers served in Hagannah under the command of Chief of Staff Yaacov Dori as the Zionists opened their military attack against the British occupation troops.[28] Members of the Office of Strategic Services taught Zionist agents the use of ciphers and codes in a secret New York City espionage school.[29] It was all very gallant and exciting, except that it ended in the expulsion of a peaceful, agricultural population from its ancient homeland and created a festering international sore that will take decades, if not centuries, to heal.

While all these events were taking place, James Forrestal, Secretary of Defense in the Truman administration, was the only cabinet member who spoke out publicly against Zionism. In the manner of Cassandra and with equal effect, he warned of the geopolitical consequences of American sponsorship of an anachronistic imperialism and colonialism that brought back memories of pith helmets and swagger sticks to Third World nations—the very nations then being assured by the State Department of America's peaceful, anti-

---

25. After two Zionist agents were arrested at the Canadian border for arms smuggling Robert Nathan, a White House assistant, got them a personal interview with FBI Director J. Edgar Hoover, who offered them his cooperation. Leonard Slater, *The Pledge*, Simon and Schuster, New York, 1970, pp. 75-6. Hank Greenspun, now a rich Las Vegas and Colorado publisher, was convicted of stealing cases of rifle barrels for Israel from a U.S. Naval Supply Depot in Hawaii, yet neither he nor any other American Jewish gunrunner guilty of similar charges ever spent a day in jail. *Ibid.*, pp. 75, 198-9. The only one who did go to prison for illegally obtaining arms for Israel was Charlie Winters, a Protestant. *Ibid.*, p. 309. William Horowitz, who was deeply involved in these unlawful operations, is now a banker and a member of the Yale Corporation, the governing body of Yale University. *Ibid.*, p. 59.
26. *Ibid.*, p. 22 ff.
27. *Ibid.*, p. 309.
28. *Ibid.*, pp. 101-3.
29. *Ibid.*, p. 117.

imperialist, anti-colonialist intentions. The vituperation Forrestal received from press and radio was one of the factors which led to his suicide.[30]

Dean Acheson, at that time Under Secretary of State and extremely active in foreign affairs, chose not to support Forrestal and obediently executed Truman's pro-Israeli policy, although he later frankly admitted it was against the "totality of American interest" in the Middle East.[31] Some twenty years after the fact, Acheson also explained that Truman did not, as British Foreign Minister Bevin had charged, commit the United States to Israel in order to woo the Jewish vote. According to Acheson, Truman's pro-Israel stand was due almost entirely to his friendship with Eddie Jacobson, his erstwhile partner in a short-lived haberdashery business in Kansas City.[32]

From the birth of Israel up to the present, a blind, unquestioning pro-Zionist ideology has so permeated and dominated American thought that, whenever the discussion has turned to the Middle East, leaders in every walk of public life abandon all reason and judgment, not to mention their intellectual integrity.[33] The same educators who insist on the

---

30. See footnote 42, p. 310.

31. Dean Acheson, *Present at the Creation,* Norton, New York, 1969, p. 169. The news media never criticized Acheson for his pusillanimity in refusing to fight for the Middle Eastern policy he believed in. But it hailed him for his courage when he made the memorable statement, "I will not turn my back on Alger Hiss."

32. *Ibid.* A leading Jewish scholar does not exactly agree with the Acheson theory. Howard Sachar asserts that Truman was also attracted to the Israeli cause by the pressure of such important American Jews as Governor Herbert Lehman of New York, Jacob "Jake" Arvey, the Chicago political boss, and David Niles, Roosevelt's and Truman's Special Assistant for Minority Affairs. *The Course of Modern Jewish History,* p. 471.

33. As one writer put it, "Zionist propaganda in this country has been so powerful, so contemptuous of constraints . . . that the few voices raised in criticism of it have scarcely been heard." *San Francisco Examiner, Book Week,* May 23, 1965, p. 15. Actually the only voices that have spoken out loudly and clearly against Zionism were those of the handful of Jews who belonged to the American Council for Judaism. The Council, which once made the dramatic but futile gesture of giving $3,000 to Palestinian refugees, lost 80 percent of its membership a year after Israel was established. In June 1967, many of its most prominent members were supporting Israel as devotedly as the most outspoken Zionists. Yaffe, *op. cit.,* pp. 186–8 and *Commentary,* August 1967, p. 70. The leitmotiv of Jewish anti-Zionism springs from the fear that Zionism in the long run will augment rather than diminish anti-Semitism.

desegregation of American schools have solidly supported Israel, which has segregated schools for its Arab minority.[34] The same churchmen and laymen who preach the separation of church and state, the equality of the sexes and opposition to any racial or religious tests for marriage have stood four-square for Israel, where church and state are one, where interfaith marriages are forbidden and where women who worship in synagogues are segregated behind screened-off galleries.

The same "One Worlders" who founded the United Nations have had only good things to say for the Zionist diplomacy that has flaunted almost all UN resolutions on Israel.[35] The same "decent" liberals who believe in the self-determination of peoples and the peaceful arbitration of international disputes have given their unstinting approval to a nation founded on old-fashioned, blood-and-iron tactics of conquest and the military dispersion of the natives. The same editorial writers who adulate leaders of anti-colonialist and socialist nations transformed Egypt's late President Nasser, the anti-colonialist, socialist leader par excellence, into a latter-day Hitler. The same opinion makers who called South Vietnam's Vice-Premier Ky a butcher applauded—whenever Israeli foreign policy so dictated—the arch reactionary King Hussein of Jordan when his Bedouin mercenaries laid down artillery barrages on Palestinian refugee camps. The same writers, painters and musicians who are horrified at the slightest restriction of artistic expression have had nothing but praise for a country which officially banned the music of Wagner and Richard Strauss.[36] The same pacifists who fought the draft so bitterly in the United States clamorously applaud a government which not only drafts all able-bodied males between eighteen and twenty-six for twenty-six months, but unmarried women of the same age for twenty months.[37]

As the 1967 replay of the periodic Arab-Israeli conflict approached, the liberal-minority establishment seemed to lose all contact with logic and rationality and lapsed into a kind

---

34. Israel has 296 public schools for Arabs only. *1969 World Almanac,* p. 526.

35. When the UN turned sharply against Israel in the Zionism equals racism vote, American liberals obediently turned against the UN.

36. *San Francisco Chronicle,* June 18, 1966, p. 34.

37. *1969 World Almanac,* p. 526.

of babbling schizophrenia. The nation's foremost advocate of nonviolence, Martin Luther King, Jr., demanded America use force, if necessary, to keep open the strait of Tiran, which Nasser had ordered closed to ships bringing strategic war materials to the Israeli port of Elath.[38] Members of peace groups threw down their placards and demonstrated with war groups.[39] Senator Wayne Morse, the Senate's leading dove, stood up and said the United States Navy should sail into the Gulf of Aqaba "with flags flying." [40] The late Robert Kennedy, although busy establishing an anti-war image for the following year's presidential race, came on almost as strongly.[41] The ideological flip-flop of America's most prominent intellectuals and politicians was so complete, the Orwellian doublethink and doubletalk so incredible,[42] that it could not altogether escape the attention of the less fanatical news organs.

The warm feelings of American Jews toward Israel are understandable. But their totalitarian dedication to Zionism has created a grave conflict of interest in regard to their duties and responsibilities as American citizens. French and Russian officials, who are allowed some free expression on the issue, have already called into question the double loyalty of Zionists and Zionist supporters.[43] In America, however, the following questions must still be asked—and answered—in silence: How American is the American citizen who has forced

---

38. *New York Times,* May 28, 1967, p. 4. Both sides of the strait, which separates the Red Sea from the Gulf of Aqaba, were Arab territory. But at the north end of the Gulf of Aqaba lay Elath, a small Israeli port, the shipping point for Israel's trade with the East since the shutdown of the Suez Canal.

39. *Time,* June 2, 1967, p. 11.

40. *Ibid.*

41. *New York Times,* May 24, 1967, p. 16.

42. It was even more incredible after the 1973 flareup of the perennial war. There was the edifying spectacle of Bella Abzug, the superdovish Representative from New York City, returning from Israel waving a handful of atrocity photographs and Senators Edward Kennedy and Walter Mondale voting to give Israel the same napalm and anti-personnel bombs that had so outraged them when used in Vietnam. *Miami Herald,* Dec. 26, 1973, p. 7A.

43. In an article in *Le Monde,* René Massigli, former French Ambassador to London, wondered about the loyalty of French Jews, particularly after their indifference to the attack on French President Pompidou by American Jews. *New York Times,* March 2, 1970, p. 15.

through a foreign policy that in a few short years has made the United States, once their firm friend, the enemy of most of the world's 115,000,000 Arabs and many of the world's 474,000,000 Moslems? [44] How American is the American citizen who has knowingly promoted and financed a program of military adventurism that gives Communist propaganda mills an unheard-of opportunity to discredit America in the Middle East, an area that contains two-thirds of the world's proven oil reserves and where the United States has a multi-billion-dollar petroleum investment? [45]

Today, as a consequence of American connivance in the genesis of Israel, Russia has become the champion and friend of the Arabs, once the most anti-communist people on earth. The Soviet navy, with almost as many vessels as the United States Sixth Fleet, patrols the Eastern Mediterranean and has even penetrated the Red Sea and the Indian Ocean. As one report stated in 1968, "The defeat of the United Arab Republic by Israel, jubilantly treated as a defeat for Russia, actually has proved also to be a disguised blessing for Moscow. The Soviets are now gradually taking over both the Republic of Yemen and the larger Republic of South Yemen created by Britain's walkout from Aden . . . the United States is go-

44. Although anti-Semitic acts are not tolerated in the U.S., anti-Arabic acts are. In 1966, King Faisal of Saudi Arabia, one of America's few remaining friends in the Middle East, was officially snubbed during a visit to New York City. Mayor Lindsay refused to give him an official reception for fear of offending his Jewish constituency. *New York Times,* June 24, 1966, p. 1. Lindsay was even more discourteous during the visit of French President Pompidou in early 1970. He not only refused to greet Pompidou, but ran off to Washington and remained there while the French president was in New York. In Chicago, Madame Pompidou was spat upon, jostled and cursed by Jewish pickets who were not afraid to create a serious incident with America's oldest ally in order to vent their spleen on France for selling fighter bombers to Libya. *New York Times,* March 3, 1970, p. 28. When Premier Golda Meir of Israel arrived in New York in late 1969, Lindsay treated her to a modern version of a Roman triumph.

45. Or had before the U.S. support of Israel greatly accelerated the nationalization of oil by various Middle Eastern countries. American military aid to Israel was directly responsible for the 1973 oil embargo which spurred inflation, quadrupled the OPEC cartel's price for oil and triggered a worldwide economic recession. Today the U.S. gets a small but vital percentage of its oil from the Middle East. But by 1980 it may have to import 50 percent of its oil, at which time the friendship of the Arab states will assume an even greater strategic significance. In 1970, before the oil embargo and the oil price hike, the net benefit of America's Middle Eastern oil investment to the U.S. balance of payments was $1.5 billion.

ing to discover with astonishment that it has lost its entire power structure from the Mediterranean to Southeast Asia." [46]

The policy which has already cost America the friendship of the Arab world and the respect of the Moslem world may also carry a much higher price. The Middle Eastern conflict is a chronic infection which at any moment can flare up into a nuclear confrontation between Russia and the United States. It was pointed out earlier that the liberal-minority coalition will only lend its full support to a war in behalf of liberal goals and minority interests. As these two necessary requirements are now present in the Middle East, American intervention is not only possible but probable. It took several years to draw the United States into World Wars I and II, largely because at the outbreak of each war the liberal-minority coalition was divided on the question of intervention or at least the rate and amount of intervention. Today, the coalition is solidly united on the Middle Eastern war and can be counted upon to agitate for the immediate dispatch of an American expeditionary force at the least sign of serious trouble for Israel.

The news media are already geared for the task and behind the news media stand the war lobbies and their political acolytes. The B'nai B'rith, a secret society which describes itself as a religious and charitable organization and which exists on tax-deductible contributions, has demanded that both major political parties pledge "in specific terms" support for appropriate arms and economic aid to guarantee Israel's political and territorial sovereignty.[47] Already 59 Senators and 238 members of the House of Representatives have gone on public record in calling for the Arab nations to settle with Israel on Israel's terms.[48]

A preview of what the news media have in store for the American people in the approaching Middle Eastern showdown was provided by its coverage of the 1967 "Six-Day War." [49] Even though the Israelis launched a combined air,

---

46. *San Francisco Examiner and Chronicle,* April 7, 1968, Sec. A, p. 11.
47. *San Francisco Chronicle,* May 14, 1968, p. 16.
48. *New York Times,* May 11, 1969, p. 16E.
49. It was a six-day battle or a six-day campaign, but the Arab-Israeli war was already twenty-one years old when it took place. If present-day

land and sea assault on Egypt, Jordan and Syria on the morning of June 5, 1967, it was several days before the American public was told who attacked whom. There were press, radio and television correspondents all over the Middle East, all primed for the outbreak of hostilities. But still no one seemed to know what was going on.[50] The strategy was obvious. Israeli aggression was to be concealed as long as possible, so Israel could conquer as much territory as possible. On the other hand, when Egypt and Syria were the first to attack in 1973, the media immediately branded the Arabs as the aggressors.

The news media offered further proof of their cringing Zionist bias by soft-pedaling the previously mentioned Israeli assault on the *Liberty,* an unarmed American communications ship. Thirty-four American sailors were killed and seventy-five wounded in an hour-long attack on a bright, sunlit day. In the course of the operation, the Israelis managed to shoot away a special American flag, so large (five by eight feet) as to practically rule out a case of mistaken identity.[51] After the facts came to light, not a single important public figure in America raised his voice in protest, a strange and unique silence in a nation which used to be so concerned with the freedom of the seas and the safety of its shipping. As has been noted, the sinking of the *Maine* in Havana harbor in 1898 was a *casus belli.* The attack on the *Chesapeake,*

---

headline writers had been alive in the fourteenth century, and had been as pro-English as they are now pro-Zionist, they probably would have described the battle of Crécy, which opened the Hundred Years' War between England and France, as a "One-Day War."

50. To this day, many Americans actually believe that the Egyptians started the battle. Both during and after the June 1967 fighting, very few stories of Arab suffering appeared in the press, even though the city of Suez was practically destroyed by bombs, artillery shells and napalm and its population of 268,000 reduced to 10,000. In Ismailia nearly every building was leveled and almost the entire population of 100,000 forced to vacate. *Time,* May 17, 1971, p. 28. One can well imagine what the news media would have done if the agony of Ismailia had been visited on Tel Aviv or Haifa.

51. *National Review,* July 11, 1967, p. 720 and *Time,* June 23, 1967, p. 16. The real reasons for the attack have, of course, never been published. The best guess is that the Israelis did not desire the presence of electronic eavesdroppers while the attack against the Arabs was in progress. The intercepted radio commands might have destroyed the illusion that the Israelis were fighting a defensive war.

which cost only three American lives, led to Jefferson's embargo on all foreign commerce.[52] The sinking of the British-owned *Lusitania,* which carried one hundred thirty-nine Americans to the bottom, almost brought about a declaration of war against Germany. But a direct attack against an American naval vessel by a foreign power in 1967 produced neither indignation nor retaliation.

The American press was equally reticent in its handling of the "Lavon affair." In 1954, Israeli secret agents were preparing to bomb and burn down various American installations (including the American library) in Cairo, Egypt, and blame the Egyptians. The idea was to further poison American-Arab relations and manufacture more American sympathy for Israel. The plot was uncovered in time and the principal agents arrested. Eventually the Israeli cabinet had to admit Israel's involvement and it then underwent some important reshuffling.[53] But still the American news media and the State Department did not consider the plot worthy of serious or extended comment. The Lavon affair can be viewed as an abortive dress rehearsal of what can be expected of Israeli cloak-and-dagger diplomacy in the future.

If there were ever a reason for the American Majority to regain control of American foreign policy it would be to undo the catastrophic damage that Zionism has inflicted upon the American posture in the Middle East. By aligning itself with Israel, a state created by the wholesale eviction of the Palestinian population, the United States, so frequently reproached in the past for moralizing and overmoralizing its foreign policy, now reveals itself to be a nation of immoralists.

The hypocrisy of the American Ambassador to the United Nations, Arthur Goldberg, himself a Jew and a Zionist,[54] abstaining and temporizing during the 1967 Israeli *coup de main,* while the overwhelming majority of delegates was calling for a cease-fire and the withdrawal of all troops to the pre-attack frontiers, will not be quickly forgotten, particularly by those who once believed that the United States

---

52. *Ency. Brit.,* Vol. 22, p. 761.
53. Safran, *United States and Israel,* p. 236.
54. Goldberg was a Zionist supporter while in private law practice. Litvinoff, *A Peculiar People,* p. 59.

stood for the rights of all peoples, including Arabs, to self-determination. Neither will President Johnson's solemn promise a few days before the renewed outbreak of hostilities that the United States would oppose any change in the frontiers of Middle Eastern nations.[55]

When the smoke had cleared away and the frontiers of three Arab countries had again been pushed back by armed force—Egypt's all the way to Suez—Johnson did not bother to eat his words. He simply chose to ignore them. Just as conspicuously silent were the Protestant and Catholic churches, even though more thousands of Arab Christians now swelled the ranks of those who had already been driven from their homes by previous Israeli aggression.[56] Christian attitudes toward the Holy Land were not exactly those of the Crusades.

What has happened in the Middle East since the end of World War II offers a valuable object lesson on the nature and extent of minority power in the United States. The national interest required the safeguarding of the huge American oil investment, the encouragement of area-wide political stability to restrain Russian military and economic penetration, and the presence of friendly, pro-American, anti-communist governments.[57] But all this has been given up for the sake of a numerically inconsequential American minority. Even Moslem Turkey and Iran, which should be the real bastions of American power in the Middle East, are drifting away into anti-Americanism as the United States puts more of its strategic eggs in the basket of Israel, a nation whose very presence keeps the area in constant ferment and disequilibrium. The rapprochement of Egypt with the United States and Israel will do nothing to end this ferment since the causes of it, the existence of Israel and the dispossession of the Palestinians, still remain.

In the conquest and settlement of Palestine, the Israelis

---

55. *Time*, June 2, 1967, p. 11.

56. The young Sirhan Sirhan was one of these refugee Arab Christians. The young presidential aspirant, Robert Kennedy, was one of the leading American Christians. The two met in the basement of the Hotel Ambassador in Los Angeles at 12:16 A.M., June 5, 1968.

57. Even as late as 1970, no Arab state permitted the existence of a Communist party within its borders. Israel has two Communist parties.

have imitated the work of their remote forebears by making the desert bloom and transforming vast stretches of sandy waste into fertile farm lands and fruitful orchards. Their brilliantly executed desert campaigns will rank in military history with those of Joshua, Tancred, Saladin, Lawrence, Allenby, Montgomery and Rommel, and have come close to the fulfillment of Biblical prophecy. All that is lacking is the Messiah.

But those who are caught up in desert politics—not only American Jews but Zionists and Zionist supporters everywhere—should beware of mirages. For the first time since A.D. 135, Jews have become a majority in a Jewish state—and those who make up this majority have been transformed into something which is almost the opposite of the historic Jewish image. Also transformed is the ex-majority of Palestine. After years of exile, poverty and defeat, the Palestinian Arabs, the Middle Eastern "wretched of the earth," are as racist, as hungry for heroism and as obsessed about their homeland as their Zionist counterparts. These Palestinian exiles and the populations of the neighboring Arab countries which shelter them may be far behind the Westernized Zionists technically and economically. But they are not spear-carrying natives. They may not be able to make their own advanced weapons, but they know where to get them.

And so the Mideast crisis deepens, for Jews, for Arabs and for the world. Jewish nationalism begets Arab nationalism, Jewish racism begets Arab racism, Zionism begets anti-Zionism, Semitism begets anti-Semitism.[58] At best, the conflict will sputter along for decades, laying waste the physical if not the spiritual resources of the entire area. At worst, it

---

58. A century before the birth of modern Israel, Dostoyevsky provided an inkling of present-day events in the Middle East by speculating on what would happen if the Jewish minority in Russia became the majority. "How would they [the Jews] treat them [the Russians]?" he asked. "Would they permit them to acquire equal rights? Would they permit them to worship freely in their midst? Wouldn't they convert them into slaves? Worse than that: wouldn't they skin them altogether? Wouldn't they slaughter them to the last man, to the point of complete extermination, as they used to do with alien peoples in ancient times, during their ancient history?" *The Diary of a Writer*, trans. Boris Brasol, Scribner's New York, 1949, Vol. 2, pp. 644–5.

might detonate a nuclear war, in which minuscule Israel could hardly escape annihilation.

For the United States to have aided and abetted the dispossession of the greater part of the Palestinian population is an act of barbarism. For American Jews to continue to edge the United States into the Middle Eastern imbroglio, where America has everything to lose and nothing to gain, is an act of sheer ingratitude to the nation which has given them more wealth, freedom and power than any other in the long sinusoidal curve of their history.[59]

In 1973, J. William Fulbright publicly stated: "Israel controls the Senate. The great majority of the Senate of the U.S. —somewhere around 80 percent—are completely in support of Israel; anything Israel wants."[60] This was a sensational charge, coming as it did from the respected chairman of the Senate Foreign Relations Committee. Yet it was carefully buried in the back pages of the newspapers.

In the winter of 1973–74, when long lines began to form in front of gas pumps and thousands of American workmen were laid off their jobs, the politicians continued to vote for "anything Israel wants." Everyone but the real culprit was blamed for the oil shortage. Every solution but the obvious one was recommended. The media cooperated fully in this massive deception, which was an unforgettable example of totalitarian mind bending.

It was a pathetic and shameful sight to watch Americans being duped into accepting sacrifice after sacrifice, even the possibility of the supreme sacrifice, for a racial dream that was not their own.

---

59. Israel refused to sign the 1975 Sinai agreement unless American technicians were interposed between the Israeli and Egyptian armies, thereby setting the scene for an incident which could get the U.S. into a war on Israel's side with minimum resistance and maximum speed.

60. *Miami Herald*, April 22, 1973, p. 32A. After saying this, Fulbright, in spite of being an erstwhile idol of the media and having served in the Senate for five terms, was handily defeated for reelection in 1974, as was Representative John Rarick, the only outspoken anti-Zionist in the House. The two gentlemen who beat them then voted 100 percent with the Israeli lobby.

Chapter 36

The United States and Africa

O F ALL THE SEVEN continents, with the exception of Antarctica, Africa should be of the least concern to the United States. It is far removed geographically. It has few strategic resources or raw materials—despite its abundance of uranium, diamonds, gold, chrome, tin, cocoa and rubber— which the United States cannot find elsewhere or produce artificially. No African nation or combination of them could possibly offer a serious military threat to America in the foreseeable future. The possession of all or parts of Africa by Russia or some other non-African power would probably present the conqueror with as many debits as credits. Yet, in spite of all these perfectly good reasons for keeping a proper distance, the United States is being steadily drawn deeper into African affairs. The cause, as in the Middle East, is domestic minority racism. But this time the racism is of a different and darker vintage.

Before World War I, Africa could be accurately described as a wholly-owned subsidiary of Europe. After World War II, when Europe was weary and bleeding, when the anti-imperialist promises of the Atlantic Charter and the United Nations had come home to roost, when liberalism was triumphant throughout the West, Africans both white and black decided the time had come to strike for self-government. They were as surprised as anyone when most of the colonial powers quickly and obediently capitulated. Only in Algeria, Madagascar, Kenya, Zanzibar and the Congo was independence achieved by wars of attrition or by considerable amounts of bloodshed.

Africa's pigmentation spectrum, viewed geographically from north to south, is sallow or dark white at the top, black in the center and black, brown and white at the bottom. Nothing will be said in this chapter about Egypt and the other Arab and Moslem nations of North Africa. They are only African by geography. Their religion, culture, history and racial composition—as well as their anti-Zionism—make them a part of the Middle East.

Africa's middle stratum is comprised of forty independent nations, almost all of them less than twenty-five years old.[1] These new black states, whose frontiers are often artificial and rarely correspond to tribal boundaries,[2] have not produced a striking record of political stability during their brief life span. Political and military coups, tribal feuds, massacres and civil wars have done nothing to disprove the Negro's historic incapacity for self-government.[3] Once a tribal clique or political caucus takes over, it follows the familiar diplomatic pattern of playing the West against the East in order to squeeze every last penny out of foreign aid. Having removed whites from political control and having made the carrying on of business and commerce extremely difficult and the growth of heavy industry all but impossible, the new black leaders had no choice but to persuade whites to return if the new nations were to be saved from total collapse. Without whites, most of black Africa would quickly

---

1. The count increased by two in 1975, when Portuguese Angola and Mozambique, the continent's two last colonies, were granted independence by Portuguese army dissidents who substituted a radical dictatorship of the left for a paternal dictatorship of the right. Whites promptly fled Mozambique en masse, while Angola exploded into civil war.

2. There are 2,000 tribes in black Africa, and in the Nigerian civil war some 1,000,000 members of the Ibo tribe of Biafra were killed between 1967 and 1969, *New York Times,* Nov. 23, 1969, p. 1.

3. In the new African states there were seven military takeovers, two bloody army coups, a tribal massacre, 100,000 civilian dead and a million refugees—all in the year 1966. *San Francisco Sunday Examiner, This World,* Jan. 8, 1967, p. 22. In thirty-one of these states (as of 1967), no government had been voted out of office, although all pretend to follow democratic forms. *Time,* March 31, 1967, p. 29. In the forty states, there have been thirty military coups since 1960, and two, Dahomey and Burundi, have had eight coups each. *New York Times,* June 14, 1970, p. 1.

revert, as has already happened in large areas of the Congo,[4] to the primitive Iron Age cultural level in which it languished before the advent of the colonial era.

Now that they have achieved independence—a purely nominal independence that has "hardly touched the personal life of most Africans"[5]—the black nations seem more interested in imitating white nations than in developing their own gifts and competencies. African art is in a state of steep decline,[6] and despite impassioned statements about *négritude* (American Negroes call it "soul"), the black elite builds itself ornate homes and government buildings in the Western style, speeds around in late-model Cadillacs, satiates itself on the cheaper and coarser forms of Western culture, attempts, and occasionally succeeds, in marrying *declassé* European women, and leaves the African masses to shift for themselves.[7] The late philosopher of African nationalism, Frantz Fanon, could not abide this new Negro bourgeoisie and accused it of almost as many crimes as he attributed to the white colonialists.[8]

There were only a few areas in Africa where black nationalism met strong white resistance. One was Kenya, where sixty thousand whites, a 0.6 percent minority in a total population of 9,948,000, fought and survived eight years of Mau Mau terror, only to yield to black rule at the insistence of the British government. Today, black leader Jomo Kenyatta,

---

4. *New York Times,* Oct. 22, 1969, p. 2.

5. John Hatch, *A History of Postwar Africa,* Praeger, New York, 1965, p. 404.

6. Traditionally, African artists have concentrated on sculpture. Today, most of the wood carving and bronze casting is "clumsy, imitative and mass-produced." The decorative arts have also deteriorated. There is some literature—in European languages or newly grammaticized African dialects —but almost no reading public. Smith Hempstone, *San Francisco Chronicle, This World,* Feb. 4, 1962, pp. 21–2.

7. A highly informative description of day-to-day living in new African nations is found in Thomas Molnar, *Africa: A Political Travelogue,* Fleet, New York, 1965.

8. Frantz Fanon, *The Wretched of the Earth,* trans. Constance Farrington, Grove Press, New York, 1963. See especially the chapter, "The Pitfalls of National Consciousness." Fanon, a Negro psychiatrist from Martinique, was so anti-American he criticized the "jazz howl" of American Negroes and described the U.S. as a "monster in which the taints, the sickness and the inhumanity of Europe have grown to appalling dimensions." *Ibid.,* pp. 243, 313.

an ex-Mau Mau, has become a tribal dictator. One of his first acts was to maltreat and persecute the Somali tribesmen in his domain and the 140,000 Indians, many of whom later migrated to England. The whites, skeptical of Kenyatta's promises of equal treatment, are selling their farms and leaving in droves.[9]

Rhodesia was scheduled to follow the same pattern of decolonialization. But having watched the disestablishment of the whites in Kenya and 75,000 other whites in Northern Rhodesia (now Zambia), 220,000 white Southern Rhodesians, a 5 percent minority in a total population of 4,530,000, seceded from Britain and asserted their independence.[10] Presently a pariah among nations, abandoned by its mother country and subjected to sanctions and boycotts imposed by most of the world's white and colored nations, Southern Rhodesia still manages to endure.[11] Its principal support comes from South Africa, where 3,563,000 whites, an 18 percent minority in a population of 19,618,000, direct the destinies of Africa's most modern, most prosperous and most civilized nation.

The story of South Africa began in 1652 with the landing of the first Dutch pioneers. In many ways the country's development paralleled that of the United States. The settlers were Protestants of Northern European descent who usually brought their families with them, so, except at the earliest pioneering stages, there was a minimum of racial mixing. The enemy of the colonists was not the native African, but the British, who harried them almost from the very beginning and took the colony from Holland by force during the Napoleonic wars when the Dutch were active allies of France. Forty years later, to escape from British rule, twelve thousand Dutch-descended Afrikaners went northward in the 1835 "Great Trek," a march which compares in heroism and fortitude to the Mormon migration to Utah.

9. Population statistics from *1969 World Almanac,* Hatch, *A History of Postwar Africa* and Molnar, *Africa: A Political Travelogue.*
10. Rhodesia was formally proclaimed a republic in 1970.
11. In 1972 the Rhodesian team, after being invited to the Olympic games, was ejected because of a threatened black boycott. A few days earlier General Idi Amin of Uganda had ordered 50,000 Asians to quit his country in 90 days. The Uganda team stayed in the Olympics.

The low point in Afrikaner fortunes came in the Boer War (1899–1902), a war for independence that failed.

But the Afrikaners' defeat was not final. Chased from the battlefield, they retreated to the ballot box, and as South Africa moved from colonial to commonwealth status, their political hopes brightened. In 1948, the Afrikaners outvoted English-speaking whites and set up a white supremacist government.[12] In 1961, they led South Africa out of the British Commonwealth and made it an independent republic.

South Africa hopes to solve its almost insoluble racial problems by means of apartheid or the separate development of races, a milder approach than *baaskap*, which is absolute domination by whites.[13] The blacks, forbidden to intermarry with whites and now living in segregated communities, are eventually to have their own territories (Bantustans) with full cultural and some political freedom, and their contacts with whites will be limited to the economic sector.[14] South Africa's white liberal element, largely of British and Jewish origin, opposes apartheid and favors giving full rights, including the voting franchise, to nonwhites.[15] The Communists,

---

12. Afrikaans-speaking whites, who also include some descendants of early German and French settlers, number 2,000,000. English-speaking whites, who include some Europeans of non-British origin and 100,000 Jews, number 1,500,000. Allen Drury, *A Very Strange Society*, Pocket Books, New York, 1968, p. 29 and Molnar, *op. cit.*, p. 166.

13. Drury, *op. cit.*, p. 98.

14. One such Bantustan, the Transkei, already exists.

15. South African racial politics is both similar and dissimilar to that of the United States. There is the same liberal-minority coalition with affluent Jews at the top, impecunious Negroes at the bottom, and whites of British descent playing the liberal role. One great difference is that the dominant Afrikaner population group votes *en bloc*. Another great difference is that South African Negroes, who outnumber the whites 5.6 to 1 cannot vote, whereas American Negroes, outnumbered by whites 9 to 1, can. The British and Jewish minorities, however, still retain some political and great financial power. There is no restriction on the cash flow to Israel, and Harry Oppenheimer, Chairman of the Board of the Anglo-American Corp., is probably the world's richest Jew. In 1959, his various enterprises made a profit after taxes of $271,074,000. *Current Biography*, 1961, p. 351. Oppenheimer's De Beers Consolidated Mines and Diamond Trading Co. produces and sells 85 percent of the world's rough, uncut diamonds. "In these modern times, when price-controlling cartels have been outlawed in other industries, the survival of the De Beers monopoly is astonishing." *McCall's*, March 1969, pp. 167–8. The best gem diamonds come from Sierra Leone where a company broke the De Beers monopoly for a brief period in the early

who are now underground and most of whose leaders were or are Jews (Fisher, Goldreich, *et. al.*), call for an armed black uprising.[16]

Americans have been indoctrinated to regard South African blacks, who did not even arrive in any numbers until the late eighteenth century—150 years after the Dutch [17]—as the country's rightful owners.[18] Unlike American Negroes, the blacks who came to South Africa came voluntarily, first in search of land, then in search of jobs. South African blacks further differ from American blacks in that they speak several different languages and are divided by fierce tribal loyalties which impede the organization of a united anti-white political front.

In the past several decades the United States, under pressure from liberal-minority lobbies and the news media, has developed a deep and disturbing concern for South African blacks, as it has for blacks in every part of Africa. The concern is described as disturbing because previous American efforts in behalf of African Negroes have been, to say the least, counterproductive. Before the Civil War, white Americans founded the state of Liberia on Africa's west coast to serve as a national homeland for emancipated slaves. Small groups of ex-slaves made the voyage to Liberia, where they formed the country's aristocracy, numbering twenty thousand when last counted in 1945. But Liberia had little or no attraction for American Negroes generally, whether slave or free, and after the Civil War the migratory trickle came to an end.[19] Sixty-five years later, Liberia was formally censored by a League of Nations committee for permitting the existence of slavery and forced labor. Both the President and Vice-President had to resign in the ensuing scandal.[20]

Although pretending to be a democracy, modern Liberia has actually been governed by a succession of president-

1960's, until Oppenheimer persuaded the Sierra Leone Parliament to stop the competition.

16. Drury, *op. cit.*, pp. 96–7 and Molnar, *op. cit.*, pp. 166–7.
17. Drury, *op. cit.*, p. 16.
18. The latest census shows 12,750,000 blacks, 1,859,000 colored (mixed) and 561,000 Asians, mostly Indians.
19. *Ency. Brit.*, Vol. 13, pp. 994–6.
20. *New York Times*, Dec. 6, 1930, p. 38 and June 7, 1931, p. 5.

dictators. The constitution has racial qualifications for citizenship, restricting it to Negroes or persons of Negro descent.[21] Liberia also happens to be one of the most backward African states, principally because it was never a colony and consequently only rarely exposed to white industrial methods and modern technology.[22]

In the aftermath of World War II, the power and influence of American "public opinion" was a great source of encouragement to the native African's precocious demands for independence. Belgium was forced to give up the Congo before there were nearly enough qualified Negroes to administer it. As the country relapsed into tribal anarchy, the United States contributed 40 percent of the $400 million spent by the United Nations "peace-keeping" mission (1960–1963). In the course of the almost interminable bush wars and insurrections which ravaged the Congo for two decades, both loyal and rebel Congolese troops mutilated, butchered, and occasionally cannibalized more than a few Americans, including missionaries and nuns.[23] Even so, the American press continued to support the occasionally pro-Russian, always black racist, Congolese government and carried on a bitter editorial and headline campaign against Moise Tshombe, the one pro-Western Congolese politician of stature. Tshombe, after being driven into exile, was kidnapped and flown to Algiers where he died in prison.

In the light of recent events and present trends, it must be said that Darkest Africa is becoming dark again and American foreign policy is hastening the process. The plantations, industrial installations, public utilities, mining companies and large commercial establishments only remain

21. *Ency. Brit.*, Vol. 13, p. 996.
22. Almost as backward is part-black Ethiopia, the only other nonwhite country in Africa with a fairly continuous history of independence, only briefly interrupted in recent times by the Italian occupation (1936–1941). Molnar, *op. cit.*, pp. 223 ff, and Hatch, *op. cit.*, pp. 185–6.
23. "The Congolese government denied charges that its troops had killed at least 11 Europeans and raped 30 white women, but its own interim minister made the most astonishing charge of all—that Congolese had eaten several white settlers in Lubumbashi, formerly Elisabethville." *Life*, July 21, 1957, p. 34. It might be added that some cannibals were not primitive natives wearing loincloths, but "men and women schooled and dressed in the European way." Molnar, *op. cit.*, p. 30.

in operation as long as there is white supervision and white money. The blacks who are trying—in vain—to replace the white technocrats are Western-trained intellectuals, a species of imitation white men as abhorrent to their own people as they are unrespected by their former masters. The real Africa and the only authentic black culture are not to be found within the city limits but out in the bush in the tribal compounds. If white liberals, white churchmen, white capitalists *and* communists, and the black intelligentsia would leave the black tribesman to his own devices, he would be free to pursue and develop the way of life which suits him best and makes the best use of his uniquely different cultural and artistic gifts.

But they will not leave him alone. Western nations continue to receive, indoctrinate and return to their native countries a black elite which, wittingly or unwittingly, carries home a colonialism of white thought, white attitudes and white institutions that weigh more heavily on the black soul than the now extinct economic colonialism of the white imperialist. Even the Arab and Moslem states of North Africa attempt to meddle with black destinies by proposing a continental pan-Africanism, apparently forgetting that many blacks have more animosity toward Arabs than toward European whites. It was the Arabs who managed the African slave trade long before the arrival of the Europeans and it was the Arabs who kept it alive long after the Europeans had outlawed it.[24]

Highly sensitive to liberal and black lobbying, the United States keeps aiding, abetting and financing "Western model" African republics which invariably turn out to be travesties of the political, economic and social institutions they laboriously mimic. These new black states supplement the larger strategy of eventually forcing Rhodesia and South Africa to adopt black rule. Although Joseph Conrad's *Heart of Darkness* probably offers the best clue to the black African's future, America prefers to base its African policy

---

24. Some Arab traders continue to do a flourishing business in black slaves according to a report made to a meeting of the International Council of Women in Teheran, Iran, in 1966. Observers have estimated that as many as 125,000 blacks a year are still being sold on the slave block.

on Marxist prophecy, the anti-white palaver of Sartre and the racial fantasies of Frantz Fanon.[25] Ignored is the historical record which is replete with evidence that Negroes in Africa, Haiti, the United States and South America have a congenital allergy to the higher expressions of Western civilization, including Western styles of government.

Apart from the Middle East, there is no area on earth where American foreign policy is as rigged against the American Majority as it is in Africa. Instead of strengthening relations with South Africa, whose resources, military capability and political stability make it the only nation on the continent that can be counted on as a trustworthy and effective ally, the United States deliberately adopts a policy that ranges from moral indignation to outright hostility. Rhodesia, an oasis of Northern European civilization in an almost totally black environment, might expect some sympathy from the United States, if only for the reason that Rhodesians are English-speaking and of British descent. But America joins the United Nations in boycotting Rhodesia.

Unbelievable as it may seem, the more a population of any African nation differs racially and culturally from the American Majority, the more that nation is likely to receive American support and American largesse. The more the population approaches the racial composition of the Majority, the more coolly it will be treated, often to the point of open enmity. The white (Mediterranean) racial layer of North Africa has fallen under the ban imposed on anti-Zionist Arabs, though a temporary waiver has been granted to Egypt and its mulatto leader, Sadat. The white (Northern European) racial component of South Africa has fallen under the ban imposed for more than a century on the American South.

---

25. Sartre's preface to Fanon's tract, *The Wretched of the Earth,* is one of the most vituperative and extensive slurs in the history of racial invective. It is a sign of the times and of the pressures of the times that the most rabid perpetrators of anti-white racism are accepted as respectable members of the white intellectual fraternity.

Chapter 37

The United States and the Western Hemisphere

GEOGRAPHICALLY, THE Western Hemisphere is divided into two continents, North and South America. Geopolitically, it is divided into Latin America (South America, Central America and Mexico) and Anglo-America (the United States and Canada). Latin America is primarily tropical or subtropical in climate; Catholic in religion; Spanish, Portuguese or Indian in language; Latin, Indian or Negro in culture (in varying proportions); and Mediterranean, Mongoloid or Negroid in race (in varying mixtures). The present population of the twenty-two independent nations and four European dependencies of Latin America is 254,706,000, as against Anglo-America's 234,645,000.[1] But by the year 2000, Latin America may have a population of 600,000,000, in comparison to Anglo-America's 325,000,000.[2]

In the time of Columbus, there were sixteen million Indians in the New World, fifteen million in Latin America.[3] When their palefaced conquerors arrived, they were subjected to two different ordeals and styles of conquest. The English,

---

1. The Caribbean area has been omitted from this census. Because of their racial or cultural affiliations, however, the larger islands, including Puerto Rico, are treated in this chapter as belonging to Latin America.

2. Latin American population projection from John Gunther, *Inside South America,* 1967, p. 121.

3. *Ency. Brit.,* Vol. 12, pp. 200, 203.

Dutch, Germans and Scandinavians parleyed and traded with the Indians, before they fought them, killed them and drove the remainder west, ultimately on to reservations. But they rarely mated with them and hardly ever married them. The sexual abstinence could be attributed to strong feelings of racial solidarity, accentuated by the color differences, and to the fact that many were settlers, which meant they had brought along their wives and families.

A much higher proportion of the Spanish and Portuguese migration, whose members were more concerned with military glory and fortune-hunting than farming, were bachelors. Of a darker shade and noticeably shorter than the Northern Europeans, they were less separated from the Indians by physical traits.[4] They also happened to be confronted with a greater number of Indians, who were more attractive and more civilized than the nomadic redskins of the northern plains and forests. When the slave ships unloaded their human cargoes, Latins persisted in their miscegenation while Northern Europeans, with some exceptions in the American South, remained true to their segregated mating habits.[5]

Centuries of racial blending in Latin America have produced many different population groups. In Mexico and Peru, where there were advanced Indian cultures, the mestizo element is Spanish-Indian. In Brazil, considerable numbers of Negroes as well as Indians generated more complex racial shadings—Portuguese-Indian, Negro-Indian, Portuguese-Negro and Portuguese-Indian-Negro. In the West Indies, where Negro slaves replaced the Indians who died off in the sixteenth century, many islands are almost totally black, and in Cuba and Puerto Rico the mulatto share of the population is predominant with pure Negroes and pure whites in the minority.[6]

---

4. The reference here is to the racial type of most of the soldiers, prospectors, administrators and priests from Spain and Portugal. Their leaders, the *conquistadores,* exhibited many Northern European physical traits. See p. 74.

5. In contrast to the practice in Latin America, the mixed offspring of Southerners were hardly ever legitimized.

6. Both the capitalist census takers in Puerto Rico and the communist census takers in Cuba seem somewhat color blind. In the early 1960's, less

In the more remote Andean nations, Ecuador and Bolivia, and in Guatemala, pure Indian strains are still in the majority. In Paraguay, Guarani, an Indian dialect, is an official state language. In Argentina, Uruguay and Costa Rica, where the paucity of mineral resources drew settlers instead of prospectors, the population is overwhelmingly white. Complicating the racial picture throughout Latin America are enclaves of Germans and Japanese in Brazil; Germans in Chile; Jews in Argentina;[7] Dutch in Surinam; French in French Guiana, Martinique and Guadeloupe; and Indians (from India) in Guyana, formerly British Guiana.

Economic wealth and social prestige in Latin America generally vary according to the whiteness of one's skin. In Central America, Costa Rica, the only white nation, is by far the most advanced and most prosperous. Haiti, with the longest continuous history of independence of any Negro country anywhere, is the least prosperous and least advanced of any New World nation, except for a few new black independencies in the smaller Caribbean islands. In South America, Chile, Uruguay and Argentina in spite of the Latin penchant for dictatorship or army rule are on a higher plane of civilization than states where Negro or Indian elements predominate.

Whatever aristocracy remains in Latin America is based almost entirely on an unsullied and uncontaminated white family tree. Politics in many areas has long since passed into the hands of mestizos, but mestizos on the light side, who marry on the light side and whose descendants eventually qualify for "certificates of whiteness." Although there is no

---

than 20 percent of the Puerto Rican population was classified as nonwhite and in Cuba one-eighth of the population was described as Negro and one-seventh as mulatto. Any visitor to either country can quickly gauge the reliability of these statistics, whose exaggerated pro-white bias is additional proof of the social value attached to the white label. In Cuba "the proportion of the population with some Negro ancestry is much higher than the figures indicated," states the *Ency. Brit.*, Vol. 6, p. 875.

7. The Migdal brothers, Lithuanian Jews, ran the vicious and lucrative white slave trade in Argentina, which was finally brought to an end by the Jewish community itself. Argentine inflation has raised havoc with Jewish small business, but the Jews in Buenos Aires still represent the richest and most influential Jewish minority in Latin America. Sachar, *The Course of Modern Jewish History*, pp. 510 ff.

official or legally sanctioned racial discrimination in Latin America, it can be seen, felt and sensed everywhere.

Neither the Indians nor the Negroes played any considerable part in the early stages of Latin American independence movements.[8] It was the Creoles, the native-born whites—some with a touch of the mestizo—who in almost every case first organized and led the armies that fought the Spanish regulars.[9] There was a moment in the 1820's when the new Latin American states might have banded together in a federation on the United States model. But the two principal leaders, Bolívar and San Martín, fell out. From that day on Latin America has been divided by petty provincialism and a never-ending succession of revolutions, military dictatorships, clerical and anti-clerical juntas and men on horseback. Venezuela has had more than a hundred revolutions in 150 years; Bolivia 179 changes of government in 126 years. Paraguay had thirty-nine different heads of state between 1870 and 1954.[10] It was this continuous political and economic ferment that caused Latin America, once a century or more ahead of Anglo-America, to fall more than a century behind.

Latin America, it should be recalled, once included Florida, Louisiana and its vast hinterland, and almost limitless expanses of geography in the American Southwest and Far West. After acquiring Louisiana by purchase and parts of Florida by force, the United States attempted to erect a diplomatic wall around the remainder of the Western Hemisphere in the form of the Monroe Doctrine (1823).

In solemnly proclaiming that the New World was closed to further colonization by European powers, America helped

---

8. Juárez, the great Indian revolutionary of Mexico, did not come to prominence until the middle of the nineteenth century, almost four decades after two white priests, Hidalgo and Morelos, had launched the drive for Mexican independence.

9. The Creole leaders seem to have inherited the courage of the *conquistadores,* but not their attitudes. Bolívar, who had a touch of Indian, married his sister to a Negro general. San Martín with his black hair, black eyes and olive skin once publicly announced he was an Indian. O'Higgins, the liberator of Chile, was the illegitimate son of an Irishman and a Chilean woman of mixed ancestry. Gunther, *Inside South America,* pp. 134–7 and 332–3.

10. *Ibid.,* p. xvi.

to safeguard the newly acquired freedom and independence of the Latin American countries which had seceded from Spain. But as American aggression against Mexico increased and as Texas, New Mexico, Arizona, California and parts of Colorado and Wyoming were incorporated into the United States, Latin Americans could be forgiven for equating the Monroe Doctrine with Yankee imperialism. It appeared as if the United States wanted to isolate the Western Hemisphere from Europe, not for the high-minded purpose of protecting the New World against the machinations of the Old, but to treat Latin America as European nations were beginning to treat Africa.[11]

Not until the 1930's did Franklin Roosevelt's Good Neighbor Policy attempt to soothe the ruffled feelings and hurt pride resulting from Latin America's century-long exposure to "gringo" dynamism. The expropriation of hundreds of millions of dollars of American investments and property by Mexico's revolutionary government was forgiven and forgotten, and a new soft key approach to Latin American relations inaugurated. In the late 1940's, the Organization of American States was formed, of which the United States was only one of twenty-three (now twenty-two) member nations, each with an equal vote in the Council. Two decades later, President Kennedy's Alliance for Progress added grants and loans to American investments as a means of building up Latin America's lagging economy. But in spite of these conciliatory steps, an era of hemispheric good feeling was as far away as ever.

Meanwhile, the United States was forced to take cognizance of stepped-up Soviet activity south of the border. The Russian subversion of Guatemala was checkmated by an American-instigated uprising which sent Jacobo Arbenz,

---

11. In the mood of the times, William Walker, doctor, lawyer, newspaper editor, freebooter and native of Nashville, Tennessee, briefly carved an independent "republic" out of Mexico's Lower California and Sonora, and later with fifty-six followers took over Nicaragua. If he had not crossed the path of Cornelius Vanderbilt's economic interests—the Commodore wished to build a Nicaraguan canal—Walker might have eventually become the emperor of Central America instead of dying before a Honduran firing squad in 1860. Albert Carr, *The World and William Walker*, Harper & Row, New York, 1963.

the first Soviet puppet in the New World, packing in 1954. However, the failure of the United States to prevent the Sovietization of Cuba stands as one of the gigantic blunders of American diplomatic history. The events represent a classic cautionary tale of how American national security is damaged when the liberal-minority coalition impinges its political and social dogmas upon the conduct of foreign affairs.

Until *The New York Times* discovered him and his small band of ragtag guerrillas in Cuba's remote Sierra Maestra mountains in 1957, Fidel Castro was an unknown, clownish and down-at-heel revolutionary. But a series of interviews with *New York Times* correspondent Herbert Matthews, whose reporting of the Spanish Civil War had been a monument of non-objectivity,[12] painted a hero-size portrait of Castro as an idealistic, "anti-communist" patriot with "no animosity toward the United States and the American people."[13] Matthews' prettifications also contained the flat statement, "But there is no communism to speak of in Castro's 25th of July movement. . . ."[14] Earl Smith, who was America's Ambassador to Cuba at the time, stated that after Matthews' interview was published, arms, money and support for Castro poured in from all sides.[15]

Inevitably, President Eisenhower himself fell under the *Times* spell,[16] refusing to sell the legitimate Cuban government badly needed arms even when Castro's insurrection assumed threatening proportions.[17] Ambassador Smith was ordered to urge President Batista, the Cuban strongman, to

12. For Matthews' pro-Loyalist bias, see Hugh Thomas, *The Spanish Civil War*, pp. 233, 388.

13. Quotations from Matthews' front-page stories in *New York Times*, Feb. 24–26, 1957.

14. *Ibid.*

15. Herbert Dinsmore, *All The News That Fits*, Arlington House, New Rochelle, N.Y., 1968, p. 185.

16. *Ibid.*, p. 177. At a press conference at Grinnell College (May 13, 1965), Eisenhower made it clear that "Herbert Matthews . . . almost single-handedly made Castro a national hero." He went on to say that John Kennedy, when senator, had told him that Castro was following in the footsteps of Bolívar.

17. The delivery of fifteen airplanes which Cuba had already bought and paid for was stopped by the State Department. M. Stanton Evans, *The Politics of Surrender*, Devin-Adair, New York, 1966, p. 380.

retire.[18] On January 1, 1959, Batista fled to Portugal and the Castro forces triumphantly entered Havana. American diplomacy had incomprehensibly taken the lead in replacing a sworn friend with a sworn enemy.

After Castro had seized control of Cuba, prominent liberals rushed into print to add further touches to Matthews' panegyrics. William Benton, one of the most influential members of the Democratic party and onetime Senator from Connecticut, wrote that Latin America appeared to be the "area of the world least menaced by a Soviet or Chinese military threat (even through Cuba)." [19] C. Wright Mills, one of the nation's leading sociologists, wrote "Fidel Castro's no communist and never has been." [20] Mills then went on to say that Castro would never allow Russia to set up bases in Cuba and, besides, Russia did not want such bases.[21]

In 1961, when Castro announced publicly that he had always been a Marxist-Leninist and had only concealed his Communist ties in order to grease the wheels of revolution,[22] Matthews was still writing about Cuba for *The New York Times,* later being promoted to chief editorial writer for Latin American affairs. In this post, his supervisor was John Oakes, the *Times* editorial director and the son of George Ochs-Oakes, founder Adolph Ochs' brother.[23] Even after

18. Evans, *op. cit.,* p. 379. For a full discussion of the general situation by a Cuban-American participant, see Mario Lazo, *Dagger in the Heart—American Foreign Policy Failures in Cuba,* Funk & Wagnalls, New York, 1968.

19. From the preface of Benton's book, *The Voice of Latin America,* Weidenfeld & Nicolson, London, 1961, p. xii. If Benton was so unknowing about foreign affairs, he had no business as an Assistant Secretary of State in 1945–1947. The multimillionaire publisher of the *Ency. Brit.,* which was cited by the Federal Trade Commission for using deceptive pricing and bargain claims (Associated Press report, July 1, 1961), Benton started his career as a radio huckster. His deodorant commercials set a standard for banality seldom matched in the history of the advertising profession.

20. *Listen, Yankee!* Ballantine Books, New York, 1960, p. 103.

21. *Ibid.,* pp. 94–5.

22. *Ency. Brit.,* Vol. 5, p. 44. It must be galling for William Benton to read in his own publishing venture a complete refutation of his predictions concerning Russian intervention in Cuba.

23. Dinsmore, *op. cit.,* p. 179. In 1967, Matthews grudgingly admitted that Castro was a Communist, but said that he became one in 1960, a statement which does not agree with Castro's. A Soviet agent as far back as 1948, Castro operated with the Communists in Colombia during the armed uprising which cost 1,000 lives. Lazo, *op. cit.,* pp. 141–6. Matthews, who as a

Castro had expropriated $1 billion of American property and set up an orthodox Communist state, complete with mass purges and forced collectivization of agriculture, the liberal-minority arbiters of foreign policy kept evincing their friendship for the Cuban revolution, although they were having doubts about Castro himself.

Since the very men who had been most mistaken about Castro and most insistent in forcing their mistaken views on the government were, in the Kennedy administration, raised to important decision-making positions, it is not astonishing that American-Cuban relations proceeded from bad to worse. The White House specialist in Latin American affairs was the minority intellectual, Richard Goodwin, a Kennedy speech writer. Another minority intellectual who had much to do with diplomatic dealings with Castro was Arthur Schlesinger, Jr., the author of the administration's 1961 White Paper on Cuba. In an outburst of ringing cliches, Schlesinger described how the "hemisphere rejoiced at the overthrow of the Batista tyranny, looked with sympathy on the new regime and welcomed its promises of political freedom and social justice for the Cuban people." [24]

There followed a farce of contradictions. On April 17, 1961, the White House intellectual general staff, suddenly reversing itself, sent a force of 1,500 American-trained and American-equipped Cuban exiles to invade Cuba. But at the very climax of the Bay of Pigs landing, the Kennedy administration, overly concerned about the cool reaction of the news media, lost its nerve and canceled all but the first of the covering air strikes. [25]

The nuclear confrontation with Russia, which came after this shameful exhibition of American indecision and weakness, culminated in what the press regarded as a Kennedy "victory," although no conclusive proof has been offered that the Russians ever removed *all* their missiles and warheads

---

foreign correspondent in Europe in the 1930's affected a grey fedora, beige gloves, matching spats and malacca walking stick, remained on good terms with his employers until the very end. Mrs. Arthur Sulzberger was the godmother of his only son. Gay Talese, *The Kingdom and the Power*, 1969, p. 463–4.

24. Evans, *op. cit.*, p. 381.
25. *Ibid.*, pp. 385–6.

from Cuba. On the contrary, there is evidence that many missiles remain, along with other advanced Soviet weapons, in the vast network of Cuba's underground installations.[26] Kennedy's diplomatic triumph, it so happened, did not include the right of on-site inspection.

There is also little doubt that Kennedy made a secret agreement with Khrushchev concerning the inviolability of Cuba. By allowing the installation of a permanent Soviet military base only ninety miles from Florida and by promising not to invade Cuba,[27] the President not only pigeonholed the Monroe Doctrine, he reversed it. The United States, once committed to preventing European intervention in the New World, had in effect become the protector of a Russian satellite state in the strategic Caribbean area. That Cuba was also a training camp for revolutionary cadres whose mission was to spearhead armed Communist uprisings in Latin America and incite racial violence in the United States made Kennedy's Cuban policy all the more inexcusable.[28]

Since dominant population groups of Northern European descent are almost non-existent in Latin American countries, which means the racial ingredient of representative or genuinely democratic government is missing, whatever political and economic stability there is will probably continue to be provided by dictators, benevolent or malevolent. Among them will certainly be a number of Castros, who will ride into power on the misery, ignorance and superstition of the

---

26. In a 1964 interview, Castro's sister, Juanita, said, "In Cuba there are long-range ballistic missiles which are well camouflaged." A year before, Representative Donald Bruce of Indiana stated, "there are forty or more Soviet missiles still in Cuba today and the highest officials in the U.S. government know it." Evans, *op. cit.,* pp. 403–6. It is not clear what type of missile Representative Bruce had in mind. There is no question that Soviet SA-2 anti-aircraft missiles are present in Cuba—144 of them according to *Time,* July 27, 1970, p. 17. But Washington is more concerned about the installation of such missiles in Egypt than in Cuba. According to *U.S. News & World Report* (March 9, 1970, p. 48), there are 165 Soviet combat planes in Cuba, 500 anti-aircraft missiles, 300 tanks, 100 self-propelled guns and 200 troop carriers.

27. In 1964, Castro declared: "There is to be no invasion of Cuba by the U.S. That is formal. It is binding on the U.S. government under any president, any government. . . . When Khrushchev proposed that there be no invasion of Cuba, Kennedy said yes." Evans, *op. cit.,* p. 401.

28. *Ibid.,* pp. 406–7.

illiterate masses, using the tested communist strategy of playing on racial animosity in the name of class war.

But, whenever a socialist or Marxist-oriented strongman appears, it is to be hoped that the United States will not, as in Cuba, first help him crush the pro-American opposition and then make him into a dangerous enemy by turning against him. The lessons of Yugoslavia and the falling out of Russia and China should not be lost. With the proper diplomatic and economic finesse, Communist Cuba, having no Russian army poised on a contiguous frontier, could almost certainly be lured or pressured into a Tito-esque neutrality.

Unless the internal convulsions of a Latin American country lead to a major threat to America's national security on the Cuban model, the United States might do well to stand aloof. The Monroe Doctrine should be removed from the diplomatic dead file and dusted off. But it should only be implemented in the event of direct foreign interference in Latin American affairs and never again used as a pretext for old-fashioned Yankee intervention. Whatever else the United States does in Latin America, it should no longer be identified with the losing side in civil wars and revolutions. There being very little possibility that an American-style economy will ever operate successfully in the quasi-feudal conditions of Latin America, the United States should be resigned to an endless succession of collectivist regimes. Rather than pick and choose between them according to the liberal-minority formula that totalitarians of the left are to be favored over totalitarians of the right, American diplomacy should endeavor to see that all Latin American states, whatever their politics, remain loyal to the Western Hemisphere.

The multilateral reaction to a possible Communist revolution in the Dominican Republic in 1965 represented America's new cooperative approach to Latin American relations.[29] With the approval of the Organization of American States, President Johnson ordered in 24,000 American marines, who were later joined by detachments from five Latin American countries. The occupying troops

---

29. *1969 World Almanac*, p. 510.

were then incorporated into an Inter-American Peace Force.[30] However, since the Dominican pacification helped keep the whiter elements of the country's population in power, it soon came under heavy fire from the American press.

Utopians have often envisioned a Pan-American Union, in which the United States is an equal partner, as the ideal instrument for resolving hemispheric problems and conducting hemispheric defense. But the United States has such an overwhelming industrial and financial edge over the other New World countries that it can hardly avoid the responsibility and stigma of domination. Latin American politicians may complain about American imperialism, but certainly their own countries, either alone or jointly, do not have the strength to defend the New World against Old World predators. Latin American capitalists and Marxists may complain about the Yankee business colossus, but they do little to build up the economy of their own nations.[31]

Pavlovian cries of "gringoism" should not be allowed to conceal a much more dangerous form of aggression that is now taking place in the Western Hemisphere. This is the aggression that is pointing north, not south. With much of Texas and the American Southwest reverting to a Spanish-speaking Mexican culture, with Puerto Ricans breeding as fast as Negroes in New York, and Cuban refugees crowding into Florida, it is possible that Latin Americans will soon reconquer their lost North American territories by default. The northward extension of Latin America can only weaken hemispheric security by further reducing the power of the American Majority, on whose shoulders any effective defense of the two continents must ultimately rest. Deprived of the

---

30. The chaos in the Dominican Republic was the natural aftermath of the assassination of Rafael Trujillo. The removal of other anti-communist dictators, in which American liberals played more than a passive role, has inevitably led to severe reverses for American foreign policy. The forced exile of Batista brought in Castro. The assassination of Ngo Dinh Diem (1963), the only South Vietnamese leader with the organizational ability and charisma of Ho Chi Minh, left a power vacuum that had much to do with the prolongation of the disastrous Vietnam war.

31. As of 1969, American business employed 2,000,000 Latin Americans, accounted for 12 percent of Latin America's Gross National Product and one-third of its exports, and paid more than one-fifth of its taxes. *Time*, July 11, 1969, p. 26.

leadership and fighting strength of the American Majority, the New World would stand a good chance of again becoming the possession of the Old.

Turning finally to Canada, it must be recognized at the outset that from a racial and cultural standpoint Canada is two nations, not one. The fact is that British and French Canada are as socially differentiated in the Western Hemisphere as England and France are in Europe. Frequently the tension between British-descended and French-descended Canadians has been greater than that between their parent populations abroad. There is no English Channel to keep them apart, and the religious differences are sharper, French-Canadians being more intensely Catholic and British-Canadians more pronouncedly Protestant than the French and British in the Old World.

As the original white settlers of Canada, French-Canadians like to think of themselves as the true Canadians. Recently, they have expressed these sentiments with Molotov cocktails, bombs, kidnapings and murder—a form of political activity unnerving to English-speaking Canadians. Deliberate attempts by France, particularly in the de Gaulle era, to arouse separatist feelings and promote French culture have done nothing to ameliorate the situation. Nevertheless, Canadian political unity is still preserved. One substantial cause has been the conciliatory attitude of English-speaking Canadians, who have leaned over backwards in granting the demands of 5,500,000 French-Canadians for more autonomy.

British Canada, as distinct from French Canada, has a racial mixture that approximates that of the white population of the United States. Canadians of British origin number approximately 8,000,000; German origin, 1,000,000; Ukrainian, 473,000; Italian, 450,000; Dutch, 429,000; Scandinavian, 386,000; Polish, 323,000; Jewish, 173,000; Hungarian, 126,000; Russian, 120,000. There are also some 220,000 nonwhites (Indians and Eskimos),[32] and a small Negro minority, numbering perhaps 30,000, some of them descendants of fugitive slaves who escaped from the United

---

32. *1969 World Almanac*, p. 487. The British figure evidently includes Canadians of Irish descent.

States shortly before the Civil War.[33] As Negroes everywhere, Canadian blacks are at the bottom of the social and economic ladder, even though they have had the vote and the full protection of the law, including integrated education, for more than a hundred years.[34] As Jews everywhere, Canadian Jews are concentrated in a few of the larger cities, principally Montreal and Toronto, and have a disproportionate share of the country's wealth.

The idea has now lost most of its fire, but the annexation of Canada once received a great deal of serious consideration from those few politicians in American history who deserve the name of statesmen. Over the strong objections of tens of thousands of American Loyalists who had fled north across the border, Benjamin Franklin tried to persuade the British to give up Canada in the peace talks which ended the War of Independence. Another wave of annexation fever swept the United States in the early years of Manifest Destiny,[35] some of it reciprocated by the Canadians, at that time still British colonials. Even as late as 1911, the Speaker of the House, Champ Clark of Missouri, was hailing "the day when the American flag will float over every square foot of British North American possessions clear to the North Pole." [36] Today, the anti-imperialism of U.S. politics, except in the Middle East, coupled with Canada's intensified economic nationalism and lingering resentment of the Vietnam war,[37] have postponed all thought of union.[38]

33. Many of these returned after the war ended. John Hope Franklin, *From Slavery to Freedom*, Knopf, New York, 1969, p. 377.

34. *Ibid.*, pp. 376, 380–1.

35. Before the outbreak of the War of 1812, Henry Clay told the House of Representatives, "The militia of Kentucky alone are competent to place Montreal and Upper Canada at your feet." Another nineteenth-century hawk, John Calhoun, prophesied, "I believe that in four weeks from the time a declaration of war is heard on our frontier, the whole of upper Canada and a part of lower Canada will be in our power." Beard, *The Rise of American Civilization*, Vol. 1, p. 416.

36. Samuel Flagg Bemis, *A Diplomatic History of the U.S.*, Holt, Rinehart and Winston, New York, 1955, p. 735.

37. In 1969 Canada served as a refuge for 53,000 American draft dodgers and deserters. *Times Literary Supplement*, Aug. 28, 1969, p. 2.

38. During World War II, 24.4 percent of the Americans interviewed in an opinion poll desired the annexation of Canada and 23.3 percent of the Canadians shared their view. *Fortune*, April, 1942, p. 112.

But this does not mean the thought will not come up again. The United States has invested $13 billion in Canada, as against $10 billion in Latin America. Canada is by far America's best customer, and the United States buys approximately 75 percent of all Canadian exports. Since the two nations are so economically interwoven and since Canada's English-speaking Majority has such a close biological and cultural relationship with the American Majority, it seems inevitable that the two Majorities, no matter how intensely the minorities in both countries oppose it, will draw closer together.

PART X

Prospects and Perspectives

Chapter 38

Nuclear Hypnosis

NOWHERE IN THIS STUDY, except for a few passing references in the foreign policy chapters, has any serious note been taken of that awesome new tool of warfare, the nuclear bomb. The omission was deliberate. The very word *nuclear* raises semantical perturbations which tend to emotionalize and obscure rather than clarify the meaningful discussion of any topic, particularly international relations. Secondly, in spite of its horror, nuclear war is still war and as such can best be studied in a military context. Even the non-military implications of nuclear weapons—for example, the nuclear hypnosis which blocks all realistic approaches to foreign policy—rightfully belong under the heading of psychological warfare.

Incongruously, the immediate military results of the discovery of nuclear weapons, at least up to the present writing, have been to channel war into more conventional paths.[1] In order to keep the hydrogen bomb safely deactivated, the nuclear and non-nuclear powers which have engaged in the many conflicts that have broken out since World War II have held a tighter rein on their military operations than might normally have been expected. The existence of

---

1. A rather tortuous way of making good another brilliant "prophecy" of Engels. In 1878, he wrote that military technology "had reached such a state of perfection that further progress which would have any revolutionizing influence is no longer possible . . . all further improvements are more or less unimportant for field warfare. The era of evolution is therefore, in essentials, closed in this direction." *Anti-Dühring,* p. 194.

sanctuaries,[2] the reappearance of the battleship[3] and the renewed popularity of guerrilla warfare all point to a step backward into the military past, not to an outpouring of new horrors from the arsenal of modern war technology.

It was in the early days of World War II that the same liberals and equalitarians who later posed as the fiercest opponents of atomic warfare actually started the nuclear arms race. In fact, it is understating the case to say that the concept, design, development and production of the world's first atomic bomb was from beginning to end a minority labor of love. The chronology begins with Lise Meitner, a refugee German scientist who went to Denmark in 1938 and handed physicist Niels Bohr the data of a successful fission experiment recently performed in Berlin. Bohr passed the information along until it reached Einstein, then in Princeton, who in two personal letters to President Roosevelt urged that America immediately start a full-scale bomb development program. The first letter was delivered by banker Alexander Sachs and contained the allegation (which was false) that the Germans were building an atomic bomb. As World War II progressed, Fermi, Bethe and Szilard worked out the details of the A-bomb, which was constructed under the direction of Oppenheimer. Teller and von Neumann, after assisting on the A-bomb, went on to develop the H-bomb. Meanwhile, Rosenberg, Greenglass and Sobell stole various bomb schematics and gave them to the Russians.[4]

That the atomic bomb, as well as the espionage that grew up around it,[5] was basically a minority idea is demonstrated

---

2. Hanoi and its port, Haiphong, were notable examples of unbombed or unblockaded sanctuaries during most of the Vietnam war. Even when air raids were permitted and a sea blockade was established, the U.S. air force and navy were restricted to purely military targets. In the Korean war the supply lines of the Chinese "volunteers" were off limits to General MacArthur, whose war planes were forbidden to fly over Red China.

3. The battleship *New Jersey* was recommissioned and used as a floating artillery backup for the fighting along Vietnam's coast.

4. Facts, names and dates have been taken, in most part, from Robert Jungk, *Brighter than a Thousand Suns,* Harcourt, Brace, New York, 1958.

5. One of the excuses offered by those who came to the defense of the atomic spies—and there were many who came—was that Russian scientists would have sooner or later penetrated the mysteries of nuclear energy by themselves. In answer to this, it might be stated that the secret formula for Greek fire was successfully guarded from the seventh to ninth centuries by

by the roster of names in the preceding paragraph. Every person in the list was Jewish with the exception of Roosevelt and Fermi, an Italian with a Jewish wife. German anti-Semitism had provoked a prodigious reaction from the world Jewish community, which included a number of high-ranking nuclear physicists, almost all of them educated at Germany's University of Göttingen. But it was Einstein, still considered a model of humanitarianism by the press, who was most responsible for "selling" the bomb to the American government. As the foremost promoter of the deadliest weapon of all time, the inventor of Relativity played a role in the history of warfare that would have seemed more appropriate to Basil Zaharoff, the Krupps and the other "merchants of death" who have become stock characters in the liberal-minority demonology.

The bomb was not completed in time to drop it on Germany. But the fraternity of atomic scientists who built it had few compunctions about using it against Japan, the ally of Hitler. The final decision, of course, was President Truman's. The scientist who opposed the project most adamantly was Ernest Lawrence, a member of the Majority.[6]

The racial motivations of the minority scientists who conceived and produced the A-bomb were made perfectly clear after the war when Oppenheimer, the most influential American nuclear physicist, attempted to stop the development of the H-bomb at the very moment the Russians had begun a crash program to build their own. Oppenheimer explained his change of heart by appealing to established liberal and pacifist principles. He emphasized his desire to give up "the devil's work."[7] But since he and practically all his colleagues had been pacifistic, liberal and even ultra-liberal before the appearance of Hitler, their second change of heart within a decade could more logically be attributed to a change of enemy. That Oppenheimer would have been so diligent about

the Eastern Roman Empire. To reveal any knowledge of it was not only considered treason, but sacrilege. It was Greek fire that helped the Byzantine government repulse the Arab attack on Constantinople, thereby, according to Will Durant, "saving Europe" and prolonging the life of the Eastern Roman Empire for nearly 800 years. *The Age of Faith*, pp. 424–5.

6. Jungk, *op. cit.*, footnote p. 186.
7. *Ibid.*, p. 333.

building bombs if Hitler had not been anti-Semitic, and so quick to give up his bomb work if he had not had the typical minority intellectual's soft spot for Marxism, is open to doubt.[8]

It took a great deal of effort on the part of the American government to override Oppenheimer's opposition to the H-bomb, backed up as it was by the most influential portion of the news media.[9] Of all the top-tier minority scientists, only Edward Teller and John von Neumann seemed to perceive the dangers of allowing America's nuclear technology to fall behind Russia's. Both Teller and von Neumann had had first-hand experience with communism in their native Hungary. It was the vigorous, opinionated Teller, far in advance of his colleagues in detecting Stalin's shift to nationalism and anti-Semitism, who fought most doggedly for the H-bomb program—often in the face of waves of vilification from the press.[10] As it turned out, the United States beat Russia to the H-bomb by only ten months.

Having failed to take America out of the nuclear arms race, the disarmament lobby proposed a mutual, Russian-American ban on all nuclear weapons. The Russians evinced their willingness, but refused to permit on-site inspection. Incredibly, liberal and minority intellectuals were prepared to grant this concession. Fortunately, the Joint Chiefs of Staff and a bare majority of Congress were not. The disarmament lobby then turned to other ways of reducing American nuclear preponderance—budget cuts for nuclear research and concentration on a second-strike rather than on a first-strike capability on the grounds that the notion of an American first strike was "unsettling" to the Russians.

---

8. Oppenheimer had many Communist connections, which when revealed cost him his security clearance amid a press hullabaloo that brought back memories of the Dreyfus affair. In one of his sessions with the FBI, he implicated and badly damaged the career of his erstwhile best friend, Haakon Chevalier, who although a hyper-liberal was never a Communist party member or a Soviet agent. *Ibid.*, p. 138, 298, 316, 320.

9. When the Special Committee of the National Security Council finally ordered the H-bomb program to proceed at full speed, the vote was two to one. David Lilienthal, the only minority member and the first chairman of the Atomic Energy Commission, voted no. *Ibid.*, pp. 284–5.

10. At first, Teller was treated as an outcast by his fellow Jews. Today, as the Jewish establishment turns against Russia, he is rapidly returning to favor.

As late as 1969, when Russia had almost achieved nuclear parity with the United States, the liberal-minority coalition was trying to vote down the nation's anti-ballistic missile program.[11] Even though the Russians had started their own ABM network and even though the side better equipped to destroy incoming missiles before they reached their targets would obviously have an overwhelming advantage, the political minions of the anti-Majority establishment were dead set against America's having an ABM system of its own.

In the years immediately following World War II, the arguments for nuclear disarmament were based on fear, pacifism, defeatism and vainglorious proposals for world government. The old liberal-minority fixation on Russia as the birthplace of communism and equalitarianism was an important motivating force, as illustrated in part by the well-publicized slogan, "Better Red than dead." A great deal of the disarmament propaganda originated in the White House itself. Such influential minority presidential consultants as Seymour Melman, Jerome Wiesner and Walt W. Rostow, all made policy suggestions which were to the ultimate military advantage of Russia.[12]

The present downgrading of American national security has been very effective, but nowhere as effective as in the area of civil defense. In the event of a nuclear war, the ability of America's manpower and industry to survive a series of devastating attacks will represent victory or the closest thing to victory. In plain words, if there is no lack of nuclear weapons on either side, as is now the case, the country whose people and industrial plants are more widely scattered and more deeply "dug in" will have the better chance of avoiding total defeat. Largely as the result of America's indifference and at times outright hostility to the

---

11. At the end of 1969, Russia had 1050 intercontinental missiles, 160 missiles on submarines and 150 nuclear bombers. The U.S. had 1,054 intercontinental missiles, 656 missiles in submarines and 528 bombers. The U.S. had more nuclear warheads, but Russia's were much bigger. Apart from a government which practiced far greater secrecy, Russia had the advantage of a far larger land area for the concealment and dispersal of its rocket sites. *U.S. News & World Report*, Dec. 1, 1969, pp. 64–5.

12. For a concise but comprehensive survey of the activities of the disarmament lobby, including a sketch of the principal lobbyists, see the chapter of the same name in Stanton Evans' *The Politics of Surrender*.

whole concept of civil defense, Russia's elaborate civil defense system is far ahead. Thirty million members of DOSAAF, the auxiliary of the Russian ground forces, have each received sixty-four hours of compulsory civil defense training since 1955. MPVO, the regular Russian civil defense organization, is 22,000,000 strong. Even the possibility of a gas attack is seriously considered in Russia. Approximately 30,000,000 gas masks have been issued.[13]

It is not necessary to be a general or an admiral on the Joint Chiefs of Staff to know that surprise gives an overwhelming edge in nuclear war. Yet an American president, John Kennedy, has gone on record with the statement that the United States will never be the first to launch a nuclear attack [14]—a gratuitous and comforting promise to an enemy which, as shown by the data furnished by the highly placed Russian intelligence officer, Colonel Oleg Penkovskiy, has built its entire nuclear strategy around a first strike against the United States.[15] Penkovskiy stated categorically that the Russian General Staff is not at all convinced that both sides will be destroyed in a nuclear war and believes it is quite possible to win such a war, provided it is short and does not degenerate into a long cycle of nuclear attrition. Russian strategists, he said, count on total surprise and the widespread radioactive fallout produced by Russia's bigger and dirtier bombs to mount an attack of paralyzing proportions.[16] Perhaps half the American population and most of the American industrial complex would be exposed to thermonuclear destruction, and bad Russian marksmanship rather than a highly organized system of civil defense would determine who survived and what factories escaped annihilation. Meanwhile, with its key personnel and many of its key defense

13. *Life,* Oct. 23, 1961, p. 79. European members of NATO spend from 55 cents to $2.50 per capita annually on fallout protection, as compared to 38 cents spent by the U.S. *U.S. News & World Report,* March 2, 1970, p. 10.
14. Evans, *op. cit.,* p. 262–3.
15. "When circumstances are favorable for delivering the first nuclear strike, the Soviet Union will deliver this strike under the pretense of defending itself from an aggressor. In this way it will seize the initiative." Oleg Penkovskiy, *The Penkovskiy Papers,* Avon Books, New York, 1966, p. 254.
16. *Ibid.,* pp. 72–3, 250–3.

plants safely underground, Russia would be well braced for retaliatory strikes.

But the Soviet Union, beset by a multitude of internal problems and by poor electronic guidance systems for its missiles,[17] is not ready to take this horrendous gamble. The sign that it is getting ready will probably be provided by a preventive strike on Chinese missile bases and atomic installations. It is doubtful if Russia will follow the American pattern and permit its greatest and most threatening enemy to build up a lethal nuclear stockpile. Far too fast for Russia's satisfaction, China is becoming a principal member of the world's nuclear club, which in addition to the two superpowers now includes Britain, France, India, and probably Israel. Japan, Italy, and West Germany, in spite of their peaceful protestations, would also like to belong, but hopefully will be prevented by Russian and American diplomatic pressure and by their signatures on the Russian-American sponsored nuclear non-proliferation treaty.[18] That both superpowers, having agreed to stop their own atmospheric testing, permit China and France to continue open-air experiments in order to perfect their own nuclear devices, shows a disturbing lack of concern, not only for the security of America and Russia, but for the security of the world.

If liberal-minority domination of American "public opinion" had not been so complete in the aftermath of World War II, mankind might never have had to worry about the possibility of thermonuclear war. From 1945 to 1949 the United States had an absolute monopoly in nuclear weapons. It had produced an atomic bomb four years ahead of Russia,

---

17. *Ibid.*, p. 327.
18. By March 1970, some ninety-nine nations had either promised not to produce nuclear weapons or, if they already had such weapons, not to give them to non-nuclear powers. The nuclear nations guaranteed the countries which agreed not to engage in nuclear research of a military nature full access to the peaceful uses of atomic power developed by the nuclear nations. It is to be noted that China, France and Israel have so far refused to sign the treaty. The latter country has a 26-megawatt reactor in the Negev, capable of producing a small number of atomic bombs of the Nagasaki type. The reactor is shrouded in such secrecy that most observers believe Israel already has a few bombs. *Time*, March 16, 1970, p. 10 and May 11, 1970, pp. 46–7.

and was even further ahead in the development and production of carrier systems. America's nuclear lead was not considerably narrowed until 1953 when Russia exploded its first hydrogen bomb.[19] At any time during a five to ten-year period, the United States without any fear of effective retaliation could have presented the Soviet Union with an ultimatum demanding the immediate dismantling of all its nuclear installations, thereby bringing Russia's nuclear buildup to a dead stop before it had a chance to proliferate. If Russia had ignored the ultimatum, the United States could have accomplished the dismantling on its own initiative by a massive preventive strike, not against the Russian population but against Russian nuclear facilities and missile sites. The same technique could have later been applied to any other nation foolish enough to start building a nuclear arsenal.

All during the critical first decade of the Atomic Age, there were many sensible and realistic Americans who advocated such a policy—a policy which was humanitarian in the highest sense of the word because it might eventually have saved hundreds of millions of lives. But these Americans were either never heard or, if heard, were mercilessly pilloried and then silenced. The liberal-minority cacophony of unilateral disarmament and accommodation with Russia at any price, including the sharing of American atomic research, would admit no debate.

As suggested in the beginning of this chapter, the present nuclear balance of power between Russia and the United States may actually have a calming and restraining effect on war by localizing and limiting conflicts and placing a renewed importance on such old-fashioned weapons as the rifle and such old-fashioned tactics as hand-to-hand combat. But if it does not, and if nuclear war should erupt, it is not likely that all civilization—despite the dire predictions of the doomsayers—will be utterly blotted out.[20]

19. *U.S. News & World Report,* Feb. 26, 1968, p. 84.
20. Prophets of death and desolation have been in vogue since the days of the flood and Sodom and Gomorrah. The invention of the sling, the spear, the bow and arrow and gunpowder were probably as terrifying in their day as chemical, biological and nuclear weapons have been to people of the present era.

Mankind has already survived a few ordeals which come close to the horror predicted for a future nuclear war. Carthage could not have been demolished more completely by an H-bomb than it was by Roman legions. Genghis Khan is reported to have killed 1,600,000 men, women and children in Herat, and not one person was left alive when Tamerlane passed through Bagdad.[21] The Black Death wiped out one fourth of Europe's population in 1348–1350.[22] Men have fought many wars in which no prisoners were taken and lost many sieges in which all the besieged, regardless of age or sex, were slain. Although megaton hydrogen bombs are up to a thousand times deadlier than the kiloton atomic bombs dropped on Hiroshima and Nagasaki, it is noteworthy that both of these cities are now more populated and more flourishing than they were before the atomic attacks.

Even conceding that a full-scale nuclear war would annihilate the entire population of Europe, North America and Asia, any one country such as New Zealand or even Argentina would be able to carry on twentieth-century civilization with scarcely an interruption. When it is remembered that the population of Athens was only 130,000 [23] in the Age of Pericles, human quality would seem to be a more basic ingredient of civilization than human quantity. In fact, a cynic or a hardened evolutionist might say that a nuclear war could actually save civilization by attacking the enemies which are threatening to extinguish it—the creeping urban blight, the despoliation of nature, the exponential birth rate of the genetically impoverished and all the other ecological and dysgenic disasters of the present era.

What is to be feared even more than nuclear war is the nuclear hypnosis to which the American public has been submitted for the last quarter century. First Americans are told to produce atomic bombs, then to drop them on two undefended cities in a nation already on the verge of defeat,[24]

---

21. *Ency. Brit.*, Vol. 12, p. 1001.
22. *Scientific American*, Feb. 1964, p. 114. As late as 1970, 300,000 to 600,000 East Pakistanis died in a Bay of Bengal cyclone. *Time*, Nov. 30, 1970, p. 16.
23. Only 50,000 of these Athenians were citizens. See p. 226.
24. The atomic attacks on Hiroshima and Nagasaki will always be considered a blot on American history and will be blamed on the American

then to forfeit the A-bomb's immense strategic advantages by sharing America's atomic research with Russia, then to agree to nuclear disarmament without inspection, then to scrap the H-bomb at the very moment Russia was building its own and, finally, in the name of a Strategic Arms Limitations Treaty to guarantee the Soviet Union a lead in nuclear-tipped intercontinental ballistic missiles.

But this is by no means the end. Since the nuclear policy of the liberal-minority coalition is not as selflessly humanitarian as it pretends, further shifts and reverses may be expected. Let Russian commissars start imitating the pogroms of the Czars, let there be the glimmerings of an Israeli Dunkirk in Palestine, let South Africa and Rhodesia erupt in a race war and let the blacks begin to lose, let a massive Fascist uprising take place anywhere in the Western world, let any one of these events occur and one may be certain that the disarmament lobby will quickly drop its pacifist mask and be the first to demand the thermonuclear incineration of the "enemy." [25]

The somnambulism that has surrounded the formulation of America's nuclear strategy will vanish as soon as it is acknowledged that nuclear weapons are not a partisan issue. They are not to serve as ideological whipping posts or chess pieces in a game of racial politics. Since each warhead on each missile is a Damoclean sword over the head of every foreign potentate with aggressive designs on the New World, nuclear weapons are nothing more and nothing less than the principal line of American defense.

---

people as a whole instead of the minority scientists who invented and built the bomb and the liberal-minority "humanitarians" who ordered and applauded the bombing. It was the same group that supported and applauded the 1945 air assault on Dresden, which killed 150,000 people in one night, most of them war refugees, the advance guard of the 13,000,000 Germans who fled westward from the depredations of the Red Army and the retributions of the Poles and Czechs. *Time,* June 21, 1963, pp. 30, 95–6.

25. One sign of what may be expected was a little-publicized incident which happened during the 1967 flare-up of the Arab-Israeli war. SANE (Sane Nuclear Policy Committee), which had always been in the forefront of every attempt to limit and weaken America's nuclear capability, had to cancel a peace march because so many of its members were getting ready to demonstrate for more military assistance to Israel. Dinsmore, *All The News That Fits,* p. 323.

The best way to avoid a nuclear war is to recognize that it is not nuclear preparedness which increases the chances of an H-bomb strike against America, but the defeatism, divisiveness and discord promoted by a minority-dominated mass media. The aim seems to be to destroy America's will to resist while chipping away at the primary means of resistance, the all-important nuclear deterrent. Those whose ideas and activities encourage a guerrilla war within the United States extend a standing invitation to totalitarian militarists overseas to inch their fingers closer to the nuclear button. Those who do not understand that hydrogen warfare calls for the modification not the abandonment of age-old concepts of tactics and strategy may one day invite a nuclear attack from those who do. Those who assert there can be no such thing as victory in a nuclear war are making such a victory possible—for the other side.

A Majority-dominated America would be relatively impervious to the selfish interests and special pleading which have recently involved the United States in so many fruitless and profitless foreign crusades. The national effort would be withdrawn from the worldwide defense of degenerate political regimes and outmoded ideologies, and focused on the well-being of America. And America's well-being, in a nuclear context, means an unshakable commitment to the proposition that war is the final court of appeal, not for the protection of foreign investments and foreign homelands, not for glory-seeking Gracchites or racist Messiahs in equalitarian clothing, but for a society faced with the immediate threat of disintegration and oblivion.

Chapter 39

Toward a Pax Americana

I T IS NOT, however, to America's nuclear defenses that the
Majority must look for deliverance and regeneration, but
to the defenses of the mind. There will be no end to its
dispossession until the Majority learns to reject *all*, repeat
all, the main currents of modern liberal thought, and there
can be no such rejection until the true nature of the illiberal
forces which engender and direct modern liberalism are
clearly understood. The absurdities, fallacies and contradictions of Marxism, Freudianism, the equalitarian anthropology of Boas and contemporary social democracy are not
important in themselves. What is important is how and why
they have been developed and synthesized into the most un-
bending intellectual absolutism since medieval scholasticism.

To understand what has happened to the Majority it is
first necessary to realize that the deterioration of power is as
much the result of success as it is of failure. The hard-pressed
society knows better than to let down its guard. It cannot
afford to ignore the motives and acts of its opponents. It is
aware that any abrogation of its possessions, tangible or intangible, is a loss that can only be recovered by the most
prolonged and arduous efforts. Conversely, the successful or
affluent society, by virtue of its surplus of life's necessities,
has the time to turn away from the grindstone of daily
existence. Less touched by the existential forces of the
human condition, its members have the rare and dangerous

opportunity of stretching their individualism well beyond the normal societal breaking point.

Certainly, according to any yardstick of per capita progress toward the good life, history has never recorded a more successful society than the United States from the end of the Civil War to the late 1920's. Even the incapable [1] and the incapacitated elements of the population were moving ahead, albeit slowly, and even the lowliest newcomers from Europe, in comparison with the status of those they left behind, were immeasurably better off the minute they planted their feet on American soil. And all the while every American of whatever background was being exposed to undreamed-of possibilities of self-fulfillment and self-realization by the soaring vitality of Majority imagination and enterprise.

The successful can afford to share their success, and the Majority did so with indiscriminate prodigality. With no qualifications or conditions, the laboriously accumulated privileges of Majority institutions were distributed gratis to members of other races and cultures who accepted them almost as a matter of course, often with a show of ingratitude, and then used them for entirely different purposes than they were originally intended. The new Americans began to vote, not as individuals, but as members of blocs. Many of them prospered greatly in an unrestricted economy, but they spent much of their wealth on group projects that were outside and often opposed to the national interest. They reveled in the freedom they could never win for themselves, but instead of treating it respectfully and responsibly, they took advantage of it. Their children thronged to the free public schools of a matchless educational system, where they learned enough about American civilization to criticize it, but not enough to become a part of it.

At first, many Unassimilable Minority members did try to fit into the overall Majority pattern. But how could they be good democrats when democracy had always been foreign to their historical experience? How could they begin supporting

---

1. Incapable in that they were not genetically or culturally suited to participate fully and voluntarily in a Western-style, progress-oriented industrial society.

an establishment when they had always been against all establishments? Many had been learned in the law—their religion was the law—but how remote such theological exercises were from the Anglo-Saxon common law. As for assimilation, how could they mix with others when the whole secret of their survival had been standing apart?

They toyed a little with the American Dream, but it eluded them. Their intellectuals read Locke, Jefferson, Emerson and Mill, but later came to prefer such Old World kinsmen as Marx, Freud and Boas. The Old Testament apocalyptics of Marxism had a familiar and agreeable ring. The anthropomorphic symbolism of Freud sat well with a religious people looking for a replacement for a dying, anachronistic faith. It was a godsend when Boas arrived in New York and obligingly declared that all races were equal. The Declaration of Independence had so intimated, but now it was a "scientific fact."

It did not take long to discover that these new theories were much more than intellectual playthings. They comprised a vast stockpile of doctrinal weapons made to order for a strategy of *divide et impera*. Marx had separated men not into races, but into exploiters and exploited, upper classes and lower classes—and the Majority was so separated. Freud had changed men into mindless animals, and the Majority was so animalized. In the matter of the great guideposts of Majority rule, the New Testament and the Constitution, by adding a little here and subtracting a little there, by emphasizing some words and re-interpreting others, these could be turned against the Majority and be used to produce further divisions in its already divided ranks.

Meantime, Majority members went blindly about their business, convinced that America would remake the strangers in its midst, not the other way around. Only a prescient handful rejected these environmentalist fantasies and warned of what was really taking shape behind the smokescreen of proletarian rhetoric and "progressive" legislation. But Henry Adams, Madison Grant, Lothrop Stoddard, Henry Ford, Ezra Pound, Charles Lindbergh and Carleton Putnam were voices crying in an echo chamber. All that was heard was the million-throated, liberal-minority chorus of calumny stigmatizing them as eccentric crackpots or murderous racists or both. Ezra Pound, the bitterest and most poetic of these voices, was singled out for more spectacular chastisement. For weeks the man described as "a principal founder and moving spirit of modern poetry in English"[2] was exposed in an iron cage in Pisa and then locked up for twelve years in a District of Columbia insane asylum.[3]

Even during the 1950's and 1960's, when the liberal-minority grip on the nation had tightened to a stranglehold, the Majority still could not believe it had become a people of little account in its own country. Most Majority members still had a home, a late-model car and a loaded deep freeze. But they no longer had preachers or teachers to defend the Majority cause, no literature, no theater, no press, no television, no nationwide forum of expression. As its ascendancy had gradually, almost imperceptibly, been blotted out, the Majority had been transformed into a swarm of middle-class drones, still permitted certain physical comforts but carefully isolated and quarantined from the seats of decision-making and opinion-molding. Majority industrial magnates were given a few more years or decades of limited independence within the narrow confines of their corporations—someone had to turn the wheels—but they were to keep their mouths and their minds shut. As for Majority politicians and intellectuals, they were still safe, provided they voted right and obeyed their masters' voices.

Yet all was not clear sailing for the minority side. Equalitarianism, an infectuous dogma of epidemic potential, was getting out of hand. It was predictable that the ruling race, having been leveled to equality, would be further demoted to subject status. It was understandable that the subject races, having been raised to equality, might wish to climb higher, particularly after learned professors flattered their genes and

2. *Who's Who in America*, 1969–70.
3. "It was an incredible barbarity for Americans to conceive and execute." Charles Norman, *Ezra Pound*, Macmillan, New York, 1960, p. 397. The aging Pound, it might be added, was held incommunicado in his Pisan cage, allowed no mail and forced to sleep on the cement floor. Compare this treatment to that accorded Jane Fonda and Ramsey Clark, who trafficked with the enemy in Hanoi during the Vietnam war. Ex-Attorney General Clark, now with the law firm of Paul, Weiss, Goldberg, etc., was a *defense witness* in the trial of the New Left hit man, whose bomb killed a Majority student at the University of Wisconsin.

whetted their ambitions with allusions to racial superiority. It was logical that blacks, having been told they were equal or superior to whites, would blame their social disadvantages not on any innate limitations, but on a devilish white conspiracy. It was inevitable that some blacks, having come to this conclusion, would feel they had a perfect right to avenge themselves and burn down cities and "get whitey." But the problem was that "whitey" was often a member of another Unassimilable Minority, the Jew who owned most of the ghetto tenements, department stores and retail shops.

So the Jewish dime-store owners and slum lords were sacrificed to the muggers and arsonists in urban no-man's lands, while Jewish New Leftists, on college campuses and in government agencies, continued to write the manifestos that inspired the guerrilla depredations and the scorched city tactics; and millionaire Jewish Old Leftists, holed up safely in suburbia, paid the bills. After all, it was war, and a few minor betrayals and casualties should not be allowed to detract from a victory already in sight. In any event, everyone was too committed to go backward—and a slowdown might give the Majority time to reorganize.

Time certainly was of the essence. Sensitive ears were beginning to hear rumblings and grumblings in the hinterland, in the heartland, in the South and Southwest and, most forebodingly, in the sacred groves of academe. Incredibly, the Majority was finally starting to rouse itself. To smash these stirrings of resistance, the liberal-minority general staff opened up all the old stops, the mind-deadening cacophony of Marxist and liberal dogma, the sly equalitarian appeals to minority racism, as well as a few new stops—drugs, pornography, homosexuality, the generation gap and women's liberation. Even the hippies, the special creation of the mass media, were armed with knives and time bombs. As usual, the big guns blasted the weakest spots in the Majority's defenses—the children and the young women. But they were also zeroing in on the prime target, the Majority's last redoubt, the family.

Now, if it was to save itself from spiritual extinction, the Majority had no choice but to quickly unlearn every lesson it had been taught since the beginning of its dispossession.

The dignity of the individual? The triumph of reason? The rights of man? The Majority's ancestors had been the first to develop these concepts and apply them to society. In their perverted modern form, they were the killers of society. Democracy, genuine liberalism, the common law, the free play of the imagination, the technological breakthroughs, all the great political, social and scientific achievements of Western man were now the spoils of non-Western man. History, once it had been "restructured" by the liberal-minority intelligentsia, not only became bunk but a deliberate fraud, the basic strategy of a war in which truth was the first casualty. Environment, climate, geography, economics, religion and blind chance were solemnly proclaimed to be the only possible (and permissible) creators of the past and future. Race was still the unspeakable historical determinant, although the loudest denouncers and deniers of race were, as always, the biggest racists.

The very desperation of the denials lends substance to the claim that history clusters about race; that its presence is felt in every obscure paragraph and every radiant page of the human record; that where there was no race consciousness there was no historical consciousness and where there was no historical consciousness there was chronology but no history; that archaeological diggings and yesterday's headlines both testify that the essence of history is the rise and fall of races.

To the racial historian, race is the being and the becoming of organized humanity. As race has been the controlling factor of much of the human past, so it will assume even greater importance in the future. Man's fate has now become the world's fate, which means that only a supreme effort will put a stop to the devastation of the environment, and supreme efforts can only be undertaken by large groups of men with similar political and social reflexes, by great teams not great mobs, specifically by great races. Race, the highest manifestation of the team spirit, may be nature's way of organizing men for the accomplishment of the unaccomplishable.

Just as the body rejects transplanted organs, races have the habit of rejecting transplanted ideologies. They may accept them temporarily, but the buildup of "antibodies" is unceasing. The only ideology acceptable to all races would seem to be the grand design of evolution, which will ultimately select one of them to give birth to a new species, the better-than-man.

In an age beginning to uncover the mysteries of the gene, whose frequencies and combinations are the fundamental units of character and intelligence, both of individuals and races, the race most likely to raise the *hominidae* another notch in the evolutionary scale will be the one that concentrates on the penetration of the genetic riddle. It will certainly not be the race that dissipates its energies on doctrinal crusades, seeking its salvation outside itself, allowing itself to become a hostage to fortune. This is the way back to the primeval ooze and the plasma—the way of devolution.

At this particular point in time, the race best suited to shoulder the main weight of the evolutionary burden would appear to be the Northern European. Equally adept at physics and metaphysics, induction and deduction, theory and application, equally at home in the macrocosm and the microcosm, the Northern European has managed to soar a little higher above the animal kingdom than the other divisions of mankind. At the moment, two devastating intraracial wars within a quarter century and the dispossession of the American Majority, the largest reservoir of Northern European genes, have grounded him. Permanently or temporarily, it is too early to know.

To put Northern Europeans back on the evolutionary track —to rekindle the Northern European efflorescence—is a project of monumental complexity. Of all the Northern European peoples, only a rehabilitated American Majority, mindful of the history it has made and is about to make, would have the strength and the resources to bring about a Northern European ingathering—not merely a political and economic ingathering cemented by treaties and trade agreements or by the common nationality and citizenship which might come in time, but an ingathering of race consciousness, the most lasting and tenacious of all social binding forces.

Should this pooling of the work and thought of a highly gifted but widely dispersed people ever be effected, there would be such a preponderance of power that no external predator would dare so much as touch the remotest corner of the Northern European living space, either in Europe, North America or Australasia. The minorities within this living space, no longer able to prosper from the divisions of their hosts, might finally learn to look to themselves for sustenance. Forced into unaccustomed self-sufficiency, they might well rebuild their own depleted cultures, and might gain from the experience.

Such is the shimmering prospect of a Pax Americana—a world order more encompassing than the Pax Romana and more enduring and more constructive than the Pax Britannica. The Pax Romana, though Rome was ruled in its expansionist days by patricians of Northern European descent, was never willing or able to reach far enough north to envelop the peoples of Germany and Scandinavia. Consequently, the first and best chance for European unity was lost.

The Pax Britannica, which kept the peace so long throughout so much of the nonwhite world, while establishing new white worlds in newly discovered continents, was dysgenically disastrous to Northern Europe. Britain's balance-of-power diplomacy which divided and exhausted Europe for hundreds of years was one direct cause of the grinding twentieth-century wars that so significantly lowered the genetic quality of every European state—with the British gene pool eventually suffering the greatest damage of all. Also, at the very crest of empire, Britain lost her most important possessions in North America, a racial setback of the most serious consequences. If the secession of the thirteen colonies could have been prevented—not an impossible feat for subtle eighteenth-century statesmanship—the Pax Britannica might still be the mainstay of Western politics. Instead, present-day Britain is a weary little island kingdom, whose recovery awaits a new upsurge of the unquenchable British spirit.

The Germans brought down the Pax Romana by their victories and the Pax Britannica by their defeats. At almost any time since the Middle Ages, Britain could have dampened German militarism by supporting, not opposing, the historic German mission of defending the West against the inroads of the East. But Britain appointed herself the arch enemy of European union, the same European union which would have crushed Bolshevism in the bud and forbidden the presence of Russian armies on the banks of the Elbe.

The Pax Americana, its primary task the consolidation, security and advancement of the Northern European peoples, would be the first world order whose geographical frontiers corresponded to its racial frontiers, once the minority elements were separated out and either sent back to their old homelands or established in new ones. Such a genetically based intercontinental confederation, a radically new way of bringing a scattered people together, might overcome or alleviate some of the dangers to mankind which the crypto-racism of proletarian politics seems to multiply. There would be room in the Pax Americana for Russians and other Slavs of Northern European descent, when and if the cumbersome Soviet complex fell apart of its own weight or was broken up by an invasion from the Asiatic steppes. There would emphatically be no place for the old-style exploitation of nonwhites nor the forcible adaptation of autochthonous civilizations to Northern European cultural norms.

But everything hangs on the fate of the American Majority. If its dispossession is not stopped and reversed, there will be no Pax Americana, no halt to the decline of the West, no giving the lie to Spengler. In fact, there will soon be no America. History is insistent in pointing out that when the dominant population group goes, the country goes. As is daily becoming more apparent, the dying fall of the American Majority is the dying fall of America itself.

Appendix
and
Index

APPENDIX

Explanation of Racial Census

During the debate on immigration quotas in the early 1920's, an attempt was made to determine the proportion of white Americans originating from various Old World and a few New World countries. The results, as published in *Immigration Quotas on the Basis of National Origin,* 70th Congress, 2d Session, Senate Document 259, p. 5, are given on the following pages. The right-hand columns of the table contain estimates of the racial composition of the mother country made by Carl Brigham, an associate professor of psychology at Princeton University. Brigham wanted to correlate the voluminous results of Army World War I intelligence tests with race. His findings were severely challenged, not so much for his racial estimates, but because he used them to help "prove" the intellectual superiority of American Nordics. See Carl Brigham, *A Study of American Intelligence,* Princeton University Press, Princeton, N.J., 1923, pp. 160, 190.

In general, Brigham's racial allocations are similar to those of Carleton Coon in *The Races of Europe,* the notable exception being Ireland. Here, Brigham seemed to go completely astray. He failed to include the large Irish Alpine component and apparently decided, in contradiction to most other anthropologists, that the Keltic element was more Mediterranean than Nordic. The percentages in the United Kingdom entry are Brigham's racial estimates for England. He had separate figures for the racial composition of Scotland (85 percent Nordic; 15 percent Mediterranean) and Wales (40 percent Nordic; 60 percent Mediterranean). He also had two categories for Turkey—Turkey (in Europe) and Turkey. His figures for the former are given in the table. As for the percentages omitted by Brigham, they can be obtained from Coon's *The Races of Europe* or from racial studies by European anthropologists.

WHITE POPULATION OF U.S. BY COUNTRY OF ORIGIN AND RACE

Country of Origin	% of White Population		% LIGHT WHITE Nordic	% WHITE Alpine	% DARK WHITE Medit.
	1790	1920			
Austria	*	0.9	10	90	
Belgium	1.5	0.8	60	40	
Czechoslovakia	0.1	1.8			
Denmark	0.2	0.7	85	15	
Estonia	...	0.1			
Finland	*	0.4			
France	1.9	1.9	30	55	15
Germany	7.4	16.3	40	60	
United Kingdom	77.0	41.4	80		20
Greece	...	0.2		15	85
Hungary	...	0.6	10	90	
Ireland	4.4	11.2	30		70 **
Italy	...	3.6	5	25	70
Latvia	...	0.2			
Lithuania	...	0.2			
Netherlands	3.3	2.0	85	15	
Norway	0.2	1.5	90	10	
Poland	*	4.1	10	90	
Portugal	0.1	0.3	5		95
Rumania	...	0.2		100	
Russia	*	1.8	5	95	
Spain	1.0	0.2	10	5	85
Sweden	0.5	2.1	100		

WHITE POPULATION OF U.S. BY COUNTRY OF ORIGIN AND RACE

Country of Origin	% of White Population		% LIGHT WHITE Nordic	% WHITE Alpine	% DARK WHITE Medit.
	1790	1920			
Switzerland	0.9	1.1	35	65	
Syria, Lebanon	...	0.1			
Turkey	...	0.1		60	40
Yugoslavia	...	0.5			
All Other	*	0.2			
Canada	1.6	4.3			
Newfoundland	*	0.1			
Mexico	0.7	1.2			
West Indies	*	0.1			
All Other	*	*			

(*) Less than $\frac{1}{10}$th of 1%.
(**) See p. 541.

Estimating the Alpine component of the American white population poses the most difficult problem in determining an accurate racial census of the United States. Statistics are available for the number of Americans originating in Eastern Europe and in other predominantly Alpine areas. To arrive at these numbers one only has to follow the method used for estimating the Mediterranean component of the white population. One merely adds up the population estimates supplied by minority organizations and minority experts for population groups from these predominantly Alpine countries. Such estimates can be found in Chapter 13.

There are, however, certain European countries—Germany and France, for example—for which such statistics are not available and which have considerable Alpine components. About the only means of estimating the number of Alpines that these countries have contributed to the American population is to employ the projection method described below.

ALPINE AND MEDITERRANEAN RACIAL ALLOCATIONS

	TOTAL	ALPINE	MEDITER-RANEAN	SOURCE
ALBANIANS	60,000	60,000		DM p. 147 RE pp. 601–4
ARMENIANS	150,000	50,000	100,000	DM p. 147 RE p. 629
AUSTRIANS	1,541,000	1,387,000		PM
BELGIANS	1,370,000	548,000		PM
BULGARS	35,000		35,000	DM p. 147 RE p. 611
CUBANS	565,000		565,000	DM p. 146
CZECHOSLOVAKS	1,750,000	1,750,000		DM p. 137 RE pp. 560–2
DANES	1,199,000	180,000		PM
DUTCH	3,424,000	513,000		PM
ESTONIANS	60,000	30,000		DM p. 135 AE
FINNS	400,000	100,000		DM p. 134 AE
FRENCH	6,253,000	4,002,000	625,000	DM pp. 138–9 RE p. 522
GERMANS	27,909,000	16,745,000		PM
GREEKS	600,000	90,000	510,000	DM p. 147
HUNGARIANS	640,000	576,000		DM p. 138
IRISH	16,000,000	7,200,000		DM pp. 124–5
ITALIANS	8,764,000	1,753,000	7,011,000	DM p. 143
JEWS	5,869,000	4,695,000	1,174,000	DM p. 149 RE pp. 643–4
LATVIANS	50,000	50,000		DM p. 135 RE p. 362
LITHUANIANS	272,000	272,000		DM p. 135 RE p. 368
NORWEGIANS	2,568,000	257,000		PM
POLES	3,000,000	2,700,000		DM p. 136

ALPINE AND MEDITERRANEAN RACIAL ALLOCATIONS (*cont.*)

	TOTAL	ALPINE	MEDITER-RANEAN	SOURCE
PORTUGUESE	176,000		167,000	DM p. 147
RUMANIANS	65,000	65,000		DM p. 147
RUSSIANS	350,000	333,000		DM p. 135
SPANISH	2,138,000	107,000	1,817,000	DM p. 146
SWISS	1,883,000	1,224,000		PM
SYRIANS	151,000		151,000	DM p. 147 RE pp. 623–4
TURKS	5,000	3,000	2,000	DM p. 147
UKRAINIANS	600,000	600,000		DM p. 136 RE pp. 569–72
YUGOSLAVS	1,000,000	1,000,000		DM p. 137 RE p. 589
TOTAL		46,290,000	12,157,000	

Key: DM (*The Dispossessed Majority*); RE (*Races of Europe*);
      PM (projection method, including Carl Brigham's percentages);
      AE (author's estimate).

By taking the 1920 percentage of each national origins group, as listed in the table, and applying it against the total number of whites in 1970, it is possible to arrive at a broad approximation of the present size of each national origins group. But such mathematics does not do much to clarify the racial background of such population groups. Here it is necessary to turn to the racial composition of the mother country, as given in Brigham's figures. By applying these percentages to the 1970 total for each national origins group, it is possible to obtain an estimate of the number of Nordics, Alpines or Mediterraneans within the group.

To illustrate this projection method, the Alpine component of Americans of German extraction can be determined as follows: In the table it is found that 16.3 percent of the white population in 1920 was contributed by Germany. Taking 16.3 percent of the 1970 white population ($0.163 \times 171,222,000$) produces a figure of 27,909,000, which represents the present number of Americans of German origin. In the Alpine column of the table, 60 percent of the German population is estimated to be Alpine in race. Taking 60 percent of the number of living Americans of German extraction ($0.6 \times 27,909,000$) yields 16,745,000 as the number of American Alpines of German origin.

POSTSCRIPT: In 1973, under the direction of Tobia Bressler of the Ethnic Origins Statistics division, the Census Bureau released a misleading study entitled *Characteristics of the Population by Ethnic Origin: March 1972 and 1971*. The study purported to show that when Americans were asked to identify themselves as belonging to one of eight specific ethnic categories, they responded as follows: English, Scottish, Welsh 29,548,000; German 25,543,000; Irish 16,408,000; Italian 8,764,000; Polish 5,105,000; Russian 2,188,000; Spanish 9,178,000; French 5,420,000. The number of those who gave "Other" ethnic origins was 85,130,000. Those who reported no ethnic origin or claimed they knew of no ethnic origin totalled 17,556,000.

The first problem is to discover the ethnic origin of the Other and Not Reported categories, which amounted to 102,686,000. The 1970 Federal Census can help us in this task, since it listed 25,463,000 nonwhites. These can be subtracted from the 102,686,000, which leaves 77,223,000 whites whose ethnic origins are unaccounted for. Making allowance for perhaps 3,000,000 Jews already included in the Russian and Polish categories listed above, and omitting the Assimilable and Unassimilable white minorities already listed above, we now add all the population estimates for all the remaining Assimilable and Unassimilable white minorities in Chapters 13 and 14 of this book, and obtain a figure of 10,037,000. Subtracting this from 77,223,000 yields 67,186,000.

Since all ethnic or national origin categories have now been exhausted, except for countries with predominantly Northern European populations, who are the Americans represented by this remainder? They have to be Americans whose ancestors came from Scandinavia, the Low Countries and Canada. They must also include Majority members of English and German descent who are so well assimilated that it did not occur to them to attach any ethnic label to their ancestry.

If we now take this 67,186,000 figure and add it back to 55,091,000, the combined figure for Americans of English, Scottish, Welsh *and* German origin, we have a total of 122,277,000. Compare this figure with the 128,273,000 Majority members listed in Table V, page 60 of this book. There is a difference of only 5,996,000. This difference narrows if 20% of the 16,408,000 Irish in the Ethnic Origin study—the percentage of the Irish defined as assimilated in Chapter 13 of this book—is added to the English and German total.

It is obvious that the responses of Americans to questions about ethnic origins are much more valid when they emanate from those who have close ties with their homelands or have a high degree of minority race consciousness. For this reason the most interesting figures in the Ethnic Origin study are those which pertain to minorities. The number of Italian-Americans, the only minority figure that varies significantly from population group estimates given in previous editions, has been incorporated in the present edition of *The Dispossessed Majority*.

Ecuador, 505
ecumenical movement, 258
Edel, Leon, 239n
Edict of Nantes, 138
Edman, Irwin, 170
education, **272–89**, 300, 314, 317, 469n, campus violence, 280, 281n, 284, 287, 362n, 368, 399, 534; downgrading of Majority history, 283–84; minority influences, 274–76, 279–80, 282–83, 285–86, 288–89; also *see* desegregation
Education of Henry Adams, 328n
Egypt, 11, 70, 113, 150, 152n, 153, 193, 216, 218, 261, 442, 495, 511n; relations with U.S., 462, 490; also *see* Arab-Israeli War
Ehrlich, Jake, 411
Ehrlich, Paul, 296n
Eichmann, Adolf, 157, 382
Einstein, Albert, 157, 170, 296, 373, 520–21
Eisenhower, Dwight, 86n, 102n, 109n, 122n, 126, 131, 161, 331, 362n, 392, 411–12
Eisner, Kurt, 186
Ekaterinburg, 454n
El Greco, 229n
Elagabalus, 394n
Elath, 486
Elbe, 444, 538
Eliot, T. S., 228n, 233, 237, 246n, 260–61, 265, 285n, 329n
Elizabeth I, 456n
Elizabeth II, 283
Ellis, Havelock, 31n, 38n
Ellis Island, 136
Ellison, Ralph, 239n
Ellsberg, Daniel, 92n, 417n
Elman, Mischa, 239n
Emerson, Ralph Waldo, 532
Emir of Mecca, 477n
Encyclopaedia Britannica, 16n, 284, 378n, 509n

Engels, Friedrich, 129, 349n, 519n
England, 37n, 38n, 39, 72, 109, 116, 133, 145n, 155–56, 159, 178, 186n, 206, 226, 230, 260, 302–03, 311, 318, 350, 359n, 378, 390n, 425n, 489n, 514, 541; also *see* Britain
English, 14, 125, 201, 230–31, 304; also *see* British
epicanthic fold, 28
Epictetus, 325
Epicurean philosophy, 325
Epicurus, 324
Episcopalians, 172, 248n, 252, 255n
Epstein, Jacob, 239n
equalitarianism, 14–16, 93–94, 106, 279, 304, 312–14, 317–18, 321–22, 324n, 334, 343, 486n, 520, 523, 530, 533–34
Equity Funding, 420
Erie Canal, 127
Ernst, Morris, 161
Eros magazine, 422
Ervin, Sam J., Jr., 259n
Escobedo, Danny, 402n
Eskimos, 28, 53n, 200, 514
espionage, 108–11, 520–22
Esquire magazine, 165
Estes, Billie Sol, 412, 419
esthetics, 31n, **112–18,** 166n, 251, 472
Estonians in U.S., 135, 540
Ethiopia, 500n
eugenics, 317, 427–28
Euripides, 261
Europe, 465, 494, 507, 514, 527, 531, 537–38; also *see* various national and geographical divisions
Evans, Roland, 416n
Evans, Stanton, 508n, 511n, 523n
evolution, 38, 181, 349n, 527, 535
existentialism, 218, 262n

Persia, 476
Persians, 12, 151
Personal History, 129
Peru, 114, 504
Petri, Angelo, 144n
Petrillo, Caesar, 357
Pettitt, George, 370n
Pfeffer, Leo, 395n, 397n
Philadelphia, 237n, 245, 405
Philadelphia Inquirer, 165
Philadelphia Plan, 362n
Philips, William, 239n
Philippine Islands, 45–46, 200, 474; relations with U.S., 432
Phillips, Kevin, 122n, 125n, 184n, 210n, 331n
Philo, 151
Phoenix, Ariz., 406
Piatorgorsky, Gregor, 239n
Picasso, 234n
Picot, Georges, 435
Pierre, 117n
Pigmentation Spectrum, 29
Pike, James, 15n, 255
Pilgrims, 37, 146, 255
Pinafore, 240n
Pinckney, Charles, 442n
Pinter, Harold, 446n
Pirandello, 240
Pisa, 533
Pisani, L. F., 143n
Planck, Max, 170, 245
Plath, Silvia, 235n
Plato, 12, 31n, 70, 117, 277–78, 299–301, 324, 326, 331
Plissetskaya, Maria, 456n
Plutarch, 201
plutocracy, 232, 246
PM newspaper, 99
Pocahontas, 50
Poland, 137, 156, 160, 489n
Poles, 345n, 381n, 452, 465n, 514, 528n; in U.S., 50, 60, 129, 136–37, 357, 540
Polycrates, 447
Polynesians, 23, 28, 200; in U.S., 53, 199
Pompey, Gnaeus, 151

Pompidou, Georges, 446n, 487n
Pompidou, Mme. Georges, 487n
Pontius Pilate, 154, 293
Poor's Register of Corporations, 173
Pope family, 144n
Popes; *see* Papacy
Popper, Karl, 69
populism, 96n, 107, 312
pornography, 169n, 244, 256n, 396n, 422, 534
Portugal, 12, 55, 74, 107, 125, 444n, 495n, 503, 504n, 509
Portuguese, 156, 206, 504; in U.S., 147, 540
Possessed, The, 465n
Possony, Stefan, 170n, 182, 349n
Potemkin, Grigori, 315, 462n
Pound, Ezra, 235, 238, 329n, 532–33
Powderly, Terence, 356
Powell, Adam Clayton, 59n, 89, 256n
Powell, Enoch, 446
Presbyterians, 172, 248n, 252
Prescott, William, 75n, 114n
Pressman, Leo, 462n
Previn, André, 239n
Prince, Hal, 169, 240n
Princeton University, 284, 288
Procaccino, Mario, 407
Proditors, 108–11, 142
Professor's House, The, 237
Progressive party, 184, 309, 312, 462
Prometheus, 266n
Proskauer, Joseph, 102n
Protestant Church, 75, 89, 133, 135, 253, 255, 257, 259, 344n, 352n, 419, 491
Protestant Ethic, 344n
Protestants, 138, 172n, 173n, 178, 248n, 258, 394, 497
Protocols of Zion, 349n
Provence, Harry, 415n
Prussia, 91, 348
Psalms, Book of, 152
psychoanalysis, 170, **263–71**, 273, 530; deracinating effect

West Germany, 186–87, 343, 351n, 445, 446n, 447, 525
West Indies, 432, 504–05, 511
West, Nathanael, 238n
Western civilization, 61, 88, 111, 117, 122, 155, 157, 179, 185, 220n, 227, 232, 243, 448, 475, 502, 527, 535, 538
Western Europe, 70, 124, 131, 226, 440, 444–50, 465, 469
Westin, Avram, 168
Wexler, Paul, 257n
Weyl, Nathaniel, 78n, 87, 170n, 182–85, 268n, 270n, 336, 348n, 349n
Whigs, 106, 318, 327
White, Byron, 397
White, Harry D., 410n, 439n, 462n
White, Leslie, 15n
white race, 13, 22–25, 30, 89, 116, 139n, 194n, 203n, 219, 467, 471, 474–75, 497–98; in U.S., 53–62, 118n, 138, 183, 199n, 208–09, 221n, 242, 539–42; also *see* Nordic, Alpine and Mediterranean races
White Steed, 133n
Whitehead, Alfred N., 271n
Who's Who in American Jewry, 179n
Wiesner, Jerome, 523
Wilde, Oscar, 231
Wilhelm II, 170
Wilson, Evan, 479n
Wilson, R. J., 393n
Wilson, Woodrow, 161, 312, 319, 365, 389, 433–38, 443n, 459–60
Winchell, Walter, 166, 310n
Winkler, Franz, 271n
Winston, Harry, 176
Winters, Charlie, 483n
Winthrop, John, 256
Wirtz, Willard, 162
Wislicency, Dieter, 157n
Wister, Owen, 240n
Witness, 110
Witt, Nathan, 462n

Wittgenstein, Ludwig, 157
Wittke, Carl, 127
Wolfe, Robert, 287
Wolfe, Thomas, 235, 243
Wolfson, Isaac, 446n
Wolfson, Louis, 163n, 177, 390, 396, 418
Women's Liberation, 129n, 534
Woodstock Festival, 176n, 245n
World Council of Churches, 253n
World War I, 76n, 100n, 134–35, 161n, 170, 209, 351, 362n, 361, 447, 467, 477, 494
World War II, 14, 76, 100n, 107, 122n, 135, 157–58, 159n, 161, 237n, 283n, 308, 310n, 317n, 319n, 329, 347, 351, 357n, 363, 408, 438–42, 444, 447, 449, 453–54, 467, 471–72, 477, 491, 500, 520, 523
Wouk, Herman, 239n
Wounded Knee, 202n
Wovoka, 203
Wretched of the Earth, The, 502n
Wright, Richard, 239n
Wurf, Jerry, 357

Yaffe, James, 40n, 178n, 188n, 189n, 211n, 234n, 237n, 240n, 241n, 258n, 288n, 308n, 322n, 349n, 405n, 484n
Yagoda, Genrikh, 347
Yale University, 284n, 288, 483n
Yale, William, 434n, 435n, 436n, 477n, 478n
Yalta Conference, 108
Yamashita, Tomoyuki, 395
Yaroslavski, Emeiian, 455n
Yeats, William Butler, 133n, 231, 265
yellow race; *see* Mongoloid race
Yerby, Frank, 239n

Wilmot Robertson is a native Pennsylvanian whose family goes back to colonial times and whose forebears fought on both sides of the Civil War. The author waited for decades for a qualified Majority scholar to write this book. Having waited in vain, he decided to take on the project himself and devoted ten years to it. His credentials are long periods of study in American and foreign universities, three years' overseas service as an army officer in World War II, a varied career in journalism, advertising and small business and, above all, an overwhelming concern for the darkening tragedy of his people.